A Brief History of Chinese Civilization

Second Edition

Conrad Schirokauer
Senior Scholar, Columbia University

Miranda Brown
University of Michigan

Australia • Canada • Mexico • Singapore • Spain • United Kingdom • United States

Publisher: *Clark Baxter*
Assistant Editor: *Paul Massicotte*
Editorial Assistant: *Lucinda Bingham*
Technology Project Manager: *Melinda Newfarmer*
Marketing Manager: *Lori Grebe Cook*
Advertising Project Manager: *Laurel Anderson*
Project Manager, Editorial Production: *Katy German*
Art Director: *Maria Epes*

Print/Media Buyers: *Rebecca Cross and Doreen Suruki*
Permissions Editor: *Kiely Sisk*
Production Service: *Graphic World, Inc.*
Cover and Text Designer: *Andrew Ogus*
Photo Researcher: *Terri Wright*
Cover Image: *Shanghai Museum*
Cover Printer: *Phoenix Color Corp*
Printer: *Quebecor World*

© 2006 Wadsworth, a division of Thomson Learning

Printed in the Canada
2 3 4 5 6 7 09 08 07 06

For more information about our products, contact us at
Thomson Learning Academic Resource Center
1-800-423-0563
For permisson to use material from this text or product, submit a request online at http://www.thomsonrights.com
Any additional questions about permissions can be submitted by email to thomsonrights@thomson.com.

Library of Congress Control Number: 2005920236

ISBN 0-534-64305-1

Thomson Higher Education
10 Davis Drive
Belmont, CA 94002-3098
USA

Asia
Thomson Learning
5 Shenton Way
#01-01 UIC Building
Singapore 068808

Australia/New Zealnad
Thomson Learning Australia
102 Dodds Street
South Melbourne, Victoria 3205
Australia

Canada
Thomson Nelson
1120 Birchmount Road
Toronto, Ontario M1K 5G4
Canada

UK/Europe/Middle East/Africa
Thomson Learning
High Holborn House
50–51 Bedford Road
London WC1R 4LR
United Kingdom

Latin America
Thomson Learning
Seneca, 53
Colonia Polanco
11560 Mexico
D.F. Mexico

Spain, Portugal
Thomson Paraninfo
Calle Magallanes, 25
28015 Madrid, Spain

Dedicated to our spouses: Lore Schirokauer and David Burke

and to David and Oliver and Leo Kipton

Contents

Part Four: China in the Modern World 258

Part Five:
Building a New China 321

Preface

A new revised edition such as this demands a new preface, for there is much about this book that is new. Most significantly, what was a solo has become a duet, extending our range and enriching our sound.

Before saying something about our collaboration, we need to affirm that some things said in earlier editions still apply. Certainly the reasons for studying China are as urgent as ever and can still be subsumed under three broad headings: the richness of its long historical record, which forms such an important part of the total history of the human race and illuminates the nature of the human condition; the enduring value of Chinese cultural achievements; and the contemporary importance of the world's most populated land. Setting aside China's contemporary importance, surely some acquaintance with its civilization is required of one who would be an educated person, for to be educated means to be able to see beyond the narrow geographic, temporal, and cultural bounds of one's immediate neighborhood. Indeed, to be educated entails the ability to see oneself in a broader perspective, including the perspective of history. And in this day and age, that means not only the history of one's own tribe or state or even civilization but also ideally of all human history—for it is all our history.

That history is woven of many strands, and so we have economic and political history and the study of social structure, of thought, and of art. This text is based on the belief that an introduction to the history of a civilization requires consideration of all these facets of human activity, a general mapping out of the terrain so that the beginner may find his or her bearings and learn enough to consider in which direction to explore further, with some idea of the rewards to be gained for the effort. An introduction then is certainly not a catalog (although it should contain basic data) or a personal synthesis or summation, nor is it the proper vehicle for extending the expanding frontiers of present knowledge. Instead, it should, among other things, introduce the reader to the conventions of a field of study and attempt to convey the state of our present understanding. The basic aim of this text then is to serve as a work of orientation. Thus, for example, where applicable, the standard dynastic framework has been used to provide the basic historical chronology. We have further decided to replace the B.C. and A.D. of previous editions with B.C.E. and C.E. (Before and in the Common Era) because that seemed most appropriate for a twenty-first century (C.E.!) book on China. It also appears to have become standard, especially, but not exclusively, among students of the history of religion.

History is the study of change and continuity, and both elements are always present. Neither the people we study nor we ourselves begin with a blank slate, and our task is not to choose between change and continuity but the more challenging one of weighing change within the continuity and continuity within the change. Such a determination requires, in the final analysis, as much art as science, and no assessment is ever final. This is so not only because of the continual discovery of new evidence and new techniques (for example, in the dating of materials) but also because scholars' intellectual frameworks and analytic concepts change, and we all learn to ask new questions. Even if that were not the case, history would still have to be rewritten at intervals, inasmuch as the ultimate significance of any individual historical episode depends in the final analysis on the whole story: As long as history itself is unfinished, so is its writing.

If this is true of all history, it seems especially the case with the history of China, about which we know a great deal more now than we did just a generation ago, but the areas of our ignorance continue to be enormous. Etienne Balazs (1905–1963) once compared students of China to Lilliputians clambering over the Gulliver that is Chinese history, and his words are still apt. Indeed, one of the continuing attractions of the field is that it offers great opportunities to the intellectually adventurous and hardy to work on major problems. Our hope is that the very inadequacies of a text such as this will spur some readers on to these endeavors. Thus, for this text to succeed, it must fail: readers must come away hungry, their appetites whetted but not satiated.

A broad survey such as this is by necessity based on the studies of many scholars (indeed our pleasure in wide reading is matched only by fear of inadvertent plagiarism). No attempt has been made to list all the works consulted. The suggested readings in the Appendix have been drawn up in the hope of meeting some of the readers' needs, not of acknowledging our indebtedness, although there is considerable overlap. It is also impossible here to list all the individuals who have contributed to this textbook by offering suggestions, criticism, and encouragement or who helped by suggesting references, supplying a date or a translation for a term, and so forth, or to acknowledge individually the teachers, students, and colleagues who have influenced our thoughts about the broader problems of history and China and the teaching of these subjects. As earlier, however, the senior author wants once again to single out for special mention Professor Arthur F. Wright (1913–1976), scholar and humanist, whom he had the privilege of knowing as both teacher and friend. Similarly both of us want to express our admiration and thanks for David Keightley although only Brown had the pleasure of taking his History 116A, which brimmed with good illustrations, colorful anecdotes, and scholarly controversy and, among other things, laid the foundations for her contributions to this textbook. If it were not for that course, her career would have taken a different shape.

In recent years scholarship has been so productive, as well as specialized, that it has become virtually impossible for one person to keep up with it all, but we owe a debt to the membership, respectively, of the University Seminars at Columbia and the Michigan Center for Chinese Studies' brown bag series. Their role in keeping us informed on sinological trends has been indispensable. Furthermore, at Michigan, Bill Baxter has been an exceptionally helpful colleague and a reliable source of good cheer and of stimulating, almost daily, early China talk. At Columbia, Pei-yi Wu has been and continues to be an engaged and engaging good friend.

Although our interests remain broad, in the present edition, there is a clear temporal division of responsibility, with Miranda Brown being responsible for the first three chapters and Conrad Schirokauer for the rest. That we are very different people is obvious at first sight: one of us is young and female and charging up the tenure hill at full steam; the other unabashedly claims senior discounts on trains and planes but not in his scholarly endeavors and hopes to demonstrate, to some at least, that he is not yet quite "over the hill." That we enjoyed our collaboration augurs well for the future. We have maintained our own voices and views even as we encourage our readers to develop their own.

Acknowledgments

We need to acknowledge those who contributed so much to the previous edition of this book and its precursors but will limit ourselves here to naming those directly involved in the present edition. These include Clark Baxter, Paul Massicotte, and the entire Wadsworth team as listed on the copyright page.

Foremost among the people specifically involved in making this book possible is Michael Nylan who brought us together and remains a major force shaping our understanding of early China. We want to thank the scholars whose critical reading of parts of the manuscript saved us from many an error of commission or omission even though we did not always follow their advice. Several prefer to remain anonymous but we can and do acknowledge: Mark Csikszentmihalyi, Robert Hymes, Jeffrey Barlow, Suzanne Cahill, Craig Canning, W. Dean Kinzley, and Huping Ling.

Among those at Columbia, Li Feng also merits special mention as do the young scholars with whom Schirokauer has cotaught East Asian courses during the past few years, listed in chronological order: Jaret Weisfogel, Letty Chen, Naomi Fukumori, Katherine Rupp, Suzanne O'Brien, Nicole Cohen, Yasu Makimura, and Kerry Ross. Both of us want to thank our students for fresh perspectives and ideas with very special thanks to the Winter 2004 Asian 455 class at Michigan, good-humored guinea pigs on a test drive through all of the material presented in Chapters 1–3.

Also deserving special mention are the staff of the Starr East Asian Library at Columbia for their help with books. For help in manuscript production and reproduction we wish to thank Lenore Szekely, a graduate student of Chinese literature at Michigan, and Diana Nobile-Hernandez of the Heyman Center at Columbia. Once again, we are grateful to Yangming Chu and Rongxiang Zhang for help in obtaining permissions from China.

Our greatest debt is to our families who have lived with this book and to whom it is dedicated. Lore, also known as Mrs. Schirokauer, not only helped in innumerable direct and indirect ways but also contributed greatly to the artwork, which includes a number of her own photographs.

Miranda Brown
Conrad Schirokauer

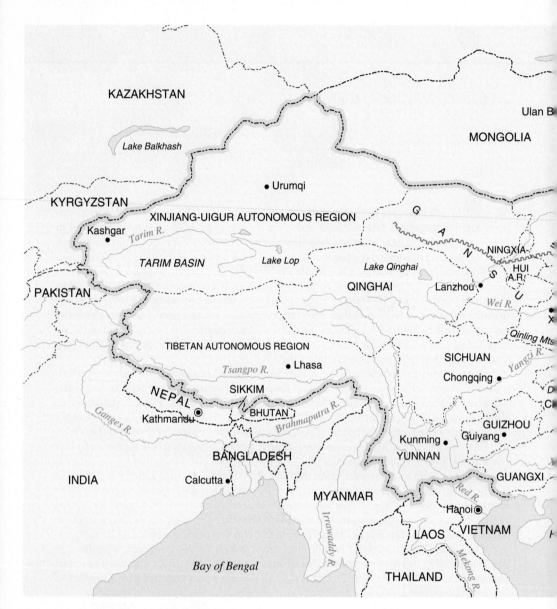

The master map shows both the agricultural regions that comprise what most scholars call China proper. It also shows the vast areas of Inner Asia and other lands beyond the Great Wall, which have only recently become incorporated into China today. Whereas the former were largely inhabited by the ancestors of the modern Chinese, who were settled agricultural peoples; the latter were inhabited by generally nomadic peoples.

With the area that now comprises China proper, the basic geographical division is between North and South. This division gave rise to two different agricultural traditions from around 5000 B.C.E. The outstanding geographical featur of the North is the Yellow River, which flows from the highlands of the West, through the alluvial lowlands of the Central Plain to empty into the sea near the Shandong Peninsula. At present, the Yellow River valley is a region of

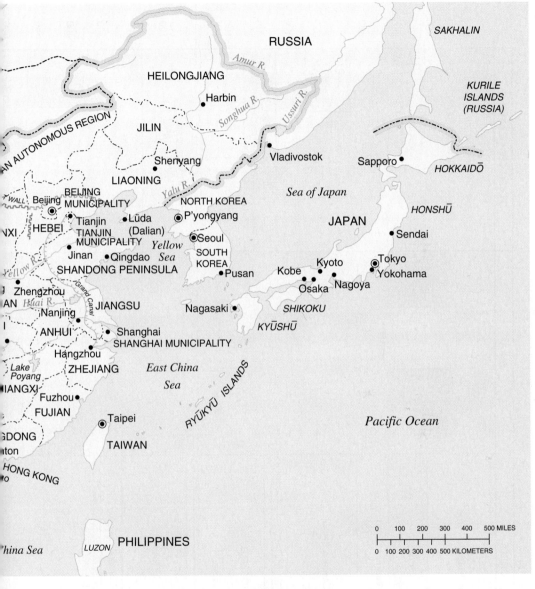

nperate climate, cold winters and warm summers, but rainfall is scarce. This is particularly true in the arid west, but the moister areas as well, the annual rainfall is extremely variable. Although the area is subject to drought, the soil fertile. It is a region suitable for growing millet, and, in moister parts, wheat and beans.

present, very different conditions prevail south of a line that runs roughly along the 33rd parallel, following the nling Mountains and the Huai River. Here, rain is abundant, and the climate is subtropical, and the soils are ached. The dominant river is the Yangzi, which is about 3,200 miles long. (Hence, the Yangzi is also called the lang jiang or 'Long River'). Once the necessary technology was developed and the land was laboriously drained er several centuries, this region proved ideal for intensive rice culture.

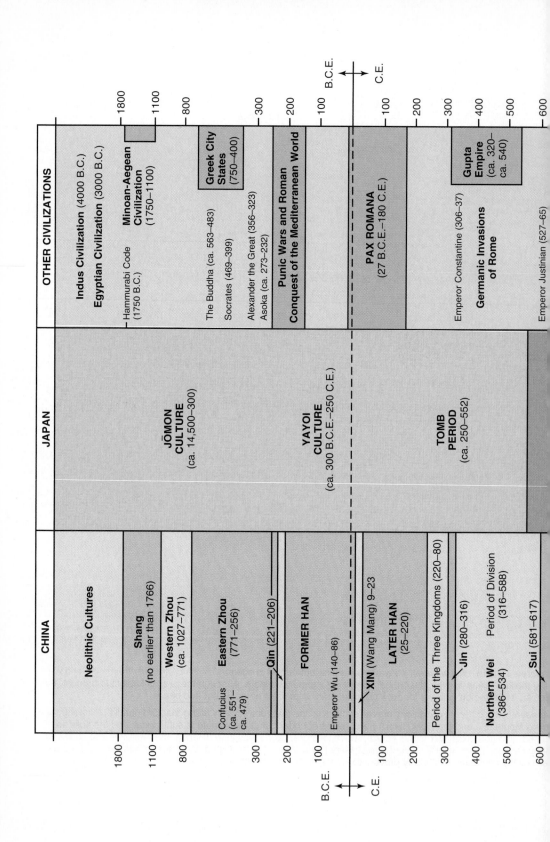

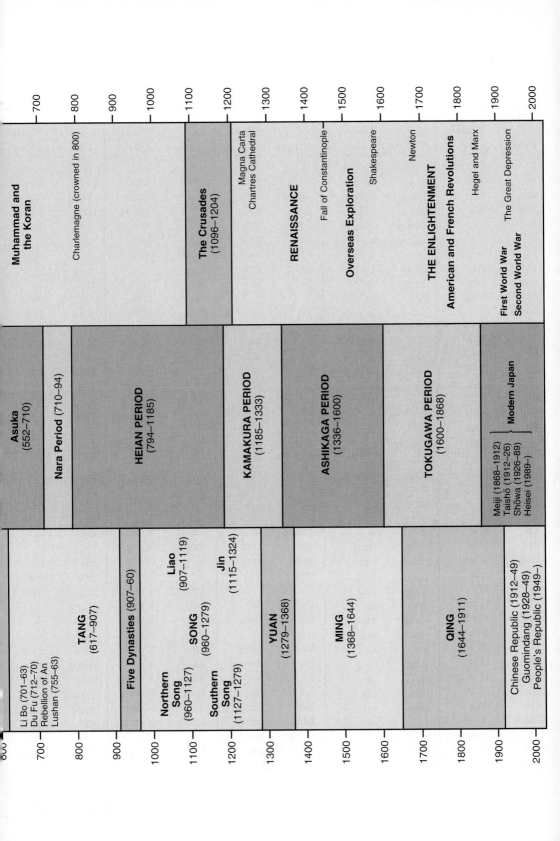

Hanyu Pinyin to Wade-Giles Conversion Table

Pinyin	Wade-Giles	Pinyin	Wade-Giles	Pinyin	Wade-Giles	Pinyin	Wade-Giles	Pinyin	Wade-Giles
a	a	chou	ch'ou	fa	fa	hua	hua	la	la
ai	ai	chu	ch'u	fan	fan	huai	huai	lai	lai
an	an	chua	ch'ua	fang	fang	huan	huan	lan	lan
ang	ang	chuai	ch'uai	fei	fei	huang	huang	lang	lang
ao	ao	chuan	ch'uan	fen	fen	hui	hui	lao	lao
		chuang	ch'uang	feng	feng	hun	hun	le	le
ba	pa	chui	ch'ui	fo	fo	huo	huo	lei	lei
bai	pai	chun	ch'un	fou	fou			leng	leng
ban	pan	chuo	ch'o	fu	fu	ji	chi	li	li
hang	pang	ci	tz'u			jia	chia	lia	lia
bao	pao	cong	ts'ung	ga	ka	jian	chien	lian	lien
bei	pei	cou	ts'ou	gai	kai	jiang	chiang	liang	liang
hen	pen	cu	ts'u	gan	kan	jiao	chiao	liao	liao
beng	peng	cuan	ts'uan	gang	kang	jie	chieh	lie	lieh
bi	pi	cui	ts'ui	gao	kao	jin	chin	lin	lin
bian	pien	cun	ts'un	ge	ko	jing	ching	ling	ling
biao	piao	cuo	ts'o	gei	kei	jiong	chiung	liu	liu
bie	pieh			gen	ken	jiu	chiu	long	lung
bin	pin	da	ta	geng	keng	ju	chü	lou	lou
bing	ping	dai	tai	gong	kung	juan	chüan	lu	lu
bo	po	dan	tan	gou	kou	jue	chüeh	lü	lü
bou	pou	dang	tang	gu	ku	jun	chün	luan	luan
bu	pu	dao	tao	gua	kua			lüan	lüan
		de	te	guai	kuai	ka	k'a	lue	lüeh
ca	ts'a	deng	teng	guan	kuan	kai	k'ai	lun	lun
cai	ts'ai	di	ti	guang	kuang	kan	k'an	luo	lo
can	ts'an	than	then	gui	kuei	kang	k'ang		
cang	ts'ang	diao	tiao	gun	kun	kao	k'ao	ma	ma
cao	ts'ao	die	tieh	guo	kuo	ke	k'o	mai	mai
ce	ts'e	ding	ting			kei	k'ei	man	man
cen	ts'en	diu	tiu	ha	ha	ken	k'en	mang	mang
ceng	ts'eng	dong	tung	hai	hai	keng	k'eng	mao	mao
cha	ch'a	dou	tou	han	han	kong	k'ung	mei	mei
chai	ch'ai	du	tu	hang	hang	kou	k'ou	men	men
chan	ch'an	duan	tuan	hao	hao	ku	k'u	meng	meng
chang	ch'ang	dui	tui	he	ho	kua	k'ua	mi	mi
chao	ch'ao	dun	tun	hei	hei	kuai	k'uai	mian	mien
che	ch'e	duo	to	hen	hen	kuan	k'uan	miao	miao
chen	ch'en			heng	heng	kuang	k'uang	mie	mieh
cheng	ch'eng	e	o	hong	hung	kui	k'uei	min	min
chi	ch'ih	en	en	hou	hou	kun	k'un	ming	ming
chong	ch'ung	er	erh	hu	hu	kuo	k'uo	miu	miu
								mo	mo
								mou	mou
								mu	mu

Pinyin	Wade-Giles	Pinyin	Wade-Giles	Pinyin	Wade-Giles	Pinyin	Wade-Giles	Pinyin	Wade-Giles
na	na			shao	shao	wa	wa	zan	tsan
nai	nai	qi	ch'i	she	she	wai	wai	zang	tsang
nan	nan	qia	ch'ia	shen	shen	wan	wan	zao	tsao
nang	nang	qian	ch'ien	sheng	sheng	wang	wang	ze	tse
nao	nao	qiang	ch'iang	shi	shih	wei	wei	zei	tsei
nei	nei	qiao	ch'iao	shou	shou	wen	wen	zen	tsen
nen	nen	qie	ch'ieh	shu	shu	weng	weng	zeng	tseng
neng	neng	qin	ch'in	shua	shua	wo	wo	zha	cha
ni	ni	qing	ch'ing	shuai	shuai	wu	wu	zhai	chai
nian	nien	qiong	ch'iung	shuan	shuan			zhan	chan
niang	niang	qiu	ch'iu	shuang	shuang			zhang	chang
niao	niao	qu	ch'ü	shui	shui	xi	hsi	zhao	chao
nie	nieh	quan	ch'üan	shun	shun	xia	hsia	zhe	che
nin	nin	que	ch'üeh	shuo	shuo	xian	hsien	zhen	chen
ning	ning	qun	ch'ün	si	ssu	xiang	hsiang	zheng	cheng
niu	niu			song	sung	xiao	hsiao	zhi	chih
nong	nung	ran	jan	sou	sou	xie	hsieh	zhong	chung
nou	nou	rang	jang	su	su	xin	hsin		
nu	nu	rao	jao	suan	suan	xing	hsing	zhou	chou
nü	nü	re	je	sui	sui	xiong	hsiung	zhu	chu
nuan	nuan	ren	jen	sun	sun	xiu	hsiu	zhua	chua
nüe	nüeh	reng	jeng	suo	so	xu	hsü	zhuai	chuai
nuo	no	ri	jih			xuan	hsüan	zhuan	chuan
		rong	jung	ta	t'a	xue	hsüeh		
ou	ou	rou	jou	tai	t'ai	xun	hsün	zhuang	chuang
		ru	ju	tan	Van				
pa	p'a	ruan	juan	tang	t'ang	ya	ya	zhui	chui
pai	p'ai	rui	jui	tao	t'ao	yai	yai	zhun	chun
pan	p'an	run	jun	te	t'e	yan	yen	zhuo	cho
pang	p'ang	ruo	jo	teng	t'eng	yang	yang	zi	tzu
pao	p'ao			ti	t'i	yao	yao	zong	tsung
pei	p'ei	sa	sa	tian	t'ien	ye	yeh	zou	tsou
pen	p'en	sai	sai	tiao	t'iao	yi	i	zu	tsu
peng	p'eng	san	san	tie	t'ieh	yin	yin	zuan	tsuan
pi	p'i	sang	sang	ting	t'ing	ying	ying	zui	tsui
pian	p'ien	sao	sao	tong	t'ung	yong	yung	zun	tsun
piao	p'iao	se	se	tou	t'ou	you	yu	zuo	tso
pie	p'ieh	sen	sen	tu	t'u	yu	yü		
pin	p'in	seng	seng	tuan	t'uan	yuan	yüan		
ping	p'ing	sha	sha	tui	t'ui	yue	yüeh		
po	p'o	shai	shai	tun	tun	yun	yün		
pou	p'ou	shan	shan	tuo	t'o				
pu	p'u	shang	shang			za	tsa		
						zai	tsai		

Source: *People's Republic of China: Administrative Atlas* (Washington, D.C.: Central Intelligence Agency, 1975), 46–47.

Wade-Giles to Pinyin Conversion Table

Each entry in the Wade-Giles column represents the initial letter or letter pair of a syllable or word. Unless otherwise indicated, conversion is accomplished simply by changing that initial letter. Where other changes are necessary or the conversion is irregular, the entire word or syllable is listed.

Wade-Giles	Pinyin	Wade-Giles	Pinyin	Wade-Giles	Pinyin	Wade-Giles	Pinyin
a	a	ch'en	chen	i	yi	p'ien	pian
		ch'eng	cheng				
cha	zha	ch'i	qi	j	r	s	s
chai	zhai	ch'ia	qia	jih	ri	shih	shi
chan	zhan	ch'iang	qiang	jo	ruo	so	suo
chang	zhang	ch'iao	qiao	jung	rong	sung	song
chao	zhao	ch'ieh	qie			ssu, szu	si
che	zhe	ch'ien	qian	k	g		
chen	zhen	ch'i	chi	ko	ge	t	d
cheng	zheng	ch'in	qin	kuei	gui	tieh	dieh
chi	ji	ch'ing	qing	kung	gong	tien	dian
chia	jia	ch'iu	qiu			to	duo
chiao	jiao	ch'iung	qiong	k'	k	tung	dong
chieh	jie	ch'o	chuo	k'o	ke		
chien	jian	ch'ou	chou	k'ung	kong	t'	t
chih	zhi	ch'u	chu			t'ieh	tie
chin	jin	ch'ü	qu	l	l	t'ien	tian
ching	jing	ch'uai	chuai	lieh	lie	t'o	tuo
chiu	jiu	ch'uan	chuan	lien	han	t'ung	tong
chiung	jiong	ch'üan	quan	lo	luo		
cho	zhuo	ch'uang	chuang	lüeh	lüe	ts, tz	z
chou	zhou	ch'üeh	que	lung	long	tso	zuo
chu	zhu	ch'ui	chui			tsung	zong
chü	ju	ch'un	chun	m	m	tzu	zi
chua	zhua	ch'ün	qun	mieh	mie		
chuai	zhuai	ch'ung	chong	mien	mian	ts', tz'	c
chuan	zhuan					ts'o	cuo
chüan	juan	f	f	n	n	ts'ung	cong
chuang	zhuang			nieh	nie	tz'u	ci
chüeh	jue	h	h	nien	nian		
chui	zhui	ho	he	no	nuo	w	w
chun	zhun	hung	hong	nüeh	ne		
chün	jun					y	y
chung	zhong	hs	x	o	o	yeh	ye
		hsieh	xie			yen	yan
ch'a	cha	hsien	xian	p	b	yu	you
ch'ai	chai	hsiung	xiong	pieh	bie	yü	yu
ch'an	chan	hsü	xu	pien	bian	yüan	yuan
ch'ang	chang	hsüan	xuan			yüeh	yue
ch'ao	chao	hsüeh	xue	p'	p	yün	yun
ch'e	che	hsün	xun	p'ieh	pie	yung	yong

Part One

The Classical Civilization of China

The first part of this book examines the beginnings of Chinese and East Asian civilization and takes the story through the Han dynasty. During this period, many institutional, intellectual, and political traditions achieved the form in which they spread both synchronically to lands beyond China and diachronically to future inhabitants of China to constitute a heritage that came to be revered as classical.

"China" in Antiquity

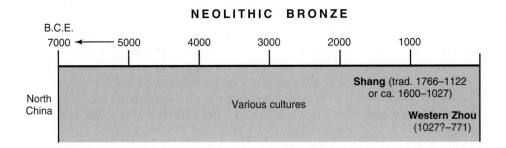

The question of when and where "Chinese" civilization began has long preoccupied scholars in China as well as in North American and Europe. Forty years ago, scholars in China and elsewhere agreed that Chinese civilization emerged from an area now known as the North China Plains (see Master Map) five millennia ago and subsequently spread through the territory that became China before disseminating throughout Northeast and into Southeast Asia. Thirty years ago, however, archaeologists in the People's Republic of China began to challenge this picture of the origins of "China" and indeed, East Asia. This chapter examines the narratives and counter-narratives of the beginnings of Chinese civilization. In doing so, it shows how archaeological discoveries and scholarly debates provide a complicated, if not conflicting, picture of origins.

The Neolithic Age

Most accounts of the origins of Chinese civilization begin with the paleontological record. The first trace of humanoid remains was discovered by archaeologists in 1965 in Yunnan Province. Based on this evidence, archaeologists have surmised that humanoids lived as long as one million years ago in Southwest China and had the use of fire. Judging from fossil remains earlier discovered near Beijing, archaeologists inferred that another kind of humanoid, the Peking man (or the *Homo erectus pekinensis*) lived about half a million years ago in North China. However, the Peking man was not an anatomically modern human, but a proto-human who used fire and worked with primitive flaked or pebble tools. Unfortunately, little else is known about the ancient inhabitants of what became China, and scholars can only speculate about the connection between anatomically modern humans and their precursors.

3

The Neolithic Age began in China about 10,000 years ago. Neolithic is a term used by archaeologists to describe cultures that use polished stone implements, as distinguished from the cruder implements of earlier ages. Neolithic cultures are also distinguished by their pottery and are often associated with agriculture and fixed human settlements. As in a number of other places on the globe, agriculture arose in China some 10,000 years ago. By recent scholarly accounts, it arose more or less simultaneously in South and North China. In the South, archaeologists found evidence of rice cultivation as well as the raising of dogs and pigs in Jiangxi Province (all geographical references are to contemporary nomenclature). Then, as now, the South provided a warm, wet climate well suited for rice cultivation. Meanwhile, millet cultivation arose in the north. In Nanzhuangtou, a village in Hebei, archaeologists discovered evidence of the earliest millet cultivation, also dating to some 10,000 years ago. As historian David Keightley recently noted, the climate of North China several millennia ago was far gentler than it is today: between around 6000–1000 B.C.E., the North China plains, now an arid and inhospitable environment, were wetter, warmer, and more temperate. And judging from the remains of Macaque monkeys, jackals, and even alligators found in the fossil record, parts of North China may have been a subtropical region with abundant water.[1]

It is important to keep in mind that the history of the early period is still very much in flux. New archaeological data and paradigms have changed and continue to change the way scholars approach the problem of the origins of Chinese civilization. As a result, it is appropriate to introduce two accounts, rather than a single, narrative account, concerning origins.

The nuclear area thesis is arguably the oldest modern narrative of the origins of Chinese civilization. It received its classical formulation in the 1960s by the American-trained archaeologist, Kwang-chih Chang (1931–2001), who later changed his mind. It held that Chinese civilization originated from a single culture of millet farmers, the Yangshao culture, in the North China Plains. Around 5000 B.C.E., this culture radiated outwards, extending from the Northeast coast all the way to present-day Qinghai in the distant Northwest.[2] Scholars have been able to track the diffusion of Yangshao culture based on the movement of Yangshao material culture, in particular, its colorful painted red or brown pottery (see Figure 1.1).

FIGURE 1.1 Painted pottery *gang* urn (bird eating fish) from North Central China, c. 3500–3000 B.C.E. This is from the Yangshao culture. In later pottery the fish design becomes increasingly abstract. (© National Museum of China.)

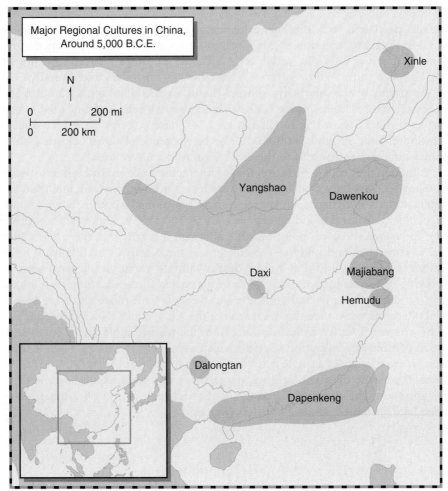

FIGURE 1.2 Map of Neolithic Age cultural sites. 🌐

A second account of the origins of Chinese civilization is called the *interactive spheres* thesis. In many ways a revision of the nuclear area thesis, it argues that the Yangshao was one culture among many in the Neolithic Age and takes into account discoveries of other cultures in various parts of China, each with its own phases. Examples of these cultures include the Daxi (5000–3000 B.C.E.), the Hemudu and Majiabang (5000–3000 B.C.E.), the Dalongtan, the Dapenkeng (5000–2500 B.C.E.), and the Xinle (7000–5000 B.C.E.) (see Figure 1.2). Each of these, as Chang pointed out in one of his last articles, had distinct styles of pottery. Artifacts from a Daxi site, located in the Yangzi River valley, have yielded pottery that is black in color with dark brown bands, sometimes with dragon designs painted on. In contrast, ceramic artifacts from Majiabang and Hemudu sites, located in Northern Zhejiang and Jiangsu on the Eastern coast, yield pottery that was brown and black. There, archaeologists have also found bone and ivory ritual artifacts decorated with or shaped in bird motifs. Unlike the millet cultivators found in Yangshao, the sites of Majiabang or Hemudu show the presence of rice farmers. In many ways, the presence of different cultures in various locations in China should come as little surprise, given its size and geographic diversity.

According to the interactive spheres thesis, around 4000 B.C.E., a number of Neolithic cultures in the North China Plains began to trade and share technology with each other. According to Chang, many of these cultures converged about a millennium later, around 3000 B.C.E. The convergence of these cultures, Chang emphasized, was to give rise to the civilization now called *China*.[3]

Although the second narrative, that of interactive spheres, has numerous merits, many scholars have challenged it. More recent accounts by archaeologists and even historians studying much later texts have questioned whether China as a single, coherent civilization did emerge as early as 3000 B.C.E. Some critics, working from the material record, point out that although it is true that there was a great deal of coherence and unity to the cultures of the North China Plains, it is important to keep in mind that a great deal of cultural variation persisted after the Neolithic Age. And indeed, judging from the material record, there were important, but distinctive, material cultures right through the Bronze and Iron Ages up until the present day. (See the discussion of the Xingan and Sanxingdui sites later in this chapter.[4]) Other critics, working from the textual angle, point out that the notion of Chinese civilization itself is a relatively recent invention. Such scholars point to the absence of a single word in *Chinese* up until the nineteenth century for *China*. Before the twentieth century, the territory that what would become China was known by the name of successive dynasties, such as the *Qin*, the *Han*—or much later, as the *Great Qing state (da Qing guo)*.[5]

The Origins of Chinese Writing

In ancient times, the place now known as China was certainly an ethnically—and linguistically—diverse area inhabited by speakers of many languages belonging to different linguistic families, ten of which have been identified by linguists. Arguably the most important language family was Sino-Tibetan, a language family that later gave rise to both modern Chinese and Tibetan. A second cluster of languages still found in present-day China was Austroasiatic, probably spoken in South China in preimperial times and later giving rise to modern languages such as Vietnamese and Khmer. The influence of Austroasiatic can still be detected through loanwords used in modern Chinese such as *Yue*, a Chinese place name (e.g., Yuenan for Vietnam), *jiang*, a term for river, and *hu*, meaning tiger.[6] A third language family that had a presence was Indo-European, a language family that, among others, gave rise to modern French, English, and Hindi. Scholars know that some Indo-European speakers lived in parts of what is now Northwest China because of the discovery of manuscripts written in an Indo-European language called Tocharian and dating from around 600 C.E. Apart from these manuscripts, evidence for the presence of Indo-European speakers comes in the form of loanwords from Tocharian. Thus, the modern Chinese term for honey (*mi*) was taken from the Tocharian word for honey.[7] In addition to Sino-Tibetan, Austroasiatic, and Indo-European, the boundaries of present-day China also included Tai-Kadia (which gave rise to modern-day Zhuang), Hmong-Mien (which gave rise to Miao-Yao),

FIGURE 1.3 The character for sun, *ri*, as found in the Shang oracle bone inscriptions.

Austronesian (the ancestor to the language still spoken by the original people of Taiwan), Altaic (which gave rise to Turkic languages and Mongol, as well as possibly to Korean and Japanese), and Xiongnu (which gave rise to the Yeniseian languages now spoken in Siberia).[8]

The origins of the Chinese script are difficult to trace. Some Chinese scholars have speculated that the earliest traces of writing predate the Shang (c. 1500–1055 B.C.E.) and can be found on Neolithic pottery fragments dating to the fifth millennium B.C.E. True, archaeologists have occasionally found pieces of pottery bearing incised or painted marks, but it is difficult to verify whether or not these marks are in fact parts of a script, because none of the marks match any of the characters found in the Shang oracle bones. There has also been speculation that the Chinese writing system was imported from outside of China. Although this is a distinct possibility, there is little evidence to date for this hypothesis. Given the paucity of evidence about the pre-Shang origins of writing, most scholars now agree that the emergence of a Chinese script probably occurred not long before 1200 B.C.E. and that it was of indigenous origin.[9]

A common myth about the Chinese script is that it, unlike our alphabet, comprises pictographs and ideograms. Pictographs are stylized pictorial representations of things, whereas ideograms are visual representations of a thing or concept through association. People who say that the Chinese language is pictographic often point to characters, such as sun, which might be construed as a visual representation of the sun (see Figure 1.3). Yet few characters, ancient or modern, are true pictographs.[10] As Figure 1.4 demonstrates, one could not tell that the early graphs represent *dragon* by merely looking at them. Early Chinese graphs, like our own alphabetic words, represent words.

Another common myth is that the Chinese script is entirely unphonetic. Although it is true that it is not as phonetic as our own, most characters have some phonetic component. Even in early China, most Chinese characters had two graphic components. One of these components represented the sounds of a word. The other component, the signifier or radical, which was used with little consistency before the first or second century B.C.E., differentiated the meaning of the graph from its homophones. As an example, consider the following characters:

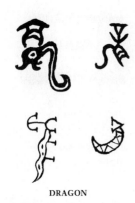

DRAGON

FIGURE 1.4 Early Chinese writing: inscriptions on bronze (heavy ink) and bone (lighter ink). (Calligraphy by Dr. Léon L. Y. Chang.)

1. *mu* 幕 "tent" (cloth radical)
2. *mu* 慕 "to long for" (heart radical)
3. *mu* 墓 "grave" (earth radical)
4. *mu* 募 "to summon" (strength radical)

In Modern Chinese, all of these four characters have the same pronunciation, because they are all read with a falling tone or pitch. In addition, they all share in common one graphic component, located at the top of the character. However, each of the four characters is distinguished by its radical, which here is located at the bottom half of the character. These basic principles are already present in the earliest known examples of writing.[11]

Although it is true that the basic principles of the Chinese script are already present in the oracle bones, the Chinese language was far from impervious to change. For one thing, the sounds of words have changed dramatically. The graph for humans, now pronounced *ren,* was pronounced as *nin* in the early Western Zhou (eleventh–tenth centuries B.C.E.). The script, furthermore, was far from standardized in the early period. Radicals were used inconsistently up through the Han dynasty (206 B.C.E.–220 C.E.). Graphs were also subject to regional variations and looked very different from each other (see Figures 1.5 and 1.6).

The Rise of the Bronze Age

The late Neolithic Era was not only a period of considerable cultural diversity but also was one of great social changes as evidenced by the material record found at Longshan cultural sites (3000–2000 B.C.E.), sites located in Northwest Henan, Southwest Shanxi, Eastern Shaanxi, and the eastern seaboard. For example, in the North China Plains, archaeologists have been struck by the differences between Longshan and the earlier Yangshao cultural sites. One major difference is the existence of town enclosures built with rammed earth at Longshan sites, implying the need of communities to defend themselves against hostile "others." Another major difference is the concentration of wealth in the graves of Longshan elites, suggesting that the distribution of wealth in Longshan society, unlike that of Yangshao society, was highly unequal.[12]

The growth of social stratification is one of a number of Late Neolithic trends that foreshadowed developments of the Chinese Bronze Age beginning around the second millennium B.C.E. Before we continue, a word about how archaeologists define the

Bronze Age in China and elsewhere is in order. As the term implies, Bronze Age cultures are characterized by the use of bronze and the rise of metallurgical technologies. They are also associated with a number of important social and political developments: as already mentioned, sharp social and economic differentiation; the rise of urban centers; and occupational specialization. Two dynasties, the Shang (c. 1500–1045 B.C.E.) and the Western Zhou (1055–771 B.C.E.), fall into the category of Bronze Age civilizations.

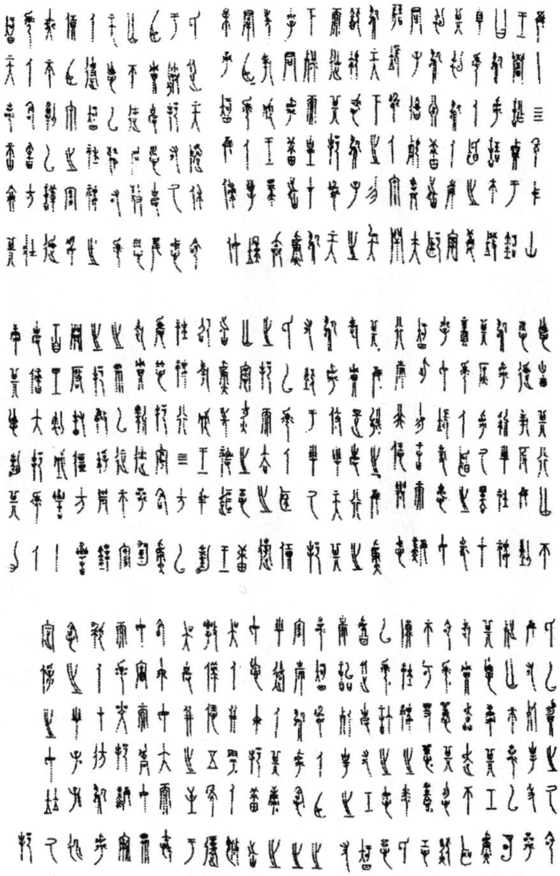

The Shang

Despite the fact that the Shang was the first civilization within present-day China known to leave written records, its origins are nevertheless murky. This is because the first surviving written records are from the latter part of the dynasty, that is, the twelfth and eleventh centuries B.C.E. Traditional Chinese

FIGURE 1.5 The first image above depicts a bronze inscription dating to the fourth century B.C.E. from the state of Zhongshan, in North China near present-day Beijing. As a casual glance confirms, the script from the Zhongshan area tended to be elongated. (© Berkeley, Society for the Study of Early China, 1997.)

accounts, based on much later records, fix the date of the Shang founding several centuries before, to 1766 B.C.E. Yet most archaeologists now think that the Shang emerged from the Longshan and other late Neolithic cultures in North and Northeast China somewhat later, by around 1500 B.C.E.[13]

The earliest evidence of the Shang comes from a site in North Central China called Erlitou, which is near modern-day Luoyang. There, archaeologists discovered foundations of large buildings, an extensive foundry, pottery, and cast bronze vessels. And from these kinds of artifacts, archaeologists have inferred that the Erlitou—or better still, the early Shang—civilization already had

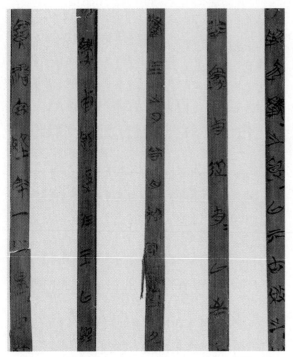

FIGURE 1.6 The image above is an example of Chu writing from South China (modern-day Hubei) on bamboo, fourth century B.C.E. Unlike the graphs from the image in Figure 1.5, the graphs here, excavated from a Southern tomb in present-day Hubei, are relatively wide and stout. (© Cultural Relics Publishing House.) ⊗

a great deal of occupational differentiation. Later Shang sites found at Erligang in Northwest China, however, hint at an even more complex state and society by the fifteenth and fourteenth centuries B.C.E. There, archaeologists found evidence that bronze vessels were even more numerous and sophisticated in design, which suggests that bronze production had by then become a large-scale enterprise. More strikingly, Erligang vessels were found outside of the Yellow River valley, which suggests that Erligang technology had disseminated widely.[14]

By the late Shang (c. twelfth century B.C.E.) written sources became available. One of the most, if not the most, important sources for our understanding of the Shang are the oracle bone inscriptions, divinatory records of the Shang kings inscribed on the backs of cattle scapulas and turtle shells. Scholars first became aware of oracle bone inscriptions in 1898 and quickly realized that they were the lost records of the Shang kings. Over time, archaeologists have collected and excavated the fragments of around 200,000 oracle bones from the area near modern-day Anyang, the site of the late Shang capital. The discovery of the oracle bones has not only greatly enhanced our knowledge of the Shang, but it has also provided independent confirmation that later accounts had some basis in history of the historical evidence of the Shang.

The oracle bone shown in Figure 1.7 records several divinations from the reign of King Wuding (1200–1180 B.C.E.). As interpreted and translated by David Keightley, the inscription confirms the king's forecast of disaster. It reads:

> [*Preface:*] Crack-making on *guisi* day [day 40], Que divined: "In the next ten days there will be no disasters." [*Prognostication:*] "There will be calamities; there may be someone bringing alarming news." [*Verification:*] When it came to the fifth day, *dingyou* [day 34], there re-

ally was someone bringing alarming news from the west. Guo of Zhi [a Shang general] reported and said: "The Tufang [an enemy country] have attacked in our eastern borders and have seized two settlements." The Gongfang [another enemy country] likewise invaded the fields of our western borders.[15]

Along with the discovery of thousands of Shang ritual bronzes, the oracle bones have provided historians with valuable clues about the lives of the Shang rulers. They reveal the degree to which ancestral worship pervaded Shang state religion and political culture. Shang kings believed that their ancestors played an active role in their daily lives and fortunes. On behalf of the Shang kings, the ancestors could intercede with the Shang deity, Di (the Lord on High) to ensure good harvests and victory in war, the former fueling the military campaigns and displays of military strength by which he asserted his power. Unsurprisingly, the legitimacy of the Shang kings was rooted in the power and influence of their ancestors. The ancestors also punish the mortal kings (sometimes with toothaches), as well as provide clues about the future.[16] For example, in one case, the King Wuding divined about the pregnancy of one of his consorts. This inscription reads:

FIGURE 1.7 Oracle bone from the reign of King Wuding (twelfth century B.C.E.). According to David Keightley, the Shang created the oracle bones by gathering cattle scapulas and turtle shells. The cattle and turtles would be killed, and the bones would be cleaned before being ritually cracked by application of heat. The cracks would subsequently be interpreted as an auspicious or inauspicious answer from the ancestors to a query. Lastly, the scapulas and shells would be inscribed with a record of the divination. (© C.V. Starr East Asian Library, Columbia University.)

> Crack-making on *jiashen* [day 21], Que divined: [*Charge:*] "Lady Hao's childbearing will be good." [*Prognostication:*] The king read the cracks and said: "If it be a *ding*-day childbearing, it will be good; if it be a *geng*-[day] childbearing, there will be prolonged luck." [*Verification:*] [After] thirty-one days, on *jiayin* [day 51], she gave birth; it was not good; it was a girl."[17]

Given the importance of ancestors, it is not surprising that the Shang paid "assiduous attention" to the treatment of the special dead.[18] The Shang elite dead, which included petty elites as well as members of the Shang royal lineage, were

FIGURE 1.8 Photograph displaying sacrificial victims found in a Shang tomb. Humans being sacrificed were decapitated and dismembered before being buried in the pits and ramps of the tomb. (From Loewe and Shaughnessy, *The Cambridge History of Ancient China*.)

buried in style: the higher the rank of the individual, the larger the tomb. The tombs of lesser elites were costly to construct and often had one ramp. Sitting at the top of the political and social hierarchy, the Shang kings were buried in massive burial chapters, dug deep in the ground and connected to the surface with four ramps.[19] In addition to being large, the tombs of Shang elites were often filled with lavish grave goods. The tomb of Wuding's consort, Lady Hao, provides a good example. In the larger scheme of things, her tomb was probably relatively modest. But when excavated in 1976, archaeologists discovered 468 bronzes, weighing together more than 1.5 metric tons; 755 jades; and 6880 cowry shells.[20] If Lady Hao's tomb was only modest, one wonders what treasures once lay in the tombs of the Shang kings, which were long ago looted by grave robbers. There is still further evidence that the Shang elites paid assiduous attention to their special dead: human sacrifice. Whereas human sacrifice was not new—the Longshan elites also sacrificed humans to accompany their special dead—the large scale of human sacrifice was something new and perhaps unique to the Shang elites. A relatively modest elite burial site, like that of Lady Hao, only had about a dozen or so victims. A particularly lavish burial site, however, could hold as many as 400 victims. Most of these were low-status young males—probably foreign prisoners of war. But there were also women and children among the victims in some tombs. In still other cases, the dead included high-status victims: royal relatives or personal dependents of the deceased, in turn accompanied by *their own* human sacrifices (see Figure 1.8).[21]

The lavish burials of the Shang elite suggest that they commanded the lion's share of wealth and human resources. They controlled a large army of labor conscripts, conscripts who represented the basis of state power: "They served in armies, built temple-palaces, excavated tombs, hauled supplies, cleared land and farmed it, and worked at the sundry tasks of production and manufacture required by the elites."[22]

The extent of the Shang elites' material resources is perhaps most clearly demonstrated by the large-scale use of costly bronzes. The bronze vessels that the elites used to drink, for banquets, and to make ancestral sacrifices required large-scale and well-organized mining and smelting industries with a forced labor pool, as well as a high degree of professional specialization. Such professional specialization is evident in the quality of Shang bronzes, which were noted for their clarity of detail and perfection of craftsmanship (see Figures 1.9 and 1.10). Bronze was worked in foundries outside Shang cities by artisans who had quarters beyond the city walls. The quarters of artisans who worked bronzes had floors of stamped earth. Although hardly luxurious, these houses were nevertheless superior to those of peasants, who lived in semi-subterranean dwellings. Bronze was a material almost exclusively reserved for the elite, as peasants continued to use stone tools and Neolithic agricultural methods.

FIGURE 1.9 This is a bronze *jue* or wine vessel, dating to the late Shang, c. 1200 B.C.E. It is 14.69 in tall and weighs 9.70 lbs. This is a common kind of ritual vessel from the Shang, one used by the political elites. (© HIP/Scala/Art Resource, NY.)

The bronze vessels of the ruling elite were cast in many forms. Some bronze forms derived from older pottery traditions. In contrast, other forms were based on containers made of more perishable materials. Still other bronze forms appear to have been new to the Shang, and these were receptacles for storing or serving various solids and liquids used in ritual ceremonies.

Characteristically, all available space on Shang bronzes is covered by decorations. One popular decoration was the forms of real and imaginary animals.

FIGURE 1.10 Bronze set (© Metropolitan Museum of Art, Munsey Fund, 1931. [24.72.1-14]. Photogtraph by Schecter Lee. © 1986 The Metropolitan Museum of Art.)

Figure 1.10 provides some examples. The pieces in this set of collected bronzes date from the late Shang or perhaps early Zhou dynasty. The set includes vessels in various styles. Most clearly visible in the illustration of the set are the heads, perhaps of rams, on the handles of the two ritual vessels at the top and the single-legged creature resembling a dragon. Some abstract forms also derive from animals. For instance, on the *gu*—the vessel in front of the set in the very center—the vertical decoration, which looks like a flower petal, is a stylized cicada. Other forms, such as the *taotie,* the most common motif on early bronzes, are still more abstract (see Figure 1.11). The *taotie,* which some scholars believe depicts a mythological being, is also presented frontally as though squashed onto a horizontal plane to form a symmetrical design. Over the centuries, various explanations of the *taotie* have arisen. In the late Zhou dynasty, some commentators described it as a covetous man banished by the Shang to guard a corner of heaven against evil monsters or, more fancifully, as a monster equipped with only a head, who tries to devour men but hurts only itself. Yet there is uncertainty about how seriously to take these explanations. One problem is that only much later, that is, during the Song dynasty (960–1279 C.E.), was the form appearing on the bronzes identified as a *taotie* at all.

Despite the impressiveness of the Shang written and material record, it is important to bear in mind that the Shang was not the only advanced material civilization within the borders of present-day China. By the thirteenth century B.C.E., bronze-casting technologies and styles from the Yellow River area spread elsewhere, prompting the development of other, very distinctive Bronze Age civiliza-

Crest   **C-horn**   **Tail** **Quill**

Lower jaw **Forehead** **Fang** **Snout** **Upper jaw or trunk** **Beak or fang** **Eye** **Leg**

FIGURE 1.11 *Taotie* design. (From William Willets, *Chinese Art, Vol. 1* [Hamondworth, England, 1958] by permission Penguin Books Ltd. and courtesy of William Willets.)

tions. Two such civilizations were discovered in the last 30 years, one centered in the Lower Yangzi River area and one centered in Southwest China.

In 1972 archaeologists discovered a new civilization when they excavated a rich tomb from Xingan in Jiangxi Province dated to around 1200 B.C.E., making it roughly contemporaneous with the late Shang kings. It is the richest Bronze Age tomb ever found in present-day China. To be sure, many of the artifacts found there, like the bronze ritual vessel shown in Figure 1.12, revealed the diffusion of Erligang or middle Shang bronze casting technologies. Yet, the artifacts were clearly not made by Shang artisans, nor were they mere copies of Shang bronzes. As Bagley argues, the bronzes were of "an undeniable local character" and thus suggest that local craftsmen had adapted the technologies and styles from the North China Plains to create products to suit local tastes.

The second civilization is that of Sanxingdui in Southwest China, which was discovered by archaeologists in 1980. Chinese archaeologists excavated there the remains of a city wall and two sacrificial deposits, which, like the Xingan site, also date to around 1200 B.C.E. The pits yielded a wealth of material culture, including several hundred bronze, jade, and gold artifacts, cowry shells, and thirteen elephant tusks. Like the artifacts found at the Xingan site, some of the material remains from the Sanxingdui site point to early contacts with the late Neolithic precursors to the Shang—and to *other* non-Shang Bronze Age civilizations from the middle Yangzi region. More interestingly, there is no evidence that the Sanxingdui artisans, unlike their Xingan contemporaries, had much contact with Shang culture.[23] In fact, much of the material culture from the Sanxingdui site strongly suggests that it represents a tradition distinct from those found in the North China

FIGURE 1.12 Bronze tripod from Xingan site, Jiangxi Province (c. 1400–1200 B.C.E.). It is 24.57 in tall with a diameter of 6.10 in and weighs 62.83 lbs. (© Asian Art & Archaeology, Inc./CORBIS.)

Plains. For example, in one of the sacrificial pits, archaeologists discovered a life-size statue on a pedestal, forty-one heads, and twenty or so mask-like items (see Figure 1.13). These masks have caught the attention of scholars because they are so different from anything found in the North China Plains, where craftsmen showed little interest making human representations.[24]

The Western Zhou Dynasty

Led by King Wu (r. 1049/45–1043 B.C.E.), Zhou armies from the West invaded the Central Plains and defeated the last Shang king in battle at Muye around 1045 B.C.E. For several millennia thereafter, the event was seen not as a simple coup d'état, but as Edward Shaughnessy has aptly put it, it represented nothing short of the will of Heaven. The following stanzas from the *Odes* (*Shi*) retrospectively commemorated the event:

> The Yin-Shang legions,
> Their battle flags like a forest,
> Were arrayed on the field of Muye.
> "Arise, my lords,
> The Lord on High looks down on you;
> Have no second thoughts."
> The field of Muye was so broad.
> The sandalwood chariots were so gleaming.
> The teams of four were so pounding.
> There was the general Shangfu.
> He rose as an eagle.
> Aiding that King Wu,
> And attacked the great Shang,
> Meeting in the morning, clear and bright.[25]

According to later Chinese historians, the reason the Shang house lost its mandate is that their rulers had failed to serve the people. As a result, Heaven (*tian*)—the Zhou's highest deity—revoked the mandate and gave it to the Zhou house, which had a healthy supply of virtuous men. But the Zhou mandate did not last. Less than 300 years later, the dynastic cycle had come full circle. Like their Shang predecessors, the last of the Western Zhou kings had neglected their responsibilities as guardians of the people. As a legend recounted by historian Sima Qian (c. 140–c. 90 B.C.E.) notes, the last of the Western Zhou kings, King You (r. 781–771 B.C.E.) had been the epitome of a bad last ruler of a dynasty. Smitten with a royal concubine of purported supernatural origin, King You spared no effort or expense in seeking to please his beloved, but all for naught. One day, however, a beacon was lit mistakenly to warn of an invasion of an alien group, the Quan Rong. And, as was customary, all the lords sworn to protect the king came to the capital, ready to fight the invaders. This spectacle caught the beloved's fancy, so the king then had the beacon lit again so that the lords would come to the capital. This occurred repeatedly, but each time the beacon was lit, fewer of the king's lords came into the capital. Finally, in 771 B.C.E., the Quan Rong did invade. The beacon was lit, but none of the lords came to assist the king. The king was killed, the capital was sacked, and the Western Zhou came to a rather inglorious end.[26]

Before we plunge into the details of the origins and development of the Western Zhou, a few words about our sources are in order. One set of sources are texts, which are most likely later in date and of unknown provenance. These include the *Odes* (*Shi*), the *History* (*Shang shu*), and the *Changes* (*Yi*). A second source for historians is the tens of thousands of inscriptions that were cast into ritual bronze vessels. Although generally more reliable than much later accounts, the bronze inscriptions too have their limitations as sources, as they tend to focus exclusively on events that brought glory to the owners. These vessels were commemorative and were often cast for individuals by the royal court in recognition of past achievements or future charges.[27] The following inscription dates to around 825 B.C.E.:

FIGURE 1.13 Bronze standing figure from Sanxingdui, Sichuan, c. 1300–1100 B.C.E. The figure stands 103.15 in. (© Cultural Relics Publishing House.)

It was the third year, fifth month, after the dying brightness, *jiaxu* [day 11]; the king was at the Zhao [Temple] of the Kang Palace. At dawn the king entered the Great Chamber and assumed his position. Intendant [*zai*] Yin to the right of Song entered the gate and stood in the center of the court. Yinshi received the king's command document. The king called out to Scribe [*shi*] Guo Sheng to record the command to Song:

> The king said: "Song, [I] command you to officiate over and to supervise the Chengzhou warehouse, and to oversee and supervise the newly constructed warehouses, using palace attendants. [I] award you a black jacket with embroidered hem, red kneepads, a scarlet demicircle, a chime pennant, and a bridle with bit and cheekpieces; use [them] to serve."

> Song bowed and touched his head to the ground, received the command, and suspended the strips from his sash in order to go out. He returned and brought in a jade tablet. Song dares in response to extol the Son of Heaven's illustriously fine beneficence, herewith making [for] my august deceased-father Gongshu and august mother Gongsi [this] treasured offertory *gui*-tureen, to use to send back filial piety and to beseech vigor, pure aid, through riches, and an eternal mandate. May Song for ten-thousand years be long-lived, truly ministering to the Son of Heaven [until] a numinous end, and [have] sons' sons and grandsons' grandsons eternally to treasure and use [it].[28]

Despite the great symbolic importance of the Zhou house to later thinkers and the existence of written records, its origins are murky. The Zhou float in and out of the Shang oracle bones, alternatively as foreign enemies, as embittered allies, and then as a powerful enemy before dropping out of the record altogether. For an explanation of the origins of the Zhou, conflicting accounts are found in later legends, such as that preserved in the *Odes*, which has it that the Zhou people were of divine parentage. A woman known as Jiang Yuan was supposed to have become pregnant by stepping into the footprint of the Lord on High (*di*), the same deity from the Shang. Subsequently, Jiang Yuan gave birth to Hou Ji or the "Lord of Millet," who was not only the Zhou founder but also was reputed to have invented agriculture. Traditional Chinese scholars, often in disagreement with each other, provide more mundane accounts of the origins of the Zhou. Some scholars state that the Zhou were from the East, in the Fen River valley of Shanxi. Others, however, insist that the Zhou were originally from a place called Bin, which is believed to have been in the West, in Shaanxi.[29] If the latter is correct, then the Zhou would have been of Western and, hence, alien origins. Along these lines, art historian Jessica Rawson has argued that the Zhou emerged from the consolidation of a group of loosely connected tribes in the Northwest. These peoples, she notes, were culturally distinct from the Shang and other peoples from the Central Plains. Judging from their emphasis on military rituals and material culture, the Zhou were part of a larger cultural milieu common to other peoples from the Northwest.[30]

The Western Zhou king, known as the "son of Heaven" (*tian zi*), did not directly rule over all of the conquered territory, which increased dramatically during the early years of the dynasty. Instead, he or his advisors initially invested members of the royal family with territory to rule more or less without interference from the Zhou king. Later, the dynasty also sought alliances with local powers. These alliances were cemented—or more accurately, tenuously held together—with fictive kinship ties. Also included, but to a much lesser degree, among the ranks of subordinate rulers were the descendants of the Shang royal house, who would reemerge, if only briefly, as a threat to the Zhou house. Given territory, the Shang descendants continued to perform sacrifices to their ancestors, perhaps to relieve the Zhou from the threat of supernatural retribution. During the early years of the dynasty, the Zhou king managed the core territory in the Zhou homeland, in the Wei River valley, while the brothers and nephews of King Wu were sent to defend and govern important territories in North and Northeast China. This arrangement set the pattern for subsequent generations. Later Zhou kings continued to charge their relatives with governing and defending a large number of territories for the Zhou house. Often, each time they charged their relatives, they would order a bronze inscription to commemorate the event.[31] As time went on, however, the bond between the main line of the Zhou house and the descendants of their kin and allies grew increasingly thin.

The relationship between the Zhou kings and the subordinate territorial authorities resembles, to a certain extent, that between lords and vassals in medieval Europe. As a result, the Zhou political system has often been identified as feudal. Nevertheless, there are major differences, such as the absence in the Zhou of subinfeudation or the phenomenon of vassals having their own vassals. Unlike their European counterparts, the Zhou appealed to bonds of kinship rather than to contractual agreements. Furthermore, the contrasts between the history of postfeudal Europe and post-Zhou make it very difficult to apply the term *feudalism* to both in the sense of a stage of development in a universal historical process. Awareness of the differences between them further serves to restrain the temptation to overinterpret the Zhou evidence, which is much more meager than that available for the student of Europe almost 2000 years later. The difficulties are further compounded by disagreements over the definition of feudalism itself. This is not the place for a study of comparative feudalism, but, in any case, post-Heian Japan presents a much richer and more fruitful field for such a study than does Western Zhou because the parallels between Japan and Europe are far more numerous.

It is important to note that from the start, the early Western Zhou rulers and their allies discovered that governing the realm was difficult. For one, political loyalty tends to become uncertain as blood ties thin. One hundred years after the Zhou conquest, the Zhou King Mu was faced with rather weak ties with relatives, who at best were second or third cousins, administering distant territories and vice versa.[32] For another, even close kinsmen could not always be counted on to be either loyal or cooperative. Not long after the Shang conquest, the virtuous King Wu died, leaving an heir, King Cheng (r. 1042/35–1006 B.C.E.), who was too young to rule. One of the younger brothers of King Wu declared himself the regent for the king, an action that proved controversial—and politically disastrous. Three of King Wu's brothers rebelled against the young king from the East, aligning themselves with the descendants of the vanquished Shang.[33] Finally, there was the threat of emerging regional powers. In the West, the Quan Rong, an alien group, invaded the capital at Chengzhou, in the East were the Xu Rong, and in the South were the Yi, who lived in the Yangzi River area. Not only were they hostile to the Zhou ruling house, but at least one of these groups was able to form a block against the Zhou, thereby uniting for a time peoples in *thirty-six* states in the Northeast, as well as Central and South China.[34]

The Odes

One of the greatest works of world literature, the *Odes,* also known as the *Classic of Poetry* or the *Book of Odes,* was created beginning in the Western Zhou dynasty. According to Eastern Zhou lore, Confucius, who will be extensively discussed in Chapter 2, selected some 300 of the odes and edited them into their present form. Later, the *Odes* became part of what many scholars came to refer to as the *Five Classics (Wu jing)*, which included the *Changes (Yi)*, the *Documents (Shang shu)*, the *Spring and Autumn Annals (Chun qiu)*, and the *Ceremonials (Yi li)*. Although there is much in the *Odes* that appeals to people of all places and times, it is important not to forget that most people did not read the odes to themselves in silence, but recited them out loud and learned them by heart. They were also probably sung in public performances or communal gatherings, not just read or recited in silence.

The *Odes* was not unique in that it was memorized and orally transmitted, but what is extraordinary about the *Odes* is that it represents a wide range of human experience for people from all walks of life. As seen earlier, it contains commemorative odes that recount the victory of the Zhou king against the Shang. There are religious hymns and the stately songs that accompanied royal, festive, and ceremonial occasions. There are prayers evoking Lord Millet (Hou Ji), the reputed ancestor of the Zhou.

In addition to these perspectives, the *Odes* represents the perspectives of peasants—perspectives unseen in Zhou inscriptions. Some songs show ordinary people at work: the men clearing weeds from the fields, plowing, planting, and harvesting; and the girls and women gathering mulberry leaves for the silkworms, making thread, carrying food hampers out to the fields for their men to have lunch. There is much about millet—both the eating variety and that used for brewing wine for use in rites. There are joyful references to granaries full of grain and to the men gathering thatch for their roofs in the off-season. Mention is made of lords' fields and private fields, and a bailiff is referred to, but the details of the system are not provided. There are also, more strikingly, odes of political protest. One compares tax collectors to big rats:

> Big rat, big rat,
> Do not gobble our millet!

Three years we have slaved for you,
Yet you take no notice of us.
At last we are going to leave you
And go to that happy land;
Happy land, happy land,
Where we shall have our place.[35]

Another tells of the hardships of military service: men constantly on the march, living in the wilds like rhinoceroses and tigers, day and night without rest. Sometimes a soldier survives the hardships and dangers of war and returns home only to find that his wife has given him up for dead and remarried. Consider the following:

We plucked the bracken, plucked the bracken;
While the shoots were soft
Oh, to go back, go-back!
Our hearts are sad,
Our sad hearts burn,
We are hungry and thirsty,
But our campaign is not over,
Nor is any of us sent home with news.[36]

Still other odes give us glimpses of the day-to-day hardships of Zhou peasants, who lived at the mercy of what was becoming an increasingly inhospitable environment:

The drought is long and deep,
Parched and barren in the landscape.
The drought demon is vicious
Like a burn, like a blaze.
Our hearts are tormented by the heat,
Our grieved hearts as if aflame.
The former ministers and their lords,
Even they do not hear our plea.
Mighty Heaven,
God on High
Why do you force us to flee?[37]

In addition to royal and peasant perspectives, the *Odes* is also famous for its love poetry, which often employs the feminine perspective:

In the wilds, there is a dead doe.
With white rushes we cover her.
There was a lady longing for the spring;
A fair knight seduced her.
In the woods there is a clump of oaks.
And in the wilds a dead deer
With white rushes well bound;
There was a lady fair as jade.

white = color of mournin.

"Heigh, not so hasty, not so rough;
Heigh, do not touch my handkerchief.
Take care, or the dog will bark." [38]

The feminine perspective in ancient China could be quite erotic or even ribald, as this ode reveals:

That the mere glimpse of a plain cap
Could harry me with such longing,
Cause pain so dire!
That the mere glimpse of a plain coat
Could stab my heart with grief!
Enough! Take me with you to your home.
That a mere glimpse of plain leggings
Could tie my heart in tangles!
Enough! Let us two be one. [39]

To be sure, with these odes, as with all poetry, much depends on the vision of the translator and interpreter. For Liu Wu-chi, the ode tells of "the tragedy of love." In the mind of another contemporary scholar, Wai-lim Yip, the first ode cited in the last paragraph is an "animated pastiche of a lovely rural seducement song."[40]

It is a truism that to translate is to interpret, and much is inevitably lost in the process. But to read is also to interpret, and in reading these odes, later literary and scholarly elites from Han times on "translated" them to conform to their own ideas of what a classic should be, namely a repository of lessons in social and political morality. And commentators worked hard to show how this should be done. For example, the ribald ode (second in the last paragraph) was transformed into a lament for the decline in ritual propriety, an indication of the decay of filial piety, because white is the color of mourning in China. Thus, in a nineteenth-century English translation by James Legge, following Chinese commentators, the ode begins:

If I could but see the white cap,
And the earnest mourner worn to leaness!
My toiled heart is torn with grief. [41]

Given the fact that Victorian elites by and large frowned upon expressions of female desire, it is not surprising that the translator would have preferred to interpret the ode in staid terms. But no matter which translation of the ode about the dead doe one selects, it is not the traditional interpretation: the *Odes* we read today is not the same as that read by traditional scholars, for *all* modern readers bring a different vision to the text. But the study of civilization cannot even begin without an attempt to understand traditional views and images. This is true of all periods, but it is especially pertinent to a consideration of antiquity, because the gap between the classical understanding of the odes and the modern is not any wider than that between the account of origins presented in this chapter and the traditional view once held by educated persons in what is now China.

Notes

1. David N. Keightley, "The Environment of Ancient China," in Edward Shaughnessy and Michael Loewe, eds., *The Cambridge History of Ancient China: From the Origins of Civilization to 221 BC* (Cambridge: Cambridge Univ. Press, 1999), pp. 35–36.

2. K.C. Chang, "China on the Eve of the Historical Period," in *Cambridge History of Ancient China*, pp. 49–52.

3. Chang, p. 59.

4. Robert Bagley, "Shang Archaeology," in *Cambridge History of Ancient China*, pp. 124–25.

5. For this view, see Lydia Liu, *The Clash of Empires: The Invention of China in Modern World* (Cambridge: Harvard Univ. Press, 2004); Laura Hostetler, *Qing Colonial Enterprise: Ethnography and Cartography in Early Modern China* (Chicago: Univ. of Chicago Press, 2001), p. 27.

6. William G. Boltz, "Language and Writing," *Cambridge History of Ancient China*, pp. 81–83.

7. Boltz, pp. 83–87.

8. William Baxter, Private communication, 2 February 2004.

9. Boltz, p. 108.

10. Boltz, pp. 109–12.

11. Boltz, pp. 118–23.

12. Chang, pp. 59–65.

13. Keightley, "The Shang: China's First Historical Dynasty," in *Cambridge History of Ancient China*, p. 232.

14. Bagley, "Shang Archaeology," p. 157.

15. Keightley, "The Shang," p. 242.

16. Keightley, "The Shang," pp. 236–37.

17. Keightley, "The Shang," pp. 236–37.

18. Keightley, "The Shang," p. 263.

19. Keightley, "The Shang," p. 268.

20. Bagley, "Shang Archaeology," pp. 194–95.

21. Keightley, "The Shang," pp. 266–67; Bagley, pp. 195–96.

22. Keightley, "The Shang," p. 282.

23. Bagley, "Shang Archaeology," pp. 121–213.

24. Xiaoneng Yang, ed., *Golden Age of Chinese Archaeology: Celebrated Discoveries from the People's Republic of China*, (Washington, D.C.: National Gallery of Art, 1999), p. 209.

25. Edward Shaughnessy, "Western Zhou History," in *Cambridge History of Ancient China*, p. 310.

26. Shaughnessy, "Western Zhou History," p. 350.

27. Shaughnessy, "Western Zhou History," p. 298.

28. Shaughnessy, "Western Zhou History," pp. 298–99.

29. Shaughnessy, "Western Zhou History," p. 299–305.

30. Jessica Rawson, "Western Zhou Archaeology," in *Cambridge History of Ancient China*, pp. 383–85.

31. Shaughnessy, pp. 317–19.

32. Shaughnessy, p. 323.

33. Shaughnessy, pp. 310–13.

34. Shaughnessy, pp. 323–25.

35. *The Book of Songs*, trans. Arthur Waley (New York, Grove Press, 1996), pp. 88–89.

36. *The Book of Songs*, p. 140.

37. *The Book of Songs*, p. 271.

38. *The Book of Songs*, p. 114.

39. *The Book of Songs*, p. 114.

40. *Chinese Poetry* (Berkeley: Univ. of California Press, 1975), p. 53.

41. James Legge, *The Chinese Classics, IV: The She King* (Reprinted Hong Kong: Hong Kong Univ. Press, 1960), p. 216.

2

Turbulent Times and Classical Thought

The Spring and Autumn Period

The Warring States Period

"The Hundred Schools"

Confucius

Mozi

Mencius

Xunzi

Laozi and Zhuangzi

Han Feizi

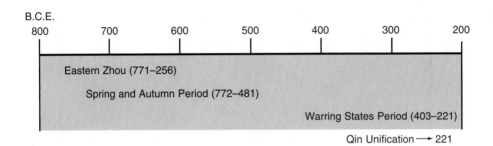

B.C.E.

| 800 | 700 | 600 | 500 | 400 | 300 | 200 |

Eastern Zhou (771–256)

Spring and Autumn Period (772–481)

Warring States Period (403–221)

Qin Unification ⟶ 221

The 550 years from 771 to 221 B.C.E., a time of major social change and political upheaval, were regarded by traditional scholars as a period of decline from the heights of the early Zhou dynasty. In this they followed the great majority of articulate, elite men who lived through these turbulent centuries and did not consider themselves fortunate to have been born in an age when great changes were underway, changes that were to lead to a stronger, more extensive, and more prosperous civilization. They could not know what the future would bring, and for them, it was a bewildering and disturbing age. Old beliefs and assumptions were challenged, prompting questions never before raised and stimulating intellectual exploration in many directions. Some of these new concepts were later abandoned; others became the guidelines for Chinese thought for centuries.

The period from 771 to 221 B.C.E. is known as the Eastern Zhou Period because the dynastic capital was in the Eastern city of Chengzhou. The Eastern Zhou is further divided into two periods: the Spring and Autumn Period (771–453 B.C.E.) and the Warring States Period (453–221 B.C.E.). The former derives from the *Spring and Autumn Annals*, a terse and opaque chronicle that covers the years after the fall of the Western Zhou capital to the beginning of the Warring States Period. The latter gets its name from the long and protracted nature of its wars.

The Spring and Autumn Period

During this period, the Zhou kingship continued to experience a decline of prestige and power. Not only were Zhou kings unable to defend themselves, but they were also increasingly at the mercy (or under the protection) of the powerful lords of "vassal" states. The last Western Zhou king (781–771 B.C.E.) had been removed and killed by a joint force led by vassal states, Shen, and the alien Quan Rong. The next ruler, King Ping, survived only after being rescued by the rulers of two pow-

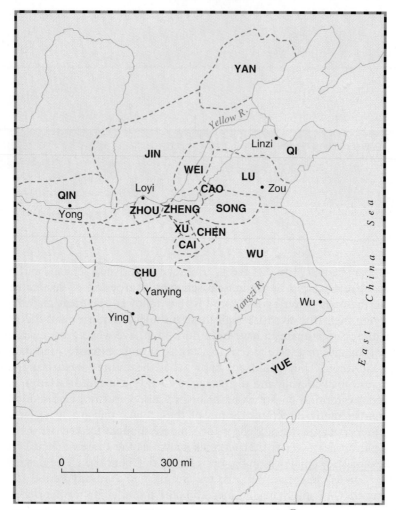

FIGURE 2.1 States of the Spring and Autumn Period.

erful states, Jin and Qi, and removed from the Wei River valley in the West to Chengzhou. In many ways, these two incidents exemplify what became the dominant trends of the Spring and Autumn Period: the decline of Zhou kingship accompanied by the rise of powerful vassal states. The most powerful of these new states included Qi in Shandong and Jin in Shanxi, as well as two powerful but culturally distinct states, Chu (in the Yangzi River area) and Qin (in Shaanxi) (see Figure 2.1).

In 667 B.C.E., a new interstate political system headed by so-called hegemons (*ba*) filled the power vacuum left by the decline of the Zhou kingship. The hegemons were the lords of the most powerful states. They were not only the custodians or caretakers of the Zhou king but were also heads of leagues of smaller and less powerful states. The hegemon would occasionally convene the rulers of allied states and make everyone take blood oaths, swearing loyalty to each other. In theory, the alliances were guaranteed by the spirit world, but, in fact, they proved to be unstable. As later records show, states that were supposed to be allied often went to war. The failure of these alliances led to an increase in tensions among the states and created a general aura of suspicion and betrayal in the sixth century B.C.E.

The best-known hegemon is Duke Wen (r. 636–628 B.C.E.), also known as Chong'er or Double Ears. Lord Wen's life story in many ways exemplifies the moral and political decline depicted by most traditional scholars, a situation in which fathers and sons were alienated while concubines and unscrupulous ministers usurped the role of proper consorts and heirs. Lord Wen, along with his elder brother, was a son of Lord Xian of Jin (r. 676–651 B.C.E.) by his proper consort. To understand his story, one must bear in mind that in early China, male members of the ruling elite often practiced polygamy but were allowed only one proper wife or consort. The other women were considered concubines. Only the children of the wife qualified as proper heirs.

Lord Xian happened in old age to be given a beautiful concubine, even though he already had two able and virtuous grown sons. Although the new concubine knew that these should succeed Lord Xian, she hoped that her own son would instead become the next lord of Qi. With this in mind she convinced her infatuated husband to order his two eldest sons killed. Although the eldest was killed, the younger, the future Duke Wen, escaped. He then spent many years wandering in foreign lands before returning to Qi and exacting revenge upon his stepmother and half-brother. Assuming the lordship of Jin, he consolidated his rule by annexing smaller states next to Jin, seizing major trade routes and salt flats, and absorbing the semi-assimilated Rong, Di, and Yi tribes. Having in his possession a large and powerful state, Duke Wen was poised to become a hegemon.

Despite political uncertainties, some important economic developments took place. One such development was the introduction of soybean cultivation, which had originated in the northwest in Manchuria. In the second half of the seventh century B.C.E., soybean cultivation spread to what is now China proper. In addition to being a rich source of protein and an important addition to the Chinese diet, this new crop plant also contains nitrogen-fixing bacteria that helped augment the fertility of the soil in which it was grown.

Another important development pointing to the future involved the taxation system. In Lu, a small state in Shandong, the ruling house enacted a reform in 594 B.C.E. that required peasants to pay land rents directly to them rather than to landlords. This represents the first example of a system of direct taxation.

Although the Spring and Autumn Period is often associated with the decline of Zhou royal power, it is important to keep in mind the fact that there were a number of important political and economic developments during this period. The first was the rise of powerful, increasingly centralized states, other than the Zhou. The second was the emergence of soybean cultivation, which not only led to improvements in diet but also increased agricultural yields. The third involved new and more efficient methods of taxation, methods that would prove indispensable to centralized states.

The Warring States Period

During the Warring States Period (453–221 B.C.E.), the trends already visible in the late Spring and Autumn Period accelerated. Some states, such as Chu and Qin, became increasingly powerful and annexed their neighbors, whereas other states, even formerly strong states such as Jin and Qi, were destroyed.

It is noteworthy that neither Chu nor Qin was located in the Central Plains, the old heartland of Zhou culture in the Spring and Autumn Period. Qin was located in Shaanxi in the Northwest, the same region from which the Zhou had emerged. Its location in the area of the Wei River provided Qin with an economic basis on which to build a strong political and military apparatus. Its location was also strategically advantageous, because the area was protected from attack by mountains whose passes were easy to defend and yet provided avenues for offensives to the east. The Qin considered their neighbors in the Central Plains less civilized than they were, merely "semicivilized," and the archaeological record confirms that the Qin were in some ways culturally distinct from the civilization in the Central Plains. For example, the dead of the Central Plains were buried in graves dug into vertical shafts in a supine position. In contrast, the Qin dead were often buried in cave-like structures and in a retroflex position. Nevertheless, it is also clear that the Qin ruling class adopted many aspects of Zhou culture, including the script and aspects of its ritual system.[1]

Like Qin, Chu had many natural advantages that favored its rise. Located in the semitropical regions of the Huai and Yangzi Rivers, Chu territory provided ideal conditions for rice cultivation. Rice and fish were staples in the diet of the people of Chu. Their technological level was on a par with that of the North: they had iron as well as bronze, made fine ceramics, and used bronze coins. Like Qin, Chu was on the fringes of Zhou culture, but also like those in Qin, the Chu elites had borrowed and adapted many practices from other elites living in the Central Plains.[2] Some notable differences between the Chu elites and their Northern counterparts included language. The language of the Chu was said to be incomprehensible to the people of the Central Plains: one source compared it to the language of birds. Another difference lay in the style of the burials of the Chu elite, which were distinctive in their use of lacquer and bright colors (see Figures 2.2 and 2.3).

One artifact of Chu culture worth mention is the *Chu ci,* an anthology of poems. Although it is impossible to date the poems precisely, the earliest may have been written as early as the fourth century B.C.E. A number of the poems, in particular, the "Li Sao" (Encountering Sorrow) have traditionally been attributed to Qu Yuan. What is striking about the "Li Sao" is the extent to which this poem offers a contrast to the *Odes.* As David Hawkes points out, in the *Odes,* which presumably originated from the North, the persona of the poet is not prominent. Out of the 305

FIGURE 2.2 Painted lacquer coffin, c. 316 B.C.E. This comes from a tomb found in Hubei (Chu territory). It is specifically from the Baoshan tomb, and it is one of three nested coffins. The privilege of having many coffins was reserved for the elite. This was probably necessary because the bodies of the elite lay in state for relatively long periods of time—anywhere from several weeks to years—before they were buried. When one considers the heat and humidity, as well as the lack of interest in any rudimentary embalming practices, it is understandable why people would have wanted to put some distance between themselves and the dead. Commoners, on the other hand, were buried as soon as they died. (© Cultural Relics Publishing House.)

odes, there are exactly three in which the bard identifies himself or herself by name. By contrast, in the "Li Sao," Qu Yuan stands very much at the forefront of the poem: he "bares his breast to us, examines his motives, admits his doubts, reveals his aspirations, argues, cites historical precedents in defense of his opinions. . . ."[3]

And indeed, by traditional accounts, the "Li Sao" is autobiographical. According to Han historian Sima Qian, the "Li Sao" relates Qu Yuan's own personal disappointments. Though loyal to his lord, Qu Yuan fell victim to slander, causing him great pain. The "Li Sao" reads:

> How well I know that loyalty brings disaster;
> Yet I will endure: I cannot give it up.
> I called on the ninefold heaven to be my witness,
> And all for the sake of the Fair One [for example, his lord], and
>   no other.
> There once was a time when he spoke with me in frankness;
> But then he repented and was of another mind.
> I do not care, on my own count, about this divorcement,
> But it grieves me to find the Fair One so inconstant.[4]

FIGURE 2.3 Lacquer cabinet and vessels. This is also from the Baoshan tomb (c. 316 B.C.E.). These contain an animal motif, although art historians are not sure whether the artists had any particular animal, or a general zoomorphic design, in mind. This is probably something that was used in everyday life. (From Xiaoneng Yang, *The Golden Age of Archaeology* [New Haven: Yale University Press, 1999], p. 334). ☺

Banished from court, Qu Yuan committed suicide in despair ("The world is impure and envious of the able/Eager to hide men's good and make much of their ills").[5] Clasping a large stone, he jumped into the Miluo River.

Along with the emergence of new major powers, the Warring States Period witnessed major political, economic, and military changes including changes in modes of warfare. During the Spring and Autumn Period armies comprising chariots and infantry amounting to no more than 30,000 men fought pitched battles staged on flat terrain. All this changed during the Warring States Period when armies composed of massed infantry may have included as many as 600,000 men, although more skeptical historians say no more than 100,000. Although more frequent than those in the Warring States Period, Spring and Autumn Period campaigns might have lasted a season but no more than one year, whereas during the Warring States Period military conflicts often lasted more than one year and sometimes as long as five years.[6] Military technology also changed as new and deadlier weaponry was developed: in addition to iron weapons from around 600 B.C.E., Warring States Period armies were equipped with new tools, such as the crossbow and lamellar armor. Finally, whereas Spring and Autumn Period armies consisted mainly of members of the ruling elite, Warring States Period armies infantry comprised all segments of society.[7]

According to some scholars, the new modes of warfare that emerged in the Warring States Period reflected social change. Spring and Autumn Period society, like that of the Western Zhou, was highly stratified. Not only were commoners (*min*) distinguished from members of the ruling elite, but within the ruling elite there were stark differences of status. Beneath the Zhou king were the nobles (*qing*), usually lords or members of a lord's immediate family. Below the nobles were the lesser aristocrats (*shi*). *Shi* is a term also later used for elites who could identify with their predecessors even though they lived in very different societies. Spring and Autumn Period *shi*, far above commoners, were usually distant descendants of and lesser relatives of lords. Many were individuals of culture, learning, and even wealth. Yet ministerial positions, like military commands, were reserved for the nobles.

In the Warring States Period, the old social hierarchies began to break down. With some luck and ability, a man of *shi* or even occasionally of humble birth could become a powerful minister or general. One famous example of a man of humble birth who rose to spectacular heights was Lü Buwei (d. 235 B.C.E.), a merchant who profited from the growth of interstate trade facilitated by the building of new roads and better communication systems (see Figure 2.4). For many years, Lü was the chief counselor of the Qin ruler and was even rumored to have been the actual father of the future First Emperor of the Qin dynasty.

Despite the possibilities for social mobility, political life in the Warring States Period was not without its dangers. According to historians, Lü was murdered by the future First Emperor of Qin. The reasons are not clear, although legend has it that he was displeased by the liberties that the minister had taken with his mother. By some accounts, the First Emperor was the illegitimate son of Lü, and by killing Lü, he unwittingly

FIGURE 2.4 These bronze tallies date to the late fourth century B.C.E., and this set was discovered in what was Chu territory. Bronze tallies exempted the bearers, in this case, a merchant, from tolls along Chu roads. Not all tallies were made of bronze; those used by lower-status individuals came in different varieties, and so many of them used cheaper materials, such as bamboo. (© National Museum of China.)

killed his own father. Most likely, however, the young ruler felt that Lü had gotten too powerful. Nor was Lü alone in this regard. A similar fate met another eminent Qin statesmen, Shang Yang (d. 338 B.C.E.), originally from Chu and famous for spearheading the reforms that brought Qin to power and for instituting harsh laws. As minister, Shang Yang reportedly had insisted that the laws apply equally to all regardless of status and followed this dictum when he punished the crown prince for an infraction of the law and had the prince's teacher branded. Later when the prince became king, he had his revenge: Lord Shang reportedly suffered dismemberment, his body torn apart by chariots pulling in opposite directions.

Qin best exemplifies the consolidation and centralization of states with Shang Yang taking the lead in advising the ruler to undertake important political and economic reforms. First, the Qin rulers instituted universal military service, thereby no doubt increasing the number of men in the Qin army. Second, in 350 B.C.E., they abolished estates maintained by nobles and divided Qin territory into *xian* or counties, which they governed directly rather than through nobles as before. This had the effect of increasing the amount of territory under their effective control while limiting the ability of nobles to rebel. Third, they established the individual household, as opposed to the estate, as the basis for taxation and military service. In addition, they prohibited more than one adult male from living in the same household. This augmented tax revenues because it increased the number of households that could be taxed and at the same time broke down large estates, the economic and military backbone of potentially rebellious nobles.

Although Qin accomplishments are certainly impressive, it is important to keep in mind that the Qin borrowed many of their techniques of statecraft from other places. For one thing, the *xian* or county system was not a Qin innovation. Instead, it originated from Chu, Shang Yang's original home state. Chu was, furthermore, a state traditionally more centralized and without strong noble clans. The Qin rulers were also not alone in their attempts to limit the power and influence of noble lineages. Lord Wen of Jin also took steps to suppress members of the nobility. He also prohibited members of the nobility from occupying high government posts and had adopted the *xian* system in 534 B.C.E.

By the end of the fourth century, Qin was poised to conquer all of China. Several developments advanced this outcome. By 316 B.C.E., Qin increased its resources without adding to its vulnerability when it conquered the state of Shu in present-day Sichuan. The conquest of Shu gave the Qin rulers two advantages. It was a region that was easy to defend, being well protected by mountains, and it was a fertile area, all the more so after the Qin rulers built the Zhengguo canal, one of the most impressive waterworks projects in the ancient world. In 312 B.C.E., Qin managed to defeat the powerful southern state of Chu at the battle of Danyang, but it had to wait until the next century for its complete triumph.

"The Hundred Schools"

The traditional designation of the Eastern Zhou as the period of a hundred schools reflects the importance later scholars accorded to the age as the formative period of Chinese intellectual history, as well as to the profusion of ideas that accompanied social and political upheaval of the times. This section will examine seven well-known texts: the *Analects, Mozi, Mencius, Xunzi, Laozi, Zhuangzi,* and *Han Feizi.* The reasons for selecting these thinkers' texts rather than others are twofold. First is the importance scholars have placed on these thinkers in the formation of what they thought were four distinct schools: the *Ru* (as termed in the Chinese classical tradition) or Confucian (the traditional European designation), Mohist, Daoist, and Legalists. (See Chapter 3 for more recent views that challenge the analytical usefulness of grouping thinkers into "schools.") Second, each of the authors of these texts grappled at length with major problems of their day such as: What are the roots of present political chaos? How can it be remedied—through a return to the traditions of a golden age or by radical cultural and political change? What is the ideal man like, and what does it mean to be human?

Confucius

Kong Qiu or Confucius is arguably the best-known Chinese thinker. Yet surprisingly little is known about his life other than the fact that he probably lived from c. 551 to 479 B.C.E., that he was a man from the state of Lu and was of good birth, and that he unsuccessfully attempted to play an important role in government. However, many contrasting legends and traditions are associated with Confucius, starting from the late Warring States Period. By most accounts, he was famous as a teacher and moral exemplar, a mentor surrounded by a retinue of disciples, some sagacious and some not, following him in his search for official employment. By other accounts, Confucius was author of the *Spring and Autumn Annals,* the political chronicle from which the period he lived in derives its name. In addition to the *Spring and Autumn Annals,* Confucius was also credited by some thinkers for editing and arranging the *Odes* (see p. 20) containing poems intoned for millennia by the educated elite.

Besides crediting him with more orthodox scholarly achievements, some accounts depict Confucius as a prophet and "uncrowned king," the author of the apocrypha, a set of Han prophetic texts. Still other images left behind by later commentators represent Confucius as a fatherless child and man unaware of his own illustrious birth. By this account, Confucius was the result of a fleeting sexual encounter between two strangers in the wild.

Modern images of Confucius also diverge. Some modern scholars regard Confucius as an egalitarian, a teacher who would accept students without regard to their class or birth. Other scholars regard him as a conservative figure clinging to old feudal institutions on the eve of radical social and political change.

One reason why images of Confucius contrast so sharply is that none of his own writing survives. Most accounts of Confucius's life, furthermore, date from long after his death. The main source on Confucius's life and thought is the *Analects,* a collection that purports to record the words and deeds of Confucius and his disciples. The authorship of the *Analects* is difficult to determine. Some portions of the text date as early as Confucius's own time whereas other portions of the text appear to have been later additions. The content of the text does not provide, as one might expect, a systematic philosophy. Rather, it is a hodgepodge of conversations between Confucius and his disciples, ethical pronouncements, and anecdotes. Many of the passages in the *Analects* are terse, cryptic, and open to multiple interpretations. Despite the difficulties of dating the text and interpreting it, scholars have managed to imagine what Confucius might have been like and what sorts of beliefs he might have held.

The *Analects* depicts Confucius as a man frustrated by his lack of recognition from rulers and by his inability to reform a world he sees descending into chaos.

Despite his frustration, the *Analects* represents Confucius as anything but an unpleasant person. We know that he enjoyed singing. His manner is described as "easygoing," and on a few occasions, Confucius is represented as having a wry sense of humor. For example, in one case, Confucius dryly notes that he has discovered that few men have a desire to learn as strong as their desire for women! Confucius is also described as a person who had strong emotional attachments. When his favorite pupil died, Confucius is reported to have been shattered and to have wailed without restraint.

The *Analects* devotes much space to describing the ethical ideal of a man. It refers to several kinds of ethical ideals, but the one most frequently cited is the *junzi*, a term that can be translated as "gentleman" or "princely man" to reflect its class connotations. In other texts, it refers to men of noble birth, either the son of a lord or even the lord himself. The use of the term *junzi* in the *Analects* reflects this history. The *junzi* is not only a man who is an ethical ideal, but he is also a cultural ideal—a man who has mastered all of the *Odes* and a man who speaks in a refined manner. Most likely, when Confucius reportedly spoke of the *junzi*, he was referring to other men like him—men of learning, culture, and noble birth. In addition to being a master of tradition and cultural refinement, Confucius claimed that the *junzi* (gentleman or princely man) is *ren* (humane, benevolent), *yi* (dutiful, righteous), and *xiao* (filial). The *junzi*, furthermore, has the power to influence positively those around him.

Confucius is famous for declaring in the *Analects* that he is merely a "transmitter," not an "innovator." Many scholars interpret that statement as proof that Confucius was "past-logged"—that he believed the only hope for the future lay with restoring past traditions. True, Confucius's reported admiration of Zhou traditions and moral exemplars is undeniable. And Confucius even claimed that the sagely Duke of Zhou, dead for more than five centuries, came to visit him in his dreams! But to say that Confucius was merely a conservative does little justice to what it means to transmit traditions. For Confucius, the gentleman was more than a passive custodian of the tradition. He was to have an active role in reinventing and updating traditions. For example, in one place Confucius observed that it was appropriate for a person of limited economic means to substitute caps made of black silk for more expensive linen on occasions when ritual propriety required their use. A gentleman could modify existing traditions because he understood the basic principles of the tradition. By doing so, he demonstrated not only active mastery of the tradition but also ensured that the tradition had continued relevance and value.

The *Analects* further depicts Confucius as an advocate of *li*, a term that encompasses the meaning of ritual, ceremony, propriety, and good etiquette. *Li* governed all aspects of elite life in early China. It prescribed not only the way one dressed, ate, or spoke, but it also dictated the manner in which a person offered sacrifices to ancestors, how he mourned, and the way in which he was buried. For Confucius, adherence to *li*, in particular the *li* of the Zhou, was the basis of good social order. According to him, a man or woman was not only supposed to execute properly the *li*, but it was also important to have the right attitude when executing the *li*. For example, in mourning, a son was not only supposed to mourn and bury his father or mother according to the rules of *li*, but he was also supposed to mourn them with the utmost sincerity. Another important aspect of Confucius's thinking about *li* has to do with his view that the *li* were invaluable for inculcating people with a respect for hierarchy. In one place in the *Analects,* he complained about a family who offered sacrifices in a manner befitting only the king of Zhou. Such an act, he felt, was symptomatic of a larger problem of his time: people were not fulfilling their proper social roles, such as lord, subject, peasant, or merchant. Lords should act as lords, whereas subjects should act just as subjects and thus should *not* usurp the privileges or power of lord. In this sense, Confucius was apparently resisting the incredible social upheavals of his own time. This was a time when high official positions were no longer reserved for men of high birth but were increasingly given to men with ability, regardless of obscure birth.

Mozi

Mo Di, later known as Mozi ("Master Mo"), was probably of obscure origins and humble birth. He lived from approximately 470 to 391 B.C.E. According to some accounts, he was from the state of Song; by other accounts, he was, like Confucius, a native of the state of Lu. Very little else is known about him, although scholars have made interesting guesses about his background. Some think Mozi had a criminal past because of his surname, which also means tattoo, as criminals in ancient China were often tattooed as punishment.[8] Others believe that Mozi had been a low-status artisan or carpenter, which might explain his apparent interest in the practical utility of traditions.[9] By one Han account, Mozi was once a follower of Confucius or one of his disciples.[10] And judging from his impressive grasp of ritual protocol and the virulence of his attacks on Confucius's followers, this seems quite plausible. What is known about Mozi mainly comes down to us in the form of the text called the *Mozi,* which purports to record his treatises or speeches. The *Mozi* lacks subtly or adornment. Its language hammers at a point repetitively with a kind of relentless logic. Despite its lack of aesthetic appeal, the *Mozi* was highly influential, not only as a challenge to traditional ways of thinking, but also in the development of logic and rhetoric in early China.

Mozi's frustrations with the present age are clearly voiced in the text. And one might go so far as to argue that Mozi was the earliest thinker to provide a systematic explanation for the chaos of his age. According to Mozi, the basic reason why governance so often failed and why there was incessant warfare in his day had to do with the human tendency to be partial. Men tended to be partial to their own kin or to their own states, and because of this, they sought benefit for their own families and states at the expense of others. Not surprisingly, strife and warfare often resulted. Rulers also suffered from partiality—partiality to their own relatives and especially to sexually attractive men. Because of their partiality, many rulers only elevated such men for powerful positions. The problem, then, is that, because all important government posts are filled with close relatives and sexually attractive men, there are few capable men in office. "If a government is rich in worthy men," Mozi observed, "then the administration will be characterized by weight and substance; but if it is paltry in such men, then the administration will be a paltry affair."[11]

Mozi's diagnosis begged the question of what was to be done. Whereas it was relatively easy for him to suggest that rulers needed to employ more men of real merit, the problem of encouraging the population to transcend the altogether human tendency to favor one's own family or state remained. In a characteristically strident tone, Mozi replied that the latter problem was not difficult to resolve. All that had to be done was to make men and women understand that the interests of others ultimately coincided with their own. "If a man were to regard the states of others as they regarded their own, then who would raise up his state to attack the state of another? It would be like attacking his own. . . . If men were to regard the families of others as they regard their own, then who would raise up his family to overthrow that of another? It would be like overthrowing his own. Now when states and cities do not attack or injure one another, is this harm or a benefit to the world? Surely it is a benefit."[12]

In relation to the *Analects,* the *Mozi* seems quite iconoclastic. For instance, whereas the Confucius of the *Analects* also urged rulers to employ capable individuals such as him, it perhaps would never have occurred to authors of the *Analects* to disregard considerations of social status and birth entirely. Mozi, however, insisted that rulers ought to employ the "worthy," regardless of origin or birth. Mozi's suggestion that all men and women should transcend their particular affinities to their own families probably would have raised the eyebrows of the *Analects* authors, as portions of that text emphasize obligations to kin over all others.

What the *Analects* authors would have perhaps objected to most was Mozi's position on the Zhou mourning and burial customs. For them, as well as for the many later self-proclaimed followers of Confucius, prolonged mourning and generous burials were an expression of children's devotion to their parents and subjects' loyalty to their lords. But Mozi took issue with these traditional mortuary practices. Before delving into Mozi's critique of these mourning and burial practices, it would be useful to discuss what they were. Prolonged mourning or three years of mourning was a *li* (ritual, etiquette) practiced by sons of noble houses when their fathers, mothers, and lords died. When practicing three years of mourning, a son was to forego the pleasures of hearty food, alcohol, sex, and luxurious accommodations. Instead, he wore clothes of rough hemp, lived in a simple lean-to in almost total social isolation, and ate a bland porridge. Lavish burial referred to the practice of burying members of the ruling elite with a great deal of material wealth. Consider the grave of Lord Yi (d. 433 B.C.E.) in Suixian, Hubei, a lord of what was not an enormous or particularly powerful state. Lord Yi went into the next life with a large number of his personal belongings: numerous weapons, eleven *tons* of ritual bronzes, and an enormous set of bronze bells and chime stones (see Figure 2.5). Lord Yi also took with him members of his harem: twenty-one young women, ranging between the ages of thirteen and twenty-six.[13] As this case demonstrates, the practice of accompanying-in-death, although less prominent than it had been in the Western Zhou or in the Shang, still continued.

Not surprisingly, Mozi hated the mourning and burial practices of the elite. Three years of mourning, he complained, wasted the time of the ruling elite who otherwise would devote themselves to the governance of the state. What was worse, he noted, was the fact that such practices endangered the health and well-being of the mourner. Lavish burials wasted valuable resources that otherwise could be used to enrich the state and bring benefits to the masses. Because of these factors, Mozi urged rulers to adopt simpler mourning procedures and more frugal burial practices. Instead of observing an extended period of mourning, mourners, he said, "may weep going to and from the burial, but after that they should devote themselves to making a living." And in lieu of lavish burials, such as

FIGURE 2.5 This wine vessel was found in the tomb of Lord Yi of Zeng and dates to around 433 B.C.E. Constructing it must have required many resources, as it weighs 374.79 lbs. Archaeologists think that it was used to cool wine, and it has a space at the top to place ice. (© National Museum of China.)

that of Lord Yi, the ruling elite should just perform functional burials: coffins three inches thick "sufficient to bury rotting bones," shrouds thick enough only to "cover rotting flesh," and graves only deep enough so that the stench of the decaying corpse does not annoy the living.[14]

Mozi's position on mourning and burial was characteristic of his philosophy in two respects. First, Mozi's attack on mourning and burial was typical of his antitraditionalism. One must not, he urged rulers, assume that what is customary or traditional is right—to "confuse what is habitual with what is right, and what is customary with what is right." Second, his polemical stance on mourning and burial reflects his iconoclasm. Unlike the *Analects* authors, Mozi would ask himself why a given practice or custom was appropriate or inappropriate and why a given act was moral or immoral. According to Mozi, the only basis for knowing whether something was appropriate or moral was Heaven. "The will of Heaven is to me," he notes, "like a compass to a wheelwright or a square to a carpenter. The wheelwright and the carpenter use their compass and square to measure what is round or square for the world, saying, 'What fits these measurements is right; what does not fit them is wrong.'"[15] This line of reasoning, of course, raised the question of how one was to determine Heaven's will. According to Mozi, the will of Heaven is unambiguous: If a course of action is correct, Heaven will send its rewards usually in the guise of bountiful harvests and peace. If not, then Heaven will send its punishments in the guise of famines, eclipses, and other natural disasters.

Mencius

Mencius or Meng Ke is perhaps the best known self-proclaimed follower of Confucius. According to the Han historian Sima Qian (c. 145–c. 90 B.C.E.), he was a native of the state of Zou and lived from about 371 to 289 B.C.E. The main source of knowledge about Mencius's life and philosophy is a text known as the *Mencius*. The date of the *Mencius* is difficult to determine with any certainty. The *Mencius*, like both the *Analects* and the *Mozi*, actually was not the work of its reputed author. Instead, it is a collection of sayings of Mencius and reports of conversations with friends, opponents, and rulers. One crucial difference between the two texts is that the *Mencius* has far more sustained argumentation than the *Analects*.

Like Confucius, Mencius was deeply frustrated with his inability to win high office. He traveled in vain from court to court, believing himself to be the only man of his day who could reform the world. Again like Confucius, Mencius eventually abandoned his efforts to find official employment and took on students. Although ignored in his own time, he was to have a lasting impact on Chinese thought and political culture into the twentieth century. During the Song dynasty (960–1279), Mencius's theories about human nature and governance came to be accepted as authoritative.

Mencius is undoubtedly best known for his assertion that human nature is good, an assertion that has drawn characterizations of his thought as being "tender-minded," optimistic, and even naïve. Yet there is more to this statement than meets the eye. For one, Mencius is not claiming that human beings are all good or that they are born good. He is claiming that all human beings have the potential to become sages, which represents the culmination of human achievement. Mencius observed: "the sage, too, is the same in kind as other men." The major difference between sages and ordinary people was that sages were the rare individuals who developed their moral potential through long and hard study and reflection.[16] And, in fact, the sage that Mencius most often held up as a model, Shun, was a man of very humble and even foreign origins. Second, he argues that human beings have in them an innate moral sensibility, which he refers to as the "four sprouts" (*si duan*). All men, he tells one interlocutor, would experience alarm if they were to see a child fall into a well. This spontaneous feeling of alarm, according to Mencius, is the beginning or sprout of the virtue of *ren* (humaneness or benevolence) that figures prominently in the *Analects*. Similarly, the other three sprouts (feelings of shame, of courtesy, and of the sense of right and wrong) constitute the basis of duty (*yi*), reticence (*rang*), and wisdom (*zhi*). It is not enough, however, to have these spontaneous feelings. One must cultivate these feelings through study and reflection to develop one's full moral potential.

Mencius is also famous for his rebuttal to Mozi's advocacy of universal concern as the solution to societal and political woes. Mencius's rejection of this doctrine is, of course, unsurprising, given the fact that he saw himself as a follower of Confucius. Confucius, who reportedly believed that sons should conceal their father's crimes, would have frowned on the doctrine of universal concern. Mencius argued that it is impossible for a person to show as much concern for the families of others as he shows to his own. Human beings, he claims, are naturally inclined to love their own fathers and kin more than those of others. Failure to do so, he adds, would make a person no different from animals. Second, Mencius rejects the view that partiality to one's own kin is at the root of social/political problems. On the contrary, encouraging people to be good sons, brothers, and members of local communities makes for good social order. "If only everyone loved his parents and treated his elders with deference," Mencius mused, "the Empire would be at peace." This is, he states, because a humane man, a man who loves his parents, can "extend his love from those he loves to those he does not love."[17]

In addition to rebutting the doctrine of universal concern, the *Mencius* also rejects the Mohist position on mourning and burial. Generous burials and extended mourning, the *Mencius* maintained, should not be discarded. Instead, the practice should be preserved because it is rooted in human nature (*ren xing*). It sprang from the spontaneous urge to mourn that all share when faced with the loss of a loved one. As proof of this claim, the *Mencius* describes the practices of men and women in distant antiquity. When a parent died, he observed, the children would take and consign the parent to a ditch. After casting off their parents' bodies, the children passed the place where the bodies laid. There, the children found them eaten by foxes and bitten by flies. Mencius reportedly described their response accordingly:

> A sweat broke out on their brows, and they could not bear to look. The sweating was not put on for others to see. It was an outward expression of their innermost heart.[18]

Two major political doctrines that Mencius advocated were the Mandate of Heaven (*tian ming*) and the rule of virtue. According to Mencius, Heaven gave ruling houses a mandate to rule, but rulers were obliged to rule benevolently and bring benefits to the masses. If a ruling house failed to fulfill its obligations, Heaven would revoke its mandate to rule. Under these circumstances, regicide could be permissible. This had already occurred several times in the past. The last rulers of the Xia and Shang dynasties had been tyrants, and they had been replaced by worthy men who established new dynasties.

Mencius also believed that with Heaven's blessing, it would be appropriate for a ruler to cede his throne to a sage. This had happened in distant antiquity: King Yao had abdicated his throne and passed over even his son, in favor of Shun, a man whose lowly birth did not prevent him from attaining sagely virtue and wisdom. Here ancient history converged with contemporary controversy related to a political crisis that occurred within Mencius's own living memory. The king of Yan had abdicated his throne to a royal favorite, a man named Zizhi, invoking the example of Yao. This decision outraged rulers from neighboring states, who accused the king and his favorite of inverting the political order and blurring status distinctions that existed between lords and subjects. The rulers of these neighboring states thereupon invaded Yan, executed the pair, and divided among themselves its territory. Mencius certainly was aware of the controversy. But for him, finding a sage who could benevolently govern the masses was more important than preserving the existing political hierarchy. "The people are of supreme importance," he observed, "the altars to the gods of earth and grain come next; last comes the ruler."[19]

Compared to the Confucius of the *Analects*, Mencius seems to place less of a premium on preserving the existing political hierarchy. This is evident not only in his doctrine of the rule of virtue, but also in views on *li*. One episode from the *Mencius* tells of him reportedly disregarding sumptuary rules regulating burial. When his mother died, he lavished on her a thick coffin, an extravagance reserved for higher-ranking individuals. When a friend reproached his violation of sumptuary regulations, Mencius was prompted to reply that in the golden age of distant antiquity, no one made such distinctions. Men simply buried their parents in a fashion that reflected their feelings of love for their parents. Thus, for Mencius, the natural feelings that all sons share take precedence over considerations of rank and political status.

In several regards, Mencius exemplified the spirit of the Warring States Period and its shift away from a rigidly stratified society to one with greater social mobility. This is seen in his habit of speaking in terms of human beings as a class with a shared nature, in his assertion that all men shared the same potential for sagehood regardless of birth or origins, and most of all, in his belief that virtue, not birth, ultimately should determine who should govern.

Xunzi

Born in the state of Zhao around 312 B.C.E., Xun Kuang, known to posterity as Xunzi ("Master Xun"), lived in a turbulent age. Although it is not known exactly when he died, some accounts suggest that Xunzi lived to be a very old man. He witnessed not only the destruction of his native state and the states he lived in but also may have lived long enough to see the unification of China under the First Emperor of Qin in 221 B.C.E.[20]

In some regards, Xunzi was far more successful in his attempt to gain influence than Mencius. He went to the powerful state of Qi to teach at the famous state-sponsored Jixia academy, which was arguably the center of intellectual life at that time. There, he received titles and stipends for a time, but finally was forced to leave because of political difficulties. Before long, however, Xunzi was appointed as an official in the powerful state of Chu. By some accounts, he lived there until the end of his life. He was the teacher of two famous thinkers, Han Feizi (d. 233 B.C.E.) and Li Si (d. 208 B.C.E.). The latter would go on to become the notorious minister and advisor to the First Emperor of Qin (259–210 B.C.E.).[21]

Xunzi is mostly known through a work named for him, the *Xunzi*. Although it is not clear that Xunzi actually wrote the *Xunzi* in part or in its entirety, the *Xunzi* is noteworthy for its format. Unlike the *Analects* or the *Mencius*, which report the words and conversations of each master, the text of the *Xunzi* is organized into essays, each of which possess a great degree of thematic unity. It is also voluminous and systematic, a reflection undoubtedly of Xunzi's longevity.

Xunzi made himself notorious by declaring human nature to be evil. In part, this blanket statement, issued at the beginning of his chapter on human nature, was intended to catch the attention of his audience, and also it was intended to highlight his fierce disagreement with Mencius, despite the fact the both of them saw themselves as followers of Confucius. By declaring human nature to be evil, Xunzi means to say the humans lack any inborn inclination to act in an ethical manner. Left to their own devices, human beings would descend into chaos and conflict. "For a son to yield to his father or a younger brother to yield to his eldest brother, for a son to relieve his father of work or a younger brother to relieve his elder brother," Xunzi mused, "acts such as these are all contrary to man's nature and run counter to his emotions."[22]

Despite the fact that he took a rather harsh view about human nature, Xunzi was nevertheless optimistic about the potential of humans to improve themselves. And, perhaps more so than Mencius, Xunzi was committed to the idea that anyone, even the "man on the street," could achieve sagehood by transforming themselves through moral training, study, and hard work. But here again the similarities stop. Whereas Mencius saw the process of sagehood as the development of innate moral sensibilities, Xunzi saw the road to sagehood as radically transformative, comparable to carpentry: "A warped piece of wood must wait until it has been laid against the straightening board, steamed, and forced into shape before it can be straight."[23]

Like other early thinkers, Xunzi was concerned about *li.* But quite unlike any other early thinker, he created a very sophisticated theory about the origins of *li:*

> What is the origin of *li*? I reply: man is born with desires. If his desires are not satisfied for him, he cannot but seek some means to satisfy them himself. If there are no limits and degrees to his seeking, then he will inevitably fall to wrangling with other men. From wrangling comes disorder and from disorder comes exhaustion. The ancient kings hated such disorder, and therefore they established the *li* and duty in order to curb it, to train men's desires and to provide for their means of satisfaction.[24]

This passage reveals much about Xunzi's ideas about the relationship between human nature and cultural institutions. Raw human desires, he declares in no uncertain terms, give rise to chaos. The chaos caused by raw human desires created a need for the *li.* In other words, although the *li* are not themselves a part of human nature, they are necessitated by human nature. In subsequent discussions, Xunzi goes on to explain how the *li* transform raw human desires and allow for their expression in aesthetically appealing and socially productive ways. All men, according to him, experience grief when their parents die. If men were left to their own devices, they would most likely be incapacitated by their grief and be unable to go about their business. They might express their feelings for their parents by burying them with incredible amounts of material wealth and even human sacrifices. If everyone adopted these practices, states would be ruined. It follows that the *li* are necessary. They put limits on how long one can mourn; they prohibit human sacrifices, and they curtail how much wealth can be buried in the ground.

Another fascinating aspect of Xunzi's philosophy was his agnosticism. He clearly did not believe in life after death and described the dead as "the ones without consciousness." In this regard, Xunzi was not alone. The *Intrigues of the Warring States* (*Zhanguoce*), a pre-Qin text that relates court politics and warfare, also tells a tale about a dying dowager queen of Qin who gave orders for her lover to be buried with her. A friend, a courtier, of her lover thereupon went to talk the dowager out of this plan. The courtier asked her whether she believed in life after death, and she replied that she absolutely did not. Thereupon the courtier pointed out that if there was no life after death, there would be no use to burying her lover with her. But if there did happen to be life after death, she would have some explaining to do in the next life when she met up with her former husband. Satisfied with the courtier's reasoning, the dowager dropped her plans.

In addition to denying life after death, Xunzi, quite unlike Mozi, regarded Heaven as inscient. The natural world proceeds according to its own ways, oblivious to humans. It will rain or not rain regardless of whether people pray or make their sacrifices. The heavenly bodies rotate the same way whether a sage or a villain is on the throne. A well-ordered and prosperous society, in other words, depends solely on the ruler:

> Respond to nature with good government, and good fortune will result; respond to it with disorder, and misfortune will result. If you encourage agriculture and are frugal with expenditures, then Heaven cannot make you poor. If you provide the people with the goods they need and demand their labor only at the proper time, then Heaven cannot afflict you with illness.[25]

Xunzi's philosophy reflected the concerns of his time in several regards. Living in a period of political change and upheaval, the destructive potential of human beings left a deep impression on Xunzi. And yet, Xunzi was optimistic about people's potential to not only transform their own basic nature, but also to create an efficacious society through human efforts alone. Xunzi's concerns, as well as his basic attitudes about what it meant to be human, would be enormously influential for hundreds of years.

Laozi and Zhuangzi

Much scholarly attention and energy has been devoted to the task of determining exactly what Daoism (also known as Taoism) was in early China. Religious studies scholars, looking for a Chinese popular religion, like to think of Daoism as a religious movement that emphasized meditation and self-cultivation practices. Students of political thought sometimes conjecture that Daoism was the by-product of a school of statecraft, one that focused on techniques of political control. Philosophers, looking for Chinese analogues to Greek skeptical thinkers, prefer to speak of Daoism as a philosophy, one that advocated a return of men and women to harmony with nature and its underlying reality, the *Dao* (or *Tao*), an ineffable, eternal, self-activating, omnipresent reality. Regardless of what label we use for Daoism, it is undeniable that two of its texts, the *Dao de jing* and *Zhuangzi,* have been enormously influential in Asia, Europe, and North America.

Recent archaeological finds in the last decade strongly suggest that the *Dao de jing* is the older of the two. The *Dao de jing* ("The Way and Its Power") is known by a variety of names. It is known by many in the United States as the *Tao te ching,* following an older Romanization. It is also known by the title of *Laozi* (Lao-tzu) or the *Book of Master Lao,* after its putative author, Laozi, who reportedly was an older contemporary of Confucius. Laozi is a shadowy figure, whose identity was very much in doubt even by Han times.

The *Dao de jing* is a strange text. Much of it is in verse, leading some scholars, such as Harold Roth, to speculate that it was originally a meditation manual.[26] And much of it is cryptic, paradoxical, and highly suggestive and hence has been the subject of more classical commentary than any other text. It is also, not surprisingly, the most frequently translated book from China. In part, the popularity of the *Dao de jing* is due to the inscrutability of its language, which invites a multitude of interpretations. But the popularity of the *Dao de jing* also has to do with its mysterious, but powerful, messages. One such message is the inadequacy of language. As the first line of the text reads, "The Way that can be named is not the eternal Way." In other words, the totality of the Way—the way things are, as well as the way things should be—eludes codification, definition, and linguistic determination. Another of the better known themes from the *Dao de jing* is the limits of conventional notions of value. Is it better to be strong, as opposed to weak? Not necessarily, suggests the *Dao de jing*. Weak states, for instance, may outlive strong states, because lacking rich resources and wealth, they may elude attack and conquest. Is it better to be famous for one's knowledge? Again, not necessarily, as "those who know do not speak; those who speak do not know." Or—to touch upon a political theme of the text—would it be preferable, as many Warring States thinkers suggested, to educate and transform the masses to create a tightly governed and prosperous state? Again, the answer, against the conventional grain, is a resounding "no." The best rulers allow the people to return to "ignorance" or to a life of primal simplicity, one in which they are in tune with nature. And to attain this ideal, the ruler must conduct his government with great delicacy and restraint, like a cook boiling a small fish. He must not interfere with the Way and, by taking no action of his own, must allow everything to take its course.

The other well-known Daoist classic is the *Zhuangzi,* which takes its name from its legendary author, Zhuangzi (or Master Zhuang). As is the case with Laozi, little is known about Zhuangzi. In fact, some scholars doubt very much that Zhuangzi or Zhuang Zhou ever existed. The text traditional scholars attribute to him is certainly not the work of a single hand, but a compilation of different works, ranging in date from the mid-Warring States Period to the first century of the Western Han dynasty. Unlike the *Dao de jing*, which comprises short verses or paragraphs, the *Zhuangzi* contains long chapters, filled with colorful anecdotes and fanciful conversations. In some places, Confucius even appears, occasionally as a venerated teacher, and, in other places, as a fool ripe for a verbal thrashing by a famous outlaw.

Many parts of the *Zhuangzi* speak to the importance of withdrawal and reclusion, as opposed to active political engagement. In many respects, this position stands in contrast with the views found in other texts surveyed earlier in this chapter. Unlike the *Analects*, the *Mencius*, or even the *Xunzi*, the *Zhuangzi* does not brim with advice for rulers about how to better administer the realm. The wise man, to put it somewhat differently, is not an active minister, but a hermit who knows that it is better to sit fishing on the banks of a remote mountain stream.

Like many of the Warring States texts covered earlier, the *Zhuangzi* also takes a position on the value of traditional mourning rituals. But unlike the *Mozi* or *Mencius*, the *Zhuangzi* does not explicitly condemn or defend the practice. Instead, it recounts an episode from Zhuangzi's own life. Zhuangzi's wife had died. When one of his comrades, Huizi, came to convey his condolences, he found that instead of being grieved, Zhuangzi was sitting in his tub singing. This took Huizi aback, and he protested. "You lived with her, she brought up your children and grew old," said Huizi. "It should be enough simply not to weep at her death. But pounding on a tub and singing—this is going too far, isn't it?" Zhuangzi responded:

> You're wrong. When she first died, do you think I didn't grieve like anyone else? But I looked back to her beginning and the time before she was born. Not only the time before she was born, but the time before she had a body. Not only the time before she had a body, but the time before she had a spirit. In the midst of the jumble of wonder and mystery a change took place and she had a spirit. Another change and she had a body. Another change and she was born. Now there's been another change and she's dead. It's just like the progression of the four seasons, spring, summer, fall, winter. Now she's going to lie down peacefully in a vast room. If I were to follow after her bawling and sobbing, it would show that I don't understand anything about fate. So I stopped.[27]

The episode about Zhuangzi's mourning for his wife not only reveals what the authors of the text thought about traditional rites of mourning, but it also illustrates two larger points found in the *Zhuangzi*. The first has to do with the limits of conventional morality, a morality that depends upon distinctions, such as between good and bad or between true and false. For the *Zhuangzi*, drawing distinctions, especially through language, is inherently problematic, because it prevents men and women from grasping the totality of the Way. "What does the Way rely upon," Zhuangzi reportedly asks. "That we have true and false? What do words rely upon, that we have right and wrong? How can the Way go away and not exist? How can words exist and not be acceptable? When the Way relies on little accomplishments and words rely on vain show, then we have the rights and wrongs of the Ru and the Mohists. What one calls right the other calls wrong; what one calls wrong the other calls right. But if we want to right their wrongs and wrong their rights, then the best thing to use is clarity."[28] Given the limits of language and, indeed, the limits of conventional morality, the *Zhuangzi* urges men and women to stop drawing distinctions. "Discard and confuse the six tones, smash and unstring the pipes and lutes, stop up the ears of the blind musician Kuang, and for the first time the people of the world will be able to hold on to their hearing. Wipe out patterns and designs, scatter the five colors, glue up the eyes of Li Zhu, and for the first time the people of the world will be able to hold on to their eyesight.[29]

The second theme that the episode about Zhuangzi's mourning touches upon has to do with the importance of acquiring the proper perspective on matters, a theme that runs through many anecdotes found in the text. Is death better than life or freedom better than captivity? With respect to these questions, the *Zhuangzi* recounts a memorable anecdote, one drawn from history:

> Lady Li was the daughter of the border guard of Ai. When she was first taken captive and brought to the state of Qin, she wept until her tears drenched the collar of her robe. But later, when she went to live in the palace of the ruler, shared his couch with him, and ate the delicious meats of his table, she wondered why she had ever wept.

The anecdote concludes by posing a more challenging question. That is, given that freedom may not necessarily be better than captivity, how can one know that death might not be better than life—"How do I know that the dead do not wonder why they ever longed for life?"[30]

Anecdotes, such as the one about Lady Li, not only illustrate the importance of perspective but also illustrate the indeterminacy or uncertainty of human knowledge. The *Zhuangzi* brings home this point in the allegory of the dream, where the text implicitly compares humans' awareness of the world with a dreamer's perception of dreams.

> Once Zhuang Zhou [that is, Zhuangzi] dreamt he was a butterfly, a butterfly flitting and fluttering around, happy with himself and doing as he pleased. He didn't know he was Zhuang Zhou. Suddenly he woke up and there he was, solid and unmistakable Zhuang Zhou. But he didn't know if he was Zhuang Zhou who had dreamt he was a butterfly, or a butterfly dreaming he was Zhuang Zhou.[31]

To realize that human awareness is in itself indeterminate was for the *Zhuangzi* authors a great insight.[32] And indeed, the text refers to this kind of awareness as nothing but "the great awakening," one in which "we know that this is all a great dream."[33]

Han Feizi

Few Chinese thinkers are as notorious as Han Feizi (c. 280–233 B.C.E.), who was one of Xunzi's two famous pupils. His ideas survive in the *Han Feizi,* a text of fifty-five chapters reviled for millennia for its *realpolitik* outlook but appreciated for its clever arguments and colorful writing. In modern times, it has even been compared to Machiavelli's *The Prince.* Like *The Prince,* the *Han Feizi* is replete with historical anecdotes illustrating the author's point, as well as many statements that shocked readers by their cynicism and apparent lack of regard for human morality.[34]

A member of the royal house of the small state of Han, Han Fei or Han Feizi ("Master Han Fei") was destined for a career in government. But according to Sima Qian, Han Fei suffered from a stammer. And in an age when statesmen distinguished themselves through brilliant oratory rather than writing, his career suffered. Worried about the fortunes of his small home state, he admonished his royal relatives in written memorials, but all in vain. Ironically, the one ruler who did take Han Feizi's writings to heart was the young Qin ruler, who would become the first emperor of China. The Qin minister, Li Si, brought to his lord's attention the writings of his former classmate, for whom he expressed great admiration. Yet despite his admiration for Han Feizi, the young Qin ruler launched a campaign against Han in 234 B.C.E. Just before the invasion, the ruler of Han dispatched Han Feizi to Qin to plead on behalf of Han, but, following Li Si's advice, the Qin ruler had Han Fei executed. Why Li Si turned on his classmate is not clear. Some suggest he was jealous of Han Fei, whom he acknowledged to be the greater talent. Others suggest that Li Si was concerned that Han Feizi was not trustworthy. Before drinking the poison sent to him by Li Si, Han Fei composed "The Difficulties of Persuasion," a famous work in which he explored the dangers facing statesmen.[35]

Traditional scholars categorize Han Feizi as a Legalist (*fa jia*). Two other famous Legalist thinkers were Shang Yang and Shen Buhai (d. 337 B.C.E.), although little is known about their philosophies. By most accounts, Legalist ideas first emerged around the fourth century B.C.E. along with state consolidation and rationalization. Legalists emphasized practical problems of statecraft and political control over ethical concerns. Unlike Mencius, who frowned upon discussions of profit and political power, Legalist thinkers openly discussed ways in which rulers could maximize their tax revenues, enlarge their corvée labor force, and effectively wage wars. They believed that strict enforcement of law (*fa*) and a system of rewards, rather than ritual norms, would ensure good social order.

In addition to subscribing to these views, Han Feizi's advice to rulers in large part reflects his specific understanding of the political upheaval in his own time. For Han Feizi, as for Xunzi, the roots of the trouble lay in human nature. Human beings, he noted, virtually always act out of self-interest—even at the expense of good political order. Expressions of self-interest were inescapable and manifested in all human relations. This is clearly shown, Han Feizi argued, by the fact that many families kill newborn infants if they are girls because, unlike boys, girls cannot support their parents in old age. If calculations of self-interest influence the relationship of parents and child, which are based on natural bonds of affection, how much more is this the case for relationships not bound by ties of natural affection, relations such as those between lord and minister? To illustrate his point about the unreliable nature of political relations, Han Feizi frequently turned to the historical record, which was replete with examples not only of ministers betraying their lords but also of conflicts of interest arising between royal husbands and wives and between brothers.

For Han Feizi, the ills of his time required some drastic measures. Rulers, he warned, should not attempt to return to an idealized past of human government, as some thinkers proposed. To do so would be to emulate a farmer who, while working in a field one day, noticed that a rabbit dashed itself unconscious against a tree stump. That evening the farmer took the rabbit home and feasted on it with his family. The next day and every day thereafter the farmer waited by the tree stump for another rabbit. Just as foolish, according to Han Feizi, were those who believed that the accidental successes of the past would be repeated.

The enlightened ruler is free of illusions about restoring humane government, which had only worked in distant antiquity before population pressures transformed society into a world of strife. Instead, the enlightened ruler needs to be aware that human beings act out of self-interest. Therefore, he must always be on guard against his ministers, wives, male favorites, and even children. He realizes that everyone—even those who profess to love him dearly—potentially benefits from his death. The enlightened ruler furthermore, Han Feizi argues, realizes that people deceive, especially when they are aware of the desires and fancies of the ruler. As a result, the enlightened ruler conceals his own thoughts and feelings to discover those of his subjects and to keep his subjects guessing. Finally, the enlightened ruler avoids activities or favorites who cloud his judgment. "The ruler is easily beguiled by lovely women and charming boys, by all those who can fawn and play at love," complained Han Feizi, "They wait for the time when he is sated with food and wine, and ask for anything they desire, for they know that by this trick their requests are sure to be heeded."[36] For this reason, the enlightened ruler disciplines himself with his favorites and acts only to promote the worthy and capable, knowing in the long run that his chances of survival are greater if he governs in a dispassionate and impartial manner.

Later assessments of Han Feizi have been far from kind. In part, Han Feizi's rhetoric—in particular, his penchant for pithy but extreme statements—inspired harsh assessments of his philosophy. But in large part, these assessments owe much to Han Feizi's association with the policies of the Qin empire and the Legalists. Some scholars even go so far as to see Han Feizi as an advocate of royal tyranny and a theorist of authoritarianism. Yet one could argue that in many regards, Han Feizi's ideas, like those of Machiavelli, should be considered in their historical context. True, Han Feizi emphasized the importance of political control and harsh penalties, but his advocacy reflected his desire to bring unity and order to an increasingly chaotic world. Had he lived a little longer perhaps Han Feizi would have seen his dreams realized.

Notes

1. Lothar von Falkenhausen, "Sources of Taoism: Reflections on Archaeological Indicators of Religious Change in Eastern Zhou China," *Taoist Resources* 5.2 (1994): 7–8.

2. Lothar von Falkenhausen, "The Waning of the Bronze Age, Material Culture and Social Developments, 770–481 B.C.E.," in Edward Shaughnessy and Michael Loewe, eds., *The Cambridge History of Ancient China: From the Origins of Civilization to 221 BC* (Cambridge: Cambridge Univ. Press, 1999), pp. 514–525.

3. David Hawkes, *The Songs of the South: An Ancient Chinese Anthology of Poems by Qu Yuan and Other Poets* (London: Penguin Books, 1985), p. 27.

4. Hawkes, *Songs of the South*, p. 69.

5. Hawkes, *Songs of the South*, p. 75.

6. Frank Kierman, Jr., "Phases and Modes of Combat in Early China," in Frank A. Kierman and John K. Fairbank, eds., *Chinese Ways in Warfare* (Cambridge: Harvard Univ. Press, 1974): pp. 26–66.

7. Mark Edward Lewis, "Warring States Political History," in *Cambridge History of Ancient China*, pp. 620–29.

8. Burton Watson, "Introduction," *Basic Writings of Mo-Tzu, Hsün Tzu, and Han Fei Tzu* (New York: Columbia Univ. Press, 1964), p. 5.

9. A. C. Graham, *Disputers of the Tao: Philosophical Argumentation in Ancient China* (La Salle, Ill.: Open Court, 1989), p. 34.

10. Robert Eno, Personal communication,18 May, 2004. The text that makes this claim is the Han philosophical compendium, the *Huai nan zi* (c. 139 B.C.E.).

11. Watson, *Basic Writings of Mo-Tzu*, p. 18.

12. Watson, *Basic Writings of Mo-Tzu*, p. 40.

13. Wu Hung, "Art and Architecture of the Warring States Period," in *Cambridge History of Ancient China*, pp. 721–723.

14. Watson, *Basic Writings of Mo-Tzu*, p. 76.

15. Watson, *Basic Writings of Mo-Tzu*, p. 83.

16. *Mencius* 2A2, trans. D.C. Lau, *Mencius* (Harmondsworth, Penguin, 1970), p. 80.

17. *Mencius* 4A11, pp. 122–23.

18. *Mengzi* 3A5, trans. D.C. Lau, p. 105.

19. *Mencius* 7B14, p. 196.

20. Watson, "Introduction," *Basic Works of Mo-Tzu*, pp. 1–2.

21. Watson, "Introduction," *Basic Works of Mo-Tzu*, pp. 1–2.

22. Watson, *Basic Works of Mo-Tzu*, p. 164.

23. Watson, *Basic Works of Mo-Tzu*, p. 157–159.

24. Watson, *Basic Works of Mo-Tzu*, p. 89. Translation slightly modified.

25. Watson, *Basic Works of Mo-Tzu*, p. 79.

26. Harold D. Roth, *Original Tao: Inward Training (Nei-Yeh) and the Foundations of Taoist Mysticism* (New York: Columbia Univ. Press, 1999).

27. Burton Watson, *The Complete Works of Chuang Tzu* (New York: Columbia Univ. Press, 1968), pp. 191–92.

28. Watson, *Complete Works of Chuang Tzu*, p. 39. Translation slightly modified.

29. Watson, *Complete Works of Chuang Tzu,* p. 111.

30. Watson, *Complete Works of Chuang Tzu,* p. 47.

31. Watson, *Complete Works of Chuang Tzu,* p. 49.

32. David N. Keightley, "Disguise and Deception in Early China and Early Greece," in Steven Shankman and Stephen Durrant, eds., *Early China/Ancient Greece: Thinking Through Comparisons* (Albany: State Univ. of New York Press, 2002), p. 137.

33. Watson, *Complete Works of Chuang Tzu,* p. 49.

34. Keightley, "Disguise and Deception in Early China and Early Greece," p. 137.

35. Watson, *Complete Works of Chuang Tzu,* p. 47.

36. Watson, "Introduction," *Basic Works of Mo-Tzu,* p. 4.

37. Watson, "Introduction," *Basic Works of Mo-Tzu,* pp. 1–15.

38. Watson, *Basic Works of Mo-Tzu,* p. 43.

3

The Early Imperial Period

I. The Qin

Sources and Historiographical Problems

Reappraisals

II. The Han

The Formative Years

The Quality of Han Rule

The Xiongnu and Other Neighboring Peoples

Intellectual Movements

Poetry

Gender

Changes in Political Economy during the Han Period

The Fall of the Han

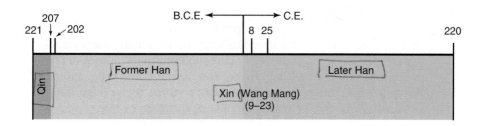

The Qin unification of China in 221 B.C.E. was the beginning of some 400 years of imperial rule, although the Qin rule was short lived. The Han built on Qin foundations and erected a more lasting political structure. Under the Han, civilization in what is now China was reshaped, and the Han state became a great imperial power comparable in achievements and historical significance to the Roman Empire (see Figure 3.2). Most historians divide the Han into two periods. The first period is the Former or Western Han (206 B.C.E.–9 C.E.), the latter name reflecting the location of the imperial capital in Chang'an in the West. This period came to an end in 9 C.E., when the regent, Wang Mang, usurped the throne and established a short-lived Xin dynasty (9–23 C.E.). By 25 C.E., members of the Liu clan wrestled control of the empire from the Xin and established the imperial capital in Luoyang in the East. This period is referred to as the Later or Eastern Han dynasty (25–220 C.E.).

I. The Qin

To most people living in Europe and North America, the Qin dynasty (221–206 B.C.E.) is famous for two monuments: the army of terra-cotta soldiers found in Xi'an and the Great Wall (of which the much later additions are still visible). It is also arguably the most notorious of all early East Asian regimes. Today, both in China as well as elsewhere, the Qin has come to epitomize authoritarian rule and imperial tyranny. The truth, however, is more complicated.

Sources and Historiographical Problems

The negative image of the dynasty is based on traditional assessments of Qin rule that emphasize three themes: the repressiveness of its rule, the harshness or severity of its institutions, and the follies of its rulers. The best exposition of the repressiveness of Qin rule is found in "The Faults of the Qin," a famous essay by the

Han scholar-official, Jia Yi (201–168? B.C.E.), who observes of the First Emperor or Qin Shihuang:

> He reached the pinnacle of power and ordered all in the Six Directions, whipping the rest of the world into submission and thus spreading his might through the Four Seas. . . . He then abolished the ways of ancient sage kings and put to the torch the writings of the Hundred Schools in an attempt to keep the people in ignorance. He demolished the walls of the major cities and put to death men of fame and talent, collected all the arms of the realm of Xianyang, and had the spears and arrowheads melted down to form twelve huge statues in human form—all with the aim of weakening his people.[1]

One infamous incident of Qin rule that Jia Yi alluded to in the preceding extract was the First Emperor's decision to burn books by a wide array of thinkers in 213 B.C.E. Jia Yi believed that this policy was intended to "keep the people in ignorance."

Most exposition of the second theme revolves around the burdens levied upon commoners through conscript labor. Conscript labor was levied upon all able-bodied adult males in the realm, usually in the form of labor or military service. Periodically the state required local officials to register the name, place of origins, status, and age of every person in the realm. With this information, the government was able to estimate the size of its conscript labor force and build large-scale public works. The best known of all public works is the Great Wall, built by linking earlier walls raised by states against each other and intended to protect the empire from hostile, nomadic groups. Restored by the Ming dynasty, it still can be seen just north of Beijing. According to Han accounts, the Great Wall was built with conscript labor.

Other important public works projects that used conscript labor include networks of roads that ran from one end of the empire to the other, as well as irrigation and transportation canals. With conscript labor, the Qin state also built a lavish mausoleum for the First Emperor. Although his tomb has yet to be excavated by archaeologists, if we believe Han accounts, it was a wonder (see Figure 3.1). According to the famous historian Sima Qian (c. 140–c. 90 B.C.E.), the 700,000 conscripts charged with building it "dug through subterranean streams and poured molten copper for the outer coffin, and the tomb was filled with models of palaces, pavilions, and offices, as well as fine vessels, precious stones and rarities." The First Emperor wanted his tomb to replicate more than his palace; he wanted to recreate the entire world within the tomb. "All the country's streams and the Yellow and the Yangzi Rivers were reproduced in quicksilver and by some mechanical means made to flow into a miniature ocean; the heavenly constellations were shown above and the regions of the earth below."[2]

The third theme in traditional accounts of the Qin focuses on the purported follies of the emperors. For example, the reason, according to Sima Qian, that the First Emperor invested great energy in his mausoleum was because he had a pathological fear of death. And by the end of his reign, like many elites, he became so obsessed with avoiding death that he sponsored futile expeditions to find immortality elixirs, including one that involved sending a score of young men and women to mythical islands. With age, his aversion to death grew so strong that none of his ministers dared to use the word in his presence. Not only did the First Emperor have a pathological fear of death, but by Sima's account, he was no less than a megalomaniac. Once, at the end of his rule, the emperor made a tour of the realm. Arriving in the East, he visited the most sacred mountain, Mount Tai, and decided to scale its heights and leave three inscriptions, which would bear everlasting witness to his achievements. Rather immodestly, one of the inscriptions, translated by Martin Kern, proclaims:

FIGURE 3.1 Terra-cotta warrior guarding the tomb of the First Emperor. Although yet to be excavated, archaeologists have discovered a complete terra-cotta army in the immediate vicinity of the tomb. (© Bridgeman Art Library.)

> The August Emperor
>   embodies sagehood,
> And after having pacified all
>   under Heaven
> He has not been remiss in
>   rulership.
> He rises early, retires late at
>   night;
> He establishes and sets up
>   enduring benefits,
> Radiates and glorifies His teachings and instructions.
> His precepts and principles reach all around,
> The distant and the near are completely well-ordered
> And all receive His sage will.
> The noble and the mean are distinguished and made clear,
> Men and women embody compliance,
> Cautious and respectful to their professions and duties.
> Distinctly demarcated are the inner and outer spheres,
> Nothing that is not clear and pure,
> Extending down to the later descendants.
> His transforming influence reaches without limit:
> May [later ages] respect and follow the decrees He bequeaths
> And forever accept His solemn warnings![3]

Yet there are reasons to doubt at least some of the stories that have come down to us about the First Emperor. True, the First Emperor may well have left three inscriptions on Mount Tai, but we must bear in mind that accounts such as Sima's were written by court historians employed by the Han victors. Jens Ostergard Petersen, for one, has questioned whether some of the repressive measures undertaken by the Qin, such as the burning of the books, really happened as conventionally understood. With respect to the burning of the books, Petersen, after careful examination of the extant textual record, concluded that the measure was far more limited than most scholars previously thought. It applied not to all philosophical inquisitions but just compilations consisting of didactic historical anecdotes, compilations that the Qin state regarded as having "fragmented form and petty concerns."[4] For another thing, many of these stories are undeniably anti-Qin and the aim is to discredit, and even slander, the Qin ruling house. Consider the following passage, also by Sima Qian, which describes the mother of the First Emperor as a nymphomaniac:

> While the First Emperor was growing up, the licentiousness of the Queen-dowager did not cease. Lü Buwei feared it might be discovered and that disaster would befall him, so he secretly sought a man named Lao Ai, who had a tremendous penis, and made him his retainer. At times he would indulge in some wild music, and have [Lao] Ai move about [in time with it], with his penis filling up the [hole of] a wheel made of tong wood. He caused the Queen-dowager to hear of this, in order to entice her. The Queen-dowager heard of it, and actually wished secretly to have him. Lü Buwei thereupon introduced Lao Ai, and had someone falsely accuse him of a crime deserving castration. At the same time [Lü] Buwei secretly told the Queen-dowager that if she could have [Lao Ai] falsely castrated, then he could be obtained to serve within [the women's quarters]. At this, the Queen-dowager secretly gave heavy bribes to the official in charge of castration, to have him [that is, Lao Ai] falsely condemned, pluck off his beard and eyebrows, and make him a eunuch. In this way he came to enter the service of the Queen-dowager.[5]

Reappraisals

Recent scholarship has presented a more balanced picture of Qin rule, acknowledging its achievements. To be sure, although Qin rule was harsh, the Qin were also responsible for the large-scale road and transportation system and the Great Walls. The achievements also include the creation of a standard script for efficient communication to replace many local scripts. In addition to standardizing the script, the First Emperor and his advisors also unified weights and measures. Acts such as these no doubt proved invaluable to subsequent generations of Han dynasty emperors, who also struggled to unify an empire prone to dissolution.

Another great, although somewhat more controversial, legacy of the Qin was its legal code. Most standard accounts emphasize that the Qin code was extensive and excessively harsh. One aspect of the code that is often criticized is the practice of collective punishment according to which the spouses, children, and often the extended family of a criminal would be punished, even put to death, if they did not each denounce the offender. The purpose of this practice was threefold. First, it was to ensure that families took responsibility for policing their members; second, it prevented family members from seeking revenge or rebelling against the state; and third, it encouraged family members to denounce, rather than to shield, each other.

Another noteworthy aspect of the Qin legal code was its control of the private conduct of its subjects. A man could not only be punished for failing to show up to do his conscript labor or for murdering his neighbor, he could also be punished for engaging in sexual relations with someone else's wife. In a similar vein, a woman could be severely punished for being rude to her in-laws, as well as for having sexual relations with a slave. The most serious offense with regard to private conduct, however, was a lack of filial piety to one's parents, an offense that was punished by execution in the marketplace.[6]

Although from our perspective, these codes seem harsh and even tyrannical, it is also important to bear in mind that they were far from arbitrary. Consider two excerpts from the Qin code:

> In trying a case, if one can use the documents to track down [the evidence in] their statements, and get the facts on the parties without an investigation by beating, that is considered superior; investigation by beating is considered inferior; in addition, intimidation is considered the worse [course of action].

> In general, when questioning parties to a case, you must first listen to everything they say and record it, with each party developing his statement. Although you may know that he is lying, there is no need to interrogate him immediately. When his statements have been recorded in their entirety and there are no explanations, then interrogate him with interrogators. When interrogating him, once again listen and record his explanatory statements in their entirety; once again, inspect the other [points] which lack explanation and reinterrogate him about them. When you have interrogated him to the greatest extent possible and he has lied repeatedly, has changed what he has said but not submitted, should the law match interrogation by beating, then investigate by beating. When you have investigated by beating, you must compose a document which reads:

> Transcript:

> Because X repeatedly changed what he has said and there were no explanatory statements, we question X by beating.[7]

As seen from these excerpts, although torture was allowed by the Qin code, it was regarded as an undesirable, last resort—to be avoided if possible and only to be used when the proper procedures were followed.

II. The Han
The Formative Years

Not long after the death of the First Emperor, rebellions broke out against the Qin. Of the rebel leaders, the most formidable were Xiang Yu (233–202 B.C.E.), a Chu aristocrat of great courage and charisma, and Liu Bang (247–195 B.C.E.), a man reputed to be of obscure origin, with little cultural refinement but personal shrewdness. According to later accounts, Liu Bang's shrewdness prevailed over Xiang Yu's courage, and by 202 B.C.E., Liu Bang, known to posterity as Gaozu, became one of the first men of obscure and nonaristocratic origin to found a major dynasty. That dynasty is called the Han, or more narrowly the Former or Western Han (206 B.C.E.–9 C.E.) to distinguish it from the Latter and Eastern Han (25–220 C.E.), also discussed in this chapter (see Figure 3.2.).

Administratively the Han built on Qin foundations, but a substantive difference between the early Western Han and the Qin lay in the degree of political centralization. Whereas the Qin attempted to rule the entire realm from the state capital, this was not feasible for the first five Han emperors. For one thing, Liu Bang had to reward the old generals and comrades-in-arms who had helped him to defeat Xiang Yu. Because of this, Liu Bang had to parcel out large territories as vassal states to his former generals or comrades-in-arms. Once firmly established, however, he regretted having given away so much territory and wished to forestall any ambitions his former generals and comrades-in-arms may have had. Under one pretext or the other, he regained control over the lands assigned and reincorporated the territory into the empire. For another thing, the empire was too vast and difficult to simply rule from the capital in Chang'an, so Liu Bang also established kingdoms in the East for members of his own clan, his many sons, and their grandsons. In many ways, one could say that the early Han had returned to the decentralized system of rule that characterized the Western Zhou.

The decentralized system of rule proved, however, to be a source of trouble. Perhaps more so than Liu Bang's old generals and comrades-in-arms, members of the imperial family with kingdoms entertained ambitions of their own. And despite rich gifts and titles from the court, by the time of the Emperors Wen (r. 180–157 B.C.E.) and Wu (r. 140–86 B.C.E.), Liu kings openly rebelled against the emperors (see Figure 3.3). Emperor Wen had special difficulty with his wayward younger brother, Liu Chang (c. 199–174 B.C.E.), also known to posterity as King Li. Liu Chang had violated sumptuary rules, using the emperor's own carriage, and he had murdered and participated in a rebellion against his brother. Nevertheless, Emperor Wen had been unwilling to punish Liu Chang because he was the emperor's last surviving brother, and the emperor loved him. Not surprisingly, it was only a matter of time before Liu Chang participated in a rebellion against the emperor. In strongly worded memorials, various statesmen, including Jia Yi, urged the emperor to punish his brother severely. Emperor Wen, Sima Qian tells, acceded, although only reluctantly, and Liu Chang was sent unceremoniously into banishment in the south in a cage. Indignant at his treatment, Liu Chang reportedly refused

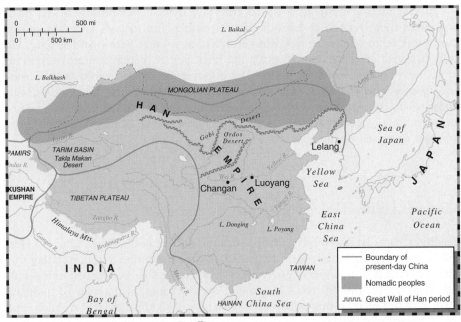

FIGURE 3.2 Map of the Han empire. 😊

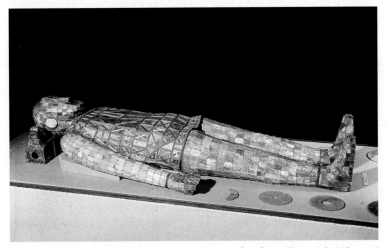

FIGURE 3.3 Jade burial suit of the Princess Dou Wan, wife of Liu Sheng (d. 113 B.C.E.). Mancheng, Hebei, 67.72 in long. The Han court bestowed jade suits only to members of the Liu clan and the highest ministers of the realm. (© Giraudon/Bridgeman Art Library.) 😊

food and water and died before reaching his destination. Hearing the news of his brother's death saddened Emperor Wen, and, again according to Sima Qian, he then made the mistake of enfeoffing Liu Chang's son, Liu An, king of Huainan, with a large territory that had once belonged to Chu.

In his turn, Liu An grew up to entertain dynastic ambitions of his own. Somewhat more refined and subtle than his father, Liu An was also well known during the reign of his nephew, Emperor Wu, as a great patron of learning. He commissioned an encyclopedic work, the *Huai nan zi,* which contains essays on topics ranging from myth to philosophy of government, geography, and astronomy. However, in 154 B.C.E., Liu An reportedly rebelled against the emperor, with hopes of superseding him. Although the truth of the charges is unclear, Liu An, along with his wife, committed suicide. His children were executed, and his territory was absorbed by the court.

The Quality of Han Rule

Traditional scholarship tends to emphasize the differences between Qin and Han rule, portraying the latter as less tyrannical and authoritarian and correlating this with differences in theories of governance. The Han ruling house, beginning with Emperor Wu (r. 140–86 B.C.E.), adopted Ru doctrines as its state orthodoxy.[8] Most scholars refer to this policy as "the victory of Confucianism." As such, one would expect that the Han dynastic house would promote traditional values associated with Confucian thinkers, such as filial piety and benevolent rule. To be sure, this explanation has a number of merits. For one thing, it is true that Han emperors supported traditions of learning scholars now retrospectively regard as Ru or Confucian, and it is also true that Emperor Wu was responsible for establishing an imperial academy. Finally, the early Han rulers did at least pay lip service to values found in the *Analects,* in particular, filial piety. From the reign of Emperor Wu on, calls to recruit "filial sons" into the imperial bureaucracy became frequent.[9]

Nevertheless, it would seem that some historians exaggerated the differences between the Qin and Han regimes, for the early Han regime was almost indistinguishable from the Qin in a number of ways. For one, Han legal institutions show great continuity with their Qin predecessors, even though Liu Bang reportedly abolished the harsh and intrusive Qin codes. Han administrative documents discovered by archaeologists in the last several decades reveal that, like its Qin predecessor, the Han state was indeed harsh.[10] Family members were punished for one individual's crimes. For example, if a man raped or engaged in illicit sexual relations with a woman, not only would he be castrated, but also his wife and the children who lived with him would be imprisoned. A woman, furthermore, who did not denounce her husband for committing a crime would also be punished, although usually somewhat less severely.

Perhaps the best example of how harsh the Han code could be is a legal case narrated in a document buried in a tomb dating to 187 B.C.E. It begins:

> The statute observes: As for those who are responsible for affairs in the county magistrate's office but whose father or mother or whose wife dies, they are allowed a grace leave of 30 days. If their paternal grandfather or grandmother dies or their natural siblings die, they are

allowed 15 days. If they are brazenly remiss in this, then they are to be shaved and made into a wall-builder or grain-pounder of the state. They are to be shackled at the feet and transported to the bureau of the salt mines in Ba prefecture [in the South West]. . . .

Next the document introduces the case of Woman A, whose husband, an army private, had died of illness. As appropriate, A and her mother-in-law named Su wailed all night next to the coffin placed in the front hall of the house before burial. This was as it should be, but:

> A and a man, B, fornicated in the chamber behind the coffin. The next morning, Su denounced A to an officer, who bound A for arrest. There was uncertainty as to what A's offense had been. . . . The [rights of inheritance] of a wife are secondary with respect to the parents of her husband. In the instance that a father or mother had died, and before they had been buried, the child had fornicated by the side of the deceased's [coffin], then the child would have been deemed unfilial. Being unfilial, he or she would have been cast off in the market place. If his or her crime had been secondary in [severity] to being unfilial, then he or she would have merited being tattooed and made into a wall-builder or grain-pounder. Had he or she been brazenly lax, then he or she would be shaved. Applying this principle to this case, the wife reveres the husband and [only reveres him] second to her father and mother. Yet A's husband died, and she was not sorrowful or grieved. She fornicated with a man by the side of the deceased's [coffin], and thus [her offense] warrants [the punishments as stipulated by] the two regulations concerning the "unfilial" and the "brazenly lax."[11]

Prurience aside, this case reveals that the Han state, like its Qin predecessor, attempted to regulate relationships between parents and children as well as between spouses and was as interested as its predecessor in penetrating into the daily lives of ordinary people and punishing what most of us now largely consider to be "personal" or "private" matters. But, on the one hand, it was, and remains, hardly unique in this respect. And, on the other, the state's actual ability to influence, let alone control, local daily life was limited in an age before the invention of paper and brush, not to speak of telephones and fax machines.

Besides being harsh, the early Han state showed great interest, like its Qin predecessor, in maintaining control over and extracting labor from the population. Many of the administrative documents discovered from Han tombs show that the state required every man, woman, and child to register their name, age, place of origin, and sex with local authorities. Each year, every able-bodied adult man and woman was required to perform service or pay for a substitute. Failure to register or perform service was seriously punished. All Han subjects were further categorized into classes, according to their status. As was the case in Qin times, high-status individuals were punished on the whole less severely than commoners or slaves. Criminal offenses, especially minor ones that did not merit death or serious mutilation, also provided the Han state with an additional source of revenue: offenders were often used in the state-owned salt and iron mines, as well as for building public works, such as city walls.

The Xiongnu and Other Neighboring Peoples

From early times the Han traded, negotiated, and fought with neighboring peoples. During the Warring States Period such contacts became quite extensive, including relations with tribal confederations in Manchuria and Korea in the Northeast, with the inhabitants of the steppes to the Northwest, and with the peoples of the South. Before the reign of Emperor Wu, Han foreign policy was generally conciliatory, but that emperor adopted expansionist policies and by force of arms asserted Han control over the Southeast, including what is now Northern Vietnam, and established Han colonies in Korea where they greatly accelerated the diffusion of Han culture into that peninsula and beyond to Japan.

It turned out that both Korea and Vietnam were suitable for the Han-style agricultural way of life and gradually adapted a Han-style government and higher culture while resisting Han political dominance. In contrast, a Han way of life was irrelevant to the people of the grasslands to the Han empire's north and northwest. The frequently antagonistic relations between the nomads of the steppe and the settled people of the plains remained a persistent problem for two millennia.

The greatest nomadic challenge that faced the Western Han emperors came from the Xiongnu, one of the nomadic groups that lived in the North and Northwest. The First Emperor reportedly had the Great Wall built as a cautionary move and had even sent out an expedition against them. In large part, the formidable military threat posed by the Xiongnu was due to effective leadership of Maodun, who became the ruler of the Xiongnu confederacy in 209 B.C.E. Under his leadership, the Xiongnu forced the Han court to make frequent conciliatory gestures, such as providing luxury gifts and sending Han princesses in marriage to Xiongnu princes. Eventually the Xiongnu leader had sufficient confidence to suggest marriage to Liu Bang's widow, the Empress Dowager, so that they could spend old age together and unite their realms. Although she was reportedly greatly insulted by such a proposal, the Empress Dowager allowed herself to be talked out of attacking the Xiongnu. Instead, she sent back a conciliatory note to the Xiongnu leader, declining his proposal on the ground that she was too old and ugly to be married!

The Xiongnu, like other nomads, were often formidable opponents because of their skill in warfare. For them war represented merely a special application of the skills of horsemanship and archery that they practiced every day in guiding and defending their flocks. It was thus not difficult for Xiongnu men to conduct the frequent raids of Han territory. In contrast, military service for a Han peasant required that he interrupt the normal pattern of his life, leave his work, and undergo special training. The mobility of the nomads was an asset not only in attack but also in defense, for traveling lightly with their flocks and tents, they could elude

Han military expeditions and avoid complete destruction or permanent control, even when the Han were able to mobilize their superior resources in manpower and wealth.

Two strategies for coping with the Xiongnu emerged in the Han court. The first, preferred by the first Western Han emperors and their advisors, was appeasement by sending Han princesses as Xiongnu brides as well as expensive gifts as payoffs. The second strategy, which was adopted by Emperor Wu, involved an aggressive stance: sending large armies into the present-day Ordos Region, Inner Mongolia, Gansu, and Han Turkistan. To maintain surveillance over these areas, he established military colonies in strategic places and pressured local rulers and chiefs to enter into tributary relations with the Han. In addition to accepting Han suzerainty, they were required to send princes to the capital, ostensibly to receive a Han education, but actually to serve as hostages. Proponents of the second strategy argued that appeasement failed on two counts. First, it did nothing to prevent Xiongnu raids on the frontiers. Second, it was expensive. To pay for his wars with the Xiongnu, Emperor Wu instituted state monopolies on salt, iron, liquor, and coinage to raise new revenues. The salt and iron industries proved to be an especially rich source of revenues for imperial coffers.

In reality, the proponents of more aggressive measures were correct at least with respect to the latter count. The costs of payoffs to the Xiongnu were high, perhaps as high as 7 percent of the total imperial budget for one year.[12] Fortunately for Emperor Wu, his aggressive strategy ultimately succeeded. By 53 B.C.E., the Xiongnu were no longer the imposing military threat they had been. By that time, the tribes had split into northern and southern federations, and it was the latter that gave its allegiance to the Han. Splitting the Xiongnu could be construed as a victory for a combination of carrot and stick. Struggles broke out between Xiongnu factions, much to the delight and satisfaction of a relieved Han court.

Intellectual Movements

Most twentieth-century assessments of Han thought have been far from kind. More charitable commentators stress the relatively conservative nature of Han thinkers, who, unlike their Warring States predecessors, rarely departed from traditional ideas in a radical way. Han thinkers developed, elaborated, and synthesized the insights of Warring States masters.[13] Less charitable commentators lament the derivative nature of Han thought, its sterility, and even its lack of intellectual rigor.[14] The most critical commentators go so far as to condemn Han thought for being fanciful, intellectual, weak, and even inherently antiscientific. The perceived lack of intellectual rigor in Han thought was so serious a problem that the Buddhist "conquest" of China was inevitable, as literati were looking for a new infusion of intellectual creativity that was found lacking in the indigenous tradition.[15] Han thought was depicted as being consumed with textual study and controversies and constrained by imperial orthodoxy.

Underlying these stereotypes are a number of scholarly misconceptions. One is that there was anything approximating a formal state ideology, "Confucian" or otherwise. True, Emperor Wu did ban self-professed *fa* masters (usually translated "Legalist"), and he did indeed promote the learning of the *Ru* (a term often translated "Confucian"). But this does not mean that he imposed a crackdown on all non-Confucian schools of thought, an impossibility because there were no organized schools of thought at that time.[16] This interpretation is also implausible, when one considers what the terms, often translated as Legalist or Confucian, actually meant in their time. *Fa jia,* for example, referred merely to experts on statecraft— and not to a school that transmitted the doctrines of certain Warring States masters. *Ru,* similarly, referred to men who were versed in the classics in general, as opposed to men who professed their loyalty to a body of doctrines or beliefs. The classics were simply from too many different sources and periods to present any single coherent worldview.[17]

The notion that Han thought was derivative, conservative, and otherwise uninspiring becomes less plausible when one considers some of its major accomplishments in historical writing and natural philosophy.

One such accomplishment was the creation of East Asia's most admired history as well as the first dynastic history. The most famous Han historian by far was Sima Qian (c. 145–90 B.C.E.), the author of the *Shiji* or the *Historical Records.* Sima Qian devoted his life to the completion of a work begun by his father, a history of his world from the legendary Yellow Emperor to his own day. His work comprised five sections: the Basic Annals, Chronological Tables, Treatises, Hereditary Houses, and Memoirs. The treatises include essays on rites, music, pitch pipes, the calendar, astronomy, the solemn *feng* and *shan* sacrifices performed at Mount Tai, the Yellow River and canals, and economics. The memoirs contain accounts of the lives of famous men, important political and military leaders, thinkers, and groups such as imperial favorites, merchants, and so forth. They also include accounts of non-Han people.

Sima Qian's work set a pattern for later histories. Its form, somewhat modified, was followed by later historians including Ban Gu (d. 92 C.E.), author of *The History of the Former Han (Han shu).* This history, which is a record of the preceding dynasty written during and sanctioned by the succeeding dynasty, was the first in a series of such dynastic histories.

One characteristic of Sima Qian's writing, which is shared by many early and later historians, is extensive quotation from original documents. Another is a careful separation between the narrative text and his own editorial comments. To be sure, Sima Qian and others could no more transcend their times and origins than could their counterparts elsewhere. The very process of selection reveals personal values and ideals. Sima Qian freely expressed his enthusiasm for political valor and virtue, his delight in clever stratagems, and his fascination with character and personality. His deep feelings give life to his prose. A fine stylist and gifted raconteur, he did not hesitate to invent dialogues or turn to poetry to convey the full force of a historical personage's feelings or personality. His flair for the dramatic is exemplified by the following account of a battle:

Tian Dan then rounded up a thousand or more oxen from within the city and had them fitted with coverings of red silk on which dragon shapes had been painted in five colors. He had knives tied to their horns and bundles of grease-soaked reeds to their tails, and then, setting fire to their tails, had them driven out into the night through some twenty or thirty openings which had been tunneled in the city wall. Five thousand of the best soldiers poured out after them. The oxen, maddened by the fires that burned their tails, rushed into the Yan encampment which, it being night, was filled with terror. The oxtail torches burned with a dazzling glare, and wherever the Yan soldiers looked, they saw nothing but dragon shapes. All who stood within the path of the oxen were wounded or killed. The five thousand soldiers, gags in their mouths so they would make no noise, moved forward to attack, while from within the city came an accompaniment of drumming and clamor, the old men and boys all beating on bronze vessels to make a noise until the sound of it shook heaven and earth. The Yan army, taken completely by surprise, fell back in defeat, and the men of Qi were able to capture and put to death its commander, Qi Jie.[18]

A second major Han intellectual accomplishment was the completion of a philosophical order to account for all reality, one that probably began late in the Warring States Period. Basic to the efforts of Han thinkers was the conviction that the world was an organic whole passing through time in identifiable phases. All phenomena, no matter how diverse, that shared any particular temporal phase were held to be interrelated in a set of extensive correspondences.

One of the texts often used by Han thinkers to draw correspondences was the *Changes* (*Yi*). The *Changes* is of uncertain authorship or date, but most scholars believe that it was an ancient divination manual. Sixty-four hexagrams and the commentaries on them form the heart of the book. Each hexagram was created by combining two trigrams, each of which consists of three lines, either broken or unbroken. Because each trigram has three lines of only two kinds, that is, broken or unbroken, only eight combinations are possible:

Combining the eight trigrams into hexagrams in turn yields sixty-four unique figures. A common method of divination was to select the appropriate hexagram by counting the stalks of the milfoil. The very concept of divination is based on the conviction that nature and man are interrelated. By identifying the *yin* with the broken line and the *yang* with the unbroken, the *Yi jing* illustrates the way this pair of concepts applies to everything. For example, the first hexagram represents heaven, all *yang*, and the second hexagram represents earth, all *yin*. The rest consist of combinations of the two.

Besides correspondences that use yin and yang, there were various versions of such correspondences, which employed Five Agents or Phases terminology and other related systems. Table 3.1 is based on the order by which the Five

TABLE 3.1 Correspondences for the Five-Agents System

Correspondence	Wood	Fire	Earth	Metal	Water
Seasons	Spring	Summer	Autumn	Winter	
Divine Rulers	Tai Hao	Yan Di	Yellow Emperor	Shao Hao	Zhuan Xu
Attendant spirits	Gou Mang	Zhu Yong	Hou Tu	Ru Shou	Xuan Ming
Sacrifices	Inner door	Hearth	Inner court	Outer court	Well
Animals	Sheep	Fowl	Ox	Dog	Pig
Grains	Wheat	Beans	Panicled millet	Hemp	Millet
Organs	Spleen	Lungs	Heart	Liver	Kidneys
Numbers	Eight	Seven	Five	Nine	Six
Stems	*Jia/yi*	*Bing/dingi*	*Mou/ji*	*Geng/xin*	*Ren/guei*
Colors	Green	Red	Yellow	White	Black
Notes	Jue	Zhi	Gong	Shang	You
Tastes	Sour	Bitter	Sweet	Acrid	Salty
Smells	Goatish	Burning	Fragrant	Rank	Rotten
Directions	East	South	Center	West	North
Creatures	Scaly	Feathered	Naked	Hairy	Shell-covered
Beasts of the directions	Green Dragon	Scarlet Bird	Yellow Dragon	White Tiger	Black Tortoise
Virtues	Benevolence	Wisdom	Faith	Righteousness	Decorum
Planets	Jupiter	Mars	Saturn	Venus	Mercury
Officers	Minister of Agriculture	Minister of War	Minister of Works	Minister of Interior	Minister of Justice

From Wm. Theodore de Bary, Wing-tsit Chan, and Burton Watson, *Sources of Chinese Tradition,* Vol. I (New York: Columbia Univ. Press, 1960), p. 199. Reprinted with permission.

Agents were thought to produce each other. Another Han arrangement was fire-water-earth-wood-metal, the sequence in which the Agents overcome each other.

The acceptance of the idea that all phenomena are interrelated in a set of correspondences gave great satisfaction. Not only did it explain everything, but also it enabled humans to feel at home in the world, part of a temporal as well as a spatial continuum. It provided both an impetus to the development of science and the basis for a sophisticated theoretical framework for explaining the world. Because it made Han investigators sensitive to phenomena that interact without apparent physical contact, it enabled them to discover and explain phenomena such as the sympathetic vibration of musical instruments and the workings of magnetism. Among the most noted scientists was Zhang Heng (78–139): mathematician (he calculated the value of pi), practical and theoretical astronomer, cartographer (he invented the grid system for map making), and inventor of a seismograph that registered the direction of earthquakes far from the capital (see Figure 3.4).

FIGURE 3.4 Mirror back. Bronze, Eastern Han dynasty, diameter 6.77 in (Metropolitan Museum of Art, New York). Mirrors have been found in many elite Han tombs, although it is not clear what their intended function was. Some of them depict the cosmos and constellations. (© A.M.S. Foundation for the Arts, Sciences and Humanities. Photograph courtesy of the Arthur M. Sackler Gallery, Smithsonian Institution, Washington, D.C.: MLS 1802.)

Poetry

Among the poetic remains of the Han are the verses collected by the Music Bureau established by Emperor Wu. These include hymns and songs for ceremonial occasions and also a group of fresh and simple folk songs. Originally they were sung to the accompaniment of instruments such as the flute, a bamboo mouth organ known as the *sheng*, the drum, the lute, or a stringed instrument that was the ancestor of the Japanese *koto*. The music has been lost, and the words alone remain. The dynasty also produced good and important poems in a form limiting lines to five words each. The most characteristic and popular form, however, was the rhapsody, a unique genre in what would be later thought of as the Chinese literary tradition. The rhapsodies (*fu*) often ran to great lengths and combined poetry with prose. There were prose introductions and conclusions, and there might be prose interludes between the streams of verse. They were frequently in the form of a poetic debate and drew on both the rhetorical tradition of the Warring States Period and on the rich metaphors and fantastic allegories of the Chu tradition. Exotic terminology, verse catalogs, and ornamental embellishments enriched the verse, but in the hands of less than a master, the form was apt to degenerate into mere ostentation and artificiality. Its thematic repertoire included royal hunts and ceremonies, landscapes, the capital, fauna and flora, female beauty, and musical instruments.

The most highly regarded Han rhapsodist was Sima Xiangru (179–117 B.C.E.), a colorful man who as a young and poor scholar eloped with the widowed daughter of a wealthy merchant. Eventually his poetic gifts were recognized by Emperor Wu, and the poet received a post at court. One of his greatest *fu* describes the imperial park. It is too long to quote in full, but the following segment, in Burton Watson's translation, is sufficiently substantial to suggest the scope and flavor of this style of verse:

> Within the park spring the Ba and Chan rivers,
> And through it flow the Jing and Wei,
> The Feng, the Hao, the Lao, and the Jue,
> Twisting and turning their way
> Through the reaches of the park;
> Eight rivers, coursing onward,
> Spreading in different directions, each with its own form.
> North, south, east, and west
> They race and tumble,
> Pouring through the chasms of Pepper Hill,
> Skirting the banks of the river islets,
> Winding through the cinnamon forests
> And across the broad meadows.
> In wild confusion they swirl
> Along the bases of the tall hills
> And through the mouths of the narrow gorges;
> Dashed upon boulders, maddened by winding escarpments,
> They writhe in anger,
> Leaping and curling upward,
> Jostling and eddying in great swells
> That surge and batter against each other;
> Darting and twisting,
> Foaming and tossing,
> In a thundering chaos;
> Arching into hills, billowing like clouds,
> They dash to left and right,
> Plunging and breaking in waves
> That chatter over the shallows;
> Crashing against the cliffs, pounding the embankments.
> The waters pile up and reel back again,
> Skipping across the rises, swooping into the hollows,
> Rumbling and murmuring onward;
> Deep and powerful,

Fierce and clamorous,
They froth and churn
Like the boiling waters of a caldron,
Casting spray from their crests, until,
After their wild race through the gorges,
Their distant journey from afar,
They subside into silence,
Rolling on in peace to their long destination,
Boundless and without end,
Gliding in soundless and solemn procession,
Shimmering and shining in the sun,
To flow through the giant lakes of the east,
Or spill into the ponds along their banks.[19]

The poet has turned the park into the cosmos, fulfilling the intent of the landscape architect who designed it. The poem, characteristically concluding with a moral or political message, ends with the emperor virtuously giving up his luxuries to benefit the people.

Gender

The reevaluation of traditional culture that began late in the nineteenth century and prevailed after the May Fourth Movement of 1919 (see Chapter 12, Part II, "Intellectual Ferment") gave rise to a dismal view of the lot of women as oppressed by *Confucianism*, a term often used as shorthand for classical elite culture. This Confucianism was denounced as a conservative, patriarchal, and highly gendered ideology that prevailed during and after the Han and dictated that women were to be subordinates to fathers, husbands, and sons; that they were to be confined to domestic affairs; and that they were to be submissive and weak. This dismal picture suited the modern agendas of missionaries and progressives bent on contrasting their vision of a modern and Westernized society with a gloomy picture of traditional society as sexually oppressive, unequal, and backward. To cite a famous example, Mao Zedong asserted that his revolution would free women from the four cords that bound them: political authority, clan authority, religious authority, and the authority of husbands.[20]

Support for this view was drawn from a limited number of passages in the classics, such as the observation attributed to Confucius in the *Analects*, "Woman and people of low birth are very hard to deal with. If you are friendly with them, they get out of hand, and if you keep your distance, they resent it."[21] Nor was Confucius the only one purportedly to have a misogynistic view of women. Along similar lines, another classical text observes: "The complaints of a woman are without end."[22]

This picture of both the ideology and the actuality is not without its problems. For one thing, it is based less on careful readings of extant sources than on passages taken out of their larger contexts. Take the just cited excerpt from the *Analects*. Commentators have been fiercely debating its meaning for millennia. Is it a general statement about women and their lack of worth or a more limited observation about male servants and young women? More to the point, however awful, this remark is mitigated by other statements attributed to Confucius in the *Analects,* passages expressing the view that women could serve as ministers to sage kings and crediting virtuous women for having played a role in creating a moral government. Similarly one should be wary of reading too much into the second passage ("A woman's complaints are without end"), often cited in isolation, ignoring the directly preceding sentence: "The virtue of a woman is without bounds." Like the first passage, this passage, when taken in its larger context, suggests a more complicated attitude toward women than one would initially think.

The textual record suggests that Han elites imagined that virtuous men were physically courageous even as children. For example, one account depicts Boyu, an ancient sage, being beaten with a stick by his mother for misbehaving. After he was beaten, he wept. According to one Han account, this took his mother aback because he had never before wept during a beating. When asked by his mother why he wept, Boyu reportedly observed, "Before, when I offended you and you beat me with the stick, I often felt pain. But today your strength could not make me feel pain. This is why I am weeping."[23] As this famous tale of filial devotion reveals, Boyu's devotion to his mother is such that he rejoices in painful beatings. His empathy for her overrode his fear of physical pain or discomfort.

Not only were virtuous men supposed to be physically courageous, but they were ideally intellectually precocious and learned. The theme of intellectually precocious and learned male children frequently recurs in Han-period texts. For example, at the age of eight, Ban Gu, the historian already encountered, was said to have been well-versed in—or even to have completely memorized—the histories and the *Odes*.[24]

Another characteristic commonly admired in men was the ability to mourn a parent or friend deeply—and in accordance with ritual dictates. For example, Ma Guang, a former army general, was reportedly a "man small of stature, cautious in mind, but when he mourned for his mother, he was devastated." Another source notes how Ma Guang mourned his mother. "His sorrow was so very deeply felt, his feelings so wounded, that his form became altered and his bones stood out."[25]

As Michael Nylan has recently shown, Han elites by and large imagined virtuous women in similar terms. Women, like men, were supposed to be physically courageous and intellectually precocious and learned and able to mourn their parents deeply. Take for example, Empress Dowager Deng Sui (81–121 C.E.), who would later become the virtual ruler of the empire. One historical record describes her as follows:

When the future empress was six years old, [her grandfather] Deng Yu doted on her, so he took it upon himself to trim her hair. Now, as he was aged and his eyesight was blurred, Deng Yu once happened to hurt her with the scissors, but she bore the pain without saying anything [because she didn't want to hurt her grandfather's feelings]. . . .

Like Boyu, Deng Sui, even as a small child, was reportedly physically courageous. So reportedly solicitous of her grandfather's feelings was she that she suppressed the rather instinctive desire to cry out. Like Ban Gu, Deng Sui was also intellectually precocious:

At the age of seven, she could handle history texts; at thirteen, the *Odes* and the *Analects*. Whenever her elder brother read the classics and commentaries, she would immediately express her ideas and pose difficult questions.[26]

Finally, virtuous women like Deng Sui mourned the passing of their parents deeply. According to her biographer, when her father died, the future Empress Dowager reportedly cried all night and refrained from eating salty vegetables for three years. She became so emaciated that her friends did not recognize her.[27]

Recent scholarship has also called into question the extent to which "Confucian"—or better still, classical elite—traditions can be called patriarchal in the sense of emphasizing a man's relationship to his father at the expense of recognizing the central importance of the mother-son bond. Han elites and, in particular, Eastern Han elites certainly recognized the central importance of the mother-son bond. Mothers were regarded as important because they represented a man's closest tie. The closeness of the mother-son bond was celebrated in Han literature as well as art. There were pictorial celebrations of the mother-son bond, for example, that of the sage Zengzi and his mother. In fact, the two were so close that they even had powers of telepathic communication. According to one second-century account, Zengzi was out of the house gathering wood in the wild when a visitor came to the house. Seeing that Zengzi was gone, the guest wanted to leave, but Zengzi's mother urged him to stay, observing that her son would soon be back. She then pinched her left arm, and at that moment, Zengzi also felt a pain in his left arm (see Figure 3.5). Upon returning, he asked his mother why her arm hurt. There were also, quite strikingly, figurines of mothers nursing newborn infants. One image expresses the ancient conception of the breast (*ying*) as the seat of "closeness" (see Figure 3.6). The closeness of the mother-son bond was also prominent in the context of mourning ritual. Eulogists wrote the most poignant inscriptions for sons who had lost their mothers. Consider the following, an inscription commissioned by a son whose mother had died in 185 C.E.:

There is a saying among men
"The humane will be long-lived."

FIGURE 3.5 Zengzi and his mother. This image is taken from the Wuliang shrine in Northeast China, a shrine that most scholars believed belonged to a locally prominent family that flourished in the mid-second century C.E. This particular site contains many depictions of historical and semihistorical episodes. Among the depictions are many that relate tales of filial sons and virtuous stepmothers. (From Feng Yunpeng and Feng Yunyuan, c. 1821. *Jin shisuo.* Reprinted: Shanghai: Shangwo Press, 1934, 3.18–19.)

They ought to enter eternal life,
Become gray and wizened without end.
Bright Heaven has no pity.
It visits upon us this cruel calamity.
Sick in her chamber, left with an incurable chronic illness,
Bitter and pained, wasted and hurt,
Grieving and saddened the filial son.
He was very fearful, very worried
That her spirit could not be raised.
There was no medicine that he did not administer to provide her.
Alas, great sorrow was this indeed!
At this, the filial son wailed out for such a long time
That her vital energies, having stopped, be restarted.
Crying out and calling, he proclaimed his grief.
He did not know his crime.
May Bright Heaven, Lord on High,
Pity the orphan left behind,
Who seeks, longs for her roaming spirit.
Does anyone know where it now resides?[28]

FIGURE 3.6 Mother and son. This figurine, excavated from Sichuan, dates to the Eastern Han dynasty. In a visually striking image, it captures the very notion of the closeness between mother and children. (© Cultural Relics Bureau of Sichuan.) 🌐

Changes in Political Economy during the Han Period

During the four centuries that spanned the founding of the Western Han and the fall of the Eastern Han, the socioeconomic configuration of the empire was transformed. Whereas early Han rulers attempted to foster economic equality in rural areas, their first- and second-century successors made few attempts to prevent social and economic stratification. The result was not only a considerable widening of the gap between the wealthy and the poor but also the weakening of central power and authority.

From the vanquished Qin, the early Western Han emperors inherited goals of economic rationalization and state building. Their efforts, however, were often thwarted by large landholders and local magnates, many of whom may have been the descendants of Warring States families who had ruled walled settlements.

TABLE 3.2 Farmer's Budget at the End of the Former Han Dynasty

Out of 100 acres to support a family of 5: total yield is 150 bushels (4500 cash) per annum

Taxes: 15 bushels (450 cash) or 10%

Food for five: 90 bushels (2700 cash) or 60%

Leftover cash = 1350 cash

Sacrifices: 300 cash

Clothes for five per annum: 1500 cash

Based on Nancy Swann, *Food and Money in Ancient China: The Earliest Economic History of China to* A.D. *25* (Princeton: Princeton Univ. Press, 1950), pp. 140–43.

Early Han emperors tried to remove them from their local bases, forcing them to relocate either to the capital or to distant frontier regions. Emperor Wu and his advisors also deployed "harsh officials" to various localities through the empire. Armed with directives, these officials eagerly prosecuted the local elites as well as errant members of the imperial families.

Like their Qin predecessors, the founders of the Western Han realized that the fate of their dynasty was linked to the fortune of small peasant landholders. Here more than humanitarianism or philanthropy was at work: there were also solid fiscal reasons. Because taxes in the Han period were collected per household, not per capita, a greater number of households meant greater government tax revenues. Thus, it was in the interest of the dynasty to have as many small landholders as possible, rather than fewer and larger households maintained on large tracts of land or manors controlled by wealthy and influential masters. Furthermore, it tended to be much easier to collect taxes from small households rather than large landholders who had resources for hiding their wealth from tax collectors, or who, in many cases, were themselves the tax collectors.

The fortunes of small landholders were difficult to protect. For one thing, their fortunes were always threatened by the possibility of debt.[29] As Table 3.2 reveals, it took very little to drive a peasant over the edge. In good years, the family of a small peasant landholder would run a deficit of 450 cash or 10 percent of their total income for one year. In addition, the costs of illness, death, burial, and special government levies, such as military taxes, were not covered under this budget. Drought, illness, burial costs, and even additional government taxes could force small landholders to go under. If that happened, the landholder would have to sell his or her land to a landlord and become a tenant farmer and dependent. From the standpoint of the central government, manors meant trouble: manors not only entailed less tax revenues but also the concentration of sufficient resources to support armies capable of challenging the dynasty.

In their efforts to keep small landholders solvent, Early Han emperors tried several measures. At some points, they seized land from aristocrats, merchants, and wealthy officials and redistributed it to the poor. They also made grants of public lands to the poor, a practice that continued until the beginning of the second century C.E. These land grants were usually territories in the West and South, territories that were either underpopulated or not yet under cultivation. The situation was something like that in nineteenth-century America when the government gave away land to anyone who was willing to settle it. Another important way in which emperors and their advisors sought to improve the lot of small land-holders was to develop agricultural improvements such as ordering the repair and creation of new irrigation systems. This was necessary because drought was a persistent problem in the North China Plains, the heartland of the Han Empire. In addition, they provided subsidies to small landholders: seed grain, iron farming implements (which replaced lower-quality wooden ones), and draft animals. Finally, they put a monopoly on iron production to lower the cost of more effective iron implements.[30] All of these improvements were intended to increase the agricultural productiveness of peasant farmers and keep them out of debt.

Despite their best efforts, the Western Han court largely failed in their attempt to keep small landholders solvent. One important reason for this was the fact that the Han economy favored economies of scale. In economies of scale, operating costs go down as the scale of the operation increases. In other words, as investment in the operation became greater, the operation became more profitable. Although in theory, small landholders should have benefited from these improvements, in reality, they did not, largely because the improvements were too expensive. As seen earlier, under favorable conditions, farmers could barely break even, let alone buy cutting-edge farming equipment. Instead, these agricultural improvements only benefited landlords, who could afford to invest in them. And the landlords did in fact make use of these improvements, which resulted in them, as opposed to the small landholders, enjoying greater productivity and more profit and ultimately acquiring more *land*. Ironically, these agricultural improvements not only failed to keep peasants out of debt, but they also contributed to the increasing gap in wealth.[31]

Perhaps the most important reason why early Western Han emperors failed to keep small landholders solvent had to do with the changing nature of their power base. Early Han emperors had wanted to keep their military and economic power close to home. As such, they not only made their relatives, maternal as well as paternal, rulers of vast territories, but they also recruited them into the imperial bureaucracy. Yet, as illustrated by Emperor Wen's trouble with his brother, blood ties were far from reliable, and this was especially the case when those ties were several generations removed. Within a generation of the founding of the dynasty, Western Han emperors faced rebellions from their brothers, cousins, and even sons. As a result, by 154 B.C.E., Emperor Wu, after considerable urging, had decided to eliminate potentially troublesome relatives. But by doing so, he left a vacuum in government. To staff his bureaucracy, he had no choice but to turn to men of local prominence, wealth, and standing—in other words, landlords.

By the end of the Western Han dynasty, the consequences of bringing land-lords to power became clear, as many of them attempted to reverse state policies not to their liking. In 81 B.C.E., the court convened to discuss the merits of Emperor Wu's economic policies, in particular, the monopoly on salt and iron. The debate and its record came to be known as the "Debate on Salt and Iron" (*Yan tie lun*). On one side of the debate were officials who defended the late emperor's policies, headed by the Lord Grand Secretary, a man of mercantile background,

Song Hongyang (152–80 B.C.E.). On the other side were a group of officials, referred to only as the Ru, who attacked the late emperor's policies and who represented the interests of the landlords. The Lord Grand Secretary and his allies argued that the monopoly was necessary for the security of the empire and beneficial to the population:

> The Xiongnu have frequently revolted against our sovereignty and pillaged our borders. . . . The former emperor [Wu] took pity upon the people of the border areas who for so long had suffered disaster and hardship and had been carried off as captives. Therefore he set up defense stations, established a system of warning beacons, and garrisoned the outlying areas to ensure their protection. But the resources of these areas were insufficient, and so he established the salt, iron, and liquor monopolies and the system of equitable marketing in order to raise more funds for expenditures at the borders. Now our critics, who desire that these measures be abolished, would empty the treasuries and deplete the funds used for defense. They would have the men who are defending our passes and patrolling our walls suffer hunger and cold.

The opponents of the state monopolies, however, disagreed. The policies, they noted, sprung from the pursuit of profit. "Never," they said, "should material profit appear as a motive of government." According to these men, the results of having the wrong motives were dire, since they corrupted the morals of the peasants and led them away from the pursuit of agriculture:

> But now in the provinces the salt, iron, and liquor monopolies, and the system of equitable marketing have been established to compete with the people for profit, dispelling rustic generosity and teaching the people greed. Therefore those who pursue primary occupations [farming] have grown few and those following secondary occupations [trading] numerous. As artifice increases, basic simplicity declines; and as the secondary occupations flourish, those that are primary suffer. When the secondary is practiced the people grow decadent, but when the primary is practiced they are simple and sincere. When the people are sincere then there will be sufficient wealth and goods, but when they become extravagant then famine and cold will follow.[32]

Sang Hongyang and his allies lost the argument. Not long after, he and a number of other officials found themselves implicated in a plot to kill the powerful regent. Along with their clans, Sang and his allies were executed. And with Sang's execution came the beginning of the end of an era of dynastic expansion, court power, and policies aimed at shaping the direction of the economy.

The effects of bringing landlords to power can also be seen from the case of the imperial uncle, regent, and usurper, Wang Mang (r. 9 B.C.E.–23 C.E.). Wang Mang rose to power around 9 B.C.E. and apparently made one last effort to save the peasants and deal with the gap in wealth. In 9 C.E., he attempted to "nationalize" and redistribute land, an attempt that hearkened back to earlier calls to implement the "well-field" system, first described by Mencius, that, in addition to preventing the encroachment of landlords, would also ensure the court needed tax revenues. The well-field system, believed to have been an ancient manner of land tenure, divided land into nine squares like a tic-tac-toe board. Eight families were given use of the eight outer squares while the remaining central square was worked by all families with the grain going to the state.

In addition to attempting to implement the well-field system, Wang Mang also tried to limit large landholdings and prohibited slavery. He reintroduced government monopolies on salt and iron and instituted the so-called "Five Equalizations," policies that fixed the price of stable goods and provided government loans to farmers. Unsurprisingly, Wang Mang's policies were unsuccessful, in large part because he met with fierce resistance from powerful landlords. One of these, Liu Xiu, the future Guangwu emperor, was a descendant of the Liu imperial clan. With the support of landed interests from his local base, Liu Xiu overthrew Wang Mang, "restoring" the Han dynasty in 25 C.E. and moving the capital to Luoyang in the East (hence, the name of the Later or Eastern Han).[33] In fact, Guangwu's "restoration" represented a decisive end to attempts to save the small landholders from the encroachment of powerful landlords.

For small landholders, both developments—the unintended effects of agricultural improvements and the political rise of landlords—were disastrous. And indeed, by the beginning of the Eastern Han dynasty, independent small landholders were largely a thing of the past. Instead, more than half of the entire Han

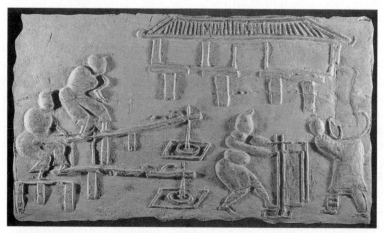

FIGURE 3.7 Hulling and husking grain. Tomb tiles such as this one provide much information on the lives of ordinary people during the Han dynasty. What is striking about these tiles is that they offer a stunning contrast to the kind of art found in North China in the same period. In Sichuan a more naturalistic perspective emerged. Many of the figures represented are in scale, and they move in real space. (© National Museum of China.)

FIGURE 3.8 Rent collection. This mural, also taken from a second-century Sichuanese tomb, provides more direct evidence of the existence of manors. This particular mural shows a rent collection scene. Here, the tenant farmers bring their rent in kind, rather than cast, to a representative of the large landholder, possibly a manager. The representative is much better dressed than the peasants bringing him the rent. (© Cultural Relics Bureau of Sichuan.)

population were now tenant farmers, and large manors had come to dominate China's economic scene. By some accounts, manors made up as much as 65 percent of the total land under cultivation.[34]

The manor system, at the heart of the emerging socioeconomic order during the Six Dynasties Period as well as during Han rule, can be summarized as follows. The owner of the manor was something of a lord, who had dependents. Dependents typically were of two kinds: tenant farmers and retainers. Tenant farmers were often former small landholders and their descendants, who had been forced by economic pressures to sell their land to a large landholder. Possessing no land of their own, they would then rent land from the large landholder. Most times, about half of their agricultural yield would go to the large landholder as rent. Retainers, on the other hand, provided military service, in return for support and protection. The relationship between these two kinds of dependents and the large landholder was certainly not equal and often not entirely voluntary.

The existence of manors is attested to not only by literary sources but also by Han mortuary art (see Figures 3.7–3.10). Some late Eastern Han tombs depict the sources of their occupant's wealth. For example, the mural shown in Figure 3.7 depicts men hulling grain. This is certainly not a representation of a small family operation, for at least three reasons. First, most peasant households would not have had four adult males because of the relatively small size of the family—on average five to six members—and infant mortality. Second, the men are depicted using sophisticated hulling machines that would have been economically out of

FIGURE 3.9 Salt mining. Some tenant farmers also mined salt and iron, as this mural depicts. The depiction of tenant farmers working the salt and iron mines of a large landholder is quite striking considering that before the end of the Western Han, salt and iron mining was monopolized by the Han state. (© National Museum of China.)

reach for small landholders on the brink of falling into debt. Third, the fact that they are using hulling machines suggests that the men represented were not producing for their own consumption. Hulling and husking removes the outer portion of the grain, leaving behind a refined, white starch, which was the food of the Han elite, not the peasantry. These reasons suggest that the men represented were the tenant farmers who rented their land from large landholders.

The Fall of the Han

Two late second-century millenarian rebellions in particular proved devastating to the Han state. The first was the Yellow Turbans (*Huang jin*) rebellion, which swept the Northeast in 184 C.E. The second was the Celestial Masters (*Tian shi dao*) movement, which is also known by a variety of names including the Five Pecks of Grains (*Wu dou mi*) or Rice Thieves (*Mi zei*). The latter, which arose during the reign of Emperor Shun (125–144 C.E.), came to control parts of present-day Sichuan, a territory the size of France. The Celestial Masters were able to hold the prefectural capital of Hanzhong for almost half a century before the warlord Cao Cao (155–220 C.E.) was able to extract a pledge of fealty from the leaders of the

FIGURE 3.10 Military stockades, second century C.E., Sichuan. One important aspect of manor life was defense. As mentioned above, retainers (*bin ke*) provided private military service to a large landholder in return for support and protection. Not surprisingly, some murals, such as this one, also show that manors were sometimes fully stocked with weapons. The reason manors had defense systems was that, by the end of the dynasty, central rule in localities had collapsed. Thus, local populations, both poor and rich, were vulnerable to attacks from bandits, as well as rebellions. (© Cultural Relics Bureau of Sichuan.)

movement in 215 C.E.[35] The movement was seriously damaging to the dynasty, not only because of the loss of a huge territory but also because Sichuan was the economic breadbasket of the empire.

Besides the military weakness of the dynasty, one reason the Celestial Masters were able to seize and hold a huge and economically important Han territory for so long was its geography. Sichuan was and continues to have one of the best natural defense systems in present-day China, because it is bordered by mountains on three sides. As such, it was not difficult for the Celestial Master armies to hold off attempts by a politically and militarily weak dynasty.

Another reason the Celestial Masters were able to hold Sichuan, much to the detriment of the Han, was the fact that the Celestial Masters were well organized. Far from being a chaotic peasant movement, once in control of Sichuan, the Celestial Masters reportedly moved to fill the power vacuum. The leaders created their own bureaucracy, one largely modeled after the Han government. But legend has it that the Celestial Masters bureaucracy had one distinctive characteristic: each bureaucracy was filled not by a single man, but by a man and wife pair. Furthermore, the Celestial Masters also created a coherent theology, one that served to cement the authority of its leaders and legitimize its rule. To be sure, most information about the Celestial Masters theology is filtered through hostile sources, and, as such, it is often difficult to separate fact from fiction. Nevertheless, judging from what our sources say, the Celestial Masters appear to have been in charge of a faith healing movement. Its origins, unfortunately, are unclear, aside from the fact that the *Dao de jing* appears to have been used by some adherents as a sacred text. Lore has it that the movement's legendary founder, one Zhang Daoling, was from the Eastern Han capital in Luoyang, and that he had previously failed to discover immortality elixirs. Having bankrupted his family in these quixotic attempts, he decided to go to Sichuan because he heard that the inhabitants there were easily duped. This is probably a baseless rumor, as the prefectural capital in Sichuan was the second largest city in the Han empire, and its inhabitants were very cosmopolitan and educated. In any event, elements of Zhang Daoling's theories about health merged with native, even non-Han, religion to form a new theology with several unusual characteristics. Among these characteristics was the belief that physical illness was the result of a sin. Conversely, the fact that a person was cured of an illness was a sign that he or she had repented. Another interesting aspect of the theology was "inherited guilt" (*cheng fu*): the idea that the sins of the parents were inherited or visited upon descendants. There was also a heavily deistic component to the theology. Heaven (*tian*) was not simply an impersonal force, but a god who punished sinners and rewarded good people. In this belief system, early death was a sign of personal or familial wickedness; longevity was a sign of personal or familial virtue.

Rebellions were not the only serious threat to the dynasty. Factional fights between eunuch cliques and members of consort clans allied with powerful bureaucrats broke out sporadically in the second century. The roots of these had to do with the fact that eunuchs, like consorts, enjoyed easy access to the emperor. Eunuchs were deliberately chosen from insignificant families to ensure that they would have no outside loyalties but would be solely dependent on imperial favor. This dependency commended them to strong-willed rulers like the founder of the Later Han; his weaker successors, however, sometimes became the instruments rather than the masters of the eunuchs. Earlier, in the Qin and during the last half century of the Western Han, individual eunuchs had become powerful, but never before had eunuchs as a group attained the prominence they achieved in the second century. They were even granted the right to perpetuate their power by adopting "sons" to create ersatz families. Not surprisingly, the power of eunuchs was resented by members of the consort clans and powerful officials. By 166 C.E., tensions came to a head, when a group of eunuchs assassinated an elderly statesman. Open fighting broke out, and eunuchs seized control of the court, executing powerful opponents and banning hundreds of powerful officials and their followers from holding office. This episode, known as the Proscription, lasted eighteen years and was responsible for eroding bureaucratic morale and local support for the dynasty.

Powerful warlords, who had strong economic bases in the provinces, also threatened imperial rule. Such men included the corpulent Dong Zhuo, who was responsible for the burning of the Han capital in 190 C.E. Besides Dong Zhuo, there was Cao Cao, a man of obscure background who held the North and who, as seen earlier, managed to pacify the area controlled by the Celestial Masters. Crafty, ruthless, and ambitious, Cao Cao had rivals. They included Yuan Shao, the scion of an old, aristocratic family; Liu Bei, a member of the Liu imperial clan; and Sun Quan, a southern warlord. The four vied for supremacy, and eventually the Yuans were eliminated. When Cao Cao died, his son, Cao Pi ended the fiction of Han rule. Cao Pi founded the Wei dynasty and state, but he failed in his attempt to reunify the empire.

Notes

1. Theodore de Bary and Irene Bloom, eds., *Sources of Chinese Tradition: From Earliest Times to 1600,* 2nd ed. trans. Daniel W. Y. Kwok (New York: Columbia Univ. Press, 1999), p. 229.

2. Yang Hsien-yi and Gladys Yang, *Records of the Historian* (Hong Kong: Commercial Press, 1974), p. 186.

3. Martin Kern, *The Stele Inscriptions of Ch'in Shih-huang: Text and Ritual in Early Chinese Imperial Representation* (New Haven: American Oriental Society, 2000), p. 17. Translation slightly modified.

4. Jens Ostergard Petersen, "Which Books Did the First Emperor of Ch'in Burn? On the meaning of 'Pai Chia' in Early Chinese Sources," *Monumenta Serica* 43 (1992): 2.

5. Derk Bodde, *Statesmen, Patriot, and General: The Shi-chi Biographies of the Ch'in Dynasty (255–206 BC)* (New Haven: American Oriental Society, 1940), p. 7.

6. Katrina McLeod and Robin D. S. Yates, "Forms of Ch'in Law: An Annotated Translation of the Feng-chen shih," *Harvard Journal of Asiatic Studies* 41.1 (1981): 111–63.

7. McLeod and Yates, "Forms of Ch'in Law," pp. 130–33.

8. Michael Loewe, "The Former Han Dynasty," in *Cambridge History of China, Vol. I: The Ch'in and Han Empires, 221 B.C.E.–A.D. 220* (Cambridge: Cambridge Univ. Press, 1986), p. 107.

9. Hans Bielenstein, "The Institutions of Later Han," in *Cambridge History of China,* p. 516.

10. A.F.P. Hulsewé, "Ch'in and Han Law," in *Cambridge History of China,* pp. 520–37.

11. Zhangjiashan er si qi hao Han mu zhu jian zheng li xiao zu, *Zhangjiashan Han mu zhu jian* (Beijing: Wenwu, 2001), p. 227.

12. Yü Ying-shih, *Trade and Expansion in Han China: A Study in the Structure of Sino-Barbarian Economic Relations* (Berkeley: Univ. of California Press, 1967), p. 64.

13. John Fairbank, *China: A New History* (Cambridge: Belknap Press, 1998), p. 62.

14. For evidence of such views, see Benjamin Schwartz, *The World of Ancient Thought,* (Cambridge: Belknap Press, 1985), p. 418; Jacques Gernet, *A History of Chinese Civilization,* 2nd ed. (Cambridge: Cambridge Univ. Press, 1999), p. 166.

15. Paul Demiéville, "Philosophy and Religion from Han to Sui," in *Cambridge History of Ancient China,* pp. 813, 828; Angus Graham, *Disputers of*

the Tao: Philosophical Argument in
Ancient China (La Salle, Ill.: Open
Court, 1989), p. 315.

16. Michael Nylan and Mark
Csikszentmihalyi, "Constructing
Lineages and Inventing Traditions
through Exemplary Figures in Early
China," T'oung Pao 89 (2003): 1–41.

17. Michael Nylan, "A Problematic Model:
The Han 'Orthodox Synthesis,' Then
and Now," in Kai-wing Chow, On-cho
Ng, and John B. Henderson, eds.
Imagining Boundaries: Changing
Confucian Doctrines, Texts, and
Hermeneutics (Albany: State Univ. of
New York Press, 1999), pp. 17–56.

18. Burton Watson, trans., Records of the
Historian: Chapters from the Shih-chi of
Ssu-ma Ch'ien (New York: Columbia
Univ. Press, 1969), pp. 32–33.

19. Burton Watson, Chinese Rhyme-Prose
(New York: Columbia Univ. Press,
1971), pp. 38–39.

20. Dorothy Ko, Teachers of the Inner
Chambers: Women and Culture in
Seventeenth-Century China (Stanford:
Stanford Univ. Press, 1994), p. 3.

21. Arthur Waley, trans., Analects of
Confucius (New York: Vintage Books,
1938, 1989), p. 216.

22. Huang Kan, ed., Chunqiu Zuozhuan
zhengyi (Shanghai: Shanghai guji,
1990), p. 1.258.

23. Cited in Wu Hung, The Wu Liang
Shrine: The Ideology of Early Chinese
Pictorial Art (Stanford: Stanford Univ.
Press, 1989), p. 184ff.

24. Anne Kinney, "Introduction," Chinese
Views of Childhood (Honolulu: Univ. of
Hawaii Press, 1995), p. 39.

25. Fan Ye, Hou Hanshu (Beijing: Zhong
hua, 1976), p. 858.

26. Cited in Michael Nylan, "Golden
Spindles and Axes: Elite Women in the
Archaemenid and Han Empires," in
Chenyang Li, ed., The Sage and the
Second Sex: Confucianism, Ethics, and
Gender (La Salle, Ill.: Open Court,
2000), p. 207.

27. Nylan, "Golden Spindles," p. 207.

28. Cited and translated in Miranda
Brown, "Sons and Mothers in Warring
States and Han China, 453 BCE–220
CE," Nan Nü 5.2 (2003): 156.
Translation slightly modified.

29. Hsu Cho-yun, Han Agriculture: The
Formation of Early Chinese Agrarian
Economy, 206 B.C.E.–A.D. 220 (Seattle:
Univ. of Washington Press, 1980),
pp. 66, 80.

30. Francesca Bray, Science and Civilisation
in China, Vol. 6: Biology and Biological
Technology Part II: Agriculture
(Cambridge: Cambridge Univ. Press,
1984), pp. 588–89.

31. Bray, Science and Civilisation, p. 591.

32. de Bary and Bloom, Sources of Chinese
Tradition, trans. Burton Watson, pp.
360–61.

33. Utsunomiya Kiyoyoshi, Kandai shakai
keizai shi kenkyū (Tokyo: Sōbunsha,
1955), p. 393.

34. Utsunomiya Kiyoyoshi, Chūgoku kodai
chūseishi kenkyū (Tokyo: Sōbunsha,
1977), pp. 19, 382. For figures, see
Chen Chi-yun, "Han Dynasty China:
Economy, Society, and State Power,"
T'oung Pao 70.1–3 (1984): 136.

35. Patricia Ebrey, "The Economic and
Social History of the Later Han," in
Cambridge History of China, pp. 628–29.

Part Two

China in a Buddhist Age

A major theme in China* and throughout East Asia during the often turbulent years discussed in this part was the gradual spread and flourishing of Buddhism in China and beyond. Concurrently, major developments in just about every sphere of human activity clearly differentiated this period from what preceded it and, in turn, laid the groundwork for the future.

Gautama Siddhartha† (c. 563–483 B.C.E.), the founder of Buddhism, was roughly contemporary with Confucius, but his teachings did not take hold in China until the collapse of the Han dynasty opened people's hearts and minds to a new and originally foreign faith. Then Buddhism simultaneously transformed and was transformed by its encounter with Chinese civilization until it came to pervade the cosmopolitan culture of Tang China and to serve as a carrier for an intensified spread of Chinese civilization to Korea and Japan.

---

*"China" is here and in the following chapters used in a purely geographic sense, stripped of the ethnographic and nationalistic connotations entailed by the term today.
†Gautama refers to his clan, and Siddhartha was the name he received at birth. He is also known as Sakyamuni (sage of the tribe). After he attained enlightenment he was called the Buddha or the Tathagata.

4

China during the Period of Disunity

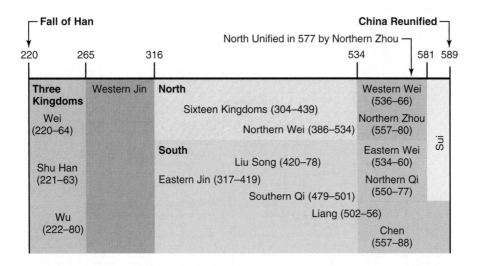

Buddhism has pride of place in our account, but this period also saw the rise of organized Daoism and is noted for the vitality of its literary and visual arts, for institutional innovations as well as political failures, for warfare and coups, but also for economic growth, especially in the South where, by the sixth century, the city now known as Nanjing (old Jiankang) had become the world's largest (see Figure 4.1). When the political center collapsed, China's intrinsic diversity came into full play.

The Fundamentals of Buddhism

Accounts of the Buddha's life were not committed to writing until centuries after his death. These narratives were the work not of dispassionate scholars but of faithful believers whose aim was to extol the great founder. Tradition has it that Gautama Siddhartha was born a prince and brought up in luxury. He was shocked into a search for religious understanding, however, when on three successive outings from the palace he encountered an old man, a sick man, and a dead man—and learned that such is the fate of humankind. On a fourth trip, depending on the source, he saw either a man laboring or a monk. He abandoned worldly pleasures to seek religious truth, studying with various masters. He then became an ascetic and practiced austerities so severe that they almost cost him his life. Ultimately he found a middle way between self-deprivation and gratification. His subsequent enlightenment under the *bodhi* (wisdom) tree, at which time he be-

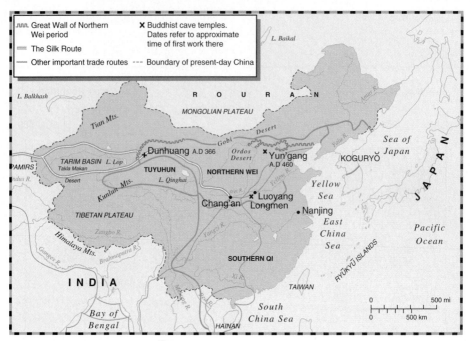

FIGURE 4.1 China c. 500 C.E. 🌐

came the Buddha, or "Enlightened One," was achieved despite the efforts of Mara, the evil one, who first sent demons to assail him and then had his daughters (Discontent, Delight, and Desire) tempt him, all equally in vain. The Buddha's success elicited a suitable cosmic response. The whole earth swayed, and blossoms rained from the heavens. After attaining enlightenment, he spent the remainder of his life teaching his disciples, a following whose growth led to the formation of communities of monks and nuns.

At the core of the Buddha's teachings are the Four Noble Truths. The first of these is that life is suffering. Like many religions throughout the world, Buddhism teaches that pain and unhappiness are unavoidable in life. The traditional response of Indian religions is to seek ways to transcend life. Death is not the answer, for in the Indian view, living beings are subject to reincarnation in one painful life after another. According to the law of karma, for every action there is a moral reaction. A life of good deeds leads to reincarnation at a higher and more desirable level in the next cycle; evil deeds lead in the opposite direction. But the ultimate goal is not rebirth as an emperor or millionaire: it is to achieve Nirvana and never be born again. Legend has it that the Buddha himself gained merit in many reincarnations before his final rebirth, and stories of his previous lives have provided rich subject matter for the artist.

The second Truth explains the first, stating that suffering has a cause that we can do something about: attachment produced by our cravings, or desires. This, in turn, leads to the third Truth: that to stop suffering, desire must be stopped. The cause of suffering must be completely understood and halted. This is accomplished by living the ethical life and practicing religious contemplation and the spiritual exercises set out in the last of the Four Truths, which proclaims the Eightfold Path: right views, right intention, right speech, right action, right livelihood, right effort, right mindfulness, and right concentration. The religious life involves vegetarianism, celibacy, and abstinence from alcoholic beverages, as well as positive religious practices. Carried to perfection it leads to release from reincarnation and to Nirvana: that is, to the absolute, the infinite, the ineffable.

There is much that is subtle in the elaboration of these ideas and in their explication by the Buddha and his followers. The doctrine that there is no ego provides an example. That which we think of as the self is merely a temporary assemblage of the five aggregates (material body, sensation, perception, predisposition, and consciousness). At any point in time an individual is a momentary cluster of qualities without any underlying unity. It is a dangerous delusion to think that these qualities pertain to some kind of permanent entity or soul: only by understanding that all is change can Buddhahood be achieved. Transmigration is likened to the passing of a flame from one lamp to another until it is finally extinguished. "Extinguished" is the literal meaning of Nirvana.

Many problems of doctrinal interpretation were left unanswered by the Buddha, for he was a religious teacher concerned with showing the way to salvation, not a philosopher interested in metaphysics for its own sake. The Buddha's concern for spreading the faith was carried on by later missionaries who undertook hazardous journeys to bring the message to distant lands. As with other religions, such as Christianity, later commentators worked out the philosophical implications of the founder's teachings, producing a mass of writings. These holy scriptures were compiled in the Tripitaka, or "three baskets," which consists of monastic rules (*vinayas*), sermons attributed to the Buddha himself (*sutras*), and later commentaries (*abhidhrma*, including *shastras*, that is, treatises). The enormity of this body of scripture indicates the vast breadth of Buddhism. It had no centralized organization or ecclesiastical hierarchy and developed in a generally tolerant atmosphere conducive to producing a rich variety of practices and beliefs.

The distinction between the Theravada sects, still predominant in Sri Lanka and Southeast Asia, and the Mahayana schools, most predominant in East Asia, developed before Buddhism entered China. *Mahayana* literally means "greater vehicle," reflecting its claim to more inclusive and powerful teachings than those of the earlier *Hinayana* or "lesser vehicle"—a term generally resented by Theravada Buddhists.

A branch of Mahayana Buddhism important for its development of doctrine was the Madhyamika (middle way) school, which taught that reality is empty or void (*sunya*). Emptiness became an absolute, underlying all phenomena. In innermost essence, everything, including the world of appearances, is Nirvana and empty. If everything is emptiness, then what is it that perceives the emptiness? One school held that the ultimate reality is consciousness; that everything is produced by the mind.

Mahayana Buddhism developed a metaphysical literature whose richness and subtlety are barely hinted at here; it also broadened the appeal of Buddhism to draw in people without the time, training, or inclination for the religious life or abstract speculation. A significant development was Buddha worship, deifying him and placing him at the head of an expanding pantheon. Other Buddhas also appeared and had their following, including Maitreya, the Buddha of the future, who exerted a messianic appeal and was often adopted as a symbol by Chinese rebel movements. Beginning in India in the first century C.E. when the first Buddhas were sculpted, statues, themselves partaking of the holy, inspired the faithful. As a Tang Period inscription puts it:

> The highest truth is without image. Yet if there were no image there would be no possibility for the truth to manifest itself. The highest principle is without words. Yet, if there were no words how could the principle be known?[1]

In addition to the Buddhas, there were numerous lesser gods, but more important than these were Bodhisattvas, who postponed their own entry into Nirvana to help other beings. Somewhat like the Virgin Mary and the saints of Christianity, the Bodhisattvas themselves became objects of veneration and worship, none more than Avalokitesvara (Guanyin in Chinese and Kannon in Japanese), famed for the shining quality of his mercy. Sometimes depicted with multiple hands and arms, Avalokitesvara is a favorite subject of Buddhist sculpture. In China this embodiment of the gentle virtues was gradually transformed into a feminine figure.

Buddhism appealed to many people in East Asia, because it addressed human suffering with a directness unmatched in their native traditions. People were variously attracted by its doctrines, magic and medicine, art, music, and ritual. For those bewildered by abstract Nirvana, there were heavens and hells. Many were comforted by the belief that one could earn merit, "the idea that there is an invisible moral order governing the universe, and that under this system one is rewarded in this life or the next for good deeds."[2] These good deeds could include sponsoring statues and contributing to temples, but also performing acts of kindness such as releasing fish (frequently by ransoming those specially caught for this purpose) or building bridges.

Spread by missionary monks who followed the caravan routes linking the northern part of India with western China, the new religion faced formidable cultural and linguistic barriers in China and might have remained simply an exotic foreign faith had not the fall of the Han set people to questioning traditional verities. During the years of dislocation and confusion that followed, China was ready for new teachings. The history of Buddhism in China cannot be understood apart from other aspects of Chinese history.

A World in Disarray

The three states (Wei, Wu, and Shu Han) into which China was divided after the fall of the Han inspired China's most beloved historical novel (see p. 203) but lasted less than half a century (see timeline at the beginning of this chapter). Wei was succeeded by the Western Jin (265–317), which unified China from 280, when it conquered Wu, until it was decimated by civil wars beginning in 304. The capture and devastation of Luoyang, the Western Jin capital, in 311 by Xiongnu rebels claiming to be the successors of the Han was followed by the fall of Chang'an in 316. Subsequently, China remained divided until reunited by the Sui in 589.

When the old world disintegrated intellectually as well as politically, thoughtful people were prompted to reexamine old assumptions and find new ways to give meaning to their lives. Whereas the collapse of the old Zhou order gave rise to classical Chinese thought, the new civilizational crisis made men receptive to a new religiosity and ultimately stimulated a cultural flowering in which the aesthetic dimension of human experience and creativity was accorded full recognition and given free play.

Intellectually there was a turning to "abstruse" or "mysterious learning" (*xuanxue*). Its most brilliant thinkers, such as Wang Bi (226–249) and Guo Xiang (d. 312), continued to accept the validity of Confucian social values, whereas their views on the ultimate problems of existence drew on Daoist texts and traditions. Wang, writing on the *Daodejing* and the *Changes* (*Yijing*), gave new depth to the concept of *wu* (non-being emphasized in classical Daoism). For him, original non-being (*benwu*) was the ultimate reality, the origin of all being, of metaphysical unity in a fragmented physical world. He was also the first to introduce two complementary concepts that were to have a long history in Chinese thought: *ti* and *yong*, usually translated "substance" and "function," and understood by Wang Bi also in the sense of latent and manifest.

In contrast to Wang Bi, Guo Xiang, author of a major commentary on the *Zhuangzi*, denied the centrality of *wu*. He understood people to be composed of three elements that they must accept: "spontaneity (a universal, natural, and impersonal force that lies within each of us); limitations in time and society (our span of life, natural endowment, and place in society); and daily renewal (an incessant state of change characteristic of all beings)." Doing so, people will "enter into a 'marvelous coincidence' with themselves and with the oneness of the world, into the mystic fusion with the immanent force that produces everything and has no beginning or end."[3]

Many refined and sensitive men turned to mystical nihilism for an explanation of ultimate reality and sought to attain it through spiritual contemplation, a "sitting in forgetfulness" so complete that forgetting is itself forgotten. To be sure, other, less sublime, ways of forgetting were not forgotten. A favorite pastime of the cultured gentleman was "pure talk." In contrast to the "pure criticism" (*qingyi*) directed against the government by Later Han scholars, *pure talk* (or pure conversation, *qingtan*) was "conversation that is highly witty, refined, and concerned with philosophical matters transcending the concerns and conventions of the mundane world."[4] There were also games of clever repartee for its own sake in which the highest honors went to the man who thought up the most adept and pithy characterization of his acquaintances.

Then there were the free spirits who venerated nature and sought naturalness in conduct, rejecting the social conventions and ideas of propriety that defined the gentleman. There ensued a burst of self-expression in the arts and in the lives of the sophisticated, who let themselves go in music, poetry, and personal attitudes. Most famous are the Seven Sages of the Bamboo Grove (third century), a group of gifted friends noted for their artistic accomplishments and their eccentricity. Wine flowed freely at their gatherings.

One man was always followed by a servant carrying a bottle in one hand and a spade in the other—equipped for all eventualities in life or death. Sometimes he drank stark naked at home. One startled visitor who found him in that state was promptly informed that his house was his pair of trousers; "What are you doing in my trousers?" the "sage" berated him. So much for Confucian propriety!

The men of this age did not invent eccentricity and unorthodox behavior, and they were certainly not the first to enjoy their cups. What was new was that they gave such conduct respectability in a world lacking a credible political as well as intellectual center.

China Divided

During the long centuries between the fall of the Western Jin in 317 and the re-unification of China by the Sui in 589, five dynasties succeeded each other in the South: The Eastern Jin, Liu Song, Southern Qi, Liang, and Chen. Together with the preceding southern state of Wu, they are known as the Six Dynasties.

Meanwhile, in the turbulent and even chaotic North, between 304 and 439 sixteen regional, overlapping short-lived kingdoms barely managed to survive their founders. Military power was paramount, and it was most effectively exercised by mounted warriors in heavy armor, firing volleys of arrows as they rushed by, steadied in their saddles by stirrups now in general use. Many fighting men came from nomadic tribes for whom, in contrast to Chinese peasants, warfare was simply a special application of the everyday skills practiced to protect their flocks.

Thirteen of the kingdoms were founded by men of "non-Chinese" background, including incompletely assimilated people living within as well as beyond "China." As Charles Holcombe has written, "This was a period of general chaos. It is not clear, however, that foreigners really invaded Chinese territories from outside during the fourth century, nor was 'Chinese' as obvious an ethnic identity then as we tend to assume that it is now."[5] Rather than continuing to think in terms of "barbarians" versus "Chinese," it is more accurate to see this as a period of "multi-ethnicity" and bear in mind the "malleability of ethnic identity."[6]

Many people sought refuge from the chaos by fleeing to the South, whereas those who remained found security in fortified citadels commanded by local strongmen. In both the North and the South, the military were the kingmakers and kings (or "emperors"), but Chinese political and literary culture was preserved and developed by the leaders of government and society.

The Northern Wei (386–534)

The most successful northern state during the fifth and sixth centuries was the Northern Wei, also known as *Tuoba* (in Chinese) or *Tabgac* (in the language of the ruling group) Wei after the nomadic tribal coalition that established the state by military force. Like similar regimes, the Tuoba realized that if they were to enjoy China's wealth on a long-term basis, they needed a political system more sophisticated than the tribal organization they brought from the steppes. In practice, this meant relying on men familiar with Chinese ways of collecting taxes, keeping records, and running a government. But the ensuing sinification had to be kept in check if the conquerors were to retain their power and something of their cultural heritage.

From early on the Northern Wei was attracted to Chinese institutions and culture. When, in 398, they built a Chinese-style capital near modern Datong (Shanxi), they are said to have brought 100,000 craftsmen to work on the project and forcefully relocated 360,000 people to populate the area. At court in the new capital, officials bearing Chinese titles performed Chinese ceremonies accompanied by Chinese music. A Chinese legal code was adopted.

The political system drew on tradition, but the dynasty also innovated. The "equal field system," established in 485, not only outlasted the Northern Wei by more than 350 years but also influenced reformers in Japan. Based on the ancient principle that all land belongs to the emperor, it provided for the allotment of agricultural holdings to each adult farmer for the duration of his or her working life. When a landholder reached old age or died, the land reverted to the state for reassignment. Exceptions were made where the nature of cultivation required greater continuity of tenure. Silk culture, for example, involved permanent planting and continuous care of mulberry trees. Although this was not the original intent, such land came to be held in perpetuity by its proprietors. In return for land, cultivators were obliged to make certain tax payments and render labor services such as road building and military service. Sinification continued apace. A watershed was reached in 493–494 when the capital was moved from the Datong area, close to the old Tuoba tribal home, south to Luoyang in the Chinese heartland, a move partly aimed as a step toward reunifying all to China. The Wei proceeded to gain control of all North China down to the Huai River but no further. In Luoyang itself major changes and improvements were made, and it was divided into regular isolated wards, an innovation adopted in the great Tang capital of Chang'an (see Figure 5.5) and continued in Tang Luoyang.

The implementation of the equal field system in devastated areas did not prevent the regime from cooperating with great landed families entrenched elsewhere. From the outset, the Tuoba rulers employed Chinese advisers and early on gained support among the Chinese elite by adopting the nine-rank system that had originated in 220 as a means for recruiting officials through local recommendation and had by the fourth century become a system for appointing men to office according to their inherited family rank. This emphasis on birth reflected the enduring power and prestige of great Chinese families of distinguished ancestry whose embodiment of Confucian traditions and lifestyle created an aura of distinction that complemented their wealth in land and connections. Their position was further strengthened by the fact that Northern Wei local officials enjoyed considerable autonomy, including the right to appoint their subordinate officials. What they lacked, however, was institutionalized military power.

The growth and triumph of Chinese influence in the end undermined the Northern Wei. During its last half century, men from distinguished families were increasingly attracted into the sinicized central government, in which Chinese was the official language. In Luoyang everyone wore Chinese dress, and even Tuoba nobles had to adopt Chinese names. Many married Chinese wives. This sinification finally alienated those Tuoba tribesmen who had not adopted Chinese ways, including the troops stationed in frontier garrisons. They expressed their displeasure in the usual way—by taking up arms. Although it hung on for close to another ten years, the dynasty never recovered from the Rebellion of the Six Garrisons (524). The Northern Wei state was split. Its legacy included the equal field system, an aristocracy of mixed ancestry from which emerged the leaders who were to unify China, and some superb Buddhist art.

Buddhism in the North

The more than 1000 Buddhist temples and monasteries that graced Northern Wei Luoyang are no more, but the sculptures of the Yungang caves near Datong and those at Longmen, eight miles from Luoyang (see Figure 4.2), although badly damaged, continue to testify to the success of Buddhism in China and illustrate the process by which the foreign religion found a new home. The creation of temples in caves, as well as the Buddhas and Bodhisattvas, were Indian in origin, but the Bodhisattva in Figure 4.3 shows Chinese artists in the process of assimilating and transforming Buddhist art. In contrast to the lovingly sensuous modeling of the naked body in three dimensions that is the glory of the Indian sculptor, the essentially linear style of the figure, with its geometric composition and frontal orientation, is characteristically Chinese. At its best, this art reproduced in metal and stone the simple piety and sweet spirituality of a religious age.

When Buddhism first reached China during the first century C.E., it was a religion of foreign merchants. Through the period of division the trade routes remained very active, because trade was as advantageous to the nomadic peoples who controlled oases and taxed caravans as it was to the buyers and sellers in the more settled regions. As life became more difficult in China, Buddhism acclimatized itself to Chinese circumstances and became more appealing to people disillusioned with the old ways. In the North devoted missionaries initially won the patronage of rough tribal leaders by using feats of magic to convince them that Buddhism was a more powerful religion than the competition. It was powerful also in other ways, for it enabled tribal chiefs to see themselves in new and grander

FIGURE 4.2 Entrance to the Buddhist cave temples at Longmen (© Lore Schirokauer.).

roles, and it appealed to alien rulers who, through their patronage of this universalistic religion, like themselves foreign to China, could create a broad and venerable base for their claims to legitimacy. And, of course, it was powerful in religious and intellectual terms, inspiring learning and art.

Political patronage was important, but to survive and prosper Buddhism also had to win a wide following among the Chinese people. In this endeavor its foreign origins were not an asset but a liability. Words and ideas, as well as artistic forms, had to be translated into Chinese terms.

Translating Buddhist texts into Chinese proved a formidable undertaking, because they were the products of a radically different culture and were written in a language totally unlike Chinese. The problems faced by the early Buddhist translators were similar to those that much later plagued Christian missionaries trying to render the Bible into Chinese. Particularly vexing was the need to introduce unfamiliar concepts at the very heart of Buddhism. Just as Christians were later to agonize over how to translate *God* into Chinese, Buddhists racked their brains over words such as *Nirvana*. One early solution was to employ Daoist terminology. This terminology had the advantage of sounding familiar. But it could also lead to a great deal of confusion, such as when the Daoist term for "non-action" (*wu-wei*) was used to express the quite different concept of Nirvana. One solution was not to translate at all but to transliterate, that is, to employ Chinese characters to

FIGURE 4.3 Seated Bodhisattva. Stone, Longmen, late Northern Wei. (Photograph © 2005 Museum of Fine Arts, Boston.)

approximate the sound rather than the meaning of the original word. Transliteration was most suitable for reproducing foreign proper names in Chinese. Furthermore, it retained or even increased the magic potency of incantations, but even in relatively modern times, Chinese readers found it difficult to divorce the characters from their meanings.

Despite these handicaps scholar-monks made good progress in their work. The greatest of the translators was Kumarajiva (350–c. 409), like many of his predecessors, a Central Asian. After arriving in Chang'an in 401, he directed a translation project staffed by some thousand monks. In a vivid comment on the translator's art, he once compared his work to that of a man who chews rice in his mouth and then gives it to another to swallow, but he and his staff produced good translations of basic Buddhist texts. They were responsible for the introduction of Madhyamika teachings, foremost among them the doctrine of emptiness (*sunyata*) that became very influential. The translations were an impressive achievement, but the transmission of ideas is always a very complex process. As Robert H. Sharf has emphasized, Chinese Buddhists understood the texts in Chinese terms, largely failing to recognize "the alterity of Indian Buddhism. . . . Like ships passing in the night, seminal features of Indian Buddhist thought simply failed to capture the attention, or at least the imagination, of the Chinese."[7]

Kumarajiva was only one of the many Central Asian monks whose missionary zeal spurred the growth of Buddhism in China. But the traffic was not all one way: Chinese also undertook the long pilgrimage to India following the merchant trade routes, by land or by sea. The monk Faxian, who made the ocean trip during 399–414, left a detailed account of his travels that serves as a prime source for the history of India during this period.

To overcome cultural barriers, early Buddhist apologists argued that their religion was basically compatible with the Chinese heritage and played down areas of potential conflict. That they enjoyed considerable success is shown by inscriptions that reveal that the pious considered the donation of an image not only an expression of their religious faith but also a demonstration of their filial piety and of their reverence for the ancestors whose souls were included in their prayers. (The idea of non-self, or non-soul, never had much currency in popular Buddhism nor was it generally taught even by well-educated Chinese monks.) Yet, not everyone was convinced by this attempt to fuse Buddhism and filiality. After all, the latter demanded the continuation of the family and thus conflicted with the celibate life of the monk and nun.

Withdrawal from the secular world left Buddhists open to charges of antisocial behavior, whereas the growth of monastic wealth and influence made the Buddhist church vulnerable to political attack. A strong competitor both for state patronage and popular support was the Daoist church. Confucians as well as Daoists instigated the persecution of Buddhism during 446–452 by the Northern Wei Emperor Taiwu (r. 424–452) and again by another Northern state during 574–578. Both aimed to destroy Buddhist monasteries and to eliminate the Buddhist religious establishment, which had grown wealthy and powerful, but no attempt was made, then or later, to suppress private Buddhist beliefs. Both persecutions ended as soon as there was a change of ruler, and the new emperor made generous amends. Buddhism had grown too strong to be crushed by government fiat; the persecutions appear to have done little permanent damage.

Religious persecution indicated tension between church and state, but this never developed into the separation of church and state so crucial in Western history. In China the state was always concerned about keeping religions in line. What became the usual pattern was exemplified by the Northern Wei when the state placed controls on the Buddhist establishment so as to prevent the monasteries from becoming havens for tax dodgers or men escaping their labor obligations, to bar fraudulent transfers of land titles to tax-exempt religious institutions, and to enforce standards for ordination and clerical conduct. This was the responsibility of a clerical bureaucracy not unlike its secular counterpart. Northern Wei emperors appointed a monk to be Chief of Monks as head of a network of Regional Chiefs of Monks. He, in turn, supervised the Buddhist orders while also looking after the interests of the religion. The great cave temples were created through a combination of official support by the court and efforts of the Buddhist clergy and laity to gain merit and glory.

Daoism—The Religion

Although it had deep historical roots, Daoism as an organized religion can be traced to the Celestial Masters of the later Han discussed in the last chapter. As indicated there, the Celestial Masters became the dominant religion of Wei, the state that was the immediate successor of the Han in the North, where the sect remained important. Well organized, it operated "inns of equity," offering travelers free meals. Each inn was supervised by a priest who could be of either sex and was also charged with explaining the *Daodejing* largely in moral terms.

As previously noted, the Celestial Masters owed much of their appeal to their activity as healers. In their case, cure of the sick was achieved through the good offices of an initiate who forwarded the afflicted person's confession, recorded in triplicate—one copy for each of the Officials in charge of Heaven, Hearth, and the Waters to share with his staff. Also of major importance were 1200 officials who were invited to enter the body of the confessing ill person.

Emphasis on healing remained a prominent feature of Daoism, whose practitioners became experts in identifying the cause of illness in the misdeeds of the patient or his progenitors and in identifying which of the countless spirits and demons was responsible for the illness, forcing it to confess and release its victim. Daoist masters also used seals and spells (some carried on the person) to battle disease and prolong life. To assist the progress of the dedicated adept there were meditation and sexual exercises. Breathing exercises to grow embryo of immortality internally and alchemy to produce elixirs externally, although not uniquely Daoist, also found a place in the Daoist repertoire.

The Celestial Masters' vision of an extraterrestrial administration occupied by paperwork much like governments operating here on earth was widely shared, as was the sect's own hierarchical organization, both probably a heritage from the time it actually governed Sichuan. This hierarchy could include the Emperor. The first Emperor to receive cosmic legitimacy through Daoist investiture was Taiwu, the Northern Wei persecutor of Buddhism. The 574–578 persecution was followed by Daoism being proclaimed the official state religion, and we will encounter further cases of the importance of political patronage when we come to the Tang and Song. Political patronage was very helpful, but the relationship between state Daoism and local practitioners is a matter of conjecture. Ultimately, Daoism depended on the credibility and potency of its message to laity and devotee alike.

For the truly dedicated practitioner, willing to spend years in study and practice, Daoism promised more than just good health:

> When he achieves salvation, the adept will wear a feathered garment, will ride on light and straddle the stars, or will float in empty space. He will have wind and light as a chariot and dragons as steeds, His bones will shine like jade, his face will be resplendent, his head will be circled with a halo, and his whole body will radiate a supernatural light as incandescent as the sun and moon. He will be able to realize all his desires and will enjoy an endless youth and a longevity equal to that of heaven and earth. Moreover, he will be able to travel a thousand *li* in a single day, and will be able to immerse himself in water without getting wet or walk through fire without getting burned. Neither beats nor weapons will have any power over him. He will command the forces of nature and the spirits.[8]

This description pertains to Great Purity (*Shangqing*), also called Maoshan (Mt. Mao) Daoism, but such aspirations were characteristic of Daoist sects generally.

Throughout the period of division and beyond, Daoist abbeys and Buddhist temples competed against each other for political patronage and vied for the support of the populace who they found were addicted to their own local cults, for "no matter whether the mountain is great or small, gods and numinous spirits are found without fail therein."⁹ The Celestial Masters' denunciation of false demons became standard fare down through the ages.

Daoists, like the Buddhists, erected statues and had pictures painted to decorate their abbeys and performed mysterious, powerful, and profound rituals. Learned practitioners developed a repertoire of texts so rich and numerous by the fourth century as to require organization and classification. The resulting "three caves" paralleled the three baskets of the Buddhists and included Linbao (numinous treasure) texts, which had begun appearing in the southeast in the 390s and were to be very influential. Key Buddhist concepts, such as karma, feature prominently in these and other scriptures. Daoists also adopted some Buddhist rituals. A popular Daoist explanation for such shared notions was that Lao Zi had traveled to India where he became the Buddha in order to convert the barbarians, and it took only a small step to make explicit that because the Dao encompassed all, it included Buddhism. Not to be outdone, Buddhist accounts depicted Lao Zi and Confucius as disciples of the Buddha and even portrayed the semidivine founders of Chinese civilization as Bodhisattvas.

After the Period of Division, the Celestial Masters faded from the scene but reappeared under the name Zhengyi (True One) around the mid-eighth century on Mount Longhu (Mt. Dragon-Tiger) in Jiangxi and continue to the present. The immediate future, however, belonged to the sect, founded in the third century, which was headquartered on Mt. Mao and sanctified by and named after three immortal Mao bothers, who are said to have come riding on white swans or cranes and landed on each of the mountain's three peaks. Mt. Mao is located in modern-day Jiangsu, west of Nanjing, capital and hub of the South.

The South

Spared the nomad incursions and warfare that plagued North China, the South enjoyed relative tranquility, despite a series of political intrigues, palace coups, and the like, which disturbed life at court. Partly through migration from the disturbed North, partly through development of the land, and building on past economic growth, the fertile area of the lower Yangzi River experienced a very substantial increase in population and productivity. Further south, Fujian now became truly Chinese for the first time as a result of increased Chinese settlement. As Chinese settlers moved in, the local aborigines were gradually either pushed back into the hills or absorbed into the Chinese population.

Rice culture was the cornerstone of the agricultural economy of the South. Sophisticated wet-field cultivation of rice took time and effort to perfect. Not only did it involve experimentation with various strains of rice, but it also entailed the construction of paddy fields and careful irrigation to keep the field wet and to maintain the water at an even temperature. When the fields were laid out on sloping ground or when terraces were constructed on hills, a complicated system of dams and reservoirs was necessary.

In the Han the Chinese developed a technique for raising seedlings in a nursery and transplanting them later into paddies when the season was right. Such early planting in nurseries greatly increased the yield, but it also increased the demands for labor. Refugees from the North helped to augment the labor supply and open up new land, making a direct contribution to the growing prosperity of the South. The enlarged labor force was, in turn, sustained by the increased rice yields obtained from wet-field cultivation, which produced more calories per acre than did Northern dry-field agriculture. In good part because of the ability of rice to support high population density, the development of the South was to be of great consequence for the future history of China.

Concurrent with thriving agriculture, the South bustled with trade and commerce—especially Nanjing, where markets could spring up anywhere, for unlike Luoyang, the southern capital was not internally divided into walled-off wards. Money and goods circulated freely in what Shufen Liu has called "a free-wheeling market economy."[10] Pottery, textiles, lacquer, bronze mirrors, and paper were produced as well as traded in the South. Especially noteworthy were the luxury goods such as pearls, ivory, coral, and incense as well as gold, silver, and slaves imported through Guangzhou (Canton) from Southeast Asia, South Asia, and even more distant lands. Buddhist texts, statues, and relics also came by sea, complementing those which reached China via the Inner Asian trade routes.

A varied commerce bespeaks a lively society—Nanjing had its merchants, artisans, beggars, and thieves, and as in the North, great families stood at the top of the social hierarchy. They controlled large estates and, combining political and economic power, dominated the governments of a succession of southern dynasties. Not only did they enjoy exemption from taxation and labor service, but they also had ready access to office and set the tone of court life. In the fifth century, they even managed to obtain legislation prohibiting intermarriage between aristocrats and commoners. Their entrenched privileges seriously hampered government efficiency. Yet they were far from invincible. For one thing, their power was constantly being undermined by intense and recurrent conflicts among themselves. Friction between émigré families and those with deeper local roots was endemic. The influence of the great families was also weakened by their lack of military power and their inability to control military strongmen of nonaristocratic background.

When Luoyang was captured by the "barbarians," its fall served to confirm the disillusionment and general pessimism felt by residents of the South. The continuing arrival of émigrés from the North reinforced this spirit. The more sophisticated turned to witty conversation, meditation, alchemy, and wine as a diversion from the depressing social and political problems of the day. It was this discontent and yearning for greater stability that made the society of southern China receptive to Buddhism. But it also served to liberate individual impulses to artistic expression, channeling energies that formerly had been devoted to philosophy and government into the secular arts. The result was an outburst of achievements in those arts that are the most highly prized and most closely identified with the Chinese gentleman: poetry, calligraphy, and painting.

Poetry

The difficult times produced some lasting poems, many of them from the brush of Tao Qian (365–427), also known as Tao Yuanming, recognized as one of China's greatest poets. After a short career in government, he retired to live the life of a country gentleman, but not without ambivalent feelings toward official life and its obligations. There is in his verse much about wine, the simple country life, books, and nature. Poems such as this have enduring appeal:

> I built my cottage among the habitations of men,
> And yet there is no clamor of carriages and horses.
> You ask: "Sir, how can this be done?"
> "A heart that is distant creates its own solitude."
> I pluck chrysanthemums under the eastern hedge,
> Then gaze afar toward the southern hills.
> The mountain air is fresh at the dusk of day;
> The flying birds in flocks return.
> In these things there lies a deep meaning;
> I want to tell it, but have forgotten the words.[11]

Tao especially loved chrysanthemums and wrote about them often; ever since, this "hermit among the flowers" has been associated with his name. The poem conveys a serene harmony with nature that is a lasting Chinese ideal and a common theme in much later Chinese poetry.

Other fine poets also wrote during this period. But there was at the same time a tendency for poets to indulge in increasingly artificial styles (for example, extreme parallelism in construction, with two lines matching each other word for word) and to exhibit their virtuosity in using an exotic vocabulary, as Han poets had in their rhapsodies. As a result, spontaneity, creative freshness, was gradually lost, and versification was already approaching a dead end when political unification from the North put an end to both the southern courts and their poetry.

More significant than poetic output per se was the development of a new attitude toward literature that grew out of a deep concern with the process of poetic creation. Formerly the poetic art had been primarily, although not exclusively, viewed as a vehicle for moral instruction, but this view was now challenged by those who emphasized free self-expression and pleasure:

> Trying the empty Nothing, and demanding Something
> Banging the silent Zero, in search of Sound.[12]

DRAGON   BOOK   GOOD

These two lines by Lu Ji (261–303) give something of the flavor of the verse of this period, when poetry was appreciated in its own right, They are from Lu Ji's rhapsody (*fu*) on literature, itself a work of high art. More generally, increased emphasis was placed on stylistic devices, exotic language, and the like. When he compiled his famous literary anthology, *Wenxuan,* Xiao Tong (501–531) based his selection on literary merit and adopted a "moderate" view on the nature and function of literature.[13]

FIGURE 4.4 Basic forms of calligraphy, from the brush of Dr. Léon L. Y. Chang. The top two characters in the "dragon" column and the top characters in the "book" and "good" columns exemplify the Li form (clerical, or official); the third and fourth characters in the "dragon" column and the second characters in the "book" and "good" columns exemplify the Zheng (also called Kai) form (regular, or standard); the fifth character in the "dragon" column and the third characters in the "book" and "good" columns exemplify the Xing form (longhand, or running); and the bottom characters in each column exemplify the Cao form (cursive, or shorthand). (Calligraphy by Dr. Léon L. Y. Chang.)

Calligraphy

Of all the visual arts, Chinese scholars traditionally have given first place to calligraphy (see Figure 4.4). Behind this high esteem lies the aesthetic appeal and the mystique of the Chinese characters themselves, along with the emphasis on literature in Chinese culture. Moreover, the development of cursive script during the Later Han turned writing into an intensely personal art, a vehicle for self-expression and a creative outlet, well suited for educated people who had been wielding the brush and working with ink since childhood. Calligraphy came to be especially valued as a means for conveying the writer's deepest self, leading a Tang connoisseur to comment that one character was sufficient to reveal the writer. The flow of the lines and the rhythm of the brush creating the abstract beauty of the whole were now far more important than legibility. Thus, Chinese appreciation of calligraphy as high art combined the pleasure and excitement associated with abstract art as well as with graphology.

"In every terrible period of human history there is always a gentleman in a corner cultivating his calligraphy and stringing together a few pearls of expression."[14] Thus wrote Paul Valery in 1915. If so, it is no wonder that calligraphy flourished during the years following the collapse of the Han, nor that the new emphasis on self-expression was particularly conducive to this art.

The greatest calligrapher of the age was Wang Xizhi (321–379), a master whose art served as a model for countless generations. He and two of his sons, also famous calligraphers, drew inspiration from Daoism, with its emphasis on the natural. They sought to express naturalism, itself an abstract quality, through pen and ink. It was a magnificent challenge and typifies the artistic strivings of the age. The effort required years of practice. Wang Xizhi is said to have destroyed everything he had written before age fifty because he was dissatisfied with it. Unfortunately, none of his original work survives. Copies exist, but none is earlier than the Song. Reproduced

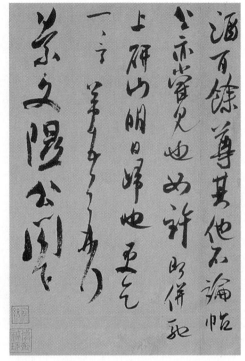

FIGURE 4.5 Portion of a letter by Mi Fei. (From *Gu Gung Fa Shu*, No. 11 [Taipei, Taiwan: National Palace Museum, 1968], p. 11b). Selected and translated by Dr. Léon L. Y. Chang.

in Figure 4.5 is a letter by a famous Song calligrapher and painter who drew inspiration from Wang Xizhi and one of his sons. The fourth line (reading right to left) is an example of the musical "continuous stroke" style for which they were famous.

Painting

The human figure remained the main subject matter of painting, although the beginnings of China's great landscape tradition can also be traced back to this period. Preeminent among the painters was Gu Kaizhi (344–407), famed for capturing with his brush the essential character of his subjects, as when, by adding three hairs to a chin, he succeeded in depicting a man's wisdom. Among the most famous of his paintings still extant, although only in the form of a later copy, is a hand-scroll illustrating a poem composed in the third century entitled "Admonitions of the

FIGURE 4.6 Gu Kaizhi, Scene 5 from *Admonitions of the Instructress to the Court Ladies.* Ink and color on silk. (© The Trustees of the British Museum.)

Instructress to the Court Ladies" in which the painted panels alternate with lines of the text. The scene reproduced in Figure 4.6 illustrates the lines, "if the words you speak are good, men for a thousand *li* will respond; but if you depart from this principle, even your bedfellow will distrust you." Presumably it is the emperor who is mistrusting the lady, although this scene has sometimes been read the other way around. The other panels also illustrate moral edicts and wifely duties. They are basically Confucian in content, although the artist himself was known for his Daoist eccentricity.

The enhanced interest taken in painting led to the development of art criticism and stimulated the formulation of the six classic principles of painting by Xie He, an early sixth-century portrait painter. Most important, but also allowing for the widest latitude of interpretation, is his first principle, which calls on the artist to imbue his painting with a cosmic vitality and sense of life. These terms have been translated by Alexander Soper as "animation through spirit consonance," where "spirit" is a translation of *qi,* the vital force and stuff of man and the universe.[15] *Qi* is also a central concept in Chinese medicine. We will encounter it again when we come to Song metaphysics and cosmology. It also figured in burial customs. The most eminent dead were fitted with jade suits to prevent the *qi* from leaking out of their bodies. Those who could not afford or were not entitled to a complete outfit were equipped with jade stoppers for ears, nose, mouth, and other orifices (see Figure 3.3). In the context of aesthetics, it is the quality that causes a painting to reverberate with life.

Xie He's second principle demands structural strength in the brushwork, demonstrating the vital link between painting and calligraphy, which used the same basic tools and techniques. It was largely in the quality of the artists' brushwork that the Chinese looked for an expression of their vital inspiration.

The next three principles require less explanation because they correspond to criteria familiar in the West. They are fidelity to the object in portraying forms, conformity to kind in applying colors, and proper planning in placing of elements—what we would call composition. The sixth and final principle is very Chinese, for it enjoins the copying of old masters. This is one aspect of the old Chinese veneration for the past. It was a way of preserving old masterpieces such as Gu Kaizhi's *Admonitions* and at the same time provided training and discipline for later artists, who by following the brushwork of a great predecessor would gain technical competence and an understanding of the medium, just as apprentice calligraphers today still begin by copying the great masters of their art, internalizing and making it their own. In neither case is there any intent to deceive.

Buddhism in the South

In the South as in the North, Buddhism made great headway, winning substantial support among the great families and the personal patronage of rulers. In contrast to the North where Buddhist missionaries had to deal with "barbarian" rulers, in the South erudite and clever monks won favor by adopting the stance and displaying the skills of the sophisticated gentlemen who dominated society. Quick-witted Buddhists became experts in pure talk and engaged also in highly abstract metaphysical discussions in which they displayed their command of the Chinese intellectual heritage.

Accorded new prominence as a model for the sophisticated Buddhist was the figure of Vimalakirti, a wealthy layman who enjoyed life to the fullest and displayed great powers of intellect and a pure and lofty personality (see Figure 4.7). Monasteries and nunneries erected in beautiful surroundings offered a peaceful, scholarly, contemplative setting to those seeking a temporary or permanent respite from the tensions and struggles of life in the world.

Even so, Buddhism did not enjoy universal approval in the South any more than it did in the North. For one thing, Daoism, well established in the South, was always available as an attractive alternative, and there was opposition from other quarters as well. Its enemies attacked Buddhism's alleged subversive effects on state and society and sought to refute its teachings. For example, Fan Zhen, a Confucian official and brilliant debater, argued against the concept of the indestructibility of the soul, now a common tenet of Chinese Buddhism, the original

FIGURE 4.7 Vimalakirti. Clay, 17.79 in high. Pagoda of the Hōryūji. (© Askaen.)

teaching of the Buddha notwithstanding. Fan Zhen argued that the soul is a passing function of the body, just as keenness is a temporary attribute of a knife. In response, Emperor Wu solicited counterarguments. He received fifty-eight refutations and only two replies supporting Fan Zhen's anti-Buddhist views. The time was not yet ripe for a major anti-Buddhist reaction. On the contrary, the full flowering of Buddhism in China was yet to come.

China on the Eve of Reunification

After the fall of the Northern Wei, the North remained unstable for another half century, but its leaders demonstrated greater political vigor than those in the South. For models on which to build their state, they relied on classical texts, especially the *The Rites of Zhou* (*Zhouli*), which describes in detail what it claims was the bureaucratic government as it existed under the revered Duke of Zhou. They did this because in the political and moral realms Buddhism and Daoism could not match the native tradition. The memory of the glories of the Han (suitably embellished) and the authority of the remote but exemplary past conveyed in classical texts held firm.

The changes that occurred between the fall of the Han and the Sui reunification were far-reaching and profound. The division of China brought with it foreign rulers and a new religion. It had stimulated a new consciousness, which found expression in literature and art. And it had accelerated the development of the South, thus altering China's economic geography.

These events are comparable to what took place in the West after the fall of Rome, but in China, unlike in Europe, the factors bringing about political integration ultimately prevailed. Buddhism was one such factor and Daoism another. Confucianism as a family ethic, as a state rationale, and as a language of government persisted even when Confucian philosophy was in eclipse. There was a shared sense of what it meant to be civilized and educated.

The ideal of political unity was never questioned. As in the creation of the first empire, reunification came from the northwest, which was again the strongest area militarily. Unification proved to be a great and difficult undertaking—and one that in the end succeeded brilliantly.

Notes

1. Helmut Brinker, "Early Buddhist Art in China," in *Return of the Buddha: The Qingzhou Discovery* (London: Royal Academy of Arts, 2002), p. 20.

2. John Kieschnick, *The Impact of Buddhism on Chinese Material Culture* (Princeton: Princeton Univ. Press, 2003), p. 157.

3. Isabelle Robinet, "Kuo Hsiang," in *The Encyclopedia of Religion* (New York: MacMillan, 1987), with some elisions and rearrangement.

4. *Sources of Chinese Tradition,* 2nd ed., Vol. 1, compiled by Wm Theodore de Bary and Irene Bloom (New York: Columbia Univ. Press, 1999), p. 390.

5. Charles Holcombe, *The Genesis of East Asia, 221 B.C.–A.D. 907* (Honolulu: Univ. of Hawaii Press, 2001), p. 124.

6. David A. Graff, *Medieval Chinese Warfare, 300–900* (London: Routledge, 2002), p. 12.

7. Robert H. Sharf, *Coming to Terms with Chinese Buddhism: A Reading of the Treasure Store Treatise* (Honolulu: Univ. of Hawaii Press, 2002), p. 19.

8. Isabelle Robinet, *Taoist Meditation: The Mao-shan Tradition of Great Purity,* trans. Julian F. Pas and Norman J. Giradot (Albany: State Univ. of New York Press, 1993), p. 45.

9. Go Hong as quoted in Susan Naquin and Chün-fang Yi, eds., *Pilgrims and Sacred Sites in China* (Berkeley: Univ. of California Press, 1992), p. 14.

10. Shufen Liu, "Jiankang and the Commercial Empire of the Southern Dynasties: Change and Continuity in Medieval Chinese Economic History," in Scott Pearce, Audrey Spiro, and Patricia Ebrey, eds., *Culture and Power in the Reconstitution of the Chinese Realm, 200–600* (Cambridge: Harvard Univ. Press, 2001), p. 46. Jiankang is the old name of Nanjing.

11. Liu Wu-chi, *An Introduction to Chinese Literature* (Bloomington: Indiana Univ. Press, 1966), p. 64.

12. Eric Sackheim, *The Silent Zero, in Search of Sound: An Anthology of Chinese Poetry from the Beginning through the Sixth Century* (New York: Grossman Publishers, 1968) p. ii.

13. David R. Knechtes, "Culling the Weeds and Selecting Prime Blossoms," in Pearce, Spiro, and Ebrey, *Reconstitution of the Chinese Realm,* p. 207.

14. Quoted in Etienne Balazs, *Chinese Civilization and Bureaucracy* (New Haven: Yale Univ. Press, 1968), p. 226.

15. Alexander Soper, "The First Two Laws of Hsieh Ho," *The Far East Quarterly* 8(1949): 412–23.

5

The Cosmopolitan Civilization of the Sui and Tang: 581–907

The Sui (581–617)

The Tang: Establishment and Consolidation

Gaozong and Empress Wu

High Tang

City Life in the Capital: Chang'an

The Flourishing of Buddhism

    Institutionally

    Aesthetically

    Intellectually

Pure Land and Chan

The Hungry Ghost Festival

Daoism

The Rebellion of An Lushan (755–763)

Li Bai and Du Fu

Late Tang

Late Tang Poetry and Culture

Collapse of the Dynasty

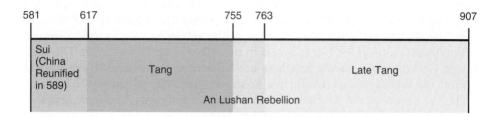

581	617		755	763	907

Sui (China Reunified in 589) | Tang | Late Tang

An Lushan Rebellion

After its reunification in 589, China remained united for approximately 300 years. During this period China became the political model and cultural center for all East Asia. Buddhism and Daoism flourished. Significant changes occurred in government and society. It was the period of classical poetry and law.

Like the Han, the Tang dynasty succeeded a powerful but short-lived regime that had accomplished the original reunification: the Sui. And like the Han, the Tang dynasty may be thought of as having very distinct earlier and later phases, although there was no comparable formal interruption of Tang rule. There are other ways, too, in which the two dynasties are similar, but the differences between them are even more instructive than their points of resemblance.

The Sui (581–617)

In 577, forty-three years after the demise of the Northern Wei, the Northern Zhou (557–581) reunified the North. Four years later the Northern Zhou general Yang Jian (541–604) usurped the throne and founded his own dynasty, the Sui, which in 589 defeated the last of the southern states. The task of then incorporating North and South into a single political system has been compared to the attempt by Charlemagne (742–814) to create a new Roman Empire in Europe. Although different in outcome, the two situations were quite comparable in terms of land area, diversity of terrain, and variety of local cultures.

Unlike the Qin, the Sui did not seek to impose a new pattern on China but adopted a policy of fusing various local traditions and amalgamating different elements. Although both Yang Jian and his strong minded, influential wife were dedicated Buddhists, the Sui also used Confucian and Daoist traditions to gain support and legitimacy. In formulating a legal code the new dynasty incorporated elements from different legal traditions, North and South, so effectively that it provided the basis for the Tang and all subsequent codes. In other respects too there was much continuity between the Sui and the early Tang, which, unlike the Han, did not repudiate the principles and policies of its immediate predecessor.

Yang Jian or Wendi (r. 581–604), the posthumous name by which the emperor is known in the histories; his wife; and their son, Yangdi (r. 604–618), came from a prominent northwestern family of mixed Chinese and steppe ancestry. Through cultural policies and marriage alliances they undertook reconciliation of the great families of the Northeast and of the South. Yangdi married a southern princess and linked North and South by completing his father's ambitious project of building a canal joining China's two great rivers, the Yellow and the Yangzi, providing the political capital in the North access to the riches of the lower Yangzi. The completed Grand Canal joined Hangzhou and Kaifeng and was linked by extensions both to the area of modern Beijing and to the Sui-Tang capital, the new Chang'an, built near the site of the old Former Han capital. Construction of official granaries helped to establish a government economic network.

The Sui devoted equal care to political consolidation and centralization. The bureaucracy was reorganized, and a tier of local administration was eliminated to make local government more amenable to central direction. Local officials could no longer appoint their subordinates as they had during the period of division, and the "rule of avoidance" prohibited an official from serving in his native place. Nor could he serve more than one tour of duty in the same locality. After this tour, usually lasting three years, he would be reassigned according to merit.

Even more important, the Sui instituted a system of recruiting officials by examination. This deprived the hereditary high aristocracy of the monopoly of power they had enjoyed during the period of division, when appointments had been made by recommendation. Although government service was opened to a somewhat wider class of people, it still remained the prerogative of the wellborn. These measures effectively reduced the ability of officials to establish a personal power base in the areas where they served, reduced the power of the great families to which they belonged, and made officials more responsive to the interests and direction of the central government.

As may be expected of a unifying dynasty, the Sui was vigorous militarily. Expeditions were sent as far south as Central Vietnam, and in the west, nomadic peoples were driven out of Gansu and eastern Turkestan. Colonies were established along the trade routes. Further afield, in Central Asia, states such as Turfan became tributaries. Envoys were exchanged with Japan. The Sui continued the militia system it had inherited from the northern dynasties and settled many troops in garrisons along the frontiers.

The dynasty's aggressive foreign policy demanded the organization and deployment of large military forces. Most costly in terms of casualties and materiel were three unsuccessful campaigns against Koguryo, the state that controlled northern Korea and much of southern Manchuria. Successive defeats placed an unbearable strain on the dynasty's resources. Insurrection and rebellion became widespread. The dynasty was doomed. It had overreached, trying to accomplish too much too rapidly. In the traditional Chinese view, however, the onus for its demise was assigned to Yangdi, who was cast as an archetypical bad last emperor, a self-indulgent tyrant—an image embellished in popular literature, which depicts him as living in luxury while his people were starving, frolicking with the numer-

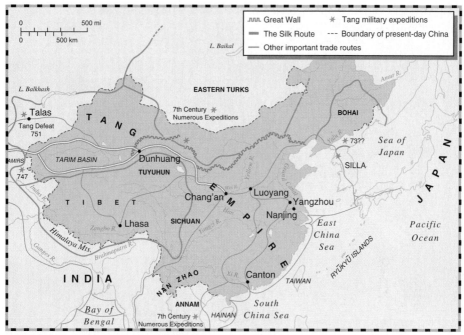

FIGURE 5.1 The Tang Empire.

ous women of his harem in a room lined with polished bronze screens to serve as mirrors, when he should have been minding the ship of state.

The Tang: Establishment and Consolidation

The Tang dynasty emerged from the struggles accompanying the disintegration of the Sui dynasty and built a great empire (see Figure 5.1). Its founder was that dynasty's top general, related through his mother to the Sui ruling house. Many of his officials had also served the former dynasty. There was no sharp break in the composition or the policy of the ruling group, but the fighting was hard and prolonged, taking up most of the reign of the founding emperor, Gaozu (r. 618–626). In 626 Gaozu's second son, a successful military commander, killed the crown prince and another brother apparently to forestall a plot against himself. He then forced his father to abdicate. Known as Taizong (r. 626–649), he directed the consolidation of the new dynasty.

Taizong's physical vigor and military prowess are suggested by the stone panels, which are more than five feet high, showing his favorite mount (see Figure 5.2). Equally vigorous mentally and wise in his knowledge of men, he became one of China's most admired rulers. His most famous Confucian minister was Wei Zheng (580–645). After Wei's death, Taizong compared his minister to a mirror used for

FIGURE 5.2 General Qui Xinggong of Emperor Tang Taizong's army removes an arrow from the Emperor's horse, Autumn Dew. Stone relief from tomb of Tang Taizong. Design attributed to Yan Liben (d. 673), 59.84 in × 58.15 in. Love of horses and excellence in horsemanship were part of the steppe legacy of the Tang royal family and northwestern elite. (University of Pennsylvania Museum, Philadelphia.)

correcting his judgment analogous to a bronze mirror for straightening out one's clothes and the mirror of the past for understanding the rise and fall of states. But, although he sought Wei Zheng's counsel on moral issues, such as the punishment of officials or the giving and receiving of gifts, the emperor did not allow him to influence major policy decisions such as those concerning peace or war.

Taizong's policies generally built on those of the Sui. He broadened the geographical composition of the bureaucracy by including men from areas other than his native Northwest, but government remained in the hands of the well-born. The most pretentious of these were the high aristocrats of the Northeast, who looked down on the "semibarbarian" northwestern families, not excluding the imperial family, even though it claimed descent from Laozi. Taizong had a genealogy compiled to define the status of families throughout China and rejected the first draft to demote one of the great Hebei lineages and promote the imperial clan to first place.

Following the Sui example, more granaries and schools were built, and a new code of criminal and administrative law was promulgated. This consisted of primary laws, meant to hold for all time, and secondary laws, open to frequent adjustment to allow for changing conditions and local variations. The central government was restructured so that its essential tasks were performed by Six Ministries (personnel, revenue, rites, war, justice, and public works), a system continued by later dynasties.

The early Tang emperors, like those of the Sui, drew on Buddhism and Daoism as well as Confucianism. Taizong gave precedence to Daoism but took care not to alienate the Buddhists. Like his predecessors he took measures to keep the religious establishments under control. Meanwhile, as Howard Wechsler has shown, the early Tang emperors, in contrast to earlier rulers, deemphasized rites centered on their own ancestors in favor of more public rituals performed by the emperor for the good of all. And they extended their own family to form a "political family" of ministers and high officials who were included in rites and granted "satellite tombs" on the vast grounds of the imperial tombs. Such tombs had also been granted in the Han, but not on a scale anything like that of the Tang.[1] The fact that in China, unlike Japan, such tombs continued to be built even in a Buddhist age is not unconnected with issues of legitimation but beyond that also reveals deep-seated differences in attitudes toward burial and perhaps even death.

Statues of foreign envoys (although now headless) still pay homage at Taizong's tomb, confirming

FIGURE 5.3 Xuanzang, a Tang monk who traveled to India in search of Buddhist scripture. Rubbing in the Schirokauer collection. Making rubbings from stone steles was a popular form of reproducing texts as well as pictures before the invention of printing and remains an inexpensive way to reproduce pictures and calligraphy. (© Lore Schirokauer)

his successful extension of Chinese power even further west than had the Han. But the Tang, like the Sui, failed in Korea. With Chinese power reaching all the way to the Pamirs and the empire at peace, travel of men and goods along the trade routes was more lively than ever. Many foreigners visited and lived in Chang'an during Taizong's reign, but the most famous traveler of the time was a Chinese monk, Xuanzang, who journeyed to India and returned with Buddhist texts and much information about foreign countries (see Figure 5.3).

The emperor was more interested in the latter than the former and even tried to persuade the venerable monk to return to lay life and become a foreign policy adviser. Xuanzang declined, and Taizong financed the translation projects to which the monk devoted the rest of his life. He also ordered Xuanzang to translate the *Daodejing* into Sanskrit for the benefit of the Indian world.

Taizong's last years were spoiled by disappointments in his sons and heirs. The crown prince became so infatuated with nomad ways, even living in a yurt, that he was finally deposed, and the emperor's favorite son was too deeply involved in intrigues over the succession to be trusted. In the end, the succession went to a weak young prince who became Emperor Gaozong (r. 650–683).

Gaozong and Empress Wu

Gaozong began as quite a vigorous ruler but suffered a stroke in 660. The remainder of his reign was dominated by Wu Zhao (625?–706?), a former concubine of Taizong's who won Gaozong's affection and engineered the removal and often murder of all rivals. After Gaozong's death in 683, two of Wu's sons reigned in succession, but in 690, no longer willing to rule through puppets, she proclaimed herself emperor of a new dynasty, the Zhou, thereby becoming the only woman in Chinese history to rule in her own name.

Gaozong showed his favor for Daoism by proclaiming Laozi "Sovereign Emperor of Mystery and Primordiality," establishing a government abbey in more than 300 prefectures, and requiring the *Daodejing* on the government examinations. Nevertheless, the content of the examination system, the guidelines for gentlemanly conduct and official policies, remained classical, and Confucian-style scholarship was sponsored by the state. In 651 an authoritative edition of the Five Classics (the *Odes,* the *Documents,* the *Rites,* the *Changes,* and the *Spring and Autumn Annals*) was completed, with each classic being accompanied by a definite commentary and subcommentary, in "a sorting out of traditions of scholarship on texts fundamental to civilized life."[2] Such a life was not considered incompatible with Buddhism or Daoism, but it was not defined in Buddhist or Daoist terms.

In contrast to Gaozong, Empress Wu, however, turned mainly to Buddhism, proclaimed herself an incarnation of Maitreya, and ordered temples set up in every province to expound the *Dayunjing,* a sutra prophesying the appearance of a female world ruler 700 years after the passing of the Buddha. Her patronage of Buddhism also extended to other temples and sects; much work was done in the Longmen caves during her reign.

Empress Wu's legitimacy was also bolstered by a genealogy compiled in 659 that listed families according to the official rank attained by their members, rather than according to their traditional inherited social standing, with the Wu family placed first. Under her rule the bureaucracy was expanded, with many new positions filled through the examination system. This opened government careers to a wider group, but in the final stage of the process, candidates continued to be judged on appearance and speech, criteria that inevitably favored the well-born. It was also normal practice for candidates to try to impress an examiner before the tests. Those who could used their family connections for this purpose; others sent samples of their verse.

Under Empress Wu, examination graduates could for the first time rise as high as Chief Minister, although the Empress preferred to bypass this office and work through the "Scholars of the Northern Gate," who formed a kind of personal secretariat. Gradually, however, during the first half of the Tang, examination graduates acquired great prestige and were promoted to the highest offices, even though the majority of officials still entered government service through other means, making use of family connections. Concurrently, government service became the most prestigious career in the empire.

FIGURE 5.4 Lady on horseback. Painted clay, Tang, 12.24 in × 15 in. Tang ladies regularly rode horses and played polo, a favorite game among the elite. (Courtesy of Karen Schlansky)

Office-holding remained a male preserve, but Tang women enjoyed more freedom than their predecessors. No doubt conditions varied according to place and social status—documents found in Turfan show women engaged in legal, financial, and religious activities—but, as Patricia Karetzky has suggested, "with dated archeological evidence, a pattern of development can be traced, and it seems to follow the trajectory of female influence at court."[3] That influence reached its zenith under Empress Wu, and, sure enough, the women depicted in paintings now become less stiff and demure. They interact more with others, are more individualized in character and expression, and, perhaps under Indian influence, are more robust. This is confirmed by figurines as well (see Figure 5.4). Art does not mirror life, but it does reflect tastes and values.

Tang power now reached its furthest geographic extent (see Figure 5.1) but at the price of constant fighting, particularly against the Tibetans. In Korea, Empress Wu

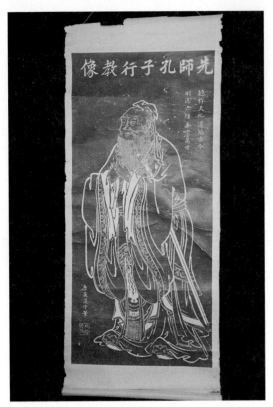

FIGURE 5.5 Portrait of Confucius propagating the teaching. Attributed to Wu Daozi (Qing?). Rubbing, 20.28 in × 43.31 in. (Schirokauer collection.)

supported the successful efforts of the state of Silla to unify the peninsula. Although China was unable to dominate the newly unified state, relations remained cordial throughout her reign. Until around 700 she remained a vigorous, although ruthless, ruler, but during her last years the empress, now in her seventies, came under the influence of sycophantic courtiers. She was deposed in 705, and the Tang was reestablished.

High Tang

The Tang reached its high point—economically, politically, and culturally—during the reign of Xuanzong (r. 713–756), also known as the "Brilliant Emperor" (Minghuang). His court must have been truly splendid. The emperor, a horse lover, is said to have kept 40,000 horses in the royal stables, including a troupe of dancing horses. Poetry and painting flourished, and horses were a favorite theme for poets, painters, and potters. The most admired of all Tang painters, Wu Daozi, lived during this period. It was later said of him that one day, after painting a scene on a wall, he walked into it, leaving only the empty wall behind. He must have been a remarkable master to have inspired this story. Unfortunately, none of his work is known to have survived, although the most famous depiction of Confucius is attributed to him (see Figure 5.5).

This is one of two portraits of Confucius attributed to Wu Daozi, inscribed on stone and distributed as rubbings. Wearing a simple cloth cap, the venerable "foremost master" is shown as a traveling teacher. Images such as this, although too far removed to testify as to the appearance of the original man or painting, had—and still have—a presence not dependent on their resemblance to the historical persons. And they are invaluable in showing how people imagined the sage and envisioned the painter's style. In 1974 a conference convened by the Taiwan Ministry of the Interior chose this rubbing to distribute to cultural sites around the world. There are even statues of the sage, modeled after this rubbing, in Tokyo and Cleveland as well as Taipei.

Political achievements under Xuanzong included reformation of the coinage, repair and extension of the Grand Canal, and the implementation of a land registration program. To carry out these measures, he employed special commissions headed by distinguished aristocrats. Men of equally imposing background also staffed the Censorate, the organ of the government charged with the surveillance of the bureaucracy. There was a tendency at this time for officials to polarize into two groups: members of the high aristocracy and those of less exalted rank. Nevertheless, factors influencing political alignments were too complex to be reduced to simple family or regional patterns.

Under Xuanzong the power of the Chief Ministers increased and a cabinet of Chief Ministers was established. Near the middle of his reign, the emperor gradually withdrew from active participation in government. From 736 to 752 government was in the hands of Li Linfu, an aristocrat who was an able minister but did not have an examination degree and was often ridiculed by those who did for his lack of scholarship. An expedition to conquer the kingdom of Nanzhao established in 738 in modern Yunnan failed, as did a second attempt in 754, leaving Nanzhao independent and free to expand.

When Li Linfu died in 752, he was succeeded by Yang Guozhong, a much less capable man, who owed his rise to the influence of his cousin, the royal concubine Yang Gueifei, China's premier femme fatale, who so captivated the emperor that he neglected all else and left the burdens of government to her relatives and protégés, unfortunately including An Lushan. In 751 An received the extraordinary honor of adoption into the imperial family in a solemn ceremony for which the rugged middle-aged "barbarian" general was dressed in diapers like an infant. This, however, this did not prevent him from rebelling four years later. The court was forced to flee to Sichuan. Along the way, loyal soldiers blamed Yang Gueifei for the country's difficulties and forced the emperor to have her strangled. Xuanzong then abdicated. The reign that had begun in such brilliance ended in disaster.

City Life in the Capital: Chang'an

Even the most casual glance at the layout of Tang Chang'an reveals that it was a planned city (see Figure 5.6). Occupying about 30 square miles, excluding the palace area, it was the largest planned city ever built and the largest enclosed by walls. Its roughly 1 million inhabitants also made it the most populous city in the world at the time. Roughly another 1 million people lived in the greater metropolitan area outside the walls.

Many cities grow in response to the social and economic needs of their inhabitants, but planned cities express the values and priorities of their builders. The essential feature of Chang'an is that it was built to be the capital of a great empire.

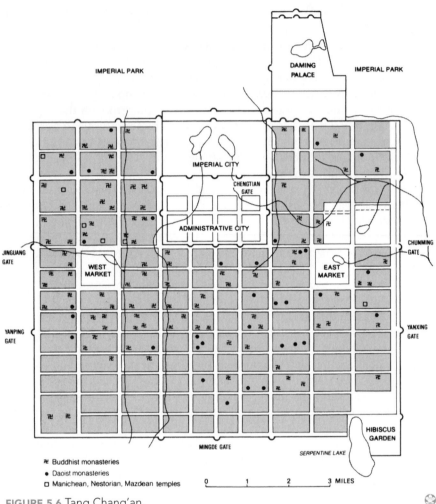

FIGURE 5.6 Tang Chang'an.

In accord with tradition, it was oriented so that both the city and the imperial palace faced south. The entire city was, in a sense, the home of the emperor. Its layout resembled that of a typical Tang house, with a service area in front and a garden in the rear. The imposing presence of the emperor and his government was further emphasized by the grand avenue that led from the main city gate to the palace and the government complex. Five hundred feet wide, enough for 45 modern traffic lanes, it was well designed to impress envoys from lesser lands with the might and grandeur of the Tang.

The people of the city lived in rectangular wards, each a self-contained unit enclosed by walls, with entry provided through a gate that was closed each night. Two friends in adjacent wards might be able to see each other's houses but would find it difficult to visit. Because it was the center of government, Chang'an was hardly the place to escape government surveillance and interference. Freedom was to be found in remote mountains and hills. Not everyone wished to rusticate in a remote village, however; many bitterly bemoaned an enforced absence from the great capital— unless, perhaps, they were posted to Luoyang, the secondary capital, or to Yangzhou, the southern metropolis.

Tang culture was cosmopolitan both in its openness to cultural influences from India and the distant west and in serving as model for the other settled societies of East Asia. Both aspects were reflected in the considerable number of foreigners who lived in Chang'an. Some were students. Among these, the most numerous were the Koreans, of whom some 8000 were said to have been in Chang'an in 640. Other foreigners were engaged in commerce, coming from as far away as India, Iran, Syria, and Arabia. The Armenoid wineseller shown in Figure 5.7 probably sold his exotic beverage in the West Market, the center for foreign trade,

FIGURE 5.7 *Armenoid Merchant Holding Wine Skin.* Pottery with three-color glaze, eighth century, 10 in × 14.65 in. Li Bai (Li Bo) was just one poet much given to this merchant's beverage. (© Seattle Art Museum, Eugene Fuller Memorial Collection, 38.6. Photo by Paul Macapia.)

where his customers could also enjoy other exotic foods and beverages and attend performances of foreign acrobats or magicians or see a foreign play.

Stylish Tang ladies sported foreign coiffures, and painters and potters had a good time rendering the outlandish features of "barbarians" from distant lands. Images of foreigners from all over Central Asia and beyond to Iran were prominent among the clay figurines manufactured in specialty shops to be used for burial with the dead. Among the tomb figures are camel drivers and grooms for the horses, examples of which can be found in almost all museum collections of Chinese art. Information concerning foreign foods, music, and customs can also be found in Tang writings, particularly poetry.

Among the amenities of the capital were the Serpentine Lake and the Hibiscus Garden in the southeast corner of the city, where newly granted degree holders celebrated their good fortune by floating wine cups on the water, and the emperor himself sometimes entered the Purple Cloud Pavilion to observe the festivities. Notably absent, however, were public buildings such as forums, baths, or stadiums found in cities inhabited by citizens rather than subjects. Nor did Chang'an boast great, monumental structures of stone or brick. The men of Tang were under no illusion concerning the permanence of stone. In their view, what endured was the written word.

As the map of Chang'an clearly shows, the city was also a religious center. To its Manichean, Nestorian, and Zoroastrian temples we can now add the abandoned Da Qin Pagoda and Monastery where a mud and plaster nativity and other Christian remains dating from around 780 were discovered in 2001. The places of worship of foreign religions testify to Tang tolerance and cosmopolitanism, but their congregations, like those of Buddhist temples during the Han, remained largely foreign. Not so were the Daoist and even more numerous Buddhist structures. Buddhist pagodas gave Chang'an its skyline, and the influence of Buddhism was everywhere.

The Flourishing of Buddhism

As a recent study puts it, the Tang saw "the emergence of China as a central Buddhist realm,"[4] home of sacred relics, of Maitreya, and of Manjusri, bodhisattva of meditation and perfect wisdom up on Mt. Wutai (Shanxi). Completely at home, Buddhism flourished institutionally, intellectually, and artistically and penetrated deeply into Chinese life. Many studies have and continue to be written about all these aspects, which we can only outline here.

Institutionally

Although the state employed Confucian ceremonies and learning whereas individual emperors might favor Daoism, what had become the most prevalent religious organization in the empire could not be disregarded. During the period of division, the southern monk Huiyuan (334–417) had asserted that monks do not bow to emperors, but in the North Buddhism had been expected to serve the state. The Tang, following the Northern Wei, restricted the number of monks and regulated the monasteries, but most emperors also patronized Buddhism as an asset for the empire even if they varied in degree of personal commitment, and Buddhist monasteries flourished economically. In the countryside they operated mills and oil presses, maintained vaults for safe deposit, issued loans for interest, changed money, and performed other banking services including pawnbroking. The temples also held much land that they cultivated with semiservile labor, rented land, and profited from their connections with wealthy patrons who sought to evade taxation by registering land under a temple name.

Urban as well as rural temples provided medical care and put up travelers. They were associated with bridge building and the domestication of sugar. As conduits for Inner and South Asian culture, they influenced Chinese material culture in many ways—including the popularization of chairs. Their grounds served as playgrounds for children and at festival time also for adults. Looking at their buildings and art and listening to the chanting of the monks satisfied people's aesthetic needs.

Aesthetically

The Guanyin shown in Figure 5.8 is a sculpture in the style seen in eighth-century Chang'an. At their very best, Tang sculptures blend Indian delight in the corporality of mass with a Chinese sense of essentially linear rhythm. It is a combination most suitable for portraying Guanyin, combining the spiritual qualities of a supernatural being with merciful concern for earthly creatures. The balance between movement and restraint, like that between the worldly and the sacred, was difficult to maintain: in later Buddhist art, corporality degenerates into obesity and the robes take on a wild, rococo life of their own.

For those seeking a temporary retreat from the world, Buddhist temples offered a serene place of contemplation:

FIGURE 5.8 Eleven-headed century, 12.48 in × 39.69 in. The sensuous quality of the body, clothed (not hidden) in diaphanous drapery, owes something to Indian influence, particularly that of the Gupta Period (320–647). (Freer Gallery of Art, Smithsonian Institution, Gift of Charles Lang Freer, F1909.8.)

> I didn't know where the temple was,
> pushing mile on mile among cloudy peaks;
> old trees, peopleless paths,
> deep mountains, somewhere a bell.
> Brook voices choke over craggy boulders,
> sun rays turn cold in the green pines.
> At dusk by the bend of a deserted pond,
> a monk in meditation, taming poison dragons.[5]

The poem is by Wang Wei (699–759), noted also for his landscape painting, music and calligraphy, all now lost. The dragons are the passions; the scene is visual yet empty.

Intellectually

Because the analysis of Tang Buddhism in terms of schools has now been questioned, it is safer to think in terms of tendencies, some of which eventually crystallized into major sects. Others, such as the proponents of the Three Stages (Sanjie), did not develop into a powerful sect but did contribute a vision of time as divided into (1) the era of true teaching, (2) the era of counterfeit teaching, and (3) the era of the decay of teaching. Although there was disagreement over exact periodization, the Tang was generally assigned to the period of decay, a view that Tang emperors naturally did not appreciate.

A tendency that became a major sect was Tiantai (Japanese Tendai), named after a mountain range in Zhejiang. Traced back to Zhiyi (538–597), it was patronized by the Sui. Mirroring that dynasty's policy of political and economic integration, Tiantai combined elements of the various doctrines and practices, seeking to combine the scholarly tradition of the South with northern pietism and meditation. The complete Truth for Tiantai was contained in the Lotus Sutra, believed to have been preached by the Buddha to 12,000 arhats (saints), 6000 nuns, 8000 Bodhisattvas, and 60,000 gods. The great god Brahma attended, accompanied by 12,000 dragons, and there were hundreds of thousands of other supernatural beings. As he talked, a ray of light emanated from the Buddha's forehead, revealing 18,000 worlds, in each of which a Buddha is preaching. This text was enormously influential in East Asia and inspired many artistic representations. Through powerful allegories such as that of a man rescued by following a mirage, it recommends the use of "skillful means" (*upaya, fangbian*) to lead people to salvation.

Tiantai doctrine centered on a tripartite truth: (1) the truth that all phenomena are empty, products of causation without a nature of their own; (2) the truth that they do, however, exist temporarily; and (3) the truth that encompasses but transcends emptiness and temporariness. These three truths all involve and require each other— throughout Tiantai the whole and the parts are one. A rich but unified cosmology is built on this basis: temporariness consists of ten realms. Because each of these includes the other, a total of 1000 results. Each of these in turn has three aspects—that of living beings, of aggregates, and of space. The result is 3000 worlds interwoven so that all are present in each. Therefore, truth is immanent in everything: all beings contain the Buddha nature and can be saved. One eighth-century Tiantai patriarch taught that this includes inanimate things, down to the tiniest grain of dust.

Like Tiantai, Huayan taught the doctrine of emptiness and the interpenetration of all phenomena, but added that all phenomena arise simultaneously in reciprocal causation. Deeply interested in doctrinal subtleties, Huayan Buddhists distinguished between *li*, which can be translated as "principle" and is formless, and *shi*, or "phenomena." One of its greatest masters was Fazang (643–712), who was patronized by Empress Wu. In a famous sermon Fazang once explained Huayan doctrine by setting up a Buddha figure surrounded by eight mirrors at the points of the compass. A ninth mirror was placed above the statue and a tenth below. When the Buddha figure was lit by a torch, each mirror reflected not only the Buddha but also all the other mirrors.

Less intellectual but very potent was the esoteric Buddhism patronized by Gaozong, consistent with his abiding interest in Daoist magic. The practitioners of this form of Buddhism, which, like Huayan, stressed the magnificence and mystery of the Cosmic Buddha (Vairocana), used mantras (mystic syllables), mudras (signs made by the position of the fingers and hands), and mandalas (pictorial representations of the cosmos—"cosmograms"). Although influential in China, it did not become a major sect there as it did in Japan, in the form of Shingon. Two other tendencies emphasized practice more than thought.

Pure Land and Chan

Jingtu (Japanese *Jōdo*), or Pure Land, derived its name from the paradise in the West presided over by Amitabha (*Amituofo* in Chinese; *Amida* in Japanese), Buddha of Infinite Light. Another great favorite of Pure Land Buddhists was Guanyin. Drawing on a long Mahayana tradition, this school emphasized faith as the means for gaining rebirth in the land of bliss. The teaching of salvation by faith was often coupled with the idea that this was the appropriate means for a decadent age. A special practice of Pure Land Buddhism was the invocation of Amitabha's name. This, if done with wholehearted sincerity, would gain anyone rebirth in the Pure Land. The popular appeal of this sect was immense, and its spiritual dimensions probably received their furthest development in the teachings of the Japanese master Shinran (1173–1262).

Chan was also very influential in Japan, so much so that in the West it is generally known by its Japanese name, Zen, but it originated in China and has affinities with Daoism. Chan masters taught meditation as the way for one to pierce through the world of illusion, recognize the Buddha nature within oneself, and obtain enlightenment. Whereas for other schools meditation was only one of many techniques, Chan rejected all other practices, such as the performance of meritorious deeds or the study of scriptures.

Chan came to be divided into "Northern" and a more radical "Southern" school founded by Huineng (638–713) who, according to The Platform Sutra of the Sixth Patriarch, became the sixth patriarch after besting his rival's poem.

> The body is the *bodhi* tree
> The mind is like a clear mirror.
> At all times we must strive to polish it.
> And must not allow the dust to collect

It was under the *bodhi* tree that the Buddha was said to have achieved enlightenment. Illiterate himself, Huineng got a monk to post his response:

> The *bodhi* tree is originally not a tree
> The mirror also has no stand.
> Buddha-nature is always clean and pure
> Where is there room for dust?

Another verse said:

> The mind is the *bodhi* tree,
> The body is the mirror stand.
> The mirror is originally clean and pure;
> Where can it be stained by dust?[6]

In contrast to the so-called Northern branch, which emphasized sitting in silent meditation and attaining enlightenment gradually, Southern Chan taught that illumination comes in a sudden flash, although only after long searching. A

Western analogy might be Newton's experience under the apple tree: he discovered the law of gravitation in a sudden flash, but he would never have done so had he not been constantly thinking about the problem, searching for a solution.

Southern Chan teachers often employed unorthodox methods to prod their disciples on the road to illumination. Their methods included irreverent or irrelevant answers to questions, contradictory remarks, and nonsense syllables—anything to jar the mind out of its ordinary rut. Some masters would strike their disciples in the belief (as with Newton) that enlightenment might come as the result of a sudden physical shock. One widely practiced technique was for the master to assign his pupils a *gong'an* (*koan* in Japanese), an enigmatic statement to be pondered until the pupil attained an understanding that transcended everyday reasoning. One famous *gong'an* asks: "What is the sound of one hand clapping?"

Chan, like some other varieties of Buddhism, was esoteric in that its teachings were fully accessible only to select lifelong practitioners, but, like the Greater Vehicle, Buddhist festivals were for everyone.

The Hungry Ghost Festival

Hungry ghosts were condemned to suffer in the lowest hells, unable ever to relieve their starvation because their needle-thin throats made it impossible for them to swallow even when food failed to burst into flames on their lips. The festival, still celebrated in East Asia today (and as Obon in Japan), is based on the story of Mulian (Maudgalyāyana in Sanskrit), a deeply filial monk who, with Buddha's help, after searching long and hard in the underworld where he encountered numerous demons, finds and rescues his mother, a hungry ghost condemned to unceasing agony by the bad karma she had accrued through her avarice and stinginess in withholding food and alms from monks.

Recounted in sacred texts but also by popular storytellers using "transformation texts" (*bianwen*) to explain and embellish what was happening in the pictures that were their stock in trade, Mulian's story underwent many variations incorporating material of diverse origin. Scholarly analysis reveals that the demons who staff the underworld include immigrants as well as native born spirits, all equally part of a single system.

Similarly the scholar can detect diverse elements and levels of meaning in the festival, performed on the fifteenth day of the seventh lunar month, long an important date in China. A major theme is the interaction of ancestors and the living, but what is perhaps most impressive is the fusion of meanings and traditions. In that fusion Buddhism, once charged with lack of family values, occupies a central place. As Stephen F. Teiser points out, the spread of the festival in China "signals the movement of Buddhist monkhood into the very heart of family religion."[7]

A document presented to Xuanzong in 739 provides for the Central Office of the Imperial Workshop to supply special bowls for the festival, and the state remained a sponsor and participant, but the festival long outlived the dynasty. This was true of Daoism as well, although it continued to benefit from direct imperial patronage. Xuanzong even strengthened the dynasty's association with Daoism by ordering statues of Lao Zi and himself to stand side by side in state-sponsored abbeys throughout the empire.

Daoism

Daoism under the Tang as summarized by Russell Kirkland was "a fairly homogenous blend of nomenclature from the Celestial Masters tradition, meditative practices from the Shangqing tradition, liturgies and social values from the Lingbao tradition, and philosophical texts like the *Daodejing*."[8] This quotation is from an essay on Sima Chengzhen (646–735), a man of distinguished family background who occupied a preeminent place in the Shangqing lineage and was an expert in ritual and meditation. Sima moved easily in polite society, associated with famous literary figures, and enjoyed a fine reputation as a writer, painter, and calligrapher. As a Daoist he emphasized gradually transforming oneself and predicted his own final release from his corporal form.

Shangqing adepts continued to journey through inner and outer space in their quest for wisdom and longevity, whereas ordinary folk too were attracted by longevity techniques, miracles, and the power of local gods: "Ordinary people are saved by the deities, statues in provincial temples take flight when threatened or act in retaliation, nasty demons are slain and good forces are harnessed to the greater prosperity not only of aristocrats but also of the common people and the wider populace."[9] The political landscape might change, but Daoism was deeply rooted in China's sacred landscape dominated by the five sacred mountains that Daoists considered the fingers of the cosmic Laozi.

The Rebellion of An Lushan (755–763)

The rebellion that drove the emperor into flight to Sichuan and created havoc in the country revealed the underlying weakness in the Tang system. Afterwards, China was never the same again. Today the thesis, first set forth by Naitō Kōnan (1866–1934), that the rebellion marked a major break in Chinese history is generally accepted, and it is only to keep the book reasonably brief that we treat both sides of this divide in a single chapter.

As usual, internal and external troubles reinforced each other. Only strong central leadership could prevent the friction between the aristocratic commissions and the regular bureaucracy from getting out of hand. Old institutions were revealed to be inadequate under new conditions. The dynasty had adopted the "equal field system" of land allotment developed by the Northern Wei as a way of bringing deserted land back under cultivation or opening up new lands, but this system proved unworkable when there was a shortage rather than a surplus of land. The breakdown of the land system brought in its train the failure of the taxation system, which was based on equal land allotments. Because most taxes were collected in kind, that is, goods rather than money, this system required a cumbersome network of transport and storage.

Similarly, the old militia system proved inadequate. The dynasty's military requirements could only be met by large standing armies composed of professional soldiers. In 747 a Tang army crossed the Pamirs, led by a Korean general who had opted for a career under the Tang. This expedition succeeded in preventing Arabs and Tibetans from joining forces, but four years later this same general suffered defeat on the banks of the Talas River near Samarkand. This momentous event not only put an end to Tang ambitions in the area but also opened to Islam what had up to then been a Buddhist-oriented Central Asia.

In 736 the Northwest had been stabilized when the pro-Tang Uighurs became the dominant power. In midcentury, however, the dynasty was challenged by an alliance between Tibet and Nan Zhao, a southwestern state in the area of modern Yunnan Province. The government's response was to create military provinces along the frontiers. These were placed under the direction of military governors (*jiedushi*) who were given logistic as well as military authority and gradually assumed other government functions. With the central army in decline, a serious imbalance of power resulted between the home army and the powerful frontier forces. An Lushan, a general of Turkish extraction, began his rebellion in control of 160,000 troops in the Northeast.

An Lushan seized both Luoyang and Chang'an and proclaimed himself emperor of a new Yan dynasty. But in 757 he was murdered by his son. The rebellion continued, led first by Shi Siming, a general of similar background, and then by his son. In the meantime, the court had fled to Sichuan, the very large (75,000 square miles) and fertile province which, ringed by mountains, is highly defensible. (During the Second World War it served as a bastion for the Nationalist Chinese.)

In 763 the court was able to regain the capital, and the Tang was saved. However, the dynasty was able to recoup only with the assistance of foreign, mostly Uighur, troops. Furthermore, it had to be content with purely nominal submission of the virtually independent "governors" in the Northeast, in the region west of the capital, in parts of Henan, and in Sichuan. Regional differences that before the rebellion had been worked out within the system now threatened to pull it apart.

Li Bai and Du Fu

The ability to write at least passable poetry was one of the accomplishments expected of a Tang gentleman and was usually required in the civil service examinations. Consequently, a great many poems—more than 48,000, by some 2200 writers—have been preserved. Naturally their quality is uneven, as would be the case if our politicians and business executives were all expected to write poetry.

Li Bai (Li Bo, 701–763) and Du Fu (712–770), China's two most beloved and admired poets, experienced both the brilliance of Xuanzong's reign and the dark times of An Lushan's Rebellion. Neither man was a political success, although Du felt this more keenly than did Li. Both enjoyed friendship and wine and composed beautiful poetry with multidimensional meanings. They were personal friends, and Du Fu greatly admired Li Bai. However, they differed greatly in personality and in their work.

FIGURE 5.9 Anonymous, *Ming Huang's* (that is, Xuanzong's) *Journey to Shu*. Hanging scroll, ink and color on silk, Tang in style but dates from Song or later, 31.89 in × 22.01 in. (© National Palace Museum, Taiwan, Republic of China.)

Like Wang Wei, Li Bai's subjects included nature, but the nature depicted in poems such as "The Road to Shu Is Steep," describing Xuanzong's flight to Sichuan (see Figure 5.9), is much more exuberant than that of Wang Wei.

Li's fondness for nature and mountains blended well with his freedom of spirit. Although he wrote poems in many forms, he preferred old-style verse, *gushi*, which, unlike the new style, *jintishi*, let poets devise their own rhythmic and verbal structure.

Li Bai was famous as the poet of wine:

> A pot of wine among the flowers:
> I drink alone, no kith or kin near.
> I raise my cup to invite the moon to join me;
> It and my shadow make a party of three.
> Alas, the moon is unconcerned about drinking,
> And my shadow merely follows me around.
> Briefly I cavort with the moon and my shadow:
> Pleasure must be sought while it is spring.
> I sing and the moon goes back and forth,
> I dance and my shadow falls at random.
> While sober we seek pleasure in fellowship;
> When drunk we go each our own way.

DETAIL FIGURE 5.9 Anonymous, *Ming Huang's Journey to Shu.*
(© National Palace Museum, Taiwan, Republic of China.)

> Then let us pledge a friendship without human ties
> And meet again at the far end of the Milky Way.[10]

The legend that, when on a nocturnal drinking expedition on a lake, Li fell into the water while trying to fish out the moon and drowned may well be spurious, but it became part of his traditional image. The Song painter Liang Kai captured this image of the slightly inebriated poet floating in space (see Figure 6.4) with an economy of means that would have pleased Li, whose verse is deceptively simple. He knew that true art does not reveal its skill.

Both poets wrote highly compressed verse, but much of Du Fu's poetry, unlike that of Li Bai, is enriched by a patina of allusions that add weight and majesty to the lines. Du was particularly effective in new-style poetry, especially regulated verse *lushi,* in eight lines with five or seven characters per line and elaborate rules governing tone and rhyme as well as verbal parallelism. Along with occasional poems and poems of friendship and wine, Du Fu is most admired for his social conscience and compassion. His sociopolitical commentary can be biting, as in two frequently quoted lines from a longer poem written shortly before the An Lushan Rebellion:

> Inside the red gates wine and meat go bad
> On the roads are bones of men who died of cold.[11]

Some of his most moving poems describe the suffering and hardships of ordinary people. One concerns the visit at night of a recruiting officer to a village where an aged grandmother informs the officer that only two males are left at home: the old man who has fled and an infant son. She tells him to take her since she can at least cook—and in the morning she is gone.

Du Fu, like his contemporaries, frequently sent poems to those close to him. The following, written while he was living near the upper reaches of the Yangzi River, is addressed to a brother living far away near the mouth of the river. The "wind in the dust" in the third line refers to the warfare that separates the two brothers:

> *To My Younger Brother*
> Rumors that you lodge in a mountain temple
> In Hangzhou, or in Yuezhou for sure.
> Wind in the dust prolongs our day of parting,
> Yangzi and Han have wasted my clear autumn.
> My shadow sticks to the trees where gibbons scream,
> But my spirit whirls by the towers sea-serpents breathe.
> Let me go down next year with the spring waters
> And search for you to the end of the white clouds in the East.[12]

In other poems Du Fu tells of life in the thatched hut he inhabited during exile in Sichuan. Often he voices his dismay at the failure of his political ambitions. His aspirations and disappointments corresponded to the experiences of many of his readers, who admired his artistry and his humanism. Perhaps for all of these reasons, he was venerated as China's foremost poet.

Late Tang

Major economic support for the dynasty came from the South. The main source of revenue was the salt monopoly, for the government controlled all but one of China's major salt-producing areas and sold monopoly salt to merchants for distribution throughout China. Dezong (r. 780–805) strengthened the dynasty's finances and also built up a large palace army. His successor, Xianzong (r. 806–820), was especially vigorous in fostering institutional renewal and in reasserting central control over some of the lost provinces. But both of these vigorous emperors relied on men directly dependent on them, the "inner court," rather than using the regular bureaucracy. The result was the emergence of eunuch power. Eunuchs commanded the palace armies and, as in the Han, formed self-perpetuating "families" through adoption. Xianzong was murdered by eunuchs, whose power grew greatly in the 820s and 830s—an attempted coup against them in 835 failed. To make matters worse, officialdom at the time was divided into bitterly hostile factions. A dispute that lasted half a century arose out of a disagreement over the results of a special civil service examination held in 808.

Dezong and Xianzong personally favored Taoism, as did Wuzong (r. 840–846), who built a Terrace for Immortals within the palace grounds so that he might "ascend into the mists and wander freely through the nine divisions of Heaven." Personally hostile to Buddhism, he could not resist the temptation to meet the state's pressing financial needs by seizing Buddhist riches. He is, consequently, best known for his persecution of the church: monastic lands and wealth were confiscated, monks and nuns were returned to lay life, and slaves and dependents were released. The emperor himself claimed to have defrocked 260,500 monks and nuns and when it was all over, the regulations allowed for only 49 monasteries with approximately 800 monks in all the empire.

Irreparable damage was done to collections of sacred texts, to the bronze statues that had been the glory of Buddhist sculpture, and to religious buildings, so that today we have only a very few Tang pagodas and halls, the largest of which is located on Mt. Wutai, Shanxi. This is similar in design to the Tōshōdaiji founded by a Chinese monk in Japan. Similarly, large-scale Tang sculpture in wood and bronze has not survived, but the more than life-size bronzes at the Yakushiji in Nara, Japan, are fine representations of the Tang international style. In China a good many stone statues survived, including a very large Vairocana Buddha just outside the caves at Longmen.

The policy of persecution was promptly reversed by Wuzong's successor, but the Buddhist establishments were to suffer another devastating blow during the enormously destructive rebellion of Huang Chao. Particularly hard hit were traditions such as Tiantai and Huayan, which focused on textual studies. Only two sects continued to flourish: Pure Land, grounded in the hearts of the people, and Chan, which took pride in its freedom from texts and patronage.

Late Tang Poetry and Culture

Poetry continued to thrive. In the 790s Han Yu (768–824) and Bo Juyi (772–846) began to write in their own distinctive and widely imitated styles. The latter was a very prolific poet, author of some 2800 pieces, and beloved wherever Chinese influence reached. His "Everlasting Remorse" is the classic poetic rendition of the tragedy of Xuangzong and Yang Guifei. Unlike Du Fu, he wrote in simple and easy language. Like Du he had a strong social conscience:

> *An Old Charcoal Seller*
> An old charcoal seller
> Cuts firewood, burns coal by the southern mountain.
> His face, all covered with dust and ash, the color of smoke,
> The hair at his temples is gray, his ten fingers black.
> The money he makes selling coal, what is it for?
> To put clothes on his back and food in his mouth.
> The rags on his poor body are thin and threadbare;

Distressed at the low price of coal, he hopes for colder weather.
Night comes, an inch of snow has fallen on the city,
In the morning, he rides his cart along the icy ruts,
His ox weary, he hungry, and the sun already high.
In the mud by the south gate, outside the market, he stops to rest.
All of a sudden, two dashing riders appear;
An imperial envoy, garbed in yellow (his attendant in white),
Holding an official dispatch, he reads a proclamation.
Then turns the cart around, curses the ox, and leads it north.
One cartload of coal—a thousand or more catties!
No use appealing to the official spiriting the cart away:
Half a length of red lace, a slip of damask
Dropped on the ox—is payment in full![13]

In other poems, he tells of his daily life, his family, and routines. He once described himself as addicted to poetry, bursting forth whenever he sees a fine landscape or meets a beloved friend: "madly singing in the mountains."[14]

Han Yu is best known for an essay reaffirming the Confucian Way, a precursor of Song Neo-Confucianism. He championed the Old Literature (or Old Culture, *guwen*) movement in opposition to the elaborate parallelism and rhetorical flourishes of more recent prose. Guwen thinkers were not the only ones dissatisfied with the literary culture of the day, but, unlike some of their contemporaries, assumed an "intellectual position that emphasized personal responsibility over the guidance of 'tradition.'"[15]

In his poetry as in his prose, Han Yu preferred the old styles, writing long poems rich in original and daring similes. A common theme in his work is the classic complaint of the Tang gentleman poet: lack of official recognition. A scholar is like a fine horse, in need of proper care if he is to flourish. The trouble with the world lies not in the lack of horses, but in the absence of a ruler who understands horses. Han Yu also showed a lighter side. He wrote an essay admonishing a crocodile and a poem about losing one's teeth.

Other major secular writers and scholars include Liu Zhiji (666–722), the first to write a critical study of history, the philosopher Li Ao (d. c. 844), and the encyclopedist Du Yu (735–812), all deserving more attention than is possible to accord them here. The same holds for the poets Li He (791–817) and Li Shangyin (812?–858). Li He had a penchant for quaint and even frankly odd language; as one Chinese critic put it: his verse has a demonic quality.

Li Shangyin, the most ambiguous of poets, wrote frequently of love, including his own love for a Daoist nun. The following untitled poem can, but need not, be interpreted allegorically. It is every bit as moving understood literally.

At eight she took a look at herself in the mirror,
Already able to paint her eyebrows long,
At ten she went out to tread on the green,
Her skirt made of lotus flowers.

At twelve she learnt to play the small zither:
The silver plectrums she never took off.
At fourteen, she was his among her relatives,
And, one imagined, not married yet.
At fifteen, she weeps in the spring wind,
Turning her face away from the swing.[16]

During the Tang, calligraphy and painting continued to be prized as the arts of gentlemen. Du Fu, one of the first poets to write on or about paintings, was keenly aware of the perishability of silk and ink. And he was right, for the poems have survived long after the paintings disappeared. Long after the Tang, Wang Wei was credited with establishing a gentleman's style of calligraphic painting in monotone, said to have contrasted with the precision of line and decorative coloring of the court style, illustrated in Figure 5.9. The coloring, blue and green, is a hallmark of Tang art, but the pleasure the artist takes in the fantastic mountains is typical of Chinese landscapists. Here, however, in contrast to later mountainscapes, nature does not overwhelm man. Instead, it provides a setting for his activities. The scene is Emperor Xuanzong's flight to Sichuan during the An Lushan Rebellion, although as Michael Sullivan has suggested, it really looks more like a pleasure excursion than a precipitous retreat after tragedy and defeat.[17] Be that as it may, this painting is probably as close as we can now get to the style of the Tang, an important reference point for later Chinese painting as well as a delightful work in its own right.

In religion and in culture, Chinese gentlemen, confident in their heritage, retained a cosmopolitan attitude. When an Arab's receipt of a prestigious decree in 850 provoked some complaints, Chen An wrote that being Chinese was not a matter of physical appearance or place of birth, but "a civilized state of mind."[18]

Collapse of the Dynasty

During its last 50 years, the Tang dynasty was weakened by conflict and divided loyalties; by mistrust between officials in the capital and military commanders in the field; and by suspicions, manipulations, and falsifications of all kinds. Even reports concerning natural disasters were falsified, as when an official assured the emperor that a plague of locusts had proven harmless because they had "all impaled themselves on thorns and brambles and died."[19] The story makes a sad litany of mismanagement, corruption, and incompetence. Meanwhile, bandit gangs, a refuge for the desperately poor and dislocated, increased in number, size, and ambition. Forming themselves into confederations, they progressed from raiding to rebellion; what had once been a nuisance now became a threat. Power, whether bandit or "legitimate," went to the strong and ruthless. Ordinary people survived as best they could the depredations of bandits and soldiers alike. Even though the dynasty made occasional gains, each rally amounted to no more than one step forward followed by two steps backward.

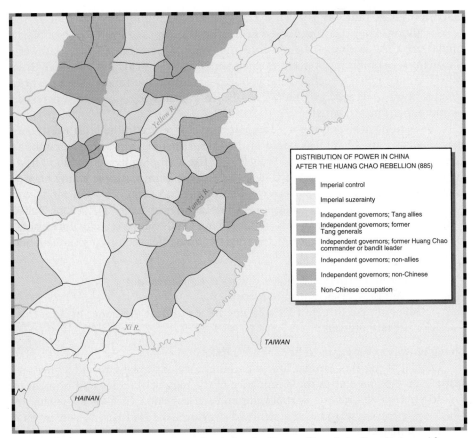

FIGURE 5.10 Distribution of Power in China after the Huang Chao Rebellion. (Adapted from Robert M. Somers, "The Collapse of the T'ang order," Ph.D. dissertation, Yale University, 1975, pp. 204–205.).

The most serious rebellion was led by Wang Xianzhi and his successor Huang Chao, who destroyed Canton (879), killing many of its foreign as well as Chinese population. He is most notorious for his brutality after he captured Chang'an in 880. Huang failed in his ambition to create a new dynasty; after his rebellion, China was thoroughly fragmented (see Figure 5.10).

The survival of the court now depended on the tolerance of and especially the competition among its neighboring rivals, including the foreign peoples who inhabited the northern borderlands. Among these, the Shatuo Turks were now the most important. Their intervention on behalf of the dynasty rescued it from destruction several times and enabled it to survive the Huang Chao Rebellion. In 905 the Shatuo Turks concluded an alliance with a people from Mongolia called the Khitan, an alliance that continued through the Five Dynasties Period (907–960). The Shatuo Turks themselves formed the second of these dynasties, called the Later Tang (923–934), which as its name implies tried to rule in the Tang tradition. They did not succeed in creating a lasting state, but a part of North China remained in foreign hands until the Ming. Meanwhile in the southwest, Nanzhao, after suffering defeats in Sichuan (829 and 874) and the Red River Valley (Vietnam, 863), declined and in 902 predeceased the Tang. After three brief regimes, it was succeeded by the Tibeto-Burman Dali Kingdom, which persisted for more than three centuries (937–1253).

The fighting at the end of the Tang, particularly severe in the Northwest, devastated Chang'an. There was panic in the streets: people screaming, scrambling over walls, and stampeding while "rebels rage like stamping beasts"; "blood flowing like boiling fountains"; severed heads; houses in flames; people eating bark or human flesh; and deserted palaces where brambles grow and fox and rabbit run wild. These are some of the images in "The Lament of Lady Qi," a long ballad composed by Wei Zhong (836–910) after Huang Chao ruined the city. Its most famous lines capture the essence of the tragic contrast between past greatness and present disaster:

> The Inner Treasury is burnt down, its tapestries and
>   embroideries a heap of ashes;
> All along the Street of Heaven one treads to dust the bones of
>   State officials.[20]

Chang'an was never again to be China's capital.

The fall of the Tang brought to an end the story of a great city and a great dynasty. It marked an end to the dominance of the high aristocracy and brought to a close a period of Chinese martial vigor and self-assertion vis-à-vis its neighbors. No Chinese empire would ever again hold sway over the Red River Valley in what is today Vietnam.

The fall of the Tang was an ending, but it was also a beginning. In considering the Late Tang and its place in history, we should keep in mind that periods when the center was weak have not fared well in the traditional Chinese histories written from the center. Focused on the deadly politics of disintegration, such accounts are apt to obscure developments beneath history's surface, pointing to a happier future. From the vantage point of the High Tang, the Late Tang appears to be a decline, but looking back from the Song and later dynasties, we can see not only major continuities but also new developments, leading to future growth and prosperity. Modern scholars therefore speak of the Tang/Song transition, aware that many later developments, in society and economy, thought, and agriculture, had their roots in the earlier period. We need to keep in mind that we are dealing with a vast and highly diverse land; that changes in the various dimensions of human activity, although interrelated, proceed at their own pace; and that periodization is a necessary analytical (and pedagogical) tool—but no more than that.

Let us end then with two inventions pointing to the future. First is the paddle-wheel boat, a Late Tang invention, but not widely used until the great burgeoning of shipbuilding stimulated by Song commercial growth. Next is the truly momentous innovation, woodblock printing, which originated, under Buddhist auspices, no later than the eighth century and was part of the Late Tang scene in the Lower Yangzi and Sichuan, but its full impact had to await the emergence of new conditions under the Song. The Tang is also the last major dynasty for which we have to rely completely on writings and records originally transmitted by hand.

Notes

1. Howard Wechsler, *Offerings of Jade and Silk: Ritual and Symbol in the Legitimation of the T'ang Dynasty* (New Haven: Yale Univ. Press, 1985).

2. Peter K. Bol, *"This Culture of Ours" Intellectual Transitions in T'ang and Sung China* (Stanford: Stanford Univ. Press, 1992), p. 79.

3. Patricia Karetzky, "The Representation of Women in Medieval China: Recent Archeological Evidence," *T'ang Studies* 17 (1999): p. 219.

4. Title and subject of Chapter 2 of Tansen Sen, *Buddhism, Diplomacy, and Trade: The Realignment of Sino-Indian Relations, 600–1400* (Honolulu: Univ. of Hawaii Press, 2003).

5. Burton Watson, *Chinese Lyricism: Shih Poetry from the Second to the Twelfth Century* (New York: Columbia Univ. Press, 1971), p. 175. Reprinted with permission.

6. *Sources of Chinese Tradition*, 2nd ed., Vol. 1, compiled by Wm. Theodore de Bary and Irene Bloom (New York: Columbia Univ. Press, 1999), pp. 496, 498.

7. Stephen F. Teiser, *The Ghost Festival in Medieval China* (Princeton: Princeton Univ. Press, 1988), p. 197.

8. Russell Kirkland, "Ssu-ma Ch'eng-Chen and the Role of Taoism in the Medieval Chinese Polity," in Livia Kohn, ed., *Handbook of Daoism* (Leiden: E.J. Brill, 2000), p. 110.

9. Livia Kohn and Russell Kirkland, "Daoism in the Tang (618–907) in Livia Kohn, *Handbook*, p. 350.

10. Liu Wu-chi and Irving Yucheng Lo, eds., *Sunflower Splendor* (Garden City: Anchor Press/Doubleday, 1975), p. 109.

11. A.R. Davis, *Tu Fu* (New York: Twayne, 1971), p. 46.

12. *Poems of the Late Tang*, translated and with an introduction by A.C. Graham (Penguin Classics). Copyright A.C. Graham, 1965. Reprinted with permission.

13. Liu Wu Chi and Irving Yucheng Lo, eds., *Sunflower Splendor* (Garden City, NY: Anchor Press/Doubleday, 1975), p. 206–207.

14. Arthur Waley, trans., *One Hundred and Seventy Chinese Poems* (London: Constable & Co., Ltd., 1918; reprinted 1947), p. 144.

15. Anthony DeBlasi, *Reform in the Balance: The Defense of Literary Culture in Mid-Tang China* (Albany: State Univ. of New York Press, 2002), p. 50.

16. James J.Y. Liu. *The Poetry of Li Shang-yin—Ninth Century Baroque Chinese Poet* (Chicago: Univ. of Chicago Press, 1969), p. 78.

17. Michael Sullivan, *The Arts of China* (Berkeley: Univ. of California Press, 1973), p. 293.

18. Charles Holcombe's summary in *The Genesis of East Asia 221 B.C.–A.D. 907* (Honolulu: Univ. of Hawaii Press, 2001), p. 51.

19. Robert M. Somers, *The Collapse of the T'ang Order* (Ph.D. dissertation, Yale Univ., 1975), p. 102.

20. Somers, *Collapse*, p. 145.

Part Three

Late Imperial/Early Modern

*S*cholars differ in how they periodize Chinese history and in the labels they use. By including more than 800 years in this section we call attention to certain continuities that set these long centuries off from what preceded them as well as what followed but by no means deny the magnitude of the changes that transformed China and are the substance of history. Although readers are invited to develop arguments for beginning "late imperial" or "early modern" later, we hesitate to break Chinese history into additional mega-periods and trust that readers will continue to find the organization of our book useful as they develop their own ideas.

Our label for this period also calls for explanation. Scholars, including particularly specialists in the last two dynasties, who emphasize continuity with the past tend to label their period "late imperial." Others, beginning with but not limited to those in Japan, prefer "early modern" as they point to similarities with early modern European history, emphasize the period's considerable continuity with its future, and cite developments that prefigured or prepared the way for future developments. At play in these discussions are various ways of defining "modern" in a post-modern age as well as a need to avoid viewing the world from a Eurocentric perspective by implying that there is only one way to be modern. We have opted for the split designation to suggest that both traditional and modern elements are to be found throughout.

6

China during the Song: 960–1279

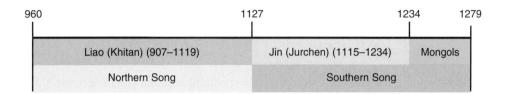

960		1127		1234	1279
Liao (Khitan) (907–1119)		Jin (Jurchen) (1115–1234)		Mongols	
Northern Song		Southern Song			

The Song (960–1279) represents a new phase of Chinese history. Although it did not equal the Tang in military power or geographic extent, this dynasty saw, in just about every sphere of human activity, the emergence of features, some of which continued into the twentieth century. Changes in state and society, in the economy, and in technology had a profound effect on China's future while new departures in philosophy and art created a heritage of classic dimensions that for centuries to come inspired and challenged thoughtful people throughout East Asia. As always, these developments were interrelated but proceeded at different tempos.

The Song, like the Tang, is bisected by a major cataclysm into an earlier and a later period.

Northern Song designates the period from 960 until 1126 when the dynasty ruled over both North and South from its capital at Kaifeng near the junction of the Yellow River and the canal system leading to the prosperous southeast and thus a location economically superior to returning to repeatedly devastated Chang'an. This "eastward shift of the political center"[1] was to remain permanent.

Southern Song applies to the dynasty after 1127 when it was confined to the South, having lost the North to the Jin, a state formed by the Juchen people from what is now Manchuria. With its "temporary" capital at Hangzhou in the lower Yangzi region, the dynasty occupied what by then was clearly the economic heartland.

The Founding

The dynastic founder was a general of what turned out to be the last of the Five Dynasties of the Tang-Song interregnum. Determined not to have his be simply the sixth minidynasty, he persuaded his fellow generals, who had helped him to power, that it was in their best interest to retire to the comfort of their estates. Although this did not prevent considerable military influence for some time, subsequent emperors and statesmen, determined to avoid the reemergence of warlords who had destroyed the Tang, saw to it that that power was placed in civilian hands. By devices such as the rotation of troops and frequent changes of command, the court prevented generals from developing personal power and succeeded in keeping commanders in line. The military profession suffered a permanent loss of status. It became a truism among the Chinese that good men are not turned into soldiers any more than good iron is wasted to make nails.

The New Elite

The old aristocratic families that had been so prominent under the Tang dynasty did not survive the violence that characterized the decline and fall of the Tang. Their demise cleared the way for the rise of new families who, ideally, based their prestige on literary learning and an elite lifestyle, their power and formal status on office holding, and their wealth on land ownership. Depending on context, they appear in the secondary literature as gentlemen or literati, scholar-officials, and landlords. Although these attributes frequently did not overlap, when all three were present they reinforced each other. Even though the spread of printing made books cheaper and encouraged the diffusion of literacy, a certain economic level still had to be reached before a family could afford to dispense with the labor of a son and pay for his education. Education, in turn, was a prerequisite for an official career, whereas office holding provided opportunities for the acquisition and protection of wealth.

Song social structure was far more complex than this, however. Then, as now, there were also the overeducated poor and the undereducated rich: the deeply learned scholar who lived a life of frugal obscurity, and the man of wealth who was not fully educated by elite standards and thus ineligible for political appointment and unwelcome in high society. The fact that learning, office, and wealth did not necessarily coincide made for considerable social variety, a variety further enhanced by contrasts between urban and rural life and by major regional differences. Furthermore, status was a function of the social group. Even a criminal (say, a salt smuggler) might enjoy high standing within his community although being despised by the official elite. It is important to remember that in premodern times the web of government rested only lightly on society and that the world of officialdom was remote from most people's lives. This reminder is necessary, because most of the historical sources stem from the world of the scholar-official, which also supplied China's historians. This scholar-official elite played a crucial role in maintaining Chinese unity, but unity should never be mistaken for uniformity.

During the Southern Song there was a shift of focus as elite families tended to concentrate less on obtaining office and more on strengthening their local roots by prudent management of their affairs and property, taking advantage of market forces in a growing economy. To quote Robert Hymes, "What was new in and after the Tang-Song transition was that the means for an elite lifestyle—wealth and the education that depended on it—became available, relatively broadly, apart from the state's extractive and redistributive mechanisms." The local elite assumed leadership roles in the construction of public works such as bridges and waterworks, in social welfare measures, in temple building, and in defense. Marriage ties with similar families helped to confirm and perpetuate their influence. They acted as powerful intermediaries between their local communities and the central state.[2]

In contrast to societies in which status is defined by ancestry, the Chinese system neither guaranteed continuity of status for these elite families nor were there laws barring the way for those trying to rise from below. Economically, movement up and down was facilitated by the ready transferability of land and other forms of wealth and by the custom of dividing estates among heirs rather than leaving them intact to a single son. Yet, once established, some local elite families could persist for generations.

To distinguish the new elite from the old, scholars, particularly those specializing in later periods, sometimes call them the "gentry," divided into the relatively large local gentry and the more restricted upper gentry of office holders or examination system degree holders eligible for office. Both were educated. Although the examinations were open to almost all men, excluding only a small minority such as the sons of criminals and the like, most candidates came from the local gentry. However, obtaining an official degree was always difficult. In the late Northern Song, roughly 100,000 men competed for about 500 degrees; that is, 1 of 200 passed. Later it got much worse, leaving candidates with little hope of earning the highest degree. Nevertheless, an examination degree remained *the* mark of elite status.

The Examination System

Founded in the Sui and increasingly prestigious during the Tang, the civil service examination system came into its own in the Song and (except under the Mongol Yuan) remained the most prestigious means of government recruitment until it was abolished in 1906. Although during the Song many men continued to enter government through other means, such as sponsorship by an official, in later dynasties the examination route represented the normal route into government service, and possession of a degree replaced pedigree as status signifier. During its long life, the system was refined and greatly elaborated, but its basic features were already clearly in evidence in the Song.

Structurally the system provided for an orderly progression through a series of tests (three during the Song, more later). These began at the local level, included a metropolitan examination given in the capital to candidates from the entire country, and culminated in a palace examination held under the personal auspices of the emperor. The Tang practices inviting candidates to bring personal influence to bear were eliminated. On the contrary, the government now went to great lengths in its attempt to secure impartiality. The papers of candidates, identified only by number, were copied by clerks before being submitted for grading so that the reader would be unable to identify the author of any paper by its calligraphy. The battle of wits between would-be cheaters and the authorities seeking to enforce honesty lasted as long as the examinations themselves and was pursued with great ingenuity by both sides. Nevertheless, despite occasional scandals, the examination system enjoyed a well-deserved reputation for honesty.

Success in the examinations required first of all a thorough command of the classics, which the candidates had to memorize. They had to be able to identify not only well-known lines but also the most obscure passages and even sequences of characters that made no sense to anyone who failed to recognize the context in which they appeared in a classic text. Tests of memory and exercises demonstrating command over formal literary styles were favored by examiners, because they made grading easier and more objective. Formal criteria were stressed in judging candidates' poems and essays. There was a persistent tendency for the examinations to turn into mere technical exercises, testing skills that revealed little about either a man's character or his administrative competence. This remained true even though the candidates were also required to discuss the meaning of designated passages from the classics and to answer questions concerning statecraft that theoretically had some bearing on the policy problems of the day.

Competition was rough. Preparing for and taking the examinations became a way of life. It has been estimated that the average age of Song candidates who completed the entire process and received the coveted *jinshi* ("presented" or "advanced scholar") degree was in the mid-30s. Because some areas, notably the southeast, were more advanced culturally and educationally than others, regional quotas were proposed, but, unlike during later dynasties, they were largely not enacted. As a result, men from the southeast predominated. Even with quotas, competition was bound to be more intense in some areas than others, but the most serious inequity was caused by the increasing importance of alternative examinations given to the relatives of officials. This, along with the special treatment accorded the numerous imperial clansmen, signified the effective abandonment of fairness during the Southern Song.

Despite its shortcomings the examination system did facilitate the careers of China's greatest statesmen during the Song and later. And it graduated administrators who shared a common intellectual heritage and recognized a common set of values, gentlemen who were scholars as well as officials. It provided a measure of social mobility and at least the appearance of meritocracy, largely determined the educational curriculum, and shaped the structure of the lives of those who aspired to a degree. It is no wonder, therefore, that the examinations themselves became a subject of profound concern and intense debate. The tradition of protest against its inadequacies is almost as old as the system itself. There were those who wished to see it abolished altogether, others who argued for reforms of various kinds, and men who felt it their filial duty to participate even though they despised preparation for the examination as unrelated to genuine study. The examination system remained a topic of political debate and scholarly controversy.

The Northern Song

From the beginning of the dynasty under Taizu (r. 960–976) and his brother, Taizong (r. 976–997), who completed the establishment of the dynasty, the Song had to tolerate a non-Chinese presence in North China. The Liao dynasty

(907–1119), which antedated the Song and had been created by the Khitan, a tribal people, held sixteen prefectures on the Chinese side of the Great Wall. To preserve their distinctiveness, the Liao created dual institutions, dividing the government into Northern and Southern Chancelleries, and produced an Inner Asian/Chinese multicultural civilization deserving fuller treatment than we can give it here. Relations between the Song and the Liao were frequently hostile, but neither state was able to subdue the other. The Song and Liao came to terms in 1005 after the Song emperor, Zhenzong (r. 997–1022), had personally taken the field against the Khitan. Negotiations led to a treaty that provided for the cession of some territory to the Song, for diplomatic exchanges, trade, and a Song agreement to send the Liao contributions in silk and silver. For the Song the cost was considerably less than would have been required to finance a military solution.

The Liao were not the Song's only troublesome neighbors. In 1038 there was a challenge from the West as the leader of the Ordos-based Tangut peoples organized the Xi Xia state, which was less successful than the Liao in containing the tensions between sinification and preservation of steppe traditions that had earlier undermined the Northern Wei and other hybrid northern states. In 1038 the Xi Xia invaded Shaanxi, and in 1044, the Song Emperor, Renzong (r. 1022–1063), signed a peace treaty with the Xi Xia along the lines of the earlier agreement with the Liao. The Xi Xia, however, remained a military problem for the Song until all of North China fell to the Jin (1115–1234).

Initially the Song had welcomed the emergence of the Jin as an ally, but the dynasty's attempt to "use barbarians against barbarians" ended in disaster. The last two emperors of the Northern Song, Huizong (r. 1100–1126) and his son, Emperor Qinzong (r. 1126–1127), were taken to Manchuria as prisoners of the Jurchen and there lived out their lives. The dynasty was able to reestablish itself in the South, but the North, homeland of Chinese civilization, remained lost. Not until the founding of the Ming dynasty in the fourteenth century was the North to come again under Chinese rule (see Figure 6.1).

Mindful of its dangerous neighbors, the dynasty concentrated its military and political attention on the North. In the South, after military conflict and political missions during the eleventh century, relations with Vietnam settled into a more or less stable pattern, with the Chinese dynasty treating Vietnam as a tributary state as it did the Dali kingdom in Yunnan. In contrast to the sixteen prefectures lost in the North and despite some wishful thinking, the prefectures once claimed in Vietnam never again became part of China. However, the Mongol Yuan dynasty was to incorporate Yunnan into the empire.

Government and Politics

The organization of the Song government basically followed that of the Tang except that the civil and military functions were strictly divided with preference to the former. Even so, the Song maintained a huge army equipped with sophisti-

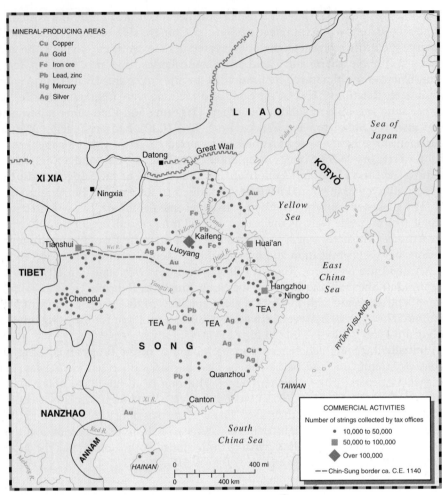

FIGURE 6.1 Song China—Political and Commercial.

cated weapons and managed to persevere for more than 300 years against a formidable succession of enemies. The maintenance and support of the military establishment was expensive, as was the financing of an expanding civilian bureaucracy. Naturally, Song scholars and officials disagreed over economic and fiscal policies much as they did over the examinations and over the linked issues of foreign and military policy.

Song politics were complicated by factionalism and infighting, usually conducted not by stable and legitimized political parties united by a common program but by factions whose members might share some common policy commitments but were more likely to be held together by personal relationships and temporary alliances. Characteristically, factions accused each other of narrow self-interest, and

FIGURE 6.2 *Five-Colored Parakeet.* Attributed to Emperor Huizong but probably painted for rather than by him, this carefully studied, realistic yet idealized, five-colored parakeet exemplifies the emperor's and the period's taste for elegance and precision. Hanging scroll, colors on silk, 20.87 in high. (© 2005 Museum of Fine Arts, Boston.)

each charged its opponents responsible for the development of factionalism itself, a phenomenon condemned by nearly everyone as inimical to the state.

Each faction sought to obtain the emperor's support. This was as crucial in practice as it was in theory, for, initially at least, the disappearance of an aristocratic counterweight served to increase the power of the throne. Still, even strong-minded Northern Song emperors tended to manipulate rather than to intimidate their officials. Those who fell out of imperial favor usually suffered nothing worse than exile. The dynasty's most imperious ruler, Huizong, harbored elevated ambitions but ended a political failure and owed his lasting fame to his aesthetics, his elegant calligraphy, and the paintings bearing his name (Figure 6.2). The dynasty did produce a number of dominant ministers, including China's greatest and most controversial reformer.

Wang Anshi

Wang Anshi (1021–1086) was not the first Song reformer. That honor went to Fan Zhongyan (989–1052), famed for defining a true Confucian as "one who is first in worrying about the world's troubles and last in enjoying its pleasures." Fan and Wang's reforms were part of a major Confucian revival that drew inspiration from shared classical ideals and was fostered by the "Old Culture" Movement (*guwen*) that had begun in the Tang (see Chapter 5, p. 129) and sought the transformation of state and society along with culture and literature. Both men sought to bring government closer to the classical ideal, and Wang, like Fan, initially commanded widespread reformist support. But Wang went far beyond his predecessor in initiating new programs. Able to promote his new policies as long as he enjoyed the support of Emperor Shenzong (r. 1067–1085), he ended up antagonizing his most illustrious contemporaries, chief among them the dynasty's greatest historian, Sima Guang (1019–1086), author of *A Comprehensive Mirror in Aid of Government* (*Zizhi Tongjian*). Other opponents included the poet and theorist of culture, Su Shi (Su Dongpo, 1037–1101), and the Cheng brothers, whose ideas became central to "Neo-Confucianism" (see later). Opposition to Wang spurred these men to some of their greatest achievements and stimulated much of "the subtle art of dissent" in poetry and painting revealed by Alfreda Murck in her admirable book.[3]

One of Wang's first acts, signaling his economic activism, was to establish a finance planning commission (1069). This, like the establishment of a state trade system (1072), was designed to save government money by breaking the monopoly on government procurement held by large merchants. It provided that the government should deal directly with small suppliers who now became eligible for government loans. Wang's willingness to innovate and readiness to delegate authority is exemplified by the "bureaucratic entrepreneurship"[4] he fostered in allowing the officials of the Tea and Horse Agency maximum discretion in operating the Sichuan tea monopoly.

Wang consistently preferred monetary transactions over dealing in commodities. Tax payments in cash were substituted for the customary deliveries of supplies to the palace (1073). Similarly, Wang instituted a tax to finance the hiring of men to perform local government service (1071), a function previously assigned to well-off local families on a rotating basis. He also increased the amount of currency in circulation. Nevertheless, there was a currency shortage brought on by increased demand.

Wang Anshi did not neglect agriculture. To save small farmers from the ruinous short-term interest rates of 60 to 70 percent charged for carry-over loans during the hard months between spring sowing and autumn harvest, he instituted farming loans ("young shoots money") with a maximum interest rate of 20 percent for the season (1069), but pressures to make money soon eclipsed the social welfare aspect of the program. To deal with the perpetual problem of faulty tax rolls and fraudulent records, Wang initiated a land survey in 1072, but that too ended in failure.

Another program organized people into groups of 10, 30, and 300 families to ensure collective responsibility for local policing, tax collections, and loan repayments and to supply men for a local security force that could also function as a military reserve. Another measure designed to cut the dynasty's enormous military expenses placed horses with farmers. In return for maintaining them, the farmers could use the horses in peacetime but were obligated to turn them over to the army in case of military need. This program failed to take into account the fact that farm horses do not make good military steeds.

A number of programs were rendered ineffective because they were sabotaged by officials and/or even used to oppress the very people they were intended to help. Reform of personnel recruitment and of management was crucial. Wang tried to obtain the men he needed by changing the examination system. He included law as a subject to be tested, assigned his own commentaries on the classics as official interpretations to be followed by the candidates in their papers, and stressed the classic known as *The Rites of Zhou (Zhou Li)*, because it provided justification for institutional reform and a government that penetrated deep into society. He also tried to circumvent the entire examination system by expanding the state university and ensuring its graduates direct entry into government. Wang realized that most of the actual work of government, particularly on the local level, was performed not by civil service officials serving a tour of duty in a county or prefecture but by a sub-bureaucracy of clerks, petty agents, and underlings who remained permanently in place. There was little to restrain these men, who shared neither the status nor the learning of the officials, from squeezing maximum profit out of their jobs. Despised as notoriously corrupt, they tended to become still more corrupt to compensate for being despised. Wang's policy was to reduce their number, improve their pay, place them under stricter supervision, and give the most capable among them an opportunity to rise into the regular bureaucracy.

Wang's personality as well as the intrusiveness of his measures made him many enemies. By 1076 he was out of office. In the middle and late 1070s, his program lost momentum, but a full reaction did not set in until the death of his imperial patron, Emperor Shenzong. Subsequently, there was an ambitious revival of reform under Huizong. Still later, individual measures similar to those of Wang Anshi were reinstituted from time to time, but no minister again tried to do so much so rapidly. His program remained an illustration of what government could do and also what it could not and should not attempt to do. Few after the fall of Northern Song shared Wang's vision of an activist government integrating state and society.

As always, political and economic developments were closely intertwined. The economic history of the period is varied and complex, but clearly the Song was a period of dramatic economic change.

The Economy

Qualitatively and quantitatively Song economic changes were so extensive that they have been called revolutionary. They occurred in all three areas of primary economic activity: industry, agriculture, and commerce (see Figure 6.1). Of this triad, industrial growth peaked during the Northern Song, whereas agricultural and commercial growth continued even after the loss of the North.

Important progress was made in the production of many commodities. Paper making and all the processes involved in book production advanced; there was progress in salt processing and notable developments in ceramics and in hydraulic engineering. Tea processing and shipbuilding gained new eminence. China developed a coal and iron industry that was the most advanced in the world. In North China deforestation provided the major incentive for coal production. Much of this coal found its way into furnaces used to smelt iron mined in an area stretching in an arc from southern Hebei to northern Jiangsu.

Much of the iron and steel went to equip an army of well over 1 million men, providing them with swords, other weapons such as arrows tipped with steel, and armor of various kinds. Iron tools, especially the *tieda,* "a pronged drag hoe that looks like an iron-toothed rake"[5] helped raise agricultural productivity. Other ferrous metal products included tools for carpenters and other workmen, consumer items such as stoves and smaller objects such as nails and needles, bits for drilling wells, and the chains used in suspension bridges. Most bridges, however, were made of stone or wood. Our illustration shows an arched bridge high enough to permit large boats to pass underneath and strong enough to support lively traffic in people and goods as well as numerous stalls. The city depicted in loving detail in Figure 6.3 is almost certainly not Kaifeng as traditionally thought, but it exemplified the growth of cities bustling with life and commerce.

Kaifeng itself originated as a commercial center and continued to function as such after it became the political capital. It housed not only government offices, garrisons, warehouses, and arsenals but also private textile concerns, drug and chemical shops, shipyards, building material suppliers, and so forth. There was also a thriving restaurant and hotel industry. In contrast to the symmetrical, planned layout of the Tang capital, Kaifeng grew organically. Lively streets replaced the old system of enclosed wards, and the population spilled beyond the city walls as its inhabitants sought relief from urban congestion.

Song city dwellers did not escape the grimmer aspects of urban life. Deadly fire was a constant threat. In Kaifeng guard stations were placed at 50-yard intervals; watchtowers were erected, each manned by 100 firefighting soldiers; and huge iron containers were kept filled with water. Despite these precautions, there were frequent and destructive conflagrations. Crime, too, was a fact of urban life. People had to be prepared for confidence men who passed lead off as gold, holdup specialists against whom merchants required special police protection, and all kinds of other petty criminals who eked out a living as best they could. For those who could not make a decent living, honestly or dishonestly, the city still offered advantages not available in the village. On special occasions, public alms were distributed. There were state hospitals and dispensaries and houses for the aged, the decrepit, and the orphaned. If worst came to worst, those dying in poverty at least had the consolation of knowing that they would receive proper burial even if they had no relatives to pay for it.

Some of the mining and manufacturing enterprises were large-scale operations employing hundreds of workers, whereas other concerns were confined to

FIGURE 6.3 The *Rainbow Bridge*, detail of Qingming Scroll by Zhang Zeduan. Hand-scroll, ink and light color on silk, mid-eleventh century, 10.04 in high. Viewers could travel at leisure through town and country as scrolls such as this were gradually un-rolled, an effect recaptured only with difficulty by the modern museum visitor who sees such a painting completely spread out in a glass case. Frequently, as here, a river pro-vides continuity. *Rainbow Bridge* resembles rainbows in both shape and color. For a cogent discussion of this famous scroll, see Heping Liu, *Painting and Commerce in Northern Song Dynasty China, 960–1126* (Dissertation, Yale University, 1997), Chapter 5. (© Collection of the Palace Museum, Beijing.)

small workshops. Various kinds of brokers facilitated commercial transactions, and numerous lines of business were organized into guilds or associations that super-vised the terms of trade and also served as intermediaries between their members and the government. As in medieval Europe, members of the same profession or guild frequently (but not always) set up shop in the same city street or district.

The growth of manufacturing and the growth of cities were sustained by an increase in agricultural yields. At the same time, the opening of new markets for rural products stimulated the development of agriculture, now called upon to feed a population of more than 100 million. The size of harvests was increased by the use of improved farm tools, advances in water control, wider application of fertilizers, and the development of new strains of rice. In the southeast it later be-came common for a rice paddy to produce two crops a year, either two harvests of rice or one of rice followed by a crop of wheat or beans grown on the paddy after it was drained.

Life in the country was hard but could be good: This is how a Late Northern Song poet describes life in his native village:

> At cock crow the whole village rouses.
> Gets ready to set off for the middle fields:
> Remind the wife to be sure to fix some millet,
> Shout to the children to shut the gate behind us.
> Spade and hoe catch the morning light;
> Laughter and hubbub mingle on the road.
> Puddles from the night before wet our straw sandals;
> Here's a wild flower to stick in the bun of your hair!
> Clear light breaks through the distant haze;
> Spring skies now are fresh and gay.
> Magnolia covers the wandering hills;
> In the empty field, a brocaded pheasant preens.
> The young people have come like racing clouds;
> Owl-like, an old man squats on his heels alone.
> The yellow earth glistens from the rain that passed;
> Clouds of dust race before the wind.
> Little by little, the whole village gathers,
> Calling greetings from field to field.
> The omens say it will be a good month;
> Let's keep on working, dawn to sundown![6]

Whether in the country or in town, economic growth rarely benefits all people equally. It does not prevent corruption ultimately at the expense of those too poor to afford bribes and presents. Nor does it preclude the wealthy from increasing the size of their holdings by taking advantage of the numerous peasants who held insufficient land to maintain their families or themselves and had to work as tenant sharecroppers or as field servants in conditions of legal inferiority. Wang Anshi's reforms notwithstanding, farmers remained burdened by inequitable taxation and exorbitant interest rates. Rural uprisings during the dynasty were rare, but there was unrest and rebellion in the 1120s. Much of the good that Huizong accomplished by building schools and sponsoring charities was undone by the heavy burden of taxation and government exactions. Especially notorious were the emperor's demands for rare plants, stones, and novelties. His reign also saw the most ambitious imperial sponsorship of Daoism.

The Religious Scene

From the outset Song emperors patronized Daoism. Then, roughly a century before Huizong, Zhezong, the emperor who personally led the army against the Liao, promoted it in a major way, sponsoring the compilation of Daoist texts, the performance of Daoist ceremonies, and the construction of Daoist edifices while claiming imperial descent from the Yellow Thearch, a mythical sage-ruler in a tradition going back to pre-Han times, and revering "heavenly texts" of supposedly supernatural provenance. The emperor patronized old sects such as the Celestial Masters and Shanqing while also bringing in new deities. Discussing Zhezong's Daoist projects, Edward L. Davis has traced the transformation of the Black Killer, a fierce god with angry eyes and unkempt hair who rides a dragon and carries a huge sword, from his origins as "the dark, militaristic god of a tenth century cult into the Perfected Lord of an eleventh century text—into a supporting minister of the Jade Emperor and defender of the Song dynasty" and noted it paralleled "the transformation of the military elite of tenth century kingdoms into the bureaucratic servants of eleventh century emperors."[7] Davis goes on to connect what was happening at court with the practices of Daoist Ritual Masters who interacted with spirit mediums and Buddhist Tantric exorcists, borrowing and competing with each other for elite patronage.

Huizong went a good deal further than Zhezong. He began by giving Daoists priority over Buddhists and ended by attempting to turn Buddhists into Daoists, even ordering that the Buddha's name be changed to "The Golden Immortal of Enlightenment." The emperor drew on practitioners from all over the empire to compile texts, and he sponsored the first printing of the Daoist cannon. In the course of time Huizong became convinced of his own elevated place in the universe, declaring himself an incarnation of the "Great Thearch of Long Life" or "Imperial Lord of the Supreme Empyrean," charged with the salvation of the realm. He was so convinced of his own sacredness that he ordered the basic five musical notes of the Chinese scale recalibrated using the length of his fingers as the standard.

Although imperial patronage of Daoism helped, its strengths were manifold. A number of new sects were established during the Song, but the most influential development occurred under Jin when Wang Zhe (1112–1370) taught that Daoism, Confucianism, and Buddhism were all three of equal value and stressed nourishing both one's nature and one's life force. The Celestial Realization sect, founded by Wang, continues today with its headquarters at Beijng's White Cloud Abbey.

Perhaps Daoism's greatest strength lay in its ability to admit local gods into its pantheon and in the vigor of its local Ritual Masters. Prominent among the latter during the Southern Song were practitioners of Thunder Rites, perhaps making effective use of gunpowder (the earliest record of the formula for gunpowder is dated 1044). With local cults proliferating in a veritable "deity explosion,"[8] gods and practitioners alike had to show that they could deliver.

Deities with sufficiently strong, enthusiastic, and influential support could hope for official recognition and an official title. A major asset of the Daoists that set them off from their competitors was their access to all the resources of a celestial bureaucracy as revealed in their sacred texts. But they did not have the field to themselves. Deeply rooted local gods promising their followers a more personal, nonbureaucratic relationship represented a countervailing trend studied by Robert Hymes, who has characterized Song religion as "the meeting point of a relatively few common assumptions, an extremely wide variety of usages, gods, rituals, and practitioners, and several organized or semi-organized bodies contending to impose order on the variety."[9]

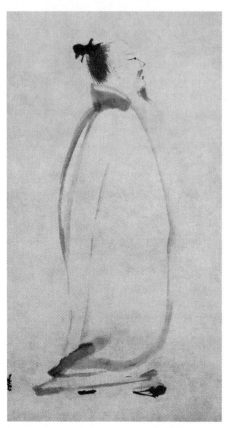

FIGURE 6.4 Liang Kai, *Li Bai*. Ink on paper, mid-thirteenth century, 31.10 in high. Chan-inspired paintings by artists such as Mu Qi and Liang Kai are mostly preserved in Japan where they continue to be influential and much appreciated. (© TNM Image Archives, http://TnmArchives.jp/.)

Some of these organizations were Buddhist, established not only by monks but also by lay leaders as Buddhism grew and flourished to such a degree that the Song has been called its "golden age." This certainly was true of Chan, which built on Tang doctrinal developments to create its own sectarian identity and developed strict and detailed monastic rules covering the entire day from how to wash your face and brush your teeth in the morning; to rules for bath, toilet, and meals; down to the directive to sleep on your right side. Chan temples became the most numerous in the land. Up north, Chan flourished, the Shaolin monastery was just one of a number of major Chan centers, and Xingxiu (1161–1246), "The Old Man of a Thousand Pines," who was also well versed in Confucianism, played a key role in the development of what remained the influential "Northern" school of Chan. Beyond China, Chan became a major presence in Korea and Japan.

The influence of Chan beyond the temple was manifold. Expressiveness and spontaneity were prized by Chan painters, some of whom worked in an untrammeled, spontaneous style developed in late-ninth-century Sichuan and best represented by Wang Mo ("ink-Wang"), who made pictures by splashing ink on silk, usually while drunk. Chan masters of this ink-splash technique dashed off their work, destroying what did not come out right, but never laboring over their art, confident that artistic inspiration, like religious enlightenment, comes in a flash. A favorite subject of Chan painters was a pair of Tang recluses wearing expressions of divine lunacy: Han Shan ("Cold Mountain"), who is famous for his poetry, and Shide, who worked in a monastery kitchen and is usually holding a broom. The finest Southern Song Chan painters were as unrestricted in subject matter as in style. For Mu Qi six persimmons could mirror the truth as faithfully as any portrait of the Buddha. Liang Kai's famous portrait of Li Bai (see Figure 6.4) suggests that he and the Tang poet were kindred spirits.

Along with Chan, a resurgent Tiantai flourished intellectually and institutionally. The prominence of Guanyin is reflected in gilded wooden figures of the Bodhisattva seated in a position of "royal ease," with one leg raised, supporting an arm. Housed in temples more delicate and refined than their Tang predecessors and now more generally capped by gracefully curved roofs, such figures were among the best products of the last phase of Buddhist art. Although not the center of focus, Guanyin is present too among the figures in the cliffs at Dazu in Siquan, just one of the places where indigenous and Tantric elements were combined into a unique local tradition. More broadly, belief in karma and the accumulation of merit came to be widely held throughout the culture.

The Confucian Revival

Confucian ceremonies, political ideals, and moral teachings had never been abandoned, but new circumstances gave the tradition new life. A major source of energy early on were advocates of literary and political reform affiliated with the *guwen* movement. Among those who turned to government, hoping to realize their ideals, were both Wang Anshi and his bitter opponent Sima Guang. Sima, rather than confining himself to a single dynasty, had the confidence and vision to do something not attempted since the Han: a study of virtually the whole of Chinese history (beginning where the *Zuo Zhuan,* a classic account of the period covered by the *Spring and Autumn Annals,* had left off). Sima's title, *A Comprehensive Mirror in Aid of Government,* reflects his focus on the state along with his conviction that an accurate account of the past is an indispensable guide for the present. Departing from precedent, he included in the finished work discussions of the discrepancies he had found in the sources and his reasons for choosing one version of an event over another. This approach was in keeping with a new widely shared spirit of rereading and rethinking old texts.

The examination system, along with the emphasis on correct understanding of tradition as a guide to politics and life, implied a commitment to education. Confucius himself had become a teacher when he failed in his search for a ruler to implement his ideas. Thus, it is no accident that the Confucian revival under the Song was accompanied by the burgeoning of schools: government schools during the Northern Song and private academies during the Southern Song. Many of these academies embraced ideas first advanced in the eleventh century but not prominent until the twelfth (see "Neo-Confucianism"). The growth of schools both stimulated and was stimulated by the spread of printing.

Poetry and Painting

Thanks to printing, a huge number of poems by more than 9000 Song authors survive. The poem quoted earlier is an example of five-character old-style verse. Many fine poems were written in the old forms including poems by Su Shi, a ver-

satile, open-spirited exponent of the centrality of cultural creativity. Su is also famous for expanding the song lyric (*ci*) form of poetry. Written to tunes, of which
only the titles now remain, it required great skill to fit the words to the music but
allowed unusual freedom in diction and used colloquial expressions. Actually Su
Shi's genius was not bound by any set form. Perhaps his most famous works are
two rhapsodies (*fu*) on the Red Cliff, site of a crucial battle fought during the
Three Kingdoms Period. Su also wrote many poems on friendship, drinking, and
nature. Like other Song poets he knew and loved the literature of the past. But he
also brought to it a critical spirit. For example, his view of the highly respected and
beloved Tang poet Meng Jiao was hardly shared by his contemporaries but will
surely strike a responsive chord in anyone who has ever labored over a poem only
to discover that the reward was not worth the effort:

> *Reading the Poetry of Meng Jiao—First of Two Poems*
> Night: reading Meng Jiao's poems,
> Characters fine as cow's hair.
> By the cold lamp, my eyes blur and swim.
> Good passages I rarely find—
> Lone flowers poking up through the mud—
> But more hard words than the *Odes* and *Li sao*—
> Jumbled rocks clogging the clear stream,
> Making rapids too swift for poling.
> My first impression is of eating little fishes—
> What you get's not worth the trouble;
> Or of boiling tiny mud crabs
> And ending up with empty claws.
> For refinement he might compete with monks
> But he'll never match his master Han Yu.
> Man's life is like morning dew,
> A flame eating up the oil night by night.
> Why should I strain my ears
> Listening to the squeaks of this autumn insect?
> Better lay aside the book
> And drink my cup of jade-white wine.[9]

Su Shi was at the center of a circle of talented friends devoted to poetry, calligraphy, and painting, the three arts of gentleman-scholars who frequently wrote
their poems on a painting, thus combining the three arts in a single work. Su himself saw a close relationship between poetry, "pictures without form," and paintings, "unspoken poems."[10] The bamboo branch attributed to Wen Tong and reproduced in Figure 6.5 illustrates what the painter can accomplish by employing
the ink and brush of the calligrapher. Bamboo was a favorite subject of painters
and poets. Sima Guang planted some in his famous "Garden of Solitary
Enjoyment" in Luoyang. Unfortunately this garden is long gone, but we have
Robert E. Harrist, Jr., to lead us through another eleventh-century garden.[11]

FIGURE 6.5 *A Broken Branch of Bamboo,* attributed to Wen Tong. Album leaf, ink on paper, 19.02 in × 12.20 in. (© National Palace Museum, Taiwan, Republic of China.) The analysis by Roger Goepper (*The Essence of Chinese Painting* [Boston: Boston Book and Art Shop, 1963], p. 134), is worth quoting in full:

> All the elements have been drawn with a single confident brush stroke: the sections of the stem and the branches with a firm and elastic writing brush (*ganbi*), the counter-pressure of whose springy tip can be felt in the hand; the leaves with a softer and limper brush (*shuibi*), which submits obediently to the slightest pressure of the hand. The interaction of the graphic forms resulting from these two techniques largely determines the general impression created by the painting, the individual elements becoming fused in a composition filled with tension and vitality. The diagonal upward movement of the stem is answered contrapuntally by the smaller twigs, while the sudden break diverts the thrust from the top left-hand corner and causes it to fade out into the largest blank space in the composition. At the same time this break introduces an element of the unexpected and exciting into the picture; it disturbs the harmonious bamboo and determines its fate, as they do with man. The fixed points of composition lie on the one hand in the knots of the stem, accentuated by small brush dashes, and on the other in the areas of radiation formed by the rhythmic play of the overlapping leaf spears.

FIGURE 6.6 Fan Kuan, *Traveling among Streams and Mountains.*
Hanging scroll, ink and light color on silk, 29.49 in × 51.02 in.
Impressive scope, strength, and dark tones have replaced the rich
colors, the clarity of line, and the decorative charm of earlier land-
scape paintings (compare Figure 5.9). (© National Palace Museum,
Taiwan, Republic of China.)

A new age evoked a new vision. The towering achievement of Song art was in landscape painting. Developing styles that first appeared during the Five Dynasties between Tang and Song, Song artists produced classic works. Fan Kuan (c. 960–c. 1030) sought to encompass the whole of nature in his work (see Figure 6.6). Here we can observe the classic Chinese perspective dividing the picture surface into three planes, one near and one distant, with the middle plane occupied by water or mist. Whereas nature in earlier paintings provided a setting for man, here man is reduced to his proper dimensions. A road invites the viewer to enter the painting and contemplate the grandeur of nature.

Fan was a northerner. In the South, masters like Dong Yuan (d. 962) and his disciple Juran (fl. c. 975) depicted the softer, more atmospheric mountainscapes of their region and founded another influential tradition. The difference between the southern and northern painters was not only a matter of tone and technique, but as Richard M. Barnhart has suggested of Dong Yuan, "The southern master appears to have wished to meditate upon the land, as a poet; the northern masters to dramatize it."[12]

The Southern Song (1127–1279)

Despite the deployment of catapults, flamethrowers, and incendiary devices made with gunpowder, the Song lost the North. The dynasty carried on under a son of Huizong known as Gaozong (r. 1127–1162), who was forced to flee from the Jurchen troops and take refuge on some islands off the southeast coast before the tide of war turned. In 1138 Gaozong designated Hangzhou as the "temporary capital," and a peace agreement with the Jin followed in 1142. The previous year had brought the death in prison of Yue Fei (1103–1141), one of China's most celebrated generals still today extolled as a hero who had paid for his patriotism with his life. Conversely, Qin Guei (1090–1155), the minister who engineered Yue's death and effected the peace, came to be despised as the prototype of the traitor. Later, iron statues representing Qin Guei and his wife in chains were placed on the grounds of Yue Fei's tomb beside Hangzhou's West Lake. In the past visitors expressed their contempt by spitting on the statues, but that is now prohibited.

In the treaty of 1142 the Song accepted the Huai River as its northern boundary, agreed to make annual payments to the Jin, and recognized the Jin as its superior. Nevertheless, relations between the two states remained uneasy. Fighting broke out again between 1161 and 1165 and again the dynasty was saved by its superior fleet, both at sea and in the Yangzi River where its maneuverable paddlewheel boats, ramming enemy vessels or using gunpowder missiles to incinerate them, carried the day. After a period of unfriendly coexistence, cold war again turned into active warfare from 1206 to 1208. This time the war came to an end only after the Song handed over to the Jin the severed head of the minister responsible for starting the war. The Jurchen state was gradually sinified during the twelfth century, adopting the examination system and other Chinese institutions, but this did not induce the Song to look any more kindly on its northern neighbor.

The Southern Song government was therefore by no means unhappy when the new Mongol power rose in the North to challenge the Jin. When the Mongols destroyed the Jin and occupied North China in 1234, the Song's situation became precarious. The dynasty held on for another 40 years, however, largely because of its maritime strength and the effectiveness of its mountain fortresses. When the end did come, it was hastened by naval treachery.

Southern Song Cities and Commerce

Politically and psychologically the loss of the North was a grave blow to the dynasty, but economically the loss was much less severe, because by this time a good two-thirds of China's population and wealth were in the South.

Trade accounted for much of this wealth. Commerce was facilitated by the use of paper money, a Chinese innovation that originated in Sichuan with the circulation of private certificates of deposit secured by funds placed in private shops. In the eleventh century, paper money was issued for the first time by the government. As long as these notes were adequately secured by goods or specie (hard cash) they worked well. However, the government could not resist the temptation to issue more paper money than it could back with solid reserves. When this became generally known, the value of the notes depreciated.

A large part of China's internal as well as foreign trade was waterborne, for it cost less to transport goods on rivers and canals than to cart them overland. China's oceangoing ships were large, capable of carrying several hundred men. They were navigated with the aid of the compass, a product of China's traditional expertise in magnetism. In other ways, too, the ships were technologically advanced. Their features included "watertight bulkheads, buoyancy chambers, bamboo fenders at the waterline, floating anchors to hold them steady during storms, axial rudders in place of steering oars, outrigger and leeboard devices, oars for use in calm weather, scoops for taking samples off the sea floor, sounding lines for determining the depth . . . , and small rockets propelled by gunpowder for self-defense."[13] Merchant ships could be converted to military use. The superiority of its navy was crucial to the Southern Song's military security.

The trading cities of the South were known for their prosperity, the fast pace of life, and the reputed frivolity and shamelessness of their inhabitants. The greatest city was Hangzhou. Situated between the Yangzi River (to which it was linked by canal) and the international ports of the southeast coast, it was a government and trade center, home of merchants and officials. Flanked by the Zhe River and the West Lake, Hangzhou was a city of bridges and canals. All kinds of merchandise, ranging from staples to luxury goods, were sold in the city. Olive, crab, ginger, water-chestnut, and orange dealers had their own guilds, as did cap makers, goldsmiths, and twine makers, among others. There were many medicine shops, among them The Ever Honest Pharmacy. The Lin Family Toothbrush Shop, Tong Family Candle Store, Niu Family Belt Store, and Xu Family Funerary Paper Shop were among the numerous family enterprises offering their wares. There were florists, fan shops, and bookstores and retailers selling pearls, jade, fine silk, and even rhinoceros hide. Among the amenities offered by the city were exquisite restaurants, tea houses, cabarets, and baths. Entertainment was also provided by a host of popular performers, chess masters, fortunetellers, acrobats, storytellers, and puppeteers as well as numerous practitioners of the world's oldest profession, ladies "highly proficient and accomplished in the use of endearments and caresses,"[14] according to Marco Polo, whose testimony on life in the city after the Mongol conquest when it was no longer the capital, is usually reliable if not necessarily based on personal observation. Outside the city, the surrounding hills with their Buddhist temples provided opportunities for pleasure excursions. A favorite pastime then as now was boating and partying on West Lake.

Quanzhou in Fujian now displaced Guangzhou (Canton) as the main port and became "the emporium of the world"[15] with a beautiful mosque to serve the Arab population and a skyline dominated by two pagodas decorated with scenes from the Ramayana, the Indian epic beloved throughout Indianized Southeast Asia. Until 1160 when monetary considerations prompted a change in policy, the government, which derived considerable revenue from foreign trade (through customs duties, licensing fees, sales and transit taxes, and so forth), encouraged overseas commerce by maintaining harbors and canals, building breakwaters, erecting beacons, operating warehouses, setting up hotels, and rewarding merchants who attracted foreign shipping to Chinese ports. Among the major imports were aromatics and drugs, textiles, minerals, and miscellaneous luxury items, and the primary exports included silks, metals (especially copper coins exported to Japan and found as far away as Somalia and Zanzibar), and ceramics. The export of the latter was actively encouraged by the government, and the discovery of Song shards not only throughout South and Southeast Asia but also in the Middle East and along the east coast of Africa attests to the wide popularity of Song products. This was the precursor of the later export trade that was to make the word *china* synonymous with *porcelain*.

Literary and Visual Arts

Song men and women were great collectors. One result was the scholarly compilation of several impressive compendia of historical and natural data. Another was Huizong's great palace art collection as well as the rare plants, birds, and animals in his magnificent and costly garden. But there were also much more modest private collections. Li Qingzhao (1094–c. 1152) has described how she and her husband used to enjoy their throve of old books and art, pawning some clothes to buy rubbings and fruit to enjoy together at home before war put an end to all that. Li's account is in prose, but she is best known for her poetry. Here she described the

FIGURE 6.7 Ma Yuan was known as "One Corner Ma" because of his tendency to concentrate his compositions in one corner. The scene of the scholar quietly contemplating and enjoying nature is charming but lacks the grandeur of Fan Kuan (see Figure 6.6).
(© National Palace Museum, Taiwan, Republic of China.)

fall festival held on the ninth day of the ninth month in a poem with allusions to her favorite poet, Tao Qian, allusions that her contemporaries, like the careful readers of our Chapter 4, would immediately recognize:

> The mists—thick clouds—sad all day long,
> The gold animal spurts incense from its head.
> Once more it's the Festival of Double Nine;
> On the jade pillow—through mesh bed curtain—
> The chill of midnight starts creeping through.
> At the eastern hedge I drink a cup after dusk;
> Furtive fragrances fill my sleeve.
> Don't say one can't be overwhelmed:
> When the west wind furls up the curtain,
> I'm more fragile than the yellow chrysanthemum.[16]

Other Southern Song poets wrote widely on themes too numerous to list but include eloquent complaints on the government's peace policy: "Stabled horses die of obesity; strings unstrung break on the bow."[17]

Painters who lived after the period of monumental masters such as Fan Kuan knew that the classical achievement could not be repeated. One solution was to paint a part of nature rather than the whole, for example, a branch to represent the tree. One who did this was Ma Yuan (c. 1160–c. 1225). Figure 6.7 shows a gentleman-scholar communing with nature. Ma was greatly appreciated in Japan, as was Xia Gui (c. 1190–1230).

FIGURE 6.8 Xia Gui, *A Pure and Remote View of Rivers and Mountains.* Section of hand-scroll, ink on paper, 18.27 in high. Many have imitated Xia's style, but very few were able to achieve the subtlety and strength of his brushwork animating the austerity of his composition. (© National Palace Museum, Taiwan, Republic of China.)

A Pure and Remote View of Rivers and Mountains (see Figure 6.8) is a masterpiece in which the artist made the most of the musicality of the hand-scroll as a temporal as well as visual medium.

Song ceramics also represent a classic achievement, combining the vigor of earlier pottery with the grace of later ware. As in painting, there were major differences between northern and southern styles, reflecting in this case not only different tastes and a varied clientele but also differences in the chemical composition of the clays used by potters. Song wares include stoneware and porcelain, vessels covered with a slip (clay coating) that has been carved away to produce a design, and vessels covered with enamel or decorated with a painting. Colors run from white and grays to black, as well as various hues from lavender to olive. Perhaps most prized is the celadon, blue-green ware often decorated with a crackle (network of fine cracks) formed by the glaze cooling more rapidly than the vessel (see p. 135). Some of this exquisite ware was made especially for the imperial household, and such pieces are fitting representatives of Song refinement and elegance.

"Neo-Confucianism"

It was the great strength of the new Confucianism that it was at once a creed that gave meaning to the life of the individual, an ideology supporting state and society, and a philosophy that provided a convincing framework for understanding the world. It conceived of the world as an organic whole and itself constituted an organic system in which each aspect reinforced the other in theory as well as in practice.

Education remained at the forefront. One of the most famous academies was the White Deer Grotto Academy, and it was primarily through private academies that the new way of thought was perpetuated. At the famous White Deer Grotto Academy, headed for a time by Zhu Xi (1130–1200), students were exposed to a heavy mixture of moral exhortation and scholarship so that they might emerge both virtuous and erudite. Like dedicated teachers everywhere, committed Confucians were forever pleading with their students to forget careerist considerations such as passing examinations and to concentrate on the serious business of learning and self-improvement.

The guidance of a mentor was believed to be extremely important, but for the sake of those who lived in remote places without teachers, Zhu Xi and Lu Zuqian (1137–1181) compiled *Reflections on Things at Hand* (*Jinsi lu*), an anthology that drew on the writings of the four Northern Song thinkers who came to be considered the founders of a new Confucian philosophy, Zhou Dunyi (1017–1073), the brothers Cheng Hao (1032–1085) and Cheng Yi (1033–1107), and Zhang Zai (1020–1077). *Reflections,* which became enormously influential in Korea and Japan as well as in China, deals with many matters of practical concern ranging from guidance on how to manage a family to advice on when to accept political office and when to decline. It includes discussions of political institutions and behavior. Its main emphasis, however, is on self-perfection, which alone makes all the rest possible.

The authors of *Reflections* carefully distinguished their teachings from those of Buddhism and Daoism and attacked the Buddha and Lao Zi. Yet, even the staunchest Confucian was not immune to the attractions of Chan, and interest in Daoism remained high. It is therefore not surprising that Song Confucians were influenced by these two traditions even as they sought to undermine them by creating the sophisticated philosophy often known in the West as "Neo-Confucianism" but not referred to by any one designation in China or East Asia generally.

The intellectual atmosphere was further enlivened by Confucians who rejected theoretical speculation and insisted that the true vocation of a scholar lay in concentrating on matters of practical statecraft. But by narrowing their intellectual focus, these thinkers also narrowed their appeal at a time when fewer men looked to the state for a solution of society's ills and their own careers. In contrast, many found Zhu Xi's classic formulation of Neo-Confucianism persuasive, and some accepted it as an identity that, to quote Peter K. Bol, "could provide social and moral guidance in their role as the elite of a local society relative to which they could be powerful, and it provided moral and political justification for their autonomy from a government relative to which they felt powerless."[18]

Zhu Xi's deep and broad impact did not come until after his death. Neither he nor his four Northern Song predecessors were accepted as orthodox in their own day. It was not until the second quarter of the thirteenth century that Zhu's teachings received official recognition and his commentaries on the *Four Books* were officially accepted. Of these four core texts, revered repositories of fundamental truth, only the *Analects* had been part of the Confucian cannon through the ages. The other three, *The Mencius, The Great Learning,* and *The Doctrine of the Mean* (the last two are chapters from the *Rites-Liji*), remained subjects of controversy for most of the Song Period.

It was characteristic of East Asian thinkers that they did not present their ideas in systematic treatises but as commentaries on the classics, in miscellaneous writings (including letters), and in conversations recorded by disciples. This made the study of their ideas very demanding but also encouraged successive generations of scholars to reinterpret texts in their own way. Neither in the Song nor later was Neo-Confucianism a monolithic philosophy.

Song thinkers, like earlier Chinese philosophers, found it congenial and fruitful to think in terms of complementary opposites, interacting polarities such as inner and outer, substance (*ti*) and function (*yong*), knowledge, and action. Perhaps they were particularly attracted to this mode of thought because it enabled them to make distinctions without doing violence to what they perceived to be an ultimate organic unity. In their metaphysics they naturally employed the ancient *yin* and *yang,* but more central to their thought was the conceptual pair *li* and *qi.*

This *li,* not to be confused with the term for rites written with a different character, is frequently translated as "principle" or "pattern." Because the Chinese word does not distinguish between singular and plural, *li* can also be understood as a network of principles. Indeed, the accepted Song etymology of the word was that it originally signified veins running through jade. Each individual *li* is part of the entire system, and in the philosophy of Cheng Yi and Zhu Xi, this system constitutes the underlying pattern of reality. In this view nothing can exist if there is no *li* for it. It is characteristic of the Confucian cast of mind that this applies as much to the realm of human conduct as it does to the physical world. The *li* of fatherhood has the same ontological status (order of being or order of reality) as the *li* for mountains. No distinction is made between the former, which is defined in moral terms, and the latter, for the world of moral action and that of physical objects is held to be one and the same. Both are comprehensible and equally "natural."

Qi, which we already encountered in our discussion of painting in Chapter 4, is an even more difficult word to render into English. It is the vital force and substance of which man and the universe are made. It is energy, but energy that occupies space. In its most refined form it occurs as a kind of rarefied ether, but condensed it becomes the most solid metal or rock. Zhu Xi envisioned the world as a sphere in constant rotation, with the heaviest *qi* held in the center by the centripetal force of the motion. *Qi* then becomes progressively lighter and thinner as one moves away from the center. This explains why the air at high altitude is thinner than that at sea level.

It was theoretically possible to construct a philosophy based on either concept. Zhang Zai based his theories entirely on *qi,* whereas Zhu Xi's contemporary Lu Jiuyuan (1139–1193) asserted that *li* alone exists. Cheng Yi and Zhu Xi, however, accepted both as irreducible entities, although *li* had logical and ontological (but not temporal) priority over *qi.* In Zhu Xi's system *li* was further identified with the Supreme Ultimate (*taiji*), which had formed the basis of Zhou Dunyi's metaphysics. In this way *li* was elevated to a level superior to *qi.* Nevertheless, in the actual world *li* never occurs without *qi*. This very important doctrine enabled the Song philosophers to accept Mencius's theory of the essential goodness of humankind and to explain man's frequent departures from that goodness: people were composed of good *li* and more or less impure *qi*. The ancient sages were born with perfectly pure *qi*: they were born perfect. But ordinary folk have to cope with more or less turgid *qi*: we must work to attain perfection.

The way for ordinary people to attain perfection is by truly grasping the *li*, but because these are found within everyone as well as out in the world, there was disagreement over the proper method of self-cultivation. Zhu Xi generally stressed the "investigation of things," by which he meant primarily the study of moral conduct and especially the timeless lessons contained in the classics. Consequently his school was associated with an emphasis on scholarly learning, even though it by no means ruled out more inner-directed endeavors such as silent meditation and reflection. Lu Jiuyuan, in contrast, foreshadowing the teachings of the major Ming dynasty philosopher Wang Yangming, stressed inner illumination. For him, without the reader's innate understanding, even the classics remain without meaning. The truth is within: he once went as far as to say, "The classics are all footnotes to me."

The Song philosophers gave the old concept of *ren* (humaneness) a new metaphysical dimension. Zhang Zai proclaimed, "All people are my brothers and sisters, and all things are my companions."[19] In keeping with this ideal was a new growth in secular charities. Meanwhile, high-minded moral seriousness, demands for vigilance against selfish desires, and ideal selflessness were repeatedly challenged by real life politics, by market forces that obeyed no moral laws, and by social change as people went about their daily affairs guided more by notions of decency than by moral perfection. This is borne out by the family-oriented *Precepts for Social Life* by Yuan Cai, who earned the highest examination degree in 1163.

Values and Gender

In Confucian theory widows should not remarry, but Song widows did so regularly, and if necessary went to court to protect their property rights. Similarly, theoretically women were not permitted to divorce their husbands, but in the Song, although the system still favored husbands, wives could initiate divorce and easily remarry. Li Qingchao, for one, remarried after being widowed, but when the marriage did not work out, she petitioned for divorce. Whether married, divorced, or widowed, women controlled the dowries they brought into the marriage and could use them as capital. This could amount to a considerable estate, because Song dowries were larger than those in the Tang, thereby compensating, as Robert Hymes suggests, for the decline of value of a bride's pedigree.[20] The stone portraits of two Song ladies in Figure 6.9 suggest the self-assured grace of women wealthy enough to patronize the Buddhist establishment.

FIGURE 6.9 Two Song ladies. Cave 165, Maijishan, Gansu. These portraits in stone convey something of the character of their subjects. The Buddhist caves at Maijishan have escaped much of the destruction seen at Longmen, Yungan, and other sites. Sculpture remained associated with religion, whereas painting could be religious or secular. (Courtesy of Michael Sullivan and Dominique Darbois.)

Although girls did not study for the examinations, they were not excluded from literacy. On the contrary, many families took joy and pride in a well-educated daughter or daughter-in-law. With men now admired for their learning, taste, and refinement rather than their martial qualities, there was a trend for elite women and men increasingly to resemble each other. At the same time, there was a countertrend to accentuate or even invent differences. This is apparent in the slender women that inhabit poetry and painting as well as in the development of women's medicine as a distinct field of specialization (there was no corresponding category of male medicine), emphasizing female vulnerability.

The most visible change in women's appearance was in their feet. The practice of footbinding probably originated among court dancers during the Five Dynasties Period and spread first to dancing courtesans and then among the Song upper classes. Under later dynasties it became prevalent among the elite and was also widely practiced in other social strata. It continued well into the twentieth century. Its purpose was to restrict the growth of the feet. The procedure may not have been fully developed in the Song, when the toes of young girls may have been bent upwards. But in its mature form, the feet of young female children were wrapped tightly in bandages about two inches wide and ten feet long. Over a period of time, the four toes of each foot were bent into the sole, and the sole and heel were brought as close together as possible. The great toe was left unbound. The result was thought to enhance a woman's grace and attractiveness. Footbinding was not part of a Confucian social program, but it was tolerated by a society supposedly governed by Confucian values.

The spread of footbinding suggests that the influence of courtesans on standards of feminine beauty reached deeply into elite society. The same was true of their song lyric poetry (*ci*), which circulated widely and was emulated by the wives and daughters of the elite to the consternation of moralists who would keep women focused on family and home. Cheng Yi reports of his mother that "she loved literature but did not engage in flowery composition. She considered it wrong for present-day women to pass around literary compositions, notes, and letters."[21] Instead, she set an example in running her family, kind but firm with servants and children. Female literacy was an asset to be used to educate the children.

Similarly the Neo-Confucians sought to channel, not suppress, women's managerial skills. The ideal was for wives to run the household, including the family's finances, leaving the husband free to pursue his studies and to deal with the outside world. This could be, and later was, interpreted literally to entail the seclusion of upper class women at home. That interpretation came later, but it roots are in the Song. The Neo-Confucian ideal also demanded the wife's total identification with her married family. First, women were praised for using their dowry for the sake of their new family; then efforts were made to change marriage and property laws, efforts that were to come to fruition during the Yuan.

The End

Among the reasons for the Southern Song's ability to sustain itself for a century and a half were the geographic defensibility and the prosperity of the South as well as the government's ability to command acceptance as the legitimate regime and to perform the traditional functions of government. However, it also suffered from internal ills: unstable imperial leadership (the first three emperors ended their reigns by abdicating), factional divisiveness in officialdom, a general decline in government effectiveness, and a lack of confidence in the government's ability to solve society's problems.

The government's monetary policies eventually produced rampant inflation, and a shrinking tax base resulted from the decline of small landholders and tax evasion by those who held much land. To deal with the latter situation, an ambitious land reform program was launched by Chief Councilor Jia Sidao (1213–1275) during the 1260s. Large landowners were required to sell to the government a portion of their holdings, which the government then managed itself. The economic gains thus realized, however, were counterbalanced by the disaffection of the wealthy and powerful at a time when the state required maximum unity against the Mongol threat.

The government had its troubles, but the dynasty continued to inspire loyal devotion to the end—and even beyond. Not only did men sacrifice their lives in its defense even after the cause was hopeless, but there were also others who remained loyal even after its demise. This was a new phenomenon in Chinese history, and, as with so many Song innovations, set a precedent for later ages.

Notes

1. F. W. Mote, *Imperial China, 900–1800* (Cambridge: Harvard Univ. Press, 1999), pp. 17–20.

2. Robert Hymes, in Denis Twitchett and John W. Chaffee, eds., *The Cambridge History of China, Vol. 4: Sung China* (forthcoming) (draft p. 126).

3. Alfreda Murck, *The Subtle Art of Dissent: Poetry and Painting in Song China* (Cambridge: Harvard Univ. Press, 2000).

4. Term coined by Paul J. Smith. Cf. his *Taxing Heaven's Storehouse: Horses Bureaucrats, and The Destruction of the Sichuan Tea Industry, 1074–1224* (Cambridge: Harvard Univ. Press, 1991).

5. Li Bozhong, "Was There a Fourteenth Century Turning Point? Population, Land, Technology, and Farm Management," in Paul J. Smith and Richard von Glahn, eds., *The Song-Yuan-Ming Transition in Chinese History* (Cambridge: Harvard Univ. Press, 2003), p. 156.

6. Qin Guan, in Kojiro Yoshikawa, *An Introduction to Sung Poetry*, trans. Burton Watson (Cambridge: Harvard Univ. Press, 1967), pp. 16–17.

7. Edward L. Davis, *Society and the Supernatural in Song China* (Honolulu: Univ. of Hawaii Press, 2001), p. 80.

8. Robert Hymes, op. cit. (draft p. 103).

9. Robert Hymes, *Way and Byway: Taoism, Local Religion, and Models of Divinity in Sung and Modern China* (Berekeley: Univ. of California Press, 2002), p. 21. Reprinted with permission.

10. Susan Bush, *The Chinese Literati on Painting: Su Shih (1037–1101) to Tung Ch'i-ch'ang (*1156–1636) (Cambridge: Harvard Univ. Press, 1971), p. 25.

11. Robert E. Harrist, Jr., *Paintings and Private Life in Eleventh-Century China: Mountain Villa by Li Gonglin* (Princeton: Princeton Univ. Press, 1998).

12. Richard M. Barnhart, "Tung Yiian," in Herbert Franke, ed., *Sung Biographies— Painters,* Münchener Ostasiatische Studien, Vol. 17 (Wiesbaden: Franz Steiner Verlag, 1976), p. 141.

13. Mark Elvin, *The Pattern of the Chinese Past* (Stanford: Stanford Univ. Press, 1973), p. 137.

14. R. E. Latham, trans., *The Travels of Marco Polo* (Baltimore: Penguin Books, 1958), p. 187.

15. Angela Schottenhammer, *The Emporium of the World: Maritime Quanzhou, 1000–1400* (Leiden: Brill, 2001).

16. Eugene Boyang, trans., in Kang-I Sun Chang and Haun Saussy, *Women Writers in Traditional China: An Anthology of Poetry and Criticism* (Stanford: Stanford Univ. Press, 1999), p. 94.

17. Liu Wu-chi, *An Introduction to Chinese Literature* (Bloomington: Indiana Univ. Press, 1966), p. 119.

18. Peter K. Bol, "Neo-Confucianism and Local Society, Twelfth to Sixteenth Century: A Case Study," in Smith and Glahn, *Song-Yuan-Ming Transition,* p. 245.

19. Wing-tsit Chan, *A Source Book in Chinese Philosophy* (Princeton: Princeton Univ. Press, 1963), p. 497.

20. Robert Hymes, in *Cambridge History of China,* Vol. 5 (forthcoming).

21. Wing-tit Chan, trans., *Reflections on Things at Hand: The Neo-Confucian Anthology compiled by Chu His and Lü Tsu-ch'ien* (New York: Columbia Univ. Press, 1967), pp. 180–81.

The Mongol Empire and the Yuan Dynasty

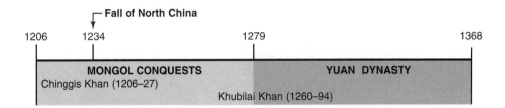

Fall of North China

| 1206 | 1234 | 1279 | 1368 |

| MONGOL CONQUESTS | YUAN DYNASTY |
Chinggis Khan (1206–27)
Khubilai Khan (1260–94)

The Mongols are famed as the world's foremost conquerors, creators of the largest empire in the history of the planet (see Figure 7.1). They established their supremacy over most of Eurasia, including Russia and Persia, all of Central Asia, China, and Korea. Mongol armies reached as far West as the Adriatic; in the East they took to ships to attack Japan and Java. Even those lands that, like Japan, preserved their independence were affected by the Mongol challenge. For a time, communication between East and West was facilitated by Mongol domination and encouragement of trade. But the Mongol territory was too vast, local cultures were too various and deeply rooted, and the centrifugal forces were too strong for the Mongol Empire to last very long. Ultimately the empire disintegrated, leaving a much disputed legacy.

Chinggis Khan: Founding of the Mongol Empire

Temujin, the future Chinggis Khan (c. 1167–1227), was the son of a Mongolian tribal chieftain. When his father was killed, the boy was forced to flee and spent a number of years wandering. Eventually he returned to his tribe and began his career as a world conqueror by avenging the murder of his father. Gradually he gained ascendancy in the hierarchy of tribal chiefs, forming a new nomadic federation in a process that gave rise to a new sense of Mongol ethnic identity that came to include not only those who had considered themselves Mongols earlier but also anyone who had been with Chinggis at this founding time.

Chinggis was almost forty by the time he established his leadership over all the Mongol tribes, which, at a great meeting held in 1206, recognized him as the supreme ruler, the Chinggis Khan. As supreme ruler he unified the tribes, organized them into a superb fighting force, and started them on the road to world conquest. Unifying the tribes was a difficult task because they were widely dispersed and also because the tribesmen were excellent fighters, jealous of their in-

169

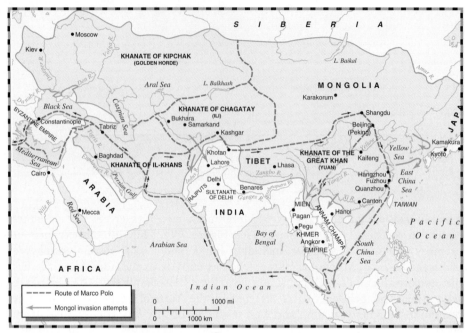

FIGURE 7.1 The Mongol Empire, 1294. ☯

dependence. It required great determination, political skill, knowledge of men, and manifest ability to lead and weld these tribal groups into a people. It also required ruthlessness, drive, military skill, and courage. Apparently Chinggis Khan had these qualities. He was able to obtain the support of the hardy tribesmen. Equally significant as a testament to his personal power was his ability to attract a following of *nökhör,* "companions," who, renouncing all other ties to clan or tribe, gave their patron their sole and complete loyalty. Many of Chinggis Khan's best generals were *nökhör.*

It does not detract from Chinggis Khan's personal achievement to note that more impersonal forces were also at work, inducing the Mongols to unify and attack the settled peoples who sometimes broke off trade vital to the steppe nomads. Particularly serious was a drop in climactic temperature that reduced the amount of grass available to feed the animals vital for Mongol subsistence.

Clans and tribes remained the basic units of Mongol organization, but at a higher level the people were also bound together by loyalty to the Great Khan and by a law code (*jasagh*) first promulgated in 1206 and later expanded. Also transcending tribal divisions was the army, organized on a decimal system in units of tens, hundreds, and thousands. An elite corps, which grew to 10,000 men, formed its core. At the height of the campaigns, the total army may have numbered nearly 130,000 men. It was joined in those campaigns by almost an equal number of non-Mongol warriors, the forces of other peoples who joined the Mongols after 1205 rather than attempt to resist the whirlwind.

The Mongol army was a superb force in its overall direction, organization, and the toughness and ability of its individual fighting men. These fighters lived in the saddle: they could even sleep on horseback while their horses marched. When necessary they withstood great privation and endured all kinds of hardship. They were able to cover enormous distances at great speed, changing mounts several times in the process. The Mongol horses too were very hardy, able to endure extremes of climate, and in winter to find food by digging it out from under the snow or stripping twigs and bark from trees. Moreover, on the command level, the Mongols achieved masterly feats of planning and carrying out their operations. Their enemies were defeated as much by the Mongols' rapid movements and the precise coordination of their far-flung armies as by their ferocity and superb tactical discipline.

Whatever the Mongols could not use they destroyed. That was the fate of cities that resisted: their women and children were enslaved, and the men were either killed or used as living shields in the next battle or assault on a city. Mongol brutality left terror in its wake. Even for Europeans, who lived in a far more military culture than that of China, the encounter with Mongol arms was an overwhelming experience that could only be explained in supernatural terms. According to *The Chronicle of Novgorod*, "God alone knows who they are and whence they came."[1] In Russia, Poland, and Hungary the merciless Mongols appeared as manifestations of God's wrath and their cruelties as acts of divine punishment meted out to sinners.

By the time of his death in 1227, Chinggis Khan had established Mongol supremacy in Central Asia, begun the offensive against Russia, destroyed the Xi Xia, fought the Jin, and captured Beijing. His headquarters remained in Mongolia with Karakorum as the capital, although it did not become a major city with a city wall and permanent buildings until 1235. This was the work of Ögödei (r. 1229–1241), who as Great Khan inherited the richest part of his father's empire. According to Mongol custom, however, other portions had been assigned to Ögödei's brothers, who ruled over three major khanates in Turkestan, Russia, and Persia.

The death of Chinggis Khan and the division of his patrimony did not diminish the momentum of Mongol conquests: in 1231 Mongol troops crossed the Yalu River into Korea and continued their advance in North China, taking Kaifeng in 1233 and Luoyang in 1234. Also in 1234 they completed the destruction of the Jin. In 1236–1238 they took Sichuan. The Dali kingdom fell in 1252–1253. Mongol armies were equally successful in the West, where they seized Kiev in 1240 and Baghdad in 1258. In 1241 a Mongol army was on the Adriatic. And then they turned back. Western Europe was spared, not because the Mongols were beaten in battle or awed by the Western defense—they had already thoroughly defeated the largest army in Europe by far, that of King Bela of Hungary— but by a command decision of the Mongol general. The exact reason for the turnabout is not known, but geography most likely played a role: the vast number of horses required by the Mongol army needed great open plains on which to graze.

The Mongols developed a courier system to link their empire; couriers could cover up to 200 miles a day. They also had a written language based on that of the

Uighurs. They were bound by the *jasagh* laws. Where complex political institutions existed, as in China and Persia, the Mongol laws were grafted on to the local culture, but the Mongols lacked a formalized system of succession as well as an organized political system capable of molding their vast and diverse conquests into a lasting unity.

Under Chinggis Khan's grandson Khubilai (1215–1294), who became Great Khan in 1260, the conquest of the Southern Song was completed in 1278. In 1264, early in his reign, Khubilai transferred the capital from Mongolia to Beijing, and in doing so tacitly relinquished the Mongol claim to rule the entire world. Once again the political balance of East Asia was dominated by China, although this time not by Chinese.

China under the Mongols: The Early Years (1211–1260)

Almost half a century passed between Chinggis Khan's first attack on territory traditionally Chinese (1211) and the beginning of Khubilai's reign. By the twelfth century the Jin had, through its examination system and other policies, developed strong claims that it, rather than the Southern Song, was the legitimate successor to the Northern Song, whose culture it did much to continue. As already noted, people living under the Jin also developed their own form of Daoism and contributed importantly to Buddhism. Unfortunately for the dynasty, the Mongol advance put an end to "High Jin,"[2] the forty years of peace from 1165 to 1206 that saw the dynasty's greatest achievements. The Mongol invasion of North China was a catastrophe for many ordinary farmers as well as for members of the elite such as Yuan Haowen, whose poems of "death and disorder" from 1233 to 1235 attest both to Jin literary sophistication and to the devastation of those years.

In their military operations against the Jin as well as the subsequent civil administration of North China, the Mongols made use of non-Mongols, particularly Khitan leaders who were traditionally hostile toward the Jin and also Chinese who felt no great loyalty toward the Jurchen. The services of such men were essential to the Mongols, operating as they were in unfamiliar terrain and outnumbered by their enemy. Indeed, the service of men of non-Mongol background was indispensable, as the Mongols themselves numbered only around 1 million people. Thus, non-Mongol military leaders were accepted as *nökhör* and granted the privileges that went with that status, including the receipt of lands to rule.

Among the non-Mongols in the service of the Khan, Yelü Chucai (1189–1243) was the most outstanding. As a sinicized Khitan of royal Liao lineage and a first-place examination graduate under the Jin, Yelü was well equipped to mediate between the Mongols and their Chinese subjects. Summoned to Mongolia by Chinggis Khan in 1218, he became influential as a court astrologer and is said to have played a role in the Mongol decision to stay out of India. But his real prominence came under Ögödei when he was able to persuade the Khan to reject the proposal by a group of Mongols that all the territory conquered in North China be turned into pasturage. This was a serious proposal consistent with the Mongol way of life and with the crucial need for great quantities of horses if the Mongols were to retain their power. Other nomadic peoples, most recently the Jurchen, although much less involved than the Mongols in maintaining power outside China, had pondered the same alternatives. In the end, Yelü's position prevailed. He persuaded the Khan, not by appealing to Chinese theories of government, but by demonstrating the profits to be gained through an orderly exploitation of a settled and productive population. Yelü was thereupon, in 1229, placed in charge of taxation and created a tax system staffed by civilian officials.

Rising eventually to highest office, he worked hard to fashion a centralized administration along Chinese lines but achieved only partial success. For example, he failed in his attempt to subject privileged non-Chinese in North China to the same taxes imposed on the Chinese population. He did obtain enactment of a census, but he could not dissuade Ögödei from granting lands to supporters, who were beyond the government's fiscal control. In this case his proposal would have affected Chinese as well as non-Chinese leaders whose self-interest was at stake. The division of China into large-scale and loosely controlled military commands continued throughout the Mongol period; these commands later evolved into the large provinces into which China was divided during the Ming and Qing.

Yelü rescued Chinese scholars from captivity and found positions for them, including posts as tutors to Mongol nobles, but always faced stiff opposition. Toward the end of his life he suffered increasing setbacks. Throughout his career he appealed to Mongol greed. In the end he was outbid by Central Asian merchants who argued that Yelü's centralized tax system was less lucrative than opening China to tax farming with the right to collect taxes going to the highest bidder. Any amount the contractor collected in excess of what he owed the government was his to keep. This arrangement appealed to the rapaciousness of both the government and the tax farmer and resulted in the most ruthless measures to exact ruinously high taxes. Despite Yelü's protests that this was a short-sighted policy harmful to the people who produced the wealth, in 1239 a Muslim businessman was granted the right to collect taxes in North China. At the time of Yelü Chucai's death in 1243, it looked as though his work was coming undone. He did not live to see how Khubilai Khan went about creating a Sino-Mongolian state.

Khubilai Khan and the Early Yuan

In 1271 Khubilai Khan (r. 1260–1294), following the transfer of the capital to Beijing, adopted Yuan ("The Origin") as a Chinese-style dynastic name, explaining in an edict that it is derived from the principle of "Great Origin" (*qianyuan*), the first hexagram of the *Changes*. Thereby the Yuan became the first dynasty named not after a place or the founder's original fiefdom but for a potent and auspicious idea. Chinese court ceremonials were adopted. Chinggis Khan now received a posthumous Chinese title (Taizu), and Khubilai himself appears in the Chinese histories under the name of Shizu. Previous khans had preferred to live among their herds and tents instead of taking up permanent residence in the capital and spent as much time hunting as they did looking after government operations. Khubilai, in contrast, spent most of his time in Beijing or in the summer capital at Shangdu in Inner Mongolia. He was careful to give at least an appearance of ruling in a Chinese manner while engaged in "a delicate balancing act between ruling the sedentary civilization of China and preserving the cultural identity and values of the Mongols."[3] Among measures designed to accomplish the latter were a prohibition against Mongols marrying Chinese, his own practice of taking only Mongol women into the palace, and a policy of discouraging Mongols from associating with Chinese. That he also saw himself as a universal ruler is indicated by an unsuccessful attempt to propagate a new alphabet that he hoped could become a universal script. On the other hand, he did not try to devise a uniform code of law applicable to all the different peoples under his rule, and the Yuan remained the only Chinese dynasty lacking such a code.

Khubilai's first priority was to make himself truly master of all China, completing the military conquest initiated by his grandfather and continued by Chinggis Khan's successors. The subjugation of the Southern Song was difficult, for resistance was stiff, and the Mongols had to learn new techniques to operate successfully in the South. They were finally victorious, assisted by the defection of much of the Song navy. When the Southern Song fell in 1279, the Mongols became the first nomadic conquerors to rule all of China (see Figure 7.1). By this time gunpowder warfare was well established. Mongol soldiers carried side arms resembling miniature cannons, whereas Yuan and Song ships fired bombards at each other.

The fall of Southern Song did not bring an end to warfare. Although Khubilai's empire was China based, his ambitions were not confined to China. He sent an expedition against Japan in 1274, and, after he was master of all of China, organized a second, more massive attack in 1281. Both attacks failed. Plans for a third attempt were never carried out. This was largely because in the 1280s Mongol forces were occupied with operations in Southeast Asia, where repeated attacks were made on Vietnam and Burma. In 1281 and again in 1292 the Khan's fleet attacked Java. These expeditions forced local rulers into ritual submission but did not expand the territory under actual Yuan control. At the same time Khubilai could not afford to neglect the inner Asian frontier, where he was repeatedly challenged by Ögödei's grandson, Khaidu. Khubilai and his successors concentrated on securing Mongolia. This they accomplished but at the cost of giving up their ambition to dominate Central Asia.

Within China a significant number of men remained loyal to the old dynasty, continued to employ Song terminology, and dreamed of a Song restoration while refusing to serve the new power. For their part, Mongols relegated southerners to the lowest category in their fourfold division of society along ethnic lines. Highest status was accorded to the Mongols. Next came persons with special status (*semuren*). These were Mongol allies, largely from Central Asia and the Near East, such as Turks, Persians, and Syrians. They played an important role in government financial administration, often served as managers for Mongol aristocrats, and enjoyed special privileges as financiers. Organized into special guilds, they financed the caravan trade and loaned out money at usurious rates. The third status group, although termed *hanren*, which usually means "Chinese," included all inhabitants of North China at the time of the Mongol conquest of the Jin: those of Khitan, Jurchen, or Korean family background as well as ethnic Chinese. Finally, at the bottom, were the 80 percent of the Chinese population who lived in the South, the *nanren* or "southerners," also referred to by the less-neutral term *manzi*, that is, "southern barbarians" even though the most cultured scholars lived in the South. The fourfold division of society was expressed in the recruitment and appointment of government officials, in the conduct of legal cases, and in taxation.

Most Chinese literati resigned themselves to the new order and accepted the Yuan as the recipient of the Heavenly Mandate, but others remained unreconciled even though Khubilai had placed Chinese Confucians in high advisory or educational posts and had shown himself so receptive to their advice that he even had his son and heir educated in the Confucian manner. The emperor was also a generous patron of Chinese arts and letters, but he refused to reinstitute the civil service examinations and continued to give top priority to expensive military campaigns. To avoid dependence on Chinese officials, Khubilai employed foreigners, including Muslims, Tibetans, Uighurs, and other Central Asians, and even men from the Far West such as the Persian astronomer Jamal al-Din and, quite probably, the Venetian Marco Polo.

Khubilai made a start in the reconstruction of the shattered economy of the North, but the South remained the main economic region. One policy that the Yuan adopted from their Jin and Song predecessors was the use of paper money. Concerned with not disrupting economic life, Khubilai even provided for conversion of Southern Song paper money into that of the Yuan and made paper money the sole legal currency. As long as the paper currency was well backed, this policy was a success despite the slow inflation that set in after 1280. In other areas too, including the rehabilitation and extension of the Grand Canal, Khubilai's regime accomplished much. He displayed an ability to learn and to adjust to new circumstances in administrative as well as in military matters. What he could not do was to construct a system that would run smoothly of itself, and, unfortunately for the dynasty, there was not to be another Khubilai Khan.

The Yuan Continued, 1294–1355

Although the Yuan accomplished more than traditionally hostile Chinese historians would later admit, it never achieved the strength and longevity of a major Chinese dynasty. Lacking a tradition of orderly succession, the dynasty was troubled by numerous succession disputes. During the 40 years after Khubilai's death, seven emperors came to the throne, often with accompanying bloodshed and murder. After 1328 men from the Mongolian steppe no longer played a major role in these struggles. Earlier, in 1307, the Mongolian homeland had been reduced to a province under civil administration. But the elimination of the steppe as a power base did not alleviate internal tensions. Nor was the dynasty able to devise a lasting formula for balancing the diverse elements in government and society.

Court politics were dominated by factionalism, which found expression in fluctuating government policies. Personnel policies were a particularly sensitive area. Not until 1313 was an imperial edict issued, reviving the civil service examinations based on the Confucian classics and the commentaries of Zhu Xi, as was to remain the case for the duration of the system. The first tests were given in 1315. Although the curriculum was a major concession to the Confucian literati, the system favored the Mongols and their non-Chinese allies, who were given simplified examinations. Even so, degree holders occupied less than 2 percent of government posts. Under these circumstances some Chinese, hungry for office, could not resist the temptation to assume non-Chinese names.

In 1335 Bayan (Chancellor from 1333 to 1340), as part of a program to restore the political system as it had operated under Khubilai Khan, obtained an imperial decree canceling the examinations. This was consistent with his policy of reinforcing ethnic separation and appointing officials on the basis of lineage and practical experience. He managed to cut costs, but gained the enmity of all who viewed the reinstitution of the examinations as a step toward the normalization of government and as an opportunity for personal advancement.

Bayan was overthrown by Toghtō (d. 1356), who served as Chancellor from 1340 to 1344 and again from 1349 to 1355. Toghtō revived the examination in 1342. Although degree holders enjoyed great prestige, the examinations did not regain the prominence they had enjoyed during the Song. Still worse from the Chinese scholar's point of view was the persistent Yuan policy of according military officials supremacy over civilian officials.

A major problem during the 1340s was the Yellow River, which broke its dikes, flooded, and, most disastrously, began to change its course away from its previous outlet south of the Shandong Peninsula. One part of the river now flowed north of the Shandong Peninsula; another emptied into the Grand Canal, putting it out of commission. Not only did this cause great dislocation and suffering to the inhabitants of the affected areas, but it also threatened the economic survival of the dynasty by interrupting shipments of grain from the South. The only alternative to the Grand Canal route was by sea, but the maritime route was in constant danger from an increasingly bold and assertive pirate, Fan Guozhen. Clearly a massive effort was required for the government to reestablish control over the river or over the sea route, and it lacked the resources to do both. Given the choice, Toghtō decided to concentrate on the more immediately threatening and more manageable inland problem. Furthermore, rather than settle for a superficial and temporary solution, he proposed the digging of a new channel for the Yellow River south of the Shandong Peninsula. Although his plan ran into political opposition, this great feat of hydraulic engineering was successfully carried out during Toghtō's second administration. Under the direction of a Chinese engineer it was completed with the labor of 150,000 civilians and 20,000 troops.

The Yellow River problem was solved, but the cost was high, for it strained to the utmost the economic resources of the government and the people. An excessive issue of inadequately backed paper money produced growing inflation, which added its toll to the hardships of the population already suffering from government exactions. In mid-century the government was beset by dire problems, but these were much more severe in the north than in the south.

The Economy

Recent demographic studies conclude that the population of China dropped by around 30 percent from 108 million in 1220 to 75 million in 1229, rose back to 87 million by 1252, but amounted to only 67 million in 1381. Although warfare accounts for much of the initial drop, factors that were out of government control also took their toll during "the calamitous fourteenth century," to use the title of Barbara Tuchman's famous book. As John Dardess reminds us, "from Iceland and England at one end of Eurasia to Japan at the other, societies were suffering plagues, famines, agricultural decline, depopulation, and civil upheaval. Few societies were spared at least some of these symptoms. China was spared none of them."[4] Global cooling produced harsh winters. Repeated floods and droughts in North China were also related to the severe weather. The epidemics of mid-century China, disasters China shared with the rest of Eurasia, probably were a consequence of the new ease of travel for disease as well as for people.

Like the Yellow River problem, these natural disasters affected everyone in the land but some more than others. Regional and local developments, such as the silting up or widening of a river, often governed the rise and fall of market/temple towns in the Southern Yangzi basin, which was much less hard hit than the North by the destruction wrought by warfare and nature. The Mongol conquerors did not disturb the class structure of South China, nor did they inflict permanent damage on the southern economy. There the ceramics and silk industries continued to flourish, and a new cotton industry also developed. (Cotton culture may have been borrowed from the aboriginal inhabitants of China's southern provinces; a species of cotton was cultivated in Western Yunnan by the third century C.E. However, cotton did not become important economically until the Yuan.)

In the Yangzi basin the spread of advanced farming techniques from the lowlands to the highlands as well as better techniques for drying fields, turning marshes into fertile farmland, were among the agricultural advances that linked the Yuan to the Song on the one hand and prepared the ground for what was to follow in the Ming on the other. Current research suggests that while the Southern Yangzi basin did not escape all harm, the fourteenth century was hardly calamitous for this vital region, which was confirmed as the most productive in the empire.

Society

Some Mongol social policies, such as creating hereditary families of artisans, appear to have had little lasting effect on Chinese social structure. But for the history of women and thus the family, this was a crucial period marked by numerous twists and turns as policies changed to take into account Mongol and Chinese views, which in certain cases and times strongly diverged, pulling in different directions, but in other cases pulled in the same directions.

A striking example of divergence is the levirate, practiced by the Mongols and other nomadic people, providing for men to inherit their brother's widows. It seems that this practice was well suited to life on the steppe, but it was regarded with abhorrence by the Chinese. Conversely, an example of convergence is the Mongol concern for having males as heads of household so that they would be available for military service, which was consistent with Neo-Confucian views on the priority of sons over daughters in inheritance. This entailed placing the wife's property under the jurisdiction of the family she married into. An official measure dated 1313 states:

> Regarding dowry lands and other goods that a woman brings into her marriage: henceforth if a woman who has once been married wishes to remarry, regardless of whether she is divorced while her first husband is alive or living as a widow after her husband has died, all the dowry property and other assets she originally brought into her marriage should be taken over by the family of her former husband. She is absolutely not permitted to take them away with herself, as was formerly done.[5]

This passage comes from a recent work by Bettine Birge, who goes on to point out that actual practice no doubt lagged behind changes in law. However, the direction of change was to be confirmed under the dynasties that succeeded the Yuan, and the actual situation of the majority of women did change.

Religion

The Mongol tolerance of foreigners also extended to foreign religions. The early khans liked to sponsor religious debates at their courts, and under the Mongols all religions were granted tax exemption. Nestorians and Muslims and Christians and Jews were welcome. Integral Perfection Daoism got a temporary boost after Qiu Chuji (d. 1227) visited Chinggis Khan in Central Asia, but in the end the intense competition for official patronage was won by the proponents of Tibetan Buddhism. After gaining the submission of Tibet, the Mongols used a prominent Tibetan abbot to rule on their behalf over this mountainous land, where the dominant religion was an amalgam of Indian Buddhism and the native Bon religion. Known as Lamaism, after the Tibetan word designating a monk, this religion was more sophisticated and universal than the native shamanism of the Mongols. The Mongol rulers were impressed by the Lamaist formulae and charms infused with magic power to cure or harm, and they were attracted to the Tibetan religion as a form of Buddhism practiced by a hardy, nonagricultural people like themselves. In 1260 a Mongol lama was established as State Preceptor, and in 1261 he was given responsibility for the entire Buddhist clergy. Khubilai's successor continued to favor Lamaism, and as a result of imperial munificence, there was a proliferation of Buddhist art. Much of this art showed Tibetan or Nepalese influence, but it never won the esteem of students of Chinese art. A very different expression of official favor took the form of an edict, issued in 1309, stipulating that anyone striking a lama would have his hand cut off and that an offender would lose his tongue for insulting a lama. However, the conversion to Lamaism of the Mongols who remained on the steppe did not take place until the sixteenth century.

Lamaism had little impact on the Chinese population whose religious life and institutions showed a great deal of continuity with the past. Shanqi Daoism continued to be strong on Mt. Mao, whereas another sect claimed succession from the Celestial Masters. Pure Land Buddhism had a vast following, and Chan remained influential, beginning with Yelü Chucai, who turned to Chan after the fall of the Jin. During a period of monastic training under Xingxiu, "The Old Man of a Thousand Pines," Yelü acquired a profound knowledge of Chan.

Many people belonged to the lay Buddhist societies that had developed under the Southern Song. As summarized by Daniel Overmyer,

> By the Yuan period these sects were characterized by predominantly lay membership and leadership, hierarchical organization, active proselytism, congregational rituals, possession of their own scriptures in the vernacular, and mutual economic support.[6]

The southern Yangzi basin was an area of vigorous religious and economic activity. There Buddhist temples displayed their power to attract people and wealth and thus stimulated as well as participated in the growth of towns, centers of religion and commerce.

Cultural and Intellectual Life

Although some earnest scholars saw it as their mission to promote the Way by serving (and civilizing) the Mongols, others found withdrawal from active politics morally preferable and the demands of study and/or self-cultivation more compelling and fulfilling. Private academies with their Neo-Confucian curriculum offered an attractive alternative to government service, as did local activism. Followers of Zhu Xi drew confidence from their claim to be continuing a tradition that Zhu Xi had firmly rooted in the work of the ancient sages and that provided ample food for thought about issues such as the proper balance between internal moral cultivation and scholarly study.

A local tradition that was to have great influence on the Ming founder was that of Jinhua (Wuzhou), 125 miles south of Hangzhou, where Neo-Confucians found room for the appreciation of literature, on the one hand, and practical considerations of governance and reform on the other—two strands that had at times appeared as alternatives to rather than as elements within Neo-Confucianism. Most significantly, the leaders of this movement "used the Neo-Confucian style of self-cultivation to define a style of leadership that valued moral independence, individual responsibility and scholarly authority."[7]

The South remained the center of intellectual life, but the North also contributed in many ways. For example, the great mathematician Zhu Shijie drew on both northern and southern mathematical traditions. His *Introduction to Mathematics,* although long lost in China, became very influential in Japan, but his stature as not only the Yuan's but also China's leading algebraist is based on *Mirror of the Four Elements* (preface 1303), a book nonetheless remarkable for being long neglected. Little is known of Zhu's life other than that he came from the North and taught in Yangzhou around 1300, but the preface to his book suggests that he had quite a following and why:

> People come like clouds from the four quarters to meet at his gate in order to learn from him. . . . By the aid of geometrical figures he explains the relations of heaven, earth, men and things (technical terms for the algebraic notation). . . . By moving the expressions upward and downward, and from side to side, by advancing and retiring, alternating and connecting, by changing, dividing, and multiplying, by assuming the unreal for the real and using the imaginary for the true, by employing different signs for positive and negative, by keeping some and eliminating others and then changing the positions of the counting rods, by attacking from the front or from one side, as show in the four examples—he finally succeeds in working out the equations and the roots in a profound yet natural manner. . . .[8]

Zhu would probably have been a mathematician under any circumstances, but other talented men, who in more normal times would have taken up a political career, now found an outlet in poetry and painting. Yuan paintings often contain an element of self-portraiture, although rarely was this as explicit as in *Emaciated Horse* (Figure 7.2) by the Song loyalist Gong Kai (1222–1307), who belonged to the generation that experienced the change of dynasties. His painting expresses the self-image of the Chinese scholars who found themselves condemned to live in a world that did not respect their talents or prize their values; a world in which, as indicated in the poem Gong added to his painting, the stables of the former dynasty remained empty. The horse, long a symbol of the scholar-official, was an especially fitting symbol for the neglected Confucian living under a conqueror who prided himself on his horsemanship. The very gauntness of Gong's haggard horse brings out the essential strength of its splendid physique. To those who understood its meaning, the painting was an eloquent, proud, and poignant statement of a bitter shared fate.

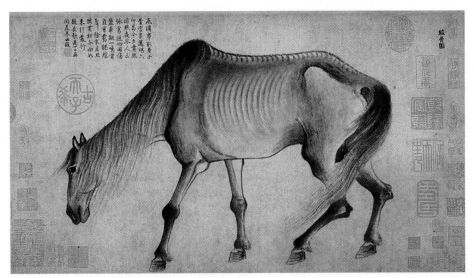

FIGURE 7.2 Gong Kai, *Emaciated Horse*. Hand-scroll, ink on paper, 22.44 in × 11.81 in. The very gauntness of Gong's haggard horse brings out the essential strength of its splendid physique. (© Abe Collection, Osaka Municipal Museum of Fine Arts.)

The uncertain times prompted a good number of educated men to make a living by pursuing occupations that brought them into close daily contact with ordinary, common people. Some became doctors, others took up fortune-telling, and still others turned to the theater for their livelihood. Great dramas were produced as well as powerful paintings.

"Northern" Drama

The performance arts had a long history in China. Early shamanistic religious dances, performances of music and acting staged for the amusement of the imperial court; "ballets" such as the Tang poet Bo Juyi's favorite, *Rainbow Skirts and Feather Jackets;* and possibly Indian influences form part of the background of Chinese drama that first emerged during the Song and reached its classic form during the Yuan. Equally important to the emergence of mature Yuan music drama was the heritage of popular entertainment, including the various theatricals staged for the benefit of the inhabitants of Song Kaifeng and Hangzhou (both of which had thriving theater districts), featuring not only performances by live actors but also puppet shows, acrobats, and shadow plays, genres with their own histories. In the puppet theater some puppets were on strings, others were on sticks, still others were controlled by explosive charges, and some productions featured "live puppets," that is, children manipulated by a "puppeteer." In the shadow plays, the audience observed silhouettes of figures manipulated behind a screen and in front of lights.

Among the precursors of the Yuan drama, none are more important than the storytellers who had enlivened the Song urban scene. In Song Hangzhou they were numerous enough to form "guilds." Set up in their stalls, they recited their stories, sometimes to the accompaniment of musical instruments. Each man had his specialty: realistic stories, stories of ghosts and the miraculous, religious tales, or stories based on historical episodes. Their art consisted not of simply relating an old story but making it come vividly alive by dramatic modulations of the voice and other dramatic devices. Cyril Birch tells of a fairly recent practitioner of the art who "in one breath could produce seven distinct sounds to represent in realistic fashion the screams of a pig in the successive stages of its slaughter."[9] Thus, the development of the theater did not inhibit the continuing flourishing of the art of the storyteller, but this art did leave its mark on the formal conventions not only of the theater but also of the novel, and it influenced the content as well as the form of both of these popular genres.

Chinese drama always involved music and never lost its character as a performance art, although in the Yuan northern performance and southern literary traditions converged to produce the written opus that came to define the genre after undergoing considerable editing, in the course of which much was lost:

> The taming of a ragged physical format, the regularization of shape and style, was paralleled by the suppression of the equally chaotic and unbounded world the text represented. In a harnessing of both behavior and presentation, regicide, forced abdication, bloody retribution, and unleashed sexual desire and predation were winnowed out, just as miswritten characters or misunderstood passages were rewritten.[10]

The plots of many of the plays still extant are based on earlier materials. Historical episodes such as the marriage of the Han palace beauty Wang Zhaojun to a Xiongnu chieftain; the political and military ploys devised by Zhuge Liang and his contemporaries of the Three Kingdom Period; the tragedy brought on by East Asia's most famed femme fatale, Yang Gueifei; the story of Xuanzang's pilgrimage to India; and other historical and semihistorical events provided the Yuan dramatists with some of their most effective and popular themes. And the plays for their part did much to fix in the popular mind colorful, larger-than-life images of these personages, creations of the poetic imagination embellishing the more prosaic historical accounts.

Theatergoers also enjoyed dramatic renditions of old love stories, such as that of the beautiful Yingying and a student named Zhang recounted in the celebrated thirteenth-century play *The Romance of the Western Chamber* by Wang Shifu. In adapting the old tale to the stage, Wang did not hesitate to rework his materials for greater theatrical and literary effect. Thus, the play makes skillful use of Yingying's mother's refusal to honor her promise to marry her daughter to whomever would rescue them when they are surrounded by rebels. Yingying, already greatly attracted to the young rescuer, now gives him her heart. And the injustice of the mother's act also transforms Nurse Huaining from an obstacle into a highly resourceful ally. To please his audience, the playwright departs from the Tang version of the story and has the drama end with the couple overcoming all obstacles to their happiness, including Yingying's mother. After Zhang passes his examinations, they are united in marriage. Love triumphs in the end. This happy resolution is characteristic of the genre, for these plays were designed to appeal to an audience not only of connoisseurs but also of ordinary people with little or no formal education, who desired happy endings.

The repertoire of the Yuan theater included many plays expressing a longing for justice. Some featured that model of official rectitude and wisdom Judge Bao (based on a real official, Bao Zheng [999–1062], a champion of justice who repeatedly uncovers even the most ingenious deceptions of the wicked. Prominent among the villains of such plays are greedy and unscrupulous officials who subvert the moral order they are theoretically committed to uphold. Among the heroes are Robin Hood-like figures, outlaws who have right on their side even as they defy the state and its laws. (Many of these heroes also appear in the Ming novel *The Water Margin,* see Chapter 8). No doubt many members of the audience derived vicarious pleasure from witnessing the punishment of venal and corrupt officials resembling those who in real life went uncorrected. The plays do not deal with contemporary events in any obvious way nor do they directly cast aspersions on the regime. Yet one wonders what a Mongol spectator would have made of the scene in *Autumn in the Palace of Han,* in which the playwright described the hardships facing Wang Zhaojun among the "barbarians" when she will have only "tasteless salted flesh" to eat and for drink "clabbered milk and gruel."[11]

The plays were written for standard actors' roles: leading man, leading lady, villain, and so on. The characters too can be classified into easily recognizable types such as the faithful lovers of *The Romance of the Western Chamber,* the corrupt officials and wise judges of the courtroom dramas, the uncouth but virtuous outlaws, and the beautiful, talented, and strong-minded courtesans. Most plays consisted of four acts between which short interludes, or "wedges," could be inserted. Because stage props were few, characters regularly made speeches of self-identification. The playwrights also used occasional recapitulations, carryovers from the tradition of the storyteller.

Music played an important part in the theater. The songs or song sequences in each act were in a single mode or key. The lute and zither were the standard instruments of the Yuan northern drama. In contrast to the mellow, refined music of the southern drama that reached its height under the Ming, the Yuan sound was vigorous and spirited. The Yuan drama's roots in the tradition of oral narrative are also revealed in the assignment of all arias to a single performer. Thus, in *Autumn in the Palace of Han,* only the emperor sings.

The products of the Yuan playwright frequently achieved high literary excellence. Dialogue written in the spoken language of the time lent an earthy freshness to texts, which at times included bawdy vulgarisms that no respectable Confucian scholar of later times would have allowed to flow from his brush. Such language contributed to the bad repute in which the Yuan drama was held in polite circles under later dynasties, until it was appreciatively rediscovered in the twentieth century. What was valued by the critics were the plays' poetic passages, particularly the lyric songs (*sanju*), which rank with other major forms of Chinese poetry in their technical intricacy, musical subtlety, and employment of various poetic devices, including the effective use of imagery. Just as connoisseurs judged paintings by the quality of their brushwork, critics focused on the merits of the poetry in the plays. Thus, a fifteenth-century critic praised the poetry of Ma Zhiyuan, author of *Autumn in the Palace of Han,* as resembling "a phoenix gliding and singing in the highest clouds."[12]

The Romance of the Western Chamber is beloved for its poetry. In it Yingying herself is deeply moved when Zhang sings to her of love, and "word follows word like the endless dripping of a water-clock."[13] Here Zhang's song was accompanied by his zither, but the *sanju* were sung without accompaniment. In the great plays the poetry is an integral part of the work, contributing to dramatic development. Thus, the recurrent image of the moon, which appears more than fifty times in the poetry of *The Romance of the Western Chamber,* helps to give the drama unity and depth. It is present, of course, when after a long courtship, the lovers are united. Then, "the bright moon, like water, floods the pavilion and terrace."[14]

The lovers have to suffer through a long period of separation and uncertainty before their union is made permanent at last, but they are fitting representatives of an essentially optimistic and life-affirming theater that combined high art with wide appeal to all classes.

Painting

In contrast to the theater, in which individuals from all kinds of backgrounds participated and which had something for everyone, elite painting was a much more esoteric pursuit. But whereas literary men later disdained the drama as plebeian, the achievements of the great Yuan painters were admired by all later connoisseurs.

The distinction between the professional who sells his wares to the aesthetically naive and the amateur who paints for himself and his friends did not originate in the Yuan but was confirmed by those critical of the taste of the Mongol court. Professional artists continued to take pride in the perfection of their techniques and the excellence of their craftsmanship. Gentlemen-amateurs, no less serious about their art, found in brush and ink a vehicle for self-expression and for the cultivation of self as in Gong Kai's horse.

The most famous Yuan horse painter was also the outstanding exception to the rule that the gentleman-artist avoided the imperial stable. Zhao Mengfu (1254–1322) held high office under the Mongols and paid the price in lost friendships and inner conflict. Later Chinese scholars, although not approving of his career, were compelled to recognize the force of his genius as a major painter and one of China's truly great calligraphers. Indeed, his paintings of horses were so prized that forgeries abound. Zhao's work is illustrated here not by a horse but by a landscape painting (see Figure 7.3), which exemplifies a deliberate archaism that appealed to the Yuan literati.

As is apparent in *Autumn Colors on the Qiao and Hua Mountains,* Zhao's archaism demanded the complete rejection of the aesthetics of his immediate pre-

FIGURE 7.3 Zhao Mengfu. *Autumn Colors on the Qiao and Hua Mountains.* Hand-scroll, ink and colors on paper, dated 1296, 36.6 in × 11.18 in. Here Zhao has discarded developments in perspective and ignored size relationships in his attempt to recapture an earlier noble simplicity. (© National Palace Museum, Taiwan, Republic of China.)

decessors. No trace can be found here of the styles of Ma Yuan and Xia Guei, and there is a deliberate, consistent avoidance of prettiness. Zhao and his contemporaries, somewhat like the Pre-Raphaelites of nineteenth-century England, tried to return to the rugged honesty of an earlier age and to unlearn the lessons of the classic period of their art. The Chinese painters, however, were more ready than the Pre-Raphaelites to sacrifice surface beauty for the sake of attaining what Zhao called "a sense of antiquity" (*guyi*). They also differed in that they conceived of their art in terms of calligraphy: both painting and calligraphy served the purpose of writing down on paper or silk the ideas the gentlemen had in their minds. In the two paintings reproduced in Figures 7.2 and 7.3, the unused space does not serve as a horizon, nor does it contribute to the overall composition. Therefore, the use of this space for calligraphy does not disturb the painting. In a sense the painting, too, is calligraphy just as, in another sense, the calligraphy is painting.

Now, as earlier, calligraphy was prized as a revelation of the lofty character of its cultivated practitioner, an emphasis that made for variety in style in painting as in writing. The master painters of the Yuan did not share a uniform style nor did individual artists necessarily limit themselves to a single style. There is, for example, a famous anecdote, recorded in the late Ming, concerning the painter Ni Zan (1301–1374), who one night, while inebriated, painted bamboos that a friend next day criticized for not looking like bamboos. Exemplifying the Yuan literati painter's

FIGURE 7.4 Ni Zan, *The Rongxi Studio.*
Hanging scroll, ink on paper, dated 1372, 13.98
in × 29.41 in. This painting exemplifies Ni Zan's
calligraphic talents and the cool restraint of his
unpeopled landscapes. (© National Palace
Museum, Taiwan, Republic of China.)

disdain for representation, Ni laughed and replied, "Ah, but a *total* lack of resemblance is hard to achieve!"[15] Yet, Ni often painted ordinary bamboos. Bamboos, which, like the gentleman-scholar, bend before the wind but do not break, were a favorite subject of the literati painters, who could also find Daoist significance in the fact that the center of this plant is hollow, that is, empty. In the painting shown in Figure 7.4, Ni, like Zhao Mengfu, has avoided all painterly tricks. He achieved a calm, bland poetry. This aesthetic of the cool and clean is also found in the white and in the blue-and-white ceramics of the age.

At the opposite stylistic pole from Ni Zan are the paintings of Wang Meng (c. 1309–1385), especially his later work (see Figure 7.5). Whereas Ni Zan works in monochrome, Wang delights in bright colors. In the painting of Ni, nature is stable and empty, but Wang fills his space with natural forces surging around the abodes of his recluses and threatening to burst forth beyond the borders of the painting. Perhaps this was an appropriate statement for a period when social and political forces in China were about to burst through the Yuan dynastic framework.

In considering the cultural achievements of the Yuan, it is worth noting that foreign influence did not enter the world of the literati painters. Conversely, no appreciation or even an awareness of their art is to be found in the literature of the European visitors, such as Marco Polo and his successors of the fourteenth century. Although there was a Catholic archbishop in Beijing and relations across the great Eurasian land mass were often cordial, these relations had a low priority on both sides of the world, for the distances were enormous, and Europe as well as China was faced with far more immediate challenges and opportunities in politics, economics, art, and thought closer to home. In many respects China was ahead of Europe at the time. Literati painting of the type prized in the Yuan was not even considered worthy of note by Europeans before the nineteenth century, and it was not until the twentieth century that people in the West learned how to see and value these paintings.

Rebellions and Disintegration

By the middle of the fourteenth century the dynasty was threatened by popular rebellions as well as by the growing independence of its own regional commanders. People caught in a seemingly hopeless situation increasingly put their hopes in charismatic leaders and

FIGURE 7.5 Wang Meng, *The Forest Grotto and Juqu.* Hanging scroll, ink and colors on paper, 16.73 in × 27.05 in. This painting employs "unraveled hemp fiber" and S-shaped strokes. (© National Palace Museum, Taiwan, Republic of China.)

messianic teachings. Under a leader who claimed descent from the Song imperial line, the White Lotus Society attracted the miserable: dismissed clerks, deserters from the Yellow River project, peddlers, outlaws, the idle, and the displaced. Known as the Red Turbans after their headdresses, these people turned to open rebellion in 1352, and for the next three years much of Central and South China was lost to the Yuan. Under Toghtō's leadership, the dynasty was able for the time being to put down this challenge, ultimately employing forces composed mainly of Chinese soldiers.

Because of court politics, Toghtō was dismissed in 1355, ousted just as he was conducting what promised to be a siege of a town on the Grand Canal seized by a former salt smuggler who, in leading a major rebellion, had seized a town on the Grand Canal and proclaimed a new dynasty. Under Toghtō, the government maintained control over its military forces by taking great care in the making of appointments, by separating command and supply functions, and by generally exercising central leadership, but after his fall no other political strongman appeared to prevent the formation of regional power centers.

Between renewed rebellions and concessions made by the government to various commanders supposedly defending it, the central government itself deteriorated to the point where it was just one more local power. During the last twelve years of the Yuan, the issue was not so much the survival of the dynasty as the determination of its successor. The dynasty had the misfortune to rule during a time when the floods, plagues, and famines that tormented the people and fueled rebellion were beyond the powers of government control. John Dardess concluded,

> The various late Yuan regimes all tried seriously to alleviate these disasters. None ignored them. Yuan medical and food relief efforts, by all appearances, were both conscientious and sophisticated. . . . It might well be that the long term cumulative effects of such repeated natural calamities were too great for any government to handle and that if normal conditions had prevailed in China, the Yuan dynasty might have lasted much longer than it did.[16]

As it turned out, the future belonged neither to the regional commanders nor to the rebel Song regime in the North, but to an organization led by Zhu Yuanzhang (1328–1398) in the South. Zhu had been born into a poor family and as a youth served as a novice in a Buddhist monastery. Later he became a beggar and eventually was drawn into the Red Turbans, where he rose to become a military commander. After the defeat of the Red Turbans, he became a leader of his own rebel organization. In contrast to the Red Turbans, who had directed their animosity as much against local landlords as against the dynasty, Zhu undertook reconciliation of the local elite. By abandoning the messianic radicalism of the earlier rebels and by demonstrating his intention to reconstruct the traditional kind of imperial government, he was able to gain valuable support among the gentry. Although some of the Chinese elite remained faithful to the Yuan and one of the most valiant and loyal defenders of the dynasty was a Chinese general, Zhu Yuanzhang could not be stopped. By 1368 it was all over: the Mongol court fled to Mongolia, and a new dynasty, the Ming, was established with its capital at Nanjing. Early in his reign Zhu Yuanzhang, known posthumously as Taizu, issued an order proscribing unorthodox religious sects, foremost among them the same White Lotus sect that had inspired his own campaign to power.

Although traditionally they had a bad reputation, the Mongols accomplished the reintegration of the North and the integration of Yunnan into the Chinese body politic and allowed the South Yangzi basin to continue its economic development. The effect of the Mongol period on Chinese political culture is more complex: scholars have looked to this period to explain the contrast between the rather benign government of the Song and the more authoritarian rule of the Ming. The Mongols had set an example of strong imperial rule and, in their declining years, had provided a lesson of what could happen in the absence of strong central direction. The lesson was not lost on the Ming founder.

Notes

1. R. Mitchell and N. Forbes, trans., *The Chronicle of Novgorod 1016–1471,* 3rd Series, Vol. 25 (London: Camden Society, 1914), p. 64.

2. Hoyt C. Tillman and Stephen H. West, *China under Jurchen Rule: Essays on Chin Intellectual and Cultural History* (Albany: State Univ. of New York Press, 1995), p. 4.

3. Morris Rossabi, *Khubilai Khan: His Life and Times* (Berkeley: Univ. of California Press, 1987), p. 115.

4. John W. Dardess, in Herbert Franke and Denis Twitchett, *The Cambridge History of China,* Vol. 6 (Cambridge: Cambridge Univ. Press, 1994), p. 385.

5. Bettine Birge, "Women and Confucianism from Song to Ming: The Institution of Patrilineality," in Paul J. Smith and Richard von Glahn, eds., *The Song-Yuan-Ming Transition in Chinese History* (Cambridge: Harvard Univ. Press, 2003), p. 235.

6. Daniel Overmyer, "Chinese Religion— An Overview" in Mircea Eliade, ed., *The Encyclopedia of Religion,* Vol. 3 (New York: Macmillan, 1987), p. 282.

7. Peter Bol, "Neo-Confucianism and Local Society, Twelfth to Sixteenth Century: A Case Study," in Smith and von Glahn, pp. 166–67.

8. Joseph Needham, *Science and Civilization in China,* Vol. 10: *Mathematics and the Sciences of the Heavens and the Earth* (Cambridge: Cambridge Univ. Press, 1959), p. 47.

9. Cyril Birch, trans., *Stories from a Ming Collection: The Art of the Chinese Story-Teller* (New York: Grove Press, 1958), pp. 10–11.

10. Stephen W. West, "Texts and Ideology: Ming Editors of Northern Drama," in Smith and von Glahn, pp. 329–30.

11. Cyril Birch, ed., *Anthology of Chinese Literature,* Vol. 1 (New York: Grove Press, 1965), p. 483.

12. Chung-wen Shih, *The Golden Age of Chinese Drama: Yuan Tsa-chü* (Princeton: Princeton Univ. Press, 1976), p. 160.

13. Shih, *The Golden Age of Chinese Drama,* p. 192.

14. Shih, *The Golden Age of Chinese Drama,* p. 159.

15. James Cahill, *Hills Beyond a River: Chinese Painting of the Yüan Dynasty, 1279–1368* (New York: Weatherhill, 1976), p. 175.

16. Dardess, *The Cambridge History of China,* pp. 386–87.

8

The Ming Dynasty, 1368–1644

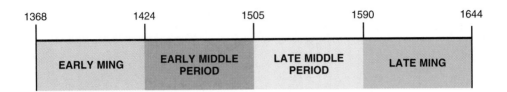

1368	1424	1505	1590	1644
EARLY MING	EARLY MIDDLE PERIOD	LATE MIDDLE PERIOD	LATE MING	

The Ming, the last native Chinese dynasty, reincorporated northern territories separated from the rest of China for almost two and a half centuries and for a short time even reestablished rule over what is now northern Vietnam. The stability of the regime and the general prosperity of the people, as well as notable achievements in literature, philosophy, and the arts, demonstrated the continued vitality of the Chinese tradition and its capacity for growth and transformation. When, toward the end of the Ming period, the first modern Europeans arrived in China, they found much to admire.

The Early Ming (1368–1424)

The Early Ming was a period of vigorous Chinese military resurgence abroad and assertion of imperial autocracy at home. The dynastic founder, Zhu Yuanzhang or Taizu (see Table 8.1), ruled for 30 years (1368–1398) and left a deep imprint on the reigns that followed. For his era name he chose Hongwu, "grand military achievement," and his military accomplishments were certainly impressive.

By the end of his reign, the Ming controlled all China, dominated the frontier region from Hami, in Xinjiang, north through Inner Mongolia and into northern Manchuria, and, beyond that, had won the adherence of Korea as well as various Central and Southeast Asian states that sent tribute (see Figure 8.1.)

Chengzu (r. 1402–1424), the third Ming emperor, often referred to by his reign name, Yongle ("perpetual happiness"), personally led five expeditions against the Mongols, intervened in Annam (now northern Vietnam), which he incorporated into the empire, and, most spectacularly, sent out great maritime expeditions marking China as the world's premier naval power.

Taizu was a harsh, suspicious, and autocratic ruler. In a move to weaken the bureaucracy and ensure that it not speak with a single voice, he abolished the position of Chancellor. Ministers now had to kneel before the emperor, whereas in the Song they had stood and in the Tang they had sat in the imperial presence. As F. W. Mote has pointed out, it was typical of Taizu that "while the emperor was

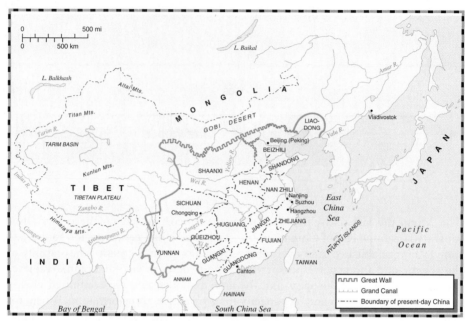

FIGURE 8.1 Ming China, middle sixteenth century.

determined to produce a universal code that could be minutely followed, he undermined that intent by constantly issuing laws which met immediate needs and which often contradicted the Great Ming Code."[1] Taizu insisted on deciding personally even matters of secondary importance. A very hard worker, he went through stacks of memorials: in one period of ten days he is reported to have perused 1660 memorials dealing with 3391 separate matters. In 1382 he appointed four grand secretaries to help him with this workload, but it was not until later in the dynasty that the Grand Secretariat developed into an institution.

Taizu energetically furthered the work of reconstruction and of relief for the poor, some of whom were resettled, and he established a tax system. But he overreached in aiming at "nothing less than the ethical and behavioral transformation of the entire population of China in accordance with ancient mores laid out in the Confucian canon."[2] To reform the people he ordered placards set up in all villages admonishing people to behave virtuously. Government regulations were posted on village kiosks along with the names of evildoers deemed deserving of public humiliation. Localities were ordered to set up schools for commoners, people and deities were registered, and unacceptable gods were banned.

To control the countryside and provide a check on officials, Taizu established the *li-jia* as a basis for labor-service and local security. Under this system, every ten families in an area constituted a *jia*, and ten *jia* formed a *li*. Each household was required to post a notice on its door indicating the names, ages, and occupations of its members, and all members of a *li* were responsible for each other's conduct. However, overlapping systems of authority made for inefficiencies as "the urgent concern with corruption overrode careful hierarchy."[3] Sarah K. Schneewind further points out, "The new dynasty could not create local social institutions by fiat, but competed for resources with local subjects and clergy, and with its own representatives."[4] Even under the Taizu the local forces more than held their own, and that was still more the case later.

Taizu reestablished the imperial university, founded many schools, and reinstituted the civil service examinations. Confucianism again became the official state doctrine. But the emperor rejected the antiauthoritarian aspects of the thought of Mencius and had 85 sections (about one-third of the text) expurgated before accepting *The Mencius* as a legitimate book. Merciless in exterminating those who stood in his way or were suspected of doing so, Taizu obtained information through a secret service provided with its own prison and torturing apparatus. Officials who displeased the emperor were subjected to beating in open court. Always painful and terribly humiliating, the beating was sometimes so severe that the victim died. *The Cambridge History* singles out 1382 to 1392 as "years of intensifying surveillance and terror."[5]

Chengzu (or Yongle) was as vigorous and severe as his father but did not hesitate to pursue a far more aggressive foreign policy and to move the capital from Nanjing to Beijing. This he did after defeating his nephew, the second emperor, in a massive civil war. He went on to rebuild Beijing into a magnificent city. To assure Beijing's supplies, Chengzu reconstructed the Grand Canal, "the world's longest manmade waterway" compared by Shih-Shan Henry Tsai to a route linking Florida and New York.[6] Just as harsh as his father when it came to purging real or suspected opponents, he was better educated than Taizu and more generous in his patronage of Confucianism. Not only did he hold more frequent civil service examinations, but he also sponsored major scholarly projects. The most grandiose of these was the compilation of a huge literary treasury, which employed more than 2000 scholars and when completed in 1408 resulted in a compendium of 22,877 rolls, or chapters. Under Chengzu the complete, unexpurgated *Mencius* was also once more made available. He also sponsored the compilation of a new Daoist cannon and venerated a number of Daoist deities.

It is sometimes said that the Ming reaction against the hated Mongols led to an overreaction against all things foreign, but this is not entirely true. Not only did the Ming continue Mongol institutions such as the system of hereditary military households and employing their own Mongol soldiers, but they also followed a broad cultural policy.

Thus, Chengzu not only sponsored a great compendium of Song Neo-Confucianism but also patronized the publication of Buddhist works, including a new edition of the Tripitaka. After the death of his wife, he had a Buddhist monastery near Nanjing repaired and built there an octagonal porcelain pagoda nine stories tall, more than 276 feet high. It remained standing until it was destroyed in 1854 during the Taiping Rebellion.

Maritime Expeditions (1405–1433)

Chengzu, reversing Taizu's policy of avoiding maritime expansion, sent a number of trusted eunuchs as envoys to Southeast Asia before launching seven great maritime expeditions under the command of Zheng He, a Muslim eunuch. The first of these included 27,800 men, 62 or 63 large ships, and 255 smaller vessels, and the third was of similar dimensions, far larger than the seventeen vessels and 1500 men who participated in the second and largest of Columbus's expeditions (1493–1495). They visited not only various areas of Southeast Asia but also the Indian Ocean, Arabia, and the east coast of Africa. These voyages were unique in their scope and official sponsorship, but the technology that made them possible had previously been employed in private ventures not considered worth recording by official historians. Thus, it is interesting to observe that on their first voyage the expedition had dealings with Chinese settlers in Sumatra. Reportedly they also defeated a Chinese "pirate" in those waters, killing 5000 men and bringing the leader back for execution in Beijing.

The Chinese sources, composed by scholars hostile to the undertaking and ever ready to attribute self-interest to a usurper emperor, emphasize Chengzu's desire to find the nephew from whom he had seized the throne but who had eluded capture. More broadly they may be viewed as an aspect of early Ming military and political assertiveness, for they effectively demonstrated Chinese power and brought tributary envoys to the Ming court such as the King of Borneo, who died in China in 1408 and was buried outside Nanjing, where his grave can still be seen. It is recorded that as a result of the fourth voyage, nineteen countries sent tribute.

Foreign envoys coming to render submission enhanced the court's glory and prestige. Also forthcoming from foreign lands were exotic objects and animals. The emperor was particularly delighted by giraffes, represented in Beijing as auspicious *qilin* or "unicorns." Most probably trade was also a motive for the voyages; we know that ships of the first voyage carried silk and embroideries on board. And trade was a major factor in inducing foreign lands to send envoys to China. On the Chinese side, however, the Ming court never looked upon trade as something intrinsically worthwhile.

From the official Chinese point of view, these expeditions did not have an economic rationale. Furthermore, their eunuch leadership did not win them friends among Confucian officials. When Chengzu died, they lost an enthusiastic supporter, although his successor Xuanzong (r. 1426–1435) did send out one last expedition.

Just as the expeditions can be seen as part of a general Early Ming assertiveness toward the rest of the world, their abandonment forms part of a broader pattern as the dynasty trimmed its ambitions and abandoned the attempt to annex Annam (1426). An incentive for maintaining an ocean navy was removed with the completion, in 1417, of a system of locks that maintained a water level sufficiently high to allow the grain vessels supplying the capital to use the Grand Canal throughout the year. No longer was the capital dependent on sea transport about six months a year. Furthermore, the crucial land frontier once again demanded military attention: fighting Mongols was a vital enterprise, whereas ocean expeditions were a luxury.

In the absence of a strong naval effort, Chinese waters became the domain of pirates and smugglers, a situation not ameliorated by the dynasty's regulations to control and curb maritime trade. For example, already during the Yongle period, the Japanese had been officially limited to one tribute mission every ten years, composed of only two ships with a maximum of 200 men (later raised to 300) to call at Ningbo (Zhejiang Province). These regulations were not always enforced, for private Chinese interests as well as the Japanese stood to profit by the trade conducted on these occasions. But the regulations illustrate the dynasty's negative attitude toward relations with maritime countries.

The Early Middle Period (1425–1505)

The seventy-five years of the Early Middle Ming were, on the whole, a time of peace, stability, and prosperity, under emperors less ambitious for military glory and personal power than Taizu and Chengzu. Xuanzong (1426–1436) abandoned the Ming effort to control Annam but did lead one expedition against Mongol raiders in the North. The Mongols were particularly troublesome under his successor, Yingzong, whom they actually captured and held prisoner for a year. On his return he endured six and one-half years of confinement in a palace in the capital while his brother, Taizong, remained on the throne, but then was able to conduct a second reign (see Table 8.1). In the 1460s and 1470s there was a revival of Chinese military strength. The Great Wall was strengthened and extended for 600 miles to protect the northern border of Shaanxi. The wall as it stands today owes much of its imposing mass and extent to the Ming.

To save himself from drowning in paperwork, Xuanzong relied on the Grand Secretaries to screen memorials, draft edicts, and the like. This informal group of two to six officials became increasingly influential during the last quarter of the fifteenth century. At the same time eunuch influence increased. Eunuchs enjoyed unique opportunities for informal, relaxed conversation with emperors who often turned to them for advice and entrusted them with important missions. Because elites did not castrate their sons, eunuchs invariably came from humble families without political influence and were thus entirely dependent on imperial favor. Going a step further than his predecessors, Xuanzong established a school for eunuchs, but this did not prevent the continuing hostility of Confucian officials, who tended to criticize even honest and able eunuchs as a matter of principle.

Ming emperors believed in doing things on a grand scale. For example, in 1425 the court reportedly had 6300 cooks in its employ, preparing meals not only for the considerable palace population but also for government officials on set occasions. Xuanzong was very fond of Korean food and sent eunuchs to Korea to bring back, among other things, virgins, eunuchs, and female cooks. He also took an active interest in the arts and was probably the only emperor after Huizong of

TABLE 8.1 Ming Emperors

Temple Name	Era Name	Era Dates
Taizu	Hongwu	1368–1399
Huizong	Jianwen	1399–1402
Chengzu	Yongle	1403–1425
Renzong	Hongxi	1425–1426
Xuanzong	Xuande	1426–1436
Yingzong	Zhengtong	1436–1450
Taizong	Jingtai	1450–1457
Yingzong (restored)	Tianshun	1457–1465
Xianzong	Changhua	1465–1488
Xianzong	Hongzhi	1488–1506
Wuzong	Zhengde	1506–1522
Shizong	Jiajing	1522–1567
Muzong	Longqing	1567–1573
Shenzong	Wanli	1573–1620
Guangzong	Taichang	1620–1621
Xizong	Tianqi	1621–1628
Sizong	Chongzhen	1628–1645

NOTE: The Ming founder initiated the practice followed by all subsequent emperors of retaining a single era name (*nianhao*, literally "year designation") throughout his reign. Normally the era name remained in use until the end of the Chinese lunar year in which the emperor died. Transposing the Chinese dates into the Western calendar, it turns out that all except three Ming emperors (Chengzu, Muzong, and Shenzong) died during the year preceding the change in reign name. (For example, Taizu died on June 24, 1398, but Hongwu was used through January 5, 1399. Huizong was enthroned on June 30, 1398, but the era name remained Taizu for the remainder of that lunar year.

Ming emperors are often known by their era names rather than by their posthumous temple names. To comply with the style of most English language materials, we will refer to Ming emperors by their temple names but use era names for the emperors of the Qing (1644–1911).

the Song to be a gifted painter and poet. Among the noted painters who served for a time at his court was the flower and bird specialist Bian Wenzhi (c. 1356–1428). Another famous painter was Dai Jin (1388–1462), who worked in the Ma-Xia tradition of the Southern Song. His artistic talents did not, however, save him from dismissal when he painted the coat of a fisherman red, a color reserved for the garments of officials. Returning to his native Zhejiang, he became a leader in what was known as the Zhe school of painting.

Xuanzong's reign is also known for its bronzes and especially for its porcelain. Under the Ming, private kilns continued to produce ceramics in traditional styles, but it was the imperial kilns, turning out vast quantities of vessels in many different shapes, that stood at the forefront of technical and artistic development. Whereas the Yongle period is noted for its white porcelain, by Xuanzong's reign blue-and-white ware had come into vogue and reached its classic peak (see Figure 8.2).

During the following reign the imperial kilns enjoyed a monopoly of blue-and-white porcelain, protected by an order prohibiting its private sale. But this could not be maintained for very long. Ming blue-and-white porcelain had such appeal that it soon stimulated imitation and went on to win admiration not only in East Asia but in distant lands such as Persia and Holland. The porcelain of each reign had its own characteristics. During the fifteenth century, its color range was broadened when white porcelains were decorated by painting them with various enamel colors. The five-colored enamels made during the reign of Emperor Xianzong (r. 1465–1488) are particularly prized.

FIGURE 8.2 Plate with bird decoration. Blue-and-white porcelain, Early Ming, probably Xuande, diameter 19.76 in. This kind of fine ware grew so popular in the West that in English "china" became synonymous with porcelain. (© The Asia Society, Mr. and Mrs. J.D. Rockefeller Collection, photograph by Lynton Gardiner.)

The Early Middle Period came to an end with the death of Xiaozong (r. 1488–1505), a model of Confucian propriety and a rare monogamist among the Ming emperors. His was generally a calm reign, but after more than 130 years, the dynasty was beginning to show signs of deterioration. The trends that would trouble government during the sixteenth century were already at work beneath the surface.

The Later Middle Period (1506–1590)

During this period, which includes most of the sixteenth century, the government suffered from inadequate imperial leadership, but the political system still showed a capacity for reform.

Wuzong, who reigned from 1506 to 1521, devoted his time and energy to sports, entertainments, sex, and drink while neglecting government and allowing eight eunuch "tigers" to run wild. Unclear and overlapping administrative jurisdictions, present from the beginning of the dynasty, as well as conflicting interests reaching up to and down from the highest levels of government worked against government efficiency. In his study of the endemic and widespread violence in the capital region David Robinson traces patronage networks that connected court eunuchs, local officials, and men of force who, depending on shifting circumstances, "often effortlessly changed hats from garrison soldiers to enterprising local bandits, from military retainers on the staff of provincial governors and local magnates to rebel leaders. In many cases services rendered and reputation acquired in one capacity directly increased one's value in another."[7] In 1510, faced with drought and government incompetence, bandits turned into rebels, creating havoc as far south as the Yangzi and reaching from the ocean west to the Taihang mountains. It took the government two years to suppress the rebellion, but it did not go beyond restoring the previous situation.

For the remainder of the Later Middle Period the center remained weak. Under Shizong, the Jiajing emperor (1522–1567), the arts flourished but government did not. This emperor became engrossed in increasingly longer Daoist ceremonies. By the end of his reign, there were ceremonies that continued for twelve or thirteen days and nights. He was followed by Muzong (r. 1567–1572), who is said to have devoted his five years on the throne more to his private pleasures than to public business. Next came Shenzong, the Wanli Emperor (r. 1573–1620), who was a minor until 1590.

Grand Secretaries and eunuchs now wielded great power while a decline in government honesty and efficiency was apparent both in the capital and in local government. The local elite increasingly avoided taxation and frequently moved to cities and towns. Then, as now, the lure of social, cultural, political, and economic opportunities was a major attraction of urban life. As absentee landlords, they often succumbed to the temptation to charge high rents, allocate taxes unfairly, and charge exorbitant interest on mortgage loans.

From early on, the tax system left a great deal to be desired. According to Martin Heijdra,

> The tax and corvee system as it was conceived in the late fourteenth century had many internal contradictions: it hovered uncertainly between land-based and population-based criteria for tax collection; it was not designed to accommodate changed in the population over time. . . .[8]

Inequalities in taxation hurt the government as well as peasants, but there were also reformers. Most notable was Hai Rui (1513–1587), who had a reputation for uprightness, courage, and concern for the common people. As a magistrate he reassessed the land to make taxes more equitable, wiped out corruption so effectively that government clerks were reduced to poverty, and himself led a life of exemplary frugality. His refusal to toady to his superiors earned him powerful enemies, and he came close to losing his life when he submitted a scathing memorial that, among other things, charged the emperor with neglect of government and excessive indulgence in Daoist ceremonies. During the Ming one did not denounce an emperor with impunity: in prison Hai Rui was tortured and condemned to death by strangulation. He was saved only by the death of the emperor. On his release from prison he resumed his career but was forced into retirement when he offended powerful families by forcing them to return lands they had seized illegally. Late in life, in 1585, he was recalled to office, and after he died he was idealized as the perfect official incarnate. About four centuries later, in the 1960s, Hai Rui became the focus of a major controversy (see Chapter 14).

A very different kind of reformer was Zhang Juzheng (1525–1582), who dominated government during the reign of Muzong and for another ten years during Shenzong's minority. He has been described as a Confucian Legalist, for he was convinced that strong and strict government was ultimately for the people's benefit. Efficiency and control were the hallmarks of his policy. Among his achievements were a repair of the Grand Canal, reform of the courier system, new regulations designed to strengthen central control over provincial officials, and a reduction in the total number of officials. He eliminated eunuch influence from the Six Ministries, prevented censors from abusing their authority, and tried to reform the provincial schools.

To improve government finances, Zhang directed an all-China land survey (1581) and extended to the whole country the "single whip method of taxation," previously tried in Zhejiang and Fujian. This replaced once and for all the Two Tax System first instituted during the Tang. Implementation remained incomplete, but, in principle, the new method provided for the consolidation of tax obligations into a single annual bill.

Another important innovation was the use of silver as the value base for tax assessment. Although Zhang thereby recognized the importance of silver, which had become widely used in commercial transactions, he based his monetary policy on high-quality copper coins because silver, unlike copper, had to be imported and was therefore of uncertain supply. But he could not prevent the continued popularity of silver, and ultimately, as we shall see, Zhang's apprehension about depending on a foreign supply of silver turned out to be well founded. The silver *tael* (ounce) remained the standard monetary unit into the twentieth century.

Zhang was also troubled by what was happening in the civil service examinations. Ever since Taizu had lent imperial favor to an essay form composed of eight rigidly stipulated sections and known as the "eight-legged essay," the tendency had increasingly been to judge papers on the basis of form rather than content. This eased the task of the examination readers but threatened to turn the examinations into mechanical exercises. Zhang, who served as an examiner in 1571, wanted the questions to emphasize current problems and the answers to be graded on content. But in his contempt for "empty" theorizing, he went beyond this and ordered the suppression of private academies. These he also considered undesirable, as potential breeding grounds for political associations and as holders of tax-exempt land. However, the decree banning academies (1579) did little permanent damage to these institutions.

Zhang Juzheng made many enemies. They had their revenge after his death, when his family property was confiscated and his sons were tortured. But he left the regime in sound financial condition at a time when it was incurring heavy military expenditures, fighting Mongol invasions between 1550 and 1570 and maintaining military preparedness thereafter. The government's fiscal health at this time reflected the general economic strength of sixteenth century China.

Economy and Society

Peace and stability made for prosperity. During the first century of the Ming, northern agriculture was rehabilitated. Taizu discriminated against the people in the Yangzi delta who had resisted him when he was founding the dynasty, but by the fifteenth century this area resumed its economic growth. The Southeast remained China's most populous and prosperous region. The gradual spread of superior strains of rice, which had begun during the Song, permitted a steady increase in China's population, which rose from 65 to 80 million in the fourteenth century (well below that of the Song) to about 150 million by the end of the sixteenth. The introduction in the sixteenth century of new crops from the Americas laid a foundation for still further population increases that were to follow in the Qing.

Although it is difficult to find major breakthroughs or radically new technologies or industries, change was so substantial that scholars speak of a "second commercial revolution." There was an increase in interregional trade in staples as well as an increase in the growing of cash crops, most notably cotton in the Yangzi delta, where grain now had to be imported. Although this was not the original intent, the Grand Canal was kept going in large part by the private trade of private merchants and also by the seamen who serviced the official boats. Suzhou, located near the juncture of the Grand Canal and the Yangzi River, emerged as a major economic and cultural center.

An increased use of money and participation in an impersonal market influenced the behavior of rich and poor even as the growth of commerce increased class differentiation. In addition to Suzhou, Nanjing, Yangzhou, and Hangzhou, numerous smaller cities prospered. Among the important industries of the period were the porcelain and ceramic kilns centered in Jiangxi, the cotton manufacture of Nanjing, and the silk weaving in Suzhou.

Enthusiastic customers for silk and porcelain were found not only domestically but overseas in Europe and Japan. As payment for these prized commodities, silver flowed into China from Japan and increasingly from Spanish America through Manila, fueling a truly global trade network. Silver also financed a flourishing domestic market. Hebei remained the center of iron manufacture, and Anhui was known for its dye works. Indigo and sugar cane, along with cotton, were important cash crops grown for the market. A well-known seventeenth-century technical manual, *Creations of Man and Nature,* offers impressive evidence of the inventiveness of Chinese craftsmen.

Much of what happened was beyond the government's purview. At the local level the central government was represented by the magistrate, who in theory was responsible for everything that happened in his district. He was supposed to supervise tax collection, provide public security, administer justice, and see to the economic as well as moral needs of the population. However, because his staff was small and the average Ming district had a registered population of more than 50,000, the magistrate's control and influence were restricted.

Local society operated according to its own rhythms, with its patterns influenced and affected by government to be sure, but not determined by it. Particularly important was the role of the local gentry elite, the magnitude of whose influence has induced a Japanese scholar to write "gentry rule," that is "indirect regional rule that went beyond the boundary of mere tenant-landlord relations" and included political rule (administering justice, mediating quarrels, maintaining public order, administering relief, etc.), cultural rule (education, culture, guidance of public opinion, etc.), and economic rule (control of the market, etc.).[9] This characterization no doubt needs qualification, but the gentry did preside over provincial life and gave it much of its tone.

There is no reason to believe that regional variations in social structure and economic relationships were of lesser magnitude in the Ming than later because they reflect differences between ecosystems as well as local traditions. A major development in the most economically advanced regions was for "descent groups" (groups larger than a family descended from a common ancestor) to organize into "lineages" with shared ceremonies and assets (usually land). In her exemplary study of a county in Anhui, Hilary J. Beattie found that the local gentry dated back to the Early Ming, that gentry lineages were formally organized in the sixteenth century, and that they were able to survive the rebellions and upheavals of the late years of the dynasty and even the great nineteenth-century Taiping Rebellion.[10] They were able to accomplish this by maintaining solid economic roots in local land ownership and by investing their income in education. Education, in turn, secured their local status, in addition to providing the requisites for competing in the civil service examinations. Members of the gentry who succeeded in becoming officials used their political influence and their economic assets to benefit the lineage, but the gentry were able to sustain themselves even during periods lean in examination success. This suggests that local social and economic status was the primary source of their power and that there was greater continuity in the family background of the local elite than there was among that much smaller subgroup of their members capable and fortunate enough to gain access to a career in the imperial bureaucracy.

Among the means used to secure lineage cohesion were the periodic compilations of genealogies. These not only fostered a sense of historic continuity among lineage members but also identified the individuals belonging to the lineage. Prominent gentry lineages also maintained ancestral halls and graveyards and conducted ceremonial sacrifices to lineage ancestors. Not infrequently, the income from lineage land was used for these purposes. Lineage solidarity was also maintained by general guides for the conduct of the members and by formal lineage rules. One penalty for severe infractions of these rules was expulsion. The contrast in status between the local elite and the government underlings who served in the sub-bureaucracy is revealed by the stipulation found in many lineage rules that any member sinking to the occupation of government clerk or runner be promptly expelled. The gentry lineages also profited from participation in a complicated network of marriage relationships.

The general trend was for the strongest lineages to develop in the Southeast, but the present state of research is not sufficient to attempt a social/historical map or timeline. Similarly, although we know that there were bondservants on landed estates in the sixteenth century as well as tenants and hired workers, the situation was complex (for example, bondservants could also be landlords), sources are unequally distributed, and geographic parameters are as yet unclear.

Literacy and Literature

Along with prosperity came an increase in literacy, not only among the well-educated and ambitious but also among the more humble and less sophisticated. Bookshops did a brisk business selling collections of model examination papers used by candidates to cram for tests as well as encyclopedias, colored prints, novels, collections of short stories, guides that explained the classics in simple language, and books of moral instruction illustrated with tales of wrongdoing and retribution.

The audience for wood block prints was even wider than that for books. Although it was the Japanese who developed the colored wood block print to its highest aesthetic form, the colored print originated in China. The earliest extant Chinese colored print formed the frontispiece of a Buddhist sutra dated 1346, but the best prints were produced in the seventeenth century and included five-color illustrations of erotica.

Some gifted men turned to literary careers after failing to advance through the examination system. Two such men were Feng Menglong (1574–1646) and Ling Mengqi (1580–1664), authors of widely read anthologies of short stories. Both men were also dramatists and scholars. Feng's interests ranged particularly widely; for instance, he wrote books on gambling as well as on Confucianism. But he is most famous for publishing *Stories, Old and New*, three collections of colloquial short stories based on the promptbooks of the storytellers, who had long formed part of the urban entertainment. Liu Wu-chi's description of the subject matter of Feng's stories reveals their diversity:

> Their range includes: quasi-historical tales of kings and generals, faithful friends and filial sons; romantic yarns of strange lands and peoples; supernatural stories of marvels and prodigies, spirits and ghosts, Buddhist monks and Daoist immortals; realistic stories of scandals in monastic establishments; daring exploits of brigands and thieves; murders, lawsuits, and court trials; domestic tragedies and bloody revenges; social comedies and family reunions.[11]

Ling, son of a noted publisher and scholar, rewrote and retold the stories in the two collections he published, both entitled *Striking the Table in Amazement at the Wonders.*

The Novel

The novel, like the short story, was only gradually freed from its antecedents in the oral tradition of storytelling, with the eliminating of extraneous material and refining of crudities. It remained essentially episodic in structure and often included poems. Despite the literary excellence and subtlety of works written by and for the educated elite and the interest they stimulated among Late Ming scholars, even the greatest novels did not gain Confucian legitimacy as high literature. In Japan the novel was an honored part of literary culture, but in China reading a novel was a surreptitious pleasure indulged in by students when their teacher was not looking—or vice versa. Many novels of the Ming period retold old stories or embellished historical episodes; others were adventure stories, serious or comic; and still others were pornographic. The four major novels that have come down to us from the Ming are *The Romance of the Three Kingdoms, The Water Margin* (translated also as *All Men Are Brothers*), *Journey to the West,* and *The Plum in the Golden Vase* (also translated as *The Golden Lotus*).

The Romance of the Three Kingdoms (*Sanguozhi yanyi*) was first published in 1522, although it may have been written in the late Yuan. It is a fictionalized account of the conflict between Wei, Wu, and Shu in the third century C.E. In its pages the gifted but badly flawed character of Cao Cao, the martial heroics of Guan Yu, and the strategic genius and devoted loyalty of Zhuge Liang come vividly alive. It is no wonder that ordinary people in China formed many of their perceptions of history from this and other novels. This literature was also popular in Korea and Japan where *The Romance of the Three Kingdoms* was widely read and much loved. The tale remains popular throughout East Asia even in our age of videos and DVDs.

A different kind of history supplied the materials for *The Water Margin* (*Shuihuzhuan*). Based on a Yuan play, it is set in the closing years of the Northern Song and recounts the deeds of 108 bandit heroes driven by the cruel corruption of a decadent government to take justice into their own hands, outlaws who champion the oppressed and avenge the wronged. Numerous episodes, rendered in everyday speech, tell of feats of strength and daring, clever stratagems, and acts of savage but righteous vengeance. The novel's theme did not endear it to the political authorities, and during the Qing dynasty it was officially proscribed. However, it continued to be sold under the counter and enjoyed a broad readership. Among the eminent twentieth-century leaders who read it with profit as well as delight was the young Mao Zedong.

The third major Ming novel, *Journey to the West* (*Xiyuji*, translated also as *Monkey*), first published in 1592, describes the trip to India of the Tang monk Xuanzang (see Figure 5.3). The trip is transformed into a fantastic journey, a heroic pilgrimage, and a tale of delightful satire and high comedy. Monkey is one of three supernatural disciples assigned by Buddha to accompany the priest and protect him from the monsters and demons that threaten him along the way. Many times Monkey saves the day, for he is endowed with penetrating, although mischievous and restless, intelligence and has acquired many magical gifts: he can somersault through the air for leagues with the greatest of ease, has the power to change into all kinds of shapes, and can transform his body hairs into a myriad of monkeys. Over his ear he wears a pin, which becomes an enormous iron cudgel when needed. The novel can be enjoyed as sheer fantasy, or for its satirical accounts of the bureaucratic organization of Heaven and the underworld, or as a religious allegory.

Either the authors of these three novels are obscure, or the attribution of authorship is itself in doubt. The identity of the author of *The Plum in the Golden Vase* (*Jinpingmei*) is even more obscure, and for good reason, because no respectable gentleman would have wanted his name linked to an erotic novel condemned by the Chinese as pornographic. In its 100 chapters, *Jinpingmei* gives a detailed account of the dissipations of a wealthy lecher. It offers a naturalistic tableau of amorous intrigues within the household and beyond, of drinking parties, and of sumptuous feasts and portraits of go-betweens and fortunetellers, doctors and mendicants, singing girls, and venal officials, and so on. After a life of sex without love, the hero, reduced to an empty shell, meets a fitting death, and the novel rolls on for another twenty chapters to recount the unraveling of the household.

Drama

In the Ming, drama in the southern style reached its peak. It differed from the northern drama (discussed in the preceding chapter) in language, form, and music. Southern plays were much longer, running to forty and more scenes, and the songs, accompanied by the bamboo flute, were assigned to choruses as well as to the leading players. The result has been described as an "undulating cavalcade"[12] composed of scenes varying in length, number of players, and importance. Because of the length of the plays and the familiarity of the audience with their plots, performances of Ming drama, as of Japanese Nō, came to feature selected scenes from a number of plays rather than a single one played all the way through. The authors were often sophisticated literary men, writing as much for their peers as for the wider public, who at times were more concerned about achieving literary excellence than creating effective theater. Ming playwrights were prolific: some 1200 titles are still known.

Acknowledged as the greatest Ming playwright was Tang Xienzu (1550–1616), who earned a *jinshi* degree but had a frustrating official career. In his *The Dream of Han Tan* a young man falls asleep as he is trying to prepare a meal of millet. He then sees his whole life in a dream: he comes in first in the *jinshi* examination, performs great deeds, is slandered and condemned to death, is cleared, and then is promoted. As he is about to die, he wakes up to discover that the millet on the stove is nearly ready to eat. This makes him realize that life itself passes as rapidly as a dream. Tang wrote three other dream plays, and a dream also features importantly in his most admired work, *The Peony Pavilion*. This long play of fifty-five scenes centers on a love so strong that it is able to bring the dead back to life.

Other well-known Ming plays were written on the theme of love. A perennial favorite was the disastrous love of the Tang emperor Xuanzong for Yang Guifei. The repertoire also contained plays on more contemporary matters. One of the last southern masterpieces was *The Peach Blossom Fan*, completed in 1699 and depicting the end of the Ming half a century earlier. In it the conflict between traitorous villains and loyal heroes is intertwined with the story of the love shared by a loyal young scholar and a virtuous courtesan. Southern dramas continued to be performed and written, but toward the end of the eighteenth century there arose a new form of theater, based more broadly on popular taste. This was Peking Drama, famed for its actors and singers more than for its writers. Its repertoire consisted largely of adaptations of older works.

Painting

The most notable center for painting in the Later Middle Ming was Suzhou, where the Wu school flourished from about 1460 to 1560. Famed for its poetry, painting, calligraphy, drama, and garden retreats, conceived and designed as miniature replicas of vast nature, Suzhou offered a place of refuge for sophisticated people fleeing the uncertainties of political life, a place where the literati could pursue their own interests in peace, the home of the gentleman cultivating his artistic talents apparently without regard for money or career as well as of the professional artist like Tang Yin (1470–1524) who, combining the "education of the upper class and the material needs of the lower,"[13] enjoyed the patronage of the wealthy for whom he painted commemorative paintings such as one celebrating the eightieth birthday of a virtuous widow who, although reportedly poor, brought up two sons by herself. Between commissions, Tang, like his compeers, supplemented his income by painting fans for a wider market, including, but hopefully not limited to, those who aspired to acceptance as cultivated gentlemen. Then, as now, other producers and consumers of a vibrant visual culture satisfied their own tastes with little regard for the latest theories or fashions current among elite (or would-be elite) sophisticates.

Designations such as "Zhe school" and "Wu school" are Chinese classifications based on the artist's residence, style, and/or social status. Unfortunately for

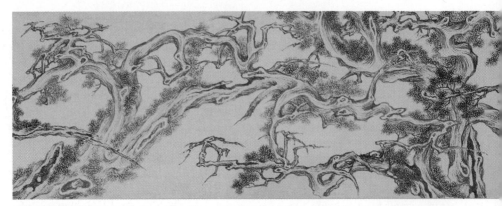

FIGURE 8.3 Wen Zhengming, *The Seven Junipers of Changshu*. Section of hand-scroll, ink on paper, 142.52 in × 11.34 in. (© Honolulu Academy of Arts, Gift of Mrs. Carter Galt, 1952 [1666.1].) In the rhapsody *(fu)*, which Wen added to his painting, he invites the viewer on a flight of the imagination:

the modern student, these criteria did not always coincide: not all amateurs resided in Suzhou, some professionals adopted "amateur" styles, and so forth. However, in stylistic terms, the Zhe school declined in the sixteenth century. Its most characteristic contribution to Chinese art was the continuation of Southern Song academic painting. For fresh departures, one must turn to Suzhou.

The man whose work stands at the beginning of the Wu tradition was Shen Zhou (1427–1509), who was also a talented poet and calligrapher. He lived in comfort on an estate about ten miles out of town and loved to paint the local landscape. Although deeply influenced by Yuan painting, he gradually developed a style of his own that conveyed a genial warmth and a sense of ease and naturalness.

Wen Zhengming (1470–1559) studied painting under Shen Zhou and befriended Tang. He admired and frequently took as his model Zhao Mengfu, the great Yuan painter, but was too talented an artist to follow one model only. Nor did he spend a lifetime perfecting a single style or refining a single vision. Instead he worked in many different manners during his long and productive life. Some of his paintings contain references to painting styles going back to the Tang, styles previously revived during the Southern Song and the Yuan. Such multiple historical references were among the qualities most admired in his work by Ming and later connoisseurs. It is not possible to illustrate the work of an artist like Wen Zhengming with a single "representative" painting, but *The Seven Junipers of Changshu* is one of his most distinctive and powerful (see Figure 8.3).

Wen's inscription states that he was copying Zhao Mengfu, but this is "copying" at its most creative, for what it shares with the Yuan painter is the power of its abstraction and the expressiveness of its brushwork. It also shares a love for the old: the trees were originally planted in 500 C.E., and four were replaced in the

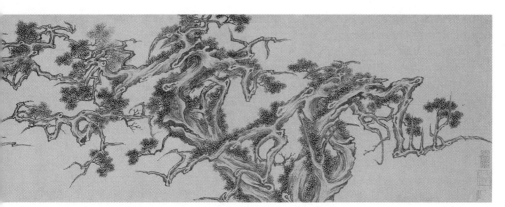

Like creaking ropes the junipers dance to the wail of the wind, conjuring up a thousand images: split horns and blunted claws, the wrestling of the dragon with the tiger, great whales rolling in the deep, and giant birds who swoop down on their prey. And now, like ghosts, they vanish, now reappear, vast entangled forms. (Tseng Yu-ho, in Richard Edwards, *The Art of Wen Cheng-ming* [1470–1559] [Ann Arbor: Univ. of Michigan Museum of Art, 1976], p. 122.)

eleventh century. But here the accent is not on venerable age, but on strength and an explosive vitality that cannot be contained by the edges of the paper.

Poems on paintings, as in the case of *Junipers*, remained common, and some poems were paintings in words:

> A slim bending egret,
> Flies to alight on a riverbank.
> Like a patch of snow that does not melt,
> It dots the emerald of the river sky.[14]

The author of this poem, Zhou Saizhen (fl. 1496), by birth and marriage belonged to the upper stratum of Ming officialdom. Apparently her poem "Encouraging My Son to Study and Abstain from Wine" did not fall on deaf ears, for he was awarded the *jinshi* degree in 1496. Zhou was one of a number of talented and sophisticated Ming women whose poems often express the grief of separation, loneliness, and/or the melancholy of the seasons.

Ming Thought: Wang Yangming

Like Wen Zhengming's junipers, Ming thought could not be confined within its traditional frame. It was Wen's and Zhou's contemporary, Wang Yangming (Wang Shouren, 1472–1529), who opened up new intellectual vistas within Neo-Confucianism. Unlike the gentlemen-painters of Suzhou, Wang had a very active official career. At its low point he suffered two months in prison and a beating of 40 strokes followed by exile in Guizhou, but he subsequently served with great

courage and distinction both as a civil administrator and as a military commander, rendering outstanding service by suppressing rebels.

Ming thinkers had to cope with the problems of living a Confucian life in a
world that remained stubbornly un-Confucian. Despite the state's official support
for Confucianism, Chinese government and society were as far from resembling
the Confucian ideal as ever. How was one to live a proper life in a society that was
not right and proper, amid the venality of officials, the social changes induced by
economic expansion, and the continuing politicization of government administration? They also had to redefine the role of the educated gentleman as the growth
of commerce created a new prosperity, new sources of power, and, de facto, new
value systems. At the same time, the spread of literacy undercut the monopoly of
classical thought, classical culture, and the status of those with a classical education. Moreover, there was a sense that in a postclassical age perhaps the only way
the scholar could make a personal contribution was through specialization, recognizing that the traditional aim of universal knowledge was no longer attainable. In
an effort to define their personal and social roles, the educated were forced to return to the question of the nature of their own nature:

> Was it static or dynamic, metaphysical or physical, an abstract ideal
> or an active force, a moral norm or a trans-moral perfection? . . . How
> was the individual to understand that nature in relation to his actual
> self and his society?[15]

The issue at stake was not purely intellectual. It involved a quest not only for
knowledge but also for wisdom and sagehood.

For Wang Yangming the essential insight came suddenly at the age of 36 after
a period of intense thought while in exile in Guizhou. His experience has often
been likened to the sudden enlightenment sought by Chan Buddhists. Like Zhu
Xi's contemporary, Lu Jiuyuan, Wang identified human nature with the mind-
heart (*xin*), in turn identified with principle (*li*). For Wang, as for Lu, *li* alone exists. Everyone is endowed with goodness and has an innate capacity to know good
(*liangzhi*). Self-perfection consists of "extending" this capacity to the utmost.
Everyone can attain perfection because we are all endowed with the gold of sagehood. People may differ quantitatively in their abilities, but qualitatively they are
the same, just as the gold in a small coin is in no way inferior to that in a large one.
Thus, Wang took it very calmly when a disciple reported going out for a walk and
finding the street full of sages. That was only to be expected. However, there is
need for strenuous effort to refine the gold by eliminating the dross, that is, "selfish desires." Sagehood does not come easily.

External sources of doctrinal authority, including the classics, repositories of
the words and deeds of the sages, have only a secondary, accessory function.
According to Wang Yangming, "If words are examined in the mind and found to
be wrong, although they have come from the mouth of Confucius, I dare not accept them as correct."[16] Conversely, if the mind finds them correct, it does not
matter if the words have been uttered by ordinary folk. The truth is in and of the
mind. It remains one whole because the mind and *li* are universal.

As is the case for all Confucians, the knowledge that concerns Wang Yangming is at once metaphysical and moral. It is not to be grasped by abstract intellectualization but must be lived. What is true of sensory knowledge holds for all knowledge: a person can no more know filial piety without practicing it than he can know the smell of an odor or understand pain without direct personal experience. Knowing and acting are inseparable, two dimensions of a single process: "Knowledge in its genuine and earnest aspect is action, and action in its intelligent and discriminating aspect is knowledge."[17] A man may discourse with great erudition and subtlety on filiality, but it is his conduct that will reveal his depth of understanding. To employ a modern example, a person who "knows" smoking is bad for him but persists in the habit reveals that he does not really "know" this with his whole being. A perfectly integrated personality is, of course, a mark of the sage.

Wang Yangming had an abiding influence because he spoke to some of the persistent concerns of East Asian thinkers and activists. One may, for example, detect in Mao Zedong's discussions of the relationship between theory and practice overtones of the Ming philosopher's insistence on the unity of knowledge and action. One reason for his influence is that he was the kind of thinker who opens many doors rather than laying down a rigid system.

Religion

Both Buddhism and Daoism had by now permeated Chinese culture, including popular festivals and medical practices. On the Buddhist side, we can cite the popularity of *Journey to the West* in many genres and for various audiences. Meanwhile among the literati the *Laozi* and *Zhuangzi* continued to delight and inspire. An example of the Daoist religious influence is Wen Zhengming's painting, for his seven junipers represent the seven stars of the Northern Dipper, important in Daoism, and depict an actual group of trees in the grounds of a Daoist temple not far from Suzhou.

Imperial patronage remained important. Shizong (1521–1566) was such a generous patron of Daoism that he has been called "The Daoist Emperor." Like so many of his subjects he turned to Daoists for ways to preserve and prolong life (although ingesting immortality medicine had cost two of his predecessors their lives). Shizong raised Daoists to the highest positions of state and neglected government in favor of Daoism. Hai Rui was jailed when he tried to persuade the emperor to give up further investigations into attaining immortality.

Daoists often formed alliances with eunuchs, but that eunuch ascendancy did not necessarily harm Buddhism is indicated by their power during the reign of Wuzong, a fervent Buddhist who in 1507 personally ordained 40,000 monks. As Chün-fang Yü has indicated, the history of Ming Buddhism falls readily into three periods.[18] As in other respects, the Ming began with a period of state activism with the government undertaking control of the number of monks and supervision of temples and monasteries. This was followed by a middle period of decline in spiritual vigor and rigor, although Buddhist institutions continued strong. Finally, the Late Ming, beginning with the Wanli reign period

(1573–1615), experienced a revival. An example of a new intensity was the four years Hanshan Deqing (1546–1623) devoted to copying a sutra in his own blood mixed with gold, invoking Amitabha after each word.

Deqing, who was ultimately recognized as a Chan patriarch, was typical in his serious study of and writing on a wide range of Buddhist texts. He also wrote commentaries on Daoist and Buddhist classics. A number of outstanding Late Ming Buddhist masters were similarly open to and learned in other teaching while remaining Buddhist at heart.

Both the fervor and the willingness to cross boundaries in search of intellectual and spiritual fulfillment were characteristic of many areas of Late Ming thought and behavior. An extreme form of Confucianism is demonstrated notably by the celebration of young women whose filial devotion induced them to slice their own flesh, hoping to cure an ailing parent.

Ming Thought after Wang Yangming

Some of Wang Yangming's followers and disciples led courageous but quite conventional lives of public service, self-cultivation, and teaching, but others developed the more radical implications of his thought. Wang Yangming taught that the mind in itself is above distinctions of good and evil, an idea with a strong Buddhist flavor and compatible with Daoist ideas. The tendency to combine Confucianism, Buddhism, and Daoism was a very old one now given new vitality. Present in Wang Yangming, it was carried further by Wang Ji (1498–1585), who freely employed Buddhist and Daoist terms, valued Daoist techniques of breath control, but remained a Confucian in his rejection of empty abstract speculation and in his moral values.

Wang Ji and Wang Gen (1483–1541) are considered the founders of the Taizhou branch of Wang Yangming's teaching, named after Wang Gen's native prefecture where he established a school. Wang Gen was born into a family of salt producers and remained a commoner throughout his life. In 1552 his enthusiasm for the teachings of the sage prompted him to build himself a cart such as the one he imagined Confucius to have used. He then rode in it to Beijing to present a memorial. He attracted much attention in the capital until persuaded by fellow disciples of Wang Yangming to return south, where he remained a vigorous and fervent popular teacher, attracting a good many commoners as students.

In their personal conduct as well as in their teachings, the more radical followers of Wang Yangming stretched the parameters of Confucianism to the utmost and went beyond the limits tolerated by the state. He Xinyin (1517–1579) was a courageous defender of free discussion in the academies and so devoted to all humanity that he turned against the family as a restrictive, selfish, exclusive institution. His unorthodox ideas, courageous personal conduct, and reputation as a troublemaker eventually helped land him in prison, where he died after being beaten. Li Zhi (1527–1602), another controversial figure, carried the individualism implicit in Wang Yangming's philosophy to the point of defending selfishness. A thorough nonconformist, he denounced conventional scholars who, he claimed, lacked an authentic commitment to the core values of Confucianism. In 1588 Li

Zhi shaved his head and became (at least in appearance) a Buddhist monk. But he continued to offend the literati; in 1590 local gentry organized a mob that demolished the temple where Li was staying. Imprisoned in 1602, he committed suicide. Until a modern revival of interest in his ideas, he was best known as an editor of *The Water Margin,* and the novel's opposition to the establishment accords very well with Li's own attitudes.

Meanwhile, Jiao Hong (c. 1548–1620) went beyond earlier theorists who had considered Confucianism, Buddhism, and Daoism as independent and complementary. Instead he saw the three teachings as forming a single teaching so that each could help explain the others.

The significance of He, Li, and Jiao may lie not so much in their intellectual influence, which was limited, but rather in demonstrating the limits to which Ming thought could be stretched. Li Zhi shocked not only members of the official establishment but also activist Confucians, who were dismayed by the radical subjectivism of this line of thought and appalled by the Buddhistic notion that human nature was beyond good and evil.

At the same time, others struggled with how to contain social change and restore what they considered a proper relationship between state and society and yearned for a simpler age such as an Early Ming, which they idealized. Timothy Brook has described the "panicked indignation" of Late Ming writers:

> Many became obsessed with the extent to which Chinese society had grown away from what they were trained to believe it had originally been: an agrarian realm where superiors knew their responsibilities and inferiors their places. But, they felt, people no longer stayed put: class distinctions had become disturbingly fluid; the cultivation of wealth had displaced moral effort as the presiding goal of the age.[19]

And he goes on to say:

> However artificial, the classical status hierarchy of gentry, peasantry, artisanate, and merchants may have seemed in the opening years of the dynasty, by the end of the Ming it was nothing but a quaint trope invoked by a few censorious gentry authors to mourn the erosion of what they deemed to be their near-hereditary claim to elevated status.[20]

Dong Qichang and Late Ming Painting

Dong Qichang (1555–1636) was a major painter and calligrapher, the leading connoisseur of his generation, and China's foremost art historian. Many of the ideas of Dong and his circle were not new, but he gave them their final authoritative expression. The key to his analysis was the division of painters into Northern and Southern schools resembling the Northern and Southern branches of Chan Buddhism. The assignment of a painter into one group or the other was not based on geography but on the man's social standing and on his style. A "Northern" painter was defined as a professional who stressed technical excellence and fine

FIGURE 8.4 Dong Quichang, *The Qingbian Mountain*. Hanging scroll, ink on paper, dated 1617. 26.38 in × 88.58 in. Natural forms are tilted, compressed, and juxtaposed, not to represent nature but to emphasize the painting's formal organization and the interplay of light and dark. (© Cleveland Museum of Art, 2003. Leonard C. Hanna, Jr. Bequest, 1980.10)

craftsmanship to produce handsome paintings of maximum visual appeal. In contrast, "Southern" painters were literati, men of wide reading and profound learning for whom painting was an experience of self-expression, a chance to allow their genius and sensibility free play, much as in calligraphy. Dong traced these two lines all the way back to the Tang and cast Wang Wei as the founder of the Southern tradition. He also included painters of his own dynasty in his analysis. Furthermore, Dong and his friends affirmed their affiliation with the Southern tradition.

Self-identification with a tradition of amateurism did not preclude the study of earlier masters. Dong himself was influenced in calligraphy by Zhao Mengfu and Wen Zhengming and greatly admired the master painters of the Yuan. But he emphasized the need to "unlearn," and a painting such as his picture of the Qingbian Mountains (see Figure 8.4) has only a faint resemblance to its purported tenth-century model. Nor is there in this painting any desire to represent mountains as they actually appear to the eye or to define the depth relationships between them by clearly placing them one behind the other. The effect of Dong's theories and art on seventeenth-century painting is suggested by Wang Yuanqi (1642-1715), a famous painter who in 1700 became the chief artistic advisor to Emperor Kangxi and who described Dong as having "cleansed the cobwebs from landscape painting in one sweep."[21]

In the final years of the Ming there were artists painting in a number of different styles, many playing on earlier modes. A painter who took as his point of departure the classic Song landscape but turned it into an expression of his own fantastic imagination was Wu Bin (c. 1568–1626): Figure 8.5 shows a landscape that never was nor ever could be. Paintings such as this suggest both some of the potentialities and some of the dangers inherent in Ming individualism. In the seventeenth century, the dynasty, like the painting, found itself balanced on too narrow a base.

Late Ming Government (1590–1644)

A conspicuous feature of the last fifty years of the dynasty was the inadequacy of its emperors. When Zhang Juzheng died in 1582, Emperor Shenzong, then not quite nineteen, determined that during his reign no minister would again dominate the government, but soon the emperor himself ceased to bother very much with government. From 1589 to 1615, a period of more than 25 years, he did not hold a single general audience, and from 1590 to his death in 1620, he only conducted personal interviews with Grand Secretaries five times. Nor, except on matters of taxation and defense, did he respond to memorials. As a result much government business was simply left undone. He was particularly remiss in personnel matters. By the end of his reign, not only were the offices in the capital seriously understaffed, but it has also been estimated that as many as half of the prefectural and district posts were also unfilled. Whereas at the start he had punished officials who criticized him in their memorials, during the last 20 years he largely ignored even them. Some high officials withdrew from their posts without authorization—they too were ignored.

FIGURE 8.5 Wu Bin landscape. Hanging scroll, ink and light color on paper, 38.78 in × 120.47 in. (© Asian Art Museum of San Francisco, Gift of the Avery Brundage Collection Symposium Fund and the M.H. de Young Memorial Museum Trust Fund, B69D17. Used with persmission.) James Cahill has said it best: "Solids evaporate into space, ambiguous definitions of surface unsettle the eye as it moves over them, and the towering construction of spires and cliffs, like the creation of some titanic, demented sculptor, balances on an absurdly narrow base." (James Cahill, *Fantastics and Eccentrics in Chinese Painting* [New York: The Asia Society, 1976], p. 36.)

The emperor did take an interest in military matters. From the 1580s on there was fighting in the southwest against various tribal peoples as well as against the Thais and especially against the Burmese. In the 1590s there were campaigns in Inner Mongolia, and large Ming armies fought a Japanese invasion of Korea. These military actions were generally successful but enormously expensive. Also costly but not as successful was the Ming military effort in Manchuria, where the Manchu chief Nurgaci founded a state and fought the Ming to a draw (see Chapter 10).

The political deterioration that marked the decline of the Ming did not escape the attention of earnest Confucians who saw it as their duty to protest forcefully against political abuses and to object against un-Confucian conduct such as the refusal of Zhang Juzheng to retire from office to observe mourning on the death of his father. Early in the seventeenth century, the Donglin Academy, founded in 1604 in Wuxi northwest of Suzhou, became a center for such "pure criticism," which cost many Donglin men their lives. Conflict between pro-Donglin and anti-Donglin factions lasted through the final thirty years of the dynasty.

Emperor Xizong (r. 1620–1627) was peculiar even by Late Ming standards. He "did not have sufficient leisure to learn to write"[22] but spent all his time on carpentry, creating many pieces of fine furniture, which he lacquered himself. Factionalism, which in the absence of strong imperial leadership had flourished under Shenzong, now turned vicious. Wei Zhongxian (1568–1627), a very capable and equally unscrupulous eunuch, gained power due to his influence over the emperor. Wei purged all opponents, foremost among them the members of the Donglin faction, six of whom died in prison after torture. One of these men, Zuo Guangdou, in his notes to his sons left vivid descriptions of agonizing pain and suffering, which he interlaced with exclamations of his fervent devotion to the emperor, such as "my body belongs to my ruler-father."[23] Like He Xinyin and Li Zhi, Zuo demonstrated his Confucian selflessness even to the point of death, but his martyrdom, unlike theirs, testifies to the persuasiveness of a kind of Confucian authoritarianism in which even a carpenter-emperor could command the loyalty others might think due, if at all, only to a sage. To the end, the dynasty retained the loyalty of most of its officials.

Not content with actual power, Wei also thirsted for public recognition. He heaped honors on himself and even had a nephew take the emperor's place in performing sacrifices in the imperial temple. He also encouraged a movement to have temples housing his image built throughout China. But he did not survive Emperor Xizong for long, and the temples perished shortly after the man. The succeeding emperor, Sizong (r. 1627–1644), attempted reform during his reign, but the lack of a consistent policy is suggested by the high turnover of the regime's highest officials: from 1621 to 1644 the presidents of the Six Ministries were changed 116 times.

Bureaucratic infighting and corruption was something the dynasty could no longer afford, for during the reign of Shenzong the earlier fiscal surplus had been turned into a mounting deficit. But the trouble went deeper:

> The Ming fiscal administration was in essence built on the foundation of a grain economy. With its diversified rates and measurements, self-supporting institutions, regional and departmental self-sufficiency,

divided budget, separate channels of cash flow, numerous material and corvee labor impositions, and local tax captains, the fiscal machinery was grossly unfit for a new monetary economy. . . . However, [these unsatisfactory features of the Ming fiscal administration] would not have been so appallingly evident had not the wide circulation of silver thoroughly changed the nation's economic outlook. The archaic fiscal structure became more outdated than ever because it was set against the background of a mobile and expanding economy.[24]

The wide circulation of silver also left China vulnerable to inflation when silver imports, largely from the Spanish Americas through Manila, were interrupted.

The delicate balance between the central government and the local elite was upset when the dynasty made too many concessions to the gentry. Too much was given away; too many fields were removed from the tax rolls. Large landowners were able to find tax shelters through various manipulations, and only peasant freeholders remained to pay taxes. Locally resentment against the gentry grew, and the shortage of funds forced the dynasty to neglect vital public works. Grain stored for emergency use was sold off. Even the postal system was shut down. Finally, the regime failed to pay even its most strategically placed troops: when the end came, the capital garrison had not been paid for five months.

Military deserters and dismissed postal employees were among those who took the lead in forming the outlaw gangs that appeared first in Northern Shaanxi and then spread from there. As they grew in size and strength, they progressed from disorganized raiding to more ambitious objectives. Two groups emerged as the most powerful. One, established in Sichuan, was led by Zhang Xianzhong (c. 1605–1647), a leader notorious for his brutality. The other was led by Li Zicheng (c. 1605–1645), a former postal attendant, whom the official sources depict as a cruel but dedicated leader, and who, in the twentieth century, came to be celebrated in the People's Republic as a hero. In 1644 Li Zicheng seized Beijing, and the Ming emperor committed suicide, but Li proved unable to found a new dynasty, for he had not taken the necessary ideological and administrative steps to win over the members of the scholar-official elite. For them he represented at best an unknown force, and no one could rule China without their cooperation. This was understood by Li's most powerful and capable competitors even though they came from Manchuria. When they built their dynasty, they made extensive use of Ming precedents.

Notes

1. Frederick W. Mote, *Imperial China 900–1800* (Cambridge: Harvard Univ. Press, 1999), p. 570.

2. John W. Dardess, in Paul J. Smith and Richard von Glahn, eds., *The Song-*

Yuan Ming Transition in Chinese History (Cambridge: Harvard Univ. Press, 2003), p. 123.

3. Sarah K. Schneewind, *Community Schools and Improper Shrines: Local*

Institutions and the Chinese State in the Ming Period, 1368–1644 (Ph.D. dissertation, Columbia Univ., 1999), p. 101.

4. Schneewind, *Community Schools and Improper Shrines,* p. 120.

5. Frederick W. Mote and Denis Twitchett, eds., *The Cambridge History of China, Vol. 7: The Ming Dynasty, 1368–1644,* Part I (Cambridge: Cambridge Univ. Press, 1988), pp. 149–81.

6. Shih-Shan Henry Tsai, *Perpetual Happiness: The Ming Emperor Yongle* (Seattle: Univ. of Washington Press, 2001), p.121.

7. David Robinson, *Bandits, Eunuchs, and the Son of Heaven: Rebellion and the Economy of Violence in Mid-Ming China* (Honolulu: Univ. of Hawaii Press, 2001), p. 97.

8. Martin Heijdra, "The Socio-Economic Development of Rural China during the Ming," in Denis Twitchett and Frederick K.W. Mote, eds., *The Cambridge History of China, Vol. 8: The Ming Dynasty, 1368–1644,* Part 2 (Cambridge: Cambridge Univ. Press, 1998), p. 477.

9. Shigeta Atsushi, as discussed in Mori Masao, "The Gentry in the Ming: An Outline of the Relations between the Shih-ta fu and Local Society," *Acta Asiatica* 38 (1980): 31–53.

10. Hilary J. Beattie, *Land and Lineage in China: A Study of T'ung-ch'eng County, Anhwei, in the Ming and Ch'ing Dynasties* (Cambridge: Cambridge Univ. Press, 1979).

11. Liu Wu-chi, *An Introduction to Chinese Literature* (Bloomington: Indiana Univ. Press, 1966), pp. 216–17.

12. K'ung Shang-jen, *The Peach Blossom Fan,* trans. Chen Shih-hsiang and Harold Acton (Berkeley: Univ. of California Press, 1970), p. xiv.

13. Anne De Coursey Clapp, *The Painting of T'ang Yin* (Chicago: Univ. of Chicago Press, 1991), p. 46.

14. Norman Kutcher, trans. in Kang-I Sun Chang and Haun Sausy, eds., *Women Writers of Traditional China: An Anthology of Poetry and Criticism* (Stanford: Stanford Univ. Press, 1999), p. 170.

15. Wm. Theodore de Bary and the Conference on Ming Thought, *Self and Society in Ming Thought* (New York: Columbia Univ. Press, 1970), p. 12.

16. Wing-tsit Chan, trans., *Instructions for Practical Living and Other Neo-Confucian Writings* (New York: Columbia Univ. Press, 1963), p. 159.

17. Wing-tsit Chan, *A Source Book in Chinese Philosophy* (Princeton: Princeton Univ. Press, 1963), p. 681.

18. Chün-fang Yü, "Ming Buddhism" Chapter 14, in *Cambridge History, Vol. 8.*

19. Timothy Brook, Communication and Commerce," in *Cambridge History, Vol. 8,* p. 579.

20. Brook, p. 580.

21. Quoted in James Cahill, *Fantastics and Eccentrics in Chinese Painting* (New York: The Asia Society, 1967), p. 22.

22. Quoted in Arthur W. Hummel, ed., *Eminent Chinese of the Ch'ing Period,* Vol. 1 (Washington, DC: GPO, 1943), p. 190.

23. Quoted in Charles O. Hucker, "Confucianism and the Chinese Censorial System," in David S. Nivison and Arthur F. Wright, eds., *Confucianism in Action* (Stanford: Stanford Univ. Press, 1959), p. 208.

24. Ray Huang, "Fiscal Administration during the Ming Dynasty," in Charles O. Hucker, ed., *Chinese Government in Ming Times* (New York: Columbia Univ. Press, 1969), pp. 124–25.

9

East Asia and Modern Europe: First Encounters

The Portuguese in East Asia

The Jesuits in Japan

The Impact of Other Europeans

The "Closing" of Japan

The Jesuits in China

The Rites Controversy

The Decline of Christianity in China

Trade with the West and the Canton System

Key Dates

1514	Portuguese Reach China
1543	Portuguese Reach Japan (Shipwreck)
1549	St. Francis Xavier Lands in Kyushu
1571	Spanish Conquest of Philippines
1601	Matteo Ricci Received by Emperor of China
1614	Persecution of Christians in Japan
1630	Japan Closed to Foreigners
1700	300,000 Christian Converts in China
1742	Pope Decides against Jesuits in Rites Controversy

The early contacts between post-Renaissance Europe and China had nothing like the impact of those that were to follow in the nineteenth century. The introduction of European firearms into sixteenth century Japan merely hastened the unification of the country, accelerating but not changing the course of history. Similarly, the introduction of Western mathematics and cannon making failed to stop the decline of the Ming. More important was the trade nexus that brought silver flowing into China, but, channeled through the Chinese community in Manila, this entailed minimal personal or cultural contact.

However, the story of these early relations can be conceived as an overture setting the tone, introducing basic themes, and establishing the harmonics of the history to come. At the same time these contacts helped set the stage for that history, because the failure of the early intermediaries to build viable bridges of mutual understanding made it all the harder to do so later when China and Japan had to deal with a Europe transformed by the French and Industrial revolutions.

As in more modern times, there were interconnections between Western encounters with China and with Japan. Because the experience of the Jesuits in Japan influenced their approach to China, what happened in Japan can help us understand this period of Chinese history. In both cases the story begins with the Portuguese.

The Portuguese in East Asia

The pioneers of European global expansion were the Portuguese, who reached India in 1498, China in 1514, and Japan in 1543. Having wrested control of the seas from their Arab rivals, they established their Asian headquarters at Goa (1510), a small island off the coast of West India. They then went on to capture Malacca (1511), a vital center for the lucrative spice trade, located on the straits which separate the Malay Peninsula from Sumatra (see Figure 9.1).

It was the desire to break the Arab spice monopoly that supplied the economic motive for this initial European expansion. Spices were highly valuable relative to their bulk and weight. Easily transported and fetching a high price, they formed an attractive cargo. And there was an assured market for them in Europe, where they added flavor to an otherwise dull diet and made meat palatable in an age when animals were slaughtered in the fall for want of sufficient fodder to sustain them through the winter. They were also used in medicine and in religious ceremonies.

FIGURE 9.1 Eastern Europe and Asia in the sixteenth and seventeenth centuries.

Prospects for trade were hampered, however, by the fact that Europe, needing pepper and other spices from Asia, had no European commodities of equal value that could be marketed in Asia. Lacking access to silver, the Portuguese initially financed themselves by a mixture of trade and piracy, taking advantage of their superior ships, weapons, and seamanship. They derived income from transporting goods from one Asian country to another: Southeast Asian wares to China, Chinese silk to Japan, and Japanese silver to China. They used their profits from this trade to purchase spices and other products for European markets. But before this trade could prosper, they had to secure entry into China and Japan. This posed problems quite different from those they had encountered in seizing a small island off the coast of politically divided India or in driving the Arabs from Malacca.

In China they got off to a very bad start. Not waiting for official permission to trade, they engaged in illegal commerce and even built a fort on Lintin Island, located at the mouth of the river that connects Canton to the sea. Their unruly behavior did not endear them to the Ming authorities and served to confirm the opinion that these "ocean devils" were a new kind of barbarian. The outrageous behavior of the Portuguese traders was further embellished by the Chinese imagination.

When the Portuguese bought kidnapped Chinese children as slaves, the Chinese concluded that their purpose was to eat them. The Chinese long continued in the firm belief that they were dealing with barbarous child-eaters. More than just a popular rumor held by the ignorant, this belief found its way into the official history of the Ming dynasty.

The first Portuguese envoy to China not only failed to obtain commercial concessions, but he also ended his life in a Cantonese prison. It was a most inauspicious beginning. But the Portuguese would not leave, and their superiority on the seas made it impossible for the Chinese to drive them out. In 1557 an arrangement was reached, permitting the Portuguese to establish themselves in Macao in exchange for an annual payment. There the Portuguese administered their own affairs, but the territory remained under Chinese jurisdiction until Macao was ceded to Portugal in 1887.

The Jesuits in Japan

Trade and booty were not the only objectives of the Europeans who ventured into Asian waters. Missionary work was also important: mid-sixteenth-century Goa boasted some eighty churches and convents. From the beginning, the missionary impulse provided a strong incentive as well as religious sanction for European expansion, and it was the missionary rather than the trader who served as the prime intermediary between the civilizations of East Asia and the West from the sixteenth to the twentieth centuries.

Among the early missionaries, the great pioneers were the Jesuits, members of the Society of Jesus. Founded in 1540, this tightly disciplined religious order formed the vanguard of the Catholic Counter-Reformation. They were the "cavalry of the church," prepared to do battle with Protestant heretics in Europe and/or the heathen in the world beyond. Along with its stress on martial discipline and intensive religious training, the Society was noted for its insistence on intellectual vigor and depth of learning. The latter included secular as well as sacred studies, and the ideal Jesuit was as learned as he was disciplined and devout.

In 1549, less than ten years after the founding of the Jesuit order, St. Francis Xavier (1506–1552), one of the original members of the Society, landed on Kyushu, the most accessible of Japan's four major islands. This was just six years after the Japanese had first encountered Europeans, some shipwrecked Portuguese who had landed on the island of Tanegashima. Xavier was well received and was soon able to establish relations with important men in Kyushu. First impressions on both sides were favorable. The Japanese were impressed by the strong character and dignified bearing of the European priests. The Jesuit combination of martial pride, stern self-discipline, and religious piety fitted well with the ethos of sixteenth-century Japan, nor did the Christian religion seem altogether strange.

On the contrary, Christianity, when initially brought to Japan from Goa, seemed like just another type of Buddhism. Some of its ceremonies were similar, and it was difficult for the early priests to convey the subtleties of theology, to explain the difference between God and the cosmic Buddha, for example, or to distinguish Paradise from the Buddhist Pure Land. At last the Jesuit fathers concluded that the devil, in all of his malicious cleverness, had deliberately fashioned Buddhism to resemble the true faith so as to confound and confuse the people.

The initial meeting of the Jesuits and the Japanese was facilitated by similarities in their feudal backgrounds. In Japan, the Europeans found a society that resembled their own far more than did any other outside Europe. "The people," wrote Alessandro Valignano (1539–1606), "are all white, courteous and highly civilized, so much so that they surpass all the other known races of the world."[1] Only the Chinese were to receive similar praise—and, indeed, to be regarded as "white." Donald F. Lach has summarized the qualities the Jesuits found to admire in the Japanese: "their courtesy, dignity, endurance, frugality, equanimity, industriousness, sagaciousness, cleanliness, simplicity, discipline, and rationality."[2] On the negative side, besides paganism, the Jesuits were appalled at the prevalence of sodomy among the military aristocracy and the monks. They criticized the Japanese propensity to commit suicide and also found fault with the "disloyalty of vassal to master, their dissimulation, ambiguity, and lack of openness in their dealings, their bellicose nature, their inhuman treatment of enemies and unwanted children, their failure to respect the rule of law, and finally their unwillingness to give up the system of concubinage."[3] Nevertheless, the similarities between Japanese culture and their own gave the Jesuits high hopes for the success of their mission.

In their everyday behavior the Jesuits tried to win acceptance by adapting themselves to local manners and customs, as long as these did not run counter to their own creed. "Thus," Valignano observed, "we who come hither from Europe find ourselves as veritable children who have to learn to eat, sit, converse, dress, act politely, and so on. . . ."[4] They learned how to squat Japanese style, learned to employ the Japanese language with its various levels of politeness, and mastered the art of tea—the Jesuit dwelling was usually equipped with a tea room so that their guests could be properly entertained. C. R. Boxer has pointed out that the Christian monks came from a land with rather different standards of personal cleanliness: "Physical dirt and religious poverty tended to be closely associated in Catholic Europe where lice were regarded as the inseparable companions of monks and soldiers."[5] But in Japan the devoted monks even learned to wash, a major concession to Japanese sensibilities. Still there were limits: Valignano could not bring himself to endorse the Japanese custom of taking a hot bath every day. That would really be going too far!

Careful attention to the niceties of etiquette was required of the Jesuit fathers in their strategy of working from the top down. It was their hope to transform Japan into a Christian land by first converting the rulers and then allowing the faith to seep down to the populace at large. The purpose of their labors was not to Europeanize Japan or China but to save souls. They realized that the enthusiastic support of the ruling authority would be an invaluable asset, whereas without at least the ruler's tacit approval they could do nothing.

This approach met with considerable success in Kyushu, where they converted important local lords, who ordered their people to adopt the foreign faith. Although there were numerous cases of genuine conversion, some lords simply saw the light of commerce, adopting a Christian stance in the hope of attracting the Portuguese trade to their ports. On at least one occasion, when the great Portuguese ship did not appear, they promptly turned their backs on the new faith. The Jesuits themselves became involved in this trade and also in politics. For seven years they even held the overlordship of Nagasaki, granted to them by a Christian lord.

Xavier and the monks who came after him realized that real progress for their mission depended on the will not only of local Kyushu lords but also of the central government. Xavier's initial trip to Kyoto came at an unpropitious time—the city was in disorder. But Nobunaga (1532–1584), the first of Japan's three great unifiers after a century of division, soon became a friend of the Jesuits. Attracted by their character and interested in hearing about foreign lands, perhaps he was also happy to talk with someone not part of the hierarchical order that he himself headed. This personal predilection coincided nicely with reasons of state. It was consistent with his hostility toward the Buddhist orders and with his desire to keep the trading ships coming in. Hideyoshi (1536–1598), Nobunaga's successor, was at first similarly well disposed toward the foreign religion. He liked dressing up in Portuguese clothes, complete with rosary, and once said that the only thing that kept him from converting was the Christian insistence on monogamy.

The political and economic success of the Jesuits helped the spread of Christianity, but power, or the semblance of power, always entails risks. There was the danger that the ruler might perceive the activities of the monks not as assets bolstering his own position but as liabilities, actual or potential threats to his authority. A portent of future disaster came in 1587 when Hideyoshi issued an order expelling the monks. Eager to encourage trade and not really feeling seriously threatened, he did not enforce the decree, but it foreshadowed the persecutions that were to begin in earnest 36 years later.

Meanwhile, there was a surge of popularity for things Western, for instance, "Southern barbarian screens," showing the giant black ships of the foreigners and the foreigners themselves (see Figure 9.2).

Other scenes, based on paintings from Europe, depicted various barbarian topics: the battle of Lepanto, an Italian court, European cities, and maps of the world, not to mention religious subjects. Whereas some artists painted European subjects Japanese style, others experimented with Western perspective and techniques of shading to produce three-dimensional effects. Western motifs were not limited to painting. Western symbols were widely used in decoration: a cross on a bowl, a few words of Latin on a saddle, and so forth.

The Impact of Other Europeans

Despite the order of 1587, Western influences continued to enter Japan. The situation was further complicated when the Portuguese were followed by other Europeans. The first of these to reach Japan were the Spanish, whose conquest

FIGURE 9.2 "Southern Barbarians" in Japan. Namban screen. (© Freer Gallery of Art, Smithsonian Institution, Washington, DC. [F1965.22].)

of the Philippines (named after Philip II) was completed in 1571. To the Japanese, Manila presented a new source of profitable trade, but the colonization of the Philippines also alerted them to the imperialist ambitions of the Europeans and revealed connections between Christian evangelism and colonialism. With the arrival of the Dutch and English Protestants in the early 1600s, there were also Europeans in Japan who broke the link between trade and missionary activity and did their best to fan Japanese suspicions of their Catholic rivals. Now, as later, the "West" did not represent a single interest, nor did it speak with a single voice.

The Spanish empire differed from that of Portugal in kind as it did in scale. Whereas the Portuguese maintained themselves by the proceeds from the inter-Asia trade, the Spanish commanded the precious metals of the New World, especially the silver that reached China by way of Manila to pay for Chinese silks. The immediate effect on Japan of the coming of the Spaniards was to complicate the situation of the Jesuits. The Spanish were every bit as committed to the missionary enterprise as were the Portuguese, but they patronized Franciscan monks rather than Jesuits. The first Franciscan arrived in Japan from Manila in 1587. Much less well informed about conditions in Japan than the Jesuits, the Franciscans were less discreet in their work. They rejected the Jesuit strategy of working from the top down, and, instead of associating with the elite, worked among the poor and forgotten, the sick and miserable—those at the very bottom of society. The Jesuits did not disguise their contempt for the ignorance and poverty of the Franciscans, the "crazy friars" (*fraile idiotas*) as they called them, and these sentiments were heartily reciprocated by the friars, who scoffed at Jesuit pretensions.

The "Closing" of Japan

It was an omen of things to come when, in 1597, Hideyoshi crucified six Franciscan missionaries and eighteen of their Japanese converts after the pilot of a Spanish ship driven ashore in Japan reportedly boasted about the power and ambitions of his king. Like Nobunaga and Hideyoshi, Tokugawa Ieyasu, the third and last of Japan's three unifiers, was at first friendly to the Christians, but he too turned against them. In 1606 Christianity was declared illegal, and in 1614 he undertook a serious campaign to expel the missionaries.

By 1614 there were more than 300,000 converts in Japan. The destruction of Christianity was long and painful. Tortures, such as hanging a man upside down with his head in a pit filled with excrement, were used to induce people to renounce their faith. Before it was all over, more than 3000 persons were recognized as martyrs by the Vatican, of whom fewer than seventy were Europeans. Others died without achieving martyrdom. From 1637 to 1638 there was a rebellion in Shimabara, near Nagasaki, against a lord who combined merciless taxation with cruel suppression of Christianity. Fought under banners on which Christian slogans were written in Portuguese and led by some masterless samurai, it was a Christian version of the rural uprisings characteristic of the century of warfare before Nobunaga. In its suppression, some 37,000 Christians lost their lives.

Persuasion as well as violence was employed in the campaign against Christianity. Opponents of Christian dogma argued that the idea of a personal creator was absurd and asked why, if God were both omnipotent and good, he should have tempted Adam and Eve and devised eternal punishment in Hell for non-Christians even though they led exemplary lives. According to Christian teaching, even the sage emperors Yao and Shun would end in hell. The First Commandment was attacked as leading to disobedience of parents and lord; a loyal retainer should accompany his lord even into hell.

Such arguments suggest that the Japanese saw Christianity as potentially subversive, not only of the political order, but of the basic social structure, for it challenged accepted values and beliefs and demanded a radical reappraisal of long-revered traditions. Its association with European expansionism posed a threat from abroad, and, as exemplified by the Shimabara Rebellion, it also harbored the seeds of radical disruption at home. Thus, the motivation for the government's suppression of Christianity was secular, not religious. The government was not worried about the state of its subjects' souls, but it was determined to wipe out a dangerous doctrine.

New restrictions followed. The Spaniards were expelled in 1624, one year after the English had left voluntarily. In 1630 Japanese were forbidden to go over-

FIGURE 9.3 *A Dutch Dinner Party.* Prints such as this satisfied the public's curiosity about the strange customs of the Westerners—and may or may not have been accurate portrayals. Color print, 12.99 in × 8.66 in. (© Charles E. Tuttle & Company, Tokyo.)

seas or to return from there or to build ships capable of long voyages. The Portuguese were expelled after the Shimabara Rebellion on the grounds of complicity with that uprising. When they sent an embassy in 1640, its members were executed. The only Europeans left were the Dutch (see Figure 9.3), who kept other Europeans from trying their luck in Japan until the English and Russians challenged Dutch naval supremacy in the late eighteenth and early nineteenth centuries. In 1641 the Dutch themselves were moved to the tiny artificial island of Deshima in Nagasaki Harbor, where they were virtually confined as in a prison. The annual Dutch vessel to Deshima was all that remained of Japan's contact with Europe, but it sufficed to spark the growth of "Dutch Learning" there.

Japan's closing was far from complete. Trade and diplomatic contacts with Korea and the Ryukyu Islands continued. Japan refused to participate in the Qing tribute system, but this did not prevent an annual average of almost twenty-six Chinese ships from coming to Nagasaki.

The Jesuits in China

Xavier had hoped to begin the work in China himself, considering that this was not only a great project in itself but also a major step in the Christianization of Japan, providing an answer to the question he was constantly asked there: "If yours is the true faith why have not the Chinese, from whom comes all wisdom, heard of it?"[6] Xavier died before he could reach his goal, and three further Jesuit attempts to enter China also failed. Then Valignano established a special training center in Macao so that missionaries could study the Chinese language and culture in preparation for work in China. As elsewhere, it was Jesuit policy in China to concentrate on gaining the support and, if possible, the conversion of the upper classes. To this end, they once more went as far as possible to accommodate themselves to native sensibilities and ways of doing things.

Again, the strong character and attractive personalities of the first missionaries were of great importance in gaining them entry. The outstanding pioneer was Matteo Ricci (1551–1610). A student of law, mathematics, and science, he also knew a good deal about cartography and something of practical mechanics. Once in the East, he was able to master the Chinese language and the classics. Slowly Ricci made himself known in Chinese officialdom, impressing scholars and officials with his knowledge of mathematics, astronomy, and cartography; his command of Chinese classical learning; and his prodigious memory. At last in 1601, after eighteen strenuous years, Ricci was received in an imperial audience and won permission for himself and his colleagues to reside in the capital. (By this time they had discarded the Buddhist robes worn by Jesuits in Japan and had adopted the gowns of Confucian scholars that were more acceptable to the Chinese.) In Beijing he was able to win over and convert a number of prominent men. By the time Ricci died in 1610, the mission was well established in the capital and accepted by the government. Ricci's body was laid to rest in a plot donated by the emperor.

During the period when the Japanese were persecuting Christians with increasing ferocity, the Jesuits in China labored fruitfully, building on the foundations laid by Ricci. They were particularly successful in demonstrating the superior accuracy of European astronomical predictions. Thereby they succeeded in displacing their Muslim and Chinese competitors and established themselves in the Bureau of Astronomy, an important and prestigious office. Jesuit gains in this area were solidified by the work of Adam Schall von Bell (1591–1666), a German Jesuit who was a trained astronomer and served as chief government astronomer in Beijing. Schall von Bell also assisted in casting cannon for the Ming, although it did not save the dynasty.

The Jesuits made some notable converts among the literati, particularly during the troubled years of the declining Ming. Most notable was Xu Guangqi (Paul Hsu, 1562–1633), who translated Euclid's *Elements* and other works on mathematics, hydraulics, astronomy, and geography, thereby becoming the first Chinese translator of European books. With the help of such men, Western science and geography were made available to China, but European influence remained limited. Thus, when Li Zhi (1527–1602), one of the most forceful and independent Late Ming thinkers, met Ricci, he was impressed with the Jesuit's personality but saw no merit in his proselytizing mission.

The triumph of the Manchus (discussed in Chapter 10) did not seriously disrupt Jesuit activity. Schall von Bell was retained by the new dynasty as their astronomer. He was followed by the Belgian Jesuit, Ferdinand Verbiest (1633–1688), the last of the trio of great and learned missionary fathers. Verbiest, like Schall von

Bell, cast cannon and in other ways won the favor of the new dynasty's greatest emperor, Kangxi. A good account of Jesuit activities at court comes from the emperor's own brush:

> With Verbiest I had examined each stage of the forging of cannons, and made him build a water fountain that operated in conjunction with an organ, and erect a windmill in the court; with the new group. . . . I worked on clocks and mechanics. Pereira taught me to play the tune "Puyanzhou" on the harpsichord and the structure of the eight-notescale, Pedrini taught my sons musical theory, and Gheradini painted portraits at the Court. I also learned to calculate the weight and volume of spheres, cubes, and cones. . . .[7]

The Emperor accepted the Jesuits' science with alacrity and took their quinine for the sake of his health. He also discussed religion with them, but here they were less successful: "I had asked Verbiest why God had not forgiven his son without making him die, but though he had tried hard to answer I had not understood him."[8] In China, as in Japan, the fathers found it most difficult to explain the central tenets of their faith to people with very different ideas about the nature of the universe and of the divine.

The high point for early Catholicism in China came in the middle years of Kangxi's reign, but by 1700 there were no more than 300,000 Christians in China, roughly the same number as in much smaller Japan a century earlier. In both cases the missionaries were there on sufferance, dependent on the good will of the authorities. And in China, as earlier in Japan, divisions between the Europeans themselves strongly contributed to their undoing.

The Rites Controversy

The controversy that brought an end to the missionary activity in China centered on the Jesuit policy of accommodation, which was opposed by rival orders, particularly and vigorously by the Dominicans. It revolved around the question of the proper attitude a Christian should adopt toward Confucianism, its doctrines, and its practices. This kind of dispute also undermined the Jesuits in Vietnam but not in Japan, where Catholic fathers of all orders agreed in their condemnation of Buddhism and Shinto and in their absolute refusal to allow their converts to have anything to do with such heathen religions.

In China, however, the basic strategy used by Ricci and followed by his successors was to accept the teachings of Confucius, "the prince of philosophers." They argued that they had come not to destroy Confucius, but to make his teachings complete, capping his doctrines with the truths of revealed religion. Like Chinese thinkers intent on using Confucius in new ways, the Jesuits also discarded and condemned previous interpretations and commentaries on the classics. They attacked Neo-Confucianism and developed new theories of their own. In their enthusiasm for the classics, the Jesuits turned Confucius into a religious teacher.

Some members of the order went as far as to trace the origin of the Chinese people to the eldest son of Noah. The most extreme even claimed to find Christian prophecies in the *Changes*. Meanwhile, the Dominicans held that the ancient Chinese were atheists and argued against the Jesuit portrayal of Confucius as a deist. The resulting literature greatly influenced Western understanding of Chinese philosophy. At its best it was a serious effort by Europeans to understand Chinese thought in what they believed to be universally valid terms.

The status of Confucius and the acceptability of the classics were major issues for missionaries operating in a society dominated by the Confucian examination system. Even more troublesome, however, was the related problem posed by Confucian observances. Were the ceremonies in veneration of Confucius, held in the temples of Confucius throughout the land, acts of religious devotion and therefore anathema to a Christian? Or were they social and political in character, secular expressions of respect for China's greatest teacher? Even more important, what about the rites performed by every family in front of the tablets representing its ancestors? Was this a worship of the departed spirits and thus the most iniquitous idolatry? Or did these acts of commemoration for one's forebears merely convey a deep sense of filial piety? Were the two kinds of ceremonials civic and moral in nature, or were they religious, and therefore sacrilegious? Consistent with their stand on Confucianism, the Jesuits claimed the ceremonies were nonreligious and therefore permissible. The Dominicans disagreed.

The issue was fiercely debated, for much was at stake. Theology aside, it is easy to see the practical reasons for the Jesuit standpoint. To exclude Christians from performing the ceremonies for Confucius would be to exclude them from participation in Chinese political life. Worse still, to prohibit the ritual veneration of ancestors would not only deprive Chinese Christians of their sense of family but would make them appear as unfilial, immoral monsters in the eyes of their non-Christian fellows. If the advocates of Christianity rejected the classics and insisted on this kind of nonconformist behavior, it would be turned into a religion subversive of the Chinese state and society. Suffering persecution and widespread condemnation, Christianity would be unavailable to many souls, who would thus be deprived of their chance for salvation.

But the Dominicans could muster strong counterarguments. Why should a church that condemned Protestant Christianity condone Confucian Christianity? The issue was not the acceptability of Christianity to the Chinese but whether the salvation of souls would be fatally jeopardized by tolerating false Confucian doctrines. In their eyes, nothing could be allowed to interfere with the Christian's sacred duty to maintain the purity of the faith.

The Decline of Christianity in China

The question, "When does Christianity cease to be Christianity?" was to reappear in the nineteenth century and is not all that different from the question, "When does Marxism cease to be Marxism?" which agitated some thinkers in the twenti-

FIGURE 9.4 A lady's portrait in Western-style costume (inspired by Daiyu). Anonymous, mid-eighteenth century. (© Palace Museum, Beijing.)

eth century. Such questions are never easy to resolve, and perhaps only true believers need grapple with them. Be that as it may, in the papacy, the church had a source of authority that could rule on what was acceptable and what was not. The process of reaching a decision was complicated and involved.

What is important here is that the outcome went against the Jesuits. In 1704 the pope condemned Chinese rituals, and in 1742 a decree was issued that settled all points against the Jesuits. This remained the position of the Catholic Church until 1939. Grand and powerful emperors such as Kangxi, however, resented Rome's claims of authority over their subjects and saw no reason to abide by the papal judgment as to what was fitting for their realm. They naturally favored the Jesuit point of view. In the end, the pope would send only those missionaries the emperor of China would not accept, whereas those already in China had to choose between expulsion for defying the emperor or excommunication for defying the pope.

Some missionaries did remain in China after the break, including the Jesuit Giuseppe Castiglione, who served as court painter for half a century, from 1715 to 1766. Among other things, he designed a miniature Versailles for the Summer Palace, destroyed in the nineteenth century. Michael Sullivan has described his fusion of artistic traditions as a "synthetic style in which with taste and skill and the utmost discretion, Western perspective and shading, with even an occasional hint of chiaroscuro, were blended to give an added touch of realism to painting otherwise entirely Chinese in manner."[9] Figure 9.4 shows a painting in the European manner done at the Chinese court. Just as Louis XV of France sometimes amused himself by having his courtiers and their ladies assume Chinese dress, the Qing emperor Qianlong enjoyed exotic Western costume on occasion. Meanwhile a Western perspective appeared in color prints intended for a broad popular market.

Regardless of the Rites Controversy, the Christians also had opponents in China itself, motivated by the usual combination of self-interest and conviction.

There was no Chinese counterpart to Nagasaki: instead, the view of foreigners in Canton and the surrounding area, the part of China most exposed to the Europeans, at this time was already negative. Christianity was proscribed in 1724. Some churches were seized, and other acts of persecution occurred, but the suppression of Christianity was not as thorough as that which had taken place in Japan. This was probably because there was no Chinese equivalent to the Shimabara Rebellion—at least not yet. Not until the nineteenth century did the potential of Christianity as an ideology of peasant rebellion become evident in China. By the end of the eighteenth century, the number of Chinese converts had been reduced to about half what it had been at the beginning of the century.

Western contact did influence some areas of intellectual life, such as astronomy and cartography, but remained peripheral, far removed from the mainstream of Chinese intellectual life. There was no revolution in thought or art. Those of the Qing elite who came in touch with things Western rarely progressed much beyond the appreciation of European exotica, such as clocks and other mechanical devices. Ricci himself lived on as the patron saint of clockmakers. The influence was much stronger in the other direction, for the Jesuit reports on China were well received in Europe and helped to create the image of an ideal China dear to the philosophers of the European Enlightenment.

A major difference between the course of events in China and Japan was that in China trade considerations did not influence government decisions concerning missionary policies.

Trade with the West and the Canton System

After 1683, the Qing, recognizing that the flourishing maritime trade with Southeast Asia was of great economic importance to coastal communities and posed no security problems for the empire, basically left its management to local authorities. Although Kangxi instituted some restrictions on foreigners trying out the Chinese market, it was Qianlong who restricted them to Canton, where a special area was set aside for the warehouses (called "factories") of the foreign traders, who were allowed to reside there but not to bring their wives and settle down (see Figure 9.5).

There were other restrictions under this Canton System (1760–1842). In all their transactions foreign traders were required to deal with a group of Chinese merchants who had been granted a monopoly of foreign trade. These merchants belonged to the Cohong, an association of firms (or *hong*) established for that purpose. In theory the Cohong was composed of a maximum of thirteen *hong*, but in practice there were only seven or eight such establishments, supervised by an imperial official who usually squeezed a good deal of personal profit out of his position. Each foreign ship was placed under the responsibility of a particular *hong*, which handled not only commercial matters but also saw to it that duties were paid and that the foreigners conducted themselves properly.

FIGURE 9.5 The Canton waterfront, c. 1760. Artist unknown. One of four panels creating a panorama of the waterfront. Notice the flags of Western nations in front of their respective warehouses. Gouache on silk, 29.02 in × 18.78 in. (© Peabody Essex Museum, Salem, MA.)

Under this system, the foreigners were not granted direct access to Chinese officials, nor were there any provisions for government-to-government relations. On the British side, the prime agent was the East India Company, which, under government charter, enjoyed a monopoly of trade between England and China and governed much of India, an arrangement not challenged until the nineteenth century, when the idea and forces of free trade triumphed.

The Qing taxed foreign maritime trade more heavily than that of Chinese ships, but both were administered separately from the tributary system of conducting foreign relations. Consequently, when Macartney, in 1793, and Lord Amherst, in 1816, came to China to try to expand trade and open European-style diplomatic relations, they ran head-on into a well-established dynastic practice that the Qing court saw no reason to change. The system continued to operate until China faced a Europe that could no longer be contained.

Notes

1. C.R. Boxer, *The Christian Century in Japan* (Berkeley: Univ. of California Press, 1951), p. 74.

2. Donald F. Lach, *Asia in the Making of Europe, Vol. I: The Century of Discovery* (Chicago: Univ. of Chicago Press, 1965), p. 728.

3. Ibid.

4. Quoted in Boxer, *The Christian Century in Japan,* p. 214.

5. Ibid.

6. A.H. Rowbotham, *Missionary and Mandarin* (Berkeley: Univ. of California Press, 1942), p. 46.

7. Quoted in Jonathan Spence, *Emperor of China* (New York: Alfred A. Knopf, 1974), pp. 72–73.

8. Spence, *Emperor of China,* p. 84.

9. Michael Sullivan, *The Meeting of Eastern and Western Art* (New York: New York Graphic Society, 1973), pp. 66–67.

10

The Qing Dynasty

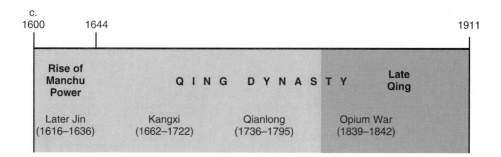

c. 1600	1644			1911
Rise of Manchu Power		QING DYNASTY		**Late Qing**
Later Jin (1616–1636)	Kangxi (1662–1722)	Qianlong (1736–1795)	Opium War (1839–1842)	

In this chapter we will consider the Qing Dynasty (1644–1911) to around 1800. This was a century and a half of major achievements: the state reached its greatest geographical extent (Figure 10.1); the economy grew, as did the population; scholars and artists were productive; and popular culture flourished. In terms of cultural and political sophistication and the dynamics of economic development, China was comparable to the most advanced societies on earth, including Europe, whose "great divergence"[1] into sustained industrial growth was still to come. But by 1800 the Qing had seen its best days, even if no one could yet imagine that it was to be China's last dynasty.

The establishment of the new dynasty was a momentous event, but by no means did it represent a radical break with the past. Social and cultural transformations tend to be more gradual than political change, and, given the limitations of seventeenth-century communication and transportation technology, the new rulers could not have refashioned China had they wanted to. In recognition of the considerable continuity between the Qing and its Ming predecessor (1368–1644), scholars interested in the long view frequently include both under the rubric "late imperial" China.

The Founding of the Qing

As we have seen, a major theme in Chinese history is the interaction between the Chinese and their nomadic and seminomadic neighbors whose way of life made them formidable horsemen and fierce warriors. One military alternative was the kind of static defense that induced the Ming dynasty to rebuild The Great Wall into the impressive structure it is today. In the northeast, the Ming relied on the Willow Palisades, a barrier formed by lines of willows and a deep trench fortified by military checkpoints.

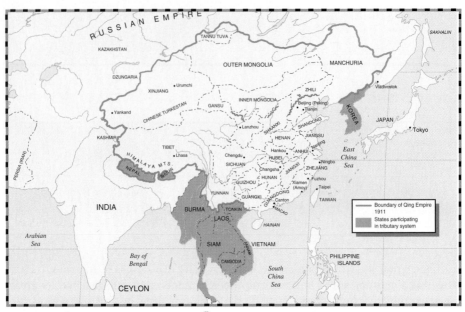

FIGURE 10.1 The Qing Empire, 1775.

Beyond the Willow Palisades lay Manchuria, home of the Jurchen, who spoke a language related to Korean but not to Chinese. Although the Jurchen traced themselves back to the Jin Dynasty (1115–1234) that had once dominated north China, they had long been divided into tribes. In the north they subsisted by hunting and fishing, but in the south, where they were in contact with Chinese speakers, they farmed, raised livestock, and took pleasure and pride in their horsemanship and hunting skills. The ethnic origins of the inhabitants of the agricultural lands of Liaodong and southern Manchuria were diverse. They were not necessarily descended from Chinese settlers, but they spoke Chinese and by and large were Chinese culturally. There was also a major Mongolian presence in Manchuria, and the Mongol influence on the Jurchen was strong.

To bring the various peoples of Manchuria into a state and create a regional power took Nurgaci (1559–1626), clan and tribal chief, more than twenty-five years as he fought, negotiated, and married his way to leadership and power. To facilitate building of the state, he ordered the creation of a script, based on Mongolian, to write the Jurchen language. Originally favored by the Ming, Nurgaci continued to send tribute to Beijing until 1609, but in 1616, he declared himself Emperor of the Later Jin. In 1625, Nurgaci established his capital at Shengyuan but died the following year. It was his son, Hong Taiji (r. 1626–1643), who created a new ethnic identity called "Manchu" and envisioned a broader empire. Defeated by Ming cannon in a battle in 1626, the Manchus made good use of Chinese artillery experts they captured in a 1629 invasion of North China that came close to Beijing. As a result, two years later Manchu forces were able to employ the new weapons effectively. At the same time Hong followed a policy of centralization of power and the use of Chinese officials to build a state capable of conquering and ruling Ming China.

In 1636, while remaining "divine khan" to his tribal subjects, Hong Taiji signaled his ambition to rule China by founding the new "Qing" (pure) dynasty. Nothing in the Chinese tradition stipulated that the imperial house had to be ethnically Chinese. From the beginning, the new dynasty drew support from an alliance with Mongols and Chinese speakers, mostly from Manchuria. This was reflected in the organization of its armies into "banners," each with its own colors. By the time of the conquest, there were eight Manchu banners (278 companies), eight Mongol banners (120 companies), and eight "Chinese" banners (165 companies). Membership in the banners was hereditary. After the conquest, they were stationed in garrisons strategically located throughout the empire. There the bannermen lived apart from the local population under a general who reported directly to Beijing.

After Li Zicheng overthrew the Ming, the key to the military situation was in the hands of the Ming general Wu Sangui (1612–1678), whose army guarded Shanhaiguan, the strategic pass between the mountains and the sea that formed the eastern terminus of the Great Wall. When Wu threw his lot in with the Manchus, Li Zicheng's fate was sealed.

After the Manchus entered the capital, Beijing, in June 1644, the Qing ruler announced he had come to punish the rebels, buried the deceased Ming emperor and empress with full honors, and claimed to be the legitimate successor of the old dynasty. To consolidate and expand their control, the new rulers needed the support and participation of Chinese officials and the tacit assent of the Chinese populace. Even before they gained the capital, the dynasty sought to draw on the talents of Chinese scholars and reassure the Chinese elite by holding its first examinations.

Also before the conquest they formed a political system that balanced an Assembly of Princes and High Officials composed almost exclusively of Manchus with traditional Chinese institutions such as The Six Ministries (personnel, revenue, rites, war, justice, and public works), and the Censorate, charged with reporting on the conduct of the civil service with the right and duty also to criticize the emperor.

Despite such reassuring measures, the subjugation of the rest of China, especially the South, involved long and bloody warfare, including a terrible ten-day massacre in Yangzhou that left the city's gutters filled with corpses. After the capture of Nanjing, which Ming loyalists had made their capital, the Qing emperor forced all men to shave the forward portion of their heads and braid their hair in back into a long queue (pigtail). The Manchus were not the first to force their hair style on their subjects; the Ming had done the same in Vietnam.

After the fall of Nanjing, the Qing still faced prolonged resistance. For some forty years warfare, banditry, and peasant uprisings, along with periods of starvation and epidemics, took a heavy toll. From 1646 to 1658 much of the southeast coast was controlled by Zheng Chenggong (1624–1662), the son of a Chinese pirate-adventurer and a Japanese mother, widely known as Coxinga. From 1661 to 1669, to deprive Zheng of support and supplies, a seventeen-mile strip along the coast, extending from Zhejiang to the Vietnamese border, was completely cleared of people. Barriers, guard posts, and watch towers were erected to prevent anyone from entering. Originally based in Xiamen (Amoy), Zheng moved to Taiwan (Formosa) from which he expelled the Dutch in 1662. His son held out against the Manchus, who finally subdued the island in 1683 and placed it under the administration of Fujian Province. By then the Southwest, too, was pacified, but only after the War of the Three Feudatories (1673–1681), one of whom was Wu Sangui, who had created a practically autonomous state for himself in Yunnan and Guizhou.

In their new empire, the Manchus, who comprised only about 2 percent of the population, and their Mongol associates formed a conquest elite who were conscious of their non-Chinese heritage, forbidden to intermarry with the Chinese, and distinguished from them in dress, family rituals, diet, and lifestyle. For example, Manchu women were not allowed to have bound feet. An inner circle of this elite dominated the inner court and exercised profound influence on government throughout the life of the dynasty.

Along with claiming to be heirs of the Ming and recipients of Heaven's Mandate, Qing emperors, as Manchus, concurrently asserted the claim to rule as khans. In addition, they demonstrated an ability to draw on Buddhist traditions to make their rule acceptable to people beyond the Great Wall. Ritual observances, the rulers solemnly acting like rulers, demonstrated that they were meant to be rulers. Potent symbolism was a major component of Qing authority and power.

China proper was divided into eighteen provinces, which were further subdivided into circuits, prefectures, and counties, but Inner Asian affairs were handled by the Court of Colonial Affairs using the peoples' own languages and appealing to their own political traditions. The emperors themselves regularly studied Mongolian, Manchu, and Chinese. Although the trend was toward increasing bureaucratization, Inner Asians saw themselves as subjects of a universal empire. But China was the Center.

Early Qing Thinkers and Painters

Although many literati accepted service under the new dynasty, the most original work came from the brushes of men who refused to serve the Qing. Among those who in these turbulent times found tranquility in a Buddhist monastery was Hongren (1610–1663; see Figure 10.2), who "represented the world in a dematerialized cleansed vision . . . revealing his personal peace through the liberating form of geometric abstraction."[2]

Although Hongren had his followers, other painters who lived through the change of dynasties were too individualistic to attract followers or perpetuate styles. One such was Zhu Da, also called Bada Shanren (c. 1626–1705), whose personal behavior was distinctly odd: he sang and laughed frequently but refused to speak. His painting was equally unusual: surging landscapes, huge lotuses, and birds and fishes with the eyes of a Zen patriarch. His hand-scroll *Fish and Rocks* (see Figure 10.3) begins with a section (not shown here) done with a dry brush, and the brushwork becomes wetter as the painting proceeds. Although there are references to the Ming dynasty and himself in the poems on and in the painting, the work remains enigmatic. Zhu Da had to wait several centuries for his fame, but he exemplifies the self-expression favored by the aesthetic theory of his time, which regarded representation as crude and unworthy of gentlemen amateurs even if the distinction between amateur and professional was one more of theory than of practice.

Like Zhu Da in the world of painting, Wang Fuzhi (1619–1704) had no followers in his own time, but late in the dynasty came to be admired as a philosopher who gave primacy to *qi* and as a student of history who emphasized the fact that institutions and policies of one age or culture were not necessarily applicable to another. Another Ming loyalist with trenchant political views that had to wait for centuries for a hearing was Huang Zongxi (1610–1695), who complained that in antiquity the people had been the master, the prince the tenant, but that now the situation was reversed. "Thus he who does the greatest harm in the world is none other than the prince."[3] Among the policies advocated by Huang was restoring pre-Ming strong chief ministership, institut-

FIGURE 10.2 Hongren's masterpiece, *The Coming of Autumn,* displays a marvelous sense of structural depth. Hanging scroll, ink on paper, 48.19 in high. (© Honolulu Academy of Arts, Gift of Wilhelmina Tenney Memorial Collection, 1995 [No. 2045.1]).

ing tax and land reforms, increasing the authority of local officials, and strengthening education, including the creation of independent schools.

Huang's most influential work was a great compendium of Ming thought still widely used. The writings and teachings of Huang's contemporary, Gu Yanwu (1613–1682), made a deep impression on mainstream Qing scholarship. Objecting to the abstract speculations of Song and Ming philosophers, Gu insisted on what he considered real and practical learning, solidly based on scholarship in the original sources rather than on later commentaries. He himself wrote important studies on historical geography and inscriptions but is most famous for work in historical phonetics. His essays, collected under the title *Records of Daily*

FIGURE 10.3 *Fish and Rocks*, Zhu Da (Bada Shanren, 1624–c. 1705), Qing Dynasty. Note the water plants and lotuses on the left and the strange rock that invites speculation. Section of hand-scroll, ink on paper, 62.01 in × 11.49 in. (© Cleveland Museum of Art, John L. Severence Fund [1953.247].)

Knowledge (Rizhilu), discuss government, the examination system, and economics as well as the classics and history and show a range and critical spirit representative of the best of seventeenth-century thought. As summarized by Kai-wing Chow, "His statecraft essays addressed a wide range of issues from political structure, excessive number of degree holders and problems of overcentralization, to taxation and monetary policy."[4] Gu was influential in founding Qing philological scholarship and what came to be known as "evidential learning." Subsequent Qing scholars contributed greatly to textual scholarship.

Not all painters of the early Qing were eccentric or even persistently loyal to the Ming. Outstanding among the more orthodox painters were four artists all named Wang, among whom Wang Hui (1632–1717) was the most gifted. One of his paintings is a rendition of Fan Kuan's *Traveling among Streams and Mountains* (see Figure 6.6). His *Summer Mountains, Misty Rain* (Figure 10.4) is representative in that Wang here follows the style and composition of the masters of the Song and Yuan in "an almost magical composite" to create a painting very much his own. Wang himself formulated his agenda and expressed his aspiration: "I must use the brush and ink of the Yuan to move the peaks and valleys of the Song and infuse them with the breath-resonance of the Tang. I will then have a great synthesis."[5]

In 1691 Wang Hui received an imperial command to supervise the painting of a series of scrolls commemorating Kangxi's southern tour. He was only one of a number of painters and other men of talent to enjoy the patronage of Kangxi and in turn enhance the aura of the throne and the glory of its occupant.

The Reign of Kangxi

Kangxi was on the throne from 1662 to 1722 and actually ruled from 1668 on. As already noted, he was able to complete the Manchu conquest of China and did so in campaigns fought largely by Chinese troops under Chinese generals. After the

FIGURE 10.4 *Fishermen Returning Home,* third and last panel of *Summer Mountains, Misty Rain* (1668), Wang Hui (1632–1717). Hand-scroll, ink on paper, 19 in × 17 in. (© Asian Art Museum of San Francisco, Gift of the Tang Foundation. Presented by Nadine, Martin, and Leslie Tang in celebration of Jack C. C. Tang's sixtieth birthday [B87D8]. Used by permission.)

TABLE 10.1 The Qing Emperors

Beginning with the Ming period emperors used a single era name (*nianhao,* literally "year designation") throughout their reigns. Consequently, the emperors are often referred to by their era names rather than by their formal posthumous temple names, although these are also employed in the scholarly literature.

Era Name	Temple Name	Personal Name	Era Dates
Shunzhi	Shizu	Fulin	1644–1661
Kangxi	Shengzu	Xuanye	1662–1722
Yongzheng	Shizong	Yinzhen	1723–1735
Qianlong	Gaozong	Hongli	1736–1795
Jiaqing	Renzong	Yongyan	1796–1820
Daoguang	Xuanzong	Minning	1821–1850
Xianfeng	Wenzong	Yizhu	1851–1861
Tongzhi	Muzong	Zaichun	1862–1874
Guangxu	Dezong	Zaitian	1875–1908
Xuanzong	None	Puyi	1909–1911

incorporation of Taiwan, he allowed people to return to the southeastern coast and turned his military attention to China's borders in the North and West. In the Amur River region his army destroyed a Russian Cossack base. This success was followed by the Treaty of Nerchinsk, signed with Russia in 1689, which settled frontier problems between the two great expansive empires and regularized relations between them. It also removed the threat of a possible alliance between the Russians and a confederation of Western Mongols. Against the latter, Kangxi personally led his troops in 1696–1697 and won a great victory.

Around the middle of the seventeenth century, Western Mongols had intervened in the political-religious struggles taking place in Tibet and had remained as conquerors. In 1720 Kangxi's armies entered Tibet and installed a pro-Chinese Dalai Lama (the spiritual and secular ruler of Tibet). This was the first but not the last Qing intervention in Tibet.

Kangxi's martial exploits reflected his identification with his forebears and his desire to preserve a Manchu way of life, which he saw as essential for maintaining Manchu supremacy. Another expression of this feeling was his zest for great hunts. To help preserve Manchu distinctiveness, one of the first acts of Kangxi's reign was the closing of Manchuria to Chinese immigration. Kangxi was very much the Manchu, but he was by no means anti-Chinese. Kangxi maintained a strict balance between Manchus and Chinese in the top central administrative posts, and in the provinces, generally, a Chinese governor was counterbalanced by a governor-general, usually placed over two provinces, who was a Manchu, a Mongol, or a Chinese bannerman. Banner garrisons continued to be the main source of security. The emperor also used his Chinese bondservants, who managed the imperial household and the emperor's personal treasury. They also performed confidential tasks such as sending in secret reports on conditions in the provinces.

Kangxi was a vigorous man. He rose well before dawn each day to go through a great stack of memorials before receiving officials, beginning at 5 A.M. (later changed to 7 A.M. to accommodate officials not living near the palace). His personal tours of inspection in the south are famous. To show his benevolence, he reduced taxes and forced Manchu aristocrats to desist from seizing Chinese lands. He was also a man of wide intellectual interests, including, as we saw in Chapter 9, Western learning. He won the affection of many Chinese literati by holding a special examination in 1679 and not only patronized artists but also sponsored the compilation of the official Ming history, a great phrase dictionary, a giant encyclopedia, and an exhaustive dictionary of Chinese characters. He gave special support to the philosophy of Zhu Xi.

Yongzheng

Kangxi was one of the most successful emperors in all of Chinese history, but he was unable to provide for a smooth succession. Although he had fifty-six children, only one son was by an empress. He was designated heir apparent but disappointed his father, who complained that he was "dissolute, tyrannical, brutal, debauched."[6] He also showed signs of mental instability, and in the end Kangxi placed him in confinement but failed to appoint a successor. The claim that fourteen years later he named his fourth son on his deathbed looks very much like a later fabrication. During these years, various sons, suspicious of each other and each backed by his own political faction, conspired and maneuvered for the succession. The result was that after Kangxi's death, the throne was seized in a military coup by the fourth son, who became Emperor Yongzheng (r. 1723–1735).

Yongzheng censored the record of his accession and also suppressed other writings deemed inimical to his regime or hostile to the Manchus. Like his father, he used military force to preserve the dynasty's position in Mongolia. When Tibet was torn by civil war from 1717 to 1728, he intervened militarily, leaving a Qing resident backed by a military garrison to pursue the dynasty's interests. After the dynasty came to an end in the twentieth century, this provided a basis for Chinese claims of sovereignty over Tibet.

Yongzheng was a tough, hard-working ruler bent on effective government. During the early Qing the emperor had been assisted by the Grand Secretariat, a six-man board composed of three Manchus and three Chinese, but under Kangxi the Grand Secretariat lost its influence. In a move toward greater efficiency and control, Yongzheng created a five-man Grand Council whose members linked the inner court with the outer bureaucracy, headed by the chiefs of the six ministries. By expanding the number of officials entitled to submit secret memorials and sending them confidential replies, he operated his own channel of communication apart from the general bureaucracy and managed local government activities in unprecedented detail.

The emperor saw the need for administrative and fiscal reform and restructured the financing of local government to free magistrates from dependence on private and informal funding. Active in tax reform, he simplified the system of tax registers by combining the land and personal service taxes. This and other measures, along with strong imperial oversight, led to increased government efficiency, although in the long run effective reform below the county level proved unattainable.

Yongzheng's reign was despotic, efficient, and vigorous. By the simple device of sealing the name of the heir-apparent in a box kept in the throne room, he was able to assure that on his death there would be no struggle over the succession. Thus, he prepared the way for what was to be the dynasty's most splendid reign, that of Qianlong.

Qianlong

During Qianlong's reign (1736–1795), the Qing achieved its greatest prosperity. Expansion into Central Asia reached its greatest extent (see map, Figure 10.1). This was partly the result of Qing diplomatic skill in practicing "divide and rule" policies, their ability to work with local leaders and manipulate inner Asian symbols of authority, and the sheer power of their armies. The Qing also took advantage of the disunity and declining strength of the Inner Asian peoples. The weakening of these peoples has been subject to various interpretations. According to Morris Rossabi, the most plausible explanations include the diminishing importance of the international caravan trade in an age of developing maritime commerce, a trend toward the development of sedentary societies marked by urbanization, and Russian expansion that reduced the area to which tribes could flee in retreat, thereby reducing their mobility.[7]

Under Qianlong, Chinese Turkestan was incorporated and renamed Xinjiang. To the West, Ili was conquered and garrisoned. This brought into the empire Muslim leaders, including followers of the activist Naqshbandiyya order, difficult to convince as to the legitimacy of Qing rule. The Qing also dominated Outer Mongolia after finally defeating the Western Mongols. Its policy there was to preserve Mongol institutions, but it allowed Chinese merchants to enter and exploit the people, thus reinforcing the anti-Chinese animosities of the animal-herding Mongols. It is no accident that after the Qing fell in the twentieth century, the Mongols promptly declared their independence.

Throughout this period there were continued Mongol interventions in Tibet and a reciprocal spread of Tibetan Lamaism in Mongolia. Qianlong fought two wars of bloody repression against the Tibetan minority in western Sichuan. He again sent armies into Tibet and firmly established the Dalai Lama as ruler, with a Qing resident and garrison to preserve Qing suzerainty. Other than that, no further attempt was made to integrate Tibet into the empire after the manner of Xinjiang. To foster the loyalty of Mongols and Tibetans, Qianlong drew on the Buddhist tradition. Six tangkas (Tibetan religious paintings) survive, portraying the emperor as Manjusri, bodhisattva of compassion and wisdom. Tibetan records often refer to him by that name.

Further afield, military campaigns against Vietnam and Burma and over the Himalayas into Nepal forced local rulers to accept Qing hegemony and render tribute. Qianlong's expansion involved millions of square miles and brought into the empire non-Chinese peoples, such as Uighurs, Kazakhs, Kirghiz, and Mongols, who were at least potentially hostile. It was also a very expensive enterprise. The dynasty enjoyed unprecedented prosperity and managed in the mid-1780s to accumulate a healthy financial reserve, but its resources were not inexhaustible. Yet Qianlong delighted in the glory and wealth. He built a sumptuous summer residence, partly of Western design, and undertook grand tours of the empire. In his policy toward the literati, he combined Kangxi's generous patronage of scholarship with Yongzheng's suspicion of anti-Manchu writings. The greatest project he sponsored was the *Complete Library of Four Treasuries* (*Siku quanshu*), employing 15,000 copyists working twelve years to produce 3462 complete works in 36,000 volumes. This "final affirmation of the unity of knowledge and power in Chinese history"[8] preserved many books but also merged with a campaign to ferret out and suppress writings offensive to Manchu sensibilities.

Some 80 percent of Qianlong's officials were Chinese, but the emperor was much concerned that Manchus not become Chinese. To this effect he ordered compilation of Manchu genealogies and histories, promoted study and use of the Manchu language by Manchus, and insisted on adherence to all customs that set Manchus apart from Chinese down to the details of feminine adornment. Three earrings in each ear were mandatory for Manchu ladies, and woe to her who made do with just one in the Chinese manner. Qianlong's measures standardized Manchu lore and practices; they reaffirmed Manchu identity but rendered the tradition inflexible.

Eighteenth-Century Governance

The eighteenth century was generally a time of prosperity, when institutions functioned as smoothly as they ever had. A system of state and local granaries ensured adequate and affordable food supplies. In the rich Lower Yangzi region, local elite-run lineages constructed and operated lineage and community granaries, but elsewhere government assumed a more active role in providing these sources of emergency food. In the eighteenth century it also performed formidable feats of information gathering and coordination over the breadth of the land.

The state's concern for upholding popular morality was expressed in the promotion of village lectures based on edifying imperial pronouncements and its compilation of an officially sanctioned pantheon of local gods and spirits, although it tolerated others as long as they were not considered downright subversive. It also fostered schools. As in the case of community granaries, in the more advanced areas education was left to local initiative, but in outlying provinces officials played a more active role. Thus, a dedicated eighteenth-century governor of Yunnan provided the leadership for establishing 650 schools for the instruction of the numerous minority peoples of the province.

When the system operated effectively, as in the eighteenth century, state and society formed a continuum without a fixed boundary. Although local gentry might resist tax collection and examination candidates resent the bitter competition that left them little hope for success, essentially officials and elite shared a broad spectrum of values and ideas, pushing them to cooperate rather than compete and to work in harmony rather than conflict. As a recent study puts it:

> Because the state understood the art of ruling to include shaping people's moral behavior, it was inclined to be meddlesome, authoritarian, and censorious. But at the same time, because only people who freely choose to do the right thing can be said to have high moral standards, the state accepted and even promoted initiatives among its subjects that it saw as likely to make people take their moral and social agency seriously.[9]

Eighteenth-Century Literati Culture

Following the lead of Gu Yanwu, but without his breadth, Qing scholars engaged in "evidential learning," rejected philosophical speculation, and relied on careful textual study to reveal the meaning of the classics:

> If only they [those who seek the Way] correct primary and derived characters, discern their pronunciation, read the explanations and glosses, and master the commentaries and notes, the meaning and principles will appear on their own, and the Way within them.[10]

Scholars of evidential learning made important, even iconoclastic, discoveries concerning the questionable historicity of parts of such canonical texts as the *Changes,* the *Documents,* and the *Rites (Liji).* One effect was to undermine the examination system orthodoxy, but the concentration on philology (historical linguistics) easily led to the view that textual studies alone were truly "solid" (in the sense that they avoided abstract speculation) and "practical."

Yan Yuan (1635–1704) was one prominent scholar who focused on practice and condemned both quiet meditation and book learning as standing in the way of true self-cultivation, which should lead to the practice of classical virtues and rites, thereby engendering the capability of changing the world. He studied military science and medicine and emphasized rigorous adherence to classic rites, specific guidelines on how to reform society and conduct one's life. During the eighteenth century scholarly and social interests converged as performance of classic and expensive rites became "an emblem of sociocultural superiority."[11]

Yan's chief disciple Li Gong (1659–1733), like many of his peers, expounded his teachings in the form of commentaries on the classics. A major eighteenth-century thinker was Dai Zhen (1723–1777), who made important contributions to linguistics, astronomy, mathematics, and geography as well as philosophy. Like most of the creative seventeenth-century thinkers, he rejected the metaphysical existence of *li,* which he considered simply the pattern of things. He also disputed Zhu Xi's dualistic theory of human nature, insisting that it contradicts the teachings of Mencius that human nature is one whole and all good and that moral perfection consists in fulfilling one's natural inclinations.

Dai Zhen shared his age's faith in philology, but this was not true of his contemporary Zhang Xuecheng (1738–1801), who strongly disliked philological studies and sought meaning in the study and writing of history. Zhang is perhaps most famous for his thesis that "the six classics are all history," by which he meant that they are not "empty" theoretical discussions but that they document antiquity and illustrate the *Dao.* A scholar must not stop at the facts but get at the meaning. Zhang once compared a work of history to a living organism: its facts are like bones, the writing is like the skin, and its meaning corresponds to the organism's vital spirit.

Along with history and philosophy, another subject of perennial concern to Chinese scholars was the function and value of literature—and the criteria by which it should be judged. The poet Yuan Mei (1716–1797) held that the purpose of poetry is to express emotion and that it must give pleasure; he rejected the didactic view, held by Zhang Xuecheng, among others, that it must convey moral instruction.

Yuan's poetry and prose reflect the life of a talented, refined eighteenth-century hedonist, unconventional within the bounds of good taste, and marginally aware of the exotic West. One of his prize possessions was a large Western mirror much admired by his female pupils.

Among Yuan's less conventional works are a cookbook and a collection of ghost stories. His interest in ghosts was shared by his friend, the painter Le Ping (1735–1799), the youngest of the "Eight Eccentrics of Yangzhou," a man who claimed to have seen the apparitions he painted. The brush of Li Shan, another of these famous eight artists, created the lotus that graces the cover of our book.

Literati women, as well as men, continued to write poetry. They disdained the verse of courtesans highly popular in the Late Ming and increased poetry's thematic scope. Although "the lovelorn poems of lonely ladies" remained popular, Susan Mann emphasizes the "growing number of poems exploring other domains of feminine sensibility: education and the acquisition of learning, spiritual development and the rewards of old age, female friendship and its intimacies, parental heartache and its intermittent release in joy and pride."[12] Furthermore, to have a published female in the family was now a source of pride.

In the eighteenth century, painters of various schools developed their manners and styles: professionals working in the meticulous and mannered "Northern" style, eclectics drawing on diverse traditions and models, and individualists striving, sometimes excessively, for originality. An unusually interesting and prolific artist was the painter Gao Qipei (1660–1734). Even in the Song dynasty and earlier, artists had experimented with unconventional materials instead of using a brush, but none had gone as far as Gao (see Figure 10.5).

Qing painters and scholars generally perceived themselves as latecomers in a long and revered tradition. As such they faced a dilemma similar to that of painters, poets, and composers of our own time who no longer feel they can contribute to the traditional lines of development in their arts, that is, be another Rembrandt or Beethoven. What had been valid for one age could not serve another. Thus, some literati artists cultivated the notion that the epitome of art was non-art, that is, the deliberate cultivation of innocent awkwardness. Unusual behavior was tolerated, and it became quite acceptable to sell one's paintings.

Both Gao and Le did so without jeopardizing their "amateur" status. Meanwhile, openly professional artists, who did not claim literati status, sold their work to ordinary, unsophisticated folk who appreciated bright colors and verisimilitude. Colored woodblock prints also appealed to a wide audience, as did popular drama and vernacular literature. The latter, in particular, reached new heights.

Fiction

Many of the dynasty's best writers and thinkers were men who had failed in the examination route to success, an experience that probably helped them to view society with a measure of critical and even satiric detachment. The examinations them-

FIGURE 10.5 *Tiger Seen from Above* (c. 1700), Gao Qipei (1660–1734). Ink and colors on paper, 20.24 in. × 41.46 in. At the upper right, Gao Qipei wrote the following text: "Life with the fingers from the man from outside the Shanghai gate." Beneath it are several red stamps. (© Rijksmuseum, Amsterdam [AK-RK-1991-10]).

selves were a favorite target. Pu Songling (1640–1715) wrote this account of the seven transformations of a candidate in the provincial examination:

> When he first enters the examination compound and walks along, panting under his heavy load of luggage, he is just like a beggar. Next, while undergoing the personal body search and being scolded by the clerks and shouted at by the soldiers, he is just like a prisoner. When he finally enters his cell and, along with the other candidates, stretches his neck to peer out, he is just like the larva of a bee. When the examination is finished at last and he leaves, his mind in a haze and his legs tottering, he is just like a sick bird that has been released from a cage. While he is wondering when the results will be announced and waiting to learn whether he passed or failed, so nervous that he is startled even by the rustling of the trees and the grass and is unable to sit or stand still, his restlessness is like that of a monkey on a leash. When at last the results are announced and he has definitely failed, he loses his vitality like one dead, rolls over on his side, and lies without moving, like a poisoned fly. Then, when he pulls himself together and stands up, he is provoked by every sight and sound, gradually flings away everything within his reach, and complains of the illiteracy of the examiners. When he calms down at last, he finds everything in the room broken. At this time he is like a pigeon smashing its own precious eggs. These are the seven transformations of a candidate.[13]

This examination was held in a labyrinthine compound, with the candidates housed in individual cells where they had to spend the night. It was an eerie place sealed off from the rest of the world, for during an examination session the great gates remained firmly shut: if a man died during the examination, his body was wrapped in straw matting and thrown over the wall. Thus, it was a perfect setting for numerous tales of ghosts, usually the spirits of jilted maidens come to wreak vengeance on the men who had done them wrong.

As David L. Rolston points out, "neither landscape painting nor traditional Chinese fiction is structured around the use of the convention of fixed perspective or viewpoint so important in western painting or fiction."[14] *The Scholars* (*Rulinwaishi*), a novel by Wu Jingzi (1701–1754), is a good case in point. Characterized by Shang Wei as "a literati novel driven by conflicting impulses toward irony and the Confucian moral imagination,"[15] it satirizes the examination system, catches in its net an assortment of human follies, and unveils the intricacies of social life in vignettes of the pompous and the ignorant, the unworldly scholar and those who cheat him, and the hypocrite and other unsavory types even as it struggles with "the question of how a literatus can live a meaningful life in a time of disenchantment."[16] Although it is episodic in organization and somewhat uneven in quality, it incorporates certain technical advances in the art of storytelling, notably in the way it allows its characters to reveal their personalities gradually rather than labeling them at the very start.

China's most beloved and exhaustively studied novel is *The Dream of the Red Chamber (Honglou Meng)*, also translated as *The Story of the Stone*. Like *The Scholars,* it offers priceless insights into Qing society, this time from the vantage point of a large, eminent family in decline. With rich detail and a cast of hundreds, it reveals how such a family was organized and how it functioned, the relationships between the generations and the sexes, the lives of women, and the status of servants, and it does all this with fine psychological characterizations based on the personal experience of the author, Cao Zhan (d. 1763). But it is far more than a novel of manners. Conscious of its own fictionality, it prompts the reader to contemplate the distinction between the real and the unreal and to ponder the nature of love and desire. C. T. Hsia has written that "it embodies the supreme tragic expression in Chinese literature"[17] and that "the ultimate tragic conflict lies in a tug of war between the opposing claims of compassion and detachment."[14] In the twentieth century this novel stimulated a mountain of serious scholarship and was finally admitted to the world of high literature.

A Buoyant Economy

During the initial forty cataclysmic years after the founding of the Qing, warfare, destruction, dislocation, and cold weather combined to bring widespread hardship, famine, disease, and population decline. But then both the economy and the population revived and went on to reach new heights. By the end of the eighteenth century, the Chinese population was around 300 million, about double what it had been around 1600. More people lived in China than in Europe. The century saw an increase in life expectancy and an all-around improvement in standard of living.

In agriculture, increased production and commercialization went hand in hand. Yields improved with the geographical spread of crops, such as specialized strains of rice suitable to local conditions, and with improved irrigation techniques and better fertilizers, such as soybean cakes. Production was also significantly increased by the introduction of new plants from the Americas: sweet potatoes, peanuts, tobacco, and corn. These could be grown on land previously left uncultivated as unsuitable for traditional Chinese crops.

An increase in the food supply induced people to refrain from female infanticide, thereby spurring population growth. A rising population spurred demand. The economy became more complex with the expansion of markets for commercial crops such as tea, sugar, cotton, hemp, and tobacco, and for other products of agricultural activity, most importantly mulberry trees for feeding silkworms. Rice was grown commercially not only to supply cities and towns but also for sale to farmers who had converted rice paddies to more profitable cash crops.

The developments in agriculture had their counterparts in manufacturing. The products of China's kilns were world famous; Chinese ceramics were copied in Europe and Japan. Brewing, papermaking, mining, and metal working industries thrived. China led the world in silk and cotton textile production. The demand for raw cotton exceeded what could be grown in China, so it was imported from India by way of Thailand. Until the 1770s, Chinese shipping predominated not only in coastal trade but also in foreign shipping, as Chinese junk owners took advantage of the monsoons and engaged in business dealings with a thriving overseas Chinese community. By the end of the eighteenth century Chinese shipping no longer dominated, but China's maritime trade with the West continued to contribute to Chinese well-being.

Throughout the century the balance of overseas trade was in China's favor, as it had been ever since the sixteenth century, when China became the world's "sink" for silver, which flowed in from Japan and the Spanish colonies of Mexico and Peru to pay for Chinese textiles and ceramics. To quote William Atwell, writing of the 1570s:

> Within a short time Chinese silks were being worn in the streets of Kyoto and Lima. Chinese cottons were being sold in Filipino and Mexican markets, and Chinese porcelain was being used in fashioning homes from Sakai to London.[18]

Although this trade was disrupted by the troubles of the seventeenth century, silver imports resumed after trade restrictions were lifted in 1683. The silver flow declined in the 1720s and again at mid-century, but it rose again after 1760. The demand for silver in China and China's ability to absorb the silver without triggering inflation attest to the productivity of the Chinese economy and to the absence of a market for European products in China.

Eighteenth-century China, like all large countries at this time, was primarily agricultural, but Beijing remained the world's largest city until London surpassed it in around 1800. Nanjing and Suzhou prospered as centers of the silk industry and handicrafts—more than seventy different handicraft trades enlivened Suzhou. Increased trade fostered growth of market towns linked by empire-wide merchant groups and serviced by a sophisticated banking system. As William T. Rowe has concluded, "the uniquely efficient water-transport system and marketing mechanism of preindustrial China allowed it to overcome the barriers of long distance and low technology, and to develop a national market by mid-Qing, even though in Europe and elsewhere such a development may have been conditional upon the advent of steam-powered transportation."[19]

Despite the spread of a "national market," generalization about China's local social and economic foundations remains difficult and potentially misleading, because conditions varied greatly from area to area then as they do today. Economic growth and transformation were most evident along the coast and along the major river arteries, with the Yangzi and Pearl River delta areas profiting most from the new prosperity.

Social Change

One consequence of economic growth was that, at least in the economically advanced parts of China, the market often prevailed over traditional status considerations. It was a time of both great riches and striking poverty, of increased opportunities for some but distress for others. Among the winners were the prosperous merchants of the major cities. The salt merchants of Yangzhou grew so wealthy from their government monopoly that some thirty of them even maintained their own theatrical troupes to entertain at banquets. A rich material culture provided for luxurious living for the wealthy. Meanwhile, the losers included impoverished Manchu bannermen as well as Chinese, giving rise to a vigorous discussion on the causes of poverty. Memorialists asked whether it was a result of insufficient productivity or of faulty distribution and inquired into the causes for the rise in rice prices, the roles of granaries, and so forth.

The uncertainties of the market were matched by those of the examination hall, where the vast majority of candidates had little hope for success. The civil service was not expanded to keep pace with the growth of the population or the economy or to accommodate the growing number of thwarted candidates, many of them superbly qualified. The average candidate had little hope for success, and those who did succeed were worried by the very real danger of downward mobility, because no amount of tutoring could make examination success hereditary.

Already in the Song there had been men who spent a lifetime taking examinations—when the emperor asked his age, one such man replied, "fifty years ago twenty-three." Now the aged candidate became a stock figure in literature. The government even relaxed standards for men older than 70 so that, past retirement age, they could at least enjoy the psychological satisfaction of receiving a degree. In an effort to weed out candidates, new examinations were introduced. Thus, in 1788 the reexamination of provincial and metropolitan graduates was introduced. That brought the total minimum number of examinations required for the final degree to eight, not counting a final placement examination. By this time the criteria for judging papers had become exceedingly formalistic. Candidates spent years practicing highly complex, artificial "eight-legged essays" required in the examinations, and bookshops did a thriving business selling model answers. In the meantime, the old battle of wits between examiners and cheaters remained a draw (see Figure 10.6).

Fear of decline in status and wealth, the dynamics of local society and economy including competition for resources, and the emphasis on family values in classic texts all contributed to the increasing prevalence, especially in the Southeast, of lineages, many of the largest of which dated to the Ming (see pp. 201–202). Those who could made it a practice to place promising boys with kinsmen located in places where examination competition was less stiff than at home. In fields such as education and maintenance of granaries, lineage activism was welcomed by some officials and thinkers as supplementing government activity, but the local power of lineages set limits on what a government official could do, and lineage conflicts generated much violence.

Below the lineage and throughout the realm in practice, as in theory, the basic social unit was the family, but the ideal joint family with "five generations under one roof," including the nuclear families of brothers, required a degree of wealth seldom enjoyed by commoners. The family was normally headed by the senior male, although a widowed matriarch could be the major force. Age prevailed over youth, but men generally outranked women.

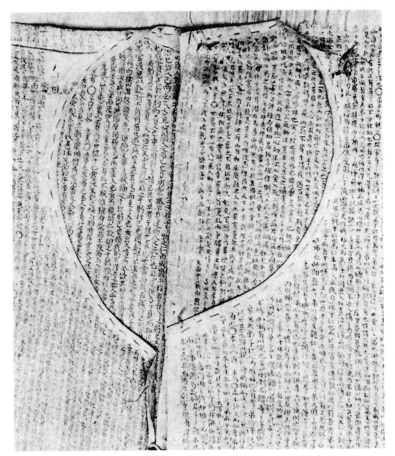

FIGURE 10.6 *A Cheating Shirt.* Before entering the examination compound where they were to spend three days and two nights, candidates underwent a thorough body search. Absolutely forbidden to bring anything with writing on it, the wearer of this undershirt clearly hoped to beat the system. (© Fujii Museum, Kyoto, Japan. Photograph by Lore Schirokauer.)

The "interior" world of the household was regarded as the women's sphere, whereas men dealt with the external world. Marriages were arranged by and for families, with the bride becoming a member of her husband's family and subject to supervision and discipline by her mother-in-law. Giving birth to a child, preferably a boy, raised her standing in the family, and, in the end, "the lonely disaffected young bride became the pillar of the joint family as a mother-in-law" and "the girl who shrieked her childhood away in agony as her foot bones were crushed grew up to insist on binding her daughter's feet."[20] Women as well as men accepted prevailing norms. Dorothy Ko has pointed to the common saying "a plain face is given by heaven, but poorly bound feet are a sign of laziness" as evidence "that a pair of nicely shaped small feet represented the triumph of individual willpower and effort."[21]

We should note here the variety of lifestyles in a land as vast as China. There were regional differences: small feet were more common in the south than in the north and were a mark of status and prosperity in both regions. Poor and low-class women had hard lives but normal feet. There were differences between urban and rural and between rich and poor. Within China proper, in the south and southwest there were many ethnic minorities with their own ways, and beyond the Great Wall non-Chinese traditions prevailed.

Ecology

The population continued to increase even though Chinese families took various measures to limit the number of children. People married young but practiced sexual abstinence in the early years of marriage when living with their parents. Infanticide, especially female infanticide, as well as neglect, also reduced the number of offspring. Still the population grew. With more people there was mounting pressure related to land. As an official put it in a memorial to Yongzheng, "while the population increases daily, the land does not."[22] Under Yongzheng the government actively pursued a policy of land reclamation, whereas under Qianlong market forces encouraged the maximum spread of agriculture up into the hills, with terraces all the way to the summits, and out into the hinterlands. In 1793 Hong Liangji (1748–1809), whose main focus was on problems of consumption, became the first official to warn against excessive population growth.

These developments changed the balance between the human and the natural environment. Deforestation, which began long before this period, became more acute. "The earth was loose; when the big rains came, water rushed down from the highlands and mud and silt spread out below. Fertile areas near the mountains were repeatedly covered with sand and were abandoned."[23] Another result of a long-term trend toward deforestation was the shortage of wood that already in the sixteenth century prompted salt extractors to shift from boiling to less effective solar evaporation. In the sixteenth and seventeenth centuries, highland and lowland communities frequently fought over woodlands to the point that the state had to intervene. As more accessible forests were cut down, the primary sources of timber were increasingly distant from the center; Guizhou in the southwest and the Yalu region in the northeast became the major suppliers.

The environmental history of much of China and East Asia is complex, because there were major differences within as well as between regions, and much remains to be learned. But a start has been made, revealing the frequently complex interrelations among technology, commerce, climate, government policies, and social practices. Indications are that major parts of China were heading into environmental crisis by the late eighteenth century as forests disappeared, soil eroded, and rivers silted and flooded, rendering human life more dire and condemning to extinction animals deprived of habitat. However, the worst was still to come. As Kenneth Pomeranz has shown, China, environmentally as well as economically, did not yet compare unfavorably to Europe, which was able to avoid intensified land use by exploiting the ecological "windfall" provided by the New World.[24]

Dynastic Decline

Merchants played a major role in financing Qianlong's wars, but as the expense of military campaigns far beyond the bounds of China proper mounted, the resources of even the prosperous Qianlong regime were strained, while laxity and corruption were rendering government less effective and more expensive. The execution of fifty-six provincial officials between 1774 and 1784 failed to alleviate, let alone solve, the problem. The most notorious offender was Heshen (1750–1799), a handsome and clever young Manchu guards officer, who, for reasons unknown, won and retained the aging emperor's complete trust for twenty-three years, during which he built a network of corruption and amassed an enormous fortune. Although bitterly detested, he could not be removed, for he never lost Qianlong's confidence and affection. An attack on Heshen implied an attack on His Majesty's own judgment and suggested the presence of factionalism. Perhaps Qianlong was especially sensitive to any signs of factionalism because his father, Emperor Yongzheng, had written a strong critique on this subject. Like his political authority, the moral and intellectual authority of the emperor were beyond question.

Qianlong abdicated as emperor after his sixtieth year so that he would not rule longer than his illustrious grandfather, but he continued to dominate the government until his death in 1799. Only then was Heshen removed.

As always, the common people bore the burden of extravagance and corruption. As a result, many of them joined in the White Lotus Rebellion (1796–1804). At its height it affected Sichuan, Hubei, Henan, Gansu, and Shaanxi. The rebellion drew its following by promising the coming of Maitreya (the Buddha of the future), a restoration of the Ming, and the rescue of the people from all suffering. It gained momentum as it attracted the destitute and displaced and proved the power of its cause. The ineffectiveness of the dynasty's response assisted the movement: government generals used the occasion to line their own pockets and bannermen proved their total incompetence. Not until after Heshen's fall did the government make real headway. A new, very capable commander was appointed, disaffected areas were slowly taken back from the rebels, and militia bands organized by the local elite proved effective in putting down insurgency.

The tendency of the government to tinker and elaborate rather than reform and innovate suggests a dangerous hardening of the institutional arteries just as China's place in the world was about to change.

Notes

1. The term is taken from Kenneth Pomeranz, *The Great Divergence: China, Europe, and the Making of the Modern World Economy* (Princeton: Princeton Univ. Press, 2000).

2. James Cahill, *The Compelling Image: Nature and Style in Seventeenth-Century Chinese Painting* (Cambridge: Harvard Univ. Press, 1982), p. 183.

3. W. Theodore de Bary, trans., *Waiting for the Dawn: A Plan for the Prince (Huang Tsung-hsi's Ming-i Tai-fang lu)* (New York: Columbia Univ. Press, 1993), p. 92.

4. *RoutledgeCurzon Encyclopedia of Confucianism*, Xinzhong Yao, ed. (London: RoutledgeCurzon, 2003), p. 233.

5. Chin-sung Chang, *Mountains and Rivers, Pure and Splendid: Wang Hui (1632–1717) and the Making of Landscape Panoramas in Early Qing China* (Ph.D. dissertation, Yale University, 2004), pp. 118, 126, with the quotation as translated by Wen Fong in Wen Fong, et al., *Images of the Mind: Selections from the Edward L. Elliott Family and John B. Elliot Collections of Chinese Calligraphy and Painting at the Art Museum, Princeton University* (Princeton Art Museum, 1984), p. 184.

6. Jonathan D. Spence, *Emperor of China: Self-Portrait of Kang-hsi* (New York: Alfred E. Knopf, 1974), p. 128.

7. Morris Rossabi, *China and Inner Asia— From 1638 to the Present Day* (New York: Pica Press, 1975), pp. 139–40. Rossabi does not think Buddhism was a major factor, although it may have contributed to the decline (pp. 140–41).

8. R. Kent Guy, *The Emperor's Four Treasures: Scholars and the Rise of the State in the Late Ch'ien-lung Era* (Cambridge: Harvard Univ. Press, 1987), p. 37.

9. R. Bin Wong, Theodore Huters, and Pauline Yu, "Introduction: Shifting Paradigms of Political and Social Order," in Huters, Wong, and Yu, *Culture and State in Chinese History: Conventions, Accommodations, and Critiques* (Stanford: Stanford Univ. Press, 1997), pp. 4–5.

10. Wang Mingsheng (1725–1798) as translated in Benjamin A. Elman, "Social Roles of Literati in Early to Mid-Ch'ing," Chapter 7 of *The Cambridge History of China, Vol. 9, Part 1: The Ch'ing Empire to 1800*, Willard J. Peterson, ed. (Cambridge: Cambridge Univ. Press, 2002) p. 395.

11. William T. Rowe, "Social Stability and Social Change," in *Cambridge History*, Vol. 9, Part 1, p. 531.

12. Susan Mann, "Women, Families, and Gender Relations" Chapter 8 in *Cambridge History,* Vol. 9, Part 1, p. 447.

13. Quoted in Ichisada Miyazaki, *China's Examination Hell,* trans. Conrad Schirokauer (New Haven: Yale Univ. Press, 1981), pp. 57–58.

14. David L. Rolston, *How to Read the Chinese Novel* (Princeton: Princeton Univ. Press, 1990), p. 14.

15. Shang Wei, *Rulin Waishi and Cultural Transformation in Late Imperial China* (Cambridge: Harvard Univ. Press, 2003), p. 279.

16. Wei, *Rulin Waishi and Cultural Transformation,* p. 285.

17. C.T. Hsia, *The Classical Chinese Novel* (New York: Columbia Univ. Press, 1968), pp. 246, 264.

18. William Atwell, in Frederick W. Mote and Denis Twitchett, eds., *The Cambridge History of China,* Vol. 7 (Cambridge: Cambridge Univ. Press, 1988), p. 587.

19. William T. Rowe, *Hankow: Commerce and Society in a Chinese City, 1796–1889* (Stanford: Stanford Univ. Press, 1984), p. 62.

20. Susan Mann, "The Education of Daughters in the Mid-Ch'ing Period," in Benjamin A. Elman and Alexander Woodside, eds., *Education and Society in Late Imperial China, 1600–1900* (Berkeley: Univ. of California Press, 1994), p. 21.

21. Dorothy Ko, *Teachers of the Inner Chambers: Women and Culture in Seventeenth-Century China* (Stanford: Stanford Univ. Press, 1994), p. 171.

22. Han Liangfu, as quoted in Robert B. Marks, *Tigers, Rice, Silk, and Silt: Environment and Economy in Late Imperial South China* (Cambridge: Cambridge Univ. Press, 1998), p. 291.

23. Quoted from the Gazetteer for Chengde (Hunan) in Peter C. Perdue, *Exhausting the Earth: State and Peasant in Hunan, 1500–1850* (Cambridge: Harvard Univ. Press, 1987), p. 88.

24. See Note 1. Another major factor in Europe's "great divergence" was the proximity of coal to the center of textile production, whereas in China they were far apart.

Part Four

China in the Modern World

*I*n the nineteenth century the whole world came to feel the might of Europe, where intellectual, political, and economic forces at work since the Renaissance were producing unprecedented wealth and power. This process was accelerated in the late eighteenth century by the Industrial and French Revolutions, gaining momentum with the emergence of new technologies, new appetites, new ideas, new values, and new problems setting off tremors that were to reverberate throughout the globe. It was a tumultuous period of intense economic competition, stringent national rivalries, bitter class conflicts, and sharp clashes between old and new values and ideas. Yet few Europeans questioned the superiority—moral, intellectual, economic, and political—of their civilization or, indeed, of their century.

A major development still with us was that the nation-state won unprecedented and enthusiastic acceptance as the "natural" and uniquely legitimate political entity worthy to be the primary object of political loyalty. Although just what constitutes a "nation" remained ill-defined; nevertheless, the nation-states were able to mobilize human and natural resources to an unprecedented degree, as demonstrated in World War I, which, triggered and fueled by nationalism, brought an end to Europe's global predominance while destroying Czarist Russia and Austro-Hungary, Europe's last old-style multinational empires.

Nineteenth-century nationalism prompted European patriots to revolt against foreign rule, and it also glorified commercial, military, and cultural expansion abroad. Consequently, Qing China faced external challenges to the dynasty and to the society and civilization on which it was built. At the same time, it had to deal with an uprising unprecedented in scope, intensity, and bloodshed. The two chapters in this part deal with how China met these challenges and take us through the collapse of the dynasty and its aftermath. We begin in the middle of the eventful and pivotal nineteenth century. Although in terms of European and even global history, the century came to a close with the First World War, the pivotal event in East Asia occurred twenty years earlier, for the Sino-Japanese War radically affected Korea, China, and Japan.

The West was never uniform, nor its course of events smooth. It helps to place East Asian turbulence in perspective if we keep in mind that the forces of nationalism and republicanism erupted in revolutions on the European continent in 1830 and 1848, that in 1839 English Chartists took to the streets demanding political reforms, that warfare played a crucial role in the creation of Italian and German national states (completed by 1870), that Americans slaughtered each other in civil war, and that bitter fighting and strife marked the transition from Napoleon III, through the Paris Commune, to the establishment of the conflicted Third Republic in France (1870). The violence of the nineteenth century is matched only by that of its successor.

11

China: Internal Crises and Western Intrusion

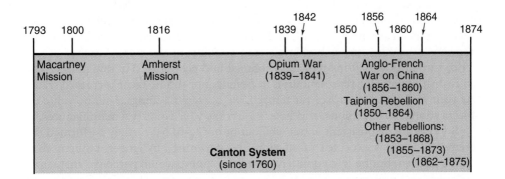

1793	1800	1816	1842 1839	1856 1850	1864 1860	1874

Macartney Mission	Amherst Mission	Opium War (1839–1841)	Anglo-French War on China (1856–1860)
			Taiping Rebellion (1850–1864)
			Other Rebellions: (1853–1868)
	Canton System (since 1760)		(1855–1873)
			(1862–1875)

Nineteenth-century China was beset by internal and external difficulties, each contributing to the severity of the other. Opium, for example, came from abroad, but the fact that its spread in China was made possible by official corruption and by the appeal of the drug to bannermen did not bode well. The Qing now faced long-term problems that would have taxed the ingenuity and energy of even an honest and effective government. Foremost were the problems created by population pressures, for the population continued to increase in the nineteenth century as it had in the eighteenth. By 1850 the number of inhabitants in China had risen to about 430 million, without any comparable increase in productivity or resources. As the pressures of the struggle for survival strained old humanistic values to the breaking point, it left little room for honesty, let alone charity. Life became brutish and hard. As ever, the poor suffered most, and they were legion, for the uneven distribution of land left many people landless, destitute, and despairing. The situation was made worse by government neglect of public works.

Emperor Jiaqing (1796–1820) tried to remedy the government's financial problems by cutting costs and selling official posts and titles but was unable to solve the underlying fiscal and economic problems, reform the bureaucracy, or help the people, who ultimately supplied the funds. Emperor Daoguang (1820–1850) continued his father's policy of frugality but could not stem the decay. Internal pressures were building, but external crisis preceded internal eruption.

The Opium War (1839–1841) and Its Causes

Before turning to the opium crisis that triggered the war, we need to consider the long-range factors that made it a turning point in China's foreign relations. Underlying the tensions between China and the West was the incompatibility of the Chinese and Western views of themselves and the world. Both were supremely self-confident and proud of their own civilizations. Both were narrowly culture-bound. Thus, when the Macartney mission arrived in Beijing in 1793 with the hope of broadening the terms of trade and initiating treaty relations, the presents sent to Emperor Qianlong by England's George III were labeled as "tribute" by the Chinese. Qianlong responded to the English monarch by praising his "respectful spirit of submission" and, in the gracious but condescending language appropriate for addressing a barbarian king residing in the outer reaches of the world, turned down all his requests, political and economic. He saw no merit in the British request for representation in Beijing, nor did he favor increased trade: "As your Ambassador can see for himself, we possess all things. I set no value on objects strange or ingenious, and have no use for your country's manufactures."[1]

Sources are inconsistent about whether or not Lord Macartney performed the ceremonial kowtow expected of inferiors and performed by emperors themselves toward Heaven, but he was confident that the Chinese would perceive "that superiority which Englishmen, wherever they go, cannot conceal."[2] The English sent another mission to China in 1816, headed by Lord Amherst, but he was not granted an audience at court.

The British motive for coming to China remained primarily economic. In contrast to China's self-sufficiency and Emperor Qianlong's disdain for foreign products, there was a Chinese product in great demand in Britain. This was tea. First imported in tiny quantities in the late seventeenth century, tea was initially taken up as an exotic beverage with medicinal properties, then popularized as a benign alternative to gin, and finally was considered a necessity of English life. The East India Company, which enjoyed a monopoly of trade with China until 1834, was required by Act of Parliament to keep a year's supply in stock at all times. Tea imports reached 15 million pounds in 1785 and double that amount in the decade preceding the Opium War. Not only did the East India Company depend on the income from the tea trade, but the British government also had a direct stake in tea, because about one-tenth of its entire revenue came from a tax on Chinese tea. Not until the 1820s did the Company begin experimenting with tea growing in India, and it was many years before Indian tea would provide an alternative to the tea of China. The importance of Chinese tea extended even to American history: it was Chinese tea that was dumped from East India Company ships in the famous Boston Tea Party (1773).

The British problem was how to pay for this tea. There was no market for British woolens in China, and the "singsong" trade in clocks, music boxes, and curios was insufficient to strike a balance of trade. Until the last third of the eighteenth century, the sale of British imports covered 10 percent or less of the cost of exports, with the rest paid for in cash and precious metals. Unable to find anything European that the Chinese wanted in sufficient quantity, the English turned toward India and the "country trade" between India and China, conducted under East India Company license by the private firms of British subjects. Money obtained in Canton by the "country traders" was put on deposit there for the Company against bills of exchange on London. In this way, England, India, and China were connected by a trade-and-payments triangle.

FIGURE 11.1 *Opium Smokers.* Those who could afford to do so indulged in high-quality opium prepared for them by servants at home. The less affluent had to prepare their own. But the least fortunate were left to smoke opium ash or refuse on rudimentary benches in shoddy surroundings in dismal opium dens. (© Mansell/Timepix Collection [838558].)

Until 1823 the largest commodity imported to China from India was cotton, but this volume never reached the amount necessary to balance the trade. That feat was accomplished with opium. Opium had long been used for medicinal purposes, but the smoking, or more accurately, the inhaling of opium fumes through a pipe, began in the seventeenth century. The spread of the practice was sufficient to provoke an imperial edict of prohibition in 1729, but this and subsequent efforts to suppress use of the drug were unsuccessful, and opium consumption continued to increase. Distributed partly through older salt-smuggling networks and protected by the connivance of corrupt officials, use of opium spread steadily and proved particularly attractive to soldiers and government underlings. The drug was habit forming and its effects were debilitating (see Figure 11.1).

Withdrawal was excruciatingly painful. Over time the addict developed a tolerance for opium and needed more and more of the drug to achieve a "high." Thus, to pay for tea, the Chinese were sold a poison. Because private country traders brought the opium to China, the East India Company disclaimed responsibility for the illegal traffic in China. At the same time, however, it profited from the sale of opium in India. However, within India, where the British, as the paramount power, felt a certain sense of responsibility, consumption of opium for nonmedicinal purposes was strictly prohibited.

The Chinese market for opium developed at such a pace that the balance of trade was reversed. During the 1820s and 1830s large quantities of silver seem to have left China to pay for opium imports. This caused an increase in the number of copper coins needed to buy a specific amount of silver, thereby destabilizing the Qing monetary system. What began as a public health problem now became a fiscal problem as well. In 1834, the East India Company's monopoly of the China trade was abolished by the British government. This opened the gates of trade still wider on the British side, resulting in an increased flow of opium to China and an increased flow of silver out of China.

Abolition of the Company's trade monopoly was a victory for English advocates of free trade, who were as antagonistic to restraints on trade abroad as at home. The immediate effect in China was to put an end to the system of Cohong-Company relations in Canton. Now in place of the Select Committee of the East India Company, an official of the crown represented the British side. To initiate the new relations, Britain sent out Lord Napier as First Superintendent of Trade with instructions to establish direct contact with the Qing viceroy, to protect British rights, and to assert jurisdiction over Englishmen in Canton. To accomplish these aims, he was ordered to use a moderate and conciliatory approach. Napier, however, more ambitious than diplomatic, immediately took an adamant stand on the issue of direct communication with the viceroy. He violated Chinese regulations by not waiting in Macao for permission to proceed to Canton and by sending a letter rather than petitioning through the *hong* merchants. With neither side willing to back down, the impasse developed into a showdown. All Chinese employees were withdrawn from the British community, food was cut off, and trade was stopped. Napier finally withdrew to Macao, where he died. This all took place in 1834. Unfortunately, in the ensuing lull, no progress was made toward finding a new modus vivendi between the two sides.

For a brief moment the Chinese considered legalizing opium, but in 1836 the emperor decided on suppression. In doing so, he sided with the Spring Purification Circle of reform-minded literati officials, who were seeking influence in government decision making. Thus, an "Inner Opium War," to use James M. Polachek's formulation, developed parallel to and intertwined with the external conflict.[3]

Opium dealers and addicts were prosecuted with great vigor, and imprisonments and executions were widespread, with the result that the price of opium dropped precipitously. This program was well under way when the vigorous and determined reformer Lin Zexu (1785–1850) arrived in Canton in March 1839. As imperial commissioner, he was charged with stamping out the drug trade once and for all.

Lin conducted a highly successful campaign against Chinese dealers and consumers. He also severely punished corrupt officials who had connived in the trade. To deal with the foreign source of the opium, he appealed to Queen Victoria: "Suppose there were people from another country who carried opium for sale to England and seduced your people into buying and smoking it; certainly your honorable ruler would deeply hate it and be bitterly aroused."[4] He also admonished the foreign merchants, and he backed moral suasion with force. He demanded that the foreigners surrender all their opium and sign a pledge to refrain from importing the drug in the future at the risk of confiscation and death. To effect compliance, he used the same weapons of isolating the foreign traders employed successfully in 1834 against Napier. Elliot, the British Superintendent of Trade, took a fateful step in response when he ordered the British merchants to turn their opium over to him for delivery to the Chinese authorities. By this act he relieved the merchants of large amounts of opium they had been unable to sell because of the efficacy of the Chinese prohibitions, and he made the British government responsible for eventual compensation. No wonder that the merchants enthusiastically dumped their opium: 21,306 chests were delivered to Lin Zexu. It took twenty-three days to destroy it all.

In England, firms interested in the China trade exerted great pressure on the government for prompt and vigorous military action. Lin, meanwhile, pleased with his victory, continued to press Elliot on the issue of the pledges, but here he did not succeed. The Superintendent of Trade argued that it was against British law to compel the merchants to sign the pledges and that the imposition of the death penalty without the benefits of English judicial procedure was also contrary to British law. What was at stake here was the issue of British jurisdiction over British subjects, a source of Anglo-Chinese friction since 1784, when the British had refused to submit to Chinese justice. The issue came to the fore again in the summer of 1839, when a group of English sailors killed a Chinese villager in the Canton hinterland. Refusing to turn the men over to Lin Zexu, Elliot tried them himself, but when they were returned to England the men were freed, because the home court ruled that Elliot had exceeded his authority.

The first clash of the war took place in November 1839, when the Chinese tried to protect one of the only two ships whose captains had signed the bond despite Elliot's stand and who now wanted to trade. When a British ship fired a shot across the bow of the offending vessel, the Chinese intervened with twenty-one war junks, which, however, were no match for the foreign ships. In December, trade with the British was stopped, and on January 31, 1840, a formal declaration of war was announced by the governor-general of India, acting in the name of the home government.

In June 1840, the British force, consisting of sixteen warships, four armed steamers, twenty-seven transports, a troop ship, and 4000 Irish, Scottish, and Indian soldiers, arrived in China. First the British blockaded Canton, and then they moved north. Lin and his associates remained confident of victory, holding that the British, like their maritime pirate predecessors, depended on the spoils of war to finance their military operations and thus had grossly overextended themselves.

The British were fired on at Xiamen (Amoy) while trying to deliver a letter from Prime Minister Palmerston under a white flag of truce, a symbol the Chinese did not understand—just one example of mutual cultural misunderstanding. They then seized Chusan Island, south of the Yangzi estuary, and Dinghai, the chief city there. The main body of the fleet sailed another 800 miles north to Beihe, near Tianjin, where Palmerston's letter was accepted. By this time the emperor had lost confidence in Lin Zexu, whose tough policy had led to the military retaliation.

Lin was dismissed, disgraced, and exiled to Ili in Central Asia. His place was taken by the Manchu prince Qishan (d. 1854), who, in September 1840, by flattery and accommodation, got the British to return to Canton for further negotiations. When these came to naught, the British resumed military operations, with the result that in January 1841 Qishan was forced to sign a convention that provided for the cession of Hong Kong, payment of an indemnity to Britain, equality of diplomatic relations, and the reopening of Canton. Both Qishan for the Qing and Elliot for the British thought they had done very well, but neither government accepted their work. The Chinese emperor was indignant at how much had been conceded, whereas Palmerston fumed that Elliot had demanded too little. The reactions of the Chinese and British governments showed all too clearly how far apart they still were. Caught in the middle were the negotiators. Like Lin Zexu earlier, now Qishan came to feel the imperial displeasure: his property was confiscated and he was sent to exile on the Amur. Elliot too was dismissed; his next position was as consul-general in Texas.

In the renewed fighting, the British besieged Canton in February 1841, but the siege was lifted on payment of a ransom of 6 million Spanish silver dollars. However, before their departure, the British experienced the growing hostility of the local population. They were attacked by a body of troops organized by the local gentry. Although militarily ineffective, the attack was an indication of popular sentiment, and its results were embellished by hard-liners to support their advocacy of continued intransigence toward the British. In August, Elliot was relieved by Pottinger, and the last phase of the war began when the British moved north, occupying Xiamen in August and Dinghai in October. Reinforcements were sent from India, increasing the naval force and bringing troop strength up to 10,000. With this force, Pottinger continued the campaign, advancing up the Yangzi until his guns threatened Nanjing. There on August 29, 1842, the treaty that ended the war was signed. It was a dictated peace imposed by the Western victor on the vanquished Chinese.

The Treaty of Nanjing and the Treaty System

The Treaty of Nanjing (together with the supplementary Treaty of the Bogue, October 1843) set the pattern for treaties China later signed with the United States and France in 1844, established the basic pattern for China's relations with the West for the next century, and supplied the model for similar treaties imposed on Japan. The Canton System and the Cohong monopoly were abolished. Five ports—Canton, Xiamen, Fuzhou, Ningbo, and Shanghai—were opened to British trade and residence. Britain received the right to appoint consuls to these cities. The treaty also stipulated that henceforth official communications were to be on a basis of equality.

The Qing was forced to pay an indemnity of 21 million Spanish silver dollars. Of this, 12 million was for war expenses, in keeping with the European practice of forcing the loser to pay the costs of a war. Another 6 million was paid as reparations for opium handed over to Commissioner Lin, and the remaining 3 million went to settle the debts owed by the *hong* merchants to British merchants.

An important provision of the treaty established a moderate Chinese tariff of from 4 to 13 percent on imports, with an average rate of 5 percent. The Chinese, whose statutory customs had been even lower, did not realize that by agreeing to this provision they were relinquishing the freedom to set their own tariffs. On the British side there was the conviction that, as Adam Smith had taught, the removal of constraints on trade would benefit all by allowing everyone to concentrate on what he did best.

The British, having acquired an empire in India, with all the burdens of government that it entailed, did not seek to create another in China. Trade, not territory, was their aim. But they did demand and obtain a Chinese base. Hong Kong Island, at that time the site of a tiny fishing village, was ceded to them in perpetuity. Well located and with an excellent harbor, it developed into a major international port.

The issue of legal jurisdiction over British subjects was settled by the Treaty of the Bogue, which provided for extraterritoriality—that is, the right of British subjects to be tried according to British law in British consular courts. Having only recently reformed their own legal system, the British were convinced of its superiority. There were precedents in Chinese history for allowing "barbarians" to manage their own affairs, but in the context of modern international relations, extraterritoriality amounted to a limitation on Chinese sovereignty.

The Treaty of the Bogue also provided for most-favored-nation treatment. This obliged China to grant to Britain any rights China conceded in the future to any other power. Its effect was to prevent China from playing the powers off against each other. It meant that once a nation had obtained a concession, it was automatically enjoyed by all the other states granted most-favored status. In the 1844 treaties, the United States and France gained this status. In the American treaty, China agreed to allow for the maintenance of churches in the treaty ports and to treaty revision in twelve years, whereas the French won the right to propagate Catholicism.

The status of the opium trade was left unsettled in the original treaties. An agreement to outlaw smuggling did not slow down the growth of the traffic, which was legalized under the next round of treaty settlements, 1858–1860, and opium even functioned as a kind of money. From the annual 30,000 chests before the Opium War, the trade expanded to reach a high of 87,000 chests in 1879. It then declined as Chinese production of opium increased. British opium imports were down to about 50,000 chests when, in 1906, the Qing took strong measures against the drug. British imports finally came to a stop in 1917, but opium smoking remained a serious social problem until the early 1950s.

For China, the treaties solved and settled nothing. A particularly ominous development was the permission granted for foreign gunboats to anchor at the treaty ports, for when additional ports were opened, foreign powers had the right to navigate China's inland waterways. Today, with the benefit of hindsight, it is apparent that the cumulative effect of the treaties was to reduce China to a status of inequality unacceptable to any modern nation.

Although it is now universally regarded as a milestone, the treaty settlement did not seem so to the Qing authorities who, as John Fletcher has shown, had made many of the same concessions as recently as 1835 in reaching a settlement with the tiny Central Asian state of Kokand. This treaty involved an indemnity, a tariff settlement, the abolition of a merchant monopoly, and a special position exceeding that of most-favored-nation status and seen by the Qing as simply a case of "impartial benevolence."[5] From the vantage point of Beijing, Hong Kong seemed as remote as Kokand.

Foreign policy remained deeply imbedded in political conflicts, revealing deep lines of division in the body politic. When the Manchu-led centralizers, who advocated peace, came into power, they purged their opposition so thoroughly that Chinese scholar-officials of various intellectual persuasions found common ground in pressing for open discussion in official channels, administrative decentralization, and a policy of determined resistance against the foreigners. Few men had any inkling of the dimensions of the challenge facing the empire. For example, Wei Yuan (1794–1857), author of the influential *Illustrated Treatise on the Sea Kingdoms* (first version, 1844), limited himself to incorporating new information into old categories, and felt no need to break with tradition. Despite his geopolitical orientation, he persisted in underestimating the British threat.

Under the circumstances, the best that experts could suggest was for China to acquire "barbarian" arms and to employ the old diplomacy of playing off one barbarian against another. Less well-informed officials suggested that future military operations take advantage of the supposed physical peculiarities of the barbarians, for example, their stiff waists and straight legs, which made them dependent on horses and ships, or their poor night vision.

Internal Crisis

The encroachments of the foreign powers were ominous, but the internal crisis was even more dangerous. Government leadership remained totally inadequate. Earlier, Emperor Daoguang's partial success in reforming the official salt monopoly system had not compensated for his failure to reinvigorate the Grand Canal or Yellow River managements. The Grain Transport Administration was "in effect a free-wheeling taxation agency that preyed upon officialdom and populace alike."[6] By 1849 the Grand Canal was impassable. From then on, tax grain had to be shipped by sea. The abandonment of the canal cost thousands their jobs. Emperor Daoguang did not live to see the Yellow River disaster of 1852. Since 1194, the greater river had flowed into the sea south of the Shandong Peninsula, but now it shifted to the north, spreading flood and devastation over a wide area.

The next emperor, Xianfeng (1851–1861), was nineteen when he inherited the throne and proved equally incapable of dealing with an increasingly menacing situation. Even while rebellion threatened the dynasty, a major scandal involving bribery and cheating shook the examination system.

Famine, poverty, and corruption gave rise to banditry and armed uprisings, as had so often happened in the past. The most formidable threat to the dynasty came from the Taiping revolutionaries. To aggravate the crisis, the dynasty also had to contend with rebellions elsewhere. In the border regions of Anhui, Jiangsu, Henan, and Shandong, there was the Nian Rebellion (1853–1868) led by secret societies, probably related to the White Lotus Society. There was also a Muslim rebellion in Yunnan (1855–1873) and the Dongan Rebellion in the Northwest (1862–1875). Yet it was the Taiping who came closest to destroying the Qing in a civil war that, in terms of bloodshed and devastation, was the costliest in human history. It is estimated that more than 20 million people lost their lives.

The Taiping Rebellion (1850–1864)

The founder of the Taiping movement was a village schoolteacher named Hong Xiuquan (1814–1864), who belonged to the Hakka, ethnically a Han subgroup, which many centuries earlier had migrated from the north to the southeast, where they remained a distinct ethnic group. Originally, Hong hoped for a conventional civil service career, and four times went to Canton to participate in the civil service examination, only to fail each time. In 1837, shocked by his third failure, he became seriously ill, and for forty days was subject to fits of delirium during which he experienced visions. These visions he later interpreted with the aid of a Christian tract he picked up in Canton, where Protestant missionaries had made a beginning in their effort to bring their faith to China. He also received some instruction from an American Southern Baptist missionary. On the basis of his limited knowledge of the Bible and Christianity, he proceeded to work out his own form of sinicized Christianity.

Central to Hong's faith was his conviction that in his visions he had seen God, who had bestowed on him the divine mission to save humankind and exterminate demons. He also met Jesus and was given to understand that Christ was his own elder brother. This recasting of Christianity into a familistic mode had appeal for Hong's Chinese audience but dismayed Western Christian missionaries, who were further appalled by Hong's claims that he himself was a source of new revelation.

The emphasis in Taiping Christianity was on the Old Testament—on the Ten Commandments, not the Sermon on the Mount. Hong's militant zeal in obeying the first commandment by destroying "idols" and even Confucian ancestral tablets soon cost him his position as a village teacher. He became an itinerant preacher among the Hakka communities in Guangxi, gaining converts and disciples among the downtrodden and dispossessed, whom he recruited into the Association of God Worshippers. To the poor and miserable, he held out a vision of the Heavenly Kingdom of Great Peace (*Taiping tianguo*), an egalitarian, God-ordained utopia.

In keeping with both Christianity and native traditions, Taiping Christianity stressed a strict, even puritanical, morality. Opium, tobacco, gambling, alcohol, prostitution, sexual misconduct, and foot binding were all strictly prohibited.

Women were made equal to men in theory and, to a remarkable extent, also in practice. Consonant with both Christian egalitarianism and native Chinese utopian ideas was a strong strain of economic egalitarianism, a kind of simple communism. Property was to be shared in common, and in 1850 the members of the Association were asked to turn over their funds to a communal treasury that would provide for everyone's needs.

The Taiping land program was based on a system of land classification according to nine grades found in *The Rites of Zhou,* long a source of Chinese radical thought. The idea was that everyone would receive an equal amount of land, measured in terms of productivity of the soil. Any production in excess of what was needed by the assignees was to be contributed to common granaries and treasuries. The system did not recognize private property.

The basic political structure was a unit of twenty-five families consisting of five groups of five families each. The leaders of these and larger units were to combine civil and military duties and look after the spiritual welfare of their people by conducting Sunday religious services. The Taiping developed their own hymns, primers, and literature, which served as the subject matter for a new examination system open to women as well as men. Similarly, there were female as well as male military units. Marriages took place in church and were monogamous.

What stood in the way of realizing this utopia were the "demons," mostly Manchus. By July 1850 the Association had attracted 10,000 adherents, primarily in the remote and neglected province of Guangxi. In defiance of the Qing, they now cut off their queues, the long braids of hair hanging down from the back of the head, which had been forced upon the Chinese by the Manchus as a sign of subjugation. Because they also refused to shave the forepart of their heads, the government called them the "long-haired rebels." Millenarian religious beliefs, utopian egalitarianism, moral righteousness, and hatred of the Manchus proved a potent combination when fused into a program of organized armed resistance. In November 1850 there were clashes with government troops, and on January 11, 1851, Hong's thirty-seventh birthday, his followers proclaimed him "Heavenly King," thus formally defying the Qing.

At this stage, the Taiping enjoyed good leadership. One of the outstanding secondary leaders was Yang Xiuqing, originally a charcoal burner, who was a talented organizer and strategist. Starting from their base in Guangxi, the Taiping forces made rapid military progress. One of their favorite tactics in attacking cities was to use their contingent of coal miners to dig tunnels to undermine the defending walls. The incompetence of the government forces also helped. As the Taiping armies advanced, they picked up strength. It has been estimated that their number reached more than 1 million by the time they took Nanjing in 1853.

After such a quick advance, with their ranks swollen by new adherents only partially versed in Taiping tenets, it was time to call a halt and consolidate. The movement had formally been proclaimed the Heavenly Kingdom of Great Peace in 1851. Now, with its capital at Nanjing, the leaders attempted to turn it into a solid regime. To continue military operations, two expeditions were sent out. A small force was dispatched north and came within twenty miles of Tianjin before suffering reverses and defeat. Large forces went west and enjoyed considerable success until 1856, but they too were eventually defeated.

Taiping treatment of Westerners was cordial but clumsy. The regime lost much good will by employing condescending language and expressions of superiority not unlike those used by Beijing. After the British failed to obtain Taiping recognition of their treaty rights, they decided on a policy of neutrality, and the other powers soon followed suit. This remained the policy of the foreign powers through the 1850s.

A turning point for the Taiping regime came in 1856 in the form of a leadership crisis they could ill afford. Yang Xiuqing had increased his power to the point of reducing Hong to a mere figurehead. Yang, too, went into trances, and claimed to be acting on God's orders, but he was unable to convince the other leaders. When he overreached, they turned on him. Yang, along with his family and thousands of followers, was killed, but no strong successor appeared to take his place. By the time Hong's cousin Hong Rengan (1822–1864) came into prominence in 1859, it was too late to restructure the regime. Hong Rengan was the most Westernized of the Taiping leaders but had neither the time nor the power to build the centralized and modern state he had in mind. His leadership lasted only until 1861. Hong Xiuquan himself was immersed in his religious mission, occupied in writing elaborate comments on the Bible, and was totally lost to the world.

Failure of its leadership was one source of Taiping weakness. Inadequate implementation of stated policies was another. Practice did not conform to theory. For example, Hong Xiuquan himself, as well as other Taiping leaders, kept numerous concubines despite the Taiping call for monogamy. Moreover, there were many missed opportunities: the failure to strike before the dynasty could regroup; the failure to cooperate with secret societies and other opponents of the regime who did not share the Taiping faith; and the failure to cultivate good relations with the foreign powers.

To make matters worse, Taiping revolutionary ideas repelled all those Chinese who identified with the basic Confucian way of life and understood that the Taiping program was not merely anti-Manchu but anti-Confucian and thus subversive to the traditional social order. Consequently, the Taiping leaders not only failed to recruit gentry support, but they also antagonized this key element in Chinese society. To the literati, rule by "civilized" Manchus was preferable to rule by "barbarized" Chinese.

Zeng Guofan and the Defeat of the Taiping

What ultimately prolonged the Qing dynasty's life was a new kind of military force organized by Zeng Guofan (1811–1872), a dedicated Confucian and a product of the examination system. Unlike the old armies organized under the Qing banner system (see p. 237), Zeng's army was a strictly regional force from Hunan, staffed by officers of similar regional and ideological background personally selected by him. They, in turn, recruited soldiers from their own home areas or from members of their own clans. A paternalistic attitude of officers toward their men, a generous pay scale honestly administered, careful moral indoctrination, and common regional ties all helped to produce a well-disciplined force high in morale.

Qing statesmen were aware that strong regional armies such as Zeng's threatened the balance of power between the central government and the regions and were ultimately dangerous to the authority of the dynasty. But the traditional armies of the regime had proved hopelessly inadequate, and the Manchu rulers had no choice but to trust their defense to Zeng. Although organized in Hunan, where it began its operations, the army also fought the Taiping in other provinces. It was not always victorious: twice Zeng suffered such serious reverses that he attempted suicide. But in the long run a well-led and highly motivated army, honestly administered and true to its purpose, proved superior to the Taiping forces.

The dynasty also benefited from the services of two other remarkable leaders: Zuo Zongtang (1812–1885) and especially Li Hongzhang (1823–1901), whose Anhui Army became the strongest anti-Taiping force. After the treaties of 1860, the Western powers sided with the regime that had made such extensive concessions to them, and Western arms were of great assistance, particularly to the Anhui Army. An American adventurer was succeeded by a British officer as leader of 4000 or 5000 Chinese in the "Ever Victorious Army." Meanwhile, French officers commanded the "Ever Triumphant Army," composed of Chinese and Filipino mercenaries. Customs revenues helped loyalists purchase foreign arms and steamers and establish arsenals.

After a series of victories, the loyalist armies laid siege to Nanjing. When the situation became desperate, Hong Xiuquan relied on divine intervention, ordering the starving people to eat manna. According to a Taiping general, "The Sovereign himself, in the open spaces of his palace, collected all sorts of weeds, which he made into a lump and sent out of the palace, demanding that everyone do likewise."[7] The same source attributes Hong's subsequent fatal illness to his eating of these weed concoctions. Shortly after Hong's death, on July 19, 1864, the city fell to an army commanded by Zeng Guofan's brother. As had happened often in this bitter war, the fall of Nanjing was followed by a bloodbath. Hong's son managed to flee, but was discovered in Guangxi and executed. The Taiping, once so close to victory, were completely eradicated. Similarly, the loyalist forces succeeded in quelling the Nian, Muslim, and other rebels.

The Taiping's example was to inspire future revolutionaries, whereas conservatives continued to admire Zeng Guofan. That others were restless and defiant is suggested by the famous life-size self-portrait of Ren Xiong (1820–1857), who served in a military headquarters but did not rest easily with his choice (see Part Opener Figure). Painted in Shanghai, which was beginning to assume its role as a major meeting place between China and the West, this original, unsettling work of art mirrors the stress of its time and foreshadows future conflict and distress.

China and the World from the Treaty of Nanjing to the End of the Taiping

As we have seen, the Treaty of Nanjing established a pattern but satisfied neither side. Frustrated in attempts to negotiate locally, the British demanded direct representation in Beijing. They also pressed for treaty revision, because the opening of the new ports had not led to the anticipated increase in trade. Behind the demands for freer trade was the persistent belief that only artificial restrictions prevented the development of a giant market in China for British textiles and other products.

One cause of friction between the English and the Chinese was the repeated postponement of the opening of Canton because of the strong antiforeign feeling of its people. The continuation of the opium trade did not help matters, nor did the development of a new commerce in Chinese laborers. These men were often procured against their will, crowded into dismal "coolie" vessels, and transported as contract laborers to work the plantations of Cuba and Peru. The boom set off by the discovery of gold in California in 1848 also brought Chinese immigrants to the United States, but they came as free laborers, their passage organized by Chinese merchants. By 1852 there were 25,000 Chinese in the American West, and by 1887 there were twice that number in California.

There were some efforts for cooperation during these years, as the foreign powers sided with the dynasty rather than with the Taiping. With Chinese consent, the British set about suppressing piracy. More important was the establishment of the Foreign Inspectorate of Customs in Shanghai in 1854 after the Qing officials had been ejected by rebels. The Inspectorate became responsible for the collection of tariffs and the prevention of smuggling. By the new treaties of 1858, its authority was extended to all treaty ports. It remained an important source of support for the dynasty during and after the Taiping Rebellion.

Nevertheless, there was more discord than harmony, and in 1856 war broke out once more. The immediate cause of war was the Arrow Affair. The Arrow was a Chinese-owned but Hong Kong registered vessel which, although flying the British flag, was boarded by Chinese officials, who seized twelve Chinese men whom they charged with piracy. When the viceroy returned the men but refused to apologize and guarantee that it would not happen again, the British responded by seizing Canton. There was a lull in the fighting while the British were occupied fighting a war in India set off by the Mutiny of 1857. When the war in China was resumed in December 1857, the English were joined by the French.

As in the first war, the Europeans again moved north, and in Tianjin the British and French negotiated the Treaties of Tianjin, providing for permanent residency of diplomats in Beijing, the opening of ten new ports, foreign travel throughout China, reduction of inland transit dues, an indemnity, and freedom of movement for all Christian missionaries. However, hostilities resumed after the British envoy discovered that the Qing planned to exchange ratifications in Shanghai rather than Beijing. Although the Chinese defeated the British at Taku, where the river leading to Tianjin enters the sea, victory went to the allies who entered Beijing, where Elgin, the British commander, vented his anger by burning down the imperial summer palace of around 200 buildings northwest of Beijing. In October the Conventions of Beijing were signed to supplement the Treaties of Tianjin, which now also took effect. In addition to the usual indemnity, China was forced to open eleven new ports, to grant rights to travel in the interior, and to allow foreign envoys to reside in Beijing. In 1860 the French also surreptitiously inserted into the Chinese text a provision granting missionaries the right to buy land and erect buildings in all parts of China.

The peace agreements were secured through the mediation of the Russian ambassador to Beijing, who used the opportunity to consolidate the gains Russia had made to date and to obtain new concessions for his country. Under Peter the Great and Catherine the Great, Russia's land empire had expanded into the area west of the Pamirs then known as Russian Turkestan, and in 1851 Russia obtained trading privileges and the right to station consuls at Kuldja and Chuguchak (Dacheng) in the Ili region of Chinese Turkestan (now Xinjiang) east of the Pamirs. Now areas southwest of Kuldja and Urga (Ulan Bator) in Outer Mongolia were also opened to them, but, having suppressed Muslim rebellions, the Qing were able to retain their position in Central Asia.

Meanwhile, Russia made massive gains in the northeast. In the Amur region Nikolai Muraviev, governor-general of Siberia, began putting pressure on the Qing in 1847. In 1860, the entire area north of the Amur was ceded to the Russians, who also received the lands east of the Ussuri River, which were incorporated into the Russian Empire as the Amur and Maritime Provinces. In the latter, Muraviev founded Vladivostok ("Ruler of the East" in Russian). Russia also now received most-favored-nation status. The gains Russia made at this time remain a source of conflict between the Russians and Chinese.

II. 1870–1894

The Post-Taiping Revival

Self-Strengthening—The First Phase

Self-Strengthening—The Theory

The Empress Dowager and the Government

Education

Economic Self-Strengthening

The Traditional Economic Sector

Missionary Efforts and Christian Influences

Old and New Wine in Old Bottles

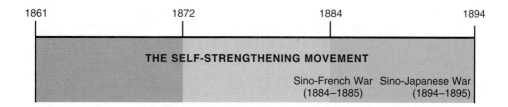

THE SELF-STRENGTHENING MOVEMENT

1861   1872   1884   1894

Sino-French War   Sino-Japanese War
(1884–1885)   (1894–1895)

The Post-Taiping Revival

During the Tongzhi Period (1862–1874), Zeng Guofan, Li Hongzhang, and other leaders in the victory over the Taipings sought to cope with the dislocations wrought by warfare and to revive the dynasty by launching a program of Confucian reformism: expenses and taxes were cut in the ravaged south, relief projects were instituted, public works projects were initiated, land was reclaimed and water was controlled, and granaries were set up. As always, agriculture had priority.

An aspect of the revival dear to its Confucian sponsors was a strengthening of scholarship by reprinting of old texts, founding of new academies, opening of libraries, and the like. Examination system reform was similarly a high priority, as was the elimination of bureaucratic corruption. Questions dealing with practical issues of statecraft were introduced, and attempts were made to limit the sale of degrees and offices. By such measures the reformers sought to raise the level of honesty.

However, the reforms did not penetrate to the crucial lower level of the bureaucracy—many county magistrates continued to gain office through purchase—and nothing effective was done to curb the rapacity of the solidly entrenched and notoriously corrupt sub-bureaucracy of clerks and underlings. Furthermore, with the leadership for the reforms coming primarily from provincial governors, the dynasty was powerless to reverse the trend toward regionalism. The disruption of old bonds with the central government removed many of the political constraints on local wealth and power and set in motion a restructuring of local society that ultimately proved dangerous for both the state and the social order.

Self-Strengthening—The First Phase

The aim of the Self-Strengthening Movement was to fortify the Qing through selective borrowing from the West. It began in the Tongzhi Period with a focus on military modernization and international relations and was expanded in its middle phase (1872–1885) to encompass transportation (shipping and railways), communications (telegraph), and mining. Finally, after China's defeat by France in 1885, it was further broadened to include light industry.

During the first phase, Li Hongzhang created gun factories in Shanghai (1862) and Suzhou (1864), established an arsenal in Shanghai with Zeng Guofan (1865), and founded another in Nanking (1867). In 1870, Li also expanded machinery works first built in Tianjin in 1867. Another leader in Fuzhou founded a shipyard with machinery from France that had a shipbuilding and a navigation school attached, one teaching French and the other English.

With the emperor being a minor, foreign policy was largely under the direction of Prince Gong, who expressed the regime's order of priorities thus:

> The situation today may be compared (to the diseases of a human body). Both the Taiping and the Nian bandits are gaining victories and constitute an organic disease. Russia, with her territory adjoining ours, aiming to nibble away our territory like a silk worm, may be considered a threat at our bosom. As to England, her purpose is to trade, but she acts violently, without any regard for human decency. If she is not kept within limits, we shall not be able to stand on our feet. Hence she may be compared to an affliction of our limbs. Therefore we should suppress the Taiping and the Nian bandits first, get the Russians under control next, and attend to the British last.[8]

It was apparent to Prince Gong that new approaches to foreign policy were required to meet these objectives. In 1861, to deal with the foreign powers and related matters, he sponsored the establishment of the Zongli Yamen (Office of General Management) as a subcommittee of the Grand Council to supervise a number of offices (see Figure 11.2). Because its influence depended on that of its presiding officer and his associates, it was most influential during the 1860s, when Prince Gong was at the height of his authority. An important innovation introduced by the Zongli Yamen was appeal to international law, using Henry Wheaton's *Elements of International Law*, a standard text translated by the American missionary W. A. P. Martin.

Prince Gong, recognizing that Chinese officials would be at a disadvantage in dealing with foreigners unless they had a better understanding of foreign languages and learning, was instrumental in having the Zongli Yamen establish a school for foreign languages and other nontraditional subjects in 1862. The language staff was foreign and included Martin, who became the school's president in 1869. By that time astronomy and mathematics had also been introduced, despite the objections of the distinguished Mongol scholar General Secretary Woren (d. 1871), who memorialized: "From ancient down to modern times your slave has never heard of anyone who could use mathematics to raise the nation from a state of decline or to strengthen it in time of weakness."[9] Woren was not alone in his objections to this extension of "barbarian" influence.

Nevertheless, similar schools were established at Shanghai, Canton, and Fuzhou. Foreigners were relied on to run both the military and educational es-

FIGURE 11.2 Three members of the Zongli Yamen and statesmen of the Tongzhi Period. Left to right: Shen Guifen, President of the Ministry of War; Dong Xun, President of the Ministry of Finance; Mao Changxi, President of the Ministry of Works. (© Hulton-Deutsch Collection/CORBIS [HU038080].)

tablishments. In this way the foundations of self-strengthening and modernization were laid, but the emphasis remained heavily military. This was true even of Feng Guifen (1809–1874), an advocate of learning from the barbarians, who had the audacity to propose that examination degrees be presented to men demonstrating accomplishment in Western mechanical skills.

During the 1860s an important area of Chinese cooperation with the foreign powers was the Maritime Customs Service. Its first director, Horatio Nelson Lay, had acquired a fleet of eight gunboats for the Chinese in England. Although these were paid for by the Chinese, he arranged that the captain of the fleet should receive all his orders through and at Lay's own discretion. This was unacceptable to the Qing, and there were protests. China's first effort to acquire a modern navy ended with disbandment of the little fleet, and Lay was pensioned off. Matters improved, however, when Robert Hart succeeded Lay in 1863. Hart's attitude was the opposite of Lay's. He insisted that the customs was a Chinese service and that Chinese officials were to be treated as "brother officers," and he gave the Qing government well-intentioned and frequently helpful advice on modernization, while building the service into an important source of support for the dynasty.

Cooperation between the Qing and the powers produced the first Chinese diplomatic mission to the West, which was headed by the retiring American minister to Beijing, Anson Burlingame, on Robert Hart's recommendation. For a multiethnic Confucian state like the Qing to employ a trusted foreigner on such an important mission did not appear as extraordinary as it would have later, after nationalism took hold. Accompanied by a Manchu and a Chinese official, Burlingame left China in 1867 for a trip to Washington, several European capitals, and St. Petersburg, where he died. Carried away by his own eloquence, he told Americans that China was ready to extend "her arms toward the shining banners of Western civilization."[10] In Washington, he concluded a treaty rather favorable to China.

The most important negotiations for treaty revision were conducted in Beijing by the British. These culminated in the Alcock Convention of 1869, which included some concessions to the Chinese on duties and taxes, and stipulated that, under the most-favored-nation clause, British subjects would enjoy privileges extended to other nations only if they accepted the conditions under which those privileges had been granted. It also allowed China to open a consulate in Hong Kong. These concessions may appear minor, but the English merchant community felt threatened by them, and their opposition proved strong enough to prevent ratification of the convention.

A fatal blow to the policy of cooperation came in 1870 in Tianjin. A Catholic nunnery there had made the mistake of offering small payments for orphans brought to the mission. Rumors spread that the children had been kidnapped and that the sisters removed the children's hearts and eyes to make medicine. The tense situation erupted into violence. A mob took the life of the French consul and twenty other foreigners, including ten nuns, in what came to be known as the Tianjin Massacre. The powers mobilized their gunboats. Diplomacy finally settled the issue, largely because France's defeat in the Franco-Prussian War in the same year deprived France of military power and forced the French to concentrate on domestic problems.

Self-Strengthening—The Theory

Confucian pragmatism was nothing new. Willingness to adopt new means to strengthen and reform the state had animated a long line of Confucian scholars from the Song on, and, as it became clear during the early years of the nineteenth century that the Qing was in serious trouble, some scholars turned against philology to focus on what today would be called policy studies. The *Anthology of Qing*

Statecraft Writing (*Huangchao jingshi wenbian*), published in 1827, is a case in point. It is a collection of essays on social, political, and economic matters written by Qing officials and published by He Changlin (1785–1841), with the actual work done by Wei Yuan. Concern for reform and willingness to take a hard, critical look at financial and political institutions characterized the writings of leading intellectuals, and Wei Yuan began to merge these concerns with an interest in the West. The first person to see the West as a source for solving the problems it had created was Feng Guifen, who urged China to use "barbarian techniques" against the "barbarians," the hallmark of the Self-Strengthening Movement.

Although self-strengthening was well established by the 1870s, its classic formulation came in 1898 from the brush of Zhang Zhidong (1837–1909), a governor-general and practitioner of self-strengthening. Like Sakuma Shōzan earlier in Japan, Zhang wanted to preserve traditional values while adopting Western science and technology. The idea was that Chinese learning would remain the heart of Chinese civilization, whereas Western learning would have a subordinate, supporting role. This was expressed in terms of the traditional Neo-Confucian dichotomy of *ti* (substance) and *yong* (function): Western means for Chinese ends. The basic pattern of Chinese civilization was to remain sacrosanct, but it was to be protected by Western techniques.

Conservative opponents of self-strengthening feared that Chinese civilization would be contaminated by borrowing from the West, because ends cannot be separated from means. In the Confucian formulation, *ti* and *yong* are aspects of a single whole. The Confucian tradition had always been concerned with means as well as ends, and generations of scholars had insisted that the Way did not consist merely of "empty" abstractions, but concerned practical realities. There was no essence apart from application. And there was a great deal more to the West than mere techniques. It was fallacious to believe that China could merely borrow techniques from the West without becoming entangled in manifestations of Western culture. If China went ahead with efforts to adopt Western techniques while preserving traditional culture, the best that could be hoped for would be an uneasy compartmentalization. To preserve tradition in a period of modernization, the country would have to be protected from the kind of radical social reappraisal hailed in Japan by champions of "reason" such as Fukuzawa Yukichi.

The contrast with Japan is instructive, for there social change was sanctioned by an appeal to nationalism as symbolized by the throne, whereas in China Confucianism was much too closely associated with the social structure to allow for a similar development. Meiji Japan demonstrated that elements of Confucianism were compatible with modernization, but also that modernization involved changes reaching into the very heart of a civilization.

The Empress Dowager and the Government

The dominant figure at court from the mid-1870s until her death, just three years before the demise of the dynasty, was the Dowager Empress Cixi (1835–1908) (see Figure 11.3). The intelligent, educated daughter of a minor Manchu official, she en-

FIGURE 11.3 The Empress Dowager Cixi (1835–1908) seated on the Imperial Throne. Scholars, too, grew long fingernails to show the world that they worked with their minds, not their hands. (Courtesy Arthur M. Sackler and the Freer Gallery of Art, Smithsonian Institution [SC-GR2.56].)

tered the palace as a low-ranking concubine and had the good fortune to bear the Xianfeng emperor his only son. After that emperor's death, she became coregent for her son, the Tongzhi emperor, whom she dominated. It was also rumored that she encouraged him in the debaucheries that weakened his constitution and brought him to the grave in 1875 at age nineteen. She then manipulated the succession to place on the throne her four-year-old nephew, the Guangxu emperor (r. 1875–1908) and continued to make the decisions even when he ostensibly assumed the imperial duties in 1889. At first Prince Gong had provided a counterforce, but his power declined in the 1870s, and in 1884 he was removed from the government altogether.

The Empress Dowager was a strong-willed woman, an expert in political infighting and manipulation. One of her most reliable supporters was the Manchu bannerman Ronglu (1836–1903), to whom she gave important military commands. Yet, it was an anomaly to have a woman in control of the court, and her prestige was not enhanced by rumors that she was responsible for the murder of her rivals. Corruption in high places also took its toll. The powerful eunuch Li Lianying (d. 1911) was totally loyal to his mistress but also totally corrupt, using his influence to amass a fortune. Cixi herself accepted payments from officials and misspent funds. The most notorious case of financial abuse was her use of money intended for the navy. The Navy Department, established in 1885, became a branch of the imperial household, and China's most famous and magnificent "ship" was made of marble (see Figure 11.4).

Cixi's prime political aim was to continue in power. She had no aversion, but neither did she have any commitment, to the policy of selective modernization advocated by the champions of self-strengthening, and her understanding of the West was very limited. It was to her immediate political advantage to avoid dependence

FIGURE 11.4 On the shore of Kunming Lake, the Marble Pavilion has become a popular recreational site attracting ordinary Chinese visitors as well as foreign tourists—the kind of folk it was intended to exclude. Summer Palace, Beijing. (© Lore Schirokauer.)

on any single group of officials and to manipulate a number of strong governors-general who had gained in power while suppressing the Taiping Rebellion. These indispensable provincial administrators could no longer be controlled by the court at will, but, fortunately for Beijing, they remained absolutely loyal to the dynasty. The governors-general operated their own political and financial machines and commanded substantial military forces, but they were still dependent on Beijing's power of appointment. Major policy decisions continued to be made in Beijing. The central government was also strengthened financially by receipts from the Maritime Customs. Thus, the West helped to preserve the dynasty even as it was undermining its foundations.

Most powerful of the governors-general was Li Hongzhang, from 1870 firmly established in Tianjin, where he commanded an army, sponsored self-strengthening efforts, and successfully avoided transfer. A protégé of Zeng Guofan, he shared his master's devotion to the dynasty, but not his Confucian probity. From his headquarters, not far from Beijing, Li dominated China's policy toward Korea, but he could not control its foreign policy elsewhere. Arguing for the priority of maritime defense, he objected to overemphasis on inner Asia and unsuccessfully opposed two military campaigns conducted there during the 1870s.

In the next decade he failed to prevent the war of 1884–1885 with France over Vietnam. In this war, fought not only in Vietnam but also on Taiwan and the Pescadores, the Qing suffered the destruction of the Fuzhou dockyards as well as the loss of the fleet built there. Because the defeated dynasty was forced to relinquish all claims to Vietnam, Li was vindicated, but his opposition to going to war against France earned him the denunciations of his enemies, who castigated him as an arch traitor.

Li, however, survived these attacks and remained the most important patron of self-strengthening, now broadened to include light industry in the hope for better results.

Education

Crucial to every phase was the need for officers, managers, and technical personnel such as scientists and engineers. The fastest way to fill this need was to send students abroad. However, the success of this approach was mixed. The most extensive effort of this sort was made between 1872 and 1881, when 120 students were sent to the United States under the supervision of Yung Wing (Rong Hong, 1828–1912), Yale class of 1854, and the first Chinese to graduate from an American university. The boys were between fifteen and seventeen years old, young enough to master new subjects, but also immature and easily swayed by their foreign environment. To assure continued Confucian training, they were accompanied by a traditional Confucian mentor. Nevertheless, they soon adopted American ways, participating in American sports, dating and in some cases eventually marrying American girls, and in a few instances even converting to Christianity. Yung Wing himself married an American and ended up living in Hartford, Connecticut. The mission had been launched with the backing of Zeng Guofan and Li Hongzhang, but Li withdrew his support when the students were denied admission to West Point and were fiercely attacked by Beijing officials for neglecting their Confucian studies. The mission, poorly managed from the start, was abandoned. Among its participants were some of the first, but by no means the last, Chinese students who, during their overseas stay, became alienated from their culture.

The obvious alternative to study abroad was to supply instruction in modern subjects at home. This was the purpose of the language school established by Prince Gong and other schools at several arsenals and the Fuzhou dockyard. By 1894 a telegraph school, a naval and military medical school, and a mining school were also in operation. The curricula of these schools typically encompassed both the classical studies required for success in the examination system and the new subjects. Because command of traditional learning remained the key to entry into government service, the students naturally tended to concentrate on that, for otherwise their career opportunities were very limited. The most famous graduate of the Fuzhou dockyard school was Yan Fu (1853–1921), who was sent to England to continue his studies at the naval college in Greenwich, but after returning home to China was unable to pass the provincial examination and gained fame not as an admiral, but as a writer and translator.

It did occur to some reformers to broaden the content of the examinations and allow candidates credit for mastering modern subjects, but suggestions along such lines encountered formidable opposition, because they affected the Confucian core of the civilization. A minor concession was finally made in 1887. Three of some 1500 provincial examination candidates might now be granted that degree after being examined in Western along with (not in place of) traditional subjects. They would then be eligible for the highest examination (the *jinshi*) on the same terms as the other candidates!

Economic Self-Strengthening

The accomplishments of the second phase of self-strengthening included a shipping company, textile mills, the beginnings of a telegraph service, and the Kaiping Coal Mines. Li Hongzhang took the lead in sponsoring and protecting the new ventures. During the first phase, the new factories, arsenals, and other enterprises, run by officials with the help of foreigners, had suffered from bureaucratic corruption and poor management. To avoid this, Li enacted a policy of "government supervision and merchant operation." Capital came from both the public and private sectors. Private financing was very much desired, but capital was scarce, and other forms of investment were more lucrative and prestigious. Private investment came primarily from Chinese businessmen residing in the treaty ports and familiar with modern-style business ventures and techniques.

The records of these companies were mixed. The China Merchants Steam Navigation Company is a good example. When private capital proved insufficient to finance the company, Li Hongzhang put up the rest from public funds. To help the company make a go of it, Li secured for the shipping line a monopoly on the transport of tax grain and official freight bound for Tianjin. He obtained tariff concessions for the company and protected it from its domestic critics and enemies. In exchange, Li exercised a large measure of control, appointing and dismissing its managers, employing its ships to transport his troops, and using its payroll to provide sinecures for political followers. He also used its earnings to buy warships. To advance his policy in Korea, Li had the company lend money to the Korean government.

In the end, the investors made money and their political sponsor benefited, but, after an initial spurt, the companies stagnated. Moreover, they failed to train Chinese technical personnel and were plagued by incompetent managers, nepotism, and corruption. Even their political sponsors exploited the companies, regarding them as sources of patronage and revenue rather than as key investments for the modernization of the country. By the mid-1890s, there was a modern sector in the Chinese economy, but it was largely limited to the periphery of the empire, where Chinese merchants were able to hold their own successfully against foreign competition.

The Traditional Economic Sector

Although the new enterprises proved disappointing, developments in the traditional sector were hardly encouraging. Chinese tea merchants, despite sophisticated institutions and techniques adequate to sustain dominance of the domestic market, found it increasingly difficult to compete internationally against tea growers in India and Sri Lanka (Ceylon). The large-scale producers in these countries had an advantage over the small Chinese growers in their ability to sustain a high-quality product by investing in fertilizer, replacement bushes, and labor at the crucial picking time. Furthermore, the elaborate structure of the Chinese collection system, which worked so well internally, was too unwieldy to organize an adequate response to international competition. After 1887, with the decline of exportation of tea, raw silk became China's main export. In the mid-1890s China was the world's largest exporter of silk, although by 1904 Japan had supplanted China in this role.

Beyond the treaty ports and their immediate hinterlands, the penetration of foreign imports appears to have been slow and their impact varied. Statistics are hard to find, and there is no consensus about the ways in which the world economy interacted with forces already at work in the Chinese countryside. Thus, Philip C. C. Huang's study of an area of North China where farmers had been growing cotton for a long time remains controversial as well as suggestive. According to Huang, because cotton brought a better price than grain but, being susceptible to drought, also entailed larger risks, the gap between the successful rich and those pushed into poverty by failure increased. Combined with population pressure and an absence of other opportunities for employment, this set in motion an invidious process of *agricultural involution,* a term first applied by the anthropologist Clifford Geertz to Java, where poor peasants worked the land for marginal and diminishing returns. According to Huang, while the men farmed, their wives and daughters supplemented family income by laboring at spinning wheel and loom, often at less than subsistence wages. Whereas spinning was practically eliminated by machine-made thread, the low prices paid to the weavers kept the price of native cloth below that of the factory-made product, which had to be shipped into the interior. "The world economy thus did not undermine the rural economic system or stimulate new departures but accelerated processes already underway. The incorporation of Chinese agriculture into the world economy telescoped and greatly accelerated change in the small peasant economy."[11]

Missionary Efforts and Christian Influences

The Western presence in nineteenth-century China was no more confined to trade and politics than it had been during the Late Ming encounter. Once again, missionaries were drawn to China, but now there were Protestants as well as Catholics. An early Protestant arrival was Robert Morrison of the London Missionary Society. He reached Canton in 1807, learned the language, brought out a Chinese-English dictionary and a Chinese version of the Bible (later used by the Taiping), founded the school where Yung Wing received his early education, and set up a printing press. Other missionaries, many of them Americans, brought modern medicine and other aspects of Western secular knowledge to China.

The missionaries made a notable effort in education: by 1877 there were 347 missionary schools in China with almost 6000 pupils. Such schools helped spread knowledge about the West as well as propagate the religion. A notable missionary-educator was W. A. P. Martin, who contributed to the Self-Strengthening Movement and became the first president of Beijing University. The first foreign language newspaper published in China was a missionary publication, and missionaries also contributed to scholarship. Outstanding among the missionaries who became sinologists was James Legge, a master translator who rendered the Chinese classics into sonorous Victorian prose. In this and other ways, missionaries with varying degrees of sophistication and self-awareness served as cultural intermediaries.

As indicated by the growth of their schools, the missionaries met with some success, but their strength was largely in the treaty ports, and the results were hardly commensurate with their efforts. By the end of the century, the number of Catholic missionaries in China had climbed to about 750, and there were approximately half a million Catholics in China, up from around 160,000 at the beginning of the century. The Protestants had less success. In 1890 there appear to have been only slightly more than 37,000 converts served by roughly 1300 missionaries, representing forty-one different religious societies. The Tianjin Massacre of 1870 had demonstrated the potential fervor of antimissionary sentiment, and nothing happened to reduce hostilities during the next quarter century.

The reasons for the poor showing of Christianity are many and various. They include difficulties in translation and communication analogous to those that plagued Buddhist missionaries a millennium and a half earlier. The most important concepts of Christianity, such as sin or the Trinity, were the most difficult to translate, but none was more so than the most sacred idea of all, the idea of God. Agreement on how to translate *God* into Chinese was never reached; three versions, one Catholic and two Protestant, remained current. As before, differences in culture compounded the difficulties in communication.

Nineteenth-century missionaries, however, also encountered problems that they did not share with their predecessors, for the Chinese associated Christianity with both the Taiping Rebellion and the unequal treaties. The former showed Christianity as subversive to the social and political order, whereas the latter

FIGURE 11.5 *The [Foreign] Devils Worshipping the Incarnation of the Pig [Jesus].* This print employs a homonym for the transliteration of 'Jesus' to depict Christ as a pig. (From *China and Christianity* by Paul A. Cohen [Cambridge: Harvard Univ. Press, 1963]. Courtesy Department of East Asian Studies, Harvard University.)

brought the missionaries special privileges. Both were resented. Furthermore, the aura of power also attracted false converts, individuals attracted by the possibilities of a treaty port career, and opportunists seeking to obtain missionary protection for their own ends. Popular resentment of the missions was fired by scurrilous stories and bitter attacks (see Figure 11.5). This hostility was encouraged by the elite, who saw in Christianity a superstitious religion that threatened their own status and values.

It was no accident that anti-Christian riots often occurred in the provincial capitals during examination time, when they were filled with candidates committed to the status quo. Here there is an interesting contrast with the situation in Japan, where 30 percent of Christian converts during the Meiji Period were from samurai backgrounds. Christianity served the spiritual needs and provided a vehicle for social protest for samurai who found themselves on the losing side of the Restoration struggle. As a result, in the 1880s and 1890s a prestigious native clergy was developing in Japan, and Christianity remained more influential than the slow growth of the churches would indicate. In post-Taiping China too, Christianity continued to appeal to people dissatisfied with the status quo, and it counted among its converts some notable protesters, including Sun Yat-sen. But the elite remained hostile, and the real cutting edge of protest was to be elsewhere: too radical for the nineteenth century, Christianity turned out to be insufficiently radical for the twentieth.

In the meantime, missionaries contributed to the Western perception of China. Working in the treaty ports, dealing not with Confucian gentlemen but with men on the margin of respectable society, the missionaries frequently developed a negative view of China and its inhabitants, an image that was the reverse of the idealistic picture painted earlier by the Jesuits.

Old and New Wine in Old Bottles

In this difficult age, as in most, there were artists and poets whose aim was "transcending turmoil"[12] by working within the rich tradition to which they were heirs. Their accomplishments can give much pleasure, but others more directly convey a sense of the anxieties and hopes of an age. For example, the poetry of Wang Pengyun (1848–1904), an official who served as a censor, sounds notes of uncertainty, apprehension, and regret in an age of dynastic decay.

> *In Reply to a Poem from Cishan, Thanking Me for the Gift of Song and Yuan*
> *Lyrics I Had Had Printed (To the Tune "The Fish Poacher")*
>
> Now that the lyric voice wavers in wind-blown dust
> Who is to speak the sorrows of his heart?
> Two years of carving, seeking from each block
> The truest music of the string unswept,
> Only to sigh now
> Finding my grief in tune
> With every beat that leaves the ivory fret!
> I sigh for the men of old
> Pour wine in honor of the noble dead:
> Does any spirit rhymester
> Understand my heartbreak?
> The craft of letters
> Furnishes kindling, covers jars:
> True bell of tinkling cymbal, who can tell!
> Du Fu,* who lifelong courted the perfect phrase
> —Did his verse help him, though it made men marvel?
> Take what you find here,
> See if an odd page, a forgotten tune

*For discussion of Du Fu, see Chapter 5.

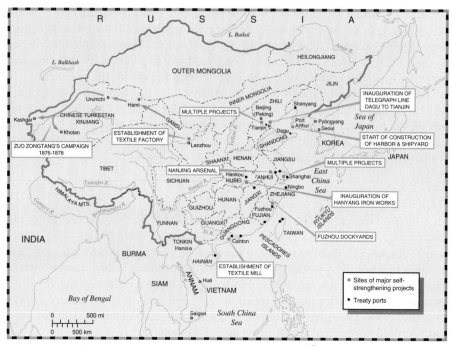

FIGURE 11.6 China During the Self-Strengthening Period.

Still has the power to engage your mind.
My toiling over
I'll drink myself merry, climb the Golden Terrace,
Thrash out a wild song from my lute
And let the storms rage at will.[13]

Late Qing writers were much given to writing sequels, new versions, and paro-dies of China's classic novels, often at great length. *The Dream of the Red Chamber* was a favorite (see the discussion in Chapter 10). Publication of *The Dream of the Green Chamber* (about a brothel) in 1878 was preceded by *A Precious Mirror for Judging Flowers* (1849), a homosexual romance. *Quell the Bandits* (1853), character-ized by David Der-wei Wang as anticipating China's modern political novel,[14] plays off *The Water Margin*, the classic novel recounting the deeds of 108 bandit heroes driven by the cruel corruption of a decadent government to take justice into their own hands (see Chapter 8). Such works, for all their flaws, looked toward the future.

A literary man and political reformer hopeful of the future was Huang Zunxian (1845–1905), who spent 1877 through 1879 in Tokyo as part of the Chinese legation. A collection of his poems describing Japan was published by the Zongli Yamen in 1879. He also wrote a history of Japan and served as a diplomat in San Francisco, Singapore, and London. Rejecting the conventional poetic gen-res, he sought to preserve tradition through innovation.

Among those who welcomed the winds from the West were a small group of remarkable men, some with experience abroad in official or unofficial capacities. Guo Songdao (1818–1891) was China's first minister to England and the first Chinese representative to be stationed in any Western country. Wang Tao (1828–1897) spent two years in Scotland assisting James Legge in his translations and also visited Japan. One of the founders of modern journalism in China, he favored the adoption of Western political institutions as well as science and technology. Another remarkable man was Zheng Guangyin (1842–1921), a famous scholar-comprador, modernizer, and writer. Such men were interested in Western "substance" (not just "function"), while remaining committed to the Confucian tradition.

Important for the future were a number of younger men whose formative years fell into this period, although they did not become influential until the late 1890s. There are three names in particular to which we will return: Yan Fu, born in 1853; Kang Yuwei, born in 1858; and Sun Yat-sen, born in 1866. The discussion of their ideas must wait, however, for it was not until China was jolted by her defeat in the Sino-Japanese War that they came to the fore.

III. Foreign Relations

Continued Pressures
Vietnam and the Sino-French War of 1884–1885
Korea and the Sino-Japanese War of 1894–1895
The Treaty of Shimonoseki (April 1895)

Continued Pressures

Western pressures continued to affect China's foreign relations in the twenty years before the Sino-Japanese War, but the nature of these pressures began to alter. The initial conflicts had been over Western efforts to open trade and diplomatic relations with China proper; in the 1870s and 1880s foreign intervention in lands constituting peripheral areas of the empire or traditionally tributary states were the major causes of friction (see map, Figure 11.6). Even as Japan was engaged in the Taiwan expedition, the Qing government was troubled by a dangerous situation in Central Asia. In 1871 the Russians used a Muslim rebellion in Xinjiang as a pretext for occupying the Ili region, where a lucrative trade had developed. In Xinjiang itself, Yakub Beg (1830–1877), a Muslim leader from Kokand in Central Asia, obtained Russian and British recognition for his breakaway state. In response to these alarming developments, the Qing court assigned the task of suppressing the rebellion to Zuo Zongtang, who had just finished crushing Muslim rebellions in Shaanxi and Gansu. He carried out the task with great success. By 1877, the government's control over Xinjiang was being reestablished and Yakub Beg was driven to his death. After difficult and protracted negotiations, the Russians returned nearly all of Ili (1881).

This strong showing in Central Asia, an area to which the Chinese were traditionally sensitive, bolstered morale, and Chinese successes in the diplomatic negotiations that followed encouraged those who were opposed to accommodation with the West. Indeed, the success of China's Central Asian policy encouraged them to demand an equally strong policy in dealing with the maritime powers. Pressure from this source was too strong to be ignored and constituted a major factor leading to confrontation and then to war with France in 1884–1885. At issue was French expansion into Vietnam.

Vietnam and the Sino-French War of 1884–1885

North Vietnam had been annexed by the Han in 111 B.C.E., but after C.E. 939 native Vietnamese regimes prevailed, the major exception being the short period of Ming domination (1406–1426). The leader of the resistance against the Ming, Le Loi, established the Later Li dynasty (1428–1789), with its capital at Hanoi and its government organized along Chinese lines. As in Korea, the determination to maintain political independence from China went hand in hand with admiration for Chinese culture and institutions. The Chinese influence on Vietnam is what sets it apart from the other, more Indian-oriented states of Southeast Asia.

China also served as the model for the Nguyen dynasty (1802–1945), which from its capital at Hue in Central Vietnam ruled the country through a bureaucracy modeled as closely as possible on that of China. The Chinese model was powerful, yet differences in size and culture between China and Vietnam required adjustments and compromises. To give just one example, Chinese influence was much stronger on civil government than on the military, for military theory and practice in Vietnam (as in the rest of continental Southeast Asia) centered on the elephant.

Vietnam's location in a cultural frontier area provided a rich and complex culture but was also a source of political weakness. One result was that the social and cultural gap between village and bureaucracy was greater in Vietnam than in China. Another result was the difficulty the Vietnamese state experienced in its efforts to incorporate the South, which had been gradually taken over from the Cambodians (regarded by the Vietnamese as "barbarians") during the century from roughly 1650 to 1750. Under the Nguyen dynasty this continued to be an area of large landlords and impoverished peasants, a region where the central bureaucracy operated inadequately. The area also suffered from educational backwardness, with the result that very few southerners were able to succeed in Vietnam's Chinese-style civil service examination system.

Vietnam's long coastline and elongated shape, as well as the presence of minority peoples within its boundaries, further hampered government efforts to fashion a strong unified state capable of withstanding Western encroachments. French missionaries and military men had early on shown an interest in the area and had assisted in the founding of the Nguyen dynasty itself. Nearly 400 Frenchmen served the dynasty's founder and first emperor, Gia-long (r. 1801–1820). Catholicism also made headway: it has been estimated that there were more Catholics in Vietnam than in all of China. For much the same reasons as had earlier animated anti-Christian policies in China and Japan, the Vietnamese authorities turned against the foreign religion, but their suppression of Catholicism gave the French an excuse for intervention.

French interest in Vietnam increased during the reign of Louis Napoleon. In 1859 France seized Saigon. Under a treaty signed three years later, the French gained control over three southern provinces, and five years later they seized the remaining three provinces in the South. These southern provinces became the French colony called Cochin China. During 1862–1863 the French also established a protectorate over Cambodia. French interests were not limited to the South but included Central and North Vietnam (Annam and Tonkin). Treaties concluded in 1862 and 1874 contained various provisions eroding Vietnamese sovereignty, and when disorders occurred in North Vietnam in 1882, France used the occasion to seize Hanoi.

Throughout this period of increasing French penetration, the Vietnamese court had continued its traditional tributary relations with Beijing. When the French took Hanoi, the Vietnamese court responded by seeking both help from the Qing and support from the Black Flags, an armed remnant of the Taiping, which had been forced out of China and was fighting the French in Vietnam.

The Qing responded by sending troops. Considerable wavering and diplomatic maneuvering followed in both Beijing and Paris, but in the end no means were found to reconcile the Chinese wish to preserve their historic tributary relations with Southeast Asia and the French determination to create an empire in this region. The resulting war was fought in Vietnam, on Taiwan and the Pescadores, and along the nearby coast of China proper, where the Fuzhou dockyards and the fleet built there were among the war's casualties.

In the peace agreement that followed, China was forced to abandon her claim to suzerainty over Vietnam. The French colony of Cochin China and the French protectorates of Annam and Tonkin were joined by protectorates over Cambodia and (in the 1890s) Laos to constitute French Indochina. Chinese influence in Southeast Asia was further diminished in 1886 when Britain completed the conquest of Burma, and China formally recognized this situation as well. Then in 1887, China ceded Macao to Portugal, officially recognizing the de facto situation there. Thus, in the last third of the nineteenth century the foreign powers tried to gain further concessions and proceeded to establish themselves in tributary areas that had been part of the traditional Chinese imperial order, although not of China proper. In the face of this challenge, the Chinese made concessions where necessary and resisted where feasible. When areas of major importance were at stake, their policy was quite forceful. The struggle over Korea is an example.

Korea and the Sino-Japanese War of 1894–1895

Like Vietnam, Korea had adopted Chinese political institutions and ideology and maintained a tributary relationship with China while guarding her political independence. Again, as in Vietnam, differences in size, social organization, and cultural tradition ensured the development of a distinct Sino-Korean culture. In the nineteenth century, however, Korea was sorely troubled by internal problems and external pressures. The Yi dynasty (1392–1910), then in its fifth century, was in serious decline. Korea's peasantry suffered from "a skewered or concentrated pattern of landholding; small average per capita holdings; high rates of tenancy; a regressive tax structure; false registration of taxable land; extortion and illegal charges and gratuities at tax collection time; and usury, especially official usury in the management of the grain loan system."[15] There was a serious uprising in the North in 1811. In 1833 there were rice riots in Seoul. And in 1862 there were rebellions in the South.

During the years 1864–1873, there was a last attempt to save the situation by means of a traditional program of reform initiated by the regent, or Taewongun (Grand Prince, 1821–1898), who was the father of the king. The reform program proved strong enough to provoke a reaction but was not sufficiently drastic, even in conception, to transform Korea into a strong and viable state capable of dealing with the dangers of the modern world. That world was gradually closing in on Korea. During the first two-thirds of the century a number of incidents occurred involving Western ships and foreign demands. Korea's initial policy was to resist all attempts to "open" the country by referring those seeking to establish diplomatic relations back to Beijing. This policy was successful as long as it was directed at countries for whom Korea was of peripheral concern, but this had never been the case for Japan. Japan, therefore, was the most insistent of the powers trying to pry Korea loose from the Chinese orbit. In 1876 Japan forced Korea to sign a treaty establishing diplomatic relations and providing for the opening of three ports to trade. The treaty also stipulated that Korea was now "independent," but this did not settle matters since China still considered Korea a tributary. Insurrections in Seoul in 1882 and 1884 led to increased Chinese and Japanese involvement in Korea, including military involvement, always on opposing sides. But outright war was averted by talks between Itō Hirobumi and Li Hongzhang, which led to a formal agreement between China and Japan to withdraw their forces and inform each other if either decided in the future that it was necessary to send in troops.

During the next years the Chinese Resident in Korea was Yuan Shikai (1859–1916), a protégé of Li Hongzhang, originally sent to Korea to train Korean troops. Yuan successfully executed Li's policy of vigorous assertion of Chinese control, dominating the court, effecting a partial union of Korean and Chinese commercial customs, and setting up a telegraph service and a merchant route between Korea and China.

Conflicting ambitions in Korea made war between China and Japan highly probable; the catalyst was the Tonghak Rebellion. Tonghak, literally "Eastern Learning," was a religion that consisted of an amalgam of Chinese, Buddhist, and native Korean religious ideas and practices. As so often before in East Asian history, the religious organization took on a political dimension, serving as a vehicle for expressions of discontent with a regime in decay and for agitation against government corruption and foreign encroachments. Finally outlawed, it was involved in considerable rioting in 1893, which turned to rebellion the following year when Korea was struck by famine. When the Korean government requested Chinese assistance, Li Hongzhang responded by sending 1500 men and informing the Japanese, whose troops were already on the way. The rebellion was quickly suppressed, but it proved easier to send than to remove the troops.

When Japanese soldiers entered Seoul, broke into the palace, and kidnapped the king and queen, Li responded by sending more troops, and war was inevitable. It was a war that everyone, except the Japanese, expected China to win, but all parties were stunned when Japan defeated China on sea and on land. Begun in July 1894, the war was all over by March of 1895. In retrospect the reasons for the outcome are easy to see: Japan was better equipped, better led, and more united than China, a country that was hampered by internal division, corruption, and inadequate leadership in the field. Equipped with shells, some of which were filled with sawdust rather than gunpowder and commanded by an old general who lined up the fleet as though he were still organizing a cavalry charge, it is no wonder that China lost the war at sea. Furthermore, powerful governors-general considered it Li Hongzhang's war, not theirs, and were slow in participating; the southern navy remained aloof.

The Treaty of Shimonoseki (April 1895)

The war was terminated by the Treaty of Shimonoseki. China relinquished all claims to a special role in Korea and recognized that country as an independent state (although its troubles were far from over). In addition, China paid Japan an indemnity and ceded it Taiwan and the Pescadores, thus starting the formation of the Japanese empire. A further indication that the Japanese had now joined the ranks of the imperialist nations was the extension to Japan of most-favored-nation status, along with the opening of seven additional Chinese ports. Japan was also to receive the Liaodong Peninsula but, after diplomatic intervention by Russia, Germany, and France, had to settle for an additional indemnity instead. The effects of the treaty on Korea, on domestic Chinese politics, and on international relations in the area are discussed in the following chapters. Here it should be noted that the treaty marked an unprecedented shift in the East Asian balance of power, a shift from China to Japan that was to continue until Japan's defeat in World War II.

Notes

1. Franz Schurmann and Orville Schell, *The China Reader: Imperial China* (New York: Vintage Books, 1967), pp. 105–13, which reproduces Harley F. MacNair, *Modern Chinese History, Selected Readings* (Shanghai: Commercial Press Ltd., 1923), pp. 2–9.

2. John K. Fairbank, *Trade and Diplomacy on the China Coast: The Opening of the Treaty Ports, 1842–1854* (Cambridge: Harvard Univ. Press, 1953), p. 59, which quotes H. B. Morse, *The Chronicles of the East India Company Trading to China, 1635–1834*, 5 Vols. (Oxford, 1926, 1929), Vol. 2, pp. 247–52.

3. James M. Polachek, *The Inner Opium War* (Cambridge: Harvard Univ. Press, 1992).

4. Ssu-yü Teng and John K. Fairbank, *China's Response to the West: A Documentary Survey, 1839–1923* (Cambridge: Harvard Univ. Press, 1954), p. 26.

5. John Fletcher, *The Cambridge History of China*, Vol. 10, ed. John K. Fairbank (Cambridge: Cambridge Univ. Press, 1978), pp. 375–85.

6. Philip A. Kuhn, *Origins of the Modern Chinese State* (Stanford: Stanford Univ. Press, 2002), p. 56.

7. Quoted in Jonathan D. Spence, *God's Chinese Son: The Taiping Heavenly Kingdom of Hong Xiuquan* (New York: W.W. Norton, 1996), p. 325.

8. Teng and Fairbank, *China's Response to the West,* p. 48. Parentheses inserted by the translation.

9. W. Theodore de Bary and Richard Lufrano, eds., *Sources of Chinese Tradition,* 2nd ed. (New York: Columbia Univ. Press, 2000), Vol. 2, p. 238. Adapted from Ssu-yü Teng and John K. Fairbank, *China's Response to the West,* p. 76.

10. Quoted in Immanuel C. Y. Hsu, *China's Entrance into the Family of Nations: The Diplomatic Phase, 1858–1880* (Cambridge: Harvard Univ. Press, 1960), p. 168.

11. Philip C. C. Huang, *The Peasant Economy and Social Change in North China* (Stanford: Stanford Univ. Press, 1985), p. 137.

12. Claudia Brown and Ju-hsi Chou, *Transcending Turmoil: Painting at the Close of China's Empire, 1796–1911* (Phoenix: Phoenix Art Museum, 1992).

13. Cyril Birch, ed., *Anthology of Chinese Literature* (New York: Grove Press, 1971), Vol. 2, p. 294. Reprinted with permission.

14. David Der-wei Wang, *Fin-de-siecle Splendor: Repressed Modernities of Late Qing Fiction, 1849–1911* (Stanford: Stanford Univ. Press, 1997), p. 125.

15. James B. Palais, *Politics and Policy in Traditional Korea* (Cambridge: Harvard Univ. Press, 1975), p. 63.

China: Endings and Beginnings, 1895–1927

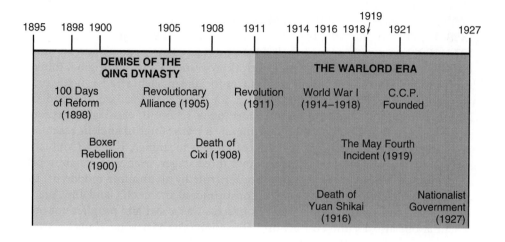

| 1895 | 1898 | 1900 | 1905 | 1908 | 1911 | 1914 | 1916 | 1918 | 1919 | 1921 | 1927 |

DEMISE OF THE QING DYNASTY

THE WARLORD ERA

100 Days of Reform (1898)

Revolutionary Alliance (1905)

Revolution (1911)

World War I (1914–1918)

C.C.P. Founded

Boxer Rebellion (1900)

Death of Cixi (1908)

The May Fourth Incident (1919)

Death of Yuan Shikai (1916)

Nationalist Government (1927)

The New Reformers

The shock of defeat allowed new voices to be heard. They differed from the proponents of self-strengthening both in the scope of the changes they advocated and in a willingness to reexamine basic assumptions. At the same time, the radicals of this generation still had received a Confucian education and had a command of traditional learning.

A major influence was Yan Fu, the one-time naval student at Greenwich, who voiced the bitter resentment of many:

> We thought that of all the human race none was nobler than we. And then one day from tens and thousands of miles away came island barbarians from beyond the pale, with bird-like language and beastly features, who floated in and pounded our gates requesting entrance and, when they did not get what they asked for, they attacked our coasts and took captive our officials and even burned our palaces and alarmed our Emperor. When this happened, the only reason we did not devour their flesh and sleep on their hides was that we had not the power.[1]

Emboldened by the more open atmosphere, Yan publicized his ideas, first in a series of essays and then in a number of extremely influential translations, notably Thomas Huxley's *Ethics and Evolution* (1898), Adam Smith's *Wealth of Nations*

(1900), and John Stuart Mill's *On Liberty* (1903). Yan argued that Western learning was needed to release Chinese energies and rejected much of Chinese tradition including even Confucius. He was especially attracted to Social Darwinism, with its dynamic view of history as evolutionary and progressive, and the hope it held out, on a supposedly modern scientific basis, for those who would struggle.

Yan Fu was no political activist, but others, notably Kang Youwei (1858–1927) and his followers Tan Sitong (1865–1898) and Liang Qichao (1873–1929), not only spread their ideas through their writings and in study groups but also tried to implement political programs. Kang, an original thinker deeply grounded in Buddhism as well as Confucianism, elaborated a highly original theory to construct a Confucian basis for ideas that went well beyond the Confucian tradition. Drawing on an unorthodox school of classical interpretation, he argued that Confucius was not merely a transmitter of ancient teachings but a prophet whose language was full of hidden meanings. Kang's Confucius saw history as a universal progress through three stages, each with its appropriate form of government: the Age of Disorder (rule by an absolute monarch), the Age of Approaching Peace (rule by a constitutional monarch), and the Age of Great Peace (rule by the people). His Confucius was a seer and prophet not only for China but also for the entire world. Tan Sitong went beyond Kang to argue that the monarchy should be replaced by a republic and attacked the traditional Confucian family distinctions in the name of *ren,* the central Confucian virtue. Neo-Confucian thinkers had earlier given *ren* a cosmic dimension, but Tan drew on modern scientific concepts in identifying *ren* with ether. Kang Youwei, too, equated *ren* with ether and electricity.

In their political program, Kang and his followers sought to transform the government into a modern and modernizing constitutional monarchy along the lines of Meiji Japan. Thanks to a sympathetic governor, they were able to carry out some reforms in Hunan, but their greatest opportunity came during the "Hundred Days of Reform" (actually 103 days, June 11 to September 20), when Emperor Guangxu asserted his authority to issue a flood of edicts aimed at reforming the examination system, remodeling the bureaucracy, and promoting modernization. It was an ambitious program, but the edicts remained more significant as expressions of intent than as indicators of accomplishment, for most were never implemented.

The reforms were initiated by moderately experienced statesmen, but later accounts exaggerated the influence of Kang and his associates and the degree to which there was, from the start, a struggle between a progressive emperor and a supposedly reactionary Empress Dowager (see Figure 11.3). However, rumors of Kang's allegedly extremist influence on the emperor helped to solidify the opposition and pave the way for Cixi, backed by General Ronglu, to stage a coup. She placed Emperor Guangxu under house arrest and turned him into a figurehead for the remaining ten years of his life.

After the coup, Tan Sitong remained in China and achieved martyrdom. Kang Youwei and Liang Qichao managed to flee to Japan, where they continued to write and work for renewal and reform. Kang, elaborating on his utopia, dreamed of a future when the whole world would be united in love and harmony under a single popularly elected government, which would operate hospitals, schools, and nurseries, administering a society in which all divisive institutions would have disappeared, including even the family. Meanwhile, Liang continued to expand his horizons as well as those of his numerous readers. Like many of his contemporaries everywhere, he championed evolution and progress, processes which he conflated and, contrary to Darwin, saw as products of human will. But this will had to serve the group. Like most Chinese and Japanese thinkers, Liang was not an individualist.

The Empress Dowager's coup sent China's most advanced thinkers into exile but did not spell a wholesale reaction against reform. She approved moderate reforms, including military modernization and reforms in education and the monetary and fiscal systems. That little was accomplished was due to the weakness of the central government and the magnitude of the problems facing the dynasty. By no means the least of these came from abroad.

The Scramble for Concessions

China's display of weakness in the war against Japan set in motion a scramble for special rights and privileges in which Russia, France, Britain, Germany, and Japan pursued their national interests and jockeyed for position in case China collapsed completely, as seemed quite likely at the time. The concessions extracted from China were economic and political. Loans were forced on the Qing, secured by tax revenues, such as maritime customs. Long-term leases of Chinese territory were granted, including the right to develop economic resources such as mines and railroads. Germany leased territory in Shandong; Russia leased Port Arthur in the southern Liaodong Peninsula; France held leases on land around Guangzhou Bay; and Britain obtained Weihaiwei and the New Territories, adjacent to the Kowloon area of Hong Kong. The powers frequently obtained the right to police the leased areas. Often they combined leaseholds, railroad rights, and commercial rights into a "sphere of interest," where they were the privileged foreign power, as, for example, Germany was in Shandong. Finally, there were "nonalienation" pacts in which China agreed not to cede a given area to any power other than the signatory: the Yangzi valley to Britain, the provinces bordering French Indochina to France, and Fujian to Japan. Russia received special rights in Manchuria.

Britain, as the prime trading nation in China, pursued an ambiguous policy, concerned to retain access to all of China but also to obtain a share of the concessions. The United States at this time was acquiring a Pacific empire. In 1898 it annexed Hawaii and, after war with Spain, the Philippines and Guam. At the urging of Britain, the United States then adopted an open-door policy enunciated in two diplomatic notes. The first of these (1899) merely demanded equality of commercial opportunity for all the powers in China, whereas the second (1900) also affirmed a desire to preserve the integrity of the Chinese state and Chinese territory. This was a declaration of principle, not backed by force; neither its altruism nor its effectiveness should be exaggerated.

The Boxer Rising

The Boxers, members of the *Yihequan* (Righteous and Harmonious Fists), developed in response to harsh economic conditions. Popular anxieties were also fueled by antiforeignism, stemming from alarm over the spread of railways, which cut across the land regardless of the graves of ancestors or the requirements of geomancy, railways along which stood telephone poles carrying wires from which rust-filled rainwater dripped blood-red. As a counterforce, the Boxers relied on *qigong* (ritualized exercise), spells, and amulets to endow them with supernatural powers, including invulnerability to bullets. In 1898 flood and famine in Shandong, combined with the advance of the Germans in that province, led to the first Boxer rising there in May of that year; but it was drought in the spring and summer of 1900 that brought many new members and wide popular support.

Originally antidynastic, the Boxers changed direction when they received the support of high Qing officials prepared to use the movement against the foreign powers. Thus encouraged, the Boxers spread, venting their rage on Chinese and foreign Christians, especially Catholics. On June 13, 1900, they entered Beijing. Eight days later the court issued a declaration of war on all the treaty powers. The Boxers were officially placed under the command of imperial princes. There followed a dramatic two-month siege of the legation quarter in Beijing, where 451 guards defended 473 foreign civilians and some 3000 Chinese Christians who had fled there for protection. The ordeal of the besieged was grim, but they were spared the worst, for the Boxers and the Chinese troops were undisciplined, ill-organized, and uncoordinated. The city was full of looting and violence, but the legation quarter was still intact when an international relief expedition reached Beijing on August 15 and forced the court to flee the capital.

During these dangerous and dramatic events, southern governors-general ignored the court's declaration of war, claiming it was made under duress. The powers, nevertheless, demanded from the Qing court a very harsh settlement. It included a huge indemnity (450 million taels, or 67.5 million pounds sterling) to be paid from customs and salt revenues. Other provisions required the punishment of pro-Boxer officials and of certain cities, where the civil service examinations were suspended. The powers received the right to station permanent legation guards in the capital and to place troops between Beijing and the sea. The Boxer rising also provided Russia with an excuse to occupy Manchuria, where some Russians remained until Russia's defeat by Japan in the war of 1904–1905.

The Boxer rising became a source of literature focusing on one of its leading figures, Sai Jinhua (1874–1936), who was a courtesan, the concubine of a Chinese diplomat in Europe, and supposedly the mistress of the German field marshall who commanded the allied forces occupying Beijing. Depraved strumpet to some, selfless heroine to others, she fills both roles in *A Flower in a Sea of Sins* (*Niehai hua,* 1907) by Zeng Pu (1872–1935).

Winds of Change

Between 1895 and 1911, the modern sector of the Chinese economy continued to grow, but it was dominated by foreign capital. Extensive railway concessions were granted to the treaty powers, and Chinese railroads, like that linking Beijing and Hankou, were financed by foreign capital. Foreigners also controlled much of China's mining and shipping and were a major factor in manufacturing, both for export (tea, silk, soybeans, and so on) and for the domestic market (textiles, tobacco, and so on). Modern banking was another area of foreign domination, prompting the Qing government in 1898 to approve the creation of the Commercial Bank of China as a "government operated merchant enterprise." Two more banks were formed in 1905 and 1907.

Except for railways and mines, foreign investments were concentrated in the treaty ports. It was also there that Chinese factories gradually developed, taking advantage of modern services and the security found in foreign concession areas. Chinese enterprises were particularly important in textile manufacturing. Most remained small (by 1912 only 750 employed more than 100 workers), but they were an important part of China's economic modernization. It was during this time that Shanghai became China's largest city.

In Shanghai and, to a lesser extent, in other treaty ports, changes in social structure occurred. During the last five years of the dynasty there emerged a bourgeoisie, "a group of modern or semi-modern entrepreneurs, tradesmen, financiers, industrial leaders, unified by material interests, common political aspirations, a sense of their collective destiny, a common mentality, and specific daily habits."[2] There were also the beginnings of an urban working class, who at times expressed their resentment over terrible working conditions by going on strike. In the city, too, the old family system lost some of its economic underpinnings, and an audience receptive to new ways of looking at things developed.

There were now 170 presses supplying 2 to 4 million readers for the "depravity," "chivalric/court case," "exposé," and "science fantasy" novels studied by David Der-wei Wang. More often than not they took a jaundiced view of those in power, although few were as blunt as the prostitute in the depravity novel *Nine-tailed Turtle* who tells her customer, "The whole of officialdom is just like a big whorehouse."[3] In *The New Story of the Stone* (1908), Wu Jianren (1866–1910) brings back the main protagonist of *The Dream of the Red Chamber,* and at one point has him arrested as a dissident, but also takes him to "The Civilized World," filled with technological wonders, a utopia (unlike Kang Youwei's) not to be taken as actually attainable.

Meanwhile, out in the real world a strong influence on provincial affairs was exercised by a semimodern urban elite composed of merchants and bankers (more or less traditional), military and professional men (among them journalists) trained in modern methods, and absentee landowners, an elite whose interests and even values often differed from those of the landed gentry on the one hand and from the central government on the other. The very definition of elite status was changed forever when the examination system was abolished in 1905, putting an end to a key institution that had linked government and society, thought and action, and the local and the central for well over a thousand years.

The government had taken this radical step not only in recognition of the need for more modern specialists, but also to secure the loyalty of graduates of new schools by reassuring them in their career expectations.

Stirrings of Protest and Revolution

Some were caught off balance by the winds of change and others trimmed their sails, but there were also those who looked to the future with hope and organized attempts to induce further changes. An early and notable example was the formation of the first anti-footbinding movement in 1894, which resulted in a law banning the practice in 1902. However, even in the cities the law was largely ignored. Footbinding persisted longest in rural areas, and old women with bound feet can still be seen in remote areas. Other expressions of public opinion included a flurry of criticism at what appeared to be a maneuver to depose the emperor (1900), protests at Russia's refusal to leave Manchuria (1903), a boycott against the United States protesting exclusionary immigration laws (1905), and a boycott against Japan (1908), as well as movements to regain railway rights.

Readers of the political press that emerged after 1895 were now exposed to articles and cartoons linking dissatisfaction with the government to resentment against foreign exactions (see Figure 12.1). Politically, the defeat of 1895 not only opened the way for radical reformism but also set Sun Yat-sen (1866–1925) on the path of revolution. Sun was born into a Guangdong peasant family, received a Christian education in Hawaii, and studied medicine in Hong Kong. He founded his first revolutionary organization in 1894. Throughout his life overseas, Chinese communities remained an important source of moral and financial support. Over the years he elaborated his "Three Principles of the People"— nationalism, democracy, and the people's livelihood. He called for the overthrow of the dynasty and the establishment of a republic, principles broad enough to attract the varied and loosely organized membership of Sun's Revolutionary Alliance (Tongmenghui), formed in Tokyo in 1905 by the merger of a number of revolutionary groups. His supporters now included students, many from elite families.

Many looked to political revolution to solve China's ills, but some more radical voices sought social revolution as well. One such was the pioneer feminist Qiu Jin, born in 1877 and executed as a revolutionary in 1907. In 1904, shortly after she had left not only the husband her family had selected for her but also a son and a daughter, she wrote the following poem:

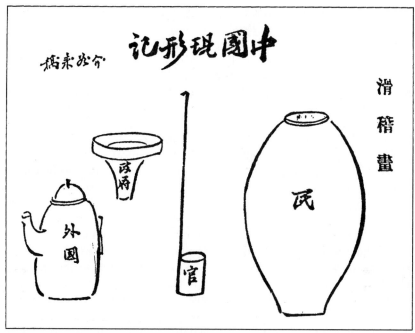

FIGURE 12.1 "A record of the situation in China." Cartoon in *Shibao*, August 26, 1907. The ladle in the center represents officials scooping from the jug of the people (on the right) and pouring their resources through a government funnel into the foreigners' teapot. (From *Print and Politics: "Shibao" and the Culture of Reform in Late Qing China*, by Joan Judge [Stanford: Stanford University Press, 1996], p. 184. Reprinted courtesy Stanford University Press.)

Regrets: Lines Written en Route to Japan

Sun and moon have no light left, earth is dark;
our women's world is sunk so deep, who can help us?
Jewelry sold to pay this trip across the seas,
Cut off from family I leave my native land.
Unbinding my feet I clear out a thousand years of poison,
With heated heart arouse all women's spirits.
Alas, this delicate kerchief here
Is half stained with blood, and half with tears.[4]

Eleventh-Hour Reform

The abolition of the examination system was the most drastic of a series of reforms by which the Empress Dowager hoped to save the dynasty after the failure of the Boxers. Some, like the drive against opium, accomplished much, but the program as a whole failed to inspire officials to change their ways. The momentum was all downhill. In *Modern Times: A Brief History of Enlightenment* (*Wenming xiaoshi*, 1905) Li Boyuan (1867–1906), a widely read author of exposé novels, depicts officials whose venality is matched only by the ignorance and arrogance of purveyors of the new Western learning. According to David Der-wei Wang, "Li Boyuan saw in this campaign for reform and modernization less a promise of new economic and political structure than an omen of collective self-delusion, incompetence, and procrastination."[5]

Frequently, measures taken to save the Qing ended up undermining it. The educational reforms are an example. By 1911 even remote provinces boasted new schools, teaching new subjects and ideas. Students also studied abroad in record numbers, especially in Japan where, by 1906, there were at least 8000 Chinese students, many supported by their provincial governments. There, away from home, they enjoyed new personal and intellectual liberty. Even those who did not manage to complete their education drank in the heady wine of new ideas. From the writing of the highly influential Liang Qichao, many learned about the major events of world history and were introduced to Western social and political thought. The example of Japan was itself a powerful influence, as were books translated from Japanese. More books were translated into Chinese from Japanese than from any other language. Many Japanese loanwords entered the Chinese language, thus reversing the flow that had taken place more than a millennium earlier.

Chinese students thus learned about Western history, law, science, and logic, became convinced of the truths of Social Darwinism, and were inspired by the visions of nationalism. As non-Chinese, the Manchus were an obvious target. The Japanese example showed that nationalism was compatible with the preservation of elements of traditional culture, but a commitment to nationalism entailed a willingness to jettison those elements of tradition that failed to contribute to national development. Toward the end of the decade students became increasingly restive and revolutionary.

Manchu political reform included restructuring the government along modern lines and developing a constitution. After a study mission abroad (1905–1906) and subsequent deliberations, in 1908 the government announced a nine-year plan of constitutional reform, beginning with provincial assemblies in 1909. Although elected on a limited franchise, these assemblies, as well as the central legislative council convened in 1910, became centers of opposition rather than sources of popular support.

Nothing was more urgent than the creation of a modern military, but here too the reform program backfired. The new forces proved unreliable because they were either influenced by new, subversive ideas or were loyal to their commanders rather than to the throne. The main beneficiary of military modernization turned out to be Yuan Shikai, who, after his service in Korea (see p. 292), had advanced his career by siding with Cixi in her coup and by standing firm against the Boxers. He became commander of the New Army in 1895 and, as governor-general of Chihli (pinyin: Zhili) from 1901 to 1907, continued to build up the army with which he retained ties even after he was dismissed from the government in 1909.

The government had some foreign policy success, especially in reasserting sovereignty over Tibet, but failed to emerge as a plausible focus for nationalism. Not only was it handicapped by its non-Han ethnic origins, but also at this critical juncture, there was general confusion and disorganization after the Empress Dowager and Emperor Guangxu both died in 1908. Because the Emperor had seemed to be in good health, there were rumors that his death one day before that of the Empress Dowager was caused by poison. The rumors were never proven, but this was not a propitious way to start a new reign. The new emperor was an infant, and the regent was inept but bitterly resentful of Yuan Shikai, who was fortunate to be allowed to retire in 1909.

The Revolution of 1911

In its program of modernization, the dynasty was handicapped by its financial weakness. This became painfully apparent in its handling of the railway issue. To regain foreign railway concessions, a railway recovery movement was organized by provincial landed and merchant elites, who created their own railway companies. The Qing government, however, wanted to centralize, and in 1911 decided to nationalize the major railway lines. Lacking the necessary financial resources, it was able to do so only by contracting foreign loans, inevitably with strings attached. The loans and the subsequent disbanding of provincial railway companies caused a furor, nowhere more so than in Sichuan, where the local investors felt cheated by the price the government was willing to pay for their shares. Provincial interests resented the threat to provincial autonomy. Nationalists were indignant over the foreign loans that financed the transaction. This was the prelude to revolt. The insurrection that set off the revolution took place when a New Army regiment mutinied in Wuchang on October 10. The mutiny was carried out by men only very loosely connected with the Revolutionary Alliance, the main revolutionary organization in the land. Its leader, Sun Yat-sen, was traveling in the United States raising money, but rushed home when he heard the news.

After the October 10 incident, province after province broke with the dynasty. It turned for help to Yuan Shikai, who had served as Grand Councilor and Foreign Minister in 1907–1908 but had been dismissed after the death of his patron Cixi in 1908. Yuan was the obvious man to turn to, for he enjoyed foreign support as well as the loyalty of China's best army, and he had prestige as a reformer. However, he was not about to sacrifice himself for a losing cause, but he was not strong enough to impose his will on all of China. The revolutionaries had in the meantime formed a government at Nanjing with Sun Yat-sen as provisional president. A compromise between Yuan and the revolutionaries was clearly called for if China was to avoid prolonged civil war and the nightmare of direct foreign intervention. An agreement was reached. The Manchu child-emperor formally abdicated on February 2, 1912, bringing an end not only to a dynasty but also to a political system whose foundations had been laid in 221 B.C.E. China now became a republic.

II. From Yuan Shikai to Chiang Kai-shek

Yuan Shikai

The Warlord Era

Intellectual Ferment

Intellectual Alternatives

Cultural Alternatives

Marxism in China: The Early Years

The GMD and Sun Yat-sen (1913–1923)

GMD and C.C.P. Cooperation (1923–1927)

The Break

Establishment of the Nationalist Government

Yuan Shikai

After the Qing abdication, Sun Yat-sen stepped aside, and Yuan accepted the presidency of a republic with a two-chambered legislature. He also agreed to move the capital to Nanjing, but once in office he evaded this provision, and Beijing remained the capital of the Republic. In the absence of well-organized political parties or deep-rooted republican sentiment among the public, there was little to restrain Yuan from rapidly developing into a dictator. To be sure, elections were held in February 1913 with about 5 percent of China's population entitled to vote.

The Guomindang (GMD or Nationalist party), the successor to the Tongmenghui, was the largest party in the new parliament. Yuan, however, was not about to share power. He bullied the elected parliament, and in March 1913, Song Jiaoren (1882–1913), architect of the constitution and leader of the parliamentary GMD, was assassinated on Yuan's orders. That summer Yuan forced a showdown by ordering dismissal of pro-Nationalist southern military governors. When they revolted in what is sometimes known as the Second Revolution, Yuan crushed them easily. For the next two years, the other military governors remained loyal, but Yuan remained dependent on military authority.

Yuan basically sought to continue the late Qing program of centralization, but to do so he had to struggle against the forces of reformist provincialism as well as revolutionary nationalism. Often the two combined, because to finance a program regarded with suspicion by provincial interests, Yuan needed funds, and, in the absence of a radical social revolution, this meant obtaining foreign loans. This move antagonized nationalists because the loans came with foreign strings and "advisors." The *Shibao* cartoon rang truer than ever (see Figure 12.1).

In 1915, taking advantage of the great powers' preoccupation with World War I, Japan presented China with the notorious Twenty-One Demands, divided into five groups: (1) recognition of Japanese rights in Shandong; (2) extension of Japanese rights in Mongolia and Manchuria; (3) Sino-Japanese joint operation of China's largest iron and steel company; (4) agreement that China was not to cede or lease any coastal area to any power other than Japan; and (5) provisions that would have obliged the Chinese government to employ Japanese political, financial, and military advisors, to give the Japanese partial control over the police, and to purchase Japanese arms. Yuan managed to avoid the last and most onerous group of demands, which would have reduced China to a virtual Japanese satellite. However, with the other powers preoccupied in Europe, Yuan was forced to accept Japan's seizure of Germany's holdings in Shandong, grant Japan new rights in southern Manchuria and Inner Mongolia, and acknowledge her special interest in China's largest iron and steel works, which had previously served as security for Japanese loans. The domestic result was a wave of anti-Japanese nationalist outrage, which expressed itself in protests and boycotts.

Yuan made no attempt to harness nationalist feelings to his own cause but prepared for restoration of dynastic rule with himself as emperor. According to an American advisor to Yuan, China was not ready for a republic. Yuan probably was not off the mark in believing that bringing back the emperorship would follow the preferences and meet the expectations of the vast majority of China's population, but he did nothing to tap or mobilize mass support or to mollify the resentment of the educated. He just went ahead. The new regime was proclaimed in December 1915, to begin on New Year's Day. Hostility to the new dynasty was so overwhelming that in March 1916 Yuan gave way and officially abandoned his imperial ambitions. He never regained his old prestige and died in June of that year, a failure.

The Warlord Era

After the fall of Yuan Shikai, the pattern of Chinese politics became exceedingly complex, as military men came to the fore. In 1917 there was even a two-week restoration of the Qing. In August of that year China, under the premier and warlord Duan Qirui (1865–1936), entered World War I by declaring war on Germany. During the next year the Chinese government received loans of some 145 million yen from Japan (the Nishihara loans), ostensibly to strengthen the Chinese ally, but actually siphoned off to support Duan's military and political plans.

Although a national government ruled in Beijing, actual power lay in the hands of regional strongmen (warlords) who came to dominate civil administration in the areas under their control largely through force of arms and who struggled with each other to enlarge or protect their holdings. They constantly made and unmade alliances with each other, while the foreign powers (especially Japan and the Soviet Union), fishing in these troubled waters, sought to play the warlords off against each other for their own benefit.

Some of the warlords, including Duan, had been generals under Yuan Shikai; others had begun their careers as bandits and more or less continued to behave as such. One of the most notorious was the "Dog-Meat General" of Shandong, with his entourage of White Russian guards and women. A huge brute of a man, greedy and cruel, he decorated his telegraph poles with the severed heads of secret society members. Other warlords showed a genuine interest in social welfare and education and tried to build up their areas economically, but they lacked the vision and organization to clear a way for the future. Conditions varied widely, but for many these were years of great insecurity and suffering.

Internationally, the 1920s were peaceful, but China's sovereignty was more impaired than ever. Its customs and salt revenues were committed to paying foreign obligations, and tariffs were kept artificially low. China's major cities were designated as treaty ports, some—most notably Shanghai—with foreign concession areas under foreign jurisdiction. In these enclaves foreigners led privileged lives. They also continued to enjoy extraterritoriality wherever they went. Although the foreigners' economic impact should not be exaggerated, both commercial travelers and missionaries used British steamers to travel inland on waterways, policed if necessary by foreign gunboats, to service churches and clinics. Foreigners were everywhere. Their presence was politically offensive and profoundly degrading.

Economically, the modern sector expanded during the global postwar boom so that 1917–1923 has been called "the golden age of Chinese capitalism."[6] The influence of the world economy on China expanded, with, for example, the sale of kerosene spreading into interior villages. Over all, these economic developments were insufficient to destabilize the economy enough to bring about either a fundamental breakdown or a breakthrough to growth. However, economic activity can never be separated from other aspects of life. We may speculate that with the state too weak to exert pressure, the examination system no longer in place to reward Confucian learning, and the old paternalistic ideology tarnished, there was increasingly little to prevent former gentry families from turning into landlords pure and simple. If so, this suggests fragmentation of the social fabric analogous to the political fragmentation produced by the warlords. Meanwhile, the shattering of the old world was most visible in the intellectual arena.

Intellectual Ferment

It did not take the fall of the Qing to produce iconoclasm and protest. Revolutionary ideas had already been current among Chinese students in Tokyo and were discussed in magazines and schools in China itself. We have already noted the begin-

nings of feminism. In China, as in Japan, radicals were drawn to the teachings of anarchism—especially the ideas that the state is inherently oppressive and that natural human social tendencies can create a just society. The abolition of the examinations and the collapse of the Qing opened the floodgates to new ideas but destroyed neither the respect accorded scholars and intellectuals nor their commitment to society and their sense of their own importance.

A major landmark was the founding in 1915 of *New Youth*, the journal that came to stand at the core of the new intellectual tide. In the first issue, its founder, Chen Duxiu (1879–1942), issued an eloquent call for the rejuvenation of China, accompanied by an equally strong denunciation of tradition. The new intellectuals castigated Confucianism as being responsible for all that was found wanting in the old state and society, for stifling human creativity and suppressing women, and for standing in the way of freedom and progress. Few were convinced by Kang Youwei, who tried to cast Confucianism in a new role as the official state religion. Unsuccessful in his earlier attempt to construct a Confucian justification for modernization that would persuade scholars grounded in the classics, he now failed to make Confucianism acceptable to those whose primary loyalty was to the nation. He was not the only intellectual whom time passed by as ideas once considered radical appeared conservative in a changed world. Confucianism was not destroyed, but it was put very much on the defensive.

New Youth opposed not only the traditional teachings but also the language in which they were written. The journal opened its pages to Hu Shi (1891–1962), a former student of the American philosopher John Dewey and China's leading champion of the vernacular language (*baihua*). Hu Shi argued that people should write the spoken language, not the language of the classics, and that the vernacular should be taught in the schools. He praised the literary merits of the old novels written in the vernacular, which had long been widely read but had not been considered respectable. The campaign for the vernacular was a success, although classical expressions had a way of creeping into the vernacular, and newly borrowed terms stood in the way of easy comprehension. Nevertheless, the new language was both more accessible and more modern than the old. Introduced into the elementary schools in 1920, it was universally used in the schools by the end of the decade.

New Youth was also the first magazine to publish Lu Xun, pen name of Zhou Shuren (1881–1936), who became China's most acclaimed twentieth century writer. Although Lu Xun had gone to Japan to study medicine, he then decided to devote himself to combating not physical ailments, but China's spiritual ills. His bitter satire cut like a sharp scalpel, but a scalpel wielded by a humanist who hoped to cure, not kill. The protagonist in "A Madman's Diary" (*New Youth*, 1918) discovers the reality underneath the gloss of "virtue and morality" in the old histories: a history of man eating man. He ends with the plea, "Perhaps there are still children who have not eaten men? Save the children. . . ."[7]

Chen Duxiu and many other intellectual leaders taught at Beijing University. Their ideas found a ready following among the students at this and other universities. On May 4, 1919, some 3000 students staged a dramatic demonstration in

Beijing to protest the assignment at the Versailles Peace Conference of Germany's former possessions in Shandong to Japan, even though China, like Japan, had entered World War I on the allied side and sent labor battalions to France. The students were outraged. Their demonstrations became violent. The house of a pro-Japanese minister was burned and another minister was beaten badly. In clashes with the police one student died. There were arrests followed by more protest, a wave of strikes, and a show of merchant and labor support for the students. In the end the government had to retreat. Those arrested were released, and those who had ordered the arrests were forced to resign. China never signed the ill-fated Treaty of Versailles.

The May Fourth incident came to symbolize the currents of intellectual and cultural change first articulated in *New Youth* and gave rise to the broader term "May Fourth Movement" (c. 1915 to early 1920s). After the incident, there was a new sense of urgency. What had been a trickle of protest became a tide of attacks on just about every aspect of Chinese culture in a total rejection of the past—including basic institutions such as the family. Simultaneously, the movement introduced a host of new and radical ideas. New journals appeared, and there was much heady and excited talk, but also action, as young people spurned arranged marriage and engaged in increased social action, including organizing labor unions. The May Fourth movement had long-term revolutionary consequences, both in what it destroyed and in what it introduced. In the short term, although the current of nationalism ran deep and strong, there were intense disagreements over the future direction of Chinese culture, and a tremendous variety of ideas, theories, and styles swelled the eddies of intellectual and cultural life.

Intellectual Alternatives

Europe's self-destruction in war and the failure of liberal principles at Versailles prompted Liang Qichao to turn back to the Chinese tradition in the hope of synthesizing the best of China and the West, with Chinese elements predominating. An important debate began in 1923 between the proponents of science and those of metaphysics, involving different evaluation of Chinese and Western cultures. Among the advocates of the latter were proponents of scientism, who believed that science holds the answers to all problems and that the scientific is the only method for arriving at truth. Their opponents argued that science is applicable only to a narrow field of study and that moral values have to be based on deeper metaphysical truths that by their very nature are beyond the reach of scientific methodology. Because similar problems agitated the West at this time, Chinese thinkers drew on the ideas of classic European philosophers such as Immanuel Kant and also on the thought of contemporaries with widely different methodology and results. For example, some promoted the ideas of John Dewey (1859–1952), the American pragmatist who would replace "absolute truth" with truths that worked as solutions to problems; but others turned to Henri-Louis Bergson (1859–1941), the French exponent of vitalism, a doctrine centering on life as a force that cannot be explained in material terms.

Those who identified with the Chinese tradition further drew on the insights of Neo-Confucianism and Buddhism, particularly the former. One of the most noteworthy defenders of tradition was Liang Shuming (1893–1988), who put his Confucian principles into action by working on rural reconstruction. Another was Zhang Junmai (1887–1969), later the leader of a small political party opposed to both the Communists and the Nationalists. Other philosophers such as Feng Yulan (Fung Yu-lan, 1895–1990) and Xiong Shili (1885–1969) drew on Neo-Confucian thought, but the trend of the times was against them.

Among the champions of science and Western values were the scientist Ding Wenjiang (1887–1937) and the father of the vernacular language movement, Hu Shi. Hu Shi was a leading liberal who advocated a gradualist, piecemeal problem-solving approach to China's ills in the face of attacks both from the traditionalists on the right and from the left. His message increasingly fell on deaf ears, for his approach required time, and time was precisely what China lacked. More often than not, this included time to digest the heady dose of new intellectual imports or, for that matter, to study the old traditions in depth.

Cultural Alternatives

Qi Baishi (1863–1957), probably the most beloved painter of the century, was singularly unaffected by the turmoil of the times. Qi began as a humble carpenter and did not turn to painting until his mid-twenties, but his industry and longevity more than made up for a late start. It is estimated that he produced more than 10,000 paintings. Qi was a great admirer of the seventeenth-century individualist Zhu Da, but followed his own inner vision. He was not given to theorizing but did express his attitude toward representation: "The excellence of a painting lies in its being like, yet unlike. Too much likeness flatters the vulgar taste; too much unlikeness deceives the world."[8] His works show, to quote a Chinese critic, "a loving sympathy for the little insects and crabs and flowers he draws" and have "an enlivening gaiety of manner" so that "his pictures are really all pictures of his own gentle humanism"[9] (see Figure 12.2).

There were other painters and calligraphers who remained uninfluenced by the West, but many felt that the new age required a new style. Among those who tried to combine elements of the Chinese and Western traditions were the followers of a school of painters established by Gao Lun (Gao Jianfu, 1879–1951). Gao sought to combine Western shading and perspective with Chinese brushwork and was also influenced by Japanese decorativeness. He sought to bring Chinese painting up to date by including in his works new subject matter, such as the airplanes in Figure 12.3.

In Shanghai, meanwhile, a small group of artists tried to transplant French style bohemianism into that international city. Xu Beihong (1895–1953), for ex-

FIGURE 12.2 *Grasshopper and Orchid Leaves*, Qi Baishi (Qi Huang, 1863–1957). Although Qi also painted landscapes and portraits, he excelled in depicting the humble forms of life, such as rodents and insects, with a loving and gentle humor reminiscent of the haiku of Kobayashi Issa. Ink on paper, 12 in × 8.46 in, signed Baishi. (Courtesy Far East Fine Arts, Inc. San Francisco [http://www.fareastfinearts.com].)

ample, affected the long hair and general appearance popular in the artists' quarter of Paris. When he returned from that city in 1927, Xu also brought back a thorough mastery of the French academic style. Somewhat more advanced in his Western tastes was Liu Haisu (1896–1994), founder of the Shanghai Art School (1920), where he introduced the use of a nude model. This was also one of the first schools to offer a full course of instruction in Western music. Liu was inspired by French postimpressionists such as Matisse and Cezanne. Later, however, Liu returned to painting in a traditional manner, and Xu, too, abandoned his Western dress for a Chinese gown. Today Xu is perhaps most appreciated for his paintings of horses (see Figure 12.4).

Modern Chinese literature had its origins in the novels of the late Qing. A very popular but superficial genre was "butterfly" literature, named after poems inserted into a novel, comparing lovers to pairs of butterflies. Between 1910 and 1930, around 2215 such novels offered a literate but unlearned public amusement and escape. Also, going back to the late Qing there was a steady and swelling stream of translations. Lin Shu (1852–1924), the most famous and prolific early translator, rendered into classical Chinese the novels of Charles Dickens, Walter Scott, and others in an opus that grew to some 180 works. Thanks to the labors of Lin and other translators, soon examples of all the major European literary traditions as well as that of Japan were available in translation.

The May Fourth movement had a strong effect on literature. The intellectual revolution was accompanied by a literary revolution. This brought with it experiments, such as those of Xu Zhimo (1896–1931), who modeled his poetry on English verse, complete with rhyme. More widespread was a tendency toward romantic emotionalism, an outpouring of feelings released by the removal of Confucian restraints and encouraged by the example of European romanticism. One strain, as analyzed by Leo Ou-fan Lee, was the passive-sentimental, presided over by the hero of Goethe's *The Sorrows of Young Werther*, read in China and Japan as "a sentimental sob story." The

FIGURE 12.3 *Flying in the Rain*, Gao Lun (Gao Jianfu), 1932. Chinese painters, like writers and intellectuals throughout East Asia, devised different ways to combine traditionalism and modernism in style and subject matter, but lyrical landscapes with airplanes bouncing through the sky are rare anywhere. Ink and color on paper. (© Art Museum, Chinese University of Hong Kong, China.)

subjectivism of these writers was not unlike that of the writers of "I novels" in Japan. Another strain was dynamic and heroic. Its ideal was Prometheus, who braved Zeus's wrath and stole fire for mankind. Holding a promise of release from alienation, it was compatible with a revolutionary political stance. For Guo Moruo (1892–1978), once an admirer of Goethe, Lenin became beyond all else a Promethean hero. Perhaps the strongest expression of Promethean martyrdom came from Lu Xun, "I have stolen fire from other countries, intending to cook my own flesh. I think that if the taste is good, the other chewers on their part may get something out of it, and I shall not sacrifice my body in vain."[10]

Controversies and rivalries stimulated the formation of literary and intellectual societies as like-minded men joined together to publish journals advocating

FIGURE 12.4 *Standing Horse*, Xu Beihong, 1935. (© Xu Beihong Memorial Gallery, Beijing, China. Used by permission.)

their causes and denouncing the opposition. Revolutionaries were not alone in arguing that literature should have a social purpose, but as the years passed without any improvement in Chinese conditions, the attractions of revolutionary creeds increased. Writers of revolutionary persuasion such as the Communist Mao Dun (Shen Yanbing, 1896–1981) depicted and analyzed the defects in the old society and portrayed the idealism of those who were out to change things. Such themes appeared not only in the work of Communist writers like Mao Dun, but also in the work of the anarchist Ba Jin (Li Feigang, 1905–), best known for his depiction of the disintegration of a large, eminent family in the novel appropriately entitled *Family* (1931), a part of his *Turbulent Stream* trilogy (1931–1940). Such works provide important material for the student of social as well as literary history.

Marxism in China: The Early Years

Marxism was not unknown in China but had little appeal before the Russian Revolution. The few who were drawn to socialism were attracted more by its egalitarianism than by concepts of class warfare. The writings of Marx and Engels offered the vision of a perfect society, but their thesis that socialism could only be achieved after capitalism had run its course suggested that Marxism was inappropriate for a society only just entering "the capitalist stage of development."

The success of the Russian Revolution (1917) changed all that. Faced with a similar problem in applying Marxism to Russia, Lenin amended Marxist theory to fit the needs of his own country and thereby also made it more relevant to the Chinese. His theory that imperialism was the last stage of capitalism gave new importance to countries such as China, which were the objects of imperialist expansion and the places where capitalism was particularly vulnerable. Also most significant was Lenin's concept of the Communist party as the vanguard of revolution, for now party intellectuals could help make history even in a precapitalist state.

Furthermore, Marxism was modern and claimed "scientifically" valid doctrines. It shared the prestige accorded by Chinese intellectuals to Western and "advanced" ideas, even as its proponents opposed the dominant forms of economic and political organization in the West. A Western heresy to use against the West, it promised to undo China's humiliation, and its converts were persuaded that the doctrine of "dialectic materialism" assured that Communism was the wave of the future. Thus, China could once again be in the forefront of world history. The Russian Revolution demonstrated that it worked.

Li Dazhao (1888–1927), professor and librarian at Beijing University, was initially attracted by its promise as a vehicle for national revolution, whereas Chen Duxiu turned from science and democracy to Marxism as a more effective means of achieving modernization. Others were drawn to it for a mixture of reasons, high among them the promise it held for solving China's ills. By the spring of 1920, when Grigorii Voitinsky arrived in China as an agent of the Communist International (Comintern), a core group of Marxist intellectuals was available as potential leaders for the organization of the Chinese Communist Party (C.C.P.) that took place the following year.

At its first gathering in July 1921, the C.C.P. elected Chen Duxiu as its Secretary General. Despite considerable misgivings, the party submitted to a Comintern policy of maximum cooperation with the GMD. A formal agreement was reached in 1923, which allowed C.C.P. members into the GMD as individuals, subject to GMD party discipline. The C.C.P. leaders found it difficult to accept the Comintern's theoretical analysis of the GMD as a multiclass party, but submitted to Comintern discipline and the logic of the situation where the few hundred Communists were outnumbered by the thousands of GMD members and had little contact with the masses. This initial period of cooperation lasted until 1927. The C.C.P. grew, but the GMD remained the senior partner.

The GMD and Sun Yat-sen (1913–1923)

After the failure of the "second revolution" of 1913, Sun Yat-sen was again forced into exile in Japan, where he tried to win Japanese support for his revolution. After the death of Yuan Shikai, Sun was able to return to China and establish a precarious foothold in Canton, where he depended on the good will of the local warlord. Denied foreign backing from Japan and elsewhere, Sun was also handicapped by the weakness of the GMD party organization, which was held together only loosely, largely through loyalty to Sun himself. The success of the Russian Revolution provided a striking contrast to the failure of Sun's revolution. Sun was also favorably disposed to the Soviet Union (U.S.S.R.) by its initial renunciation of Czarist rights in China. This corresponded to a new anti-imperialist emphasis in his own thought and rhetoric, after the end of Manchu rule had not led to a marked improvement in China's position in the world. Also, he was impressed by the mass nationalism of the May Fourth Movement.

Sun was therefore ready to work with the Communists and in 1923 concluded an agreement with the Comintern that concurred with Sun's view that China was not ready for socialism and that the immediate task ahead was the achievement of national unity and independence. Through this pact, Sun received valuable assistance and aid. Under the guidance of the Comintern agent Mikhail Borodin (originally named Grusenberg), the GMD was reorganized into a more structured and disciplined organization than ever before, while General Galen, alias Vassily Blyukher (or Blücher), performed the same service for the army. Sun made some minor ideological compromises but did not basically depart from his previous views.

GMD and C.C.P. Cooperation (1923–1927)

For both sides this was a marriage of convenience. At first it worked. The GMD gained guidance and support. C.C.P. members rose to important positions in the GMD, and the party grew. A good example of a C.C.P. leader occupying an important GMD office is Zhou Enlai's (1898–1976) service as chief of the political department of the Whampoa Military Academy under Chiang Kai-shek (1887–1975). Here the cream of the GMD officer corps was trained and prepared to lead an army to reunify China and establish a national regime.

The C.C.P. devoted itself mainly to organizing the urban labor movement, which had already won its first victory in the Hong Kong Seamen's Strike of 1922. Shanghai and Canton were particularly fertile grounds for labor organizers, because in these cities the textile and other light industries continued their pre–World War I growth, assisted by the wartime lull in foreign competition. Of some 2.7 million cotton spindles in China in around 1920, 1.3 million were in Chinese-controlled factories, and 500,000 were owned by Japanese. In Chinese and foreign plants alike, wages were very low, working hours long (averaging nine and one-half hours in Shanghai and up to thirteen in the provinces), and all-around conditions remained very harsh. Under these circumstances, the C.C.P.'s work met with substantial success. It gained greatly by its leadership during and following the incident of May 30, 1925, when Chinese demonstrators were fired on by the police of the International Settlement in Shanghai, killing ten and wounding more than fifty. A general strike and boycott followed; in Hong Kong and Canton the movement held out for sixteen months. The strike did not achieve its goals, but C.C.P. party membership increased from around 1000 in early 1925 to an estimated 20,000 by the summer of 1926.

Sun Yat-sen did not live to witness the May 30 incident, for he died of cancer in March 1925. He was an energetic speaker and tireless visionary, glorified as the father of the revolution, but he left no clearly designated heir and an ambiguous ideological legacy. His last major statement, "Three Principles of the People" (1924), stressed the first principle, nationalism—now directed against foreign imperialism—and provided for self-determination for China's minorities. The second principle, democracy, contained proposals for popular elections, initiative, recall, and referendum, but full democracy was to come only after a preparatory period of political tutelage. He emphasized the need for a disciplined people and believed that the Chinese people had too much freedom, not too little. The state would be a republic with five branches of government: legislative, executive, and judicial (as in the West), plus an examination branch to test applicants for government posts and a censorial branch to monitor government officials and control corruption, as under the emperors.

Finally, the principle of the people's livelihood was aimed at both egalitarianism and economic development. It incorporated a proposal by the American reformer Henry George (1839–1897) to tax the unearned increment on land values to equalize holdings. An additional refinement was a land tax based on each landowner's assessment of the value of his land. To prevent underassessment, the state was to have the right to purchase the land at the declared value. Beyond that, Sun had a grandiose vision of "building the wealthiest, most powerful and happiest nation on earth,"[11] but his plan for Chinese industrialization was unrealistic. More realistic was a proposal for state ownership of major industries, but he remained critical of Marxist ideas of class struggle.

After Sun Yat-sen's death, Wang Jingwei (1883–1944) was well placed to succeed to the GMD leadership, for he had been associated with Sun in Japan and was considered a revolutionary hero for his attempt to assassinate the Manchu Prince Regent in 1910. But in 1926 it became apparent that he had a formidable challenger in Chiang Kai-shek. In 1923, Sun had sent Chiang to Moscow to study the Soviet military. On his return to China, Chiang became head of the Whampoa Military Academy, where he was highly successful, esteemed alike by the Soviet advisors and by the officer candidates.

While Wang Jingwei loosely presided over the GMD, the C.C.P. steadily gained influence in the party, much to the alarm of the GMD right and of Chiang Kai-shek. In March 1926, Chiang decided to act: he declared martial law, arrested Soviet advisors, and took steps to restrain the C.C.P. influence in the GMD, yet managed to retain the cooperation of both the C.C.P. and of its Soviet supporters, whose assistance he needed for the military unification of the country. This he began in the summer of 1926 by launching the Northern Expedition (see Figure 12.5), setting out with his army from Canton. Although there was some heavy fighting against warlord armies, the force made rapid headway on its march to the Yangzi, and some warlords decided to go over to the Nationalist side. In the fall of 1926, the Nationalist victories enabled them to shift the capital from Canton to more centrally located Wuhan. There, Wang Jingwei headed a civilian government but could not control Chiang and his army.

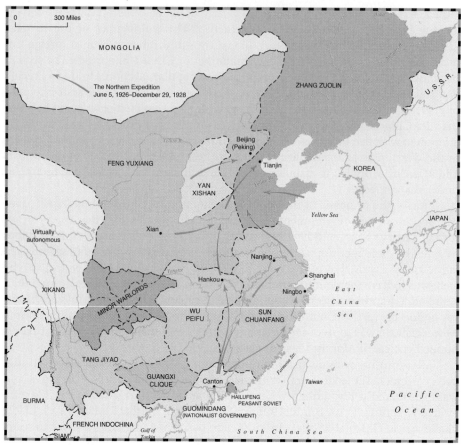

FIGURE 12.5 China and the Northern Expedition, 1926–1928. 🌐

The Break

On its march north to the Yangzi, the army was assisted by popular support, and nowhere was this support more enthusiastic than among the Communist-led workers of Shanghai, where the General Labor Union seized control even before the arrival of the troops. Elsewhere, too, there was an increase in labor activity. This alarmed Chinese bankers and industrialists, who, ready to support a national but not a social revolution, financed the increasingly anti-Communist Chiang Kai-shek. In April 1927, Chiang finally broke with the C.C.P. completely by initiating a bloody campaign of suppression in Shanghai, which then spread to other cities. Union and party headquarters were raided, those who resisted were killed, and suspected Communists were shot on sight. C.C.P. cells were destroyed, and unions were disbanded in a devastating sweep that left the urban C.C.P. shattered.

The C.C.P.'s emphasis on city factory workers was entirely consistent with Marxist theory, but the majority of the Chinese people continued to work the land. Marx, as a student of the French Revolution, despised the peasantry as "the class which represents barbarism within civilization."[12] But Lenin, operating in a primarily agrarian land, assigned the peasantry a supporting role in the Russian Revolution. The C.C.P., although it concentrated on cities, had not neglected the peasants. Beginning in 1923, China's first modern peasant movement was organized by Peng Pai (1896–1929), and by 1927 the C.C.P. was at work in a number of provinces, most notably Hunan, where the young Mao Zedong (1893–1976) wrote a famous report urging the party to concentrate on rural revolution and predicting, "In a very short time . . . several hundred million peasants will rise like a mighty storm, like a hurricane, a force so swift and violent that no power, however great, will be able to hold it back." In another famous passage in the same report, he defended the need for violence, saying, "A revolution is not a dinner party."[13]

In Hunan, as in other rice areas, tenancy rates were high, and the poorer peasants were sorely burdened by heavy rental payments and crushing debts. Tenants had few rights and faced the recurring specter of losing their leases. It was, as Mao saw, a volatile situation, fraught with revolutionary potential. But the Chinese party and its Soviet advisors remained urban-minded.

After Chiang's coup, the C.C.P. broke with him but continued to work with the government at Wuhan, which also broke with Chiang, but still depended for military support on armies officered largely by men of the landlord class, the prime object of peasant wrath. In this situation Comintern directives were wavering and contradictory, reflecting not Chinese realities but rather the exigencies of Stalin's intraparty maneuvers back in Moscow. The end result was that in June the C.C.P. was expelled from Wuhan. Borodin and other Soviet advisors were sent back to the U.S.S.R. The C.C.P. entered into a difficult period of regrouping and reorganization.

Establishment of the Nationalist Government

After Chiang Kai-shek's coup in Shanghai, he established a government in Nanjing, which remained the capital until 1937. The Northern Expedition resumed in 1928, by which time the Wuhan leaders, bowing to the inevitable, had made their peace with Chiang, as had a number of warlords whose forces now assisted the Nationalist drive north and actually outnumbered Chiang's own troops. In June 1928, after a scant two months of fighting, Beijing fell. China again had a national government, but the often only nominal incorporation of warlord armies into the government forces meant that national unification was far from complete. Warlordism remained an essential feature of Chinese politics until the very end of the Republican period in 1949.

In 1927 anti-imperialist mobs attacked British concessions in two cities, and violence in Nanjing left six foreigners dead, a number wounded, and foreign businesses and homes raided. Such incidents were officially attributed to Chiang Kaishek's leftist rivals. The powers concluded that he was the most acceptable leader, who would negotiate rather than expropriate their holdings. Chiang's victory re-assured all the powers except Japan, which had plans of its own for Manchuria and Inner Mongolia. Japan had restored its holdings in Shandong to Chinese sover-eignty in 1922 but now sent troops to Shandong, claiming they were needed to protect Japanese lives and property. In 1928 they clashed with Chinese soldiers. Still more ominous was the assassination that year of the warlord of Manchuria, Zhang Zuolin, by a group of Japanese army officers who acted on their own, hop-ing this would pave the way for seizure of Manchuria.

The Japanese officers did not get their way in 1928, but their act was to serve as a prelude to the Japanese militarism and expansionism that threatened China during the 1930s, even as the Nanjing government tried to cope with warlords and revolutionaries at home, in its attempt to achieve stable government.

Notes

1. Quoted in James Reeve Pusey, *China and Charles Darwin* (Cambridge: Harvard Univ. Press, 1983), p. 50.

2. Marianne Bastid-Bruguiere, "Currents of Social Change," in John K. Fairbank and Kwang Ching Liu, eds., *The Cambridge History of China* (Cambridge: Cambridge Univ. Press, 1980), Vol. 2, pp. 558–59.

3. David Der-wei Wang, *Fin-de-siecle Splendor: Repressed Modernities of Late Qing Fiction, 1849–1911* (Stanford: Stanford Univ. Press, 1997), p. 216.

4. Quoted in Jonathan D. Spence, *The Gate of Heavenly Peace: The Chinese and Their Revolution, 1895–1980* (New York: Viking, 1981), p. 52. Reprinted with permission of Jonathan Spence.

5. Wang, *Fin-de-siecle*, p. 223.

6. Marie-Claire Bergere, in John K. Fairbank, ed., *The Cambridge History of China* (Cambridge: Cambridge Univ. Press, 1983), Vol. 12, pp. 745–51.

7. Joseph S. M. Lau and Howard Goldblatt, *The Columbia Anthology of Modern Chinese Literature* (New York: Columbia Univ. Press, 1995), p. 15.

8. See the biographical entry for Ch'i Pai-shih in Howard L. Boorman, ed., *Biographical Dictionary of Republican China* (New York: Columbia Univ. Press, 1967–71), Vol. 1, pp. 302–304. Qi's statement is quoted on p. 302.

9. Michael Sullivan, *Chinese Art in the Twentieth Century* (Berkeley: Univ. of California Press, 1959), p. 42.

10. Quoted in Leo Ou-fan Lee, *The Romantic Generation of Modern Chinese Writers* (Cambridge: Harvard Univ. Press, 1973), p. 74.

11. Quoted in David Strand, "Calling the Chinese People to Order: Sun Yat-sen's Rhetoric of Development," in Kield Erik Brødsgaard and David Strand, eds., *Reconstructing Twentieth-Century China: State Control, Civil Society, and National Identity* (Oxford: Oxford Univ. Press, 1998), p. 155, citing Lu Fangshan, *Zhu Zhixin yu Zhongguo geming* (*Zhu Zhixin and the Chinese Revolution*) (Taibei: Sili dongwu daxue, 1978), p. 236.

12. Karl Marx, quoted in Lucien Bianco, *Origins of the Chinese Revolution, 1915–1949*, trans. Muriel Bell (Stanford: Stanford Univ. Press, 1971), p. 74.

13. Mao Tse-tung, "Report on an Investigation on the Peasant Movement in Hunan," in *Selected Works of Mao Tse-tung* (Peking: Foreign Language Press, 1967), Vol. 1, reprinted in Ranbir Vohra, *The Chinese Revolution: 1900–1950* (Boston: Houghton Mifflin, 1974), pp. 115–17.

Part Five

Building a New China

*T*he Nationalists and their Communist enemies and successors, although bitter enemies, agreed on the need to build a new China. Both wanted their country to be strong economically and militarily and to be a world power, universally respected. However, they clashed vehemently on what that new China should look like, how it was to be achieved, and who should lead it. By the beginning of the twenty-first century, it was clear that a new China was indeed being born, but its present and future compatibility with either vision remains unclear.

China under the Nationalists

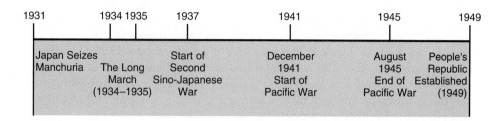

1931	1934	1935	1937	1941	1945	1949

Japan Seizes Manchuria	The Long March (1934–1935)	Start of Second Sino-Japanese War	December 1941 Start of Pacific War	August 1945 End of Pacific War	People's Republic Established (1949)

For most of the world the 1930s were bleak and somber years, and they led into global warfare. The Chinese Nationalists faced formidable obstacles to realizing their vision of turning China into a strong and modern state. In considering China during this period, we need to bear in mind not only that external military and economic forces constrained China's freedom to act but also that in the wake of the Great Depression, people in many lands, desperate for vigorous action, accepted dictatorship of one kind or another as the most effective way of pulling a nation together. It was not in Italy and Germany alone that fascism was viewed as the wave of the future. In Japan, militarists seized power from the political parties, and in China, too, the military gained in power and prestige.

The Nanjing Decade

From 1927 to 1937, the Nationalist government in Nanjing avoided war with Japan, but these were hardly peaceful years. Even after the completion of the Northern Expedition in 1928, the government actually controlled only the lower Yangzi valley. Elsewhere it was dependent on the unreliable allegiance of local powerholders. In 1930 the government secured its authority in the North after waging a costly campaign with heavy casualties against the combined armies of two warlords. Nanjing was strengthened by this victory, but still lacked the power to subdue the remaining warlords once and for all. That some of these could claim to stand for national goals reinforced the strong tendency of the Nationalists to give the highest priority to building military strength, even before Japan's seizure of Manchuria and the threat of further Japanese aggression made such a policy imperative.

At home, the Nanjing regime had to deal with warlords and Communists. The government's policy toward the warlords was to temporize, to try to prevent the formation of antigovernment warlord coalitions, and to settle for expressions of allegiance until it could establish central control. Its power and prestige were increased when it defeated a rebellion in Fujian in 1933–1934 and especially after it obtained control over Guangdong and the submission of Guangxi in 1936. Its campaigns against the Communists provided occasions for the dispatch of central government troops into warlord provinces, especially after the Communists began their Long March in 1934 (see later), and similarly the Japanese threat proved useful in eventually bringing certain warlords into line. Thus, the trend favored Nanjing, but the actual balance between central and local power varied widely in different parts of China. The tenacity of the warlord phenomenon in certain regions is illustrated by Sichuan, in parts of which warlords remained powerful even after the Nationalists moved their wartime capital to that province. Similarly, Xinjiang, in the far west, remained virtually autonomous.

The Nanjing Decade—Domestic Policies

The regime's military emphasis was reflected in government spending, with 60–80 percent of the annual outlay going to military expenses and debt service. The latter amounted to about one-third, reflecting heavy government borrowing, but military considerations were also paramount in civil projects such as road and railway construction. Taking the place of the ousted Russian military advisors were a series of German military men, who tried to introduce German military doctrines (including concepts of military organization not necessarily suitable to the Chinese situation) and helped arrange for the import of German arms and munitions. In 1935, at the height of their influence, there were seventy German advisors in China, but their number decreased after Germany and Japan signed the anti-Comintern pact in December 1936. The last German advisors were recalled in 1938. Noteworthy within the army were the graduates of the Whampoa Military Academy, particularly those who completed the course during Chiang Kai-shek's tenure as director, for they enjoyed an especially close relationship with their supreme commander.

During 1931, Whampoa graduates formed the Blue Shirts, a secret police group who pledged complete obedience to Chiang Kai-shek. They and the so-called CC clique (led by two Chen brothers trusted by Chiang) were influenced in ideology and organization by European fascism. The Blue Shirts were greatly feared because of their spying and terrorist activities, including assassinations. The CC clique, too, had considerable power but failed in its prime aim, which was to revitalize the Guomindang. After the split with the Communists in 1927, the Guomindang purged many of its own most dedicated revolutionaries. One result was that young activists, often from the same modern schools that had earlier supplied recruits for the Guomindang, were drawn to the Communist party. Another result was the creation within the ruling party of an atmosphere attractive to careerists who, concentrating on their own personal advancement, were disinclined to rock the boat. Meanwhile, Chiang saw to it that the party remained just one of several centers of power.

The deterioration of the party was a particularly serious matter, because the Nanjing government suffered from factional politics and favoritism as well as from bureaucratic overorganization, which spawned departments with overlapping functions and countless committees grinding out lengthy reports and recommendations, detailing programs that consumed vast quantities of paper but were rarely implemented. Coordination was poor. It sometimes happened, for example, that government censors suppressed news items deliberately issued by the government itself. The conduct of official business lumbered along unless quickened by the personal intervention of Chiang Kai-shek, whose power was steadily on the increase. His power was based on the loyalty of the military, the Blue Shirts, and core partisans such as the CC clique; on the financial backing of bankers and businessmen (including the relatives of Chiang's wife); and on Chiang's manipulation of various political cliques and factions. The Soong family deserves special mention, for it included not only Sun Yat-sen's widow, who was politically inactive during the 1930s, but also the decidedly active wife of Chiang Kai-shek, another sister who married the notoriously corrupt H. H. Kung, and T. V. Soong, a brother who was a reformist finance minister. Chiang was indispensable but lacked the charisma to inspire his officials, who feared rather than loved him. Nor did he have the gift of eloquence with which to rouse the people had he so desired. Negative sanctions, such as the executions sporadically ordered by Chiang when an exceptionally flagrant case of corruption was brought to his attention, were not enough: the regime lacked drive and direction.

The regime was also weak ideologically. Sun Yat-sen became the object of an official cult, but his ideas were not further refined or developed. Nor was political tutelage enacted. Instead, the emphasis was shifted toward a revival of Confucianism. In contrast to Sun's admiration for the Taiping, Chiang sought to emulate Zeng Guofan, who in his day had crushed the Taiping by revitalizing Confucian values. Chiang's regard for Confucius and Zeng was already apparent during his days at Whampoa, but it became even more obvious in 1934 when he launched an extensive program to foster traditional values known as the New Life Movement. He exhorted the populace to observe four vaguely defined Confucian virtues and spelled out the criteria for proper behavior in detailed instructions. The people were to sit and stand straight, eat quietly, refrain from indiscriminate spitting, and so forth, in the hope that they would thus acquire discipline. It did not work. Officials and commoners continued to act much as before. The government never did devise an ideology able to arouse the enthusiasm of its own personnel, command the respect of the people, or convince intellectuals. Censorship clearly was not the answer, although even foreign correspondents were subjected to it, with some complaining that China was worse than Japan.

Local government under the Nationalists was equally ineffective. They restructured county government and established four bureaus charged with education, construction, public security, and finance and even attempted to reach down below that level by assigning officials to the wards into which they divided the counties; but they failed to wrest control over taxes and local security from the entrenched local elite, who, in practice, continued to wield actual power. Like its predecessors, the Nanjing regime failed to mobilize the financial or human resources of the village. With income from land taxes remaining in the provinces, the government was financed primarily from the modern sector.

Despite early links with the business community, the Guomindang tended to treat business as a source to be exploited for revenue rather than as an asset to be fostered as a component of national strength. During 1928 and 1929, China at long last regained the tariff autonomy lost in the Opium War, but this was of little help to China's industries, because exports were subjected to the same tariffs as imports, and imported raw materials were taxed as heavily as were finished goods. In 1933, heavily in debt to the banks, the government took control of the banking system in a move that benefited the treasury but not the private sector. Overall, the modern sector grew during the first ten years of Nationalist rule, but only at roughly the same pace as during the years between the fall of the Qing and the establishment of the regime in Nanjing.

During the early 1930s, the traditional agrarian sector of the economy, which accounted for most of China's production and employed the vast majority of its people, was affected by severe weather conditions, the exactions of the tax collector piling on surtax after surtax (later changed to special assessments), and the decline in commodity prices brought on by the Great Depression. Not only climate, but also taxation and exposure to international markets varied widely, making generalization very risky. Even in provinces such as Jiangsu and Zhejiang, firmly controlled by the government, taxes paid by one district often far exceeded those paid by another. When the international price of silk collapsed, peasants dependent on sericulture, such as those of Wuxi County in Jiangsu, were badly hurt. Parts of the north were no better off. Statistics for parts of northern China indicate that by 1934–1935 nearly half of the peasant households were farming less than 10 mu (1 mu = 0.167 acres), when 15 were needed for subsistence, reflecting a deepening agrarian crisis. Everywhere, because the government did nothing to change the status quo in the villages or on the land, the poorest and the weakest suffered most. Like so much legislation promulgated during those years, a law passed in 1930 limiting rents to 37.5 percent of the harvest was not enforced. Payments of 50 percent were common and 60 percent was not unusual. Programs for developing cooperatives and fostering rural reconstruction were organized, but their benefits rarely filtered down to the rural poor. In 1937 there was a price recovery, and harvests were good, but by that time millions had suffered bitter poverty and despair.

Chiang Kai-shek and his supporters wanted to unify the country and stabilize society. They wished to consolidate the revolution that had brought them into power, not expand it. Consequently, they put a premium on suppressing forces pushing for continued revolution and were intent on destroying the Communists, who maintained that the revolution was unfinished and proclaimed their determination to lead it to completion. To Chiang Kai-shek nothing was more urgent than the elimination, once and for all, of his old enemies. For the C.C.P., too, these were crucial years.

The Chinese Communists, 1927–1934

The Shanghai massacre and the subsequent suppression of the C.C.P. and its associated labor movement effectively eliminated the party as an urban force, altered its geographical distribution, and profoundly affected its strategy and leadership. For some years it remained unclear just what direction it would take. Neither the Comintern in Moscow nor its Chinese followers were willing simply to write off the cities. Urban insurrection was tried but failed: the Canton Commune (December 1927) met with profound popular apathy and lasted only four days. The use of armed force to capture cities such as Changsha in Hunan in 1930 also failed. Although no one was ready to say so, at least in public, Moscow clearly did not have the formula for success. Meanwhile, in China various groups and factions contended for power and the adoption of their policies.

One of these groups was the C.C.P. military force, reorganized in the mountains on the Hunan-Jiangxi border, where, in the spring of 1928, Zhu De (1886–1976) joined Mao Zedong, who had arrived the previous fall. In command of some 2000 troops, the two men laid the groundwork for the Red Army, with Zhu in military command and Mao in charge of political organization and indoctrination. As Mao was to say in 1938, "Political power grows out of the barrel of a gun. Our principle is that the Party commands the gun; the gun shall never be allowed to command the Party."[1] Through indoctrination, the recruitment of soldiers into the party, and the formation of soldiers' committees, Mao secured the control of the party over the army. On the military side, Zhu and Mao emphasized guerrilla warfare, which put a premium on mobility and surprise, rapid retreats to avoid battle with superior enemy forces, lightning strikes to pick off small contingents of the enemy, and constant harassment to keep the enemy off balance.

Essential to this type of warfare is popular support to provide intelligence, supplies, and recruits, as well as cover for guerrillas under enemy pursuit. Peasant participation and support were secured by redistributing land and furthering the revolution in the countryside.

This strategy focused on the development and expansion of rural C.C.P.-controlled bases. In the early 1930s there were a number of such areas, with the largest in Jiangxi, where the founding of the Chinese Soviet Republic was proclaimed in December 1931. The basic agrarian policy was "land to the tiller," involving the confiscation of large holdings for reassignment to the poor, with "middle peasants" left largely unaffected. But there was a good deal of disagreement over definitions, as well as wide variations in the degree of local implementation of the program. In Jiangxi, Mao and Zhu were strong, but they had by no means won complete acceptance of either their program or their leadership, even after party headquarters were moved from Shanghai to Jiangxi in recognition of the new

FIGURE 13.1 China, 1930–Spring 1944. The Long March. 🌐

C.C.P. power center, a defeat for those oriented toward the Comintern in Moscow. Factionalism continued to threaten party unity, but the most severe challenge was external.

Chiang Kai-shek's first three "annihilation campaigns," in 1930–1931, helped strengthen rather than weaken the C.C.P., as the Red Army employed its tactics to good effect, capturing weapons, men, and land. The fourth campaign, 1932–1933, again ended in defeat for the Nationalists. In the fifth campaign, begun late in 1933, Chiang, on German advice, changed his strategy. Deploying some 750,000 men supported by 150 airplanes, he surrounded the Jiangxi Soviet and gradually tightened the circle of his blockade. When, in the fall of 1934, their situation became untenable, the Communist forces abandoned their base, broke through a point in the blockade manned by former warlord armies, and began their Long March (see Figure 13.1).

The Long March

When the Communists left Jiangxi, their first priority was survival, and their destination was unclear. That was settled in January 1935 at an important conference held at Zunyi in Guizhou, where it was decided to proceed to Shaanxi, where a small soviet was already in place. In Shaanxi the C.C.P. would be out of easy reach of Guomindang armies. They would be able to act on their declaration of war against Japan and might even hope for some aid from the U.S.S.R. At Zunyi, Mao gained a new prominence, although he did not actually control the party until the 1940s.

The March itself was a heroic vindication of Mao's belief in the power of human will and determination. In just over 1 year, the marchers covered some 6000 miles, traversing snow-covered mountain passes where they froze in their thin clothes and crossing treacherous bogs and marshes. To the hardships provided by nature was added the hostility of man, for there was rarely a day without some fighting. At one point they had no alternative but to cross a mountain torrent spanned by a thirteen-chain suspension bridge from which the enemy, armed and waiting on the other side, had removed the planks.

The six- or seven-day crossing of grasslands in the Chinese-Tibetan border region was a terrible ordeal. Here heavy rainfall and poor drainage had created a waterlogged plain on which green grass grew on multiple layers of rotting grass beneath. First a vanguard was sent to chart the way, and in the central grasslands they could find no place dry enough to sleep, so the marchers had to remain standing all night long, leaning against each other. The rest of the army followed through the slippery, treacherous terrain, trudging on despite hunger and fatigue, trying to ward off rain and hail and survive the unbearable cold of the nights. As the men and women carried only a very small amount of grain, they subsisted mostly on wild grasses and vegetables eaten raw because there was no firewood for cooking. Sometimes the vegetables turned out to be poisonous, and the stagnant water reportedly smelled of horse's urine.

The marchers succeeded in overcoming this and other obstacles. Some of the women even gave birth. But less than 10% of about 100,000 who set out from Jiangxi completed the March. Some were left behind to work in various areas, but many more perished. The losses were only partially offset by new recruits who joined along the way. After completion of the March, the Communists, led from Mao's headquarters in the caves of Yan'an, were about 20,000 strong, including those already in Shaanxi.

The survivors of the March emerged toughened and filled with a sense of solidarity forged by shared hardships. There was also heightened self-confidence—a conviction that the movement would surmount all obstacles. Something of this spirit is conveyed in a poem Mao wrote shortly before reaching Shaanxi:

> Lofty the sky
> and pale the clouds—
> We watch the wild geese
> south till they vanish.
> We count the thousand
> leagues already travelled.
> If we do not reach
> the Great Wall we are not true men.
> High on the crest
> of Liupan Mountain

Our banners billow
in the west wind.
Today we hold
a long rope in our hands.
When shall we put bonds
upon the grey dragon?[2]

The saga of the Long March remained a source of heroic inspiration for decades. The last veteran of the March did not leave the stage until Deng Xiaoping died in 1997.

United Front and War

With the Communists in Shaanxi, Chiang remained as determined as ever to crush them, but their call for a united front against Japan had special appeal for the troops of Marshal Zhang Xueliang, who had been ordered to end resistance against the Japanese in Manchuria in 1931 and move south with his armies to Xian. Zhang's forces were less than enthusiastic in fighting the C.C.P. To breathe life into the anti-Communist campaign, Chiang Kai-shek flew to Xian in December 1936. But he had misjudged the situation. Instead of pledging themselves to renewed anti-Communist efforts, Marshal Zhang and some of his men seized Chiang and held him prisoner for two weeks while his fate was negotiated. Exactly what transpired is not clear, but the C.C.P., agreeing with Stalin's policy of forming a worldwide united front against fascism, intervened with Marshal Zhang. Chiang was finally released after agreeing to terminate his campaign against Yan'an and lead a united front against Japan. He was at the time China's most distinguished military man, the leader of the government recognized as legitimate at home and abroad and the heir to the mantle of Sun Yat-sen. Even his enemies saw him as the only man possessing the political, military, and ideological authority to lead China in an effort to stop the Japanese.

Following Chiang's 1936 success against Guangdong and Guangxi, the formation of the Chinese united front in 1937 dismayed Japanese army officers intent on dominating China. Ever since 1933 there had been a constant danger that an unplanned military incident might escalate into a major war. This is, in effect, what happened when the Chinese held firm and refused further concessions after a clash between Chinese and Japanese soldiers on the Marco Polo Bridge outside Beijing in July 1937. Thus began the second Sino-Japanese war that in 1941 merged into World War II, although this is not what Japan intended in 1937.

The fighting went badly for the Chinese. By the end of July the Japanese were in possession of Beijing and Tianjin, and in August Japanese forces attacked Shanghai, the main source of Nationalist revenue. Here Chiang used some of his best German-trained troops in three months of heroic and bloody fighting with very heavy casualties. After Shanghai fell, the Chinese retreated in disarray, failed to take a stand at Wuxi as planned, but poured into Nanjing, which fell in December. The Nanjing Massacre followed. Japanese soldiers, backed by their superiors, went on a rampage, terrorizing people, killing and raping, burning, and looting for seven weeks. Sixty years later the number of people who perished remains a matter of bitter contention—as though sheer numbers can measure the horror. The figure inscribed in the memorial erected in Nanjing (1985) is 300,000, but "whether 200,000 or 240,000 people were killed does not alter the dimension of the horror."[3] How and why it happened and the lessons to be drawn therefrom continue to generate intense controversy and stimulate reflection. The Japanese acquired a reputation for terrible cruelty, which stiffened the Chinese determination to resist and continued to cast a pall long after the war.

After Nanjing, the Japanese maintained and continued their offense, taking Canton in October and Wuhan in December, whereas Chiang, refusing to submit, adopted a strategy of "trading space for time." As the war escalated, so did the Japanese government's aims and rhetoric. What had begun as a search for a pro-Japanese North China turned into a holy crusade against the West and Communism. In 1938, unable to obtain Chinese recognition of Manchukuo, the government of Prime Minister Prince Konoe Fumimaro (1891–1945) declared Chiang's regime illegitimate and vowed to destroy it. In November Konoe proclaimed Japan's determination to establish a "New Order in East Asia" to include Japan, Manchukuo, and China in a political, economic, and cultural union, a bastion against (Western) imperialism and against Soviet Communism. Those who did not see the light were to be brought to their senses by force. Originally, in the summer of 1937, Japanese plans had called for a three-month campaign by three divisions, at a cost of 100 million yen, to destroy the main Chinese force and take possession of key areas while waiting for Chiang to ask for peace. But by the following spring they were preparing orders for twenty divisions and had appropriated more than 2.5 billion yen with the promise of more to come and no end in sight.

The Nationalist government moved its wartime capital to Chongqing in Sichuan. Many refugees followed the government to the southwest (see Figure 13.2). Not only universities but also hundreds of factories were transported piecemeal to help the war effort in Chongqing, where Chiang held on gamely. Before the Japanese attack on Pearl Harbor (December 1941), China obtained financial assistance from the United States and U.S.S.R., and Stalin sent some pilots to be stationed in Gansu Province. During 1939–1941 Chongqing was bombed repeatedly. Not until August 1941 did help come in the form of the Flying Tigers, volunteer American pilots who were later incorporated into the Fourteenth U.S. Air Force, commanded by General Claire L. Chennault. However, the West's support remained primarily moral, and the U.S.S.R. alone sent some official assistance. Meanwhile, during 1939–1941, fighting on the ground was limited to skirmishes, with both sides working to consolidate their positions.

In 1940 the Japanese established a puppet regime in Nanjing headed by Wang Jingwei, the erstwhile follower of Sun Yat-sen and leader of the left wing of the Guomindang. However, like a similar regime established earlier in Beijing, it was all too clear to the Chinese populace that the Japanese were pulling the strings.

FIGURE 13.2 *Refugees Crowding onto Train Bound for Guilin*, Cai Dizhi. Chinese refugees escaping from Japanese-occupied territory followed the Chinese Nationalist government southwest to its temporary wartime capital in Chongqing. Scenes like this were common in 1937–1938. Woodcut. (From *Woodcuts of Wartime China, 1937–1945*, Yonghau lingxin, ed. [Taiwan: L. Ming Cultural Enterprises, Dist.])

Expansion of the War into a Pacific War

A major Japanese foreign policy concern during the 1930s was relations with the U.S.S.R. During 1938–1939 there were several military clashes in the border area along Russia's frontier with Korea and Manchukuo. In these operations, quite large in scale and involving the deployment of armor, Japan was defeated. During 1937–1940 there were three military confrontations along the Russian frontier with Korea and, far more serious, along the Mongolian border with Manchukuo. These operations, which increased in scale, involved the deployment of armor, artillery, and aircraft. The Japanese fought well, but the Soviets proved to be more than a match. The last and most severe conflict cost Japan 180,000 men and resulted in an armistice.

Japan was caught off guard diplomatically when Germany, without any warning, came to terms with the Soviet Union in August 1939. Japan was therefore neutral when World War II began in Europe shortly thereafter. However, the dramatic success of the German blitzkrieg strengthened the hands of those in Tokyo who favored a pro-German policy, and in September 1940, Konoe signed the Tripartite Pact, forming an alliance with Germany and Italy.

The Germans again surprised the Japanese in June 1941 when Hitler invaded Russia. Some army men wanted Japan to join the attack on the U.S.S.R. As Alvin D. Coox pointed out, they saw this as a way out of the China impasse, "apparently convinced that the best way to climb out of a hole was to widen it."[4] However, the navy wanted to advance into the oil- and mineral-rich south. Officially, Japan claimed its mission to be the creation of a "Greater East Asian Co-Prosperity Sphere," but the underlying perception was that the resources of Southeast Asia were essential for Japan's economic security.

Konoe hoped that, armed with the Tripartite Pact, he would be able to reach his aims without going to war with the United States, but the American government was becoming increasingly alarmed over Japanese expansion. When in the summer of 1941 Japan moved troops into southern Vietnam, the United States, Britain, and Holland (then in control of the East Indies [modern Indonesia]) retaliated by applying the economic sanctions they had withheld in 1931. An embargo on scrap iron was serious, but the crucial product cut off from Japan was oil.

America and Japan were on a collision course. To quote Michael A. Barnhart, "The Japanese Empire was determined to retain the rights and privileges it considered necessary for its economic and political security. The United States thought these rights and privileges contrary to its own deeply held principles and to the survival of what were now in effect its allies in the struggle against global aggression."[5]

The United States was determined that Japan should withdraw from China as well as from Indochina. For Japan, this would have meant a reversal of the policy pursued in China since 1931 and the relinquishment of the vision of primacy in East Asia. Dependent on oil and rubber from Southeast Asia, the Japanese were in no position to carry on protracted negotiations. They had to fight or retreat. It is a bitter irony that Japan now prepared to go to war to attain the self-sufficiency that its proponents of total war had once considered a precondition for war.

When it became clear to Konoe that the situation had reached an impasse, he resigned, to be followed by General Tōjō Hideki (1884–1948), prime minister from October 1941 to July 1944. When last-minute negotiations proved fruitless, the Japanese decided on war as the least unpalatable alternative. It began on December 7, 1941, with a surprise attack on Pearl Harbor, in Hawaii, that destroyed seven American battleships and 120 aircraft, and left 2400 dead. With the United States and Japan at war, Hitler, too, declared war against the United States, but German-Japanese cooperation during the war remained limited.

The Course of the War

At first the war went spectacularly well for Japan. By the middle of 1942 Japan controlled the Philippines, Malaya, Burma, and the East Indies. Japan was also in charge in Indochina (officially under the jurisdiction of Vichy France) and enjoyed

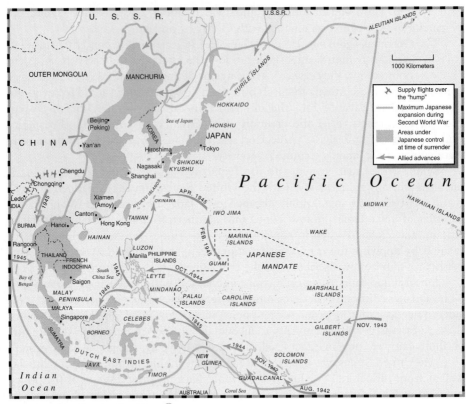

FIGURE 13.3 The Pacific War. 🌐

the cooperation of a friendly regime in Thailand. However, contrary to hopes in Tokyo, the United States, far from being ready to negotiate a quick peace, mobilized for full-scale war.

In June 1942 Japan suffered a major defeat in the battle of Midway, 1200 miles northwest of Hawaii (see Figure 13.3). The Americans, taking advantage of advance knowledge of Japanese movements obtained from breaking the Japanese secret code, destroyed many Japanese planes and sank four Japanese aircraft carriers while losing only one of their own. Three more years of intense warfare, including bloody hand-to-hand combat, lay ahead, but the American use of aircraft carriers and the extensive deployment of submarines, which took a tremendous toll on vital Japanese shipping, were two of the factors contributing to Japan's ultimate defeat. Another was the island-hopping strategy whereby American forces seized islands selectively for use as bases for further advances, bypassing others with their forces intact but out of action. One consequence of this strategy was that although the Allies wanted Japan to remain bogged down in China, China itself was not a major war theater.

China at War

The conviction that eventually the United States would enter the war sustained Chiang Kai-shek during the long years when China faced Japan virtually alone. When this did happen after Pearl Harbor, it buoyed the spirit of the Chinese, now allied with the one country powerful enough to crush Japan. More material forms of support were soon forthcoming, although there was never enough, because in 1942 Japan cut off Chongqing's last land route to its allies by seizing Burma and closing the Burma Road. Thereafter, supplies had to be flown in from India to Yunnan over the Himalayas (the "hump"). In addition, China ranked low in the American war effort. The Allies decided first to concentrate on the defeat of Germany, and the island-hopping strategy adopted against Japan largely bypassed China, although the Allies appreciated the fact that vast numbers of Japanese troops that otherwise might have been used elsewhere were engaged in China (see Figure 13.3).

The top American military man in China was General Joseph Stilwell, who in 1942 became Chiang's chief-of-staff as well as commander of American forces in the China-Burma-India theater. Stilwell was a fine soldier, but Chennault disregarded his warnings against building airbases that were unprotected by ground troops, bases from which, in early summer 1944, heavy bombers attacked industrial facilities in Kyushu and Manchukuo, airfields in Taiwan, and oil refineries in Sumatra. However, Stilwell was proven right when later that summer Japan launched their Ichigo (Number One) campaign into Hunan and Guangxi and captured the airfields. A heavy blow for the Guomindang, it proved a hollow victory for the Japanese.

Stilwell had high regard for the ordinary Chinese fighting man but scarcely concealed his irritation and impatience with the inefficiencies and corruption he encountered in Chongqing and his disgust at Chiang's policy of preparing for a postwar showdown with the C.C.P. rather than joining in a single-minded effort against the Japanese enemy. The relationship between the two men deteriorated until Chiang requested and received Stilwell's recall in 1944.

Stilwell was replaced by General Albert Wedemeyer, who was more friendly to Chiang but equally critical of conditions in the Chinese army, which were, by all accounts, horrendous. Induction was tantamount to a death sentence. Those who could possibly afford to do so bribed the conscription officer. The remainder were marched off, bound together with ropes, to join their units, often many miles and days away. Underfed and exhausted, many never completed the trip. Those who did found that food was equally scarce at the front, and medical services were almost completely lacking.

Misery and corruption were not unique to the military. Even in times of famine (as in Henan during 1942–1943), peasants were sorely oppressed by the demands of the landlord and the tax collector, whereas the urban middle class suffered from mounting inflation, which had reached an annual rate of 40–50 percent between 1937 and 1939, climbed to 160 percent for 1939–1942, and mounted to an average of 300 percent for 1942–1945. By 1943 the purchasing power of the salaries paid to bureaucrats was only one-tenth what it had been in 1937, whereas teachers

FIGURE 13.4 Jiang Qing (left) and Mao Zedong in Yan'an, 1960. After the Long March and during the war, the Chinese Communist Party leaders lived and worked in the Yan'an caves. (© Revolutionary Workers Online.)

were receiving 5 percent of their former earnings. The result was widespread demoralization of the military and civilian populations under Nationalist control. The secret police were unable to root out corruption. Government exhortations and the publication of Chiang Kai-shek's book *China's Destiny* (1943) failed to reinvigorate ideological commitment to the government and party.

A major reason for the wartime deterioration of the Guomindang was that Japan's seizure of the eastern seaboard and China's major cities deprived the Nationalists of the great business centers of eastern China (especially Shanghai). In Sichuan, they were dependent on the elements in society that were most resistant to change and reform. Moreover, Chiang, hoarding his strength for the coming showdown with the C.C.P., was unwilling to commit his troops to battle with the Japanese more than was absolutely necessary. As a consequence, he missed whatever opportunity existed for building a modern Chinese force with American assistance and for translating anti-Japanese nationalism into support for his own regime.

The shortcomings of the Chongqing government were highlighted by the accomplishments of the Communists, headquartered in Yan'an (see Figure 13.4). From 1937 to 1945, the party expanded its membership from roughly 40,000 to more than 1 million, and its troop strength increased tenfold to an estimated 900,000, not counting guerrillas and militiamen. Furthermore, the Communists enjoyed widespread peasant support in northern China, where they established themselves as the effective government in the countryside behind the Japanese lines. The Japanese, concentrated in the cities and guarding their lines of supply, did not have the manpower to patrol the rural areas constantly and effectively.

In the areas nominally under Japanese control, the Communists skillfully pursued policies to fuse national resistance and social revolution. The key to their ultimate success was mass mobilization of the peasantry, but the mix of policies and the pace of change varied according to local conditions. Carefully avoiding premature class warfare, they frequently began by organizing the peasants to wage guerrilla war, enlisting support from the village elites for the war effort and manipulating them into going along with rent and interest reduction. Building up their military power, they enlisted elite support even as they undermined elite power.

Crucial was the creation of new mass organizations led by poor peasant activists, who, freed from the exactions of landlords and given a voice in government, became enthusiastic supporters of the party and government. The peasant associations and local party branches took the lead in effecting changes in taxation and reducing rent and interest payments, thus destroying the economic foundations of the old system. Similarly, new energies were released by organizing women and young people in an attack on traditional family authority. Actual or potential rivals such as secret societies or bandits were attacked and eliminated. The twin lessons of nationalism and revolution were brought home to the people through indoctrination programs and a campaign to combat illiteracy, conveying new ideas to the peasantry even as they gained access to the written word, shattering the old monopoly on learning.

The Japanese patronized puppet armies and even tolerated trade with the Guomindang-controlled areas of China, but the Wang Jingwei regime was too obviously controlled by the Japanese ever to gain credibility. At best, life in occupied China went on as usual, but Japanese arrogance alienated many Chinese. Humane behavior on the part of some individuals was overshadowed by acts of cruelty that evoked Chinese hatred and resistance. An example is the notorious "kill all, burn all, destroy all" campaign carried out in 1941 and 1942 in parts of northern China in retaliation for a C.C.P. offensive. Implemented literally, the Japanese hurt the C.C.P. badly, but they also helped turn apolitical peasants into determined fighters.

The policies and record of the C.C.P. also helped to attract urban intellectuals. To ensure discipline and preserve the cohesion of the movement, swollen by new adherents, the party under Mao (now firmly established as leader) organized a rectification campaign to assure "correct" understanding of party ideology and to bring art and literature into line. Art for its own sake or for self-expression was condemned, and those guilty of being insufficiently mass-oriented were induced to confess their faults. Many were sent to work in villages, factories, or battle zones to "learn from the masses."

The C.C.P. emerged from the war stronger than it had ever been before. The outcome of the civil war that followed was by no means obvious to observers at the time, but it is one of the ironies of the war that the Japanese, who proclaimed that they were combating communism in China, instead contributed to its ultimate victory.

Japan at War

Well before Pearl Harbor, the effects of the continued war in China were felt by the Japanese people as militarization and authoritarianism increased at home. The National General Mobilization Law of 1938 strengthened the power of the prime minister at the expense of the Diet, and the government began to place the economy on a war basis, with rationing, economic controls, and resource allocations administered by a technological and bureaucratic elite drawn from the most prestigious universities. Getting the various centers of economic and political power to pull together remained a problem, but a precedent was set for government to direct the economy, institutions for this were founded, and Japan gained a cadre of economic and social bureaucrats.

The war entailed a greater role for government not only in industry and commerce but also in agriculture. The war years were hard on rural landlords, already hurt by the Depression, whereas ordinary tenant farmers benefited from measures to control inflation, such as rent control (1939), as well as government efforts to increase production by allocating fertilizer. In the last years of the war, the government paid much larger bonuses to farm operators than to landlords with noncultivated land, who emerged from the war much weakened. As Ann Waswo has shown, "in purely economic terms and in terms of local political influence, ordinary farmers made significant gains."[6] As ever, war proved a potent catalyst for change.

In October 1940, the political parties were merged into the Imperial Rule Assistance Association, which, however, did not become a mass popular party along the lines of European fascism, but served primarily as a vehicle for the dissemination of propaganda throughout Japan. Similarly, labor unions were combined into a single patriotic organization. Great pressures were exerted to bring educational institutions and the public communications media into line so that the whole of Japan would speak with one collective voice.

To effect the "spiritual mobilization" of the country, the government tried to purge Western influence from Japanese life. As one writer put it, "While the black ships that represent the material might of the West have left, a hundred years later the Black Ships of thought are still threatening us."[7] Prominent intellectuals insisted on Japanese uniqueness and exceptionalism and drew on German concepts of irony and angst, nostalgia for the past, and the aesthetics of death, subjectivity, and poetry to attack the "modern" at home and abroad. Not only were foreign radical and liberal ideas banned from theoretical discourse, but popular culture also was purged. Permanent waves and jazz, so popular during the 1920s, were now banned. Efforts were made to remove Western loanwords from the language, and the people were bombarded with exhortations to observe traditional values and revere the divine emperor. Heterodox religious sects with no ostensible political agenda were suppressed, and in a "triumph of religious stateism"[8] all religions were subordinated to the imperial cult. To mobilize the public down to the ward level, the people were formed into small neighborhood organizations.

The End of World War II

Japan's surrender on August 15, 1945, brought an end to half a century during which Japan was the dominant military and political power in East Asia. Japan's defeat also initiated a new phase in the history of South and Southeast Asia, as former colonies resisted the return of Western colonial masters. On the broader international scene, the war left the United States and the Soviet Union as the two giant powers who maintained a presence in East Asia and had the capacity to influence events in that part of the world. And the bombing of Hiroshima and Nagasaki had demonstrated just how dangerous a place that world could be.

An immediate result of the war was that Japan had to relinquish not only Manchuria and other areas seized since 1931 but also all lands acquired since 1895, most notably Taiwan and Korea. China had preserved its national independence, but the end of the war did not lead to demobilization and peace. The country that had been at war for four years before Pearl Harbor did not attain peace until four years after Japan's surrender.

Before turning to the civil war between the C.C.P. and Guomindang, let us pause briefly to consider the half century during which Taiwan was under Japanese rule.

Taiwan

When Japan acquired Taiwan as its first colony in 1895, it did so with many of the same objectives that subsequently prompted it to seize Korea, and the Japanese implemented many of the same policies in both colonies. Consequently, the inhabitants of the island shared many of the experiences of their fellow colonials, but, in the final analysis, the differences between Taiwan and Korea, then as now, loom at least as large as the similarities.

One difference was that in 1895 the people on Taiwan were given two years in which to decide between staying on as Japanese colonials or moving to the mainland as subjects of the Qing. The latter choice proved attractive to a good number of the local elite. This included men who had staked their future on the examination system, for by the time of the Japanese takeover, the "gentrification"[9] of what had once been a frontier elite was well advanced. To serve their needs, between 1860 and 1893, fourteen academies had been established on the island, which only in 1885 had been elevated to provincial status.

The departure of 6400 people, about 2.3 percent of the population, no doubt removed some potential leaders of resistance, but, as it was, the Japanese occupation began with five months of fighting. The Taiwanese, however, lacked coordination. The "Republic of Taiwan," declared by the last Qing governor, lasted only twelve days. Until 1902 the Japanese faced occasional scattered attacks. Even after Japanese authority had been firmly established over the Han (ethnic Chinese) population (2,890,455 according to the 1905 census), armed clashes continued with Taiwan's original inhabitants (estimated to be 122,000 in 1909), who occupied the central highlands and continued to lose ground as they had under the Qing. It was their misfortune that their forest contained camphor trees. Camphor, turned into a government monopoly by Japan, was a prime export, in great demand for use in the manufacture of smokeless gunpowder.

As in Korea, in Taiwan the governor-general was the supreme administrative and judicial authority. Until 1919 he was a military man, but from 1898 to 1906 civil administration was in the hands of Gotō Shimpei (1857–1929), a medical man responsible for much of the basic framework of the Japanese colonial system.

A major objective, accomplished by 1905, was for Taiwan to pay for itself despite continuing heavy government expenditures. To rationalize their administration, the Japanese conducted a land survey and a census. As they also did later in Korea, the colonial authorities relied heavily on the police for a wide range of services, including tax collection, agricultural, hygiene, water supply, and sanitation service, but in Taiwan, unlike Korea, the Japanese controlled these matters by cleverly adapting an old Chinese system of mutual responsibility (*baojia*), under which the population was organized into groups of (theoretically) a hundred households, each composed of units of ten. In contrast to the ineffectiveness of this system on the mainland, in Taiwan the *hokō* system (pronouncing the term the Japanese way) became the instrument by which the state reached down into the villages to affect each individual, something beyond the ability of all Chinese mainland governments before 1949. Only the Han population was organized in this manner.

The *hokō*, along with earlier guard units composed of Han settlers and acculturated aborigines, supplied the manpower for a local militia who acted as police auxiliaries. They not only provided security and surveillance, but also undertook road repair and even railroad maintenance, as well as contributing to various rural campaigns. They also constituted a heavy burden for the population, who, in addition to the regular taxes, were saddled with *hokō* dues and had to supply labor when needed. Although nominally the *hokō* leaders were elected by the households, the system was controlled by the police, which came to include 20–30 percent Taiwanese, but remained firmly under Japanese command.

The Japanese developed the Taiwan economy, but did so to meet their own needs and serve their own purposes. A central bank (The Bank of Taiwan, 1899) issued currency and sought to manage the economy. By the time Japan acquired Taiwan, it was an exporter of tea and sugar as well as camphor, but the sugar industry was faltering. The Japanese changed that, turning Taiwan into a major producer of sugar, able to fulfill their domestic needs and thus saving foreign exchange that otherwise would have gone for sugar imports. Along with tea, the Japanese also fostered rice cultivation and initiated irrigation projects. They also did much to develop the network of roads and railways and improved the harbors for ocean shipping. Modern postal and telegraph systems were established. Beginning with Gotō, they were also very active in public health. The death rate was reduced, and by 1945 the population had just about doubled.

Consumer industries included food processing, logging, and textiles, but not until Japan began preparing for total war did heavy industry get started. The completion of the Sun Moon Lake Electrical Generation Plan (1935) was a milestone. Aluminum, textiles, iron, cement, and chemical industries grew in what nevertheless remained an essentially agrarian economy.

As in Korea, there were local people of wealth and education who worked with the Japanese-dominated establishment. Here too the Japanese were ambivalent about colonial education. True, schools were established, but initially there were only lower-level and inferior schools for the Taiwanese, in contrast to the higher levels of education available to Japanese who settled in Taiwan. In 1928, an imperial university was established in Taipei, but it had three times as many Japanese students as it did Taiwanese. In 1945 there was only one Taiwanese professor on its faculty.

As shown by the establishment of the university, in Taiwan as in Korea, there was a relaxation of control in the 1920s followed by the severity of the 1930s. In the 1920s, Japanese liberals talked of eventual assimilation, and there was a temporary and limited loosening of the colonial reins, with greater tolerance for Taiwanese to express their own views at home as well as in Tokyo. In 1921 a Taiwanese intellectual even demanded the abolition of the *hokō* system. Although some changes were made, it was not abolished until two months before Japan surrendered in 1945. To follow Siomi Shunji's analysis, from 1895 to 1920 the police were the prime movers, but during the next quarter of a century they were a background force.[10]

Stimulated by developments in China and Japan, there was a quickening of intellectual life in Taiwan and among Taiwanese in Tokyo, with movements to forge a new and modern culture and to write in the vernacular about current concerns. The main character of the first novel written by Lai Ho (1894–1943), often considered the father of modern Taiwanese literature, was a Taiwanese vegetable seller whose small manual scale for weighing out his sales was broken in two by Japanese policemen. A central issue facing Lai and a new generation of younger writers trying to forge a Taiwanese identity was that of language, as classical Chinese was rapidly becoming obsolete, and the new literary language that gained currency on the mainland after the May Fourth Movement was based on a vernacular incomprehensible to the people of Taiwan. Lai Ho himself was really most at home in classical Chinese, which he had to translate into the local vernacular.

One solution was to write in Japanese. From the start, the Japanese had encouraged people to learn Japanese, and by the 1930s there was a substantial audience for writers such as Wu Cho-liu (1900–1976), whose *An Orphan of Asia* expressed a sense that Taiwan had been abandoned by its Chinese parents and never become a full-fledged member of the Japanese household in which it now found itself. The problem of defining Taiwan's place in the world was to persist long after the Japanese were gone.

As in Korea, during the 1930s and especially during the war, there were campaigns to have Taiwanese adopt Japanese names and worship at Shinto shrines, but these did not make them into first-class subjects of the Emperor. Taiwanese men did fight in the imperial army, and Taiwanese living on the China coast enjoyed status as Japanese subjects, forming an imperial vanguard much as Korean settlers did in Manchuria. However, many Taiwanese suffered under the heavy hand of Japanese rule. Like the people in Japan itself, they were totally surprised by the defeat of Japan but welcomed reversion to Chinese rule, even though they had not been consulted.

Civil War and Communist Triumph, 1946–1949

When Japan surrendered, Chiang Kai-shek, with American concurrence, directed Japan's generals in China to submit only to Nationalist forces. To enable the Guomindang armies to accept the Japanese surrender, the United States transported them by water and by air to those parts of the country then occupied by Japan. However, they were not allowed into Manchuria until January 1946.

Manchuria had been occupied by the U.S.S.R. during the last days of the war, and the Soviets, intent on harvesting the Japanese military and industrial assets there, did not completely withdraw their troops until May 1946. By that time they had allowed the C.C.P. to gain substantial control of the Manchurian countryside. Chiang Kai-shek, determined to recover the territory where the Japanese had begun their aggression in 1931, disregarded American warnings against overextending his forces and dispatched almost half a million of his best troops to Manchuria.

During the year or so immediately after the war, the Nationalists appeared to have superior resources, at least on paper. Recognized as the legitimate government of China by all the Allies, including the Soviet Union, they had three or four times as many men under arms as their Communist rivals and enjoyed a similar advantage in armaments. They were, therefore, in no mood to make concessions to the C.C.P. The Communists, on the other hand, had become battle-hardened through the war, with well-established support in the countryside and high morale. Their leaders, too, were convinced that victory would ultimately be theirs in the coming struggle. Against this background, in December 1945, President Truman sent General George C. Marshall to China to attempt to mediate between the two parties. Given their history of conflict, divergence of views, and confidence in their respective causes, the American initiative was probably doomed from the start. Marshall's efforts were also undercut by American support of the Nanjing government, even though President Truman stipulated that large-scale aid to China was contingent on a settlement. As during Mao's visit to Chongqing in August through October (see Figure 13.5), there was a show of cordiality, but the Marshall mission produced only a brief breathing spell before fighting broke out in earnest in mid-1946.

Initially, until July 1947, the Guomindang armies enjoyed success, even capturing the wartime C.C.P. capital at Yan'an. However, these were hollow victories. Like the Japanese before them, in northern China and Manchuria the Guomindang controlled only the cities in the midst of a hostile countryside. Moreover, the military efficacy of the armies was undermined by the rivalries between their commanders, by Chiang Kai-shek's penchant for personal decision making even when he was far removed from the scene, and by his abiding concern for preventing any possible rival from amassing too much power. Also much in evidence were the harshness and corruption that had sapped the soldiers' morale during the war against Japan and were even more demoralizing now that they were supposed to fight fellow Chinese.

In other respects too, far from stimulating reform, the defeat of Japan resulted merely in the transfer to the rest of China of the ills that had been incubating in wartime Chongqing. A nation badly in need of political, economic, and social reconstruction was subjected to a heavy dose of autocracy and to a galloping inflation. Liberal reformers, disillusioned by the corruption and alarmed at the prospect of civil war, tried to rally the opposition. One leader of this non-Communist opposition to the Guomindang was Wen Yiduo (1899–1946), a professor at Qinghua University on its wartime campus in Kunming who tried to encourage those who hoped for a rebirth of democracy and greater freedom to criticize the government. However, the Guomindang responded to these calls for

FIGURE 13.5 Mao Zedong (left) and Chiang Kai-shek exchange toasts at Chongqing during a welcoming party for Mao Zedong. August–October 1945. (© Bettman/ Corbis [BE046254].)

reform by assassinating the critics. In 1946, Guomindang agents assassinated Wen Yiduo himself just after he gave a fiery eulogy for one of his murdered colleagues. Wen's death shocked China and served to expose the depths to which the ruling group had sunk in its desperation to retain power.[11]

Intellectuals and students were not the only ones disenchanted with the regime, for many suffered from the arrogance of the Nationalist soldiers and the rapacity of those with political connections. The situation was particularly bad in Taiwan, where carpetbaggers from the mainland enriched themselves at the expense of alleged Taiwanese "collaborators"—a convenient charge against any uncooperative Taiwanese who had done well during the preceding half-century of Japanese rule. When the Taiwanese rioted in protest in 1947, the Nationalist government responded with brutal and bloody repression. The exact number of casualties is not known; however, Taiwanese leaders in exile claimed that more than 10,000 were killed.

The government, inefficient as well as autocratic, proved unable to halt rapidly accelerating inflation that threatened all those whose incomes did not keep up with rising costs. Toward the end, people in the cities had to carry enormous bundles of paper money on their daily rounds of shopping for the necessities of life.

In the C.C.P. areas, in contrast, a disciplined and well-organized political and military leadership offered credible leadership. Unlike the Guomindang, which promised reform only after the fighting was finished, the C.C.P. implemented one change after another. A crucial and impressive demonstration of their expertise in mass mobilization took place in Manchuria, where they made the most of the window of opportunity granted them by the Soviet Union before it withdrew. Here,

FIGURE 13.6 *Seizing the Landlord and Transporting His Movable Property.* Dongbeizhibao, October 9, 1947. Energized by the Chinese Communist Party's campaign for land redistribution, local populations reversed the traditional power structures. (From *Anvil of Victory: The Communist Revolution in Manchuria, 1945–1948,* by Steven Levine. Courtesy Columbia University Press.)

once their military presence was established, they were able in a mere eighteen months to transform indifferent, suspicious peasants into ardent participants in and supporters of the party and of the military campaigns directed by the brilliant general Lin Biao (1907–1971). Cooperation was secured by a mixture of hope and fear that varied with groups and individuals. Party cadres led a series of carefully orchestrated campaigns attacking and systematically displacing the old local elite that could no longer summon support from a provincial or regional elite undermined and compromised during the preceding fourteen years of Japanese rule. The campaigns culminated in land redistribution (see Figure 13.6), which revolutionized the local power structure.

The contrast between C.C.P. dynamism and Guomindang decay helps explain not only the outcome but also the unexpected rapidity of the course of events. The military turning point came in July 1947 when Communist armies attacked along several fronts in northern China. In Manchuria, Lin Biao commanded a campaign that put the Guomindang forces on the defensive and ended in October 1948 when they were completely routed. During that same month and into November, the last great battle of the war was fought at the strategic city of Xuzhou on the Huai River where the Beijing-Nanjing Railway line joins the Longhai line that runs from Shaanxi to the sea. Around half a million men on each side were involved in this battle, generally known as the Battle of Huai-Hai after the Huai River and the Longhai Railway. When it was all over, the Nationalists, under Chiang Kai-shek's personal command, had lost 200,000 men and no longer had any way to supply their forces to the north. In January 1949, Nationalist generals surrendered Beijing and Tianjin. Throughout the campaigns, the Communist army gained not only military advantages from its victories, but also captured valuable military equipment and supplies and increased its manpower as Nationalist soldiers defected or surrendered and were incorporated into the People's Liberation Army.

During 1949 the Communists continued their advance. They crossed the Yangzi in April, took Nanjing the same month, and were in control of Shanghai by the end of May. On October 1, Mao Zedong, in a great ceremony in Beijing, formally proclaimed the establishment of the People's Republic of China. There was still some fighting in the south, but clearly the C.C.P. had won control of the Chinese mainland. Meanwhile, Chiang Kai-shek and the Nationalists took refuge on Taiwan and vowed continued resistance.

The triumph of the Communists in 1949 began a new chapter in China's long history. It was the result of a long revolutionary process that had started well before the founding of the C.C.P., but in terms of the party's own programs and goals, the revolution had only just begun.

Notes

1. Stuart R. Schram, *The Political Thought of Mao Tse-tung* (New York: Frederick A. Praeger, 1963), p. 209.

2. Jerome Ch'en, *Mao and the Chinese Revolution* (New York: Oxford Univ. Press, 1965), p. 337.

3. Joshua A. Fogel, Introduction to *The Nanjing Massacre in History and Historiography*, ed. Joshua A. Fogel (Berkeley: Univ. of California Press, 2000), p. 6.

4. Alvin D. Coox, in Peter Duus, ed., *The Cambridge History of Japan, Vol. 6: The Twentieth Century* (Cambridge: Cambridge Univ. Press, 1988), p. 324.

5. Michael A. Barnhart, *Japan Prepares for Total War: The Search for Economic Security, 1919–1941* (Ithaca: Cornell Univ. Press, 1987), p. 234.

6. Ann Waswo, in *The Cambridge History of Japan, Vol. 6*, p. 104.

7. Kamei Katsuichiro, quoted in Kevin Michael Doak, *Dreams of Difference: The Japan Romantic School and the Crisis of Modernity* (Berkeley: Univ. of California Press, 1994), p. 101.

8. Sheldon Garon, *Molding Japanese Minds: The State in Everyday Life* (Princeton: Princeton Univ. Press, 1997), pp. 84–87.

9. Robert Gardella, in Murray A. Rubinstein, ed., *Taiwan: A New History* (Armonk, N.Y.: M.E. Sharpe, 1999), p. 180.

10. Hui-yu Caroline Ts'ai, *One Kind of Control; The Hokō System in Taiwan Under Japanese Rule, 1895–1945* (Ph.D. Dissertation, Columbia Univ., 1990), pp. 494–95, citing Shunji's essay as translated into Chinese by Chou Hsienwen in *T'ai-wan yin-hang chi-kan*, comp. T'ai-wan Yinhang Ching-chi Yenchiu-shih (Taipei: Bank of Taiwan), Vol. 5, No. 4 (1953), pp. 267–68.

11. For the eulogy, in which Wen Yiduo attacked Chiang Kai-shek personally and predicted that the Guomindang leaders would meet the same fate as Mussolini and Hitler, see Pei-kai Cheng and Michael Lestz with Jonathan D. Spence, *The Search for Modern China: A Documentary Collection* (New York: W.W. Norton, 1999), pp. 337–38.

China under Mao

I. Consolidation and Construction Soviet Style, 1949–1958

Government and Politics

Foreign Relations and the Korean War

Economic Policies

Thought Reform and Intellectuals

II. The Revolution Continued, 1958–1976

The Great Leap Forward

The Sino-Soviet Split

Domestic Politics, 1961–1965

The Great Proletarian Cultural Revolution: The Radical Phase, 1966–1969

The Winding Down, 1969–1976

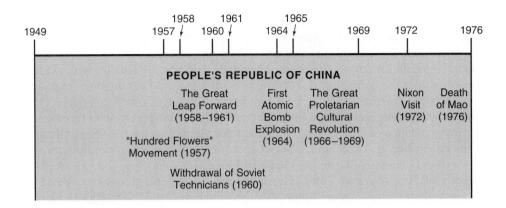

| 1949 | 1957 | 1958 | 1960 | 1961 | 1964 | 1965 | 1969 | 1972 | 1976 |

PEOPLE'S REPUBLIC OF CHINA

The Great
Leap Forward
(1958–1961)

First
Atomic
Bomb
Explosion
(1964)

The Great
Proletarian
Cultural
Revolution
(1966–1969)

Nixon
Visit
(1972)

Death
of Mao
(1976)

"Hundred Flowers"
Movement (1957)

Withdrawal of Soviet
Technicians (1960)

When Mao Zedong proclaimed the establishment of the People's Republic on October 1, 1949, it marked a watershed in the history of modern China. After a century of internal disintegration and foreign aggression, China made a new beginning under leaders deeply committed to the revolutionary transformation of the nation. Mao and his associates were determined to create an egalitarian society and make China strong and prosperous.

In taking control of the entire country and then restructuring Chinese society, the new leaders faced problems as immense as China itself. They were dedicated Marxists, and in their march to power had brilliantly adapted the foreign ideology to Chinese conditions. The challenge that now awaited them of transforming China in the spirit of that ideology proved a formidable one, and the course they took was anything but smooth.

The People's Republic of China (P.R.C.) began with an initial period (1949–1952), during which the regime consolidated its rule and forged the basic framework of a new sociopolitical order. This was followed by a period of Socialist Construction (1953–1958), initiated by the first Soviet-style five-year plan—begun in 1953, but not published until 1955.

Government and Politics

Following the example of the Soviet Union (U.S.S.R.), the Chinese formed parallel government and party structures with high party officials appointed to top government posts. Thus, Mao headed the party as Chairman of the Chinese Communist

347

Party (C.C.P.) Central Committee and, until 1959, was also officially head of state. High party members also held positions of leadership in various quasi-official organizations such as trade unions; and, as earlier, party members served as political commissars in the army, which reported to the Military Affairs Commission headed by Mao.

Administratively, China was divided into provinces, which remained the primary political subdivisions after an additional governmental level between the provinces and the central government was tried but discarded. The three most highly populated metropolitan areas, Shanghai, Beijing, and Tianjin, were placed directly under the control of the central government, and "autonomous regions" were created in areas inhabited by a significant number of minority people. One such "autonomous region" was Inner Mongolia. (The new government recognized the independence of Outer Mongolia, where the Mongolian People's Republic had been established in 1924, under Soviet sponsorship.) The other autonomous regions were Guangxi, Ningxia (southeast of Inner Mongolia), and the vast western regions of Xinjiang and Tibet. The latter was incorporated into the People's Republic after Chinese troops entered that mountainous land in October 1950, but Tibet did not receive autonomous region status until 1965. Aside from their strategic importance, the Inner Asian territories were significant because the government had to deal with the interests and sensitivities of their ethnic minorities.

A major step toward realization of the egalitarian aims of the revolution was taken in 1950 with the promulgation of a marriage law that gave women political and economic equality as well as equal rights to divorce. Women were free to participate in the workforce and pursue careers, although, in practice, this did not release them from their traditional household responsibilities.

An important factor in making the new system work was the cohesiveness of the Party leadership forged during years of struggling side by side. The only political conflict to erupt openly was an attack on Gao Gang, the C.C.P. leader in Manchuria who was accused of separatist ambitions. Additional factors were Gao's ties with the Soviet Union and the issue of Soviet influence in Manchuria. Gao's suicide was reported in 1955. At this juncture Rao Shushi, who was based in Shanghai, was also purged. Both leaders, in charge of prime industrial centers, were accused of "operating independent kingdoms" and of forming a political alliance.

To achieve its goals, the leadership launched massive national campaigns in what became a pattern. Thus, during 1951–1952 there was a "three antis" campaign against waste, corruption, and bureaucratism, aimed at disciplining the greatly enlarged C.C.P. membership, and a "five antis" campaign against bribery, tax evasion, fraud, the stealing of state property, and the theft of economic secrets. As a result, many wealthy men had to pay heavy fines. In line with Mao's *On the New Democracy* (1940), members of the "national bourgeoisie" were initially tolerated, and only capitalists with Guomindang or foreign ties were labeled enemies of the revolution. Gradually, however, private companies were turned over to the state, although their former owners often remained as managers.

Not all drives were directed against human evildoers; there was also a concerted attack on the "Four Pests": a war against rats, sparrows, flies, and mosquitoes. Although the inclusion of sparrows was misconceived, it was partly by such campaigns that the P.R.C. achieved enormous improvements in public health. Furthermore, by involving all the people in these campaigns, the leadership not only made use of China's greatest asset (manpower) but also gave the people a sense of participation and pride in the resulting accomplishments.

Foreign Relations and the Korean War

The Communist victory was hailed with enthusiasm in Moscow and bitterly deplored in Washington. Partly for ideological reasons and partly in response to continued, even if unenthusiastic, American support for the Nationalists, the C.C.P. adopted a policy of "leaning to one side," formally aligning itself with the U.S.S.R. in a treaty in February 1950, a product of Mao's first visit to Moscow and, in fact, his first trip outside China. However, relations between the two allies were not easy, for Stalin drove a hard bargain and was slow to relinquish special interests in Manchuria and Xinjiang. Still, the relationship with the U.S.S.R. was very important to China because the Soviet Union provided a model for economic and political development as well as moral, political, and economic support.

On the American side, although some observers had taken the measure of Chiang Kai-shek, large sectors of the American public continued to view him as China's savior, a view fostered by wartime propaganda and the efforts of ex-missionaries, politicians, and other supporters. Many, in and out of government, failed to appreciate the fact that the C.C.P. were nationalists as well as Communists. All this stood in the way of easing tensions between Washington and Beijing, but it is clear that "both Chinese and American leaders were interested in and groping uneasily toward accommodation."[1] However, time ran out with the beginning of war in Korea in June 1950.

During World War II, the United States and the Soviet Union had agreed on the 38th parallel as a dividing line: north of this line Japanese forces would surrender to Soviet troops; south of the line they would submit to troops of the United States. What was not clear at the time was that this was to become a semipermanent dividing line between a Soviet-backed Communist state in the north and an American-supported state in the south. Both states harbored the ambition to rule over the entire country. These ambitions erupted into war in June 1950, when North Korea attacked South Korea.

The period of intense fighting can be divided into three main phases, each with its own subdivisions. First, from June to September 1950, the North Koreans were on the offensive, pushing the South Korean and American forces back until they established a defense perimeter around Pusan from which they could not be dislodged. The second phase began with MacArthur's amphibious landing at Inchon in September, which led to the recapture of Seoul and then to an offensive intended to unify Korea by force. Then, in November, the Chinese, alarmed by the American advance to the Yalu River, and having had their warnings ignored, sent massive "volunteer" armies into Korea. These succeeded in regaining hold of the north but were unable to win control over the south. This became clear in late May 1951, and in July of that year truce talks began, but not until July 1953 did they lead to an armistice, which, although marred by incidents, still remains in effect today.

The Korean War did not alter the international configuration of power in East Asia, but it did embitter Sino-American relations. Both sides were now more convinced than ever of the enmity of the other. In the United States, proponents of a moderate China policy were removed from influence and subjected to slander. The Nationalist regime on Taiwan was given economic and military assistance, and in 1954 the United States signed a mutual defense treaty with the government of Chiang Kai-shek. Meanwhile, American troops remained in Korea and on bases in Japan and Okinawa. The Chinese, alarmed by these developments, were confirmed of the wisdom of allying themselves with the U.S.S.R. Whereas the Chinese viewed America as an imperialist aggressor, throughout the 1950s many people in the United States, even those in high places, considered the People's Republic to be little more than a Soviet satellite.

If the Korean War merely froze the participants into their Cold War postures, it also enhanced China's international status by demonstrating the ability of its peasant army, a bare year after the triumph of the revolution, to resist the formidable armed might of the United States. Within China, the Korean War helped the government to mobilize the people under the banner of national resistance and created its share of national heroes. Above all, it meant that the revolution had now been tested in foreign as well as domestic war.

Abroad, Beijing's representatives played an important role in the Geneva Conference on Indochina (1954) and at the conference of Asian-African states held at Bandung (Indonesia) in 1955. However, the Nationalists retained the China seat at the United Nations, and the United States prevailed on most of its allies to join it in withholding recognition of the P.R.C. The buildup of Nationalist strength on Taiwan rankled Beijing, but with the U.S. Seventh Fleet patrolling the Taiwan Strait, actual fighting was limited to sporadic shelling of two Nationalist-held islands off the coast of Fujian Province.

Economic Policies

Economic matters were of central concern to the new government right from the start. It had inherited a land ravaged by war and floods, with both agricultural and industrial output badly decreased from prewar levels and the monetary system wrecked by inflation. In addition, the underlying economy had serious structural weakness. In the agrarian sector, the prevalence of small, uneconomical, scattered landholdings and uneven land ownership helped to perpetuate traditional farming techniques and discouraged investment and capital formation. The industrial sector, on the other hand, consisted primarily of light industry concentrated around Shanghai and heavy industry in Manchuria. The latter had been developed to meet the requirements of foreign capital rather than the needs of China and its people.

Any government would have had to restore and strengthen the economy, but as Marxists, China's new leaders were also committed to the transfer of the means of production from private to public ownership and the creation of an egalitarian system of distribution. Their aim was to create a socialist state with a strong proletarian (working-class) base. The necessary precondition for this was vigorous industrialization, and because this was also required for the attainment of national strength, economic ideology and patriotism pointed to the same end.

By 1952, despite the strains of the Korean War, the economy had been restored to prewar levels. Factories had been put back into operation, railway lines had been repaired, and inflation had been brought under control. In the cities, the private sector was temporarily retained and even encouraged, but control over materials and marketing, as well as wages, prices, and working conditions, was in the hands of the state. Meanwhile, in the countryside, land redistribution was carried out not by government decree but by mobilizing the suppressed fury of the rural poor.

Landlords were denounced and humiliated in public trials and at mass "speak bitterness" meetings. The more fortunate ones were allowed to retain enough land to support themselves, but many lost their lives. The campaign became associated with a general suppression of potential counterrevolutionaries during the Korean War. The end result was not only a more equitable distribution of land but also a change of village leadership, now drawn from the poor peasantry.

The achievements of the first three years of the People's Republic were viewed as merely a preamble for further socialization and economic development. A planning organization was established, as was a statistical bureau, and in 1953 China took its first modern census, showing a total population of 582,600,000 on the mainland. Although its accuracy has been questioned, this figure is accepted as a general indication of the size of China's population at the time.

China's First Five-Year Plan followed the U.S.S.R. model of economic development in stressing heavy industry, with some 85 percent of total investments going into this sector. The Soviet Union supplied technical assistance (plans, blueprints, and so forth), helped train Chinese technicians (28,000 Chinese technicians and skilled workers went to the U.S.S.R. for training during the 1950s), and sent about 11,000 of its own experts to work in China. Development was accelerated by importing entire plants from the Soviet Union. Most of what was left of the private sector was now eliminated. Control over the plants was given to professional managers and technocrats, whose prime responsibility was to carry out government economic directives. To enable them to do this, they were placed firmly in charge of their factories.

Because loans advanced by the Soviet Union amounted to only 3 percent of China's total state investments, the financing of this industrialization effort was predominantly Chinese. These funds came out of the government's budget. The government, in turn, derived much of its revenue from taxes and from the income of state enterprises. Ultimately, a considerable portion of investment capital came from agriculture, which remained the heart of the Chinese economy.

To increase output and channel agricultural surplus more effectively into capital formation, the government in 1953 began a program of more radical transformation of the pattern of land management. To replace the existing system of small fields, individually owned and worked, the government planned to collectivize agriculture by pooling land, labor, and other resources. The change was not to be accomplished all at once. First, "mutual-aid" teams, which shared labor, tools, and work animals, were organized. The next stage was to create village producers' co-operatives in which land also was pooled.

Initially, agricultural collectivization was planned as a gradual program, because the Chinese leadership wanted to avoid the terrible bloodshed and suffering that had accompanied Stalin's rapid collectivization in the U.S.S.R. Mao, however, in a major speech delivered in July 1955, drew on the experience of the Chinese as distinct from that of the Russian Revolution and reaffirmed his faith in the revolutionary spirit of the Chinese peasantry. Just as the peasantry had been in the vanguard of the revolution that gave birth to the People's Republic, it would now lead the nation to socialism. In Mao's view it was the party, not the people, that was dragging its feet. The immediate effect of Mao's speech was an acceleration in the agricultural collectivization program, so much so that it was largely accomplished within a single year (1955–1956), and the timetable for full collectivization was set ahead. This speech marked the emergence of a radical Maoist strategy of economic development. In 1957 the process of collectivization was completed.

At the end of the First Five-Year Plan, the Chinese viewed the results with considerable satisfaction. The government was now firmly in control of the industrial sector: agriculture had been reorganized; iron, coal, and steel production targets had been exceeded; industrial output doubled from 1953 to 1957; and, altogether, remarkable progress had been made on the road to industrialization. There were problems, to be sure. One was the widening gap between city and country, a problem that has plagued all industrializing countries but was of special concern in China, where the peasantry remained the majority and where the party leaders identified with it. Another problem was the reemergence of bureaucracy and the transformation of a revolutionary party into the mainstay of the establishment.

Thought Reform and Intellectuals

The leaders of the People's Republic were convinced not only of the scientific correctness of their doctrine but also of its moral rightness, and they believed that virtually everyone could be brought to share their vision and act accordingly. They were optimistic not only about the course of history but also about human nature. In keeping with tradition, they had faith that everyone could attain moral perfection, now redefined in terms of an ideal socialist person. It was their belief that given the proper environment and correct guidance, people would become self-lessly devoted to revolution and community.

Naturally, the most promising were the young, uncontaminated by the old society, and the government saw to it that they were educated in the new values. Special attention was paid to the political awareness of Communist Party members and cadres, who were relied on to set examples of personal conduct and lead the people. To further the thought reform and moral transformation of even the most unpromising individuals, the authorities devised techniques of group discussion, self-criticism, and public confession. By using the individual's own feeling of moral inadequacy and guilt and by applying external pressures, the authorities induced people to renounce old values and prepared them for conversion to the new faith. Perhaps the most famous example of such a change of heart, accomplished in the controlled environment of a correctional institute, was provided by Puyi. As an infant he had been the last occupant of the Qing throne, and more recently he had served the Japanese as puppet ruler of Manchukuo. After undergoing thought reform, he reemerged as a citizen in good standing.

Not only prominent personages but also ordinary people now spent much time in small discussion groups, analyzing their lives as well as problems or incidents at their places of work. In this way the new ideology was transmitted to the people, and they were taught to use it in analyzing everyday problems. At the same time, social pressures were applied to everyone to conform to generally accepted standards of behavior.

The thought reform of intellectuals, already a target of Mao's wartime rectification campaign (see Chapter 13), remained difficult. Highly trained and educated people were a rare and precious resource for a nation bent on industrialization and modernization. Yet few came from peasant or worker backgrounds. More serious than their class background was the persistence of traditional elitist attitudes among intellectuals, as well as their critical habits of mind. They tended to resent taking directions from party cadres less well educated than themselves. Their special knowledge and skills were needed, but could they be trusted?

With education and the media under tight party control, the arts too were meant to serve the revolution. Whereas Western style artists were taught "Socialist Realism," a style intended to inspire, not to mirror, life (see Figures 14.1 and 14.4), artists working in traditional styles (*guohua*) were accepted as furthering national glory but urged to incorporate modern subjects in their work (see Figure 14.2).

The integration of artists and intellectuals into the new society remained problematic. When, in May 1956, Mao invited writers and thinkers to "let a hundred flowers bloom; let a hundred schools contend," there was little response from intellectuals, wary of exposing themselves to attack. But in February 1957, Mao said in a speech, "On the Correct Handling of Contradictions Among the People," that nonantagonistic contradictions should be resolved by persuasion rather than force. After some further reassurance, the floodgates of criticism were opened.

Criticism was directed not only against the behavior of individual party functionaries and at specific party policies but also at the C.C.P. itself for seeking "to bring about the monolithic structure of a one-family empire."[2] Intellectuals and writers asked for independence from the party's ideological control. Academic problems should be left for professors to solve: "Perhaps Mao has not had time to solve these problems for us,"[3] one history professor suggested.

Mao had intended the campaign to rectify the party, but the criticism was more than he had bargained for. Weeds grew where he had invited flowers. A full-fledged anti-Rightist campaign developed, beginning in June 1957. Not only did prominent intellectual, literary, and artistic figures disappear into labor camps, but also so did more than 400,000 others, with the government announcing a target

FIGURE 14.1 *Chairman Mao Standing with People of Asia, Africa, and Latin America*, Wu Biduan (b. 1926) and Jin Shangyi (b. 1934). Notice the new artistic style of Socialist Realism. Oil on canvas, 56.29 in × 61.42 in. (Collection National Art Gallery of China, Beijing. © Jinn Shangyi. Used by permission.)

of 5 percent per organization and the campaign quickening to include a massive purge of party members and cadres. Under these pressures some saved themselves by denouncing their friends. The upshot was that people with negative entries in their files had their lives ruined. Many of the victims were not fully rehabilitated until after Mao's death. By 1958 few were left to dare object when Mao launched his Great Leap Forward.

An underlying issue was how to balance the demands for ideological purity and revolutionary fervor with the professional competence required to operate a modern state and build an industrial system. Without the former, a new elite of experts, technocrats, and managers would pursue its own aims, and the revolution would be jeopardized. Mao believed that progress toward Communist egalitarianism and the building of national strength went hand in hand, but he put his faith in Redness, often at the expense of expertise.

II. The Revolution Continued, 1958–1976

The Great Leap Forward

The Sino-Soviet Split

Domestic Politics, 1961–1965

The Great Proletarian Cultural Revolution: The Radical Phase, 1966–1969

The Winding Down, 1969–1976

By the end of the First Five-Year Plan there were indications that following the Soviet model was not producing the desired economic or social results, but there was no agreement on what should be done. Although the party establishment saw a need for only relatively minor adjustments, Mao advocated a far more radical line. In the subsequent complicated, often turbulent, years, he did not always get his way, but he did prevent the revolution from settling down into comfortable routines.

The Great Leap Forward

The Great Leap Forward was initiated in January 1958, but lost momentum the following year. After 1959 it continued, but without vigor, until it was terminated in January 1961. On Mao's initiative, the gradualism of Soviet-style central planning was abandoned in favor of reliance on the energies of the masses imbued with revolutionary consciousness. Mao believed that ideology was a force that could motivate people to heroic accomplishments. History was not confined to a series of well-defined objective stages of economic and sociopolitical development, but could be turned into a process of "permanent revolution" driven by the subjective will transforming the objective world. The P.R.C. had made use of massive manpower in labor-intensive projects all along, projects such as the building of waterways, roads, and other giant construction works. Now the glorification of labor became more intense:

> Labor is joy; how joyful is it?
> Bathed in sweat and two hands full of mud,
> Like sweet rain my sweat waters the land
> And the land issues scent, better than milk.
> Labor is joy; how joyful is it?
> Home from a night attack, hoe in hand,
> The hoe's handle is still warm,
> But in bed, the warrior is already snoring.[4]

The author of these lines, written in 1958, was Yuan Kejia (1921–), who had once been an admirer of T. S. Eliot.

All of China's human resources were to be focused in a giant leap. Through Redness and revolutionary fervor, Mao hoped to accelerate China's economic development and speed the advance toward socialism. The spirit of the people was to be the driving force for continued economic growth and social transformation. Through the catharsis of intense participation, the Great Leap Forward mobilized the emotional involvement of many people in the creation of a new order. They were made to feel that building a strong China was not something to be left to experts and technocrats; it was to be done by, as well as for, the people.

As the prime vehicle for this effort, rural communes were formed by combining the already existing cooperatives. By the end of 1958 there were 26,000 rural communes in which 98 percent of China's rural population lived. Each averaged about 25,000 people. The communes were divided into production brigades, each corresponding roughly to the traditional village, and these, in turn, were divided into production teams. The communes were intended to function as China's basic political as well as economic and social units, integrating all aspects of life. As economic units they supervised agricultural production and distribution, provided banking services, and ran small factories and machine shops, which were operated at the commune- or production-brigade level, depending on the size and degree of specialization of the plant. The communes were further responsible for police functions, and they ran schools and hospitals, provided day-care facilities and mess halls, took care of the aged, and staged plays and other entertainment. They represented an ambitious attempt to create new, large-scale communities. But they turned out to be too large, and the cadres who ran them were too far removed from the realities of farming. Their size was therefore reduced, so that by the end of the Great Leap Forward the original number of communes had almost tripled to 74,000, with a corresponding decrease in the size of their memberships. Later the communes lost many of their functions to the smaller production brigades and peasants were given greater discretion.

There was also a movement to establish communes in the cities by combining or transforming earlier street associations that included the inhabitants of one street (or of several small streets, or of a section of a large street) originally organized for security and welfare. They were now given additional responsibilities for economic enterprises as well as for educational and medical facilities. In general, the formation of urban communes involved the transfer of authority over factories from central and provincial ministries to the local party committee that controlled the communes. Some of the communes consisted of workers in one large factory, others included the residents of one part of a city, and still others, located on the outskirts of cities, included some farmland along with an urban sector. Whatever the form of urban organization, an effort was made to release women for work by establishing mess halls, nurseries, homes for the aged, and service facilities such as laundries.

To enlist popular enthusiasm and encourage local initiative, local authorities were granted substantial leeway in deciding how to implement government directives. The central government still set general economic policy and retained control over the largest heavy industrial plants, but 80 percent of all enterprises were decentralized. No longer was there to be reliance on experts in far-off Beijing making all the decisions and operating with a centralized bureaucracy as in the U.S.S.R.

As far as possible, literature and the visual arts were to be not only for but also by the people. Teams were sent out to collect the people's literature and to encourage peasants to compose poetry and otherwise participate in the creation of art. In Shanghai alone some 200,000 people participated in producing 5 million poems. Many thousands undoubtedly were exhilarated at achieving recognition in a field previously reserved for an exclusive elite.

High social as well as economic expectations were raised by the creation of the communes. According to Communist theory, the achievement of a truly communist society entails a change from paying people according to their productivity to paying "each according to his needs." In line with this, experiments were conducted in paying people approximately 70 percent of their wages in kind (produce to satisfy their needs) and the rest in cash according to their productivity. Meanwhile, impressive production targets were announced, including the goal of catching up with British industrial production in fifteen years. To the Chinese leaders, the social and economic goals seemed entirely compatible.

If the Great Leap Forward achieved some of its political and psychological goals, it also produced an economic disaster. This did not become apparent for some time; the initial statistics of production were impressive, but they turned out to have been grossly inflated. An unanticipated consequence of the Great Leap Forward was a breakdown in China's statistical services, and serious mistakes were made because the government accepted the exaggerated figures forwarded by overenthusiastic local authorities. Some projects originally pursued with enthusiasm later had to be abandoned as unworkable. Perhaps the best known was the campaign to use local villagers and materials to build and operate backyard furnaces for making iron and steel. Because this fitted in well with the policy of decentralization and relying on the masses, the plan was vigorously implemented. All over China small furnaces were set up and utensils were melted down, but the furnaces proved incapable of turning out iron of acceptable quality, let alone steel.

The most serious failure of the Great Leap Forward was in agriculture. Misconceived irrigation projects leached nutrients from the soil and mass mobilization for work projects exhausted and demoralized the people. Here, too, the government worked with misleading statistics, as local units vied with each other in reporting productivity gains. The harvest of 1958 was seriously exaggerated. Relying on faulty expectations and inflated reports, the government took so much grain that in many areas practically nothing was left for the peasants. Massive famine resulted. The number who perished is difficult to determine, but 16–27 million is a conservative estimate. The Great Leap ended in a stupendous crash.

The Sino-Soviet Split

From the beginning of the People's Republic there were areas of tension and potential conflict between China and the Soviet Union. As we have seen, the C.C.P. came to power only after going its own way, independent of Moscow. Furthermore, the Chinese leadership was as determinedly nationalistic as the Soviets, who, under Stalin, operated on the principle that what was good for the Soviet Union was good for world Communism. This equation had some plausibility as long as there was only one great Communist state in the world, but it was a thesis that the Chinese, sooner or later, were bound to challenge.

Initially, the forces holding the alliance together were stronger than those pulling it apart. These included not only ideological ties but also shared Cold War enemies. However, around the mid-1950s serious cracks in the alliance began to appear. One cause of friction was territorial. The Chinese reluctantly accepted the independence of Outer Mongolia, whose historical status resembled that of Tibet, but they were very unhappy about their northern and western boundaries with the Soviet Union. These borders had been drawn in the nineteenth century and thus formed part of the history of imperialism that China's new government was pledged to undo. As early as 1954 Chinese publications indicated the country's refusal to accept vast regions of Central and Northeast Asia as permanently belonging to the U.S.S.R.

Another source of trouble was the Chinese desire for recognition as leaders of world Communism, as suggested in Figure 14.1. After the death of Stalin in 1953, they expected that Mao would be honored as the leading living contributor to Marxist ideology and the architect of strategies to advance the cause in the Third World. Instead, Khrushchev went his own way by denouncing Stalin in a famous speech in 1956 that implied the illegitimacy of all "personality cults," including that forming around Mao. Figure 14.1 shows Mao as a world figure. Stylistically, it exemplifies a turning away from Soviet models and "the nationalization of oil painting," a term applied to "any means of imbuing oil painting with recognizably Chinese aesthetics." As illustrated here, one way of doing so was by forgoing the effects of light and shadow and favoring "flat patches of unmodulated color rather than painterly textures."[5]

Khrushchev's theory of peaceful coexistence and the U.S.S.R.'s new international stance further irritated the Chinese. Even Mao's opponents within the C.C.P. felt insulted that Chinese leaders had not been consulted before these major shifts in Soviet policy were announced. For their part, the Soviet leaders could hardly be expected to welcome Chinese claims, made during the Great Leap Forward, that their communes represented a higher stage on the road to the ideal society than anything achieved in the Soviet Union after forty years of Communist rule.

Despite efforts toward reconciliation, such as Chinese support for the Soviet suppression of the Hungarian uprising in 1956, Mao's visit to Moscow in 1957, and Khrushchev's to Beijing in 1958 and 1959, the strains in the alliance continued to mount. Contributing to this was the U.S.S.R.'s unwillingness to exploit its temporary supremacy in rocketry to support a possible Chinese attack on Taiwan, an attack that would have had no hope for success unless the United States were neutralized by Soviet threats. Khrushchev's relatively unbelligerent stance toward the United States seemed to the Chinese like a cowardly betrayal, whereas Mao's belittling of the dangers of nuclear warfare made him appear to the Soviets as a dangerous adventurer gambling with the lives of millions. No wonder the Soviets were hesitant about sharing nuclear secrets with the Chinese.

The split became unbreachable in the summer of 1960, when the Soviets withdrew their technicians from China. They even took their blueprints with them. After that, despite limited cooperation during the Vietnam War, relations remained bitter, as China and the U.S.S.R. denounced each other's policies and challenged the Marxist legitimacy of each other's revolutions. Whereas the Chinese charged that the Soviets had deviated from the true revolutionary path, Russian and East European ideologists depicted Chinese aberrations as arising from their lack of a firm proletarian base as well as an inadequate understanding of Marxism.

An aspect of this situation was the Soviet Union's support of India in its disputes with China. Relations between China and India became tense in 1959, after the Chinese, asserting their rights under international law, imposed their rule on Tibet and used their soldiers to suppress Tibetan resistance. India's welcome of Tibetan refugees, including the Dalai Lama, the spiritual and sometime secular leader of Tibet, was resented in Beijing. As it was, China and India, the world's two most populous nations, were natural rivals for Asian leadership. The resulting tensions would not have led to outright hostility, however, had it not been for a border dispute over a remote area through which China had built a road linking Xinjiang with Tibet. The result was a short border war in 1962 in which the Chinese quickly humiliated the Indian troops. The Soviet Union continued its policy of friendship with India, and China cultivated good relations with India's arch rival, Pakistan. Meanwhile, within the Communist world, China defended and allied itself with the bitterly anti-Soviet regime of Albania.

Militarily, the Soviet Union remained much the stronger of the two powers, but the People's Republic was also developing its armed strength. A milestone was reached in 1964 when it exploded its first atomic bomb.

FIGURE 14.2 *Celebrate the Success of Our Atomic Bomb Explosion,* Wu Hufan. Hanging scroll, ink and color on paper, 1965. (Shanghai Institute of Chinese Painting. © Wu Hufan. Used by permission.)

Although, as indicated by its title, the painting reproduced as Figure 14.2 was understood as celebratory, it may have been an ironic response to relentless pressures on Wu Hufan (1894–1970) to produce art that would serve the revolution and the state, for Wu was a highly sophisticated and sensitive traditional-style painter and a careful student of the paintings of the Four Wangs, who had delighted the court of Kangxi (see Chapter 10). To quote Julia F. Andrews, "As incongruous as it seems, this painting of the mushroom cloud is one of the most beautiful demonstrations of brushwork to be found during the period." She goes on to cite its "casual lively strokes and subtly varied ink tones."[6]

The bomb did not soften relations between the two Communist giants. Numerous border clashes endangered the peace between them, and both feared that the situation might escalate into full-fledged war. Beijing built an extensive system of underground shelters for use in case of an attack by air. The hostility of the Soviet Union was one of the principal factors that led to a gradual rapprochement between China and the United States during the 1970s.

Domestic Politics, 1961–1965

The failure of the Great Leap Forward led to retrenchment in domestic policies, a willingness to accept, at least for a while, more modest interim social and economic goals. It was a serious setback for Mao's personal authority as well as plans. He remained party chairman, but in December 1958 had to resign as head of the government. That post was filled by Liu Shaoqi (1898–1969), a hard-working organization man long associated with Mao. Liu had supporters in high party and government positions, but the supervision of the state's administrative machinery, including the various ministries, remained under the direction of the head of the State Administrative Council, who had the title of premier. This position had been held since 1949 by another trusted party veteran, Zhou Enlai. Zhou also served as foreign minister until 1959 and continued even after he left that post to act as China's main spokesman in foreign affairs. By all accounts, Zhou was one of the most capable and versatile of all the C.C.P. leaders, a superb political and military strategist and a truly gifted administrator and negotiator.

Another important government position was that of minister of defense. In 1959 Peng Dehuai (1898–1974), a veteran general, was ousted from this post for going too far in criticizing Mao and the Great Leap Forward. He was further accused of pro-Soviet tendencies and held responsible for overemphasizing professionalism and failing to imbue the troops with sufficient ideological spirit. His successor as minister of defense was another distinguished general, Lin Biao (1907–1971), who was favored by Mao.

Under the direction of Liu Shaoqi, the government relaxed the tempo of social change. There was now greater appreciation of expertise and less reliance on the revolutionary enthusiasm of the masses. There was an increased use of economic rather than ideological incentives: in the communes the more productive workers could earn extra work points, and in the factories there were wage increases, bonuses, and promotions to be earned, measures later castigated as "economism." Peasants, although still under the obligation to produce a fixed amount of grain for the state, were allowed small private plots and permitted to sell on the free market whatever they could grow on them.

No longer able to rely on the U.S.S.R. in the international arena, China in 1964 channeled investments into creating a "Third Front," described as "a crash program to build heavy industry in inland provinces away from the militarily vulnerable coastal and northeast areas."[7] Despite political turmoil, this effort continued until 1971, augmenting the damage already inflicted on the environment by misguided dam building and other abuses during the Great Leap Forward. From the beginning, as in the campaign against sparrows, Mao and his followers advocated and pursued the conquest of nature.

After the great exertions and the disappointments of the Great Leap Forward, there was a natural slackening not only of the pace of change but also of revolutionary fervor. This alarmed Mao, who sought to combat this trend by initiating a socialist education movement in 1962 without, however, much effect. Furthermore, there now appeared in print thinly veiled attacks on Mao himself. Among them was the historical play, *Hai Rui Dismissed from Office*, written by the deputy mayor of Beijing. In this play the sixteenth-century official (see Chapter 8) was portrayed sympathetically as an honest minister who stood up for the peasants and was dismissed by a foolish and autocratic emperor. What was implied was a critique of Mao's own dismissal, in 1959, of Minister of Defense Peng Dehuai. In November 1965 an article was published in the Shanghai press denouncing this play. Thus began the Cultural Revolution.

The Great Proletarian Cultural Revolution: The Radical Phase, 1966–1969

The Cultural Revolution was profoundly ideological and strongly political. It was cultural in the broadest sense, for it sought to remold the entire society and to change the consciousness of the Chinese people. Utopian in its aims, its results were disastrous. Its moving force was Mao himself, who was determined not to allow the revolution to drift into Soviet-style revisionism. Thus, he resolved to combat the reemergence of old patterns of bureaucratic arrogance and careerism, convinced that drastic measures were necessary to prevent the entrenchment of new vested interests in state and party and hungry to resume personal control. Now an old man, Mao was unwilling to rest on his laurels as the father of the revolution. He actively involved himself in the Cultural Revolution and dramatically displayed his physical vigor by publicly swimming some ten miles across the Yangzi River five months before he turned 74 in 1966.

The obstacles to the Cultural Revolution were formidable, because it affected the interests of a majority of party functionaries both at the center and in the provinces. But among Mao's assets were not only his unequaled prestige but also the support of the People's Liberation Army, which, under Lin Biao, emphasized guerrilla-style revolutionary spirit and fostered solidarity among officers and men by deemphasizing rank. In the summer of 1965, insignia of rank were abolished and uniforms in no way differentiated officers and men. Mao and other leaders hoped similarly to reduce or, if possible, to eliminate the distinctions and privileges of rank in society at large.

To accomplish this required the destruction of the Establishment. To carry on the battle, the country was inundated with copies of *Quotations from Chairman Mao,* the omnipresent Little Red Book cited on all occasions as the ultimate source of authority. Mao himself was glorified as never before. His sayings and pictures were everywhere; his writings were placed on family altars, his name filled the air; some villages began meetings by people holding hands and dancing to the tune of "Sailing the Seas Depends on the Helmsman, Making Revolution Depends on Mao Zedong's Thought."

The vanguard and shocktroops of the Cultural Revolution were the Red Guards, young people mostly born since the founding of the People's Republic. Mao hoped that their youthful spirit would revitalize the revolution and rescue it from sinking into comfortable revisionism. In his view it was not enough for these young people merely to read theoretical and historical works and to sing revolutionary songs. They must actually live and make revolution, so that they would be molded by direct personal revolutionary experience. As Mao had said, "a revolution is not a dinner party" (see p. 328). Going on their own "long marches" was not enough. The Red Guards were responsible for many excesses as they organized public humiliations of prominent people; administered beatings and took captives; ransacked houses; and destroyed books, art, and anything old or foreign. Many people were beaten to death or committed suicide and countless others were imprisoned or sent to labor on the land. Among the most enthusiastic participants were urban youths of questionable class background, proving to others and themselves their revolutionary purity.

Opposition to the Red Guard and the Cultural Revolution was considerable. In many places the local authorities were able to draw on popular support. There was rioting, and pitched battles were fought between rival groups, each claiming to represent the thought of Mao. Much of the information on these struggles comes from numerous posters written in large characters. Mao himself, in August 1966, wrote such a poster, "Let Us Bombard the Headquarters."

Many party headquarters were attacked, and the party was crippled. Leaders of the government, from Liu Shaoqi down, were made to confess their sins in public and then were removed from public view. Universities were closed, scientific and scholarly journals ceased publication (although nuclear development went on apace), intellectual and cultural life was disrupted, and there was turmoil in the cities. However, Zhou Enlai managed to keep the basic machinery of government working and was able to protect some from attack. Meanwhile, Mao's wife, Jiang Qing (c. 1914–1991), and Mao's secretary, Chen Boda (1904–1989), emerged as leaders of the Cultural Revolution group.

Writers and artists were prominent among the victims of the Cultural Revolution, and a narrow orthodoxy was also enforced in the other arts. Jiang Qing, herself once an actress, championed revolutionary operas. In place of traditional Chinese opera, audiences were now treated to dances on the theme, "We Are So Happy Because We Are Delivering Grain to the State," or expressing joy at the completion of an electric power plant.

The Cultural Revolution reached its most radical phase in early 1967. At the beginning of that year a dramatic series of events in Shanghai led to the triumph of a workers' movement that was able to overthrow the local party apparatus by overcoming factional divisions. In February the workers formed a People's Commune, which lasted only nineteen days, because Mao, thinking it too radical, did not endorse it. He preferred the formation of "revolutionary committees" in which the army played a leading role. With the party out of commission and the country badly divided, the army grew in importance as the single organized and disciplined institution capable of forceful action on a national scale. However, the revolution developed a new "ultraleft" intensity before the army was called in to calm things down. In the summer of 1967, hundreds of thousands demonstrated in Beijing against Liu Shaoqi and Zhou Enlai. Radicals even occupied the foreign ministry for two weeks. Outside of the capital the army killed countless numbers in clashes with opponents. The most dramatic events took place in July, when the army intervened to suppress insurgents in Wuhan. Further violence ensued else-where. Finally, in September, Mao and the leadership turned toward the army to restore order. The Red Guards were disbanded in July 1968.

Military men were prominent on the various revolutionary committees set up to administer provinces, factories, and communes as the Cultural Revolution con-tinued, increasingly under army auspices. The revolution came to an end in 1969. In April of that year, a party congress officially confirmed the new prominence of the army by adopting a new constitution designating Lin Biao as Mao's successor. An important official criterion for party membership was class background. "Bad elements," such as the descendants of landlords, rich peasants, capitalists, and "rightists," continued to face obstacles in career advancement.

Earlier, party cadres and intellectuals had been "sent down" to work the land among the peasants, and now thousands of Red Guards were similarly removed from the cities for a stint of labor in the fields. This was not only a practical mea-sure for restoring order but also had a theoretical basis in the "mass line," which embodied Mao's conviction that the people were the source of valuable ideas and that the function of leaders was to obtain these ideas from the masses, to concen-trate and systematize them, and then take them back to the masses. The function of leaders was to learn humbly from the masses and also to teach them. The idea was that leaders would identify with the common people, but the actuality was that for ten years most of China's best and brightest had to suffer physical hardship and mental anguish and despair. Some were never to make it back to the cities, and nu-merous others would never be able to make up for years lost in education and train-ing. China as a whole was to pay a heavy price for the loss of ten years of educa-tional, intellectual, and technological advances.

The Cultural Revolution saw the resumption of Great Leap Forward trends that had been discarded during the early 1960s. A policy of economic decentral-ization and provincial self-sufficiency was emphasized as consistent with the Third Front program as well as with Maoist ideology. Again, Redness was emphasized over expertise and private economic incentives, and, again, the focus was on the rural sector, which benefited from programs that extended medical care and edu-cation. Plants were built in rural areas to manufacture and repair farm machinery, produce fertilizer, or process local products, thereby diminishing the distinction between city and country. There were experiments in calculating work points for farm work on the basis of political criteria rather than in terms of an individual's productivity. Similarly, in urban factories there were provisions for greater worker participation in factory management and programs to lessen the distinction between workers and managers and between mental and manual labor.

The Winding Down, 1969–1976

Although the Cultural Revolution was officially ended in 1969, Jiang Qing and her associates retained control over the media and cultural affairs. During the next seven years radical Maoists remained influential in national politics and had some victories. Nevertheless, there was a gradual turn to moderation. The party was rebuilt, and moderate leaders reappeared. Mao himself wanted to curb the power of the military and turned against Lin Biao, whose downfall came in the autumn of 1971. Allegedly, Lin tried to save himself by staging a coup, and, when that failed, he attempted to flee in an airplane that crashed in Mongolia.

The fate of Liu Shaoqi and Lin Biao demonstrated the hazardous position of those marked for the succession, but Zhou Enlai, as usual, was on the winning side. Zhou continued as premier, and, with Mao's aging, he was more influential than ever. Army influence decreased and more moderate economic policies were adopted. There was a general relaxation of emphasis on revolutionary fervor. For example, when universities were first reopened in 1970, after a four-year hiatus, admission was based on recommendations from comrades in the candidate's work unit and the approval of the appropriate revolutionary committee, but in 1972 academic criteria for admission were reintroduced. Also in that year, the first scientific periodicals reappeared but with an emphasis on applied science. Public exaltation of Mao was toned down. There were even attacks on the Little Red Book; C.C.P. members were now urged to pursue a thorough study of Marxist writings.

During 1973–1974, Lin Biao, although dead, was further denounced in a campaign linking him with Confucius. Both men were portrayed as "political swindlers" and sinister reactionaries. Confucius was depicted as representing a declining slave-owner class, whereas Lin Biao was charged with wanting to restore capitalism, each man exerting himself to reinstate an outdated system. The campaign against Confucius and Lin Biao was a sign of the continuing influence of the Cultural Revolution leaders' attack on the past, but the ancient philosopher and modern general made a strange pair, and very likely Confucius was actually a surrogate for Zhou Enlai. The politics and ethos of the time are illustrated in Figure 14.3. The slogan spanning and dominating the entrance reads, "Workers, Peasants, and Soldiers Are the Main Force Criticizing Lin and Criticizing Confucius." Parking their bicycles and small tractors outside the gate, people have entered the compound to peruse wall posters spelling out the case against the two villains while loudspeakers, high on their poles like their counterparts everywhere, blare out announcements, slogans, and revolutionary music.

FIGURE 14.3 *Repudiating Lin Biao and Confucius,* Yang Zhixian. Like many peasant paintings, this one employs bright colors. Peasant painting exhibited in Beijing in 1973. (From *Peasant Paintings from Huhsien County.* Compiled by the Fine Arts Collection Section of the Cultural Groups under the State Council of the People's Republic of China [Peking, 1974].)

Most peasant paintings do not serve overt political campaigns but celebrate rural life and work. Their urban counterparts were paintings showing people working in factories. Many show women at work, for China was determined that women were to become fully equal with men (see Figure 14.4). In China, as in the Soviet Union, the challenges and triumphs of a socialist society were the main top-

FIGURE 14.4 *Wo shi haiyan (I am a Seagull),* Pan Jianjun (designer/artist), c. 1973. Chinese poster showing a strong, exuberant woman defying the elements to bring modernity to the countryside. (Photograph © Stefan R. Landsberger. [Chinese Propaganda Poster Pages, online exhibit, http://www.iisg.nl/~landsberger.])

ics of art and literature, depicted in a style usually designated "socialist realism," although intended to inspire, not to mirror life.

Peasant and "social realist" paintings represent a break with old styles of painting, but other artists painted new subjects in a traditional way (see Figure 14.1) or placed modern subjects in an essentially traditional setting rendered in a traditional manner, as in Qian Songyan's *Ode to Yan'an* paying homage to the place where the victory of the Chinese Communist Party was forged and the revolutionary Yan'an spirit supposedly held sway (see Figure 14.5).

During the 1960s and 1970s, workers and peasants continued to be encouraged to participate in the creation of art. There were efforts to produce collective writing and painting. Another arrangement was for part-time authors to get a day off from their factory jobs to write. Professional writers were periodically "sent down" to a factory or commune so that they would not lose touch with the people. As a matter of routine, they invited popular criticism of their work and responded to suggestions for changes. For example, before *The Golden Road* (1972) was published, 200 copies were sent to communes and factories for criticism. This novel by Hao Ran (Liang Jinguang, 1932–), 4 million copies of which were sold, dealt with the change from individual farming to the formation of mutual aid teams. In all the arts, the same themes occur over and over: the ideals and struggles of the revolution, the wisdom of Mao, the heroism of soldiers, the triumph of socialist virtue over selfishness, and the glory of work.

During and after the Cultural Revolution, Chinese relations with the Soviet Union remained tense, even though both powers supported North Vietnam in its war against the Saigon regime and the United States. Concern over Soviet intentions was heightened to alarm when the U.S.S.R. invaded Czechoslovakia in 1968 and Party Secretary Leonid Brezhnev announced that the U.S.S.R. had the right to intervene in socialist countries, which he accorded only "limited sovereignty."

Fears of a Soviet nuclear strike, actual troop deployments along the lengthy Sino-Soviet frontier, and armed clashes in Manchuria induced China to seek broader diplomatic contacts with the United States. Although Chinese personnel did assist the North Vietnamese, there was no repetition of Korea. Chinese terrain was not threatened and no massive intervention by Chinese troops took place. Meanwhile, a channel of communication was maintained with the United States through periodic meetings of the ambassadors of the two countries, held first in Geneva and later in Warsaw. The fall of Lin Biao and the emergence of Zhou Enlai increased the prospect for improved Sino-American relations.

A contributing factor on the American side was the intention of President Nixon, elected in 1968, to withdraw the United States from the war in Vietnam. As

FIGURE 14.5 *Ode to Yan'an,* Qian Songyan (1898–1985). A pagoda and a transmission station face each other across a space defined, as in traditional landscapes, by mist and clouds rendering just barely visible the entrances to Yan'an's famous caves. (Collection Conrad Schirokauer. Photograph © Lore Schirokauer.)

long as China and the United States were committed to the opposing sides of a war that was raging at full force and threatening to escalate still further, substantial improvement in Sino-American relations remained highly unlikely.

Nevertheless, a high-level Sino-American dialogue was not dependent on the actual end of the war—a shift in direction toward peace was enough. By 1971 both sides were ready to talk. A new approach to China was deemed a logical corollary of the Kissinger-Nixon concept of international balance-of-power politics. The Chinese were receptive. The Sino-American rapprochement began informally with the Chinese invitation of an American ping-pong team, whose members were personally greeted by Zhou Enlai. Then came President Nixon's visit to Beijing in February 1972 and the Shanghai Communiqué, which provided for partial normalization and paved the way for the resumption of full formal diplomatic relations in 1979. In 1971, even before the Nixon visit, the United Nations had voted to admit the People's Republic in place of the Nationalists, and the new American stance now removed the last obstacle to recognition by most countries.

Two deaths dominated the news in 1976. When Zhou died in January of that year, his enemies banned public mourning but were unable to prevent a massive gathering at the Martyrs' Memorial in Beijing's great Tiananmen Square on China's Day of Mourning in April. This expression of reverence for the late premier was tantamount to a rejection of the Cultural Revolution. Mao, aged and ailing, still had sufficient authority to designate Hua Guofeng (1920–) as Zhou's successor.

Hua was soon called upon to demonstrate his administrative talents, for in July China's worst earthquake in four centuries devastated Tangshan, an industrial and mining city 100 miles from Beijing. In old China, people would have interpreted this as a signal of further shocks to come—and they would have been right, for on September 9 Mao died. Architect of the triumph of the C.C.P., Mao presided over the successes of the revolution, but he was also responsible for its failures and for needless suffering, hardship, and dying. His passing marked the end of an era.

Notes

1. Warren I. Cohen, ed., *New Frontiers in American-East Asian Relations* (New York: Columbia Univ. Press, 1983), p. 144.

2. Quoted in Merle Goldman, *Literary Dissent in Communist China* (Cambridge: Harvard Univ. Press, 1967), p. 192.

3. Quoted in Goldman, p. 193.

4. Hsu Kai-yu, *The Chinese Literary Scene—A Writer's Visit to the People's Republic* (New York: Vintage Books, Random House, 1975), p. 227.

5. Julia F. Andrews, "The Victory of Socialist Realism: Oil Painting and the New Guohua," in Julia F. Andrews and Kuyi Shen, eds., *A Century in Crisis: Modernity and Tradition in the Art of Twentieth-Century China* (New York: Guggenheim Museum, 1998), p. 230.

6. Julia F. Andrews, *Painters and Politics in the People's Republic of China, 1949–1979* (Berkeley: Univ. of California Press, 1994), p. 303.

7. William A. Joseph, Christine P.W. Wong, and David Zweig, *New Perspectives on the Cultural Revolution* (Cambridge: The Council on East Asian Studies/Harvard University, 1991), Introduction, p. 2.

The Chinese World Since Mao

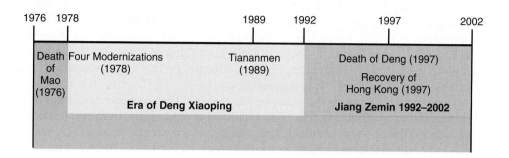

| 1976 | 1978 | | 1989 | 1992 | 1997 | 2002 |

| Death of Mao (1976) | Four Modernizations (1978) | | Tiananmen (1989) | | Death of Deng (1997) Recovery of Hong Kong (1997) | |
| | | **Era of Deng Xiaoping** | | | **Jiang Zemin 1992–2002** | |

After the death of Mao Zedong, China embarked on a profound change of course. Many of the policies of the previous quarter century were reversed, and new measures were adopted that bore scant resemblance to either those of Mao or of his more conventional opponents. The economy changed dramatically, and by 2000 China was the fastest growing country in the world, creating new problems and opportunities including well over 100 million migrant workers—assets to employers but potential liabilities to state and society as well. Many unemployed laborers returned to their villages, and two thirds of China's people continue to live in the countryside, but an estimated 150 million have moved to cities and towns in what shows every sign of a continuing pattern.

All spheres of life were affected by change, but in different ways and at different speeds. Artistic and intellectual change was most intense; changes in politics and its institutions lagged.

China's relationships to the external world, both in East Asia and beyond, also changed. One factor initially spurring China's leaders to adopt new policies was the recognition that economically and technologically it had fallen behind the impressive achievements of the rest of East Asia. That included not only Japan and Korea but also Hong Kong (returned to China in 1997) and especially Taiwan, whose twentieth century continued to be so different from that of the mainland as to call for separate treatment.

Deng Xiaoping and the Four Modernizations

After a period of adversity (1977–1978), it became clear that Mao's true successor was not Hua Guofeng, as he had intended, but Deng Xiaoping (1904–1997). Deng was a party veteran who, during the Cultural Revolution, had been removed from office and denounced as second only to Liu Shaoqi in "taking the capitalist road," but more recently Deng had enjoyed the backing of Zhou Enlai. In July 1977, Deng became first deputy premier and from 1978 on was clearly China's most powerful political figure. Blamed for all the ills of the Cultural Revolution were the "Gang of Four," led by Jiang Qing, Mao's widow, who insisted, in vain, that she had simply been carrying out Mao's directives. By November 1980 the new leadership under Deng felt sufficiently secure to put the Gang of Four on trial and have the trial televised. In January 1981 Jiang Qing and another leader were given suspended death sentences, later commuted to life imprisonment. Hua Guofeng was soon shunted into political obscurity.

Deng's program was epitomized by the slogan "The Four Modernizations," first introduced by Zhou Enlai in 1975. Directed at agriculture, industry, science, and defense, the aim was to turn China into a modern industrial state. The years since 1952 had seen considerable economic progress, but China remained an underdeveloped country. Furthermore, the Cultural Revolution had taken a heavy toll in lost educational and technological progress. Now, under Deng, merit, not revolutionary virtue, was rewarded. Professionalism and individual initiative were encouraged, and market forces were allowed greater play.

There were drastic changes in the countryside as agriculture was decollectivized. In 1982 communes lost their social and political authority, and their economic power was also curtailed. Under the "responsibility system," peasants were assigned land on contracts to produce a certain amount of grain and increasingly won the right to decide on just how to do this and to dispose of any surplus produce on the open market. The amount of land to be assigned was to depend on the number of people in each family, an arrangement that seemed new but actually resembled both the 1951 Land Reform and the "equal-field system" enacted in 486 and discarded in the eighth century! Gradually, restrictions on commercial activities were eased, and enterprising peasants did notably well.

Similar changes took place in light industry and commerce, but at a slower pace. Official enterprises were expected to justify their existence by making a profit, government regulation was decreased, and individuals were allowed to open restaurants and workshops. Under a new open door policy welcoming foreign companies, special economic zones were established, where foreign investment was encouraged. At the same time, the skylines of first Beijing, then Shanghai, and more recently even cities in the interior, were being transformed by high-rise buildings, among them international luxury hotels where the affluent traveler could savor China in luxury and at an antiseptic distance.

Mao Zedong had once seen China's large population as an asset, but even before his death it became clear that China's future would be dim if the population continued to grow without restraint. In the early 1970s, China adopted a vigorous birth-control program. Even so, the population continued to increase, topping 1 billion in 1982. In the cities, the birth rate had fallen even before severe pressures ensured virtually full compliance with the one-child-per-couple law. But this was not the case in the countryside, where children, in the absence of a public safety net, continued, with good reason, to be regarded as an asset to a family.

Industrialization and population growth put additional strains on China's already hard-pressed environment. We will return to them in our discussion of the 1990s, but note here that air and water pollution were on the rise and that land erosion had already turned the Yangzi River into a second Yellow River. In the mid-1980s topsoil loss of more than 5 billion tons annually deprived China of more soil nutrition than that produced by its entire synthetic fertilizer industry. Major programs of reforestation were one positive response, but in general the environmental degradation accelerated. The state's obligation to protect the environment did find its way into the 1982 constitution, and a body of law ensued, but environmentalism did not figure in the Four Modernizations.

From early on some, mostly elderly, party leaders objected to the pace of change, but there were also voices at the opposite end of the political spectrum calling for more rapid liberalization. They found expression in postings on Beijing's "Democracy Wall," where, for a time, people could freely state their views. Especially notable was a poster put up in December 1978 by Wei Jingsheng (1949–), a young man who worked as an electrician and had four years of army service under his belt. In his poster Wei called for democracy as a Fifth Modernization absolutely necessary for the attainment of the other four.

This was too much for Deng and the political leadership. The wall was abolished. In May 1979 Wei was arrested. Subsequently, he received a fifteen-year sentence. Instead of a fifth modernization, Deng, in March 1979, proclaimed "four cardinal principles" as guides for the future.

The Four Cardinal Principles

The four principles consisted of "the socialist road," "the dictatorship of the proletariat," "the leadership of the Chinese Communist Party (C.C.P.)," and "Marxism-Leninism and Mao Zedong Thought." In practice, as in theory, all four were vague at best. In 1981 "socialism with Chinese characteristics" was adopted as the official policy, but clearly the attainment of utopian egalitarianism receded into the distant future. The "socialist road" was to be a long one, with China deemed to be only in the "initial stage of socialism," as General Secretary Zhao Ziyang (1919–2005) put it at the Thirteenth Party Congress in 1987. That same year the mayor of Shenyang was quoted as saying, "When used to promote the development of China's socialist economy, bankruptcy, leasing, shareholding and these sorts of things are no longer capitalist."[1]

Of the other cardinal principles, the leaders took "the leadership of the C.C.P." most seriously and brooked no challenge to the political dominance of their party, which they equated with "the dictatorship of the proletariat," the orthodox Marxist label for the stage between revolution and the withering away of the state that would usher in true communism.

The status of "Marxism-Leninism and Mao Zedong Thought" was more problematic. Nineteenth-century self-strengtheners had once firmly believed in the Confucian ends they meant to serve with novel and foreign means, but China's new leaders conveyed no similar depth of conviction. To many it seemed that the official ideology commanded little more than lip service, whereas acquiring and enjoying personal wealth became the order of the day. China took on a new look as revolutionary posters and slogans gave way to commercial advertisements on billboards and in the media, clumsy at first but then "gradually transmogrified into slavish imitations of Hong Kong, Taiwanese and Japanese models." Geremie R. Barmé goes on to point out, "The world presented in such advertising was one nearly entirely divided from the ideological landscape constructed by the party." Referring to the vision projected by international consumerism and playing off Marx's denunciation of religion, he concludes, "During the early 1990's, this vision of the consumer's paradise, rather than the state religion of Marxism-Leninism and Mao Thought, became the true opiate of the masses."[2]

Intellectual Life and the Arts in the 1980s

It was a heady time, stimulated by a deluge of new ideas, forms, and styles. The period began with the "literature and art of the wounded," as artists and writers gave expression to their suffering during the Cultural Revolution. This was followed by a "search for roots," expressed not only in literature but also in films, such as *Yellow Earth,* directed by Chen Kaige (1952–), who, along with his fellow "fifth generation" director, Zhang Yimou (1952–), won international acclaim for Chinese film. One of the many writers expressing similar sentiments was Mo Yan (Guan Moye, 1956–) whose *Garlic Ballads* depicts, with great human sympathy, the bitter life of peasants suffering at the hands of arrogant party cadres. He also wrote *Red Sorghum,* in which the villains are the Japanese military in China during World War II. Made into a movie directed by Zhang Yimou, it shocked the Chinese audience but won the best picture award at the Berlin Festival in 1988.

Some writers turned more to psychological themes or to the interplay of human feelings and engaged in stylistic experiments such as the flow of consciousness technique used by Wang Meng (1934–), Minister of Culture from 1987 to 1989. Others favored the magic realism of Gabriel García Marquéz. Meanwhile, Chinese intellectuals in all fields rejoined the international intellectual community and undertook a reexamination and reevaluation of their own past. Foreign scholars too were welcomed, as at conferences on Confucius and Zhu Xi (1987) held in the philosophers' home provinces (Shandong and Fujian, respectively). Temples and monuments were restored, as were mosques and churches. Jiang Qing's revolutionary operas disappeared from the stage, and Arthur Miller was invited to help prepare a Chinese performance of *Death of a Salesman* (1985).

Now, too, the Chinese public had its first look at modern artists ranging from Picasso to Jackson Pollock. While members of the Obscure School of Poetry expressed their alienation in verse, avant-garde painters depicted faceless figures set in endless, barren space. Some determined nonconformists, such as the Dada

FIGURE 15.1 Detail view of the nonsense characters on the printed pages of the books from *Book from the Sky* (1987–1991) by Xu Bing. Mixed media installation: hand-printed books, ceiling, and wall scrolls form intentionally false letter blocks. At first glance, the writing looks like Chinese, for the characters are composed of elements found in traditional writing. They are, however, nonsense characters invented by the artist. (© 1991 Xu Bing. Used by permission of the artist.)

group of Xiamen, Fujian's largest city, sought to smash all frames. Like the original proponents of Dada in post–World War I Europe, they mocked all art. Proclaiming the end of art, they ended their 1986 exhibit by burning all the works on display, frames and all. A kindred spirit was Xu Bing (1955–), who devoted three years of hard work to compose his *Book from the Sky* that no one can read, thus challenging the viewer to reflect on the nature of writing, language, art, and life in a postmodern world (Figure 15.1).

The spirit of iconoclasm and revolt was not limited to the highbrows. Many aspects of Western popular culture found a following in China, where Japanese and Taiwanese pop tunes were widely enjoyed and rock and roll gained an ardent audience. In the mid-1980s Beijing's own Cui Jian (1961–), "the John Lennon of China,"[3] formed a rock group whose records were best-sellers, much to the puzzled dismay of the establishment.

Although raucous music and critical writings continued to find a ready hearing among students and intellectuals, the regime, guided by Deng, was concerned that matters might get out of hand, but for some ten years refrained from strong-arm measures that could alienate the intellectuals whose cooperation was needed for modernization. Thus, campaigns against "cultural pollution" (1983) and "bourgeois liberalism" (1987) were relatively mild.

Still, pressure for change mounted. An outspoken advocate of openness in government, free speech, and political pluralism was the astrophysicist, party member, and university vice president Fang Lizhi (1936–1986), who encouraged his students to campaign for genuine local elections in Anhui, where his university was located. The movement spread from Anhui. In December, some 30,000 students demonstrated in Shanghai, and there were further demonstrations in Tianjin, Nanjing, and Beijing. In response, the government removed Fang from his job and expelled him from the C.C.P. More than 1 million students were sent to spend the following summer recess in the countryside.

For some ten years Deng successfully orchestrated the pace of change, and in 1987 he had the satisfaction of seeing the Thirteenth Party Congress affirm the general directions of his policies, including the primacy of economic development. This session also marked the retirement of a substantial number of the old guard, who were generally replaced by men more inclined to "seek truth from facts," an expression found in the *History of the Han* (*Han Shu*, first century C.E.), taken up by Mao, and used as a slogan by Deng. Deng now felt sufficiently confident to resign as deputy premier although, significantly, he retained his chairmanship of the Military Commission for two more years.

Tiananmen

The policy of mild repression of demands for democracy and human rights failed to deter student activism or dampen student demands for greater freedom of speech and of the press, an end to favoritism and government corruption, the right to form their own organizations, and the right for the people to have a greater say in government. In the spring of 1989 the government was caught off guard when students demonstrated, boycotted classes, held sit-ins, and occupied Beijing's huge Tiananmen Square in their determination to be heard.

With the approach of the seventieth anniversary of the May Fourth Movement, students and officials alike were aware of the historical significance of the occasion, as was the press, now including international television as well as print media. Marches and demonstrations on May 4 quickened the movement, but did not settle anything. On May 13, two days before the state visit of Premier Mikhail Gorbachev, more than two hundred students began a hunger strike supported by thousands of Beijing residents. When Gorbachev arrived, the government had to change the program and avoid Tiananmen. By May 16, the number of hunger strikers had mounted to more than 3000. Meanwhile, as the movement gathered steam,

FIGURE 15.2 *Goddess of Democracy,* Tiananmen Square, Beijing, May 30, 1989. Radical students erected the statue to democracy, and tanks and soldiers destroyed it six days later in their violent assault on Tiananmen Square. (© Peter Turnley/Corbis [TL009252].)

students in many other cities demonstrated in support. Most alarming to the government, ordinary people, including factory workers, increasingly became involved.

Opposition within the government prevented even a mild compromise with the students, who were not well organized and did not speak with a single voice. When Deng Xiaoping asserted his leadership, the government moderates, including General Secretary Zhao, lost out. On May 20 martial law was declared, and 250,000 soldiers were brought into Beijing, where they were greeted by roadblocks and demonstrations. On May 29, in a show of determination, radical students erected a large statue of the Goddess of Democracy holding high the torch of freedom to serve as the symbol of their movement (see Figure 15.2). Cui Jian's "Long March Rock" was their unofficial anthem.

The end came early on June 4 when, shortly after midnight, columns of tanks and armored cars charged into the city and on to Tiananmen, crushing barriers and shooting anyone in the way. After the soldiers destroyed the student encampments and the statue on the square, the violence escalated. Many students and civilians were shot, and some soldiers died too. Victims of the carnage overwhelmed Beijing's hospitals, many of which were forbidden to treat civilian casualties. Nor could they or anyone else compile statistics on the numbers of dead and wounded.

Military suppression was followed by the arrest, and in some cases execution, of student leaders in the capital and elsewhere. Others found their way into exile in the

West, where some continued as leaders of a nonunified and contentious political/intellectual community. Fang Lizhi, too, found freedom abroad. In 1997, after a second imprisonment, Wei Jingsheng also found sanctuary abroad. After 1989 Chinese voices in many parts of the world presented alternatives to the ideology and policies proclaimed by Beijing. In the 1980s use of the telephone, photocopier, and fax helped undermine the government monopoly on information, which proved even more difficult to sustain with the spread of email, cell phones, and the Internet toward the end of the century. The leadership's credibility now depended not on the old ideology but on its performance, especially its economic performance.

State, Economy, and Society in the 1990s and into the New Century

An immediate result of Tiananmen was that Deng's leading protégé, General Secretary Zhao Ziyang, was forced out of office and placed under house arrest. His place was taken by Jiang Zemin (1926–). In 1992 the octogenarian Deng made a dramatic tour of the south, proclaiming his determination to continue the pragmatic economic policy. After this trip, Deng, although still considered China's paramount leader, faded into the background, allowing Jiang to establish himself and ensure a smooth transition when Deng died in 1997.

Essentially, Jiang continued Deng's policies of economic liberalization without relaxing C.C.P. control over politics and public discourse. Economic liberalism without relaxation of political control became the hallmark of Jiang's leadership and legacy. Indicative of this dual policy was his speech of July 1, 2001, declaring that capitalists should be welcomed into the Communist Party and the government's subsequent shutting down of a publication named *The Pursuit of Truth* for criticizing this extraordinary departure from Marxist practice. Jiang redefined the role of the party as representing "advanced productive forces, advanced Chinese culture, and the fundamental interests of the majority."[4]

These "Three Representations" were billed as major theoretical contributions and were seen as a bid by Jiang to gain status as a thinker before he relinquished his post as General Secretary of the C.C.P. in November 2002. He did, however, retain his position as chairman of the Military Commission without any public indication that he would relinquish that important post in the fall of 2004. Furthermore, the appointments to positions of leadership of many of Jiang's protégés suggested a wish to remain the country's paramount leader as had Deng Xiaoping after his "retirement." Meanwhile, the record of the new General Secretary, Hu Jintao (1942–), included some grounds to encourage both hard-liners and reformers, and a *New York Times* headline announced, "China's New Leader Promises Not to Sever Tether to Jiang."[5] In the fall of 2004, China had effected a smooth political transition and continuity in its basic policies.

Whatever it represented, the C.C.P. still controlled the state, but, with the state no longer "commanding" the economy, the relationship between state, economy, and society had changed. The direction of economic change remained much the same as before, although there were times of pause and hesitation. Under the direction of Premier Zhu Rongji (1928–), like Jiang an engineer by background, and a former mayor of Shanghai, the economy weathered bouts of inflation, peaking in 1988 and 1995, and the government continued to encourage foreign investment and trade, negotiating its way into the World Trade Organization in 2001.

Whereas previously people had depended on their work unit to supply everything from housing to entertainment, these functions were now privatized, with the result that in Shanghai and other eastern cities a hundred stores blossomed, a thousand restaurants contended, and advertisements urged, "buy a house and become a boss."[6] The private sector prospered and new boom towns appeared, but not everyone could become a boss.

During the early years of the new century the economic boom reached new proportions. Abroad it turned China into a major factor in determining global commodity prices, while at home there was some success in implementing banking and other policies meant to provide for a smooth landing to avert a traumatic bust.

Throughout the Jiang-Hu Period, the government reduced the scope of the state-run sector and announced its determination to continue doing so, because these enterprises were inefficient, frequently lost money, drained funds, and weakened the state banks on which they depended. However, the government had to proceed gradually because of the threat of social unrest posed by workers deprived of the security of their "iron rice-bowls." The labor market was already swollen by about 60 million peasants who were annually leaving their villages in search of better pay. The urban and rural unemployed formed a "floating population" that appeared in China's major cities looking for a day's work.

In the countryside, peasants received longer leases on their land but continued to be required to sell a quota of grain to the state, which was anxious to maintain grain self-sufficiency. At the same time, many peasants now engaged in rural industries, which came to account for 60 percent of China's industrial output but did not solve the problem of rural poverty. Like authorities of other governments at the time, those of the P.R.C. accepted a widening income gap as the price of economic growth.

Similarly in line with global trends, China moved in the direction of market economics, but the government often gave mixed political and economic signals. Heavy taxes, land requisitions, autocratic and corrupt officials, and/or severe water pollution elicited peasant petitions (70,000 in 1995) and demonstrations, some large and violent. One response was the provision for village elections "as a safety valve to let the peasantry vent their dissatisfaction." Jean C. Oi goes on to point out that different constituencies and different agendas left China "a country riddled with policy contradictions."[7]

That the new relationship between state and society is unstable and difficult to define is reflected in the proliferation of labels proffered by Western academics, including, but by no means limited to, *capitalism with Chinese characteristics, capital socialism, state-socialist corporatism, symbiotic clientism, Confucian Leninism,* and *bureaupreneurialism.* The proliferation of terms reflects the inadequacy of traditional categories as well as the blurring of the line between state and society. It also reflects the variety of relationships between state and society to be found in China. One reason is that the initiative to a considerable degree passed to local, especially county, levels. Following the penchant for fours favored in the post-Mao years, Richard Baum and Alexei Shevchenko have characterized local governments as "Entrepreneurs, Patrons, Predators, and Developers." One of their major conclusions is that the situation "augurs neither the continued potency of the central party state nor the emergence of a pluralistic civil society but the proliferation of quasi-autonomous (and potentially corrupt) local economic empires."[8]

The potential for corruption was fully realized in what Lionel M. Jensen has aptly termed a "hybrid political economy" and in "the moral confusion wrought by a contradictory ideology."[9] The country was riddled with corruption, and crime was on the increase. Nor was malfeasance by any means purely local. In August 1999 China's auditor-general reported that one-fifth of China's annual revenue had been "misappropriated," that all eighteen provincial governments were guilty, and that the Ministry of Water Resources was building luxury office buildings rather than much-needed dams and dikes.

The Environment

Industrialization and the efforts to meet the needs and some of the aspirations of a population reported to be 1.248 billion in 1998 placed great strains on the environment. Quality of both air and water posed health threats. China's major cities were shrouded in a permanent haze, and people breathed polluted air not only outside but also even indoors, where it especially threatened women cooking over stoves burning raw coal. Most coal remained untreated, and most women, although theoretically the equals of men, remained unliberated from the stove. China was well on the way to replacing the United States as the planet's foremost producer of greenhouse gases.

Water, too, can be lethal in China. All too often "the river runs black."[10] Irrigation water is often contaminated by discharge. In the case of a village in Gansu inhabited by descendants of Confucius, the village leaders were able to obtain some redress only after challenging managers of a fertilizer plant to drink some water from a stream they had poisoned. Whether a farmer near Beijing whose geese all died after imbibing poisonous water will obtain legal redress is not yet known, but at least the courts have agreed to hear his case.

Pollution is not the only water problem. In the north water tables have sunk alarmingly and water shortages are severe. The diversion of Yellow River water for irrigation has reduced the transport of silt to the sea. Instead it is deposited on the riverbed, raising it above the surrounding countryside and posing a threat of devastating floods as of old. Meanwhile, recurrent floods inundated southern regions. Not until 1999 did the government officially acknowledge that chopping down trees in the headlands of the Yangzi had something to do with this. There have been people in and out of government who were aware of the problem, but environmental policies formulated in Beijing were often ignored locally, especially when the problem mostly affected people downriver or far away.

However, the government too contributed to the destruction of the environment. In 1992 it approved a major project to dam the Three Gorges of the Yangzi River to address China's need for clean energy and flood control and to open Sichuan, China's most populous province, to oceangoing vessels. The waters of the river were diverted in 1997, and the dam is scheduled for completion in 2009. It is to be 170 meters high and run for 2 kilometers, comparable to a four-story building a mile wide, and will cost much more than the $25 billion of the very optimistic official estimate. It will displace well over 1 million people and inundate priceless cultural sites. The government discounted warnings about the potential disasters posed by the buildup of silt behind the dam, unpredictable geologic effects, the dangers of forming a lake even more polluted than the present river, and possible adverse effects downstream. Nor was it impressed by the turning of world opinion against megadams. Although energy generation and water control could be achieved more cheaply and less dangerously by a series of small dams, these would not provide maritime access to Sichuan, where Chongqing is growing into a huge metropolis.

In April 2004 Wen Jiaobao (1942–), who had succeeded Zhu Rongji as Prime Minister in 2002, surprised Chinese and foreign observes by ordering a major review and at least a temporary halt of a huge dam project on the Nu river in Western Yunnan province that would displace 50,000 people and threaten the ecology and beauty of a region selected as a World Heritage Site. Whether and to what degree increased awareness and laws can avert the worst environmental destruction remains to be seen. The example of what the wealthy nations do will be a factor. Meanwhile, in some places local gods have sometimes been enlisted to defend the local environment.

The Revival of Religion

One response to the loosening of central government reins was the reemergence of religion, condemned not only by Cultural Revolution enthusiasts but also denounced by Karl Marx himself as the "opiate of the people." Village temples to local and lineage deities were rebuilt, traditional burial practices resumed, and traditional beliefs and practices such as geomancy (*fengshui*) resurfaced. These cults and practices were still denounced as "superstition" by the political and intellectual establishment, which distinguished them from "legitimate" religions such as Buddhism, Daoism, Islam, and Christianity. As Stephen Feuchtwang attests, partly on the basis of personal observation, "In some places new religious buildings were tolerated, in others the Public Security forces periodically destroy them."[11] Much depended on local authorities and circumstances. For example, at Black Dragon Pool in northern Shaanxi the head of the officially sanctioned Cultural Management Institute also heads the temple association, and the Institute is responsible for the upkeep of the Black

Dragon god's temple and the conduct of its main annual festival, featuring a tour by the god around the dry land to bring rain.

During the Cultural Revolution there was a tendency to elevate Mao to a status far beyond that of an ordinary human, and now tens of thousands of pilgrims have visited a monastery in Hunan, Mao's native province, where:

> some pray for the safety and harmony of family members while others ask Mao to cure chronic diseases. [Members of] the latter group are given a glass of "holy water" after their prayers. Those who feel Mao has listened to their prayers thank him for the kindness received.[12]

Some mosques and churches, converted to factories during the Cultural Revolution, were returned to their congregations and became once again places of worship sanctioned and supervised by the state. Chinese Catholics remained separated from Rome, as the government refused to let them obey the pope, and neither Catholic nor Protestant missionaries were permitted into the country. Unsupervised worship in private houses was also prohibited. But the loss of credibility of official materialism provided fertile ground for those seeking something beyond the quest for wealth and the passing satisfactions of consumerism.

The state remained suspicious of religion as an alternate source of authority and potential nucleus of resistance and was particularly wary of Vajrayana Buddhism in Tibet and Islam in Xinjiang and Qinghai. But the government's concerns were not limited to peripheral minorities such as these. They were taken aback, and the security apparatus was caught by surprise, when 10,000 followers of *Falungong* quietly assembled in Beijing to protest the outlawing of their sect. Led from New York by its exiled founder, the sect, estimated by the government to have 70 million adherents, offered spiritual and physical health through dance-like *qigong* exercises and mental concentration. Its leader insisted from the start that it was nonpolitical, but the authorities were alarmed at its abilities to mobilize thousands and troubled that its followers were largely middle-aged and well-integrated members of the community, some even belonging to the C.C.P. It was outlawed, and periodic arrests and trials followed.

The suppression of religious expression and the arrest of political dissidents continued in the face of international concern over human rights. Although avoiding a second international outrage like Tiananmen, the regime continued to try to stamp out any sparks of separatism it feared might catch fire in Tibet or elsewhere. In international relations, particularly with the United States, the human rights issue continued to smolder, only to be doused by geopolitical and geoeconomic considerations. This was all the more the case when, after September 2001, China gave its support to the American war on terror.

Foreign Relations and Hong Kong

Foreign relations during the late 1970s and 1980s remained within the pattern set earlier, and China remained at peace except that conflicting ambitions in Cambodia prompted an unsuccessful invasion of Vietnam in 1979. Sino-Vietnamese relations remained tense for some time. There were border clashes in 1985, but relations improved in the late 1990s. China did not engage in any further military combat but concentrated on modernizing its military.

China's relations with the Soviet Union became more cordial, especially after the U.S.S.R. withdrew from Afghanistan in 1988, whereas the fall of Communism in Eastern Europe and the disintegration of the Soviet Union were taken by China's rulers as warnings of what could befall them and their country.

Full diplomatic relations with the United States were established on January 1, 1979. Although Chinese wariness of the only remaining superpower was balanced by American unease over an emergent giant, relations remained generally cordial while trade grew and Americans entered into joint ventures with Chinese partners. With its business community enthralled by the old Western dream of an unlimited Chinese market, the United States tolerated widening trade deficits, and in the first year of the new century agreed to forgo annual reviews of China's generally unsatisfactory human rights situation. As already noted, the next year China was admitted to the World Trade Organization.

A notable diplomatic success was the agreement signed in 1984 with Great Britain to return Hong Kong to Chinese sovereignty in 1997. China in turn guaranteed that for the next fifty years Hong Kong would retain its own laws and institutions. The People's Republic thus acknowledged the economic importance of Hong Kong, which, by the mid-1980s, had developed into a major world financial and trade center with a thriving manufacturing sector. Symbolizing the future, China's Central Bank erected the city's tallest skyscrapers (1982–1990), designed by I. M. Pei (Ieho Ming Pei, 1917–), the Chinese-born American architect who in 1983 had received architecture's highest award, the Pritzker Prize. Much younger, and not nearly as famous, was Yuen Kwok-chung (1964–), whose *Triptych* (see Figure 15.3), which was exhibited at the 1994 Hong Kong Contemporary Art Biennial Exhibition, invites the viewer to see the barcode as the true flag of Hong Kong and infers that commercial consumerism (mediated through Hong Kong?) is what links the United States and the P.R.C. The Chinese title, "study hard and make progress every day," would make a splendid slogan for a textbook, but here heightens the sardonic effect. Fortuitously, in the exhibition catalog *Triptych* is preceded by a painting titled *Perplexity* and followed by *Coiling Incense Smoke*.

Although *Triptych* represents the money-making spirit of Hong Kong and of would-be Hong Kongs further up the China coast, the city also provided a haven for the likes of the noted philosopher of "New Confucianism," Mou Zongsan (1909–1995), and highly original painters such as Irene Chou from Shanghai (see Afterword Figure A.1) and Liu Guosong from Taiwan (see Figure 15.5).

With the erosion of its old ideological base, the government of the P.R.C. could seek legitimacy from its economic performance—the success of "managed consumerism," as Richard Kraus has termed it. Or it could emphasize "orchestrated nationalism"[13]—orchestrated lest it get out of hand in demonstrations that could interfere with the conduct of foreign policy and might even threaten the established order. During the 1990s it pursued both consumerist and nationalist aims. With Hong Kong safely in the fold, the de facto independence of Taiwan remained a major irritant.

FIGURE 15.3 *Triptych 1994*, Yuen Kwok-chung (1962–). Most people in the People's Republic at this time would probably recognize the American flag as well as their own but had never seen a barcode. That, however, was a familiar symbol in Hong Kong. Acrylic on canvas, 114.17 in × 72.44 in. (© Yuen Kwok-chung. Used by permission of the artist.)

Although chafing over foreign criticism of its suppression of human rights in Tibet and elsewhere, the government of the P.R.C. was particularly troubled by Taiwan's failure to be persuaded of the benefits of its "one country–two system policy." On the eve of Taiwan's first direct presidential elections in 1996, the P.R.C. fired missiles and conducted naval maneuvers in a show of force. As the new century began, the future of P.R.C.-Taiwan relations remained very much in doubt.

Intellectuals and Artists in the 1990s and into the New Century

The P.R.C. continued to jail dissidents and did not tolerate political opposition. They allowed people to choose their own jobs but no longer guaranteed them a job. In general, the government gave people more latitude in the conduct of their lives to enjoy their electric appliances and other new possessions. People were allowed freedom of movement. The arts continued much in the spirit of the 1980s, producing a profusion of styles and agendas as well as a renewed appreciation of

FIGURE 15.4 Shanghai Museum (1996), architect Xing Tonghe. The circular building placed on top of a square recalls the tradition that heaven is round and the earth is square, and the arches on the roof resemble the handles on ancient bronzes. (© Lore Schirokauer.)

tradition, including Confucianism. An unusually satisfactory marriage of new and old was the Shanghai Museum (see Figure 15.4), by the Shanghai architect Xing Tonghe, completed in 1996 to house the city's treasures, including China's foremost collection of bronze vessels from the first dynasties. Two years later it was joined by the Shanghai Grand Theater designed by Jean-Marie Charpentier, a French architect. Paul Andreu, another French architect, designed a new airport for Shanghai, and the city's postmodernist flavor will be further strengthened if and when the new art museum to be built in collaboration with New York's Guggenheim Museum sees the light of day.

Many of those prominent in the 1980s remained productive. Wang Meng fought off his critics and advocated cultural pluralism with the market as judge. In 1992 he founded *Green Leaves,* a journal on the environment. Mo Yan published *Wine Republic.* Characterized by David Der-wei Wang as a "Swiftian satire and Kafkaesque fable," it follows a detective sent to a country where people eat children. Wang comments:

> In a world where the high and the low, the fragrant and the putrid, mingle, nobody has clean hands; the protagonist is fittingly murdered by being drowned in a manure pit at the end of the novel. Eschatology and scatology turn out to be two readings of the same reality.[14]

In 1995 Chen Kaige directed *Farewell My Concubine,* which found a warm reception overseas. The work of some of the most experimental artists was confined to their apartments, whereas the audience of others, like the computer artist Feng Mengbo, was primarily overseas. Feng, a resident of Beijing, explained the thought behind his series of paintings *Taxi! Taxi!—Mao Zedong I–III* as follows:

> In 1990, when I was still at the academy, I suddenly realized that the way Mao Zedong waved his hand at the army [of Red Guards] gathered in Tiananmen Square during the Cultural Revolution was very similar to the way people wave to hail a taxi. So I copied the image of Mao waving and put a common yellow taxicab in front of him—the kind you see everywhere in Beijing today.[15]

Mao had been taken off his pedestal and made to hail a cab! Once inside he was likely to encounter a Mao traffic safety charm. To recover from the shock would he have taken a swig of "The East is Red" health drink, thirsting for the days when this had been the anthem of the revolution?

Cui Jian, the rock star, had his ups and downs, but mostly was tolerated by the authorities and allowed to perform at home and abroad. David Fricke, critic for *Rolling Stone,* heard him in concert in 1995 and wrote:

> But just as he challenges the arthritic authority of his country's leaders, Cui tolerates no laws or limits to his music. The rumble of Chinese barrel drum fattened the surge of angular guitar grooves. Beastie-style beats, fierily Jamaican ska and the roadhouse rattle of early Springsteen collided in such anthemic fireballs as "The Other Shore," "Together we confront the same reality—Together we sing a song loudly."[16]

Listeners will need to judge the results for themselves as postmodern Chinese intellectuals engage "in a new search for a real 'hybridization' or 'hybridity' based on a dialectical synthesis beyond the old dichotomies between the traditional and the modern, the particular and the universal."[17]

One dichotomy that was breaking down was that between the thought and symbolic world of artists and writers living in the P.R.C. and those living elsewhere in a Chinese or semi-Chinese world. Whereas critics worried about the hybrid culture, the mixing of elements from different traditions continued to the point that when a joint exhibit was held in New York in 1999, it was often difficult to distinguish the works of those in the P.R.C. from the works of those outside. Mainland exiles in America, Europe, Australia, and New Zealand as well as artists and writers from Taiwan contributed to "a China defined not by geopolitical boundaries and ideological closures but by overlapping cultural and shared imaginative resources."[18]

In 2004 Xu Bing exhibited *Where Does the Dust Itself Collect,* an installation in Wales and Berlin employing dust from Ground Zero in New York to represent the dust in the poem of the Sixth Patriarch (see p. 121) to make a Zen statement. Also in 2004 the reaction of people at the Shanghai Biennal suggested that at least in that increasingly cosmopolitan city the most determinedly avant garde art had just about lost its ability to shock.

Taiwan

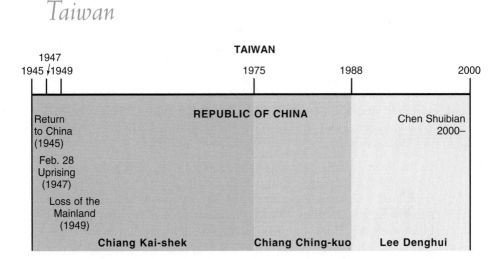

As noted earlier, Taiwan's first two years under the Guomindang-controlled Republic of China were so oppressive as to provoke the violence of 1947. One result of Guomindang actions was that the Taiwanese elite was decimated. Ironically, this removed not only resistance to the political dominance of the Nationalists but also a potential source of opposition to land redistribution and other economic reforms undertaken during the 1950s with American backing, pressure, and advice. As in postwar Japan, the end of landlordism had profound economic and social effects.

During the Japanese years, Taiwan had acquired much of the necessary infrastructure for industrialization, and many of the approximately 2 million civilian refugees who fled from the mainland also brought training and skills that contributed to the development of light industry and commerce. Capital came in part from the great sums of money the Nationalists brought over with them. Until terminated in 1966, American economic aid also helped, and once the Japanese economy had recovered, Japanese companies invested heavily. The government generally supervised and advanced development, first building up infrastructure and then fostering exports. In 1965 it created special Export Processing Zones where companies enjoyed tax incentives and were free of import taxes as long as they exported whatever they made or assembled.

Culturally, the government saw its mission as preservation of old Chinese traditions. Taiwan became the home for institutes of higher learning. The use of the local Taiwanese language was suppressed and, as in the P.R.C., instruction was in Mandarin. A museum was built to house the priceless Palace Collection the Nationalists brought with them from the mainland.

At a time when mainland artists were caught in the political storms, artists in Taiwan and elsewhere were free to explore new ways to draw on their tradition to create forms of expression suitable for the twentieth century. One of the most gifted of these was Liu Guosong (Liu Kuo-sung, 1932–), who was born in Shandong, was educated in Taiwan, established himself as a painter there, taught many years in Hong Kong, and returned to Taiwan, where he now lives.

As Liu explained, "We are no longer ancient Chinese nor modern Westerners. We do not live in the Song or Yuan society, nor in the modern European or American environment. If it is false for us to copy old Chinese paintings, isn't it the same to copy modern Western painting?"[19] Not satisfied with working in either Chinese or Western styles, Liu asserted, "'Chinese' and 'modern' are the two blades of the sword, which will slash the Westernized and the traditionalist schools alike."[20]

Liu is deeply conversant with both traditions. Chu-tsing Li describes the collage in Liu's *Metaphysics of Rocks* (see Figure 15.5) as follows:

> In the lower middle part are two pieces of collage, one large and the other small, both suggesting rock shapes. The paper is in color, but combined with some textures printed with wrinkled paper. Thus there seem to be several kinds of rocks, done with different techniques and brushwork. Yet none of them is realistic enough to resemble real rocks. But each gives us an idea of some quality of rocks, such as jutting up, having interesting textures, or showing watery surfaces.[21]

Liu went on to paint a distinctive series on the sun and moon and continued to experiment with textures and techniques and paint abstractions that suggested the metaphysics of mountains.

Under the Guomindang, the Republic of China remained ideologically committed to the reunification of China and to Sun Yat-sen's Three Principles of the People. Until ousted from the United Nations in 1971, its claim to speak for China was widely accepted abroad. At home, although the Guomindang was reformed, it remained dictatorial, refusing to share substantive power with the Taiwanese, that is, people of Chinese stock who had settled on the island before 1945. Although the native Taiwanese did win elections to local governments, real control remained in the hands of the central government. Prosperity and repression kept dissent to a minimum. Among those imprisoned on Green Island was Bo Yang (1920–), given ten years for translating an English language comic deemed insulting to Chiang Kai-shek. His acerbic critique of Chinese ways won him a wide readership on the mainland.

When Chiang Kai-shek died in 1975, there was an easy and smooth passing of power to his son Chiang Ching-kuo (in *pinyin*, Jiang Jingguo, 1910–1988). Progress was sufficient for the economy to come through both the oil crisis and the diplomatic defeats of the 1970s in good shape. As in Japan, there was a turn to more advanced technology such as computers. In 1980 the state established a science-oriented industrial park and an electronics industry.

By that time Taiwan had attained a level of per capita income second in Asia only to that in Japan. In many ways, it became a modern country. By 1979 more

FIGURE 15.5 *The Metaphysics of Rocks,* Liu Guosong. The artist uses calligraphy, brushwork, and collage. Ink and acrylic with collage on paper, 1968, 26.49 in × 27.01 in. (© Liu Kuo-sung. Used with permission of the artist.)

than one-half of the people owned a color television set and 90 percent had refrigerators. During the 1980s air conditioners became common, and cars largely captured the road dominated previously by motorbikes.

The normalization of U.S. relations with the P.R.C. meant that relations with Taiwan were formally downgraded. Semiformal relations were maintained, but the Guomindang's claim to the rulership of all of China was weakened, and those born in Taiwan who coupled demands for democratization with calls for a Republic of Taiwan found their case strengthened. Chiang Kai-shek's response had been repression, but his son alternated between jailing leaders of the opposition and instigating reform. The latter was predominant during his last two years, when martial law was revoked, press restrictions were eased, and the prohibition against opposition parties relaxed.

These reforms allowed the Democratic Progressive Party (D.P.P.) to field candidates in the election of December 1986. Inhabitants of Taiwan were, for the first time in thirty-eight years, allowed to visit relatives on the mainland. The government was confident that they would return with an appreciation for the higher standard of living they enjoyed on Taiwan. In practice, even the post-1945 newcomers came to see themselves as different from mainlanders and as having much in common with their fellow Taiwanese.

When Chiang Ching-kuo died in January 1988, he was succeeded by Lee Teng-hui (Li Denghui, 1923–), a Taiwanese with a Ph.D. in agricultural economics from Cornell who brought more Taiwanese into the top party and government posts and included fourteen holders of American doctorates in his cabinet. The emergence of a strong middle class, strong advances in education, and continuing affluence provided fertile ground for continued movement in the direction of greater democracy, whereas the ultimate nature of a Taiwanese identity remained in dispute. The GMD won the election of 1989, but the D.P.P. gained ground. Despite the P.R.C.'s show of force, Lee was victorious in Taiwan's first direct popular presidential election in 1996. However, he had to face not only D.P.P. opposition but also divisiveness within his own party that led to a major defection in 2000. In the election of that year, Chen Shui-bian (also written Chen Shui-bien or Chen Shuibian) (1951–) of the D.P.P., with 39.3 percent of the vote, defeated two rival candidates to become the Republic of China's youngest and first non-GMD president. His vice president, the women's rights advocate Lu Hsiu-lien (Lu Xiulian, Annette Lu, 1944–), was the first woman elected to that high office. Elected on a promise to put an end to widespread corruption, Chen, on assuming office, played down his Taiwanese nationalism and gave priority to domestic house-cleaning. Beijing, which had issued threatening statements before the election and had made it clear that it would not rule out the use of force if Taiwan declared independence, was quieted for the time being, but the example of a party losing an election to an opposition running on an anticorruption platform must have been distasteful, not to say unnerving, to those too deeply implicated in the mainland status quo.

The broad picture was little changed after March 2004 when Chen and Lu were reelected by less than 30,000 of 13 million votes, although 300,000 protested the election results in a demonstration that ended in violence.

Notes

1. Christopher R. Wren, "Comparing Two Communist Paths to 'Reform,'" *The New York Times*, Sept. 6, 1987, Section 4, p. 2.

2. Geremie R. Barmé, *In The Red: On Contemporary Chinese Culture* (New York: Columbia Univ. Press, 1999), p. 123.

3. Shen Tong, *Almost a Revolution* (Boston: Houghton Mifflin, 1990), p. 310, as quoted in Andrew E. Jones, *Like a Knife: Ideology in Contemporary Chinese Popular Music* (Ithaca: East Asia Program, Cornell Univ., 1992), p. 95.

4. *The New York Times*, August 16, 2001, p. A13.

5. *The New York Times*, November 21, 2002, p. A16.

6. *Xinmin wanbao* (*New People's Evening News*), Shanghai, May 11, 1994, as

quoted by Deborah S. Davis in her introduction to *The Consumer Revolution in Urban China* (Berkeley: Univ. of California Press, 2000), p. 9.

7. Jean C. Oi, "Two Decades of Rural Reform in China: An Overview and Assessment," *The China Quarterly,* No. 159 (Sept. 1999), p. 627.

8. Richard Baum and Alexei Shevchenko, "The State of the State," in Merle Goldman and Roderick MacFarquhar, eds., *The Paradox of China's Post-Mao Reforms* (Cambridge: Harvard Univ. Press, 1999), pp. 345, 349. The list of labels at the beginning of this paragraph is taken from the same source, where each label is documented.

9. Lionel M. Jensen, "Everyone's a Player, but the Nation's a Loser: Corruption in Contemporary China," in Timothy B. Weston and Lionel M. Jensen, eds., *China Beyond the Headlines* (Latham, Md.: Rowman and Littlefield, 2000), p. 42.

10. Elizabeth C. Economy, *The River Runs Black* (Ithaca: Cornell Univ. Press, 2004.)

11. Stephen Feuchtwang, "Religious Resistance," in Elizabeth J. Perry and Mark Selden, eds., *Chinese Society: Change, Conflict and Resistance* (London: Routledge, 2000), p. 171.

12. *Eastern Express,* October 5, 1955, p. 39, as quoted in Elizabeth J. Perry, "Crime, Corruption, and Contention" in Goldman and MacFarquhar, *The Paradox of China's Post-Mao Reforms,* p. 323.

13. Richard Kraus, "Public Monuments and Private Pleasures in the Parks of Nanjing: A Tango in the Ruins of the Ming Emperor's Palace," in Deborah S. Davis, ed., *The Consumer Revolution in Urban China,* p. 306.

14. David Der-wei Wang, *Fin-de-siecle Splendor: Repressed Modernities of Late Qing Fiction, 1849–1911* (Stanford: Stanford Univ. Press, 1997), p. 332.

15. Quoted in Barmé, *In the Red: On Contemporary Chinese Culture,* p. 231.

16. David Fricke, "Cui Jian: New York, The Bottom Line, Aug. 31, 1995," *The Rolling Stone,* Nov. 2, 1995.

17. Min Lin with Maria Galikowski, *The Search for Modernity: Chinese Intellectual and Cultural Discourse in the Post-Mao Era* (New York: St. Martin's Press, 1999), p. 197.

18. David Der-wei Wang, "Chinese Fiction for the Nineties," in David Der-wei Wang and Jeanne Tai, eds., *Running Wild: New Chinese Writers* (New York: Columbia Univ. Press, 1994), p. 238.

19. Quoted in Chu-tsing Li, *Liu Kuo-sung— The Growth of a Modern Chinese Artist* (Taipei: The National Gallery of Art and Museum of History, 1969), p. 32.

20. Preface *to The Way Forward for Modern Chinese Painting* (Taipei: Literary Star, 1965), pp. 3–4, quoted in program for the Hong Kong Museum of Art Exhibit "Liu Guosong, a Universe of His Own," curated by Christina Chu (Hong Kong: The Leisure and Cultural Service Department, 2004).

21. Ibid., p. 53.

Afterword

A major theme of modern history is the interaction of regional civilizations and cultures, each with its own dynamic, in an accelerating process that links us all, in varying degrees and for better or worse, in a multitude of ways, some obvious and others less apparent. The roots of contemporary globalization extend deeply into the past, but the process has reached new dimensions in our own time as history becomes increasingly world history and no country, no matter how large or powerful, has the luxury of withdrawal.

All around the globe the modern era saw the growth in power of the nation-state to a degree unprecedented by that of any institution in human history even as economic links were formed that became the precursor of the contemporary global economy. At the start of the twenty-first century, in China as elsewhere, the state's role in managing the economy was diminishing in the face of a global economic and financial system grown beyond the power of even the strongest state to control. Nevertheless, the nation-state remained the dominant military and political institution. After the events of September 11, 2001, national governments strengthened the state in its battle against terrorist enemies with radical religious and anti-globalization agendas, but at the same time they needed and sought greater international cooperation.

Both globalization and nationalism held promise of a brighter future, but both also entailed dangers. It remains very much to be seen whether sovereign states can solve global problems while being focused on local issues and while national rivalries continue to generate international dangers.

International Tensions

Despite differences in scale and relative size, Taiwan and the People's Republic of China (P.R.C.) are similar in that the two sides reject each other's political and economic systems and tell different versions of China's modern story. One side—Taiwan—has achieved much greater wealth than the other. Like Hong Kong, Taiwan is an element of "Greater China," with a standard of living dramatically higher than that of the P.R.C. itself. There is every sign that the flow of knowledge, goods, and people between Taiwan and the mainland will continue to accelerate, creating common ground and enhancing each side's stakes in a peaceful reintegration of the Chinese nation.

Although economic reintegration of China is taking place, political reintegration remains a very difficult problem. The P.R.C. insists that it wants peaceful reunification with Taiwan—but on its own terms. Meanwhile, it is willing to wait for changes to occur that will permit political reintegration, whatever those changes might be. However, it will not permit overt secession and the establishment of an independent republic on Taiwan that rejects the principle of Taiwan's belonging to "one China." The P.R.C. has made it clear that in that circumstance, it would intervene militarily to enforce its claim to Taiwan's "belonging" to China.

Under this threat from the mainland, the Republic of China on Taiwan continues to proceed cautiously in asserting its intention to move toward independence, even though its president, Chen Shui-bian, was elected on an independence platform. Other countries, meanwhile, remain nervous about the potential for conflict between the two governments. The United States, which has committed itself to defending Taiwan from encroachment or invasion from the mainland, sometimes aggravates tensions in the Taiwan Straits by selling weapons to Taiwan and implying that Taiwan is a country. This raises hackles in Beijing and reminds the P.R.C. that the United States is a main reason that what the P.R.C. sees as a purely domestic issue remains unsolved after more than half a century. However, concern about terrorism and North Korean nuclear policy, as well as economic ties, have encouraged Beijing and Washington to cooperate and keep the Taiwan issue off center stage.

Another point of friction is the tiny Senkaku/Diaoyu (or Diaoyu/Senkaku) islands in the China Sea, claimed by Japan as well as by China and Taiwan, which could provide a focus of conflict fueled by the strong popular anti-Japanese sentiment in China. In the event of domestic setbacks, the regime could be tempted to look overseas for a way to rally the Chinese people behind a government that can no longer derive its legitimacy from a now discredited ideology and depends on its performance as the champion of the nation as well as the performance of the economy.

Economic Globalization

A truly momentous development emerged in 2004 when the growth of the economy reached the point that China became a major player in global trade and finance. Japan remains the world's second largest economy, but China has become Japan's major customer, as well as the country with which the United States had the largest trade deficit. Chinese demand for crucial commodities such as oil and iron reached a level at which it became a decisive factor in setting world prices. China became more dependent on the global economy, but the global economy also became more dependent on China.

Everywhere globalization has benefited some but harmed others. It has brought unprecedented prosperity to those in a position to take advantage of new opportunities but reduced the unfortunates to dire poverty. In China, as in the United States, the gap between winners and losers has widened. Even as luxury car dealerships are being established in Beijing, Shanghai, and Guangzhou to cater to the very rich, there are people who live by foraging in garbage dumps.

In China, as elsewhere, cities are the nodes of the global system, and Chinese cities are transformed at a dizzying pace. "This is a country where everything is changing before your eyes, and a visitor can return after a year's absence and be surprised at the transformation. It has a kind of frontier character," to quote John R. Logan, who has contributed to making Chinese urbanization a "research frontier" as well. The transformation continues, but by now sleepy provincial capitals such as Changsha (Hunan) have acquired skylines and boast theme parks whereas Beijing looks and feels like any world capital dominated by high-rise buildings and choked with traffic. Gone are the bicycles that used to crowd Shanghai's Nanjing Road, as that city competes with Hong Kong in trade, manufacturing, and international panache. Aesthetically, too, the major cities are becoming global, as prominent European architects are commissioned to design buildings in the latest styles.

Contending Trends

Economic growth increases demands on the environment but also opens opportunities for more efficient use of resources. After a distinguished career of research on the Chinese environment, Vaclav Smil concludes by emphasizing "contending trends" at work "in every instance of securing China's energy and food while maintaining an acceptable quality of environment." In the light (and heat) of global warming, we should bear in mind that China is a major factor in world ecology as well as economy.

Contending trends can be found in just about every dimension of human life, including the political. On the one hand, globalization has entailed a strengthening of the rule of law, but political change has lagged behind economic change, and stability continues to have higher priority than political liberalization. Although some commentators predict democratization, Hu Jintao announced that China does not need more than one party. Globalization affects political structures and the relationship between state and society as well as just about everything, but despite the dreams of some and the nightmares of others, it does not equal Americanization.

From Sun Yat-sen through Mao Zedong and Deng Xiaoping to the present, China has sought its own "Chinese" way to build a strong, modern state and society. The imperatives of twenty-first century globalization may set certain limits but leave ample room for variation and, again, contending trends, including the meaning of "Chineseness" at the very heart of a Chinese identity. In this respect as in so many others, China is not alone: a recent book by Ambin Shi is an example of academic globalization, for he is a comparativist trained in both Chinese and American universities and conversant with trends both in the P.R.C. and abroad.

Cultural Globalization

Parallel to economic globalization, one can speak of cultural globalization, both in terms of a youth culture with shared taste in music and dress and of a global "transcultural" avant-garde of literary and visual artists, in which China is well represented. If these people have found inadequate representation in our text, we make amends herewith by including an illustration from one of the earliest of their number, Irene Chou (Zhou Luyun, 1924–), who left Shanghai for Hong Kong in 1949, but now resides in Australia. In an eloquent style very much her own, she continues to present a vision that soars beyond our normal perceptions of space and time (see Figure A.1). Among the younger generation, we could cite Ha Jin (1956–), winner of the 1999 National Book Award, who once served in the People's Liberation Army but owes his reputation to novels written in English, and Gao Xingjian (1940–), China's first Nobel Prize winner (2000), who moved to Paris in 1989.

The globalization of thought and art often encounters resistance. Neither Ha Jin nor Gao Xingjian can be published in China, and East Asian countries are hardly alone in their suspicion of the outside world. China has become much more open to ideas from abroad, but tolerance for dissent remains limited. However, the Internet and the rise of cheap and easy global commu-

FIGURE A.1 Satin Painting II Ink & Color on Satin. The title leaves viewers free to explore and understand the painting on their own. 22.8 in × 48.4 in.

nications have implications for political change that worry many of the conservative regimes in East Asia. The P.R.C. learned this in 1989, when fax machines and satellite television completely undermined its ability to control the flow of news about the Democracy Movement.

Although the government tries to filter what comes in via the World Wide Web, email can put savvy Chinese in instant touch with relatives overseas and other sources of information or exchange. Chat rooms, although censored, spread information not available in the press.

Cinema, one of the earliest genres of global influence, remained a major avenue of influence across national boundaries. Film not only told stories but represented whole peoples and ways of life. Hollywood images of American life are notorious for their portrayal of the United States as a sun-drenched suburb and, concurrently, as a nation of violent cities. The coexistence of these two images in the minds of people all over the world is proof of the vast abilities of cinema to further, or distort, understanding. The television age has simply extended this power into the homes of even the most remote communities around the globe. The influence of cinema, however, is by no means all one way. The films of major Chinese directors now play abroad and are available on videotape and DVD.

Other examples of transnational influence within East Asia and between the region and the rest of the world are legion. As Beijing prepares to host the summer Olympics in 2008, people have become passionately involved in international sports. Religion is another vast field of intense and varied interaction, as seen in the appeal of messages directed at all people by global religions such as Buddhism, Christianity, and Islam, and also in the return of many people to their local, traditional beliefs and gods. This return to local creeds and loyalties is itself a global phenomenon. As in other areas of endeavor, attempts to work out a viable balance between the local and the global remain crucial as the twenty-first century gets under way.

Notes

1. John R. Logan, ed., *The New Chinese City: Globalization and Market Reform* (Oxford: Blackwell Publishers, 2002), p. 21.

2. Vaclav Smil, *China's Past, China's Future: Energy, Food, Environment* (New York: RoutledgeCurzon, 2004), p. 214.

3. Anbin Shi, *A Comparative Approach to Redefining Chinese-ness in the Era of Globalization* (Lampeter, Wales: Edwin Mellen Press, 2003).

Appendix: Suggestions for Further Study

The literature in English on the history and civilizations of China is so extensive that careful selection is imperative for student and researcher alike. The effort here has been to suggest books that are broad enough in scope to serve as introductions to their topics, that incorporate sound and recent scholarship, that make for good reading, and that in their totality reflect a variety of approaches. This listing gives special attention to sources with well-researched bibliographies. When such sources are up-to-date and readily available, additional readings are generally not given. Please also note that the length of individual subsections depends in part on the availability of a good recent source for further readings—not on the intrinsic importance of a topic nor on the current state of research. Therefore, there may be fewer items given for a well-researched topic on which there is a recent bibliographical essay or other source of readings than for a topic on which less work has been done but for which there exists no good bibliography. Textbooks and collections of classroom readings are not included. Years given are dates of first publication. For the most part, we have not listed here books already cited in the individual chapters.

General

The website of the Association for Asian Studies (www.aasianst.org) maintains a list of the numerous websites dealing with China and the rest of East Asia. It also publishes the *Annual Bibliography of Asian Studies* online that is available in many libraries. Endymion Wilkinson, *Chinese History: A Manual* (Cambridge: Harvard University Asia Center, 1998), is the place to begin researching any topic through Qing. Keith Schoppa, *The Columbia Guide of Modern Chinese History* (New York: Columbia University Press, 2000), is the best place to begin further study of topics in modern Chinese history. The various volumes of the *Cambridge History of China* are a major resource. *China Review International* is a journal that reviews books on China in all periods and disciplines.

General Overviews and Interpretations

A book stimulating to neophyte and expert alike is Caroline Blunden and Mark Elvin, *Cultural Atlas of China* (1983, 1998). For anthropological perspectives on Chinese society and religion, Arthur Wolf, ed., *Religion and Ritual in Chinese Society* (1974), is still worth consulting but should be read in conjunction with Hymes, *Way and Byway*, cited in our discussion of the Song dynasty. For an overview on the burgeoning field of women's history, see Dorothy Ko, Jahyun Kim Haboush, and Joan R. Piggot, *Women and Confucian Cultures in Premodern China, Korea, and Japan* (2003). Also see Susan Mann and Yu-Yin Chen, eds., *Under Confucian Eyes: Writings on Gender in Chinese History* (2001).

Thomas J. Barfield, *The Perilous Frontier: Nomadic Empires and China, 221 B.C. to A.D. 1757* (1989), is a thoughtful and well-informed study of a major theme in Chinese history, but for the early period should be read in conjunction with Nicola Di Cosmo, *Ancient China and Its Enemies* (2001). Kang Chao, *Man and Land in Chinese History* (1986), is an ambitious interpretation of China's premodern economic history. Francesca Bray, *The Rice Economies: Technology & Development in Asian Societies* (1986), is an excellent introduction to rice agriculture whereas K. C. Chang, ed., *Food in Chinese Culture: Anthropological and Historical Perspectives* (1977), deals with an important (and delicious) subject. Another book that provides much food for thought, *The Retreat of the Elephants: An Environmental History of China* (2004) by Marek Elvin concerns premodern China. Unfortunately, it appeared too late for us to consult in writing our text. Language provides a key to any civilization: John de Francis, *The Chinese Language: Fact and Fantasy* (1984), and S. Robert Ramsey, *The Languages of China* (1987), are recommended.

The Arts and Literature

Sherman E. Lee, *A History of Far Eastern Art*, 5th ed. (1994), includes a consideration of Indian art that is helpful for understanding the Buddhist art of East Asia. It is a well-written, insightful, but also a demanding book. Michael Sullivan, *The Arts of China*, 4th ed. (1999), is a good survey. Also see *Three Thousand Years of Chinese Painting* by Richard M. Barnhart (1997). *Theories of the Arts in China* (1983), edited by Susan Bush and Christian Murck, is a stimulating collection of essays on a variety of important topics.

The best brief general survey of Chinese literature remains Liu Wu-chi, *An Introduction to Chinese Literature* (1966). For more detailed studies, see Victor H. Mair, ed., *Columbia History of Chinese Literature* (2001). For a concise introduction, also see J. Y. Liu, *Essentials of Chinese Literary Art* (1979). *The Indiana Companion to Traditional Chinese Literature* (1985), William H. Nienhauser, Jr., et al., eds., is indispensable but uneven (see review in *Journal of the American Oriental Society* 107 [1987] 1: 293–304). For a sensitive reading of Chinese poetry, see Stephen Owen, *Traditional Chinese Poetry and Poetics: Omens of the World* (1985). Tao-Ching Hsu, *The Chinese Concept of Theater* (1985), is multifaceted and highly informative. *The Confucian Progress: Autobiographical Writings in Traditional China* (1990), by Wu Pei-yi, offers unusually thoughtful and well formulated insights into literary and intellectual/psychological history.

When, in 1954, Joseph Needham published the first volume of his monumnetal series *Science and Civilization in China,* he began a project that continues after his death to produce well-researched, reliable, and stimulating studies of a wide range of sciences and technology. The most recent volume (1999), by Peter Golas, deals with mining. Two noteworthy contributions by Nathan Sivin, today's leading senior student of Chinese science, are *Medicine, Philosophy and Religion in Ancient China: Researches and Reflections* (1995) and *Way and the Word: Science and Medicine in Early China and Greece* (2002).

Thought and Religion

East Asian Civilizations: A Dialogue in Five Stages (1988), by Wm. Theodore de Bary, is a masterful summation that concludes by pointing to the need for both East Asia and the West to catch up with each other. For more recent perspectives, see *Rethinking Confucianism: Past and Present in China, Japan, Korea, and Vietnam,* edited by Benjamin A. Elman, John B. Duncan, and Herman Ooms (2002), and Thomas A. Wilson, ed., *On Sacred Grounds: Culture, Society, Politics, and the Formation of the Cult of Confucius* (2002). A basic resource for the student of Chinese philosophy is Wing-tsit Chan, *A Source Book in Chinese Philosophy* (1963), which covers all periods. The journal *Philosophy East and West* publishes articles on Chinese philosophy.

Donald S. Lopez, Jr., ed., *Religions in China in Practice* (1996), is an important entry into a tradition that has been been characterized as emphasizing orthopraxis rather than orthodoxy. Introductory surveys of Chinese religion are provided by Daniel L. Overmyer, *Religions of China* (1986) and Christian Jochim, *Chinese Religions* (1986). Anthony S. Cua, *Encyclopedia of Chinese Philosophy* (2003), Xinzhong Yao, ed., *Routledge Curzon Encyclopedia of Confucianism* (2003), and Livia Kohn, ed., *Handbook of Daoism* (2000), are valuable resources, and there are also good discussions on many Chinese topics in Mircea Eliade, ed., *The Encyclopedia of Religion,* in sixteen volumes (1987).

Part One: The Classical Civilization of China (Through the Han)

Early China is the leading scholarly journal focusing on this period. The essays in Michael Loewe and Edward Shaughnessy, eds., *Cambridge History of Ancient China: From the Origins of Civilization to 221 B.C.* (1999), reflect the sometimes but not always different perspectives of leading scholars summarizing research in a variety of disciplines. For Shaughnessy's own views, see *Before Confucius: Studies in the Creation of the Chinese Classics* (1997). All of David N. Keightley 's writings merit serious study. His *Time, Space, and Community in Late Shang China, ca. 1200–1045 B.C.* (2000) is highly recommended.

Poo Mu-chou, *In Search of Personal Welfare: A View of Ancient Chinese Religion* (1998), is an oustanding study as is Donald J. Harper, *Early Chinese Medical Literature: The Mawangdui Medical Manuscripts* (1998). Both are highly recommended for those interested in early Chinese religion.

Mark Lewis, *Sanctioned Violence in Early China* (1990), is an important book on a most important topic. A. C. Graham, *Disputers of the Tao: Philosophical Argument in Ancient China* (1989), is a masterly interpretative survey of early Chinese thought. Michael Puett, *The Ambivalence of Creation: Debates Concerning Innovation and Artifice in Early China* (2001), is itself highly innovative. Michael Nylan, *The Five "Confucian" Classics* (2001), is a superb introduction to some of the world's most influential texts. Also see Robin D. S. Yates, *Five Lost Classics: Tao, HuangLao, and Yin-yang in Han China* (1997). *Knowing Words: Wisdom and Cunning in the Classical Traditions of China and Greece,* by Lisa Raphals, is a fascinating comparative study. Benjamin Schwartz, *The World of Thought in Ancient China* (1985), has been described by A. C. Graham as "a lucid, accurate, agreebly written and comprehensive survey" written from the point of view of those who prefer to think of the Chinese as like ourselves" (*Times Literary Supplement,* July 18, 1986, p. 795).

For the Qin, see Martin Kern, *The Stele Inscriptions of Ch'in Shih-hwang: Text and Ritual in Early Chinese Imperial Representation* (2002). On Qin law, see A. F. P. Hulsewé, *Remnants of Ch'in Law: An Annotated Translation of the Ch'in Legal and Administrative Rules of the 3rd Century B.C., Discovered in Yün-meng Prefecture, Hupei Province, in 1975* (1985), and Robin Yates and Katrina McLeod, *Forms of Ch'in Law: An Annotated Translation of the Feng-chen Shih* (1981).

Important perspectives on the Han are provided by Martin Powers, *Art and Political Expression in Early China* (1991), and Wu Hung, *Wu Liang Shrine: The Ideolology of Early Chinese Pictorial Art* (1989). For the history of women, see Lisa Raphal, *Sharing the Light: Representations of Women and Virtue in Early China* (1998); Michael Nylan, "Golden Spindles and Axes: Elite Women in the Achaemenid and Han Empires," in *The Sage and the Second Sex, Essays on Classicism, Confucian Learning, and Feminism,* edited by Li Chenyang (2000, pp. 199–222); and Miranda Brown, "Mothers and Sons in Warring States and Han China, 453 B.C.–A.D. 220," in *Nan Nü: Men, Women and Gender in Early and Imperial China,* 5.2 (2003).

For the period's (and China's) own greatest historian, there is Burton Watson's *Ssu-ma Ch'ien: Grand Historian of China* (1958), Watson's very readable translation, *Records of the Historian: Chapters from the Shih Chi of Ssu-ma Ch'ien,* two volumes (1961), and Michael Nylan's, "Sima Qian: A True Historian" in *Early China* (23–24 [1998–99], pp. 203–246). Roger T. Ames, *The Art of Rulership: A Study in Ancient Chinese Political Thought* (1983), is a translation of a major Han text by a scholar who in collaboration with the philosopher David L. Hall went on to publish a number of studies of Chinese thought in comparative perspective. For life and poetry, also see Anne Birrell, *Popular Songs and Ballads of Han China* (1988).

Part Two: China in a Buddhist Age

Buddhism in China

The literature on Buddhism in English is rich and varied. Heinz Bechert and Richard Gombrich, *The World of Buddhism: Monks and Nuns in Society and Culture* (1984), is a well-illustrated introduction.

Donald S. Lopez, Jr., *The Story of Buddhism: A Concise Guide to Its History and Teachings* (New York: HarperCollins, 2001), is a more recent introduction. Two well-regarded books on Buddhist thought are Paul Williams, *Mahayana Buddhism: The Doctrinal Foundations* (New York: Routledge, 1989), and Roger J. Corless, *The Vision of Buddhism: The Space Under the Tree* (New York: Paragon House, 1989). Donald W. Mitchell, *Buddhism: Introducing the Buddhist Experience* (New York: Oxford University Press, 2002), focuses on the history of Buddhist ideas and religious practice.

For a brief account of Buddhism in China viewed as a rich and complex historical process of interaction between China and the Indian religion, see Arthur F. Wright, *Buddhism in Chinese History* (1959). Of all the sects of East Asian Buddhism, Chan has attracted the most attention in the West. The most scholarly translation of a key text is Philip P. Yampolsky, *The Platform Sutra of the Sixth Patriarch: The Text of the Tunhuang Manuscript* (1967). The relationship between Chan (Zen) and the arts remains as difficult to define as the religion itself, but the arts, especially painting, testify to the power of Zen even as they offer an approach to understanding. Enthusiastically recommended is Jan Fontain and Money L. Hickman, *Zen Painting and Calligraphy* (1970), a catalog of an exhibition of both Chinese and Japanese works.

Robert Ford Campany, *To Live as Long as Heaven and Earth, a Translation and Study of Ge Hong's Tradition of Divine Transcendents* (2002), is a major recent contribution to the study of Daoism during the period of disunity with a good bibliography.

Secular Developments

Studies in Chinese secular culture during the period of division include Robert Van Gulik, *Hsi K'ang and His Poetic Essay on the Lute* (1940). Richard B. Mather has translated the *Shishuo Xinyu* under the title *A New Account of Tales of the World* (1976). This very learned and meticulous translation makes available in English a major source for the study of the period's sophisticates. Three out of a projected eight volumes have been published to date of David Knechtges' monumental translation of China's oldest surviving literary anthology, *Wen Xuan or Selections of Refined Literature* by Xiao Tong (1982, 1987, 1996).

Sui and Tang

The Cambridge History of China, Volume 3, *Sui and T'ang, 580–906, Part 1* (1979), edited by Denis Twitchett, is a major resource. Arthur F. Wright, *The Sui Dynasty* (1978), remains authoritative. Charles Hartman, *Han Yü and the T'ang Search for Unity* (1986), deals with political as well as literary and intellectual history. David

McMullen, *State and Scholars in T'ang China* (1988), is a major work of scholarship that, however, may be tough going to a beginner. Peter Bol, *This Culture of Ours—Intellectual Transitions in T'ang and Sung China* (1992), is demanding and essential reading.

Tang poetry is well represented in anthologies as well as in studies of individual poets. Selecting from a number of titles is in part a matter of taste, but it is generally recognized that one of the best books by a master translator is Arthur Waley, *The Life and Times of Po Chü-i* (1949). Although not as fully biographical as Waley's book, the following studies also provide windows on Tang life: Arthur Cooper, *Li Po and Tu Fu* (1973); David R. McCraw, *Du Fu's Laments from the South* (1992); A. R. Davis, *Tu Fu* (1971); and three books by Stephen Owen—*The Poetry of Meng Chiao and Han Yü* (1975), *The Poetry of the Early T'ang* (1977), and *The Great Age of Chinese Poetry: The High T'ang* (1981). For late Tang poetry, see A. C. Graham, *Poems of the Late T'ang* (1965), and James J. Y. Liu, *The Poetry of Li Shang-yin* (1969). A leading student of Tang culture is Edward H. Schafer. Two of his finest books are *The Golden Peaches of Samarkand: A Study of Tang Exotics* (1963) and *The Vermillion Bird: Tang Images of the South* (1967). For a fascinating view of Tang China as seen through the eyes of a visiting Japanese monk, see Edwin O. Reischauer, *Ennin's Travels in T'ang China* (1955).

Part Three: Late Imperial/Early Modern

Much of the general literature considers late imperial and/or early modern as beginning in the Ming and focuses on that period; works are mostly listed there although they have implications also for Song/Yuan. One such that we think does belong here is Theodore Huters and R. Bin Wong, eds., *Culture and State in Chinese History: Conventions, Accommodations, and Critiques* (1997). For insights into the transformation of the environment, see *Sediments of Time: Environment and Society in Chinese History,* edited by Mark Elvin and Liu Ts'ui-jung (1998). The individual contributions are of high quality although some are more demanding than others. Nicholas K. Menzies, *Forest and Land Management in Imperial China* (1994), is similarly broad in scope. R. Keith Schoppa, *Xian Lake—Song Full of Tears: Nine Centuries of Chinese Life at Xiang Lake* (2002), is highly recommended as are the books by Marks and Perdue cited in our text.

A book on economic history and thought rare in its broad chronological coverage is Richard Von Glahn, *Fountain of Fortune: Money and Monetary Policy in China 1000–1700* (1990). *Kinship Organization in Late Imperial China 1000–1400,* edited by Patricia B. Buckley and James J Watson (1986), is an influential volume which, like James L. Watson and Evelyn S. Rawski, eds., *Death Ritual in Late Imperial and Modern China* (1988), exemplifies fruitful collaboration of anthropology and history.

Song China

For current scholarship, see the *Journal of Song-Yuan Studies*. Robert P. Hymes, *Statesmen and Gentlemen: The Elite of Fu-Chou, ChiangHsi in Northern and Southern Sung* (1986), is essential reading for social history, as is John W. Chaffee, *The Thorny Gates of Learning in Sung China: A Social History of Examinations* (2nd ed., 1995). Another major contribution to the relationship between state and society is *Powerful Relations: Kinship Status and The State in Sung China (960–1279)*, by Beverly J. Bossler (1998). Recommended as another major study is Thomas H. C. Lee, *Government Education and Examinations in Sung China* (1985). Village structure is analyzed in Brian E. McKnight, *Village and Bureaucracy in Southern Sung China* (1971), who is also the leading authority on Song law. Among his more recent contributions is *The Enlightened Judgments: Ch'ing-ming Chi: The Sung Dynasty Collection* (1999), translated by McKnight and James T. C. Liu. Liu's *China Turning Inward: Intellectual and Political Changes in the Early Twelfth Century* (1988) remains an important and influential study.

A stimulating discussion of the Song economy in the light of world history is provided in the first chapter of William H. McNeill, *The Pursuit of Power: Technology, Armed Force, and Society since A.D. 1000* (1982). For insights into the vital world of maritime trade, see Angela Schottenhammer, ed., *The Emporium of the World: Maritime Quanzhou, 1000–1400* (2001). Also see Billy K. L. So, *Prosperity, Regions, and Institutions in Maritime China: The South Fukien Pattern, 946–1368* (2000).

Family and Property in Sung China: Yuan Ts'ai's Precepts for Social Life (1984), Patricia B. Ebrey, trans., is a fascinating and important contribution to social history as is her book, *The Inner Quarters: Marriage and the Lives of Chinese Women in the Sung Period* (1993). Richard von Glahn, *The Country of Streams and Grottoes: Expansion, Settlement, and the Civilizing of the Sichuan Frontier in Song Times* (1987), deals with a major theme in a sophisticated manner.

Ronald C. Egan, *The Literary Works of Ou-yang Hsiu (1007–72)* (1984), examines a key literary and intellectual figure. Michal A. Fuller, *The Road to East Slope: The Development of Su Shi's Poetic Voice* (1990), is a study of the dynasty's major poet and literatus. For the study of Song poetry, James J. Y. Liu, *Major Lyricists of the Northern Sung* (1974), has the great merit of including for each poem the Chinese text, a word for word rendition, and a polished translation. A thoughtful and highly commendable book is Jonathan Chaves, *Mei Yao-ch'en and the Development of Early Sung Poetry* (1976). Chaves is also the author of the excellent and delightful, *Heaven My Blanket, Earth My Pillow—Poems from the Sung Dynasty by Yang Wan-li* (1975). Also see Julie Landau, *Beyond Spring: Tz'u Poems of the Sung Dynasty* (1994). There are a number of other worthy books on Song poetry that cannot be listed here, but we should mention a study of China's foremost woman poet: *Li Ch'ing-chao* by P'in-ch'ing Hu (1966). For readers interested in the history of music, there is Rulan Chao Pian, *Song Dynasty Musical Sources and Their Interpretation* (1967). Also recommended is Peter C. Sturman, *Mi Fu and the Art of Calligraphy in Northern Song China* (1997).

A prime source for the study of Neo-Confucian thought is Wing-tsit Chan, trans., *Reflections on Things at Hand: The Neo-Confucian Anthology Compiled by Chu Hsi and Lu Tsu-ch'ien* (1967). Among the many other contributions by Wingtsit Chan to the study of Neo-Confucianism are his translation of *Neo-Confucian Terms Explained (The Pei-hsi tzu-i) by Ch'en Ch'un, 1159–1223* (1986) and his editing of *Chu Hsi and Neo-Confucianism* (1986), a wide-ranging volume of essays by East Asian as well as Western scholars. A fine study of one of the alternatives to Zhu Xi is Hoyt C. Tillman, *Utilitarian Confucianism: Ch'en Liang's Challenge to Chu Hsi* (1982). Tillman is also author of *Confucian Discourse and Chu Hsi's Ascendancy* (1992), an important book that views Zhu Xi in the perspective of the intellectual life of his time. See also Bol's book cited under earlier under "Sui and Tang."

The Yuan

Volume 6 of the Cambridge History, *Alien Regimes and Border States 907–1368* (1994), includes chapters by the major scholars in the field as well as useful bibliographic essays. For those who would like to explore Yuan culture, there are two books that are authoritative and sensitive: Chungwen Shih, *The Golden Age of Chinese Drama* (1976), and Hok-lam Chan and Wm. Theodore de Bary, eds., *Yuan Thought* (1982), which remains the best book on its subject.

The study of Marco Polo is a field all to itself. http://www.silk-road.com/artl/marcopolo.shtml is a useful and attractive website; also see http://www.usnews.com/usnews/doubleissue/mysteries/marco.htm. A learned and delightful older study is Leonardo Olschki, *Marco Polo's Asia: An Introduction to His "Description of the World" Called "il Milione"* (1960). For other travel accounts, see Christopher Dawson, ed., *Mission to Asia: Narratives and Letters of the Franciscan Missionaries in Mongolia and China in the Thirteenth and Fourteenth Centuries* (1955). Also see Jeannette Mirsky, ed., *The Great Chinese Travelers* (1964), which includes three accounts falling into this period. For a traveler in the opposite direction, see Morris Rossabi, *Voyager from Xanadu: Raban Sauma and the First Journey from China to the West* (1992).

Ming/Qing

Before turning to the last two dynasties individually, it behooves us to mention a few books on Late Imperial China that are useful for students of either or both periods. These include the influential and still very useful collection of essays edited by G. William Skinner, *The City in Late Imperial China* (1977). Randall A. Dorgen, *Controlling the Dragon: Confucian Engineers and the Yellow River in Late Imperial China* (2001), studies an important topic. Philip C. C. Huang, *The Peasant Family and Rural Development in the Yangzi Delta, 1350–1988* (1990), and its counterpart, *The Peasant Economy and Social Change in North China* (1985), are both rich in stimulating interpretations. Francesca Bray, *Technology and Gender: Fabrics of Power in Late Imperial China* (1997), is superb.

On intellectual history, see Kang-Ching Liu, ed., *Orthodoxy in Late Imperial China* (1990), and its companion volume, which includes important work on religious history, *Heterodoxy in Late Imperial China* (2004), edited by Liu and Richard

Shek. Also see Richard Smith, *Cosmology, Ontology, and Human Efficacy* (1993). Benjamin A. Elman is a leading scholar interested in the history of thought and institutions. See his *From Philosophy to Philology: Intellectual and Social Aspects of Change in Late Imperial China* (1984) and *A Cultural History of Civil Examinations in Late Imperial China* (2000), as well as *Education and Society in Late Imperial China, 1600–1900,* edited by Elman and Alexander Woodside (1994).

Robert E. Hegel, *Reading Illustrated Fiction in Late Imperial China* (1998), discusses the physical appearance of books and the expectations of those who read them. Also see Hegel, *The Novel in Seventeenth Century China* (1981).

Ming

The Cambridge History of China, Volume 7, Part 1, *The Ming Dynasty, 1368–1644* (1988), Frederick W. Mote and Denis Twitchett, eds., is a detailed narrative history of the dynasty, and Part 2 (1998) consists of topical essays. A number of studies on social and economic history begin with the Ming but also include later history. A still useful survey of major topics complete with excellent suggestions for further reading is Lloyd E. Eastman, *Family, Fields, and Ancestors* (1988). An authoritative study of an important subject is Ray Huang, *Taxation and Government Finance in 16th Century Ming China* (1974). A real treasure house of information is the monumental *Dictionary of Ming Biography, 1368–1644,* two volumes (1976), edited by L. Carrington Goodrich and Chaoying Fang.

Wm. Theodore de Bary, *Neo-Confucian Orthodoxy and the Learning of the Mind-and-Heart* (1981), takes Neo-Confucianism from the Song to the Ming and beyond. Also see Wm. Theodore de Bary, et al., *Self and Society in Ming Thought* (1970). On Wang Yangming there are two complementary studies: Julia Ching, *To Acquire Wisdom: The Way of Wang Yangming* (1976), and Tu Wei-ming, *Neo-Confucian Thought in Action: Wang Yangming's Youth (1472–1509)* (1976). On late Ming thought, see Wm. Theodore de Bary et al., *The Unfolding of Neo-Confucianism* (1975), Edward Ch'ien, *Chiao Hung and the Restructuring of Neo-Confucian Thought in the Late Ming* (1985), and Irene Bloom, ed. and trans., *Knowledge Painfully Acquired: The K'un-chih chi by Lo Ch'in-shu* (1987).

Craig Clunas, *Pictures and Visuality in Early Modern China* (1997), and his *Fruitful Sites: Garden Culture in Ming Dynasty China* (1996) are stimulating and informative. Music as well as art was central to the culture. For music we are fortunate to have Joseph S. C. Lam, *State Sacrifices and Music in Ming China: Orthodoxy, Creativity, and Expressiveness* (1998). Literature provides fascinating vignettes of Ming life as well as insights into Ming sensibilities. For translations, see the *Indiana Companion to Chinese Literature* (see earlier under "General Works"). Andrew H. Plaks, *The Four Masterworks of the Ming Novel* (1987), is superb. For painting, see James Cahill, *Parting at the Shore: Chinese Painting of the Early and Middle Ming Dynasty, 1368–1580* (1978), and his *The Distant Mountains: Chinese Painting of the Late Ming Dynasty 1570–1644* (1982), as well as Anne De Coursey Clapp, *The Painting of T'ang Yin* (1991), which also provides insights into the social life of Ming Suzhou.

First Encounters

David E. Mungello, *The Great Encounter of China and the West, 1500–1800* (1999), is a short and highly recommended account complete with bibliography. Other books on China's relations with the rest of the world are the following: Philip Snow, *The Star Raft; China's Encounter with Africa* (New York: Weidenfeld & Nicolson, 1988); Jacques Gernet, *China and the Christian Impact: A Conflict of Cultures* (New York: Cambridge University Press and Paris: Editions de la Maison des sciences de l'homme, 1982), trans. Janet Lloyd, deserves a close reading. Also see L. J. Gallagher, trans., *China in the Sixteenth Century: The Journals of Matteo Ricci* (1953). Jonathan D. Spence, *The Memory Palace of Matteo Ricci* (1984), is a fascinating exercise in comparative history. For the later history of Christianity, see Daniel H Bays, *Christianity in China from the Eighteenth Century to the Present* (1996). For the arts, see Michael Sullivan, *Meeting of Eastern and Western Art* (1973, 1989).

Qing

The recent publication of *The Cambridge History*, Volume 9: Part 1, *The Ch'ing Empire to 1800*, edited by Willard J. Peterson (2003), reduces the number of studies that we need to list separately here. Readers should, however, be aware of the very recent work edited by Lynn A. Struve, *The Qing Formation in World Historical Time* (2004), a thoughtful collection of essays viewing Qing in terms of world history, which adopts a global perspective. Evelyn Rawski, *The Last Emperors: A Social History of Qing Imperial Institutions* (Berkeley: University of California Press, 1998), is an excellent account of the Qing as a multiethnic dynasty. Pamela K. Crossley, a leading scholar of Manchu studies, has published *Orphan Warriors— Three Manchu Generations and the End of the Qing World* (1990), a general survey titled *The Manchus* (1996), and *A Translucent Mirror: History and Identity in Qing Imperial Ideology* (1999). Also see Mark Elliott, *The Manchu Way: The Eight Banners and Ethnic Identity in Late Imperial China* (2001), and Edward J. M. Rhoades, *Manchu and Han Ethnic Relations and Political Power in Late Qing China, 1861–1928* (2000).

For demographic information, see *One Quarter of Humanity: Malthusian Mythology and Chinese Realities, 1700–2000*, by James Z. Lee and Wang Feng (1999). For the eighteenth century, see Susan Naquin and Evelyn S. Rawski, *Chinese Society in the Eighteenth Century* (1987), an ambitious synthesis and excellent source for additional references on government as well as other topics. William T. Rowe, *Saving the World: Chen Hongmou and Elite Consciousness in Eighteenth-Century China* (2001), is a major study of political thought and action. R. Kent Guy, *The Emperor's Four Treasures: Scholars and the State in the Late Ch'ien-lung Era* (1987), is illuminating on both scholars and state. Jonathan D. Spence, *Treason by the Book* (2001), and Philip A. Kuhn, *Soulstealers: The Chinese Sorcery Scare of 1768* (1990), are sophisticated, well-written accounts rich in insights on Qing political culture. Harold L. Kahn, *Monarchy in the Emperor's Eyes: Image and Reality in the Ch'ien-lung Reign* (1971), has fun showing how elusive the reality behind the image truly is.

Arthur Waley, *Yuan Mei: Eighteenth Century Chinese Poet* (1956), is a sensitively drawn portrait. Research and interpretation of the century's and China's most acclaimed novel has grown into a major industry known as "Red Studies." Two outstanding studies are Andrew H. Plaks, *Archetype and Allegory in the Dream of the Red Chamber* (1976), and Anthony Yu, *Rereading the Stone: Desire and the Making of Fiction in Dream of the Red Chamber* (1997). Also see Shang Wei, *Rulin Waishi and Cultural Transformation in Later Imperial China* (2003). Kai-wing Chow, *The Rise of Ritualism in Late Imperial China: Ethics, Classics, and Lineage Discourse* (1994), is a major contribution to intellectual history for which also see the books by Benjamin Elman listed above.

The texture of ordinary life is brilliantly conveyed by Jonathan Spence in *Death of Woman Wang* (1979). More elite women are studied by Susan Mann as quoted in our text. Also see *Under Confucian Eyes: Writings on Gender in Chinese History,* Susan Mann and Yu-Yin Chen, eds. (2001). See http://www.pem.org/yinyutang/, the Peabody Essex Museum website, for a Qing merchant house.

Part Four: China in the Modern World

Paul A. Cohen, *Discovering History in China: American Historical Writing on the Recent Chinese Past* (1984), is a thoughtful account of some of the constructs and concerns underlying American Chinese studies. Also see his more recent *China Unbound: Evolving Perspectives on the Chinese Past* (2003).

The Long Nineteenth Century (to 1911)

The Cambridge History of China, Volume 11, Part II, *Late Ch'ing, 1800–1911,* edited by John K. Fairbank and Kwang-Ching Liu (1980), remains a valuable reference with useful bibliographical essays.

Jane Kate Leonard, *Controlling from Afar: the Daoguang Emperor's Management of the Grand Canal Crisis, 1824–1826* (1996), is a study of China's internal crisis. For subsequent internal politics, see the study by James M. Polachek cited in the text. For an important perspective on early Sino-Western relations, see Jane K. Leonard, *Wei Yuan and China's Rediscovery of the Maritime World* (1984). Some of the denizens of the maritime world are studied in Dian H. Murray, *Pirates of the South China Coast, 1796–1889* (1984). For a different, comparative and less maritime-oriented perspective, see James L. Hevia, *Cherishing Men from Afar: Qing Ritual and the Macartney Embassy of 1793* (1995). Also see the same author's review article, "Opium, Empire, and Modern History," *China Review International* (10, No. 2 [Fall 2003] pp. 307–326).

Hankow: Commerce and Society in a Chinese City, 1796–1889 and *Hankow: Conflict and Community in a Chinese City, 1786–1895* (1984, 1989), both by William T. Rowe, summarized much research even as they broke new ground. Yen-p'ing Hao, *The Commercial Revolution in Nineteenth Century China* (1986), is an authoritative account of the modern sector.

On Christianity, see the book by Daniel H. Bays cited above, and for the Taiping Rebellion the book by Jonathan Spence quoted in the text is an excellent narrative account. Historians have increasingly turned to local history in their search for answers to major questions of social and political history. A fine example of the genre is Mary B. Rankin, *Elite Activism and Political Transformation in China: Zhejiang Province, 1865–1911* (1986).

The study of modern Chinese intellectual history has been deeply influenced by the brilliant writings of Joseph R. Levenson, especially his *Confucian China and Its Modern-Fate,* three volumes (1972, 1958–1965). Also see Maurice Meisner and Rhoads Murphy, eds., *The Mozartian Historian: Essays on the Works of Joseph R. Levenson* (1976). A different approach is taken by Chang Hao in his *Chinese Intellectuals in Crisis: Search for Order and Meaning, 1890–1911* (1987). An excellent example of what can be accomplished by a master in the field of intellectual biography is Benjamin Schwartz, *In Search of Wealth and Power: Yen Fu and the West* (1964). *An Intellectual History of Modern China,* by Merle Goldman and Leo Ou-fan Lee (2002), provides a useful survey. Also see Kirk A. Denton, ed., *Modern Chinese Literary Thought: Writings on Literature, 1893–1945* (1996).

Two of the leading figures during the last decade of the Qing are examined in Daniel H. Bays, *China Enters the Twentieth Century: Chang Chih-tung and the Issues of a New Age, 1895–1909* (1978), and Stephen R. MacKinnon, *Power and Politics in Late Imperial China: Yuan Shi-kai in Beijing and Tianjin, 1901–1908* (1980). Also see Joan Judge, *Print and Politics: "Shibao" and the Culture of Reform in Late Qing China* (1996).

Luke S. K. Kwong, *A Mosaic of the Hundred Days* (1984), lays some myths to rest. For newer research and analysis, see Rebecca E. Karl and Peter Zarrow, ed., *Rethinking the 1898 Reform Period: Political and Cultural Change in Late Qing China* (2002). Paul A. Cohen, *History in Three Keys: The Boxers as Event, Experience and Myth* (1987), is a good place to begin reading about the Boxer Rebellion.

Periodizations differ, reflecting different purposes and some fine books straddle our headings. A case in point is *Remaking the Chinese City: Modernity and National Identity, 1900–1950* (2000), edited by Joseph Esherick, a social historian whose other books are also recommended.

Bonnie S. McDougall and Kam Louie, *The Literature of China in the Twentieth Century* (1997), is one of the few books that treats the twentieth century as a whole. James R. Pusey, *China and Charles Darwin* (1983), is very informative on Liang Qiqao, but it may turn out that a certain social Darwinism continued throughout the century.

Part Five: Building a New China

Republican China is the subject of Volumes 11 and 12 of *The Cambridge History.* The discussions found there should be read in conjunction with *Reappraising Republican China* (2000), a collection of essays edited by Frederick Wakeman, Jr., and Richard L. Edmonds, which to some extent cast a more favorable light on the period. Also see Lloyd E. Eastman, *Seeds of Destruction: Nationalist China in War and Revolution* (1984), and his *Family, Fields, and Ancestors,* mentioned earlier. For additional readings on an important topic, see "Warlord Studies," a review essay by Diana Lary in *Modern China* (VI, No. 4 [1980]: 439–470).

The bitter rejection of tradition by the leaders of the May Fourth Movement continues to generate much controversy, and it may be too early for a general history. For a study of the post-Imperial city, see David Strand, *Rickshaw Beijing: City People and Politics in the 1920s* (1989), a masterful account of its multifaceted subject. Among the rich literature on Shanghai is Leo Ou-fan Lee, *Shanghai Modern: The Flowering of a New Urban Culture in China, 1930–45* (1999).

Thomas G. Rawski, *Economic Growth in Prewar China* (1989), is highly informative. His contention that China's economy grew from 1912 to 1937 is a valuable contribution to economic history and discourse. For business history, see Sherman Cochran, *Encountering Chinese Networks: Western, Japanese, and Chinese Corporations in China, 1880–1937* (2001). Frank Dikötter, *Crime, Punishment and the Prison in Modern China* (2002), analyzes prison policies in the pre-Communist period.

The warlord period is particularly complex. Edward A. McCord, *The Power of the Gun: The Emergence of Modern Chinese Warlordism* (1993), includes an analysis of interpretative approaches as well as a detailed study focusing on Hubei and Hunan. Prasenjet Duara, *Culture, Power, and the State: Rural China, 1900–1942* (1988), is a major influential interpretative study.

Arif Dirlik, *The Origins of Chinese Communism* (1989) is thoughtful and complex. Philip Short, *Mao: A Life* (2000) is the most comprehensive study of Mao available in English.

Jeffrey C. Kinkley, *Chinese Justice, the Fiction: Law and Literature in Modern China* (2000), is far reaching and outstanding. Also see Kinkley's *The Odyssey of Shen Congwen* (1987). Leo Ou-fan Lee, *The Romantic Generation of Modern Chinese Writers* (1981), and the same author's *Voices from the Iron House: A Study of Lu Xun* (1987), as well as the conference volume he edited, *Lu Xun and His Legacy* (1985), are highly recommended. Ralph Crozier, *Art and Revolution in Modern China: The Lingnan (Cantonese) School of Painting, 1906–1951* (1988), explores the relationship between art and politics and that between nation and province.

The People's Republic of China

An excellent account of the various approaches scholars have used in their attempts to analyze the Chinese revolution is provided by the introduction to Kathleen Hartford and Steven M. Goldstein, eds., *Single Sparks: China's Rural Revolutions* (1989). Volume 14 of *The Cambridge History* (1987), edited by Roderick MacFarquhar and John K. Fairbank, deals with the People's Republic from 1949 to 1965 and contains discussions of bibliography.

A leading student of ideological developments in China is Maurice Meisner, whose *Marxism, Maoism, and Utopianism: Eight Essays* (1982) is recommended. A major topic is examined in James L. Watson, ed., *Class and Social Stratification in*

Post-Revolution China (1984). *Popular Chinese Literature and Performing Arts in the People's Republic of China, 1949–1979* (1984), edited by Bonnie S. McDougall, is another valuable collection of essays.

Two important and very useful studies of China under Mao are John Wilson Lewis and Xue Litai, *China Builds the Bomb* (1998), and Judith Shapiro, *Mao's War Against Nature* (2001). A book that belongs on everyone's list is Richard P. Madsen, *Morality and Power in a Chinese Village* (1984). Its empirical basis is an outstanding village study by Anita Chan, Richard Madsen, and Jonathan Unger, *Chen Village: The Recent History of a Peasant Community* (1984). Its sequel, Chan and Unger, *Chen Village under Mao and Deng* (1984 and 1992), is also highly recommended. Zhang Xinxin and Sang Ye, *Chinese Lives: An Oral History of Contemporary China* (1987), edited by W. J. E. Jenner and Delia Davin, is a collection of personal vignettes—windows into life in China.

For the cultural revolution, see Roderick MacFarquar, *The Origins of the Cultural Revolution* (1974), Elizabeth Perry, *Proletarian Power: Shanghai in the Cultural Revolution* (1997), Barbara Barnouin, *Ten Years of Turbulence: The Chinese Cultural Revolution* (1993), and Heng Liang, *Son of the Revolution* (1993), translated by Judith Shapiro. The fallout of the Cultural Revolution years can be sampled in *Mao's Harvest: Voices from China's New Generation* (1983), edited by Helen F. Siu and Zelda Stern. Also see Yue Daiyun and Carolyn Wakeman, *To the Storm: The Odyssey of a Revolutionary Chinese Woman* (1985), a gripping personal account.

Orville Schell, *Mandate of Heaven: A New Generation of Entrepreneurs, Dissidents, Bohemians, and Technocrats Lay Claims to China's Future* (1994), is an account of Tiananmen and its aftermath by an experienced China observer. Tony Saich, ed., *The Chinese People's Movement: Perspectives on Spring 1989* (1990), provides analyses and includes a chronology.

A good way to keep up with current developments is in the pages of *The China Quarterly*. Economic development has first priority in Deng Xiaoping's China so *The Political Economy of Reform in Post-Mao China* (1985), edited by Elizabeth J. Perry and Christine Wong, is especially welcome. For the countryside, also see Ashwani Saith, *The Re-emergence of the Chinese Peasantry: Aspects of Rural Decollectivisation* (1987). John P. Burns and Stanley Rosen, eds., *Policy Conflicts in Post-Mao China: A Documentary Survey with Analysis* (1986), is very useful. Energy policy is the focus of a fine study of how Chinese politics operate: Kenneth Lieberthal and Michael Oksenberg, *Policy Making in China: Leaders, Structures, and Process* (1988).

One of the distinguished contributors to Jonathan Ungar, ed., *The Nature of Chinese Politics* (2002), is Andrew J. Nathan., an authority on contemporary China and author of *China's Crisis: Dilemmas of Reforms and Prospects for Democracy* (1990) and other studies. Also see *The Paradox of China's Post-Mao Reforms* (1999), edited by Merle Goldman, and R. MacFarquar. Doug Guthrie, *Dragon in a Three-Piece Suit: The Emergence of Capitalism in China* (1999), is right on track.

Jun Jing, *The Temple of Memories: History, Power, and Morality in a Chinese Village* (1996), is a superb study of a branch of the Kong clan, which claims descent from Confucius, and how they revived their tradition and built a temple to the sage. Vaclav Svil, an outstanding student of the Chinese environment, has recently published a collection from his previous writings along with his latest reflections in *China's Past, China's Future: Energy, Food, Environment* (2004). Also see Lester Ross, *Environmental Policy in China* (1988).

The arts are worth studying for their own sake as well as for what they reveal about the people who produce and support them. Julia F. Andrews, author of *Between the Thunder and the Rain: Chinese Painting from the Opium War to the Cultural Revolution, 1840–1979* (2000) and *Painters and Politics in the People's Republic of China, 1949–1979* (1994) is an art historian well grounded in history. Also see Andrews and Kuiyi Shen, *Century in Crisis: Modernity and Tradition in the Art of Twentieth-Century China* (1998), Ellen J. Laing, *The Winking Owl: Art in the People's Republic of China* (1988), and Joan L. Cohen, *The New Chinese Painting, 1949–1986* (1987).

Richard C. Kraus, a political scientist with a keen eye and ear has written *Brushes with Power: Modern Politics and the Chinese Art of Calligraphy* (1991) and *Pianos and Politics in China: Middle-Class Ambitions and the Struggle over Western Music* (1989). Yingjih Zhang, *Encyclopedia of Chinese Film* (1999), is a useful reference work. Also see Cyrus Berry, ed., *Perspectives on Chinese Cinema* (1991), and Linda C. Ehrlich and David Desser, eds., *Cinematic Landscapes: Observations on the Visual Arts and Cinema of China and Japan* (1994).

Jeffrey C. Kinkley, *After Mao: Chinese Literature and Society, 1978–81* (1985), is an analysis of the post-Mao literary world by a leading authority on contemporary literature and intellectuals. Another thoughtful and authoritative book is Perry Link, *The Uses of Literature: Life in the Socialist Chinese Literary System* (2000). For popular culture, see Michael Dutton, *Streetlife in China* (1998).

Wu Hung, *Chinese Art at the Crossroads* (2002), makes for rewarding reading, like his other books and essays such as his contribution to *Inside Out* (1998), the catalog to a notable exhibition of the works of artists who live on the mainland, Taiwan, and elsewhere. Similarly, Chinese writers from all over are included in *Running Wild: New Chinese Writers*, edited by David Der-Wei Wang with Jeanne Tai (1994). Also see *Chinese Literature in the Second Half of a Modern Century: A Critical Survey* (2000), edited by Pang-Yuan Chi and Wang, who stress here as elsewhere commonalities in Chinese writing wherever performed.

Travel accounts generally reveal as much about the traveler as they do about China, and it would be interesting to compare systematically the reports of recent visitors with those of foreigners who visited China in earlier times. Among the most engaging of the contemporary books are those by professional writers (Simon de Beauvoir, Alberto Moravia, and Colin Thubron), those by journalists with Chinese experience (Edgar Snow and Seymour Topping), and those by specialists in Chinese studies (Ross Terrill, Simon Leys, and Orville Schell). Especially noteworthy are books by those who have resided in China for a time as university teachers (Tani E. Barlow and Donald M. Lowe), journalists (Fox Butterfield and David Bonavia), or embassy officials (Robert Garside).

Taiwan and Hong Kong

The *Cambridge History* volume does not include Taiwan (which will be discussed in Volume 15). Murray A. Rubinstein, *Taiwan: A New History* (1999), is a good place to begin reading about the history of Taiwan. Important books that have appeared subsequent to publication of Rubinstein's history include Jay Taylor, *The Generalissimo's Son: Chiang Ching-kuo and the Revolutions in China and Taiwan* (2000), and Stephane Corcuff, *Memories of the Future: National Identity Issues and the Search for a New Taiwan* (2002). Among older studies expecially worth consulting, see Thomas B. Gold, *State and Society in the Taiwan Miracle* (1986), and for earlier social history, see Johanna M. Meskill, *A Chinese Pioneer Family: The Lins of Wu-feng, Taiwan, 1729–1895* (1979).

Issues of identity are also foremost in the minds of Hong Kong artists and intellectuals. See *Hong Kong Becoming Chinese,* a series published in Armonk, NY, by M. E. Sharp under the editorship of Ming K. Chan and Gerald A Postiglione.

The Sociology/Anthropology of Knowledge

Postmodernism has given new urgency to the need for students be fully aware of the human context of the work in their discipline. Archeology is no exception to this rule, but archeologists occupy a special place in China as intellectuals who work with their hands as well as minds and do so throughout a country that continues to prize history. That at least is the argument advanced by Erika E. S. Evasdottir in *Obedient Authority: Chinese Intellectuals and Their Achievement of Orderly Life* (2004), a brilliant anthropological examination of the lives and careers of archeologists in China today. Published just as we complete our work, it is a completely contemporary book that takes us back to the beginnings.

Credits

Chapter 6. 6.02: Photograph © 2005 Museum of Fine Arts, Boston **6.03:** © Collection of the Palace Museum, Bejing, China **6.04:** © TNM Image Archives, http://TnmArchives.jp/ **6.05:** © National Palace Museum, Taiwan, Republic of China **6.06:** © National Palace Museum, Taiwan, Republic of China **6.07:** © National Palace Museum, Taiwan, Republic of China **6.08:** © National Palace Museum, Taiwan, Republic of China **6.09:** Courtesy of Michael Sullivan and Dominique Darbois

Chapter 7. 7.02: © Abe Collection, Osaka Municipal Museum of Fine Arts **7.03:** © National Palace Museum, Taiwan, Republic of China **7.04:** © National Palace Museum, Taiwan, Republic of China **7.05:** © National Palace Museum, Taiwan, Republic of China

Chapter 8. 8.02: © The Asian Society, Mr. & Mrs. J.D. Rockefeller 3rd Collection, photograph by Lynton Gardiner **8.03:** © Honolulu Academy of Arts, Gift of Mrs. Carter Galt, 1952 (1666.1) **8.04:** © Cleveland Museum of Art, 2003. Leonard C. Hanna, Jr. Bequest, 1980.10 **8.05:** © Asian Art Museum of San Francisco, Gift of the Avery Brundage Collection Symposium Fund and the M.H. de Young Memorial Museum Trust Fund, B69D17. Used by Permission

Chapter 9. 9.02: © Freer Gallery of Art, Smithsonian Institution, Washington, D.C.: Purchase, F1965.22 detail **9.03:** © Rijksmuseum voor Volkenkunde Leiden **9.04:** © Collection of the Palace Museum, Bejing, China **9.05:** © Peabody Essex Museum, Salem, MA

Chapter 10. 10.02: © Honolulu Academy of Arts, Gift of Wilhelmina Tenney Memorial Collection, 1955 (2045.1) **10.03:** © Cleveland Museum of Art, John L. Severance Fund, (1953.247) **10.04:** © Asian Art Museum of San Francisco. Gift of the Tang Foundation presented by Nadine, Martin, and Leslie Tang to the Asian Art Museum in celebration of Jack C.C. Tang's sixtieth birthday, B87D8. Used by permission **10.05:** © Rijks Museum, Amsterdam, AK-RK-1991-10 **10.06:** © Lore Schirokauer

Chapter 11. 11.01: © Time Life Pictures/Mansell/Time Life Pictures/Getty Images **11.02:** © Hulton-Deutsch Collection/CORBIS **11.03:** © Cixi, Empress Dowager of China, 1835–1908 Photographs. Freer Gallery of Art and Arthur M. Sackler Gallery Archives. Smithsonian Institution, Washington, D.C., Purchase. Photographer: Xunling, SC-GR 256 **11.04:** © Lore Schirokauer **11.05:** Reproduced from *The Cause of the Riots in the Yangtse Valley: A 'Complete Picture Gallery', Hankow 1891.* Courtesy Houghton Library, Harvard University

Chapter 12. 12.01: From "A Record of the Situation of China," Cartoon in *Shibao*, August 26, 1907 **12.02:** Courtesy Far East Fine Arts, Inc. San Francisco. (http://www.fareastfinearts.com) **12.03:** © Art Museum, Chinese University of Hong Kong, China **12.04:** © Xu Beihong Museum

Chapter 13. 13.02: From Yonghua lingxin, ed., *Woodcuts of Wartime China, 1937–1945* (Taiwan: Li Ming Cultural Enterprises, Dist.) **13.04:** © Revolutionary Workers Online **13.05:** © Bettman/CORBIS **13.06:** From Steven Levine, *Anvil of Victory: The Communist Revolution in Manchuria, 1945–1948.* Courtesy of Columbia University Press

Chapter 14. 14.01: National Art Gallery of China, Beijing. Used by Permission **14.02:** Shanghai Institute of Chinese Painting. © Wu Hufan. Used by Permission **14.03:** From *Peasant Paintings from Huhsien County.* Compiled by the Fine Arts Collection Section of the Cultural Groups Under the State Council of the People's Republic of China (Peking, 1974) **14.04:** From the Stefan R. Landsberger Collection (Chinese Propaganda Poster Pages, Online Exhibit, http://www.IISG.NL/~Landsberger) **14.05:** Collection Conrad Schirokauer. Photograph © Lore Schirokauer

Chapter 15. 15.01: ©1991 Xu Bing. Used by permission of the artist **15.02:** © Peter Turnley/CORBIS **15.03:** © Yen Kwok-Chung. Used by permission of the artist **15.04:** © Lore Schirokauer **15.05:** © Liu Kuo-Sung. Used by permission of the artist

Index